THE DEMOCRATIC ACCOUNTABILITY
OF CENTRAL BANKS

The Democratic Accountability of Central Banks

A Comparative Study of the European Central Bank

FABIAN AMTENBRINK
LL D (Groningen)

·HART·
PUBLISHING
OXFORD AND PORTLAND, OREGON
1999

Hart Publishing Ltd
Oxford
UK

Published in the United States by
Hart Publishing c/o
International Specialised Book Services
5804 N.E. Hassalo St, Portland
Oregon 97213–3644 USA

Distributed in Australia and New Zealand by
Federation Press Pty Ltd
Annandale, NSW 2038
Australia

Distributed in the Netherlands, Belgium and Luxembourg by
Intersentia, Churchillaan 108
B2900 Schoten
Antwerpen
Belgium

Hart Publishing Ltd is a specialist legal publisher based in Oxford, England.
To order further copies of this book or to request a list of other
publications please write to:

Hart Publishing Ltd, 19 Whitehouse Road, Oxford, OX1 4PA
Telephone: +44 (0)1865 434459 or Fax: +44 (0)1865 794882
e-mail: hartpub@janep.demon.co.uk

British Library Cataloguing in Publication Data
Data Available
ISBN 1 84113–042–7 (cloth)

Typeset by Hope Services (Abingdon) Ltd.
Printed in Great Britain on acid-free paper
by Biddles Ltd, Guildford and Kings Lynn.

"Accountability is an elusive concept and trying to find an accurate and comprehensive definition is correspondingly difficult."

HC Select Committee on Treasury, *Accountability of the Bank of England*

"Most economists, regardless of their particular ideological biases, dwelt rigidly within a narrow definition of their discipline. They cloaked their observations in dense, neutral-sounding terminology that was opaque to non scientists. The neutral language masked the political content of economics and the social rituals of capitalism—as if all economic players were simple molecules destined to behave according to the same natural order, regardless of their political value or wealth."

W.Greider, *Secrets of the Temple*

Preface

This preface introduces a book that deserves praise for its scholarly research, perspicacious methodology in comparative public law, and persuasive conclusions on complex subjects. Six national central banking systems were studied and assessed as well as the entities emerging after the Treaty of Maastricht - the European System of Central Banks (ESCB) and the European Central Bank(ECB). The three years of collecting material, analysis and drafting must have been a formidable task for one author: projects of this scope are ordinarily entrusted to a team of experts in organisations such as the Dutch T.M.C. Asser Instituut, the French C.N.R.S., or the German Max Planck Institutes. To squeeze out of the mass of documentation constitutional, statutory and regulatory canons relevant for each of the seven organisations involved, together with pertinent practice and opinion, would have been an achievement on its own. To subject that ocean of data to incisive comparative legal, political and economic thought is an admirable exercise in scholarly interdisciplinary scrutiny. For a German lawyer to submit such a study in English as a doctoral thesis to the Dutch University of Groningen Law Faculty shows academic achievement, linguistic proficiency and professional skill.

The monograph raises the question of how far society may still consider itself to be democratic when it transfers authority to independent entities, with consequent exclusion from the making of alternative choices, for the sake of an optimal monetary policy regime.

> ". . . at the end of the day it is the electorate which must have the basic choice between different alternatives".[1]

In this context the book assesses the constitutional and statutory framework, practice and opinion of the Deutsche Bundesbank, the Banque de France, the Bank of England and the Nederlandsche Bank. Mr Amtenbrink spells out his view of consequent deformations of the democratic principle in general and democratic accountability in particular. Yet the most significant finding is the "democratic deficit" of the ESCB and of the ECB which ensues from the pertinent texts in the Maastricht Treaty, including the ESCB/ECB Statute. As a matter of legislative policy Mr Amtenbrink suggests that this deficit might be overcome by adapting the provisions of the European Union Treaty, notably on the lines of the contemporary New Zealand Reserve Bank scheme, which he describes in impressive detail. The author is aware of the difficulties that could arise from using the clumsy procedure of Art N. of the Maastricht

---

[1] Typescript of thesis, p. 380–1.

Treaty to achieve this,[2] but nevertheless puts his case with admirable skill and vigour.

The recent contentious discussion between a learned member of the ECB's Executive Board and an equally learned member of the Bank of England's Monetary Policy Committee[3] on whether to extend the accountability of the ECB to the voting record of the ECB Governing Council tends to suggest that the debate will continue. The Frankfurt institution declined to follow the example of "effective accountability" from London, on legal and policy considerations. In view of that lasting - and for the moment - overt dichotomy it may be helpful to leave room for evolution by taking the recent advice of the Bank of International Settlements:

> "First . . . great uncertainty about the transmission of monetary policy in the EMU area . . . and the price stability objective will, at least intitially, put a premium on a discretionary approach, which inherently complicates communication with the public and the markets. Secondly, a monetary policy stance that is appropriate from an EMU-wide perspective may be more difficult to explain to national audiences".[4]
> "Thirdly, when markets rely too much on central bank guidance, the central bank may be forced to comment or take action more frequently, even if the differences between data outturns and forecasts are only small".[5]

I am convinced that no matter how this public debate will end, Mr Amtenbrink's monograph will have a measurable impact on its outcome. It may provide testimony to the time-honoured wisdom of books that unite many qualities: *Habent sua fata libelli.*

Hugo J. Hahn Dr. iur. Dr h.c. LL.M Harvard
Emeritus Professor of Law
Bayerische Julius-Maximilians-Universitat Wurzburg

---

[2] Laurence Gormley/Jacob de Haan, Independence and Accountability of the European Central Bank, *in European and Monetary Union: The Institutional Framework*, Andenas, Gormley. Hadjiemmanuil & Harden, eds, 331, 339, 1997.

[3] Otmar Issing, Financial Times, 22.9.98, p 16; Willem H. Buiter, Financial Times, 24.9.98, p14.

[4] 68th Annual Report, Basle, 8th June 1998 p75.

[5] Ibid., 74.

Acknowledgements

The book is based on a doctorate conferred by the University of Groningen under the supervision of Professor Laurence Gormley and Professor Jakob de Haan. My thanks are due to them and to that institution. I would also like to thank Professor Sylvester Eijffinger, Professor Hugo Hahn and Professor John Usher who comprised the reading committee for the thesis and to Professor Ian Harden, Professor Martijn Van Empel and Professor Bernhard Kempen who acted as additional examiners for the award of the degree with distinction.

Thanks are due to my family for their support and encouragement which has been the foundation for everything I ever achieved. Moreover, I am grateful to Frea Rijnsbergen and Malcolm Jarvis for their friendship and support during their time in Groningen and thereafter. A special word of thanks must go to Walter van Straalen, who despite his own tight research schedule offered his friendship and support during crucial months of research and who acted as my paranymph primus. Finally, I must thank Nathalie Richard for her patience and strength despite the many difficulties involved with me working in Groningen and for the loving support she has given me. I could not have done it without her.

FA
November 1998

Contents

Detailed Contents

Table of Legislation

European Community

Regulations

Decisions

France

United States of America

Abbreviations

AJIL	*American Journal of International Law*
BayVBl.	*Bayerische Verwaltungsblätter*
BBankG	Bundesbankgesetz
BdL	Bank deutscher Länder
BGBl.	Bundesgesetzblatt (Federal Law Gazette)
BNL	*Banca Nazionale Del Lavoro Quarterly Review*
BTDrucks.	Bundestag-Drucksache
BVerfGE	Enscheidungssammlung des Bundesverfassungsgerichts (Reports of decisions of the (German) Federal Constitutional Court
BVerwGE	Enscheidungssammlung des Bundesverwaltungsgerichts (Reports of the decisions of the (German) Federal Administrative Court)
CFR	Code of Federal Regulations (US)
Cmd.	Command Papers (1919–1956)
CMLR	Common Market Law Reports
CMLRev.	*Common Market Law Review*
Cmnd.	Command Papers (1956–1987)
CPM	Conseil de la politique monetaire (Banque de France)
DÖV	*Die Öffentliche Verwaltung*
DtZ	*Deutsch-Deutsche Rechts-Zeitschrift*
EBLR	*European Business Law Review*
ECB	European Central Bank
ECJ	European Court of Justice
ECR	European Court Reports
ECU	European Currency Unit
EFC	Economic and Financial Committee
ELRev.	*European Law Review*
EMCF	European Monetary Co-operation Fund
EMI	European Monetary Institute
EMS	European Monetary System
EMU	Economic and Monetary Union
EP	European Parliament
ERM	Exchange Rate Mechanism
ESCB	European System of Central Banks
EuR	*Europarecht*
EuZW	*Europäische Zeitschrift für Wirtschaftsrecht*
EWS	*Europäisches Wirtschafts- und Steuerrecht*
FOMC	Federal Open Market Committee

GBl. DDR	Gesetzblatt der Deutschen Demokratischen Republik (Law Gazette of the German Democratic Republic)
HC	House of Commons (UK)
HCon.Res.	House Concurrent Resolution (US)
HJRes.	House Joint Resolution (US)
HR	Designation for bills originating in the US House of Representatives
ICLQ	*International and Comparative Law Quarterly*
JCMS	*Journal of Common Market Studies*
JORF	Journal Officiel de la Republique Française
JuS	*Juristische Schulung*
JZ	*Juristenzeitung*
LPA	Les Petites Affiches
LQR	*Law Quarterly Review*
MPC	Monetary Policy Committee (Bank of England)
NJB	*Nederlandse Juristenblad*
NJW	*Neue Juristische Wochenschrift*
NVwZ	*Neue Zeitschrift für Verwaltungsrecht*
OECD	Organisation for Economic Co-operation and Development
PA	*Public Administration*
PL	*Public Law*
PTA	Policy Target Agreement (Reserve Bank of New Zealand)
RGBl.	Reichsgesetzblatt
RDP	*Revue du droit public et de la science politique en France et à l'étranger*
RMC	*Revue du Marché commun et de l'Union européenne*
RRJ	*Revue de la Recherche Juridique*
RS	Reprinted Statutes (NZ)
RUDH	*Revue universelle des droits de l'homme*
SCon.Res.	Senate Concurrent Resolution (US)
SEA	Single European Act
SEW	Sociaal-economische wetgeving
Stat.	Statute at Large (US)
Stb.	Staatsblad
TEU	Treaty on European Union
USC	United States Code (US)
WM	*Wertpapier Mitteilung—Zeitschrift für Wirtschafts- und Bankrecht*
ZParl.	*Zeitschrift für Parlamentsfragen*

1

Introduction

I. CONTEXT

With the signing of the Treaty on European Union (TEU) in 1993 the Member States have agreed upon what may very well be described as the most ambitious European project since the signature of the Treaty of Paris establishing the European Coal and Steel Community (ECSC), and subsequently the Treaties of Rome establishing the European Atomic Energy Community (EURATOM) and the European Economic Community (EEC).[1] Indeed, given the slow-down in further political integration, the creation of an Economic and Monetary Union (EMU) and a single currency area can presently be considered as the main engine propelling the Member States into an ever closer Union.[2]

The approach taken with EMU is a diverse one, comprising elements both of co-ordination of national policies and the formulation of Community policies. The Economic Union is characterised by a close co-ordination of the Member States' economic policies on the basis of general guidelines defined by the Council of the European Union (hereafter the Council), and includes surveillance and enforcement mechanisms to ensure the durable convergence of the national economies.[3] The Monetary Union entails the transfer of authority over monetary policy from the level of the Member States to the European level and the European System of Central Banks (ESCB) because, unlike in the case of economic policy, the continued conduct of separate monetary policies by the Member States in a single currency area is impossible. The role of the central banks participating in the ESCB with regard to monetary policy changes—in many respects—from that of policy-makers to executive arms of the European Central Bank (ECB), implementing the latter's decisions in the Member States.

If there has been one particular feature about the ECB which has become the subject of discussions beyond the circles of well-informed specialists in the field, it has been the independent status of the ECB. Tellingly, this has served both proponents and opponents of EMU. Whereas in Germany it has been put to the people that the independent status of the ECB is a guarantor for a stable single currency, elsewhere, in France it has become the focus of public criticism of EMU.[4] For some

---

[1] For details cf. Chap. 3V 1.
[2] On the feasibility of this approach, cf. Chap. 5 III.
[3] Cf. Chap. 3 V 1, with further references.
[4] Cf. e.g. the information brochures published by the Federal Ministry for Finance: Bundesministerium für Finanzen, Referat Öffentlichkeitsarbeit, *Keine Angst vor der Währungsunion*, per Saldo 1/1996, 8–9.

time extensive research has been undertaken into the subject of central bank independence, in particular with regard to monetary policy, and its results on economic performance. Many economists today emphasis the importance of an independent monetary authority. Recent institutional developments in several central banks provide evidence of a global trend towards more independent central banks. The discussions on central bank independence have also heavily influenced the institutional choices for the ECB. Considering that central bankers have been at the centre of the decision-making process for most of the way, the institutional structure of the ECB may for many observers not be surprising. Yet, another aspect directly linked to independence, and often considered as an antipode to the former, has been treated as a side-issue at best, both in the general discussions on central bank independence and with regard to the ECB. This is democratic accountability. Economists and lawyers have gone to great lengths in order to develop criteria for the evaluation of the degree of independence of a central bank, whereas only recently can similar efforts be detected for democratic accountability.

Not least inspired by the sheer vigorousness of the discussions on the institutional structure of the ECB in the run-up to and during the negotiations on the TEU, in an effort to ensure the independence of the ECB, the present study sets out to examine the democratic accountability of central banks.

II. OBJECTIVE

The objective of this study may be considered twofold, comprising both an abstract and a concrete level.

On an abstract level, the study offers an explanation, rather than a generally applicable definition, of what democratic accountability amounts to with regard to central banks, first, by providing guidance for the application of the somewhat inconsistently used terminology, by describing both what accountability and the word "democratic" can represent. At the same time, criteria which can be applied in order to evaluate the existing degree of democratic accountability for a central bank are developed. Moreover, the necessity of the democratic accountability of central banks is highlighted.

On a concrete level, the present study sets out to examine the existing arrangements with regard to democratic accountability for a number of central bank systems existing today. Not least against the background of these systems, the ECB is examined. The questions to which this study aims to provide some answers are whether and to what extent the ECB is democratically accountable, and to what extent the democratic accountability of the ECB needs to be reinforced. As the responsibility for monetary policy shifts from the level of the Member States to the ECB, it needs to be observed to what extent this has an impact on the democratic accountability of monetary policy. To what extent will mechanisms of democratic accountability in the participating Member States still be applicable, and to what extent are they replaced on the European level?

III. APPROACH

In the course of this study six national central bank systems are analysed, namely the Bank of England, the Banque de France, the Deutsche Bundesbank, the Nederlandsche Bank, the Reserve Bank of New Zealand, and the Federal Reserve System (Fed), and, additionally, the ESCB and ECB. The Bundesbank has been included not only because it may be considered as the dominant central bank in Europe, but also because of its high degree of independence, which has helped it to be chosen as the blueprint for the institutional structure of the ESCB and the ECB. The Fed has also been discussed in the context of the ESCB, not least due to its decentralised structure comprising 12 Federal Reserve Banks. It is usually also regarded as having a high degree of independence. At the same time the Fed differs in important respects from other independent central banks in its relationship with Parliament. Both the Bank of England and the Banque de France have a long central bank tradition, and in both countries the approach to monetary policy has undergone remarkable changes, granting the central bank more independence in the area of monetary policy. In the case of the Bank of England these changes have only very recently taken place, and, moreover, stand for a new approach to democratic accountability. The latter has also been the reason for including the Reserve Bank of New Zealand, which in many respects has been recognised for alternative institutional arrangements for independence and democratic accountability. By including the Nederlandsche Bank not only the central bank system of the country in which this study has been produced is recognised, but the Nederlandsche Bank itself demonstrates an interesting institutional structure both with regard to its independence and accountability.

In the analysis a legal, i.e. rule-orientated, approach is taken. The basis of the analysis is formed by the legal bases of the central banks, but also any practical arrangements related thereto. Indeed, the present study aims at distancing itself somewhat from an economic, performance-orientated approach, commonly associated with the discussion on central bank independence, but also increasingly to be found in discussions on the accountability of central banks. Nevertheless, it is inherent in the nature of the subject-matter that economic, and at times also political and sociological, aspects have to be taken in consideration in order to give a complete view of the issues.

In principle, the democratic accountability of a central bank can be observed in the context of all functions which a central bank fulfils. In broad lines this includes functions related to monetary policy, services to the government and commercial banks, and banking supervision. However, the present study focuses on the democratic accountability of central banks for the performance of monetary policy, and thus for the control of the supply of money. This is justified by the prominent position which monetary policy takes, on the one side, in the activities of central banks, and, on the other side, as part of the general economic policy of the government.

In the course of this study it will be argued that a comprehensive understanding of democratic accountability of a central bank includes the participation of all three branches of government, and thus not just the executive and legislative branches.[5] Indeed, in a constitutional system which subscribes to the rule of law the actions of a central bank must in principle be subject to judicial review. It may also be understood as a counterweight to the independent position of a central bank *vis-à-vis* the executive government and Parliament.[6] Yet despite these weighty arguments, it has been chosen to leave judicial review outside the scope of this study. One of the main reasons for doing so has resulted from the observation that there simply is not a substantive body of case law for the central banks examined in this study. To be sure, this evaluation is only valid for the functions of the central bank in the area of monetary policy. In other areas, in particular banking supervision, judicial review may be considered to play a substantial role. But the judicial review of monetary policy decisions as mechanism of democratic accountability may be more of an illusory concept in practice.

Bearing in mind the particularities of the different judicial systems, the present study cannot provide the comprehensive analysis required for explaining this limited impact of judicial review in the area of monetary policy. In fact, the limited amount of literature available for a number of central banks examined in this study calls for a separate line of research into this area, in order to examine whether and to what extent the performance of monetary policy of the central bank can become subject to judicial review, if not in practice, then in theory.[7] This would amount to a comparative study not only of the different judicial systems, but also of the legal nature assigned to monetary policy decisions in the different countries. Some of the basic issues which this research would have to tackle are related to the admissibility of actions against monetary policy decisions, and the question who has standing to challenge monetary policy decisions, as well as the question to what extent such an action can be founded, bearing in mind the general nature of monetary policy decisions and the extent of discretion for the central bank resulting from that. With Daintith it can be observed that this is inherent to the nature of monetary policy objec-

---

[5] This criterion is often neglected by studies on democratic accountability of central banks, but it is recognised for example by R.M. Lastra, "European Monetary Union and Central Bank Independence" in M. Andenas/L.W. Gormley/C. Hadjiemmanuil/I. Harden (eds.), *European Economic and Monetary Union: The Institutional Framework* (Kluwer Law International, London, 1997), 289–329, 328.

[6] H.J. Hahn, *Währungsrecht* (C.H. Beck, Munich, 1990), at 305; Ch. König, "Institutionelle Überlegungen zum Aufgabenzuwachs beim Europäischen Gerichtshof in der Währungsunion", [1993] *EuZW*, 661–6, at 664 and 666.

[7] It should be noted that the Bundesbank may be considered as an exception in this respect, since a number of (German) studies deal with the contestability of monetary policy decisions. E.g. D. Coburger, "Mindestreserve- und Diskontpolitik der deutschen Bundesbank aus rechtlicher Sicht" [1989] *WM* 1005–8; H.-D. Hoppe, "Der Rechtsschutz gegen Akte der Währungspolitik" (Diss., Würzburg, 1994), with further references. Cf. also Hess. VGH, Beschluss of 22 Sept. 1986 (8 TG 1524/86) [1986] *WM* 1312, and VG Frankfurt a.M., Urteil of 19 May 1989 (VII/3 E 636/86) [1989] *WM* 1416, for two court decisions on decisions by the Bundesbank on minimum reserve requirements.

tives, constituting an obligation of *results* rather than of *means*.[8] These problem areas are basically confirmed by the few existing court decisions.[9] A separate issue is whether and to what extent conflicts between the central bank and government on monetary policy issues can become the subject of judicial review. With the coming into existence of the ESCB and the ECB in stage three of EMU, a new dimension is added to the judicial review of the participating central banks. In addition to any national arrangement on the judicial review the European Court of Justice (ECJ) when called upon by the ECB, reviews national central banks' fulfilment of obligations deriving from the EC Treaty and the ESCB Statute. Yet, similar difficulties with regard to the feasibility of review of monetary policy decisions arise in the context of the ESCB and ECB.

This study generally takes into account the legal status as existing at the end of 1997. It is presently recognised that in particular during the last couple of months in the run-up to EMU the legal bases of a number of central banks examined in this study have been amended in order to comply with the EC Treaty and the ESCB Statute.[10] This has been the case for the Banque de France,[11] the Bundesbank[12] and the Nederlandsche Bank.[13] However, since it is part of the objective of this study to provide a picture of the legal arrangements relating to the national central banks prior to the coming into existence of EMU, these institutional amendments are generally not anticipated in the analyses. Put differently, the democratic accountability of those central banks included in this study participating in the ESCB is evaluated on the basis of their respective statutes prior to any amendments which might have been necessary to comply with primary Community law. Instead, major amendments of the legal basis which have since taken place, influencing the described institutional structure,

---

[8] T. Daintith, "Between Domestic Democracy and the Alien Rule of Law? Some Thoughts on 'Independence' of the Bank of England" in Andenas/Gormley/Hadjiemmanuil/Harden (eds.), n. 5 above, 357–72, at 369.

[9] Informative in this respect are the cases existing in the USA, where the institutional structure of the Fed has been challenged in courts by members of Congress. In most cases the basic substantive legal issue was the issue of private versus public control of the Fed. However, the centre of all these decisions became the procedural question of *locus standi* of members of Congress, cf. *Reuss* v. *Balles*, 73 FRD 90 (DDC 1976) (584 F 2d 461); *Riegel* v. *Federal Open Market Committee*, 656 F 2d 873 (1981); *Melcher* v. *Federal Open Market Committee et al.*, US District Court, DC, 5 June 1986. Civ. A. No. 84–1335, 644, Federal Supplement 510; US Court of Appeals, DC, 18 December 1987, 836 F. 2d 561 (DC Cir. 1987). For an attempt by a group of private individuals cf. *Committee for Monetary Reform* v. *Board of Governors*, 766 F 2d 538; 247 US App.DC 48.

[10] For more details on this obligation cf. Chap. 4 I.

[11] Loi no. 98-357 du 12 mai 1998 hereafter referred to as Banque de France Act 1998. Those parts of the law not relating to stage three of EMU have already come into effect with the establishment of the ECB.

[12] Cf. Sechstes Gesetz zur Änderung des Gesetzes über die Deutsche Bundesbank of 22 December 1997, BGBl. I, 3274. Parts of this amendment took effect on 31 December 1997, whereas provisions relating to stage three of EMU take effect on 1 January 1999.

[13] Nieuwe bepalingen inzake De Nederlandsche bank N.V. in verband met het Verdrag tot oprichting van de Europese Gemeenschap (Bankwet 1998), Wet van 9 april 1998, Stb. 200; hereafter referred to as Bank Act 1998. Also Memorie Van Toelichting, Tweede Kamer, Vergaderjaar 1997–8, 25 719, nr. 1–3.

are pointed out in various spots throughout the study. Indeed, given the speed of developments in the area of central banks and in particular the ECB, it is virtually impossible always to take into account the latest developments. Besides, given the objective of this study to examine different central bank systems with regard to the existing institutional arrangements of democratic accountability, it would be useless to examine central banks on the basis of statutes which have already been brought in line with the EC Treaty and the ESCB Statute, and thus show a high degree of conformity. Yet, some central banks have for some time already operated under a statute which takes into account the forthcoming EMU, such as the Banque de France since 1993. With regard to the Banque de France differences compared with the previous status of the bank are highlighted. The examination of the Bank of England has to be considered as an exception to the above stated time frame in as much as the institutional changes at the bank, which have *de jure* been introduced by the Bank of England Act 1998, form the basis of the analysis. This is not least justified against the background that the UK will not participate in EMU from the outset and the fact that the new institutional arrangements at the Bank of England are not primarily designed to comply with primary Community law.

IV. STRUCTURE

The democratic accountability of central banks is observed in four main chapters, developing a picture of what democratic accountability amounts to for central banks.

Chapter 2, provides the theoretical background to the study, by focusing on the concepts of central bank independence and democratic accountability. Understanding the main theoretical arguments and the empirical evidence brought forward in favour of central bank independence is an important precondition for understanding today's institutional structure of many central banks. This understanding again forms the basis for the evaluation of the democratic accountability of the central banks. The philosophy behind the case for central bank independence is particularly important in order to understand the rigorousness with which the independence not only of the ECB, but also of the national central banks participating in the ESCB, has been implemented in primary Community law. The summary of the case for central bank independence focuses on the impact of central bank independence on inflation and economic growth, as two of the major economic arguments brought forward in favour of central bank independence. Moreover, the legal and non-legal criteria which have been developed in order to judge the degree of central bank independence are highlighted. The second half of Chapter 2 turns to the concept of the democratic accountability of central banks. The importance of the concept is explained in two succeeding steps. First, the roots of democratic accountability are traced by approaching the terminology in a broad, constitutional context.

The significance of democratic accountability in a democratic system is highlighted. This includes an examination of the EU, which forms the background against which the ECB is set up. Thereafter, the significance of democratic accountability for central banks is explained, observing both the position it has within a state and the tasks it fulfils. Having built the case for democratic accountability, the remainder of Chapter 2 focuses on explaining the terminology. Unlike central bank independence, a review of the existing literature reveals that the term "democratic accountability" is far from well defined. Indeed, discussions of the accountability of central banks are characterised by a certain degree of inconsistency in the usage of the terminology. Chapter 2 will point out why the term "democratic accountability" does not necessarily coincide with such phrases as democratic or political control and political accountability. It will be shown that a generally applicable, comprehensive definition of democratic accountability is missing. Only recently have attempts been made to explain democratic accountability in terms of criteria. Against the background of these attempts eight criteria are developed, namely the legal basis of the central bank, its monetary policy objective, its relationship with the executive government,[14] appointment and dismissal procedures, the override mechanism, the relationship with Parliament, transparency, and budgetary accountability. These criteria form the basis for the evaluation of the central banks in Chapter 4. The Chapter concludes with a closer look at the relationship between central bank independence and democratic accountability; two concepts which are often thought to be contradictory.

Chapter 3 offers an introduction to the central bank systems included in this study. Observing the complex institutional structure of central banks on the basis of criteria puts restraints on the type of information which can be included in such an evaluation without being in danger of losing sight of the main issues. Thus, general observations on the central banks are excluded so far as possible. Nevertheless, this general information facilitates the understanding of the central bank systems. Therefore, Chapter 3 provides an overview of the historic development, institutional structure, and the tasks of the banks. This overview serves the purpose of a point of reference in the course of the study, in particular for those readers not familiar with the details of the different central bank systems.

Chapter 4 returns to the focal point of this study by examining the seven central bank systems on the basis of the eight criteria developed for democratic accountability. The order in which central banks are examined, as well as the sub-headings under which they are examined in itself provides a picture of the institutional arrangements of the central banks with regard to the respective criterion of democratic accountability. Generally, a comparative approach is

[14] In the present study generally the expression *executive* government is preferred because at least in the US legal system, which is also examined in this study, the expression "government" refers to all three branches of government, including Parliament and the judiciary. Moreover, in the case of Germany, the expression *Federal* government is used to describe the executive government.

taken in examining the different central banks. Similarities and noteworthy differences are highlighted. However, the complex institutional arrangements of the different banks make it inevitable that the arrangements for each central bank corresponding with the respective criterion are examined separately. What emerges from the examination in Chapter 4 is not only an assessment of the degree of democratic accountability of each central bank, but moreover patterns of democratic accountability for central banks.

Chapter 5, the final chapter, provides more than a summary of the previous chapters. On the basis of the criteria developed in Chapter 2, and the findings of Chapter 4, it takes a new approach in defining democratic accountability as consisting of two elements: conditions and instruments. Those criteria providing the foundation on the basis of which the performance of the central bank with regard to monetary policy can be judged are considered to constitute conditions of democratic accountability. The two main conditions identified are the existence of a yardstick to measure the performance of a central bank, and, moreover, the existence of an environment which enables the institutions charged with holding the central bank accountable to obtain the necessary information to do so. Criteria providing a mechanism to penalise a central bank, once the performance has been judged insufficient, are regarded as instruments of democratic accountability. Generally, Parliament's right to change the legal basis, the (re-)appointment and dismissal procedures, an override mechanism, and budgetary accountability are regarded as criteria which can function as such instruments. In assigning the different criteria to the basic classification of conditions and instruments, a summarising look is taken at the arrangements existing for the six national central bank systems included in this study. The main themes are traced, whereby the emphasis has been put on highlighting the principal shortcomings, as well as outstanding institutional arrangements, with regard to democratic accountability. Gradually, something like a model for a democratically accountable central bank emerges from these discussions. Yet, at the same time, limits to the degree of democratic accountability, inherent to a specific institutional structure of a central bank, are pointed out.

The second major contribution of Chapter 5 is the separate evaluation of the degree of democratic accountability of the ECB as provided for in primary Community law. The newly introduced distinction is applied by evaluating the conditions for and instruments of democratic accountability for the ECB, whereby the institutional arrangements of the national central banks examined in this study and the experiences with these arrangements with regard to the democratic accountability of the banks form the background of this evaluation. What emerges from this is that the preconditions for holding the ECB democratically accountable, as well as the instruments available, are insufficient. Democratic accountability plays only a subsidiary role in the context of the ECB. For this reason a new approach to making the ECB democratically accountable is submitted, by proposing an improvement of the conditions and a strengthening of the instruments necessary for a sufficient degree of democratic accountability. At the same time it is recognised that not all improvements, in principle considered desirable, can be implemented under the existing institutional structure of the EU. This touches foremost on the role of the European Parliament (EP) in holding the ECB accountable. In this respect some of the shortcomings are an expression of the democratic deficit in the Community structure as such, rather than only a particular deficiency of the ECB.

Finally, Chapter 5 returns to somewhat broader considerations in the context of democratic accountability of central banks. It presents an index which quantifies the democratic accountability of central banks, while at the same time commenting on other recent efforts to introduce such an index. On the basis of the experiences in the present study, the limits of such an indexing along the lines of those common for the evaluation of the degree of independence of different central banks are emphasised, as certain elements of democratic accountability may be beyond the scope of such an index. Thereafter, this Chapter takes a final look at the relationship between central bank independence and democratic accountability. It is submitted that this relationship should be interpreted as a system of mutual dependencies, rather than inverse concepts, which exclude each other.

2

Democratic Accountability and Central Bank Independence—the Theoretical Background

This chapter discusses the concept of central bank independence and democratic accountability. It may seem to be an unusual approach against the background of the title of this study to commence with a summary of the discussion on central bank independence. However, due to the fact that many issues surrounding the democratic accountability of central banks can only be fully appreciated against the background of the strong case which is presented in favour of independent central banks, it is presently believed that the discussion on the latter subject-matter needs to be the point of departure.

First, the theoretical arguments and the empirical evidence brought forward in favour of central bank independence are summarised. Thereafter, the criteria applied for the evaluation of the degree of independence of a central bank are reviewed. The second half of this chapter turns to the focal point of the book with the definition of *democratic accountability* in two succeeding steps, including an examination of the terminology in a broad, constitutional context, and with regard to central banks. Thereafter, criteria for the evaluation of the democratic accountability of central banks are developed which become the basis for the evaluation of the central banks included in this study in Chapter 4.

I. CENTRAL BANK INDEPENDENCE

For some time the subject-matter of central bank independence has become the focal point of discussions notably among economists. In a number of countries the status of the central bank has been overhauled recently granting it (more) independence from government. The discussion on central bank independence has additionally been fuelled since the late 1980s by the discussions on the establishment of the European System of Central Banks and the European Central Bank as part of Economic and Monetary Union. Since, numerous publications have emphasised the necessity for the establishment of an independent European Central Bank. In plain terms: discussing central bank independence has become "fashionable".[1]

[1] A term adopted in *Independent and Accountable, A New Mandate for the Bank of England,*

Literature on the subject-matter of central bank independence is extensive and thus this section will focus on providing an overview of the main arguments in favour of central bank independence while at the same time referring to more in-depth studies where appropriate. This is followed by an overview of the criteria which are applied to measure the degree of independence of a central bank. In this context institutional preferences of the proponents of independent central banks become apparent. The (theoretical) concept of central bank independence which emerges from these considerations will be revisited on a practical level in the following chapters in the course of the examination of the current institutional settings of the central banks enclosed in this study.

1. The case for central bank independence

The majority of publications on central bank independence demonstrate a link between central bank independence and economic performance. One of the underlying reasons for this can be found in the refocusing of the discussions on the optimal monetary regime, or, in other words, on what monetary policy can and cannot achieve.[2] The concept of a monetary policy aimed at directly promoting economic growth and full employment in the long run has been put to rest.[3] The painstaking experiences with high inflation in the 1970s have redirected discussions on the objective of monetary policy to price stability. Contrary to what was earlier believed, inflation has been recognised causing considerable economic welfare losses.[4] The alleged long-term trade-off between inflation and unemployment has been found to be non-existent.[5] Instead, it has been recognised that price stability promotes real growth and employment in the long term.[6] An independent central bank in charge of monetary policy is

Report of an Independent Panel Chaired by Eric Roll, Centre for Economic Policy Research (CEPR), 1993, hereafter referred to as the Roll Report.

[2] H. Tietmeyer, "The Role of an Independent Central Bank in Europe" in P. Downes/R. Vaez-Zadeh, *The Evolving Role of Central Banks* (Central Banking Department, IMF, Washington, 1991), 176–89.

[3] Monetary policy is considered to be neutral, that is to have no effect, on real (economic) variables in the long-run. This does not rule out that it can affect growth and employment in the short-run; n. 21 below.

[4] Cf. e.g. N.G. Mankiw, *Macroeconomics* (3rd edn., Worth Publishers, New York, 1997), 166 *et seq.*, on the social costs of anticipated and unanticipated inflation.

[5] According to the findings of A.W. Phillips in the late 1950s a stable relationship between the increase in wages and inflation existed, the so-called Phillips-curve, in as much as unemployment is fuelled if nominal wages rise compared to a given level of inflation and productivity. According to this the only way to decrease the real wages, i.e. nominal wages minus inflation, and thus to promote employment is to increase inflation. In short, the Phillips-curve suggests a trade-off between inflation and unemployment; For details cf. Kredietbank, "La banque centrale idéale—I", *Kredietbank-Bulletin hebdomadaire*, vol. 48 no. 26 (1993), 1–6, at 3. On the modern Phillips curve cf. Mankiw, n. 4 above, 346 *et seq.*

[6] E.g. Tietmeyer, n. 2 above, at 178. Real economic growth stands for *nominal* growth minus inflation.

generally believed to be the best guarantor of a monetary policy aimed at price stability.

Theoretical arguments and empirical evidence on the impact of central bank independence have been gathered for a variety of macro-economic aggregates, and include, apart from the rate of inflation and inflation variability, also economic growth and its variability, disinflation costs, (*ex post*) real interest rates,[7] government deficits and unemployment.[8] The economic record of countries like Germany featuring central banks with a generally recognised high level of independence from government are often used as examples to prove the point. For the purpose of providing a short introduction to the economic discussions surrounding central bank independence the following overview of the economic impact of central bank independence will focus on arguably the two most prominent aggregates, inflation and economic growth.

1.1. Impact of central bank independence on inflation

The foremost argument put forward in favour of an independent monetary authority is that of price stability. In short, independent central banks are likely to produce lower inflation rates, increasing price stability.[9] The argument sets out from the observations on governments' temptation to use monetary policy for their own political purposes.[10] This may be the case in several ways.

Recently, the argument in favour of central bank independence has been based on the so-called *time-inconsistency* problem linked with the discretionary policies of government.[11] At the centre of this stands the problem of a lack of consistency on the part of the policy-maker. In the outset government may choose to pre-announce its future policies in order to influence the expectations of economic agents. However, at the planned time for the implementation of the policy, after the economic agents have acted in accordance with such expectations, government has to deviate from a pre-set optimal (inflation) policy due to

---

[7] *Ex post* real interest rate stands for the actually realised nominal interest rate minus inflation, whereas *ex ante* interest rate represents the expected interest rate in a given case.

[8] For an overview cf. S.C.W. Eijffinger/J. de Haan, *The Political Economy of Central-Bank Independence*, Special Papers in Economics no. 19 (International Finance Section, Department of Economics, Princeton University, Princeton, NJ,1996).

[9] Examples drawn from a wide range of publications: cf. R.C.K. Burdekin/C. Wihlborg/ T.D. Willet, "A Monetary Constitution Case for an Independent European Central Bank", *World Economy*, vol. 15 no. 2 (1992), 231–49, with references to other analyses and studies; D. Gros/N. Thygesen, *European Monetary Integration* (Longman, London, 1992), 422 *et seq.*

[10] Cf. e.g. N. Roubini/J. Sachs, Government Spending and Budget Deficits in the Industrial Countries", *Economic Policy*, no. 8 (1989), 9–132; V. Grilli/D. Masciandaro/G. Tabellini, "Political and Monetary Institutions and Public Financial Policies in the Industrial World", *Economic Policy*, no. 13 (1991), 162–212.

[11] Cf. F. Kydland/E. Prescott, "Rules rather than Discretion The Inconsistency of Optimal Plans", *Journal of Political Economy*, vol. 85 no. 3 (1977), 473–91; R. Barro/D. Gordon, "Rules, Discretion and Reputation in a Model of Monetary Policy", *Journal of Monetary Economics*, vol. 12 (1983), 101–21.

incentives which it did not anticipate at the time of the setting of the policy.[12] Rational forward-looking economic agents assume such a development, by considering the announced policy incredible, and offset the planned policy goals of the government resulting in a higher inflation rate without any of the desired long- or short-term benefits. Discretionary monetary policy is believed to lack credibility and to result in higher inflation. In an environment in which the policy-maker has committed himself to a pre-set policy such temptations do not exist to the same degree, since the costs in terms of loss of credibility which would result from a deviation from the rule are thought to be much higher than is otherwise the case. In the context of this discussion on *rules versus discretion* it has been suggested that an independent central bank which is pre-committed to a binding monetary objective is thought to overcome the disadvantages associated with the time inconsistency problem.[13] As Lippi observes:

> "embedding monetary policy into an institutionalised policy scheme that is costly to be changed, makes policy revisions more difficult and hence increases policy pre-commitment. . . . Because credibility problems arise due to a lack of a commitment technology . . . institutions which help increasing policy precommitment are likely to influence policy credibility and hence the inflation performance."[14]

A direct conflict between fiscal and monetary policy may arise where government creates money in order to inflate away nominal debts, i.e. debase government debt, arising from excessive government spending.[15] Moreover, governments which have to service a large debt are tempted to create money in order to soften the effects of servicing such a debt.[16] In fact, if the government has exclusive control over the size of the budget deficit, the central bank is condemned to financing government deficits through the creation of money, thereby fuelling inflation.[17] An independent monetary authority on the other

---

[12] J. de Haan/S.C.W. Eijffinger, *De politieke economie van centrale bank onafhankelijkheid*, Rotterdamse Monetaire Studies (Wolters-Noordhoff, Groningen, 1994), 5 *et seq.*, identify reasons for the government to change its incentives, including monetary expansion in order to increase employment and changing incentives to inflate in connection with public finances.

[13] B. Eschweiler/M.D. Bordo, *Rules, Discretion, and Central Bank Independence: The German Experience 1880–1989*, NBER Working Paper Series, no. 5597 (National Bureau of Economic Research, Cambridge, Ma, 1993), who suggest that the second-best outcome in terms of monetary policy can be achieved through central bank independence, if the policy-maker is not capable of making a commitment; more critically B.T. McCallum, *Crucial Issues Concerning Central Bank Independence*, NBER Working Paper Series, no. 5597 (National Bureau of Economic Research, Cambridge, Ma, 1996), Chap. 1, n. 5, at 302, refers to other solutions to the time-inconsistency problem, including legislative monetary rules, an exchange rate peg, a currency board, and a constitutional commitment of the policy-maker to price stability.

[14] F. Lippi, *Central Bank Independence and Credibility*, Tinbergen Institute Research Series (Erasmus University Rotterdam, 1997), at 8.

[15] Sometimes referred to as *fiscal inflation;* Roubini/Sachs, n. 10 above.

[16] Money creation leads to inflation which in return debases the real value of the government debt.

[17] Burdekin/Wihlborg/Willet, n. 9 above, 231 *et seq.*, with reference to a study by D. Masciandaro, *Central Bank Independence, Macroeconomic Models and Monetary Regimes*, mimeo (Centre for Monetary and Financial Economics, Universita Commerciale Luigi Bocconi, Milan, Italy, 1991); Eijffinger/de Haan, n. 8 above, at 5, with reference to a study by N.J. Sargent/

hand is arguably more reluctant to succumb to the needs of government budget deficit finance and thus to the creation of money. Lastra summarises the argument:

> "Inflation is a non-legislation tax, not subject to Parliamentary approval. In order to prevent the monetary financing of government deficits, the central bank should be granted independence."[18]

Another source of inconsistency is the political business cycle. Prior to elections government may chose to adjust its preferences with regard to monetary policy, thereby abandoning pre-set monetary objectives, in order to increase the benefits for the electorate in an attempt to persuade the latter to re-elect the former.[19] Theoretically, from the point of view of a balanced budget, this can only be achieved by relocating money from one area to another. However, the creation of negative benefits in the course of creating positive benefits can be avoided— in the short run—through the creation of money.[20] Therefore, governments will be tempted to put pressure on monetary authorities to create money in order to produce a pre-election economic boom. This is even more tempting in the light of the existing evidence that policies promoting employment can be implemented in the short run through the creation of money without the immediate cost of inflation.[21] This will enhance the popularity of the government with an electorate which appreciates lower unemployment but dislikes inflation.

Although the motives of the government in manipulating monetary policy differ, a common pattern emerges: governments are tempted to create money for their own political ends and in order to produce economic benefits in the short term, which eventually leads to an increase in the rate of inflation associated with the macro- and micro-economic costs. The conclusion which is drawn from these theoretical arguments is that a low rate of inflation requires a monetary policy which is delegated to an independent institution, thereby removing it from immediate government political influence.[22]

Apart from the level of inflation the variability of inflation is being linked to the degree of central bank independence. Generally, the political orientation of

---

N. Wallace, "Some Unpleasant Monetarist Arithmetic", *Federal Reserve Bank of Minneapolis Quarterly Review*, vol. 5 (1981), 1–17.

[18] Lastra, n. 13 above, at 301.

[19] The economic fluctuations arise because subsequent to the elections the government has to take anti-inflationary measures in order to overcome the effects of the previous money creation.

[20] This is also referred to as the "public choice view", cf. R.E. Wagner, "Public Choice, Monetary Control and Economic Disruption" in P. Whiteley (ed.), *Models of Political Economy* (Sage Publications, London, 1980); also T. Besley/A. Case, *Does Electoral Accountability Affect Economic Policy Choices? Evidence From Gubernatorial Term Limits* (National Bureau Of Economic Research Inc., Working Paper No. 4575, Cambridge, 1993); A. Alesina, "Politics and Business Cycles in Industrial Countries", *Economic Policy*, no. 8 (1989), 55–98.

[21] On the existence of a short-term trade off between inflation and employment, the so-called short-run Philips-Curve, cf. Mankiw, n. 4 above, 350 *et seq.*

[22] For extended discussion e.g. R.H. Hasse (ed.), *The European Central Bank: Perspectives for a Further Development of the European Monetary System* (Bertelsmann Foundation Publishers, Gütersloh, 1990), 122 *et seq.*

a government influences monetary policy and economic performance. While one, perhaps more, conservative government will give higher priority to a stable and low rate of inflation, another, more left-wing government will focus on other factors arguably—in the short run—more directly linked to social welfare benefits, e.g. level of employment, presumably resulting in higher government spending and a higher rate of inflation. In the case of regular changes of government and a central bank which pursues monetary policy according to the priorities of the government of the day the level of inflation will vary.[23] But even without changing governments the level of inflation can be exposed to inconsistent monetary policy, as the level of inflation may vary due to the political business cycle. As observed earlier, governments facing the challenge of re-election will be tempted to create a pre-electoral economic boom through the creation of money. Moreover, it has also been observed that inflation variability is positively related to inflation. The logical conclusion from this is that an independent central bank which has a positive influence on the inflation rate has the same effect on the inflation variability.[24]

Theoretical considerations on the relationship between central bank independence and the rate of inflation are backed by empirical evidence. On the basis of comparisons of the degree of independence of central banks and the inflation record of the respective country a negative correlation between the degree of independence and the inflation record has been generally acknowledged.[25]

On the contrary, empirical evidence does not provide an unambiguous proof of the theoretical finding that an independent central bank also reduces the risk of inflation variability. Although empirical evidence backs the findings on a positive correlation between the level of inflation and inflation variability, evidence for a significant negative correlation between central bank independence, which increases price stability, and inflation variability is not entirely conclusive.[26] One of the obstacles to the establishing of empirical evidence in this field is that

---

[23] A. Alesina, *Macroeconomics and Politics* (NBER Macroeconomic Annual, Cambridge University Press, Cambridge, 1988); the same, n. 20 above.

[24] Cf. Eijffinger/de Haan, n. 5 above, at 12, with further references.

[25] E.g. A. Alesina/L.H. Summers, "Central Bank Independence and Macroeconomic Performance: Some Comparative Evidence", *Journal of Money, Credit and Banking*, vol. 25, no. 2 (1993), 151–62, at 159; A. Cukierman/S.B. Webb/B. Neyapti, "Measuring the Independence of Central Banks and Its Effects on Policy Outcomes", *The World Economic Review*, vol. 6 no. 3 (1992), 353–98, at 383.

[26] For a critical overview cf. de Haan/Eijffinger, n. 12 above, 37–8, with further references. Alesina/Summers, n. 25 above, at 159, suggest that "monetary discipline associated with central bank independence reduces the level and variability of inflation", while emphasising that the results of their study are not conclusive; Cukierman/Webb/Neyapti, n. 25 above, at 383, state that the rate of turnover of the central bank governors, which they consider an important indicator for the degree of central bank independence, is an important factor in explaining inflation variability across the overall sample of countries chosen in their study (cf. also Chap. 4 I.2.2.). S.C.W. Eijffinger/E. Schaling/M. Hoeberichts, *Central Bank Independence: A Sensitivity Analysis*, Center for Economic Research Discussion Paper, no. 9710 (Tilburg University, 1997), at 12, find some empirical evidence for a correlation between central bank independence and inflation variability.

such studies rely on the comparison of the level of independence of a central bank with the country data on inflation variability of the state in which the central bank is located. Variances between different studies in the evaluation of the relationship between the inflation variability and the level of central bank independence in a given country can—among others—arise from the different interpretation of the level of independence of the central banks.[27]

1.2. Impact of central bank independence on economic growth

If an independent central bank in charge of monetary policy produces a better inflation record the question arises whether and to what extent the degree of independence of a monetary authority and its commitment to price stability influence economic growth and economic growth variability.

Some theoretical studies suggest a negative relationship between central bank independence and economic growth. According to this view, an independent central bank, following a restrictive monetary policy, produces lower inflation rates. This will increase (*ex post*) real interest rates. Since interest rates have an influence on the level of investment and thus on economic growth, a low level of inflation is thought to *decrease* economic growth.[28] On the contrary, it can be argued that there is a positive relationship between central bank independence and economic growth. An independent monetary authority faces less political pressure from government. As has been pointed out above, an independent monetary authority is not exposed to the same temptations as government, that is to abuse monetary instruments for short-term political purposes. Therefore, an independent monetary authority may produce less uncertainty about inflation, hence its conduct of monetary policy is more stable and predictable. This results in economic stability and reduced risk of unstable interest rates and consequently stimulates economic growth.[29] Economic instability, leading to high inflation rates, is considered to produce significant economic costs.[30]

With respect to *economic growth variability*, similar conclusions to those for inflation variability can be drawn. Since an independent central bank will be more hostile to high inflation rates and inflation variability, the stability of economic growth increases, thereby decreasing economic growth variability.

---

[27] Eijffinger/de Haan, n. 8 above, compare the results drawn from different measures of central bank independence.

[28] On this view cf. K. Rogoff, "The Optimal Degree of Commitment to an Intermediate Monetary Target, *Quarterly Journal of Economics*, vol. 100 (1985), 1169–90; S. Fischer, "The Role of Macroeconomic Factors in Growth", *Journal of Monetary Economics*, vol. 32 (1993) 485–512, at 509, who concludes to the contrary that a low level of inflation and a small budget deficit facilitates sustained economic growth.

[29] J.A.H. de Beaufort Wijnholds, *Van kapiteins, loodsen en rechters: de wereldwijde beweging naar centrale bank autonomie* (Inaugurele rede Groningen, 1992), at 9.

[30] Cf. Eijffinger/de Haan, n. 8 above, 13–14, with further references, who identify *inflation uncertainty* as a possible cause for the negative influence of the rate of inflation on economic growth, and, moreover, that high levels of inflation may obstruct the price mechanism, thereby harming economic growth.

Although theoretical arguments propose a positive or negative correlation between central bank independence and economic growth, most empirical evidence suggests that the level of independence has no effect on economic growth or growth variability at all.[31] On the one hand, it may be considered as a positive finding that central bank independence, though leading to lower inflation, does not have a negative impact on economic growth, since it does away with the believe that low inflation hinders growth.[32] On the other hand, this result presents some observers with a dilemma because price stability is considered to be a precondition for economic growth, yet a positive correlation between central bank independence, promoting price stability, and economic growth is not detected.[33]

2. The evaluation of central bank independence

The case for central bank independence is based on the economic performance of countries featuring central bank systems with distinct levels of independence. Theoretical arguments suggest a correlation between the level of independence and economic performance. In order to establish such a correlation, the level of independence of a central bank is used as a benchmark against which its economic performance is judged. Hence it becomes vital to define central bank independence. Providing an overview over the criteria applied for the evaluation of central bank independence serves a double purpose. First, it becomes apparent what the practical implications in terms of the institutional set-up of the case for central bank independence are. Secondly, the reader is introduced to the concept of applying criteria for the evaluation of central banks. This concept will be revisited in the second half of this chapter in the context of the definition of the democratic accountability of central banks.

A universally valid definition of central bank independence is missing. Indeed, even the choice of terminology is discussed, as some authors prefer phrases like autonomy or room for manœuvre to describe the position of the central bank.[34] This may be explained by the complexity of the institutional settings and the position in the overall constitutional system, which differ between central banks and countries. Instead, criteria have emerged on the basis of which the degree of independence of a central bank is identified and evaluated. Evaluations of central bank independence are far from being homogeneous inasmuch as different sets of criteria are applied in different studies. In spite of the different criteria, two basic approaches to defining central bank independence emerge from a

---

[31] E.g. Alesina/Summers, n. 25 above, at 159.

[32] E.g. Burdekin/Wihlborg/Willet, n. 9 above, at 233, who find "little or no costs in terms of average rate of unemployment or real output growth".

[33] Cf. Eijffinger/de Haan, n. 8 above, at 36, with further references.

[34] This already becomes apparent from the different titles of the works cited throughout this study.

study of the relevant literature, namely a legal approach and a non-legal approach.[35] Most of the studies on central bank independence in one form or another combine both approaches.

2.1. Legal approach

The majority of evaluations of central bank independence are based on an examination of the legal basis of the central bank. Both legal and economic studies focus *primarily* on the evaluation of the institutional settings of the central banks. Observations are related to institutional/functional independence, organisational independence, and financial independence of a central bank.[36]

2.1.1. Institutional independence

Generally, institutional independence describes the status of the central bank as an institution separate primarily from the executive, i.e. government, but also from the legislative power, i.e. Parliament.[37] In short, a central bank which forms part of the executive branch of government, e.g. the Treasury, lacks institutional independence. In this context the legal basis of the central bank and its position in the overall constitutional system in which it is located play a role.[38] With regard to the tasks of the central bank, institutional independence stands for the central bank's power to formulate monetary policy independently from political institutions and in particular the executive government. In other words, a monetary authority is considered to possess institutional independence when it is free to set the final goals of monetary policy. This has also been referred to as *political* or *goal* independence.[39] In this context the existence of an

[35] For an overview, cf. S.C.W. Eijffinger/E. Schaling, "Central Bank Independence: Criteria and Indices", Department of Economics Research Memorandum, FEW 584, University of Tilburg, Mar. 1992, 18 *et seq.*; G. Quaden, "Indépendance et responsabilité des banques centrales, l'expérience des banques nationales", *Reflets & perspectives de la vie economique*, vol. 30 no. 3, 133–45.

[36] E.g. Hasse (ed.), n. 22 above, 116 *et seq.*; Gros/Thygesen, n. 9 above, 419 *et seq.*; *Vers Un Systeme Européen de Banques Centrales*, Rapport du groupe présidé par Jean-Victor Louis (Editions de l'Université de Bruxelles, Brussels, 1989), 25 *et seq.*; R. Smits, *The European Central Bank—Institutional Aspects* (Kluwer Law International, London, 1997), 155 *et seq.*; K. v.Wogau (Rapporteur), *Report of the Committee for Economic, Monetary and Industrial Policy on the National Central Banks in the Perspective of the 2nd and 3rd Stages of EMU*, European Parliament, Session Documents (1.12.1993, DOC-EN\RR\240652).

[37] Smits, n. 36 above, 155–156. For more details on the position of a central bank in a constitutional system, cf. Chap. 2 III.

[38] Gros/Thygesen, n. 9 above, 421–2, refer to the legal ranking of the central bank statute as part of the political independence of the central bank and find a positive correlation between the ability to change the legal basis of a central bank and its independence, stating that the more difficult it is to change the legal basis of a central bank the more credible its position will be.

[39] Alesina, n. 23 above, on the basis of a study by Bade/Parkin refers to *political* independence. Similarly, Grilli/Masciandaro/Tabellini, n. 10 above, 186 *et seq.*, who refer to political independence and include elements described below as part of the organisational independence, such as appointment procedures; G. Debelle/S. Fischer, *How Independent Should A Central Bank Be?*, CEPR conference paper no. 392, Stanford, 1994, 3 *et seq.*, refer to *goal* independence; S. Fischer, "Modern Central Banking" in F. Capie *et al.*, *The Future of Central Banking* (Cambridge University Press, Cambridge, 1994), 262–308, 292 *et seq.*

explicit and clear legal mandate in the central bank status is often considered as an important element. To be sure, formally speaking the existence of a monetary policy objective may be considered to infringe the central bank's independence in its conduct of monetary policy. Yet it is often mentioned in the context of central bank independence because an explicit monetary policy objective, e.g. price stability, is thought to reduce the risk of political pressure on the bank, and ensures that the central bank does in fact follow an inflation-averse monetary policy.[40] This is moreover considered to be consistent with the rationale for central bank independence, since central banks charged with multiple objectives face policy choices which may require to put aside the objective of price stability.[41] In order to judge the degree of goal independence sometimes a distinction is drawn between *ex ante* and *ex post* interference by government. First, it is observed whether the central bank is free to make its decisions without *ex ante* government interference in the form of instructions, and, secondly, whether decisions are subject to (potential) *ex post* government intervention, in the form of an override mechanism.[42]

2.1.2. Functional independence

A central bank is considered to be functionally independent when it can decide freely on the application of its monetary policy instruments, such as the adjustment of interest rates and open market operations. In this context it is also sometimes referred to as *instrument* independence, characterising a central bank which is free to choose the instruments necessary in order to reach its objectives.[43] The functional independence of a central bank is restricted where it is obliged to have its actions authorised by government in advance, or where the executive government can override a decision by the central banks.

The functional independence of a central bank also excludes any obligation to provide the government with overdraft and other types of credit facilities. According to this an independent central bank has to be free to decide whether and under what circumstances it provides its liquidity.[44] Where governments as the fiscal authorities have direct or indirect access to central bank credits they are tempted to finance their expenditures through the central bank and the

---

[40] E.g. Grilli/Masciandaro/Tabellini, n. 10 above.

[41] J.O. de Beaufort Wijnholds/L.H. Hoogduin, "Central Bank Autonomy: Policy Issues" in J.O. de Beaufort Wijnholds/S.C.W. Eijffinger/L.H. Hoogduin (eds.), *A Framework for Monetary Stability* (Kluwer Academic Publishers, Dordrecht, 1994), 75–95, 82 *et seq*. Lippi, n. 14 above, at 12, considers the "policy mandate", alongside "commitment-enhancing institutional autonomy", as one of two basic elements which make up central bank independence.

[42] J.-J. Rey, "Indépendance et responsabilité: le projet de Banque centrale européenne", *Réflects & perspectives de la vie économique*, vol. 30 no. 3 (1991), 147–60, 154 *et seq*.

[43] Grilli/Masciandaro/Tabellini, n. 10 above, 188 *et seq*., refer to this point as part of *economic independence*; also A. Alesina/V. Grilli, "The European Central Bank: Reshaping Monetary Politics in Europe" in M.B. Canzoneri/V. Grilli/P.R. Masson (eds.), *Establishing a Central Bank: Issues in Europe and Lessons from the US* (Cambridge University Press, Cambridge, 1992), 49–77, 54 *et seq*.

[44] K. v. Wogau, n. 36 above, at 7; Grilli/Masciandaro/Tabellini, n. 10 above, 188 *et seq*., examine—among others—whether the credit facility of the government is automatic, whether it is only temporary, and whether it is limited as regards the amount.

creation of money. This results in a loss of central bank independence, as in that case monetary policy is subordinated to fiscal policy.[45]

2.1.3. Organisational independence

The organisational independence relates to the personnel composition of the organs of the central bank and the modalities of the appointment and dismissal of central bank officials.[46]

A number of studies concentrate on the personnel composition of the policy board of the central bank. Here, much attention is pointed towards the participation of government officials on the bank's policy board.[47] Needless to say a central bank system which features government officials with voting powers on the policy board is much more exposed to government influence, subject to the concrete arrangements, than a central bank which excludes government participation entirely or restricts it to a non-voting participation. Apart from the exclusion of direct influence of the government in the central bank, organisational independence also refers to the independence of central bank officials from government instructions.

With respect to the modalities of appointment and dismissal of central bank officials, first of all, the conditions under which a central bank official can be dismissed are evaluated. Dismissal on grounds other than serious misconduct is generally considered to be incompatible with an independent position of central bank officials, thus excluding dismissals on political but also performance-based grounds.[48]

Some authors stress the relation between the term of office and the level of independence of a central bank. The level of independence of a central bank is supposed to increase as the term of office of the appointees is longer, because central bank officials have a better chance of developing and defending independent views.[49] It has also been suggested that it is desirable to design the term of office to be longer than the average term of government, since a policy board of a central bank which is not reshuffled with every change in government results in greater consistency of monetary policy.[50] Generally, the reappoint-

---

[45] Hasse (ed.), n. 22 above, at 121. Note that this aspect is also sometimes discussed in the context of financial independence: O.Hahn, *Die Währungsbank: Behörde, Unternehmen, Autorität* (Erich Schmidt Verlag, Berlin, 1993), at 63, identifies three types of independence in this area, including restriction of financing through percentage quotas, through maximum amounts, and the lack of any such restriction.

[46] For Gros/Thygesen, n. 9 above, 420 *et seq.* and Grilli/Masciandaro/Tabellini, n. 10 above, 186 *et seq.*, these criteria form part of the political independence of a central bank.

[47] Hasse (ed.), n. 22 above, at 116; also Grilli *et al.*, n. 10 above, who refer to *political* independence.

[48] E.g. Grilli/Masciandaro/Tabellini, n. 10 above, 366 *et seq.*, who examine to what extent appointment and dismissal procedures influence the independence of a central bank. The concept of performance-based dismissal is revisited in Chap. 4 II 2.2.

[49] Eijffinger/de Haan, n. 9 above, 23 *et seq.*, with further references to corresponding studies.

[50] Roll Report, n. 7 above, at 28. However, even if the term of office of the members of the bank's policy board coincides with the term of the government, policy inconsistency due to personnel changes should not be overestimated. Not in all cases do governments stay in power for only one

ment of bank officials is thought to have a negative influence on the appointee's independence and, hence, central bank independence. Central bank official are more vulnerable to government influence for the sake of re-election.[51] However, seen from the point of view of monetary policy consistency it may be argued that the reappointment of members of the policy board has its advantages since the personnel continuity may promote a continuous approach to the formulation and/or implementation of monetary policy by the central bank.

2.1.4. Financial independence

Financial independence refers to the role which the government and/or Parliament plays in the determination of the budget of the central bank. Here, the view is taken that a central bank faced with budgetary control by government is presumably more vulnerable to pressure on monetary policies. Thus, in order to secure independence from government, it is often emphasised that a central bank should have a budget at its own disposal which is not subject to governmental approval.[52] Usually, a central bank can secure its financial assets independently from government by the issue of banknotes, open market operations and interests on assets backing compulsory deposits from the commercial banking sector.

Finally, the arrangements regarding the redistribution of central bank profits are sometimes considered as a criterion for the degree of central bank independence, whereby an independent central bank is supposed to be free in the usage of its profits.[53]

Table 1, compiled by Eijffinger and de Haan, presents the legal indices of four different studies for the central bank independence of 22 industrial countries, including the central banks which are examined in this study on the basis of the legal arrangements existing at the time.[54] In all four indices a higher value indicates a higher degree of central bank independence.

---

legislative period. Therefore, a re-elected government may very well chose to maintain its prior approach in the appointment of central bank officials.

[51] Hasse (ed.), n. 22 above, at 116.

[52] E.g. K. v. Wogau, n. 36 above, 7–8.

[53] Hahn, n. 45 above, 63–4.

[54] Cf. Eijffinger/de Haan,n. 8 above, at 23, for further details on the implications of these legal indices. According to these indices, Alesina measures the independence on a scale from 1 to 4, Eijffinger and Schaling on a scale from 1 to 5, and Cukierman on a scale from 0 to 1. LVAU is the unweighted legal-independence index. The legal indices for independence used by Grilli, Masciandaro, and Tabellini are based on separate indicators for political and economic independence. The index for political independence is shown in brackets. Their overall index ranges from 3 to 13. The extensions of the Eijffinger-Schaling index (marked in table 1 with ᵃ) are based on S.C.W. Eijffinger/M. Van Keulen, "Central Bank Independence in Another Eleven Countries", *BNL Quarterly Review*, vol. 192 (1995), 39–83. Except for Denmark, the ranges of these 7 countries refers to central bank laws adjusted during the last 10 years.

Table 1: Legal Indices of Central Bank Independence

Country	Alesina	Grilli, Masciandaro, Tabellini	Eijffinger-Schaling	Cukierman (LVAU)
Australia	1	9 (3)	1	0.31
Austria	–	9 (3)	3[a]	0.58
Belgium	2	7 (1)	3	0.19
Canada	2	11 (4)	1	0.46
Denmark	2	8 (3)	4[a]	0.47
Finland	2	–	3[a]	0.27
France[55]	2	7 (2)	2	0.28
Germany	4	13 (6)	5	0.66
Greece	–	4 (2)	–	0.51
Iceland	–	–	–	0.36
Ireland	–	7 (3)	–	0.39
Italy	1.5	5.4	2	0.22
Japan	3	6.1	3	0.16
Netherlands	2	10 (6)	4	0.42
New Zealand	1	3 (0)	3[a]	0.27
Norway	2	–	2[a]	0.14
Portugal	–	3 (1)	2[a]	–
Spain	1	5 (2)	3[a]	0.21
Sweden	2	–	2	0.27
Switzerland	4	12 (5)	5	0.68
United Kingdom[56]	2	6 (1)	2	0.31
United States	3	12 (5)	3	0.51

Source: Eijffinger/de Haan (1996)

2.2. Non-legal approach

Any evaluation of independence restricted to the legal provisions governing the central bank at some point may fall short of a profound assessment. The reason for this is that the actual degree of central bank independence may also depend upon factual circumstances rather than only legal provisions. In other words, a central bank may have *de facto* a different level of independence from that which can be determined on the basis of the central bank legislation.[57] This is

---

[55] It should be noted that the legal basis of the Banque de France has been amended since: cf. Chap. 3 III.

[56] It should be noted that the institutional arrangements regarding the Bank of England have been subject to changes since: cf. Chap. 3 I.

[57] E.g. A. Cukierman, *Central Bank Strategy, Credibility, and Independence* (MIT Press, Cambridge, Ma., 1992), 369 *et seq.*, who, apart from the legal independence of a central bank, identifies two indicators to take into account *practices diverging from the wording of the law*, including the actual turnover of central bank governors and the answers to a questionnaire sent off to central bankers; Kredietbank, "La banque centrale idéale—II", *Kredietbank-Bulletin hebdomadaire*, vol. 48 no. 27 (1993), 1–5, at 2.

recognised by some studies which introduce non-legal indices of central bank independence. Cukierman and, thereafter, Cukierman, Webb, and Neyapti measure the actual degree of independence of a central bank by considering the turnover rates of central bank governors and, moreover, on the basis of questionnaires answered by specialists on monetary policy in the different central banks.[58] While on the one hand high turnover rates, such as have been recorded for a number of developing countries, suggest a lower level of *de facto* independence, other examples, such as until recently the UK, prove that long tenures do not necessarily go hand-in-hand with a high degree of independence. Turnover rates have been considered to influence inflation and, even more so, inflation variability when comparing industrial with developing countries.[59] Overall, the actual discrepancy between the legal and the actual independence of central banks in industrial countries seems to be smaller than is the case for developing countries.

Another prominent example of discrepancies between the legal and the actual situation which influences the evaluation of central bank independence is the existence of override mechanisms in a number of legal bases of central banks which, however, have never been put to use.[60] Nonetheless, in some cases ratings of the degree of independence of a central bank have been based on such provisions.[61] Besides, the relationship between a central bank and government has often developed over the years and is hardly ever entirely reflected by the legal provisions. The personnel and the priorities of the monetary policy board of the bank may influence the level of independence.[62]

3. Conclusions

From the short overview of the economic arguments it has become apparent that the case for central bank independence is based on the assumption that a government faces monetary temptations conflicting with a sound, i.e. inflation-averse, monetary policy. In the view of the majority of commentators this conflict can only be solved by the establishment of a monetary authority which is independent from government and thus, from short-term political considerations. Hasse hits the nail squarely on the head in summarising the debate:

> "The history of monetary policy is the history of its abuse by the government. The history of monetary reforms has thus always been a chronicle of the efforts undertaken to make it more difficult for the government to gain the right to issue money, in order to avoid fiscal inflation."[63]

---

[58] See n. 25 and 57.
[59] Cukierman/Webb/Neyapti, n. 25 above, 363–7, observe that the results of the industrial countries by themselves do not offer an explanation for inflation (variability) in these countries.
[60] This is e.g. the case for the Nederlandsche Bank and the Bundesbank: cf. Chap. 4 V.
[61] Critical are Eijffinger/de Haan, n. 8 above, 58 *et seq.*, with reference to a study by Cukierman; de Beaufort Wijnholds, n. 29 above, at 3 and 9 *et seq.*
[62] Kredietbank, n. 57 above, 1 *et seq.*
[63] Hasse (ed.), n. 22 above, at 123.

Arguments in favour of central bank independence also take on a political dimension as they suggest that monetary policy should be neutral ground insulated from political influence. Politicians are believed to be less committed to a stable monetary policy and much more worried about pleasing the electorate. Indeed, it may be observed that the very nature of their position, being based on the mandate of the electorate, makes it impossible for politicians to be impartial to the short term benefits of an expansive monetary policy. Only a conservative, i.e. inflation-averse, and independent central banker is believed to provide such long-term stability.[64] Politicians are thought to lack the commitment and qualifications of experts in the field, i.e. central bankers.[65] Moreover, the political process does not provide the type of flexibility and efficiency needed for an effective pursuit of monetary policy.[66] The criteria which are used to evaluate the degree of independence of a central bank reflect this approach.[67] Institutional, functional, organisational and financial independence, as well as non-legal arrangements, all refer to the relationship between the central bank and the executive government (and Parliament) in pursuing monetary policy. The evaluation of the actual degree of independence of a central bank depends upon which criteria are applied and how their importance is weighted.

Although theoretical arguments strongly suggest that only the removal of monetary policy from the political arena can result in the pursuit of a sound monetary policy, they do not always pass the litmus test of empirical review. A majority of studies finds empirical evidence for a negative correlation between the level of independence of a central bank and the rate of inflation of the country in which it is located. Such a negative correlation has not been established for the relationship between central bank independence and economic growth.[68] Some have taken this as evidence for assuming that central bank independence is a "free lunch", meaning that it produces lower inflation while at the

---

[64] Rogoff, n. 28 above, who suggests appointing a central banker who is more averse to inflation than society as a whole. Critical of this view is J. de Haan/W. Kooi, "What Really Matters: Conservativeness or Independence?", *BNL Quarterly Review*, no. 200 (1997), 23–38.

[65] R.M. Lastra, "The Independence of the European Central Bank", *Harvard International Law Journal*, vol. 33 (1992), 475–519, at 477, with further references; the same in n. 13 above, 305–6, pointing out rightly the extensive implications which such an argument may have with regard to other economic policies.

[66] Hasse (ed.), n. 22 above, at 125, refers to a "technical argument".

[67] It should be noted in this context that the observations have focused on the arguments brought forward in favour of an independent central bank and the criteria which are applied to measure the existing degree of independence of central banks. However, these observations cannot explain why a central bank actually embodies a certain degree of independence. A number of studies by economists have developed factors such as the equilibrium or natural rate of unemployment, the stock of government debt, political instability, supervision of financial institutions, financial opposition to inflation, public opposition to inflation and other factors, which, to a different degree, influence the actual degree of independence of a central bank in a country, e.g. S.C.W. Eijffinger/E. Schaling, *The Ultimate Determinants of Central Bank Independence*, Center for Economic Research Discussion Paper, no. 9505, Tilburg University, Jan. 1995.

[68] For an overview of the empirical evidence for other economic variables, such as (*ex post*) real interest rates and the government budget deficit, cf. Eijffinger/de Haan, n. 8 above, 38 *et seq*.

same time not harming economic growth.[69] However, such enthusiastic statements may be exaggerated. First, even to the extent to which empirical evidence points towards a negative correlation between central bank independence and the rate of inflation, these findings have to be considered with care. The fact that a negative correlation between central bank independence and the rate of inflation can be detected does not necessarily permit the conclusion that they are causally linked, as other economic, political and historical factors, such as historically developed aversion of a country to inflation, may provide a starting point for an explanation.[70] This finding is supported by the inflation record of some countries which do not fall in line with the findings on the relationship between central bank independence and the inflation mentioned above.[71] Moreover, in the absence of empirical evidence suggesting a correlation between central bank independence, and real growth, the question arises why so much emphasis should be put on inflation in the first place if it does not hurt economic growth. Besides, it should be noted that while arguably a majority of commentators favours central bank independence the economic discussion on the optimal monetary policy is far from resolved.[72]

Yet the concept of central bank independence as a "free lunch" may not only raise questions in the light of the somewhat inconclusive economic empirical evidence. Central bank independence may also carry with it other costs. One line of argument against central bank independence, which is only briefly mentioned here, derives from the assumption that independence can result in a lack of co-ordination between fiscal and monetary policy since monetary policy may run contrary to fiscal policies.[73] Conflicts between fiscal and monetary policies can only be avoided through co-operation. Failure of co-operation can result in a deterioration of the economic record. Fair, for example, relates price stability not only to central bank independence but also to the co-ordination and mutual

---

[69] Debelle/Fischer, n. 39 above, at 7, with reference to Grilli/Masciandaro/Tabellini, n. 10 above.

[70] F. Heylen/A. Van Poeck, "Central Bank Independence: Only Part of the Inflation Story", *De Economist*, vol. 144 (1996), 45–61, in their theoretical and empirical analysis, point out that additional political and structural specifics of a country, such as the natural rate of unemployment and a stable government, influence the relationship between central bank independence and the rate of inflation; Burdekin/Wihlborg/Willet, n. 9 above, at 246, ask: "Is it the specific institutional arrangements adopted in such countries as Germany and Switzerland that explain these nations' correspondingly favourable inflation performance? Or are both the institutions and the good inflation records simply joint products of the underlying attitudes of political and economic leaders and of the general public in these countries?"

[71] E.g. Japan, which in the past had a good inflation record despite the fact that the Bank of Japan is generally considered to have a low degree of independence.

[72] This includes discussions on the degree of pre-commitment of a central bank (rules versus flexibility), e.g. N. Healey/P. Levine/J. Pearlman, *The Political Economy of a European Central Bank*, conference paper, 2nd ECSA-World Conference: *Federalism, Subsidiarity and Democracy in the European Union*, Brussels, 5–6 May 1994, Working Group II, at 9, and on the optimal targets, e.g. Mankiw, n. 4 above, 375–6.

[73] For details cf. e.g. P. Löwenthal, "De l'autonomie des autorités monétaires", *Reflets Perspectives de la Vie Économique*, vol. 30 no. 3, 161–9, with regard to the ECB.

reinforcement of monetary and fiscal policies.[74] Others interpret the separation of monetary from fiscal policy as a chance for the latter to become more disciplined, as fiscal policies which have the potential to damage the inflation record are likely to be offset by monetary policy measures in the form of interest rate adjustments by the central bank.[75]

Linked to this are arguments that an independent central bank may interfere with powers of a democratically elected government. This is the case where the economic objectives of a government do not correspond with the monetary objectives of an independent central bank, i.e. high employment and high economic output in the short run versus price stability and stable economic growth in the long run. Co-ordination of economic and monetary policies is also an issue in the EMU. Here, on a much larger scale, policies have to be co-ordinated on a supranational scale between the Council and the ECB.[76]

The second argument against infinite central bank independence advanced by legal and increasingly also by economic scholars is the necessity of mechanisms of accountability for a central bank. Here generally two lines of arguments can be pursued. First, from an economic point of view more recently it has been recognised in academic and central banker circles that a central bank may also be too independent to produce the optimal output. While governments may lean towards an inflationary policy, on the contrary central banks may tend to develop their aversion to inflation to a point where a stability-orientated monetary policy turns into a deflationary policy.[77] As Debelle and Fischer put it: "Without accountability to elected representatives, such as Congress, central banks run a good chance of becoming too conservative".[78] For economists producing sub-optimal monetary policy is on an equal footing with not serving the public interest, as the latter is defined through optimal economic output.

Secondly, from a legal point of view the question arises whether and to what extent independent institutions, such as central banks, fulfilling executive functions have to be subject to restraining mechanisms in order not to run contrary to fundamental democratic principles. The second half of this chapter and the chapters thereafter focus on this case for democratic accountability of central banks.

II. THE DEMOCRATIC ACCOUNTABILITY OF CENTRAL BANKS

It has emerged from the foregoing discussion that central bank independence is generally considered desirable from an economic point of view. The implica-

---

[74] D.E. Fair, *Relationship Between Central Bank and Government in the Determination of Monetary* Policy, Société Universitaire Européenne de Recherches Financières, SUERF Series 31 A, 1980, at 5.
[75] Ch. Goodhart, *The Central Bank and the Financial System* (Macmillan, London, 1995), 69–70.
[76] E.g. P.R. Masson/M.P. Taylor, "Fiscal Policy within Common Currency Areas", *JCMS*, vol. 31 (1993), 29–44.
[77] Contrary to inflation, deflation is characterised by a enduring fall in the general level of prices.
[78] Debelle/Fischer, n. 39 above, at 28.

tions for the institutional structure of the central bank and its relationship with government have been outlined. However, central banks do not perform in a vacuum in which only the economic implications of central bank independence matter. From a legal point of view central bank independence has to be justified against the background of democratic principles rather than economic performance. This is the case for both national central banks as well as in the European context the ECB. On the one hand central bank accountability is viewed as a counterweight to central bank independence and as such is often used as an argument against central bank independence. On the other hand central bank accountability may function as a justification for central bank independence. This implies that in principle it is possible to regard democratic accountability and central bank independence either as contrary or conjunct concepts.

1. The case for democratic accountability

1.1. Democratic accountability and democracy

The common notion of democracy is that of the government by the people. The principle of the sovereign power of the people by itself requires that any political power has to be legitimised through the people. The people are the holder of the *pouvoir constituant*. In a democratic system the people not only hold the power but they also exercise it; government *by* the people. As such the concept has found its way into a number of written constitutions.[79] As a form of government, democracy can be described as an organisational principle for the holding and exercise of state power.[80] In a direct or participatory democracy the people exercise that sovereign power themselves by taking all the necessary decisions through plebiscites. Since such concrete decisions constitute original exercise of sovereign power by the people, no further legitimation is required.[81] On the contrary, the representative democracy is characterised by the delegation of the sovereign power of the people to a group of representatives, i.e. Parliament, entrusted with the exercise of the state power, expressed primarily through the creation of laws. From this point of view representative democracy is a form of *legitimation of rule*.[82] The legitimation is renewed in regular intervals through (free and fair) elections. At the same instance the electorate may decide to withdraw his confidence when the representative is no longer thought to express its

[79] E.g. Germany: Art. 20 ss. 1 and 2 Basic Law (*Grundgesetz*); Art. 2 French Constitution of 1958 which, however, refers to the more abstract principle of national sovereignty.

[80] E.W. Böckenförde, "Demokratie als Verfassungsprinzip" in I. Isensee/P. Kirchhof (eds.), *Handbuch des Staatsrechts*, Vol. I (F. Müller Juristischer Verlag, Heidelberg, 1987), § 22, side note 9.

[81] P.M. Huber, "Die Rolle des Demokratieprinips im europäischen Integrationsprozeß", *Staatswissenschaft und Staatspraxis* (3) 1992, 349–79, at 353. Plebiscitarian elements can also be found in representative democracies, e.g. Art. 3 French Constitution of 1958.

[82] P. Hirst, *Representative Democracy and Its Limits* (Polity Press, Oxford, 1990), at 29, with reference to Max Weber.

will. Elections are more than a repeating legitimation of state power. They are at the same time a mechanism by which the representatives are held accountable by the electorate for their past performance. In this context the term *democratic accountability* can be defined in general as a mechanism, existing between holders of delegated power and those who have the formal power to replace them. Hence, accountability includes everything which those who have delegated the power find relevant to their decision whether to continue or withdraw its confidence.[83] Elections have to be considered as the ultimate source of democratic accountability of state power in a representative democracy, whereby democratic accountability amounts to more than the *control* of the state power, since the electorate can also *sanction* those to whom it has delegated powers by revising its delegation. In some constitutional systems this basic power of the electorate extents beyond Parliament to include (parts of) the executive. This is, for example the case in the USA, where the President as the holder of the executive power, is elected by the people through a system of state electors,[84] and—to a different extent—in France, where the President of the Republic is directly elected by the people.[85]

Nevertheless, in a representative democracy periodic elections cannot provide for a sufficient degree of democratic accountability. This is not least due to the fact that even where the executive government has this democratic coupling back either because it is directly elected by the people, or its members are elected from among the members of Parliament, the overwhelming part of the executive branch of government is outside the scope of this mechanism. However, it may be argued that by way of elections the electorate not only delegates its power to representatives, i.e. Parliament, but to some extent delegates mechanisms of democratic accountability. First, the legislator has the power to lay down the rules with which the executive branch of government complies. The Roll Report characterises this mechanism as "*ex ante* democratic control".[86] Moreover, in many constitutional systems, democratic accountability is ensured through mechanisms through which the executive branch is answerable to the legislative branch. This may be in the form of the principle of ministerial responsibility, to be found in many parliamentary democracies, where the executive government has to explain not only its own actions but also the actions of those over whom it exercises a supervisory power. But the impeachment procedure to be found in the American democracy can also be viewed as such a mechanism. The legislative holds the power ultimately to discharge the executive of its duties. In so far as the executive is not directly elected by the people, democratic accountability

---

[83] G. Vickers, "Accountability" in L.H. Browder, Jr. (ed.), *Emerging Patterns of Administrative Accountability* (Mr Cutchan Publishing Corp., Berkeley, Cal., 1971), 28–46, 28–9.

[84] Cf. Art. II s. 1 of the Constitution of the United States of America; hereafter referred to as United States Constitution.

[85] Cf. Arts. 5 *et seq.* French Constitution. On the bicephalous executive under the French Constitution; see e.g. L.M. Nguyen, *La Constitution de la Vème République* (4th edn., Les Editions STH, Paris, 1989), 85–6.

[86] Roll Report, n. 1 above, at 47.

amounts to a mechanism existing between the two holders of delegated powers, whereby the holder of powers who is directly legitimised through a popular mandate holds the other holder of power answerable. In such a system the electorate can hold the executive branch of government only indirectly accountable through the elections of the legislative branch. This system has its limits in the real world of parliamentary democracies which feature majority governments, that is where a majority in Parliament makes up the executive. In such systems the executive may hold the real power on a day-to-day basis.

Where power is delegated by the legislative or the executive branch to independent government agencies or independent bodies which are not even considered as part of a government (so-called "quangos" = quasi autonomous non-governmental organisations) these mechanisms of democratic accountability fail to a large extent, as the latter may be out of reach of such mechanisms as democratic elections, answerability to Parliament, or even control by the executive government. Majone in this context refers to "non-majoritarian institutions", characterised by a lack of direct accountability to the electorate or elected politicians, which include—among others—independent central banks.[87] It is not least this development which has raised doubts about the effectiveness of democratic mechanisms. The textbook approach to representative democracy as a "government of the people, *by the people* and for the people" has long been questioned by political scientists, who emphasise the limits of today's representative democracies and point out the differences between the theoretical concept of the *rule by the people* and political realities.[88] Government is understood as a constraint on, rather than an expression of, the will of the people. The danger of "elective despotism" in a partisan state and the inevitable rule of unaccountable officials as a consequence of big government are only two issues discussed in this context. From this standpoint representative democracy to a large extent amounts to a system of limitation and control of power.[89]

What is more, the executive government of the national state is no longer the only source of "state" power. With the transfer of sovereignty from national states to a new European legal order a new dimension is added to the discussion of democratic accountability and democracy. The penetration of the national legal order through Community law complements the existing national

---

[87] G. Majone, *Independence vs. Accountability? Non-Majoritarian Institutions and Democratic Government in Europe*, EUI Working Paper SPS No. 94/3, European University Institute, Florence, 1993, at 25, who argues that "the growth of non-majoritarian institutions is at the same time a symptom and a consequence of the failure of the interventionist and welfare policies of the past". The reasons for transferring responsibility for monetary policy to an independent institution have been observed at Chap. 2 I.

[88] On these issues see e.g. A. Barnett, "The Creation of Democracy" in P. Hirst/S. Khilnani, *Reinventing Democracy* (Blackwell Publishers, Oxford, 1996), 157–74; also P. Hirst, "Democracy and Civil Society" in Hirst/Khilnani, above, 97–116.

[89] G. Sartori, *The Theory of Democracy Revisited* (Chatham House Publishers, Chatham, NJ, 1987), at 280; also I. Harden, "Democracy and the European Union" in Hirst/Khilnani, n. 88 above, 132–43, 134 *et seq.*, who refers to "critical democracy" as a concept which "questions, limits and constrains public power".

structures by a new source of political power. Supremacy and direct effect of Community law may be considered as the two key concepts in this respect. It becomes obvious from the outset that the concept of democratic legitimation and accountability which have been developed against the background of the national state cannot readily be applied to the European level. This has to do with the fact that the very nature of the Community as a new legal order is somewhat difficult to place on a scale ranging from a federation of states to a federal state. The European Union as such does not have legal personality and, for the time being, arguably represents little more than a portrayal of the three pillars including the European Communities, Common Foreign and Security Policy, and Justice and Home Affairs. Of these three pillars only the first pillar is essentially supranational, whereas the third and large parts of the second pillar remain intergovernmental in their nature.[90] The German Constitutional Court (*Bundesverfassungsgericht*) in its controversial *Brunner* decision describes the EU as a union of the peoples of Europe, a confederation of allied states (*Staatenverbund*); a description rather than a precise definition of its legal nature.[91] At the centre of the EU structure stands the EC Treaty which has been recognised by the ECJ as the "*constitutional charter* of a Community based on the rule of law".[92] It is important to define the nature of the EU in order to determine on which level the sources of democratic legitimation and accountability have to be located. In a federation the participating national states provide the democratic legitimation and the necessary mechanisms of democratic accountability, whereas in a federal state it arises on the state but—more importantly— also on the federal level.

Observing the institutional structure of the EU confirms its structure as a half-way house. The EP does not constitute a legislature in the classical, national, sense.[93] Its role in the adoption of Community acts amounts—at best—to co-decision-making in accordance with Article 189b EC,[94] and is otherwise limited to the co-operation procedure of Article 189c EC, or reduced to consultations. Within this limited scope provided for by the EC Treaty the ECJ has recognised

---

[90]   On the second and third pillars of the EU before and after the Amsterdam Treaty cf. e.g. H.C. Posthumus Meyjes, "Nieuwe kleren voor het buitenlands en veiligheidsbeleid. Een beschouwing over de tweede pijler van het Europese Unie-Verdrag", *SEW*, vol. 45 no. 10 (1997), 365–9; J.P.H. Donner, "De derde pijler en de Amsterdamse doolhof", *SEW*, vol. 45 no. 10 (1997), 370–7.

[91]   Federal Constitutional Court, decision of 12 Oct. 1993, 2 BvR 2134/92 and 2 BvR 2159/59, BVerfGE 89, 155; reprinted in [1993] EuZW, 667; for an English translation, cf. [1994] 1 CMLR, 57 *et seq.* For more details cf. Chap. 4 I 3. Critical with regard to the terminology is T. Koopmans, "Rechter, D-mark en democratie: het Bundesverfassungsgericht en de Europese Unie", *NJB*, vol. 69 no. 8 (1994), 245–51, at 249.

[92]   ECJ Opinion 1/91 [1991] ECR I-6079, at 6080; emphasis added.

[93]   At this time it may very well be appropriate to be sceptical about the extent to which the electorate's selection of the national representatives is based on European issues, since in many cases national issues/considerations may prevail. In this respect EP elections may not always reflect the will of the people with regard to decisions in which the EP takes part one way or the other.

[94]   P. Raworth, "A Timid Step Forwards: Maastricht and the Democratisation of the European Communities" (1994) 19 *ELRev.*, 16–33, at 25, concludes that the Council takes a superior position in the co-decision procedure.

the participatory rights of the EP in the legislative procedures as "an essential factor in the institutional balance intended by the Treaty", and, moreover, as a reflection of "the fundamental democratic principle that the peoples should take part in the exercise of power through the intermediary of a representative assembly".[95] However, the real legislative function is fulfilled by the Council, which consists of the representatives of the governments of the Member States. Legislative decisions on the European level are thus by definition dominated by the executive.[96] The direct elections to the EP since 1979 and the notion of European citizenship introduced by the TEU cannot compensate for this imbalance.[97] Indeed, it may only distract from the fact that in reality the limited extent to which the citizens of the Member States participate in holding European political power accountable is mediated through national parliamentary elections, which decide on who represents the national interests in the Council in the future.[98] The legitimation of the executive governments in the Member States can be identified as the true source of legitimation of the European political power.[99] It may be argued that the founding Treaties do not introduce a separate source of legitimation, since their existence is based on ratification by the national parliaments as well.[100] Seen from this point of view democratic accountability on the European level is remote and takes place only to a very limited extent indirectly via the answerability of the Member States' executive governments to their respective national parliaments. With the extension of qualified majority voting in the Council this coupling back to the national Parliament is non-existent in the case of a Member State which is essentially outvoted. The executive government cannot be held accountable for decisions which it has not supported. The secrecy in which Council decisions are taken adds to this problem. The democratic coupling back to the citizens of the Member States may be considered weak in comparison with the extent of competences which have been transferred from the national to the European level. The lack of competence of the EP, which is the only Community institution obtaining its legitimation

---

[95] Case 138/79 *Roquette Frères* v. *Council* [1980] ECR 3333, consideration 33; recently see Case C–41/94 *Council* v. *European Parliament* [1995] ECR I–4411, on the annulment of the budget due to the absence of an agreement between the Council and the European Parliament.

[96] Cf. D.G. Grimm, "Braucht Europa eine Verfassung?", *JZ*, vol. 50 no. 12 (1994), 581–91, at 582.

[97] With regard to European Union citizenship cf. J.Shaw, "European Union Citizenship: The IGC and Beyond", *European Public Law*, vol. 3 no. 3 (1997), 413–39.

[98] In *Brunner* the German Constitutional Court refers to the EP as an additional factor within the institutional structure of the EU supporting the democratic legitimation of the EU but fails to elaborate on this line of reasoning.

[99] E.g. J.-C. Piris, "After Maastricht, are the Community Institutions More Efficacious, More Democratic and More Transparent?" (1994) 19 *ELRev.*, 449–87; see also W. Steffani, "Das Demokratie-Dilemma der Europäischen Union. Die Rolle der Parlamente nach dem Urteil des Bundesverfassungsgerichtes vom 12. Oktober 1993" in W. Steffani/U. Thaysen, *Demokratie in Europa: Zur Rolle der Parlamente*, ZParl Sonderband 1/95, Westdeutscher Verlag, Opladen, 1995, 33–49, at 41.

[100] Similarly Huber, n. 81 above, at 354. Apparently different is M. Zuleeg, "Demokratie in der Europäischen Gemeinschaft", *JZ*, vol. 48 no. 22 (1993), 1069–74 who refers to the national Parliaments and the Treaties as the two sources of legitimation of Community power.

directly from the electorate, the dominant position of the Council, and lately also the role of the Commission of the European Communities (hereafter the Commission), have been at the centre of discussions focusing on the "democratic deficit" of the EU.[101] Different solutions have been offered. Proponents of further integration advocate the reconstruction of the institutional system by making the EP a truly legislative body along the lines of the national parliaments.[102] Others, while recognising a need for greater democratic legitimation of EU institutions, rather than envisaging a federal state with institutional structures known in the Member States, advocate the strengthening of mechanisms of accountability, e.g. through enhanced transparency in Council decisions which allows for the national parliaments to hold their executive branches to account.[103] The democratic deficit has also been associated with the lack of a genuine European public opinion and political debate on the European level without which even a reinforced EP cannot substitute for the feedback of the EU to the Member States provided for by the current institutional structure described above.[104] The examination of the democratic accountability of the ESCB and the ECB has to take into account this diverse structure of the EU.

1.2. Democratic accountability and central banks

It has emerged from the foregoing discussion that the concept of democratic accountability is closely linked with the concept of democracy itself. It is positively correlated to the principle of democratic legitimation which forms the basis of any delegation of power in a representative democracy. State power requires democratic legitimation, a feedback to the electorate. In many instances this feedback is weak, since the role of the electorate is limited to electing the legislative at regular intervals and, in some constitutional systems, the

---

[101] E.g. B. Boyce, "The Democratic Deficit of the European Communities", *Parliamentary Affairs*, vol. 46 no. 4, 458–77, summarises these discussions as a controversy about democracy, integration, and efficiency. She criticises in particular the Commission for being "unelected and largely unaccountable" (at 469).

[102] E.g. Le groupe permanent pour une Europe Démocratique, "L'Europe Attend", *RMC*, no. 404 (1997), 13–15. Also see European Parliament, Resolution on the Intergovernmental Conference of 14.04.1997 (OJ 1997 C115/165), considerations 13–15.

[103] See Harden, n. 89 above, 136 *et seq.*, who calls for the "extension of the European dimension of critical democracy"; P. Holmes, "From the Single European Act to Maastricht: The Creation of the European Union" in B. Einhorn/M. Kaldor/Z. Kavan, *Citizenship and Democratic Control in Contemporary Europe* (Edward Elgar, Cheltenham/Brookfield, 1996), 54–68, at 66, who states: "The 'democratic deficit' does not exist because 'Brussels' imposes things on member governments. Rather, the Member States find the Council of Ministers to be a convenient device to ignore their own Parliaments". See T. Christiansen, "Gemeinsinn und Europäische Integration. Strategien zur Optimierung von Demokratie- und Integrationszielen" in W. Steffani/U. Thaysen, *Demokratie in Europa: Zur Rolle der Parlamente*, Zeitschrift für Parlamentsfragen (ZParl) Sonderband 1/95 (Westdeutscher Verlag, Opladen, 1995), 51–64, 60 *et seq.*, argues that integration and democratisation have to be linked in order to provide for a legitimation of a supranational power.

[104] See Grimm, n. 96 above, 587 *et seq.*, with further references both in favour and against this view; see otherwise Zuleeg, n. 100 above, according to whom such a European public opinion already exists.

head or a part of the executive. The overwhelming part of the executive branch of government falls outside the scope of direct influence by the electorate. However, it is the executive which in many instances holds a dominant position. To be sure, the executive branch of government does not *per se* lack democratic legitimation, as legitimation is mediated to the holder of delegated power through the elected and thus democratically legitimised legislative.

Daintith makes the point that the need for the accountability of central banks derives from a "broader idea of democratic responsibility, which is common to all democratic constitutions".[105] Indeed, the basic argument for the democratic accountability of central banks is that they stand for the delegation of powers to independent unelected officials and that such a delegation of power is acceptable in a democratic society only if central banks one way or the other are accountable to democratically elected institutions.[106] The doctrine of the separation of powers, the principles of ministerial accountability, and parliamentary democracy as such are invoked against extensive central bank independence.[107] Central bank accountability has been described in dramatic terms a "fundamental political or even ethical demand for democracy".[108] However, in some instances such observations amount to hardly more than catchwords which fall short of providing an explanation why central banks should be subject to mechanisms of democratic accountability.

1.2.1. The rule-oriented and functional approach

Explaining the case for democratic accountability can be done from two points of departure. First, a rule-oriented approach can be taken by identifying the legal nature of a central bank and its position within a democratic system. A second, functional approach examines the task of central banks in the area of monetary policy and the powers which have been delegated to it in order to fulfil these tasks.[109] Both the rule-oriented and functional approaches overlap to

---

[105] T. Daintith, "Between Domestic Democracy and an Alien Rule of Law? Some Thoughts on the 'Independence' of the Bank of England", [1995] *PL*, 141–55, at 147; the same in "Between Domestic Democracy and the Alien Rule of Law? Some Thoughts on 'Independence' of the Bank of England" in Andenas/Gormley/Hadjiemmanuil/Harden (eds.), op. cit., Chap. 1, n. 5, 357–72.

[106] E.g. J.W. Crow, *Monetary Policy, and the Responsibilities and Accountability of Central Banks*, The Gerhard de Kock Memorial Lecture at the University of Pretoria, Bank of Canada, Ottawa, 1993, at 7; L.W. Gormley/J. de Haan, "The Democratic Deficit of the European Central Bank", *ELRev.*, vol. 21 (1996), 95–112, at 112; R. Caesar, "Die Unabhängigkeit der Notenbank im demokratischen Staat", *Zeitschrift für Politik*, vol. 27 no. 4 (1980), 347–77, 361 *et seq.*, with further references.

[107] E.g. E. Schokker, "De autonomie van de Centrale Bank; een vergelijking tussen Nederland en de BRD", *Maandschrift Economie*, vol. 48 no. 1 (1984), 41–55, at 50, who lists all of these arguments.

[108] B.C. Briault/A.G. Haldane/M.A. King, *Independence and Accountability*, Bank of England Working Paper Series no. 49, Bank of England, London, 1996, at 7.

[109] It has been pointed out in Chap. 1 that the scope of this study is the democratic accountability of central banks with regard to monetary policy. This is not to say however that functions outside the area of monetary policy do not also constitute the exercise of powers which call for mechanisms of democratic accountability. This is namely the case where a central bank is charged with banking supervision.

some extent. On the basis of this assessment it becomes possible to determine the extent to which the central bank requires mechanisms of democratic accountability.

Generally, central banks are a creation of Parliament, either initially having been set up or subsequently nationalised by an Act of Parliament. Defining the position of such a central bank within a given constitutional system proves to be difficult with regard to both the legal nature of the institution and its relationship *vis-à-vis* the three branches of government. This is reflected by the occasional ambiguity in the description of a central bank, where its legal position is sometimes described as "independent within government"[110] or "*Neben-regierung*" (sub-government).[111] In some instances the legal nature of the central bank as such is unclear and makeshifts such as "institution *sui generis*" are used to describe its status.[112] Interestingly, such problems do not only arise in connection with one type of constitutional system. As will be seen in the chapters hereafter, this applies to parliamentary democracies as well as to American democracy. It may be considered a common feature of all central banks which do not form an integral part of the executive branch of government that they fall outside the classical three-branch system of government featuring elements of checks and balances which form an important element in the legitimation of the power delegated to these branches. In the context of this legal approach the need for mechanisms of democratic accountability of central banks derive from their exceptional position *vis-à-vis* the democratically elected legislative and the executive. In so far as a central bank holds an independent position, mechanisms of democratic accountability are required in order to legitimise the position of the central bank within the constitutional system. This view is confirmed when taking a functional approach.

The need for mechanisms of democratic accountability may also be explained through the tasks which central banks perform with regard to monetary policy. Generally, monetary policy is defined as the control of the supply of money, and as such forms part of a broader definition of economic policy which is formulated and implemented by the democratically elected executive government. The central bank does not hold a neutral position within the system of government. With respect to monetary policy a central bank performs executive functions. It executes, i.e. implements, and possibly also develops, i.e. formulates, monetary policy on the basis of powers delegated to it by the legislature. However, since these functions are not performed by the executive branch of government itself, the accountability of executive activity through the legislative is narrowed. The initial act of delegation of monetary policy to a central bank through an Act of Parliament does serve as the basic democratic legitimation of the central bank in the constitutional system. In this respect some comments on the need of democratic accountability of central banks at times have a tendency

[110] Note in particular the discussion on the Fed in Chaps. 3 and 4.
[111] Note in particular the discussion on the Bundesbank in Chaps. 3 and 4.
[112] This is the case for the Banque de France, cf. Chap. 3 III.

to overshoot the mark. For example, Briault, Haldane, and King argue that "independence delegates responsibilities for monetary policy to an ultimately unelected authority—the central bank. So making this authority accountable for its actions insures against the 'democratic deficit' ".[113] Observations like this may be misleading in as much as the reference to the central bank as an "ultimately unelected authority" can leave the impression that the central bank lacks democratic legitimation due to the fact that its principal actors, i.e. members of the decision-making bodies, are not elected by Parliament. However, if this line of argument is followed, democratic accountability could not substitute for such a lack of democratic legitimation. Indeed, a central bank that fits this description would have to be considered incompatible with democracy itself as defined above because it is inherent in a democratic system that all state power has to be founded on the sovereign power of the people. A chain of legitimation must thus exist for all state power. In the case of central banks such a legitimation can be found in the legal basis of the central bank, which, at least for all the central banks examined in this study, is an Act of Parliament. As will be argued hereafter the right to enact new legislation or amend existing legislation can function—among others—as a mechanism of *ex ante* and *ex post* control by Parliament.[114] However, it is questionable whether this initial legitimation can be taken up as an argument to explain and/or even justify the absence of mechanisms of democratic accountability. It is sometimes argued that independent central banks constitute a democratic self-restraint by the democratically legitimised legislative which recognises its own tendency to (ab)use monetary policy for its own political ends, and thus tolerates or creates an independent central bank.[115] One step further, the need for the maintenance of "the stability of the existing democratic system" is thought to legitimise the absence of democratic mechanisms.[116] The logic which runs behind this argument seems to be that central bank independence provides monetary stability which in return is a necessary condition for a stable democracy. This would lead to viewing monetary stability as an essential precondition of democracy.[117] From this hypothesis it is only a small step to elevate central bank independence into the ranks of a democratic principle. It is not entirely convincing how the absence of democratic

---

[113] See Briault/Haldane/King, n. 108 above, at 7; similarly C. Johnson, "Memorandum submitted to the Treasury and Civil Service Select Committee" in Treasury and Civil Service Committee, *The Role of the Bank of England* (House of Commons Paper. Session 1993–4 ; 98–I, vol. 2), Report, together with the proceedings of the Committee, HC Session 1993/94 (HMSO, London, 1993), 187–91, at 188.

[114] Cf. Chap. 2 II 2.2.

[115] M. Deane/R. Pringle, *The Central Banks* (Viking, London, 1993), at 320; H.H. v.Arnim, *Staatslehre der Bundesrepublik Deutschland* (Verlag Franz Vahlen, Munich, 1984), at 342, with regard to the Bundesbank; Lastra, n. 65 above, at 479, with reference to a work by J.M. Buchanan, calls this the "Robinson Crusoe" paradigm.

[116] Lastra, n. 13 above, at 307; who nevertheless supports strong mechanisms of accountability.

[117] O.Pöhl, "Towards Monetary Union" in IEA, *Europe's Constitutional Future* 38 (1990), as cited in Lastra, n. 13 above, at 307, note 18.

mechanisms can actually promote or "stabilise" a democratic system. The one-time legitimation of an independent central bank by an Act of Parliament does not unhinge the basic principle according to which all executive power has to be accountable. If monetary tasks are removed from government, which itself has to be accountable, than an independent institution needs to be accountable too.[118]

1.2.2. The European dimension

It has been pointed out that the constitutional legal order of the EU is far from static or well defined. Yet, the ECB formulates and implements monetary policy independently on behalf of all participating Member States. It will thus exercise considerable power, power which will moreover affect the Member States with a derogation or the non-participating Member States respectively.[119] Despite their participation in the ESCB the national central banks remain separate legal entities in accordance with the respective national laws. However, the participating central banks are only allowed to act in accordance with the guidelines and instructions issued by the ECB.[120] The national central banks give up their competence for the formulation and/or implementation of monetary policy, with the consequence that any existing mechanisms of democratic accountability for the conduct of monetary policy at the national level become largely ineffective.[121] These mechanisms may not become completely useless though, since the governors of the national central banks are represented on the Governing Board of the ECB where all monetary policy decisions are taken. However, whether and to what extent the governors can be held accountable for their behaviour on the Governing Board of the ECB depends to a large degree upon the institutional structure of the ESCB and the ECB, in particular the decision-making process, and is furthermore restricted by Article 107 EC on the independence of the ECB, the national central banks, and the members of their decision-making bodies.[122] Other than this potential coupling back to the level of the Member States, the democratic accountability for monetary policy in EMU will rely on any existing mechanisms on the European level and thus on the democratic accountability of the ESCB and ECB itself.

2. Defining democratic accountability for central banks

In explaining the reasons for the need for mechanisms of democratic accountability of central banks in a democratic system some basic elements of a defini-

[118] See also e.g. Crow, n. 106 above, at 7.
[119] On the differences cf. Chap. 3 V 1.
[120] Art. 14.3. ESCB Statute.
[121] F. Amtenbrink, *Anmerkungen zur demokratischen Kontrolle von Zentralbanken in der Europäischen Währungsunion*, in *Europäische Integration- Schon eine "Union des Rechts"? Zwischen Erfolgsbilanz und Balanceverlust*, Almanach junger Wissenschaftler, Hans-Martin-Schleyer-Stiftung, V.Kongreß "Junge Juristen und Wirtschaft", Essen, 29.–31. Mai 1996, 16–17, with regard to the Bundesbank.
[122] For more details cf. Chap. 4 I.

tion of the democratic accountability of central banks have already emerged. Any evaluation depends to a large extent upon the definition of the areas of examination. Where the comparison of different institutions is involved, the definition of the terminology acts as a safeguard and yardstick for an equal approach to the different systems. From the observations on the discussion of central bank independence it has become clear that any analysis stands or falls with the definition of the terminology.[123] Consequently, the present section begins with an examination of the terminology of *democratic accountability*. Although the analysis of the existing contributions on the subject of central bank accountability reveals differences in the handling of the terminology a framework of what democratic accountability stands for in the context of central banks emerges. Thereafter, a set of common criteria which function as a yardstick for the evaluation of democratic accountability and which fill out the general framework are developed. These criteria become the basis of Chapter 4 and the examination of the central banks included in this study.

2.1. In search of a definition

Discussions on central bank accountability are frequently characterised by a lack of consistency in the handling of the terminology. In describing the relationship of the central bank *vis-à-vis* executive branch and/or legislative branch of government the terms "democratic accountability", "democratic control", "political accountability" and "political control" are applied.[124] The inconsistency in the terminology raises the question whether all of these terms actually have the same meaning. In other words, does control mean the same as accountability, and are the terms "democratic" and "political" interchangeable in this context?

The dictionary describes "control" as synonymous with check, test or verifying by counter or other evidence.[125] Moreover, control may stand for the exercise of straining or guiding influence. Thus, control may also stand for a system whereby the principal basically remains in charge. "Accountability", on the other hand, describes the quality of being accountable, liable or responsible. The term "accountability" is broader as it can also stand for the quality of being reckoned or charged/chargeable.[126] According to this meaning accountability may in particular be applicable to relationships where the principle has charged somebody else with the exercise of a certain task, thereby giving up the basic

---

[123] Cf. Chap. 2 I. Observations on a correlation between central bank independence and economic aggregates to a large extent rely on the evaluation of the level of independence of a central bank. This requires a definition of central bank independence.

[124] For an example of the different applications of the terminology e.g. J. Pipkorn, "Legal Arrangements in the Treaty of Maastricht for the Effectiveness of the Economic and Monetary Union" (1994) 31 *CMLRev.*, 263–91, at 281; Gormley/de Haan, n. 106 above, 95 *et seq.*; Eijffinger/de Haan, n. 8 above, 14 *et seq.*

[125] Webster's *Third New International Dictionary* (Merian-Webster Inc., Springfield, Ma, 1986).

[126] *The Oxford English Dictionary*, Vol. 1 (Clarendon Press, Oxford, 1970).

control. Control and accountability arguably concern different standards and/or qualities. Browder describes accountability on an abstract level as a mechanism applicable in the relationship between a holder of power and those who have the power to review:

> "For the party who is accountable, the heart of the matter is to explain as rational as possible the results of efforts to achieve the specific task objectives. For the party in charge of reviewing, the major objective will be to the matching of performance and attainment levels against their expectations as expressed in the task specifications and making a determination of their level of confidence in the steward and his efforts."[127]

Transferred to the present context, the central bank constitutes the accountable party who holds the power over monetary policy and either executive government and/or Parliament is the party in charge of review.[128] De Beaufort Wijnholds and Hoogduin refer to accountability as "the degree to which central banks explain or make visible their policies to Parliament and/or the public".[129] However, it has been pointed out that accountability also refers to the decision to maintain or withdraw confidence in the holder of the power, which in a democracy basically takes the form of parliamentary elections. Accountability includes the power to sanction sub-optimal performance and as such resembles more than a review of past performance. Thus accountability also stands for the evaluation of performance as a result of which sanctions may be imposed.[130] To this end Fischer observes that "the general notion of accountability is that there be *adverse consequences* for the central bank or the central banker for not meeting targets".[131] In the light of these elements of accountability a distinction can be made between continuing control of power and remedy after abuse of power.[132] On the one hand, continuing control of power includes instruments for the *ex ante* and *ex post* control of a central bank, such as the (*ex ante*) determination of rules and (*ex post*) reporting requirements. Remedies after abuse of power, on the other hand, refers to disciplinary actions in the event of central bank misconduct. Such actions can range from repressive sanctions, such as are provided by override mechanisms, to the revising of the legal basis of the central bank.

[127] "Introduction: Emerging Patterns of Administrative Accountability—A Point of View" in L.H. Browder, Jr. (ed.), n. 83 above, at 2.

[128] In the context of the legality of central bank action, moreover, the judiciary may play a role. Cf. Chap. 1 III.

[129] de Beaufort/Hoogduin, n. 41 above, at 81.

[130] A. Dunsire, *Control in Bureaucracy: The Execution Process* (Martin Robertson, London, 1967), as cited in R. Levaggi, "Accountability and the Internal Market", *Financial Accountability & Management*, vol. 11 no. 4 (1995), 283–96, at 287. Thus, when C. Hood, "Concepts of Control over Public Bureaucracies: 'Comptrol' and 'Interpolable Balance'" in F.X. Kaufmann (ed.), *The Public Sector* (Walter de Gruyter, Berlin and New York, 1991), 347–66, at 347, describes control as the "self-conscious oversight, on the basis of authority, by defined individuals or offices endowed with formal rights and duties to inquire, call for changes in behaviour and (in some instances) to punish" he actually provides a definition of accountability.

[131] Fischer, n. 39 above, 292 *et seq.*, italics added. For more details on targeting turn to the discussion of monetary objectives as criteria of democratic accountability.

[132] Presently following a distinction made by Hirst, n. 82 above, at 29, in the broader context of accountability in a democracy.

It has become clear in the context of the evaluation of central bank independence that an examination and evaluation of a central bank cannot be founded on legal provisions only.[133] Therefore, this study needs to focus on both formal and informal arrangements in order to consider the full range of mechanisms of accountability. These different arrangements may be referred to as mechanisms of *de jure* and *de facto* accountability.

Like the terms "control" and "accountability", the terms "political" and "democratic" are applied inconsistently.[134] The words are a reference to the type of accountability exercised and/or characterise the institutions involved. In a broad context democratic accountability in the first place refers to the relationship between the electorate and the elected, i.e. the legislative branch and possibly parts of the executive. Political accountability on the other hand describes in particular the legislative–executive relationship between Parliament and the executive branch of government.[135] Democratic accountability therefore first of all refers to the accountability of the central bank *vis-à-vis* democratically elected bodies but thereafter includes any democratically legitimised institution. Thus, a central bank does not have to be directly accountable to the electorate in order to be democratically accountable. On the contrary, political accountability could either refer to the accountability of the executive government for the monetary policy to the legislative branch or to the accountability of the central bank to the executive government. To be sure, democratic accountability is not the inverse of political accountability. Rather, the notion of political accountability may be considered as somewhat narrower in scope.

It already becomes apparent from the inconsistencies in the use of the terminology that a common definition of democratic accountability of central banks is missing. In most instances accountability is explained in the context of a particular central bank system and in the course of the evaluation of that system. Nonetheless, in some instances more abstract definitions are offered, which in one form or the other often resemble the elements of accountability identified above. Daintith differentiates between *normative* and *non-normative* control.[136] Normative control includes the evaluation of performance by reference to predetermined rules, whereas non-normative control involves accountability/answerability to a body (Parliament or the electorate itself) which examines and censures regardless of any established norms, and regardless of their absence ("appropriateness regardless of legality"). Daintith differentiates between legal institutions, i.e. courts, and democratic institutions, i.e. Parliament, arguing that these institutions make divergent use of the two forms of control. Legal institutions are commonly restricted to normative control,

---

[133] Chapter 2 I 2.2.

[134] For an example of differences in the application of the terminology see e.g. de Beaufort/Hoogduin, n. 41 above, at 81; Fair, n. 74 above, 8 *et seq.*; S. Weatherill/P. Beaumont, *EC Law* (2nd edn., Penguin Books, London, 1995), 656 *et seq.*

[135] K.Featherstone, "Jean Monnet and the 'Democratic Deficit' in the European Union", *JCMS*, vol. 32 (1994), 149–70, at 151, which refers to the classic executive–legislative model.

[136] Daintith, n. 105 above, 141 *et seq.*

whereas democratic institutions apply *ex ante* normative control in the shape of legislative powers, and also make use of normative and non-normative control through parliamentary accountability. Fischer identifies three basic areas concerning the accountability of a central bank, namely the type of accountability of the central bank (responsibility to meet certain goals for monetary policy, or otherwise at least explain its conduct publicly), the addressee of the responsibility within the bank (governor and/or monetary policy board), and the organs in charge of holding the bank accountable (elected officials).[137] With regard to the last point, Van Wijk differentiates between direct and indirect accountability, whereby the former refers to the legislative branch of government, i.e. Parliament, whereas the latter refers to the executive branch of government.[138] For Mancera central bank accountability consists of two elements, that is the banks responsibility to meet targets and its requirement to explain and justify its policy to the legislature and to the public.[139]

2.2. Towards common criteria for the evaluation of democratic accountability

The different aspects of democratic accountability which have emerged from the foregoing discussion can only function as a framework. In order to examine and evaluate the degree of democratic accountability of central banks concrete criteria have to be generated taking into account the different elements of this framework. Where different central bank systems are compared with regard to their degree of democratic accountability the criteria ensure that each central bank system is approached in the same way, using the same set of criteria. This forms the basis for a comparative analysis of the different banks. The ESCB and the ECB are evaluated—among others—against the background of this analysis. However, the application of common criteria to different central bank systems, situated against different constitutional backgrounds, with different institutional settings, and occasionally somewhat different tasks in the area of monetary policy, has certain consequences. So in order to take into account the different features of each central bank the criteria have to be defined broadly since a (narrowly defined) criterion which applies in the case of one particular bank may be totally irrelevant in another case. Consequently, it is questionable whether a ranking can be assigned to the criteria.[140]

Recently, a number of studies have suggested the application of criteria for the examination of the democratic accountability of central banks. With regard to the Bank of England, the Roll Report defines general elements of democratic control of a central bank, including statutory objectives of price stability, mech-

---

[137] Fischer, n. 39 above, 292–3.

[138] H.H. van Wijk, *De Nederlandsche Bank: functie en werkterrein* (Nederlands Instituut voor het Bank- en Effectenrecht, Amsterdam, 1988), at 20.

[139] Remarks by M. Mancera (Conference proceedings), in F. Capie *et. al.*, n. 39 above, 315–22, at 318.

[140] Cf. Chap. 5 IV.

anisms through which bank and government are answerable to Parliament for their actions and with respect to the objectives, and informing the electorate through enhanced public debate.[141] Eijffinger and de Haan,[142] and, based on the former, Gormley and de Haan[143] identify five criteria, namely the ultimate objective(s) of monetary policy, precision of specification of monetary targets, statutory basis for central bank independence, override mechanisms and the appointment of bank officials, on the basis of which they evaluate the democratic accountability of central banks. Neumann bases the control of central banks on three elements, including a legal basis defining the rights and obligations of the central bankers, the appointment of governors by government, and regular reporting about policy targets and implementation.[144] Similarly, Lastra identifies three different forms of accountability, including institutional accountability, disclosure, and performance.[145] With regard to the first element, it is emphasised that accountability of a central bank should include all three branches of government in order to provide the necessary democratic legitimation. Disclosure stands for the transparency of the central bank in the operations of monetary policy, whereas performance-based accountability demands the existence of statutory goals/targets against which the performance of the central bank can be measured. Briault, Haldane, and King have taken this one step further by constructing an index of central bank accountability on the basis of four criteria following the example of indices on central bank independence.[146] First, it is observed whether the central bank is "subject to external monitoring by Parliament". Secondly, it is observed whether the minutes of meetings to decide monetary policy are published. Thirdly, it is examined whether inflation or monetary policy reports are published, in addition to central bank bulletins. Finally, the existence of an override mechanism to be applied "in case of certain shocks" is observed. Here, a distinction is drawn between "explicit" and "implicit" override mechanisms, whereby the former is supposed to refer to the existence of an "escape clause" in the legal basis of the bank, and the latter refers to central bank systems where such a mechanism "is not *a priori* excluded".

In the following sections eight criteria are developed for the evaluation of the democratic accountability of central banks taking into account the general considerations on democratic accountability of central banks and the approaches to developing criteria to be found in the literature. None of these criteria stands

---

[141] Roll Report, n. 1 above, 19 *et seq.*

[142] Eijffinger/de Haan, n. 8 above, 15 *et seq.*

[143] Gormley/de Haan, n. 106 above, 97 *et seq.*; similarly J. de Haan, "The European Central Bank: Independence, Accountability and Strategy: A Review", *Public Choice*, vol. 93 (1997), 395–426.

[144] J. Neumann, "Commenting on Beaufort Wijnholds/Hoogduin: Central Bank Autonomy—Policy Issues" in J.O. de Beaufort Wijnholds/S.C.W. Eijffinger/L.H. Hoogduin (eds.), *A Framework for Monetary Stability* (Kluwer Academic Publishers, Dordrecht, 1994), 103–7, at 104.

[145] Lastra, n. 13 above, 324 *et seq.*

[146] Briault/Haldane/King, n. 106 above, at 44–5. For more details cf. hereafter Chap. 5.

completely by itself and in many cases different criteria are interdependent. Moreover, no single criterion by itself is decisive for the degree of democratic accountability of a central bank.

2.2.1. Legal basis

The legal basis refers to the initial act which sets up the central bank as an institution, describing its structure, and its tasks and powers. This will generally be in the form of an Act of Parliament. However, a central bank may also be recognised by the constitution of the respective country. Since this study features a rule-oriented evaluation of central bank accountability, the legal basis is important in the context of all criteria listed hereafter. However, the very nature of the legal basis as an Act of Parliament may provide the basis for a mechanism of democratic accountability by itself.

Whether and to what extent Parliament can change the legal basis of the central bank is important to observe, because the possibility of changing the legal basis can function as a mechanism by which a central bank can be held accountable by the democratically elected representatives of the electorate. Indeed, it has been argued that Parliament always holds the ultimate responsibility for monetary policy since it can change the legal basis of the bank.[147] Parliament's legislative power can function as a mechanism of *ex ante* control whereby Parliament sets the rules with which the central bank must comply. However, this does not amount to more than a one time legitimation of the institution, its position and tasks by the legislator, but means little in terms of accountability. More importantly, it may also function as a mechanism of *ex post* accountability because Parliament may decide to change the legal basis of the bank as a reaction to a certain behaviour. It can exercise its power to ensure that a certain behaviour is ruled out in the future, thereby sanctioning the bank's past actions.

It is equally important to observe the nature of the legal basis. First, a constitutional recognition of the central bank, e.g. its independent position, has implications with regard to Parliament's power to change the legal basis. Proposals for changes of the position of a central bank are inevitably linked to proposals for changes of the constitution itself. Regularly, a broader consensus is required in the legislative assembly to amend the constitution. It can be argued that a constitutionally recognised central bank bears a higher degree of legitimation than would otherwise be the case for a central bank which is based on an Act of Parliament only. This is at least the case in countries with a written constitution where the doctrine of the supremacy of Parliament does not prevail.[148] A constitutional recognition may imply a recognition of the central bank as a constitutional organ alongside other institutions such as e.g. the independent

---

[147] Crow, n. 106 above, at 8, who also observes that changing the legal basis is a "clumsy" procedure.

[148] This is not the case in constitutional systems without a written constitution where the principle of parliamentary sovereignty applies, such as is the case in the UK and New Zealand; cf. Chap. 4 I.

judiciary. Criticising the institutional arrangements of a central bank which is recognised by the constitution with respect to its democratic accountability has implications beyond the scope of the institutional structure of the bank itself. It carries a more fundamental criticism of the constitutional system as such.

In order to evaluate the legal basis as a criterion of democratic accountability, besides observing the legal nature of the statute of a central bank, the procedures for changing the legal basis have to be examined. The analysis of these procedures forms the basis for the evaluation of whether and to what extent Parliament's power to change the legal basis of the central bank can actually function as a mechanism of democratic accountability. In the context of this study the relevant legislative procedures are summarised, and any observations are restricted to those on the procedures necessary for amending the legal basis of a given central bank.

The provisions on the ESCB and the ECB introduced by the TEU have considerable implications for the central bank laws of the Member States, in particular with regard to provisions relating to the position of the banks *vis-à-vis* government and/or Parliament. This has already resulted in considerable amendments in case of some central bank systems in the run-up to EMU. These changes, and those which are required at the latest at the time of the establishment of the ESCB, have to be highlighted together with any constitutional difficulties that may arise or have already arisen in the context of changing the central bank laws.

2.2.2. Monetary objectives

Generally, monetary objectives can be described as the ultimate purpose at which a central bank aims with its monetary policies and its day-to-day performance. The characteristic of the objective(s) of a central bank in the field of monetary policy has much to do with the question of what a central bank can be held accountable for.

Several characteristics of monetary objectives can be distinguished. First, the legal nature of the monetary objectives needs to be observed. Central bank objectives can be fixed, *e.g.* statutory, or subject to discretionary decisions by the central bank or the executive government. A fixed monetary objective—as will be observed hereafter—is for example to be found in the case of the Banque de France where the statute explicitly refers to price stability. The counter-example has been until recently the Bank of England, as the Bank of England Act 1946 did not include any reference to the monetary objective of the bank. Apart from the rule *versus* discretion discussion, the difficulty involved with discretionary monetary objectives relate to the democratic accountability of the central bank. Where the government, and even more so where the bank, is free to decide on the monetary objectives two problems may arise. First, it is questionable whether it is legitimate in a democratic system to leave the decision on the general guidelines of monetary policy in the hands of an independent institution which is not subject to electoral or political accountability, in the form of general elections or ministerial responsibility respectively. It can also be argued that, if not the electorate itself, then it should be at least democratically elected officials who should decide which monetary objective(s) represent the public interest. The Roll Report concludes that:

> "In a democracy, a central bank cannot both be independent *and* free to determine its own objectives".[149]

The second problem resulting from the lack of a statutory monetary objective is the difficulty in giving a fair judgement of the performance of the bank with regard to monetary policy. The government (representing the principal) may hold formal mechanisms to hold the bank (representing the agent) accountable, but it is the agent in such a case which decides what it is being held accountable for. Moreover, it is not *per se* excluded in such a case that the bank may decide to change the monetary objective, thereby readjusting its own position and possibly covering any inconsistencies in its past performance. Under such circumstances it becomes very difficult to hold the bank accountable for monetary policy, since any discretionary goalposts may be rearranged in accordance with the preferences of the bank. This is similarly the case in the relationship between Parliament and the executive government, where the latter is in charge of such discretionary decisions.

Additionally, the number of central bank objectives needs to be taken into account. Generally, *single* and *multiple* monetary objectives can be distinguished. Moreover, in the case of multiple objectives it has to be observed whether they stand on an equal footing or whether a hierarchical order exists between them. The advantage of a single objective is that the central bank is not drawn into political judgements about how to make trade-offs between multiple objectives.[150] It becomes easier for the bank to explain its own conduct, since multiple objectives require subjective policy choices by the bank. Besides, the choice of a single objective also simplifies the monitoring of central bank performance because where the central bank has to make policy choices on the basis of multiple objectives it is effectively given discretion with regard to the decision of which pursued monetary policy is carried out. This is even more the case where the central bank decides on the goals of monetary policy in the first place. From an economic point of view it may also be argued that multiple objectives reduce the credibility of any anti-inflationary monetary policy, since the markets in the light of multiple objectives will anticipate a sudden change in priorities which is believed to result in higher inflation expectations and a built-

---

[149] Roll Report, n. 1 above, at 3, emphasis added; L.Poullain, "Für eine 'demokratische' Autonomie" in D. Duwendag (ed.), *Macht und Ohnmacht der Bundesbank* (Athenäum Verlag, Frankfurt .a.M., 1973), 36–52, at 38, argues that autonomy cannot stand for a central bank which is insulated from the political will, but rather that decisions are taken rationally on the basis of prescribed goals and in accordance with the law.

[150] Roll Report, n. 1 above, at 49.

in inflation bias.[151] Where multiple objectives exist, in the attempt to make the central bank accountable for its decisions, the preferences of the Bank may be judged against the (political) preferences of the reviewing institution. The disadvantages resulting from multiple objectives may be avoided to some extent by the introduction of a clear hierarchy according to which any secondary objectives may only be pursued as long as they do not conflict with the primary objective. Yet, for some even the existence of a clear hierarchy between objectives means that the bank has to give equal consideration to all objectives, since it is in practice judged on the basis of all objectives.[152]

However, even when a central bank is charged with a statutory *and* single or primary objective, it has a large discretion with regard to the question how this objective is defined. In other words if price stability is the primary objective of the central bank, as is for example, the case for the ECB, the question arises what rate of inflation is considered to be consistent with price stability.[153] This amounts to the issue whether any existing monetary objective should be quantified, that is should be defined by specific numeric targets for reaching the objective. Like the absence of a monetary objective, the absence of an unequivocal, *quantified* objective, laid down in the central bank statute or, otherwise, in a legally binding document, may decrease the effective accountability of the bank. A quantified monetary objective may be considered as the primary yardstick by which to judge the performance of the central bank in conducting monetary policy. The objectives and plans for monetary policy announced by the central bank may not be a full substitute in this respect, since they arguably do not have the same binding effect, and since the bank may decide thereafter not to give effect to its plans.[154] The need for a quantified monetary objective for a central bank is increasingly recognised. Goodhart is in favour of a quantified and statutory objective for containing inflation, arguing that the term price stability is too vague: "It will always be possible for the Governor to say: 'Well, we have lived in a very difficult world, doing everything we can to achieve price stability'".[155] Gormley and de Haan argue that "the accountability of the Central Bank must refer to policy outcomes, so that sanctions can be imposed if certain targets are not realized", and Crow reasons that: "the clearer and more precise the purpose of monetary policy, the more readily can responsibility for

---

[151] M. Lloyd, "The New Zealand Approach to Central Bank Autonomy', *Reserve Bank Bulletin*, vol. 55 (1992), 203–20, at 209.

[152] This has been identified as one reason for excluding a secondary objective for the Reserve Bank of New Zealand, cf. Chap. 4 II 3.

[153] With regard to the different interpretations cf. J. de Haan/F. Amtenbrink/S.C.W. Eijffinger, *Accountability of Central Banks: Aspects and Quantifications*, Center for Economic Research, Discussion paper, no. 9854, Tilburg University, May 1998.

[154] E.g. the practice by the Fed with regard to the semi-annual reports on its objectives and tasks under the House Concurrent Resolution 133 before 1978: cf. Chap. 4 II.

[155] Ch. Goodhart, *Minutes of Evidence*, in Treasury and Civil Service Committee, *The Role of the Bank of England* (House of Commons Paper. Session 1993–4 ; 98–I, vol. 2), Report, together with the proceedings of the Committee, HC Session 1993–4 (HMSO, London, 1993), 1–10, at 4.

conducting monetary policy be assumed by the central bank, because the more readily can the central bank be held accountable in a credible way".[156]

Generally, different approaches can be taken in quantifying the monetary policy objective of a central bank. The (statutory) *target approach* involves a statutory obligation of the executive government to define the objective by formulating and announcing targets for monetary policy, such as a target for money growth, or inflation. The *contract approach* differs somewhat from the target approach because rather than announcing targets itself, the executive government or Parliament concludes a contract with the central bank in which concrete targets for monetary policy are determined. Instead of imposing a certain definition of the monetary policy objective upon the central bank, the executive government and the bank agree upon a definition in form of a target. This may enhance the commitment of the bank to reach the target and *de facto* creates a personal responsibility of the central bank official signing the agreement, who presumably will be the governor of the central bank. Both the (statutory) target approach and the contract approach may specify any consequences resulting from failure to meet these targets, although the only central bank examined in this study where this is presently the case takes the contract approach.[157] Both approaches may include either a point target, i.e. 2 per cent inflation, or a target range, i.e. between 0 and 3 per cent inflation, whereby in the case of the former the room for manœuvring for the central bank may be considered smaller. Similar point or target ranges may equally be applied for a monetary objective other than price stability. Together with the target it should be specified whether and to what extent certain circumstances may justify a deviation from the target. On the one hand, this approach recognises that the conduct of monetary policy is far from being an exact science and that events outside the control of the central bank, such as severe economic shocks or even natural disasters, can have a negative influence on the implementation of the monetary objective and the meeting of the targets. On the other hand, by specifying the conditions for a deviation from the target the bank is cut off from finding other reasons for not meeting the targets; responsibilities become evident.

With regard to the consequences for not meeting the described or agreed upon target, it has been suggested that the governor as well as the decision-making board as a whole should be penalised. This may take the form of dismissal or financial sanctions.[158] However, whether such an individual or collective responsibility is feasible depends upon the institutional structure of the central bank. Individual responsibility is difficult to envisage in a central bank system

---

[156] Gormley/de Haan, n. 106 above, at 112; Crow, n. 106 above, at 8.

[157] C.E. Walsh, "Optimal Contracts for Central Bankers", *The American Economic Review*, vol. 48 no. 1 (1995), 150–67; Fischer, n. 39 above, at 292: "In the optimal contract the central bank is responsible for achieving the target inflation rate, and is penalised for failing to do so". The Reserve Bank of New Zealand may be considered as the reference system for such an contract approach, cf. Chap. 4 II, with further references.

[158] Fischer, n. 39 above, 292 *et seq.*, suggests a penalty in the form of a cut in the salary. In the case of the Reserve Bank of New Zealand the governor may be dismissed, cf. Chap. 4 IV.

where the governor at best is considered to be a *primus inter pares* and where monetary policy decisions are taken collectively. Yet, where decisions are taken collectively but not unanimously a financial sanctioning of all members of the decision-making board, including those who have not supported the particular decision(s) in question, fails to assign the responsibilities adequately. The solution to this dilemma seems to be to vest all decision-making power in the governor of the bank, who is then also accountable for the conduct of monetary policy. However, such a clear allocation of responsibility within the bank requires a hierarchical structure as it may only be possible in a centralised system. More decentralised central bank systems rely on a representative participation on the decision-making board.

It is often stated that central banks (are supposed to) act in the public interest. Some central bank statutes in this respect even include an explicit reference. However, how should the public interest be defined in order to judge whether the central bank has performed properly? Providing the central bank with a clear and unambiguous monetary objective and setting concrete targets for the purpose of defining that objective may be understood as one way of formulating the public interest.[159] To be sure, from the point of view of democratic accountability what the quantified monetary objective consists of is of secondary importance. Thus, although in the majority view price stability is the favourable monetary objective, it is not a precondition for an accountable central bank. Yet, the less a central bank is bound to specific objectives the more difficult it becomes to evaluate the bank's performance, since a suitable yardstick is missing. The evaluation of central bank performance is the central element of central bank accountability and is therefore essential. If the basic argument for central bank independence is the danger of government tampering with monetary policy, then a system by which both government and the central bank commit themselves to a single and quantified objective promotes both the independence of the central bank in pursuing this objective, as well as the accountability of the central bank *vis-à-vis* the executive government and/or Parliament, *and* even the accountability of the executive government in its approach towards monetary policy. What emerges from this is that central bank independence and central bank democratic accountability may not necessarily be irreconcilable.

Where central banks are criticised for focusing single-mindedly only on inflation rather than taking into account other economic aggregates, such as growth and employment, the fact that broad monetary objectives can have a deterring effect on the accountability of central banks is often neglected. The central bank may be obliged to promote a wider range of objectives but the

---

[159] In the same direction see F.S. Mishkin/A.S. Posen, "Inflation Targeting: Lessons from Four Countries', *Federal Reserve Bank of New York Economic Policy Review*, vol. 3 no. 3 (1997), 9–110, at 82, while emphasising the element of transparency: "Where monetary policy goals and performance in meeting them are publicly stated . . . the policies pursued cannot diverge from interests of society at large for extended periods of time, yet can be insulated from short-term political considerations."

built-in ambiguity and discretion makes it at least very difficult to hold the bank accountable for these objectives as a result of which the effective implementation of these objectives cannot be safeguarded. The present observations highlight that democratic accountability is not neutral with respect to the basic structure of the monetary objective, since the latter has an influence on the degree to which a central bank can be effectively held accountable.

2.2.3. The relationship with the executive branch of government

It results from the definition of democratic accountability that the executive branch is one of the three branches which may be in charge of holding the central bank accountable. Therefore, the relationship between the executive and the central bank is one important factor in determining the level of democratic accountability of a central bank. It is especially in this relationship that the democratic accountability of a bank may be based on legal provisions as well as on *de facto* arrangements. The potential conflict between central bank independence and democratic accountability may become most obvious with regard to this criterion because where explicit provisions on the independent status exist in the legal basis they may form the background against which the relationship between the executive government and the central bank is set. For this reason central provisions safeguarding the independence of the central bank in the field of monetary policy have to be observed as part of this criterion. The examination, moreover, has to include any formal mechanisms of consultation or participation, such as regular meetings between the central bank and the Ministry of Finance/Treasury, or the participation of government officials in meetings of the policy board of the bank. Moreover, informal contacts may exist. Naturally, where such formal and/or informal arrangements exist it has to be examined whether such mechanisms promote central bank accountability by providing information on the basis of which the performance of the bank can be evaluated. In fact, such arrangements may also become channels of political influence on the central bank, which does not necessarily coincide with a high degree of democratic accountability. In this context it has to be observed whether and to what extent executive government itself is accountable *vis-à-vis* the legislative branch for its handling of the relationship with the bank because to the extent to which the executive government can influence the central bank, government itself has to be accountable to Parliament.

However, the observations on the relationship between the central bank and the executive and to some extent also the legislative branch would be incomplete without including the appointment and dismissal procedures as well as override mechanisms. Due to their importance for the democratic accountability of a central bank, these two criteria are examined separately hereafter.

2.2.4. Appointment, reappointment, and dismissal procedures

Observing the (re-)appointment and dismissal procedures for central bank officials is a reference to the very basis of accountability as a mechanism between the person who has delegated the power, i.e. appointed the official, and the person entrusted with the delegated power, and the question whether the former continues or withdraws, i.e. dismissal, his confidence in the latter.[160] Although, in order to offer a comprehensive picture of the central banks examined in this study, a full account needs to be given of the appointment and dismissal procedures, the importance of these procedures differ. Arguably the most important mechanism of democratic accountability in this context is the dismissal of central bank officials. The dismissal procedure may amount to a mechanism of *ex post* accountability where a central bank official is dismissed on grounds of bad performance. Similarly, the reappointment of central bank officials in principle can function as a mechanism of *ex post* accountability by which a central bank official could be punished for his past performance. Against the background of these procedures, the appointment of central bank officials may be considered less important for democratic accountability. It can be argued that it amounts to an *ex ante* mechanism of control by choosing the persons entrusted with the power over monetary policy. Yet, the appointment of central bank officials may be better described as a mechanism of democratic legitimation rather than accountability, and it certainly plays a larger role in the context of central bank independence.[161]

Several distinctions can be drawn in the context of this criterion. First, the institution(s) in charge of appointing, reappointing and dismissing the central bank officials need to be identified. It needs to be observed whether and to what extent other institutions apart from the executive government (in particular Parliament) take part in the (re-)appointment and dismissal procedures. Arguably the most direct form of democratic accountability be it *ex ante* or *ex post* would be provided by putting the democratically elected Parliament itself in charge of the (re-)appointment and dismissal of central bank officials. On the other hand, it may be argued that this should be left to the democratically elected executive government which is in charge of the overall economic policy. This is the approach to be found in the case of most central banks. Yet, even where the executive government is in charge a broad participation of different constitutional bodies may ensure a balance of powers. Here, differences between centralist and federalist organised countries may emerge, as in the case of the latter both the Federal and State level may participate.

A number of elements surrounding the appointment and dismissal of central bank officials arguably determine the value of the procedures for the democratic accountability of a central bank. First, the term of office has to be observed. Supporters of independent central banks emphasise the importance of long and non-renewable terms for central bank officials. Yet, this may not be the optimal from the point of view of the democratic accountability of the central bank. On the one hand, short tenures may enhance the accountability of the central

---

[160] The present criterion refers only to political appointments and thus does not include normal employees of the bank.

[161] Cf. Chap. 2 I 2.1.3., on the organisational independence of central banks.

banker *vis-à-vis* the appointing body by giving the latter a chance to review the performance of the former in regular and short intervals. In that sense it could be proposed to introduce one-year terms (e.g. ending with the presentation of the annual report and accounts) with an option to be re-appointed. However, such an approach would result in a considerable inconsistency in the management of the bank and may press central bankers into short-term considerations in order to pass the annual "performance test". Instead, the tenures could be longer but renewable and/or coincide with the electoral circle. From the point of view of democratic accountability it makes sense to have renewable terms because the organ in charge of the appointments comes into a position where it can pass a judgement on the performance of the officials by either re-appointing or replacing them by new appointments. Besides, one may observe with Spitz that non-renewable terms have the potential of providing "lame-duck officials" with the opportunity "to go their own way", without having to worry about reappointment.[162] However, the option of reappointments is not without drawbacks. Proponents of central bank independence emphasise that the possibility of reappointment makes those central bank officials interested in a continuance of their career in the bank vulnerable to potential pressure by the organ in charge of (re-)appointments. Even if a clearly defined, quantified monetary objective exists the central bankers may have the desire to bow to political pressure. This is at least the case where the organ charged with the (re-)appointment is also in charge of evaluating the performance of the central bank and—if possible—dismissing central bankers on grounds of that performance. Mechanisms of democratic accountability may be abused to pursue political interests of the executive government. Another drawback for democratic accountability is that reappointment may result in the accumulation of power in the hands of the same officials over long periods of time.

Another building block of *ex ante* control may be the existence of provisions on the qualification of appointees. The existence of certain qualifications can ensure the proper conduct of monetary policy in as much as it may be observed that the presence of experts reduces the risk of an "arbitrary use of agency discretion".[163] A similar effect may be assigned to rules which determine whether and under which circumstances central bank officials may pursue activities outside the bank.

With regard to dismissal procedures, the most important question is under what conditions central bank officials can be dismissed. It has been pointed out that a dismissal may function as a sanction for poor performance by linking the tenure of central bank officials to policy results, i.e. meeting the predetermined monetary policy target. Moreover, clear provisions on the range of activities in which a dismissed central bank official may not engage immediately after his dismissal can ensure that the dismissal does not amount to a "golden parachute",

---

[162] E. Spitz, *Majority Rule* (Chatham House Publishers, Chatham, NJ, 1984), at 29.
[163] Majone, n. 87 above, at 26.

whereby the person cashes in on his or her inside knowledge by taking up a lucrative post in the private sector. However, where the dismissal is limited to cases of malfeasance dismissal procedures do not add considerably to the accountability of the central bank. To be sure, a broad provision allowing for the unconditioned dismissal of central bank officials at any time does not necessarily add to the democratic accountability of the central bank for the conduct of monetary policy either, since such a discretionary decision may be based on political considerations rather than on monetary policy performance. Such an unconditioned right of dismissal may seem appealing, as it implies that the ultimate responsibility for monetary policy lies with the executive government which—in most instances—is directly accountable to the legislative. However, such a provision can also obscure actual responsibilities, making the central bank the scapegoat for developments which are beyond its control, or which are not part of the monetary objective(s) of the bank. Under such circumstances dismissal is an ineffective mechanism for the democratic accountability of a central bank.

Finally, it should be noted that with regard to the (re-)appointment and dismissal of central bank officials, a distinction between the different organs of a central bank, namely the executive board and the policy board, has to be made. The present study focuses on the central bank organs charged with the monetary policy decision-making. In this context, the structure of the different central bank systems, i.e. central/federal, has to be observed, as it presumably influences the structure of the policy board. It has been suggested in this context that a diversity of representation exists between centralised and decentralised systems.[164] It has been pointed out that in a more centralised central bank system the governor may be personally responsible for the performance of the central bank with regard to monetary policy and the role of any existing monetary policy board may be essentially restricted to that of an advisory body. In a more decentralised system the monetary policy decisions may be taken by a formal vote in the monetary policy board whereby the governor of the central bank can be overruled. In the first system the individual responsibility of the governor prevails, whereas the second system is characterised by the collective responsibility of the members of the monetary policy board of the bank.

2.2.5. Override mechanisms

In the context of central banks override mechanisms generally describe instruments conferred upon government in order to approve, suspend, annul or defer central bank decisions or, one step further, to issue directions for the conduct of monetary policy.[165] The existence of override mechanisms has been described as a recognition of the government's ultimate responsibility and as the "true check

---

[164] Roll Report, n. 1 above, at 61.

[165] It should be remembered in this context that the opportunity for the legislative to change the legal basis of a central bank may also be understood as the ultimate override mechanism. With the amendment of central bank legislation the "code of conduct" of the central bank is changed, leaving only Parliament itself with the power to change it again.

on an autonomous central bank".[166] In many cases, even in countries with highly independent central banks, the legal basis includes a provision on the basis of which the executive government can overrule the central bank on monetary policy issues. Override mechanisms are not only highly relevant for the evaluation of central bank independence, but also for the evaluation of its democratic accountability. Whereas from the independence point of view the existence of an override mechanism is generally considered to decrease the position of a central bank, it can (but, as will be observed hereafter, does not necessarily have to) increase its democratic accountability. In examining override mechanisms attention has to be paid to the type of override mechanism, the procedure for its application, the period of its application and the areas of central bank functions. In analysing the override mechanisms, first the type of override mechanism has to be determined. Here it has recently been suggested that a distinction should be drawn between "explicit" and "implicit" override mechanisms which may be applied in case of certain shocks, whereby the former is supposed to refer to the existence of an "escape clause" in the legal basis of the bank, and the latter refers to central bank systems where such a mechanism "is not *a priori* excluded".[167] However, as will be seen with respect to the central banks examined in this study, the types of override mechanism are somewhat more graduated than this.

The second element which has to be observed is the procedure of application of override mechanisms. The simple fact that executive government can override the central bank does not necessarily add to the democratic accountability of monetary policy. Rather, the conditions under which an override mechanism can be applied should be laid down in detail. The necessity for detailed provisions on the conditions under which the central bank can be overridden increases with the seriousness of the override mechanism. Where the central bank can be directed to implement an economic objective the role of the executive government can amount to more than holding the bank accountable for its past performance because it may take over, thereby—in the short run—establishing itself as the monetary authority by determining the monetary objectives. Where the executive government to some extent is also entrusted with holding the central bank accountable for its conduct of monetary policy, a strong override mechanism can result in a loss of democratic accountability for the conduct of monetary policy, since the executive government in that instance is both the watchman and the one being watched. Whether and to what extent this potential conflict of interest arises depends on the existence of mechanisms of accountability for the check of the organ empowered with overriding the central bank, i.e. executive government, *vis-à-vis* other democratic institutions, e.g. Parliament.[168] Thus, where the executive government is given the right to sus-

---

[166]   Crow, n. 106 above, at 9; Mancera, in Capie *et. al.*, n. 39 above, 315–22, at 319.

[167]   Briault/Haldane/King, n. 108 above, 44–5.

[168]   The Roll Report, n. 1 above, suggests a procedure whereby "the government shall be able to suspend the objective of price stability only by a public instruction of limited duration which has received approval by Parliament".

pend the monetary objective of the central bank by requiring it to formulate and/or implement monetary policy in accordance with economic objectives other than those specified in the statute of the bank, the legal basis should specify conditions under which this override may be applied and should limit the period of time in which it may be applied. The executive government should have to justify the application of an override mechanism *vis-à-vis* Parliament.[169] From the point of view of the democratic accountability not only of the central bank, but also of the executive government, the most desirable form would be to make parliamentary approval a *conditio sine qua non* for the application of the override mechanism. This may be in particular desirable where the executive is not directly answerable to the legislative branch.[170] Another, somewhat less stringent, option may be to open the application of the override mechanism to a review either by the courts or a government body, other than Parliament, charged with deciding whether the application of the override mechanism was admissible. Moreover, where a single quantified monetary objective is overridden in favour of general economic considerations of the government, the necessary yardstick for an effective evaluation of the conduct of monetary policy is abolished. This goes hand in hand with a loss of transparency in monetary policy. It results from the foregoing that at least the procedure for the application for the override mechanism itself needs to be transparent. The decision, stating the reasons for the application of the override mechanism, should be made public.

In some respects the suspension of monetary policy decisions may provide a less radical override mechanism. Where monetary policy decisions can be suspended by the executive government for a certain period of time room for consultations is provided for which may lead to a peaceful settling of the differences. On the other hand, where the suspension is limited in time the central bank can basically refuse to co-operate and thereafter take whatever decision has been suspended in the first place.

What results from these observations is that in some instances there may be a trade-off between different mechanisms of democratic accountability, such as for example between an override mechanism on one side and a single quantified monetary objective and/or transparency in monetary policy on the other side. Override mechanisms can build a bridge between the central bank and the democratically elected institutions, i.e. Parliament and executive government. The override mechanism can function as a tool to hold the central bank accountable on a continuous basis by providing the government with the ability to intervene. However, at the same time it has to be ensured that the mechanism is not used as a tool for undesired political influence by the executive government and, even where its application is justified, that it does not result in a deterioration of the democratic accountability of the central bank or monetary

---

[169] E. George/R. Pennant-Rea, *Minutes of Evidence*, in Treasury and Civil Service Committee, n. 155 above, 22–37.
[170] E.g. Chap. 4 III.2. with regard to the USA.

policy respectively in other areas, with regard to other criteria.[171] The examination of the statutory arrangements regarding any existing override mechanism has to be completed by an examination of its efficiency as a mechanism of democratic accountability in practice. It needs to be seen whether and under what circumstances override mechanisms have been applied in the past, and, if this is not the case, what the implications of a non-appliance of such mechanisms are.

With the entering into stage three of EMU override mechanisms in the statutes of the Member States' central banks participating in the ESCB are considered incompatible with the EC Treaty, namely Articles 107 and 108 EC, and the ESCB Statute. Therefore, the legal bases of the national central banks participating in the ESCB are no longer allowed to include any provisions referring to override mechanisms. This may not seem like much of a loss, bearing in mind that the responsibility for the formulation and implementation of monetary policy is transferred from the level of the Member States to the European Central Bank. Yet it needs to be examined whether the ESCB Statute provides for an override mechanism along the lines of those to be found in some Member States, and if this is not the case, whether other mechanisms substitute for this mechanism of democratic accountability.

2.2.6. Relationship with Parliament

The relationship between the central bank and Parliament has to play a major role in any evaluation of the democratic accountability of central banks. It is Parliament which has delegated the power over monetary policy to the central bank, usually through an Act of Parliament. Consequently, Parliament should also be the principal actor charged with holding the central bank accountable. It has been pointed out that where a central bank has been established by an Act of Parliament, Parliament holds the ultimate mechanism for holding the central bank accountable, that is by changing its legal basis. In order to evaluate the significance of this power as a mechanism of democratic accountability it needs to be examined whether and to what extent Parliament makes use of it.

But Parliament is not restricted to introducing new or amending existing legislation. Rather, these measures usually stand at the end of a long opinion-forming process in which Parliament reviews existing policies and legal arrangements. This equally applies to monetary policy and the central bank. Regular reporting requirements to parliamentary committees as well as *ad hoc* inquiries into monetary policy matters add to the transparency of monetary policy and may provide the legislator with the information necessary for an effective oversight. Moreover, in parliamentary democracies Parliament can make use of ministerial accountability to review the position of the executive government in holding the central bank accountable. This amounts to an indirect accountability of the central bank itself.

---

[171] Against this background Deane/Pringle, n. 115 above, at 343, reject override mechanisms.

A problem similar to that in the relationship between the central bank and executive government exists in the relationship of the central bank with Parliament. On the one hand, from the point of view of democratic accountability it is desirable that Parliament plays a major role. On the other hand it is sometimes argued that the participation of Parliament may result in an undesirable politicisation of monetary policy.[172] First, the ruling party in the executive government may hold a majority in Parliament, a constellation often found in parliamentary democracies, such as e.g. Germany and the UK.[173] Under such circumstances the executive government may use its majority in Parliament to put political pressure on the central bank which it could otherwise not do. Secondly, even without such majority constellations Parliament may still use its power to pursue its own political ends, a reproach sometimes applied in connection with the position of the US Congress *vis-à-vis* the Fed.[174] The problem with the politicisation of monetary policy is that it does not necessarily provide for an effective degree of democratic accountability. Although it is the foremost task of politicians as representatives of the electorate to pursue the public interest, which should then become the yardstick for the review of the central bank performance, this may not always be the case. Yet it is presently suggested that such "risks" involved with a meaningful role of Parliament in the democratic accountability of the central bank can be minimised through the introduction of a clear yardstick against which the performance of the central bank has to be judged. This way the possibility of politically influenced interpretations of what exactly the objective of the central bank should be is minimised. Moreover, the introduction of a clear set of rules on the conduct of this parliamentary oversight, and on the possible sanctions which may be applied, can reduce the risk of political pressure. Rather than following a self-imposed abdication from monetary policy in order to forestall criticism of the politicisation of monetary policy, Parliament should impose clear rules on itself regarding the way in which it holds the central bank accountable. The democratic accountability of the central bank to Parliament should function as a constant reminder for the bank that it exercises monetary policy on behalf of the democratically elected Parliament which, at least in the national context, has delegated—but not abrogated—these powers.

2.2.7. Transparency

In the context of this study the term transparency in general describes the openness in which a central bank conducts monetary policy. First, transparency itself could amount to a mechanism of democratic accountability. If an independent central bank has gained the confidence of the general public, a legislator, planning to change crucial central bank provisions, may face opposition from

---

[172] E.g. Neumann, n. 144 above, at 104.

[173] This is highlighted by Lastra, n. 13 above, at 327, who suggests the strengthening of minorities in Parliament as one possible solution to this problem.

[174] Cf. Chap. 4 VI.

general public. On the other hand, a central bank which does not have the general public's confidence may face the amendment of its legal basis by a Parliament which comes under public pressure.[175]

Therefore, transparency may also result in a greater accountability to the general public. It is little surprising in this context that transparency has also been recognised by proponents of central bank independence as an important element enhancing the credibility of the central bank in the financial markets.[176] Yet, while transparency provides an important link to the general public which can result in concrete action by Parliament it cannot provide by itself for a sufficient degree of democratic accountability, thereby substituting other mechanisms of accountability. In this context the potency of transparency as a constraining mechanism seems to be overestimated by some. The underlying assumption seems to be that, once provided with sufficient information, the financial markets provide an adequate mechanism of accountability in the form of a loss of credibility of the central bank in case of poor performance.[177]

Transparency is also a prerequisite for other mechanisms of democratic accountability. Whatever other arrangements on the democratic accountability of the central bank may exist they are limited in their scope without transparency because information on the central bank is crucial for the evaluation of its performance and thus for holding the bank accountable. Transparency has to be considered as the cornerstone to democratic accountability.[178] As Day and Klein note: "effective scrutiny implies effective access to information".[179] Yet, there may be a limit to access to information. In principal–agent theories asymmetric information between the principal and the agent resulting from the incapability of the former effectively to monitor and assess the actions and information provided by the latter, due to the complexity of the structure, has been identified as one of the central problems. Indeed, it has been argued that an uneven allocation of information stands in the way of a complete oversight of a public bureaucracy.[180]

---

[175] Henry Ford, Sr., as cited in W. Greider, *Secrets of the Temple* (Simon and Schuster, New York, 1987), at 55, seems to have referred to this when making his rather famous observation on the Fed: "It is well enough that the people of the nation do not understand our banking and monetary system for, if they did, I believe there would be a revolution before tomorrow morning".

[176] E.g. J. Nell, "Central Banks and the News", *Central Banking*, vol. 6 no. 4 (1996), 79–83. It has also been pointed out that a loss of credibility may also result in a decline of economic performance, as some authors—pointing towards the Bundesbank as an example—recognise a correlation between central bank credibility and the success of central bank monetary policy. E.g. Grilli/Masciandaro/Tabellini, n. 10 above, at 185.

[177] E.g. D.G. Mayes, *Accountability for the Central Bank in Europe*, conference paper prepared for the 11th Lothian Conference (A Central Bank for Europe), 19 November 1997, Whitehall Place, London.

[178] Briault/Haldane/King, n. 108 above, 10–12, while referring to transparency as part of a broader definition of accountability use the terms transparency and accountability parallel.

[179] P. Day/R. Klein, *Accountabilities: Five Public Services* (Tavistock Publications, London/New York, 1987), at 22.

[180] S. Gates/J. Hill, "Democratic Accountability and Governmental Innovation in the Use of Nonprofit Organisations", *Political Studies Review*, vol. 14 no. 1/2 (1995), 137–48, at 139, with further references.

The degree of transparency of a central bank system is determined by different factors. On a general level the whole structure of a central bank can have an influence on the level of transparency. The clarity of the legal basis, e.g. with regard to the monetary objective, and the complexity of the decision-making processes within the bank are important factors influencing the level of the overall transparency of the central bank. The more straightforward the provisions governing the central bank and the simpler its institutional structure, the more accessible the decision-making processes within the central bank become for outsiders and the easier it is to judge its performance. It may be observed with Deane and Pringle that "an open democratic society has the right to demand a broad degree of understanding of what central banks do and how they do it".[181]

Apart from these general considerations the transparency of the central bank depends upon whether meetings of the decision-making bodies of the bank are open to the public, and/or whether and to what extent these bodies, those deciding on monetary policy issues, are required to publish minutes of their meetings and/or the (reasoned) decisions they have taken.[182] Where the reasons for a certain monetary policy decision are open and the proponents and opponents of a particular decision become known it is easier to make a judgement and to hold central bank officials and, in case of a participation on the monetary policy board of the bank, government officials accountable for their behaviour. In this context it is sometimes argued by central bankers that the secretiveness of the deliberations on monetary policy is necessary for open and candid discussions on monetary policy issues and, moreover, that public meetings or an immediate disclosure of deliberations in many instances can frustrate the effective implementation of monetary policy measures decided upon in these meetings.[183]

Central banks should also be required to report at regular intervals in particular on their past performance and future plans for monetary policy in accordance with the monetary objective. This is even more important where a clear monetary objective is missing, because in such cases past statements of the central bank may be the only basis on which the performance of the bank can be judged. However, there may be a limit to the degree of transparency that such improved reporting requirements can provide for. Fischer observes that the actual degree of transparency resulting from the publication of monetary policy reports will depend on the incentives of the central bank, whereby a more dependent central bank may have a greater incentive to use the reports to make public its own views and possibly put pressure on government.[184]

---

[181] Deane/Pringle, n. 115 above, at 313.

[182] Majone, n. 87 above, at 26, concludes that transparency in the decision-making is one of the common principles to secure accountability of non-majoritarian institutions.

[183] Cf. e.g. the remarks by different central bankers in Capie *et al.*, n. 39 above, 252 *et seq.*, and Chap. 4 VII 1 and Chap. 5 I 2.1.

[184] A. Fischer, "New Zealand's Experience with Inflation Targets" in L. Leiderman/L.E.O. Svensson (eds.) *Inflation Targets* (CEPR, London, 1995), 32–52, at 38.

2.2.8. Budgetary accountability

A central bank must also be held accountable for the way in which it manages its finances. The budgetary position of a central bank is always recognised as an important indicator for the degree of independence of central banks, but sometimes neglected as a criterion for their degree of democratic accountability. This is rather surprising, bearing in mind that central banks are usually publicly-owned institutions. But even where this is formally not the case, it is recognised that the central bank fulfils public functions, in which case any profits should also belong to the public. The fact that most independent central banks finance themselves through financial market operations cannot be invoked against budgetary accountability, since at least in the case of all central banks examined in this study their legal bases include provisions on the profit distribution to the government.[185] Therefore, the central bank should be accountable for the way it manages its finances. Generally, budgetary accountability could take place *ex ante* in the form of a parliamentary appropriation process, or *ex post* in the form of a review of the accounts. With regard to the first point it can be generally observed that independent central banks usually do not depend on the government's general budget for their financing. Parliament's traditional power to approve the government general budget does not extend to the central bank and thus cannot be applied to it as an *ex ante* control mechanism, and also not as a mechanism to hold the bank accountable for past performance.[186] Only recently, in the case of the Reserve Bank of New Zealand, has a new approach been taken in giving Parliament a role in the budget of the central bank.[187]

Other mechanisms through which the central bank can be held accountable for its financial behaviour include making the finances of the bank subject to a review by a court of auditors. Where a court of auditors considers an institution independent from Parliament and government, concerns about an abuse of budgetary control to put political pressure on the central bank are secondary. Here, *ex post* budgetary accountability could even fulfil a function beyond holding the bank accountable for its budget behaviour as such. In principle it could also be applied to judge the conduct of monetary policy by reviewing the monetary policy operations of the bank. However, it will be observed that this approach is usually considered to be in contradiction to the independence of the bank with regard to monetary policy.[188] Another option is the operation of internal or external auditors to review the finances of the central bank and issue a report. Finally, the bank can be obliged to publish and/or forward to Parliament financial statements on a regular basis, which then become subject to review by Parliament. The basic problem facing all of these approaches is the absence of

[185] For details cf. Chap. 4 VIII.

[186] In this context Rogoff, n. 28 above, has proposed to use the budget as a tool to commit the banker to an anti-inflationary policy, by making it contingent on the state of the economy which supposedly influences the incentive which the central banker faces in choosing the rate of inflation.

[187] For details cf. Chap. 4 VIII 2, and Chap. 5 II 4.

[188] Cf. Chap. 4 VIII.

any clear yardstick for the evaluation of the financial behaviour of the central bank apart from common accounting practices. Therefore, the central bank is generally not restricted in the amount of money it spends nor in the type of operations which are covered by that.

3. Conclusions

It has emerged from the theoretical discussion on democratic accountability and democracy that democratic accountability and democratic legitimacy are linked. In fact, it may be argued that democratic legitimation in some respects is mediated through democratic accountability. In the *trias politicas* of governmental powers the exercise of monetary policy is commonly associated with the executive functions.[189] From a legal point of view the delegation of powers over monetary policy to an independent institution outside this system of government has to be justified against the background of the basic democratic principles. The basic case for the democratic accountability of central banks is little disputed. It is generally recognised that the nature of the tasks performed by the central bank, i.e. monetary policy, and the independent position of the central bank in many countries calls for such mechanisms. As Crow observes 'the greater the *responsibilities* assigned to the central bank, obviously the more important it is to have sound arrangements for accountability".[190] By the same token it can be said that the more *independent* a central bank is within a given constitutional system the greater the need for democratic accountability.

While the basic case for democratic accountability has been recognised, concrete definitions of what are considered to constitute mechanisms of democratic accountability for central banks vary. This can already be observed with respect to the terminology. Control forms one element of accountability, which moreover stands for remedies after abuse of power. The difficulty in generating and defining criteria results from the differences in the constitutional systems in which central banks are situated. In connection with the evaluation of different central bank systems the question arises whether there is one sole benchmark for judging central bank systems which are set in different constitutional environments.

III. ON THE RELATIONSHIP BETWEEN CENTRAL BANK INDEPENDENCE AND DEMOCRATIC ACCOUNTABILITY

There is a common perception of the relationship between independence and democratic accountability in the sphere of central banks which may be

---

[189] The trichotomy of governmental powers stands for the principle of the separation of the constitutional powers.

[190] Crow, n. 106 above, at 7, italics added.

summarised by the comments of Brentford, who refers to a "fundamental trade-off", whereby "substantial accountability rules out independence".[191] It is the inverse of this relationship, i.e. independence rules out substantial accountability, which seems to rule out the presence of both concepts at the same time. Yet, it is questionable to what extent this suggested negative correlation between independence and democratic accountability actually amounts to an inescapable pattern. Put differently, does one have to choose either an independent *or* accountable central bank?

The reason independence and democratic accountability are seemingly incompatible concepts is the tendency to overstate the importance of these concepts and the effects they have when examined apart. On the one side, the depolarisation of monetary policy through central bank independence, as often suggested by the promoters of an independent central bank, may not be such a straightforward concept. At best a central bank is not a politicised institution inasmuch as it is independent of the executive and legislative branch of government. However, a central bank does not operate in a political and social vacuum. Its decisions carry political implications in addition to economic and social ones. Central banks are in many instances more than passive bystanders who stubbornly pursue their monetary objectives. At times they can be found actively taking part in political discussions (e.g. through formal and informal channels with executive government, and the general public at large). Moreover, as can be seen in the case of the Fed, a central bank may even lobby actively among politicians and interest groups to prevent the introduction of legislation which it considers undesirable. Here, a central bank abandons the role of a neutral institution, charged with monetary policy, and becomes an active opponent of Parliament. The boundaries between the central bank as the guardian of the currency and an active political power become blurred. While an independent central bank may be insulated from outside pressure on monetary policy, this is not to say that the central bank does not exercise such influences itself. An institution which takes part in the democratic process to such an extent has to be subject to mechanisms of democratic accountability because otherwise, taking into account the magnitude of its tasks, a central bank could indeed become an unaccountable fourth branch of government. Mechanisms of democratic accountability form a prerequisite for granting a central bank independence. From this point of view democratic accountability does not in the first place constitute a restrictive mechanism limiting the independent position of the central bank, but rather a validating mechanism, legitimising the independent position of a central bank. In this respect the phrase "accountable independence" appears one-sided, as it puts the emphasis on a restrictive effect of accountability.[192]

---

[191] P. Brentford, "Constitutional Aspects of the Independence of the European Central Bank" (1998) 47 *ICLQ*, at 108; Majone, n. 87 above, at 22, suggests that the dilemma that either an institution forms part of the executive government and thus cannot be independent, or is independent but not really accountable, is caused by the traditional theories of "political control".

[192] A term applied by Lastra, n. 65 above.

At the same time promoters of strong mechanisms of accountability have to recognise that mechanisms of accountability lose their purpose where the central bank is effectively prevented from pursuing a sound monetary policy without the danger of being overridden on any grounds. The economic costs potentially resulting from a monetary policy which is determined in the political arena have been observed.[193] Besides, a dependent central bank is not *per se* also a fully accountable central bank, since this only results in a transfer of responsibility, and as the decisions are taken elsewhere also the need for mechanisms of accountability arises elsewhere, e.g. at the ministerial level.

Reflecting on the findings of this study, the discussion on the relationship between central bank independence and democratic accountability is revisited in the final chapter of this study.[194]

---

[193] Cf. Chap. 2 I.
[194] Cf. Chap. 5 IV.

3

The Central Banks—an Overview

Examining and comparing central banks with regard to their democratic accountability on the basis of criteria imposes a strict guideline for examining each system. These criteria function as a magnifying glass, highlighting the relevant features in each system. Consequently, general descriptions of the central banks have to be excluded as much as possible in order not to water down the real issues at hand. Such a concentrated analysis, however, requires the reader to have a basic understanding of the central bank systems. Therefore, an overview of the institutional structure and the tasks of the examined seven central bank systems is provided below. This overview may be considered as a point of reference for the remainder of this study.

In addition, a summary of the historic development of each central bank system is included. Not only does this summary add to the basic understanding of each system but it forms part of a comprehensive understanding of the existing mechanisms of democratic accountability. Central bank systems, and for that matter their degree of accountability, are at times the product of historic developments, reflected in the legal bases and/or the practical arrangements of the system. In this respect the ECB takes a special position as compared to the other central banks. Although it has a legal history as far as its establishment is concerned and, moreover, in many respects is influenced by the historic developments and experiences of central banks in the Member States, it does not resemble a historically grown institution in itself. This has to be recalled when analysing the degree of democratic accountability of the ECB.

I. BANK OF ENGLAND

Until recently the Bank of England carried out monetary policy under the supervision of the Treasury and, more particular, the Chancellor of the Exchequer. It was for the executive government to determine monetary policy and to be responsible for its conduct in Parliament. Consequently, economists gave the Bank of England low ratings with regard to its independence.[1] Since September 1992, following the suspension of the UK's membership of the European exchange rate mechanism (ERM),[2] new arrangements were introduced by the government to give monetary policy a more formal basis by announcing infla-

---

[1] Cf. table 1.
[2] The UK participated in the ERM between 8 Oct. 1990 and 16 Sept. 1992.

tion targets and introducing (independent) inflation reports by the Bank of England, and, eventually, by leaving the Bank some discretion on the timing of the implementation of monetary policy decisions. In 1997 the new Labour government announced considerable changes in the institutional structure of the Bank of England, introducing for the first time a statutory monetary objective and granting the Bank operational independence. The UK has effectively excluded itself from the provisions on EMU, reserving itself a right to opt into the EMU at a later time.[3] Taking into account the likelihood of a British participation in EMU by the beginning of the next century these institutional changes are important, since they bring the Bank of England closer in line with the requirements for national central banks participating in the ESCB set out in the EC Treaty and in particular Articles 107 and 108 EC.

1. Historic development

The Bank of England embraces a history of more than 300 years. In contrast to other central banks examined hereafter the history of the Bank of England to a very large extent stands for continuity.

1.1. Creation and evolution

In one respect the foundation of the Bank of England can be found in the so-called Nine Years War between England and France between 1689 and 1697. With the government's growing difficulties in financing the war a new source of financing was needed. William Paterson, a Scottish promoter and financier, first proposed the establishment of a national bank. The Bank was established in 1694 by an Act of Parliament as a joint-stock company under the title "The governor and Company of the Bank of England" and, thereafter, was granted a royal charter on 27 July 1694.[4] A Court of Directors consisting of a governor, a deputy governor and 24 other members was put in charge of the management of the Bank of England. It was elected by the holders of the Bank of England stock which came together annually in the so-called *General Courts of the Bank Proprietors.*[5] This practice of appointment continued in general until the nationalisation of the Bank in 1946.[6]

Since 1725 the Bank of England was acting as a note-issuing bank with banknotes issued in printed denominations for the first time. In the light of the

---

[3] Cf. Protocol on certain provisions relating to the United Kingdom of Great Britain and Northern Ireland, annexed to the TEU.

[4] Hereafter referred to as Bank of England Act 1694.

[5] With the gradual change of the Bank's role from a simple private corporation to a public institution, the importance of the General Courts vanished.

[6] The procedures underwent numerous changes, e.g. the rotation of chairs, the procedures of recommendation (by 1941, proposals for Directors were put to the Chancellor of the Exchequer as was the case in the appointment of J.M. Keynes).

absence of a clear mandate in the charter of the Bank the authority to issue banknotes was simply assumed.[7] From 1826 the Country Banker's Act allowed the Bank to open branches anywhere in England.

The Bank Charter Act of 1844 acknowledged the Bank's *de facto* transformation from a private corporation towards a public institution. It separated the banking operations from the note-issuing operations by obliging the Bank to hold separate accounts and to produce a separate weekly summary of both accounts. Moreover, the Bank Charter Act of 1844 tied the note-issuing to the size of the Bank's gold reserve expected for a fiduciary issue of £14 million, and endorsed a monopoly of the Bank of England as the sole note-issuing bank.[8]

The functions of the Bank of England were twofold. On the one hand, representing a private corporation, the Bank undertook business for banking customers, such as—among others—the discount market. At the same time it operated as a banker to the government, acting as its financial agent and, increasingly, advising and giving effect to the government's policies. Moreover, the Bank gradually developed into a bank of last resort.[9] The Bank was relatively independent from government in its operations for most of the time prior to its nationalisation. Nevertheless, despite the fact that the Bank of England was a joint-stock company owned by private shareholders and was therefore not part of the administrative system,[10] Congdon describes the position of the Bank of England *vis-à-vis* government as being "operationally independent from both Crown and Parliament, but . . . ultimately answerable to Parliament".[11] This assessment is based on the fact that the Royal Charters, which provided the Bank with its privileges, had to be renewed at regular intervals by Parliament which took the opportunity to review the performance of the Bank. Nevertheless, on some occasions the government wanted to tighten its grip on the Bank. One such example occurred towards the end of World War I

---

[7] P.L. Cottrell, "Bank of England" in M. Pohl/S. Freitag (eds.), *Handbook on the History of European Banks* (Edward Elgar, Aldershot, 1994), 1190–2, at 1190. It has to be noted, however, that the Bank of England was not the only note-issuing institution for a considerable time. In fact, until 1921 other bank institutions also issued notes, and in some instances even the Treasury issued banknotes.

[8] The Gold standard had been officially adopted in 1816 and was formally abolished in Mar. 1919, and reinstated in modified form in May 1925. The pound sterling was statutory defined in terms of a fixed quantity of gold.

[9] A. Cairncross, "The Bank of England: Relationship with the Government, the Civil Service, and Parliament" in G. Toniolo (ed.), *Central Bank's Independence in Historical Perspective* (Walter de Gruyter, Berlin and New York 1988), 39–72, at 42, according to whom this was mainly achieved through the development of the Bank rate as an instrument for regulating the flow of credit. But already before that (e.g. during the financial crisis following the Seven Years War between 1756–63) the Bank acted as banker of last resort.

[10] R.S. Sayers, *The Bank of England 1891–1944*, Volume 2 (Cambridge University Press, London, 1976), at 593, finds evidence that the Bank had acted more or less as a public institution since the late 19th century.

[11] T. Congdon, *Memorandum submitted to the Treasury and Civil Service Select Committee*, in: Treasury and Civil Service Committee, *The Role of the Bank of England*, (House of Commons Paper. Session 1993–4; 98–I, vol. 2), Report, together with the proceedings of the Committee. HC Session 1993–4, HMSO, London, 1993, appendix 25, 200–1.

when Prime Minister Asquith asked the governor of the Bank Cunliffe to make a written promise: "that during the War the Bank must in all things act on the discretion of the Chancellor of the Exchequer and must not take any actions likely to affect credit without prior consultation with the Chancellor". Eventually, the governor agreed to make the statement: "so long as I am governor of the Bank I shall do my utmost to work loyally and harmoniously with you and for you as Chancellor of the Exchequer . . . ".[12] Before World War II once again the government of the day wanted to ensure its control over the Bank and in 1937 the governor of the Bank at the time, Norman, declared: "I am an instrument of the Treasury".[13] Despite this gradual change in the relationship between the Bank and the government, still no statutory provisions on this relationship existed. This was bound to change with the nationalisation of the Bank of England.

1.2. Nationalisation

As part of a general nationalisation policy the Bank of England was transferred into public ownership by the Bank of England Act 1946.[14] The capital stock of the Bank of England was transferred to the Treasury through compulsory acquisition of shares by the government. The stockholders were provided with an equivalent amount of so-called Government stocks which had been issued for this occasion.[15] With respect to the institutional arrangements, the Bank of England Act in many respects gave statutory form to the previously existing arrangements in practice. Indeed, the Bank of England Act 1946 may be characterised as being affirmative, rather than innovative. Until very recently the Bank of England Act 1946 still constituted the legal basis of the Bank of England. It has been pointed out that the Chancellor of the Exchequer, and thus not the Bank of England, took the final decisions on monetary policy. The role of the Bank was effectively confined to that of an expert adviser and to implementing monetary policy according to the directions of the Treasury. Since the Treasury was effectively in charge of monetary policy the Chancellor of the Exchequer was in principle fully responsible to Parliament for the conduct of monetary policy. It is thus not surprising that the Bank of England Act 1946 did not include any reference to the monetary policy objective of the Bank. The Bank remained managed by a Court of Directors consisting of a governor, one deputy governor, as well as four executive and 12 non-executive directors.

---

[12] Cited in Cairncross, n. 9 above, at 45.

[13] Cited in F. Capie/Ch. Goodhart/N. Schnadt, "The Development of Central Banking" in F. Capie *et al.*, *The Future of Central Banking* (Cambridge University Press, Cambridge, 1994), 1–231, at 130.

[14] Bank of England Act 1946 of 14 Feb. 1946 (9 & 10 Geo 6 c27), reprinted in Lord Hailsham of St. Marylebone (ed.), *Halsbury's laws of England*, Vol. 3 (1), (4th edn., reissue, Butterworths, London, 1989), para. 1–8. Also Bank of England Charter of 1 Mar. 1946, Cmd. 6752.

[15] Ss. 1(1)(a) *et seq.* Bank of England Act 1946.

The non-executive Directors had a special position within the Court of Directors as they did not work on a full-time basis in the Bank, but commonly participated in the conduct of other—private—business outside the Bank of England. This arrangement served a specific purpose since the non-executive directors did not take part in direct operational decisions, but rather acted as expert advisers to the Bank and especially to the governor of the Bank who made use of the experiences and knowledge which the non-executive directors had in their fields of business. However, it was also recognised that the engagement of non-executive directors in business activities outside the Bank could lead to conflicts of interest and, more specifically, had the potential that certain sensitive market information could leak to the outside. Therefore, ever since the findings of the Radcliff Committee,[16] it had been accepted that deliberations involving sensitive market information, such as the change in Bank rates, should take place only between the governor and deputy governor, or, in the case of some policy matters, in the close circle of the Committee of Treasury.[17]

The Committee of Treasury was the senior standing committee of the Bank. Its name originated from the early years of the Bank's history, when its main business was done with the Treasury and the Committee of Treasury acted as an intermediary between the Bank and the Treasury. The Committee of Treasury consisted of the governor, deputy governor of the Bank and not more than seven members of the Court of Directors, who were chosen by secret ballot.[18] The Committee of Treasury constituted more than a secretariat to the Court of Directors as it also—to some extent—fulfilled the functions of an advisory committee. In fact, the Committee of Treasury was consulted by the governor for the "more important business of the bank", e.g. recommendation to the Chancellor of the Exchequer on bank rates. Moreover, the Committee of Treasury played a special role in the deliberations on policy matters which involved sensitive market information and which were kept from the non-executive Directors for the stated reasons. The Committee could take the initiative to invite the attendance of any member of the Court not present in the Committee of Treasury as well as inviting third persons from outside the Bank for "discussion of special matters". It was accepted that the governor and deputy governor were obliged to inform the Committee of Treasury concerning the affairs of the Bank of England. Due to its advisory role the Committee of

---

[16] In 1957 two External Directors were accused of having benefited from a premature leak of a change in the bank rates. Cf. Report of the Committee on the Working of the Monetary System, Cmnd. 827, Aug. 1959.

[17] E. Hennessy, "The Governors, Directors and Management of the Bank of England" in R. Roberts/D. Kynaston, *The Bank of England—Money, Power and Influence 1694–1994* (Clarendon Press, Oxford, 1995), 185–216, at 199.

[18] Three of the seven had to be members of the Court that had held the position neither of governor nor deputy governor. Moreover, only one non-executive Director could participate. Cf. Sayers, n. 10 above, Vol. 2, 630 *et seq.*, who raises doubts whether and to what extent these secret ballots had much reality. In his opinion the actual composition relied on the power of the governor and informal rules, rather than the formal secret ballot.

Treasury was sometimes referred to as an "inner Cabinet of the Bank" or even as the "Governor's Cabinet".[19]

1.3. Reform

With the change of government in 1997 the new Labour government announced major institutional changes for the Bank of England. This announcement followed more recent suggestions by two independent reports on the role of the Bank of England to grant the Bank more independence in the area of monetary policy while at the same time making it accountable for its conduct of monetary policy.[20] With the Bank of England Act 1998 these institutional changes, which on the basis of an agreement between the executive government and the Bank of England[21] operated *de facto* since, have been given a formal legal basis.[22]

2. Institutional structure

The Bank of England constitutes a single-tier system. Although since 1958 the Bank no longer has the power to set up new branches independently it continues to have five branches and three agencies. The main function of the branches and agencies is the continuing monitoring of the industrial developments of the regions.[23] The Bank of England is managed by the Court of Directors. Recently, a Monetary Policy Committee (MPC) has been established.

2.1. Court of Directors

The affairs of the Bank of England other than those related to monetary policy are managed by the Court of Directors which consists of a governor, two deputy governors and 16 non-executive directors. The term of office of the governor and the two deputy governors is five years. The term of office of the 16 Directors is four years.[24] As such the Court of Directors is supposed to represent the whole of the UK. The Court's function is to manage the Bank's affairs, other than the

---

[19] Cairncross, n. 9 above, at 63.

[20] Cf. Roll Report, op. cit., Chap. 2, n. 1; Treasury and Civil Service Committee, *The Role of the Bank of England*, (House of Commons Paper. Session 1993–4; 98–I, vol. 1 and 2), Report, together with the proceedings of the Committee. H.C. Session 1993–4, HMSO, London, 1993.

[21] Letter of the Chancellor of the Exchequer, Gordon Brown, to the governor of the Bank of England of May 1997.

[22] The Bank of England Act 1998 of 23 Apr. 1998 came into force on 1 June 1998.

[23] P.L. Cottrell, n. 7 above, at 1190.

[24] For more details on the appointment and dismissal procedures, cf. Chap. 4 IV. For a list of all governors, deputy governors and directors since the establishment of the Bank of England cf. R. Roberts/D. Kynaston, *The Bank of England—Money, Power and Influence 1694–1994* (Clarendon Press, Oxford, 1995), Appendix 2.

formulation of monetary policy. This includes in particular determining the Bank's objectives, including those for financial management, and strategies. Moreover the Court of Directors is to keep under review the performance of the Bank as a whole, including that of the Monetary Policy Committee. These functions are delegated to a standing sub-committee of the Court of Directors consisting only of the 16 non-executive directors of the Court, who do not serve in the MPC. This sub-committee—among others—keeps under review the procedures followed by the MPC, and, in particular, whether the MPC has collected the regional, sectoral and other information necessary for the purpose of formulating monetary policy.[25] In some respects this new sub-committee takes over the functions previously performed by the Committee of Treasury. The Court can also establish other sub-committees and delegate duties and powers to such a sub-committee, or delegate such duties or powers to a member of the Court or any officer, servant or agent of the Bank.[26]

The Court of Directors meets at least once a month or upon request of the governor, or in his absence the deputy governor, of the Bank. A quorum of nine members is required in order to take decisions.[27]

2.2. Monetary Policy Committee

The Monetary Policy Committee may be considered as the main institutional novelty introduced under the new arrangements for the Bank of England. As such it has similarities with the Monetary Policy Council (*Conseil de la politique monétaire*) which has been introduced as part of the new institutional settings at the Banque de France in 1993.[28]

The MPC consists of the governor and the two deputy governors and six additional members appointed on a rotational basis for a renewable term of three years.[29] Two of the six members take on an executive function, having management responsibility for monetary policy and market operations. It can be assumed that the other four members play an advisory role. Subject to the approval of the Chancellor of the Exchequer, they may engage in activities outside the Bank which do not give rise to a conflict of interests.

The MPC is charged with formulating monetary policy and, more concretely, with taking operational decisions on interest rate policy. The MPC has to meet on a regular basis at least once a month.[30] In practice these meetings take place once a month over a period of two days, normally on the Wednesday and Thursday following the first Monday each month. The first day is reserved for discussions, whereas on the second day the decisions on policy actions are

[25] s. 16 Bank of England Act 1998.
[26] Above, sched. 1, para. 10 and 11.
[27] Above, sched. 1, para. 13.
[28] Cf. Chap. 3 II 2. Already the Roll Report, n. 20 above, vol. 1, drew attention to the arrangements at the Banque de France, and proposed the creation of a Monetary Policy Committee.
[29] For more details of the appointment and dismissal procedures, cf. Chap. 4 IV.
[30] Sched. 3, para. 10 Bank of England Act 1998.

taken.[31] For any decisions to be taken a quorum of at least six, of whom two must either be the governor and one of the deputy governors, or both deputy governors is required. Decisions are taken by a majority of the votes, but the governor has a casting vote in case of a tie. The Treasury has the right to send a representative to participate in these meetings, however, without a voting right.

3. Tasks

3.1. Conduct of monetary policy

The monetary policy objective of the Bank of England is to maintain price stability and—subject to that—to support the economic policy of the government.[32] Short-term interest rates and foreign exchange interventions are considered the two main instruments of monetary policy.[33]

The Bank has operational responsibility for setting short-term interest rates. On the one hand, the Bank of England influences the liquidity of the money market by adjusting the interest rate. On the other hand, the Bank influences the liquidity through open market operations. For this the Bank holds the accounts of discount houses, holders of large stocks of commercial bills which are purchased by major banks with their surplus money. The discount houses function as an intermediary for the Bank. The latter infuses money into the market either by buying commercial bills, or by granting loans to the banks. The interest rates at which the Bank of England deals with these discount houses effect the interest rates used by the commercial banks.

The Bank of England manages the Exchange and Equalisation Account governed by the Exchange Equalisation Act 1979 which holds the overwhelming part of the official gold and foreign currency reserves of the UK. Since the exit from the ERM in September 1992 the Bank of England has implemented exchange rate operations in accordance with the instruction of the Treasury. Finally, the Bank of England issues banknotes.

3.2. Services to the government

The Bank holds the main accounts of the government, and major payments by and to the government, such as taxes and social security, are completed via these accounts. Until recently the Bank of England also managed the government debt, offering advice to the Treasury on the issue, redemption and conversion of securities, and undergoing open market operations in the government bill and

---

[31] P. Rodgers, "Changes at the Bank of England", *Bank of England Quarterly Bulletin*, vol. 37 no. 2, 241–7, at 242.
[32] For more details of the monetary policy objective of the Bank of England, cf. Chap. 4 II.
[33] For a short overview cf. The Bank of England, *The Value of Money*, (Online), available from: URL http://www.bankofengland.co.uk/value.htm (last accessed Oct. 1998).

bond markets. However, under the new arrangements these functions are transferred to the Treasury. The Bank of England continues to manage the government's stock register.

3.3. Services to commercial banks

The Bank of England acts as the lender of last resort for the financial system.
Moreover, it provides a clearing and settlement systems as all clearing banks
regulate their differences via accounts which they hold at the Bank. Besides, all
commercial banks are obliged to keep a non-interest bearing deposit at the
Bank.

3.4. Banking supervision

Until recently, the supervisory and regulatory functions relating to deposit-
taking business of banks were vested in the Bank of England, internally carried
out by the Board of Banking Supervision.[34] Under the new arrangements functions relating to the supervision of banks under the Banking Act 1987, the
Banking Co-ordination Regulation 1992, section 101 (4) of the Building
Societies Act 1986, as well as those relating to the listing of money market institutions and certain functions under the Companies Act 1989, will be transferred
to a new institution, the so-called Financial Services Authority.[35]

II. BANQUE DE FRANCE

France is one of the Member States in the European Union participating in
EMU from the outset. France also embodies a tradition of government-guided
monetary policy with the Banque de France representing something similar to
an administrative arm of the executive. This relationship was reflected in the
institutional set-up of the Bank. In 1992, the institutional structure of the Bank
was substantially amended, thereby creating a more independent monetary
authority. This basic change in policy with regard to the relationship between
the executive government and the Banque de France took place against the
background of the TEU and the prospect of the establishment of the ESCB and
the ECB.[36]

---

[34] Formerly s. 2 Banking Act 1987.
[35] s. 21 *et seq*. Bank of England Act 1998.
[36] P. Collas, "Le 'Dépeçage' de l'administration—un nouveau pas: la tentative d'autonomiser la
Banque de France", *RRJ*, 1994–2, 557–98, at 589.

1. Historic development

1.1. Establishment

As has been the case in other countries, the motive for the creation of the institution was the increasing demand for methods of raising finance for the state. In the case of France the underlying factor was the economic recession following the revolutionary period and the war between France and England.

The two Acts which effectively created the Banque de France were a decree of 18 January 1800, which established the seat of the Banque de France and the so-called *statuts fondamentaux* of 13 February 1800, which represented a charter of 26 articles established by the initial meeting of the first shareholders in a constitutive general assembly.[37] The institutional structure of the Banque de France was somewhat complex. Set up as a public corporation the Bank initially held a capital of 30 million francs composed of 30,000 shares.[38] The capital of the Bank was held by shareholders who were represented in the Assembly (*assemblée générale*). Despite its name the General Assembly did not consist of all shareholders but only drew together the 200 biggest shareholders.[39] The administration of the Bank was handed down to the General Council (*conseil général*) which consisted of 15 regents (*régents*) nominated by the General Assembly for a renewable term of five years. Three regents, nominated by the General Council, formed the Central Committee (*comité central*), which constituted the executive board of the Bank. The General Assembly also nominated three censors (*censeurs*) which had the task to monitor the execution of the statute.[40]

By law of 14 April 1803 the Bank was given the exclusive right to issue banknotes in Paris for the first time, although limited to a period of 15 years.[41] Moreover, since that time one half of the members of the General Council, including the Censors, had to be chosen from among manufacturers and

---

[37] 28 Nivose an 8 (18 janvier 1800)—Arrêté qui destine un local à l'établissement de la Banque de France. (III, Bull. I, no. 5). and 24 pluviôse an VIII (13 janvier 1800); hereafter referred to as Bank Act 1800 and of the same day: Arrêté qui prescrit la destination des fonds que recevra la caisse d'amortissement, reprinted in: J.B. Duvergier, *Collection Complète des Lois, Décrets, Ordonnances, Réglements, et Avis du Conseil d'Etat*, Tome Douzième (Paris 1826), at 72; cf. R. Dhordain/O. Clodong, *Les Banques Centrales* (deuxième tirage, Les Éditions D'Organisation, Paris, 1994), at 72, on prior attempts to establish a note-issuing bank.
[38] Arts. 1–4 Bank Act 1800. The Bank Act 1800 only refers to a "Banque publique"; cf. M. Dufaur, *La Nouvelle Organisation de la Banque de France*, Diss., Université de Toulouse, 1937, at 7, who refers to a corporation ("*société anonyme*").
[39] Arts. 10 *et seq.* Bank Act 1803.
[40] For more details on the Bank Act 1800 cf. H. Biard, *Le Nouveau Statut De La Banque De France*, thesis, Université de Paris, 1937, 15 *et seq.*
[41] 24 germinal an XI (14 avril 1803).—Loi relative à la Banque de France. (III, Bull.CCLXXI, no. 2698; Mon. du 24 germinal) reprinted in J.B. Duvergier, n. 37 above, 195 *et seq.*; hereafter referred to as Bank Act 1803, cf. Art. 1. The privilege was renewed four times until the nationalisation of the Bank in 1946. As to the crisis of the system around 1848, cf. B. Eufrun, *La Banque de France* (Berger-Levrault, Paris, 1995), 18 *et seq.*

traders.[42] Institutional reforms initiated in 1806 secured the government a certain degree of influence over the Banque de France.[43] A governor and two deputy governors were introduced to the Banque de France. They replaced the Central Committee and, in addition to the General Council, were charged with the management of the Bank.[44] In contrast to the General Council, the governor and deputy governors were appointed by the executive government. They were obliged to hold a certain number of shares.

1.2. Nationalisation

With the rise to power of the *Front Populaire* in 1936 the influence of the government over the Banque de France was systematically expanded. The first and most important amendments were implemented in July 1936.[45] The 15 regents were replaced by 20 Councillors (*conseillers*) who, together with the three censors, the governor and deputy governors, formed the General Council of the Bank. Unlike the regents, who had been selected by the General Assembly, the Councillors were deemed to represent economic and social interests and the "collective interests of the nation".[46] In fact, only two of the 20 Councillors were elected by the General Assembly and thus, by the representatives of the shareholders, whereas the majority was appointed according to a rather complex procedure involving—among others—the Minister of Finance, the National Economic Council (*conseil national économique*) and the personnel of the Bank.[47] Additionally, the General Council consisted of a number of *ex officio* members, comprising—among others—the President of the financial section of the State Council (*président de la section des finances du Conseil d'Etat*).[48] The motive behind these changes was to remove the representatives of the big private interests from the Bank, who had had great influence not only over the policies of the Bank, but at times also over the government itself.[49] The Bank Act 1936 removed the statutory limitation of the number of shareholders represented in the General Assembly and, moreover, abandoned the obligation of the governor and deputy governors under the old statute to hold a certain number

---

[42]   Biard, n. 40 above, 21 *et seq.*

[43]   Loi du 22 avril 1806, hereafter referred to as the Bank Act 1806; Dufaur, n. 38 above, at 9, observes that the Bank Act 1806 did not include provisions in case of a conflict between the governor and the General Council.

[44]   A. Plessis, "Banque de France", in M. Pohl/S. Freitag (eds.), *Handbook on the History of European Banks* (Edward Elgar, Aldershot, 1994), 204–8, at 204.

[45]   Loi du 24 juillet 1936—Loi tendant à modifier et à compléter les lois et statuts qui régissent la Banque de France, hereafter referred to as the Bank Act 1936, reprinted in Duvergier, *Collection Complète des Lois, Décrets d'Intérêt Général*, Tome Trente-Sixième (Recueil Sirey, Paris, 1936), 341–2.

[46]   Art. 9(2) Bank Act 1936.

[47]   Ibid., Art. 9.

[48]   Art. 9 III. Bank Act 1936.

[49]   J. Bouvier, "The Banque de France and the State from 1805 to the Present Day" in G. Toniolo, *Central Banks' Independence in Historical Perspective* (Walter de Gruyter, Berlin and New York, 1988), 73–103.

of shares in the Bank. This removed the last bond between the shareholders of the Bank and the governor and deputy governors. of the Bank.[50]

On the basis of these changes and additional, smaller, amendments in the following years, the government gained considerable influence over the Bank.[51] It is quite remarkable that despite all these changes the legal status of the Bank as a corporation under private law (*société anonyme*) remained formally in place.

However, the general trend towards nationalisation of the national industries at the end of the Second World War eventually also led to fundamental changes for the Banque de France. Anticipating its nationalisation the Bank took the initiative to propose a reform, at the centre of which the Bank would have been transformed into a mixed economy company, putting the State firmly into control through its ownership of half of the capital plus one share. Bouvier evaluates these proposals as an attempt "to keep up the façade" at a time when both government and Parliament were in favour of nationalisation.[52]

The Bank was nationalised on 1 January 1946.[53] The shares were transferred to the State. As the General Assembly was abolished so were the members of the General Council and the Censors who used to be elected by the shareholders.[54] Although the Bank Act 1945[55] called for the implementation of a law which would modify and complete the statute of the nationalised Banque de France, in large parts it operated under the old statute until 1972, when new legislation was implemented.[56] The Bank Act 1973 constituted a political compromise which stood at the end of fundamental differences between the government of the day and the Banque de France. The former, personified by the Minister of Finance Valéry Giscard d'Estaing, favoured total government control over monetary policy, whereas the latter, personified by the governor of the Banque de France at the time Oliver Wormse, insisted on an independent role of the Bank.[57] Yet, under the Bank Act 1973 in the field of monetary policy the Bank executed the policies of the government. The composition of the General Council changed in as much as the Councillors no longer represented different interest groups in the economic sectors, but were appointed on the basis of their professional competence. The General Council consisted of nine members, eight of whom were

---

[50] Art. 9 Bank Act 1936.

[51] On two other occasions during the 1940s the composition of the General Council was amended, cf. Eufrun, n. 41 above, at 26.

[52] Bouvier, n. 49 above, at 93, with reference to H. Koch, *L'histoire de la Banque de France et de la monnaie sous la IV République* (Dunod, Paris, 1983).

[53] 2 décembre 1945—Loi relative à la nationalisation de la Banque de France et des grandes banques et à l'organisation du crédit, titre 1, hereafter referred to as Bank Act 1945, reprinted in J.B. Duvergier, *Collection Complète des Lois, Décrets d'Intérêt Général* (Recueil Sirey, Paris, 1945), 698–702.

[54] Art. 1 Bank Act 1945.

[55] Ibid., Art. 3, according to which the composition of the General Council and the statute of the Banque de France were supposed to be modified and completed by law before 28 Feb. 1946.

[56] Loi no. 73–7 du 3 janvier 1973 sur la Banque de France [1973] JORF, 165, hereafter referred to as the Bank Act 1973, and décret no. 73–102 du 30 janvier 1973 [1973] JORF, 1248, hereafter referred to as decree 1973.

[57] Bouvier, n. 49 above, 95 *et seq*.

appointed by the Council of Ministers on a recommendation of the Minister of Economic Affairs and Finances and one of whom was appointed by the staff of the Bank. A Censor, appointed by the Minister of Economic Affairs and Finances, was put in charge of controlling the management of the Bank and in that function participated in the deliberations of the General Council with a voting right.[58] Additionally, a Consultative Council (*Conseil consultatif*) combining the representatives of the economic and financial sector was set up. The Bank Act 1973 also recognised the increased functions of the Bank since its nationalisation in the field of money and exchange markets and "credit controls".

The new legislation on banking supervision, created in 1984, specified the role of the Banque de France with regard to its regulatory and supervisory functions in the field of banking supervision.[59] Moreover, the new legislation has introduced the National Credit Council (*Conseil National du Crédit*) which acts as an advisor on the functioning of the banking and financial systems and, furthermore, at the time was given a participatory role in the formulation of monetary policy.[60] Article 4(2) of the Bank Act 1973 stated: "[t]he Bank helps to prepare and takes part in the implementation of the monetary policy that has been decided by the government *with the assistance of the Conseil National du Crédit, according to its terms of reference.*"[61]

1.3. Reform

The introduction of a new statute in 1993 may be considered as the most important institutional reform of the Banque de France since its nationalisation in 1946. In the light of the imminent conclusion of the Treaty on the European Union (TEU), introducing the provision on EMU, the French government opted for an early reform of the statute of the Banque de France, in its view, in order to comply with the institutional requirements which would eventually be imposed on national central banks under the new Article 108 EC as a condition for a participation in EMU.[62] However, the introduction of a new statute for the Banque de France was delayed, as the Constitutional Council (*Conseil Constitutionnel*) ruled certain central provisions of the new status to be uncon-

[58] Arts. 13–16 Bank Act 1973.
[59] Loi no. 84–46 relative à l'activité et contrôle des établissements de crédit [1984] JORF, 390, hereafter referred to as law on the activity and supervision of credit institutions.
[60] Art. 24 *et seq.* law on the activity and supervision of credit institutions. It constitutes a consultative body which comprises representatives of different economic groups appointed by the Minister of Economic Affairs and Finances.
[61] Translation provided in Bouvier, n. 49 above, at 99; emphasis added.
[62] Indeed, it has been suggested that the French government believed it would enhance its negotiating position with regard to membership in EMU, cf. J.-P. Duprat, "The Independence of the Banque de France: Constitutional and European Aspects" [1995] *PL*, 133–49, at 138. Whether and to what extent the Bank Act 1993 was compatible with Community law will be examined in Chap. 4 III1.

stitutional.[63] The new statute of the Banque de France finally came fully into effect on 1 January 1994.[64]

2. Institutional structure

Ever since its nationalisation in 1946 the legal nature of the Bank has been largely undetermined.[65] The Bank Act 1946 governed the transfer of the Bank's capital to the state without defining the new legal status of the former corporation under private law. The Bank Act 1973 did not introduce any clarifications as it merely referred to the Banque de France as an *institution*.[66] Article 6 of the Bank Act 1993 includes a similar provision: "[t]he Banque de France is an institution whose capital is owned by the state". Moreover, Article 32 of the Bank Act 1993 emphasises that the new statute is not intended to create a new legal entity. Rather than identifying the legal nature of the Bank, most authors simply note that the Bank is defined by its functions, or do not discuss this point at all.[67] Bouvier reflects on these attempts to define the legal nature of the Bank as follows:

> "In 1972 the question has been the object of long debate. And what do we have? The bank of issue, a 'body *sui generis*', which belongs 'to absolutely no determined juridical category': a perfect example of legal flexibility. The Banque is thus defined 'by what it does rather than what it is'."[68]

The Bank has kept its original centralised single-tier structure. It has its seat in Paris.[69] Apart from the head office the Bank features 211 branches in the 22 regions of continental France.[70] Each is managed by a director which is

---

[63] Décision no. 93–324 DC of 3 Aug. 1993]1993] JORF, 11014; for more details cf. Chap. 4 I.

[64] Loi no. 93–980 du 4 août 1993 relative au statut de la Banque de France et à l'activité et au contrôle des établissements de crédit [1993] JORF, 1147, and Loi no. 93–1444 du 31 décembre 1993 portant diverses dispositions relatives à la Banque de France, à l'assurance, au crédit et aux marchés financiers [1994] JORF, 231, as amended; hereafter referred to as the Bank Act 1993. The Bank Act 1993 is complemented by a decree by the Minister of Economic Affairs and Finances which determines some aspects of the application of the act, Décret no. 93–1278 du 3 décembre 1993 sur la Banque de France [1993] JORF, 16854.

[65] Bouvier, n. 49 above, at 98; M. Lombard, "Le nouveau statut de la Banque de France", *L'Actualité juridique—Droit administratif*, 20 juillet/20 août 1994, 491–5, at 493, with details on the discussions during the drafting of the Bank Act 1993.

[66] Art. 1 Bank Act 1973; Lombard, n. 65 above, points out that in the preparatory stages of the Bank Act 1973 it was proposed to define the legal nature as a company (*société*). However, these plans were relinquished by the government.

[67] D. Besnard/M. Redon, *La monnaie: politique et institutions* (2e édition, Dunod, Paris, 1987), at 80, refer to a public institution; Banque de France, *History, Organization, Role* (Banque de France, Paris, 1995), at 10, according to which " its legal nature is defined by its functions and, as a result, its legal status features many contrasts"; Duprat, n. 62 above, 138, with further references, who rejects the description as a "*société sui generis*".

[68] Bouvier, n. 49 above.

[69] Décret no. 73–102 du 30 janvier 1973 [1973] JORF, 1248, Art. 73.

[70] France has 26 regions including the 4 overseas areas. The regions fulfil administrative functions, including e.g. the economic development and educational matters of the area.

appointed by the governor of the Bank.[71] The central structure of the Banque de France includes the Monetary Policy Council, the General Council and the advisory bodies.

2.1. Monetary Policy Council

The Monetary Policy Council (*Conseil de la politique monétaire* = CPM) is a creation of the Bank Act 1993. It is the policy board of the Banque de France and comprises the governor, his two deputy governors and six additional members. Both the governor and the deputy governors are elected for a period of six years, renewable once. The six additional members are elected for a non-renewable term of nine years.[72]

Generally, the task of the CPM is to formulate monetary policy and to monitor changes in the money supply and its counterparts.[73] Within these broadly defined boundaries the CPM defines the operations to be carried out by the Bank. According to the non-exhaustive provision of Article 7 of the Bank Act 1993, this includes the determination of the terms and conditions under which the Bank can purchase or sell outright or under repurchase or resale agreements, lend or borrow, discount or take as collateral any debt instrument, and issue interest-bearing bills. Moreover, the CPM decides on the nature and scope of securities attached to loans granted by the Bank in the course of implementing monetary policy and determines the requirements to be imposed on credit institutions in pursuance of monetary policy, e.g. reserve requirements. The CPM meets at the request of the governor, but at least once a month. Moreover, upon request of a majority of the members of the CPM the governor is obliged to convene a meeting of the Council within 48 hours.[74]

The CPM can take authoritative decisions only if at least two-thirds of its members are present at the meeting. Provided that fewer than six members are present at a meeting all decisions are postponed and the governor convenes a new meeting with the same agenda. At that time a quorum is no longer needed. Instead, decisions are taken by a simple majority of the members present. In the case of a tie the governor has a casting vote.[75] In addition to the members of the CPM, the Prime Minister and the Minister for Economic Affairs and Finance may take part in these meetings, or may, in case of indisposition, be represented by a person specifically named and explicitly nominated to fulfil this function.[76]

The position of the governor of the Bank has been strengthened by the Bank Act 1993. According to Article 13(1) of the Bank Act 1993 he manages the Bank. He presides over the CPM and the General Council and prepares and imple-

---

[71] For a detailed examination of the structure and functions of the branches, cf. Eufrun, n. 41 above, 39 *et seq.*

[72] The procedures and conditions of their appointment is discussed in Chap. 4 IV.

[73] Art. 7(1) and (2) Bank Act 1993.

[74] Ibid., Art. 9(1), Art. 9(1) decree 1993.

[75] Bank Act 1993, Art. 9(2).

[76] For more details cf. Chap. 4 III 1.

ments the decisions made by both of these organs.[77] The governor represents the Bank *vis-à-vis* third parties and is authorised to sign all formal agreements on behalf of the Bank.[78] Moreover, according to Article 7(5) of the Bank Act 1993, the CPM may "temporarily delegate certain powers to the governor". However, such a delegation has not taken place in the past as the CPM and the governor always emphasise the collegiality of the decisions taken, and it has been suggested that such a delegation would only take place under extraordinary circumstances.[79]

2.2. General Council

The General Council (*Conseil Général*) has been left mostly unchanged by the Bank Act 1993. It comprises the nine members of the CPM complemented by one representative of the staff of the Bank who is elected for a period of six years.[80] Additionally, a so-called Censor (*Censeur*) or his alternate may attend the meetings of the General Council. In administering the Bank, the General Council decides on issues related to the conduct of the Bank's activities other than the formulation and implementation of monetary policy. It sets out the terms of employment of the staff of the Bank and manages the Bank's finances, including the allocation of funds and drawing up of the Bank's balance sheet and accounts. Moreover, it proposes the appropriation of net profits and the dividend to be paid to the State.[81]

By law the General Council is obliged to meet at least six times a year upon request of the governor. Extraordinary meetings may take place upon request of at least half of the members of the General Council or the Censor.[82] Decisions of the General Council require a quorum of at least six members and are taken by a majority of the votes of the members present at the meeting. The governor, who also presides over the General Council, has a casting vote in case of a tie.[83]

2.3. Advisory bodies

According to Article 35 of decree 1993, the Monetary Policy Council and the General Council may establish consultative bodies including individuals outside the Bank's personnel. Currently, two advisory bodies on the central level and the level of the branches exist. A Consultative Council (*conseil consultatif*) is located at the seat of the Banque de France and meets infrequently. It is made up

---

[77] Art. 13 Bank Act 1993.

[78] Ibid., Art. 13(4).

[79] This has been suggested to the author by officials working at the Banque de France.

[80] Bank Act 1993, Art. 12(1); for more details on the role and appointment and dismissal of the representative of the staff of the Bank cf. Chap. 4 IV.

[81] Art. 11(4) Bank Act 1993.

[82] Art. 9(1)–(2) decree 1993. According to the Bank's *Annual Report* the General Council met 13 times in 1995.

[83] Art. 12(2) and (3) Bank Act 1993.

of between 15 and 24 members who are appointed for a period of three years by the General Council on recommendation of the governor of the Bank.[84] Its members are chosen from among representatives of industry, commerce and agriculture.[85]

Depending on the branch's importance, between six and 17 Councillors (*conseils*) are located at each branch and are appointed by the General Council on recommendation of the governor of the Bank for a period of three years. The function of both the Consultative Council and the Councillors is to give advice and information on the economic situation and perspectives in the different sectors.[86] In general the advisory bodies have a more representative function as a result of historic developments.

3. Tasks

3.1. Monetary policy and related tasks

First of all the Bank formulates monetary policy with the ultimate goal of achieving price stability.[87] The Bank determines interest rate policy by intervening on the money market in the form of inter-bank market interventions and open market operations. This is complemented by the reserve requirements for credit institutions.

The Bank decides on the exchange rate regime and the French franc parity on behalf of the government, which formulates the framework of the general exchange rate policy guidelines. The Bank is therefore in charge of the day-to-day foreign exchange operations. It holds and manages the gold and foreign exchange reserves of France and records them as assets in its balance sheets. Subject to permission by the Minister of Economic Affairs and Finances, the Bank has the right to participate in international monetary agreements. Since its establishment in 1979 the French Franc has participated in the ERM. Furthermore, the Bank carries out additional tasks which are considered to be related to the conduct of monetary policy. These tasks include the issue of banknotes and the management of banknotes and coins.[88]

3.2. Services to government

Traditionally one of the major roles of a central bank is to act as the banker for the State, servicing its debts by means of credits and the purchase of government

---

[84] Eufrun, n. 41 above, at 38.

[85] For a current list of the members of the Consultative Committee and their origin cf. the latest *Annual Report* of the Bank.

[86] Eufrun, n. 41 above, at 38.

[87] Art. 1(1) Bank Act 1993. For more details on the monetary objective, cf. Chap. 4 II.

[88] Art. 5 Bank Act 1993. Coins are issued by the State.

securities. This was also the case for the Banque de France prior to the institutional changes in 1993.[89] The facilitation of credit was subject to an agreement between the Bank and the Minister of Economic Affairs and Finance which had to be approved by the National Assembly (*Assemblée Nationale*), and which defined the extent of credits.[90] The financing of the State through open market operations, that is the purchase of debt securities, was not subject to any regulations and thus, performed at the discretion of the Bank.[91]

Since the institutional reform of 1993, Article 3 of the Bank Act 1993 prohibits any overdraft or any other type of credit facilities in favour of the government, i.e. Treasury, or any other public body or state owned corporation.[92] Moreover, the direct purchasing of government debt instruments is excluded. Here, the Bank Act 1993 has anticipated matching provisions introduced into the EC Treaty by the TEU.[93] Outside this area, the Bank still acts as a fiscal agent to the State.[94] Among other tasks, it holds the Treasury's account, collects payments for government securities and is involved in the management of the national debt.[95]

3.3. Services to commercial banks

The Bank is in charge of safeguarding the smooth operation and the security of the payment systems. This combines the modernisation of payment methods, e.g. credit cards, the providing of banking services to commercial banks, e.g. interbank settlement systems, and risk prevention in payment systems, e.g. by means of an interbank prevention programme.[96] It organises the payment and settlement systems. Commercial banks hold accounts with the Bank which in return supplies the former with central bank money and carries out their reciprocal transactions. Moreover, it offers other services to commercial banks such as the credit register and databases on companies and cheques.

---

[89] Title II Bank Act 1973.

[90] Ibid., Art. 19.

[91] Taking into account the dependence of the Banque de France on government prior to the Bank Act 1993 this gave the government a relatively unrestricted access to credit financing; cf. W. Disch, *Die geldpolitische Konzeption der Banque de France und der Deutschen Bundesbank* (Centaurus-Verlagsgesellschaft, Pfaffenweiler, 1995), at 11.

[92] Note that the present restriction does not apply to state-owned credit institutions in the context of the provisions of liquidity by the Banque de France: Art. 3 para. 3 Bank Act 1993.

[93] According to Art. 104 EC, since 1 Jan. 1994, Member States, that is central governments, regional, local or other public authorities, or other bodies governed by public law or public undertakings, may no longer hold overdraft facilities or any other type of credit facilities with the ECB or with the central banks of the Member States. Art. 104 EC also forbids the purchase of debt instruments from the Member States by the ECB or the Member States' central banks.

[94] Arts. 15 and 16 Bank Act 1993.

[95] For more details cf. Banque de France, n. 67 above, 30 *et seq.*

[96] Art. 4 Bank Act 1993.

3.4. Banking supervision

The fourth major task of the Banque de France is related to the supervision of credit institutions. The regulation and supervision of the banking system is subject to the law on the activity and supervision of credit institutions. The tasks are shared by three committees, the Banking Regulatory Committee (*Le Comité de la Réglementation Bancaire*), the Credit Institution Committee (*Comité des Etablissements de Crédit*) and the Banking Commission (*La Commission Bancaire*).[97] The governor of the Bank chairs two of the three Committees, that is the Credit Institution Committee, which may be described in short as the authorising authority for credit institutions, and the Banking Commission, which conducts investigations into the performance of credit institutions and their compliance with the statutory requirements. Moreover, the governor is a member of the Banking Regulatory Committee, which, under the chairmanship of the Minister for Economic Affairs and Finance, represents a regulatory body charged with the fixing of provisions for credit institutions.

III. DEUTSCHE BUNDESBANK

Any evaluation of the democratic accountability of central banks, in particular when including the newly established ESCB, has to consider the Bundesbank. The Bundesbank was not only arguably the single most influential central bank in Europe in the past, but has been considered as the raw model for the ECB. This is to a large extent due to its widely recognised anti-inflationary track-record over the last four decades which is not least attributed the Bundesbank's independent position within the German system of government. Thus, examining the democratic accountability of the Bundesbank is interesting against the background, first, of its reputation to constitute one of the most independent central banks existing, and, secondly, because it constituted the reference system for the ESCB and the ECB.

1. Historic development

The history of monetary institutions in Germany is closely linked to political developments over the years and some of today's features of the Bundesbank can more easily be understood with some knowledge of these developments.

In the nineteenth century about 140 different coins and notes were in circulation on the territory of the different German states, including foreign and

---

[97] The law on the activity and supervision of credit institutions also established two advisory body, namely the National Credit Council (*Le Conseil National du Crédit*) and the Advisory Committee (*Comité Consultatif*), which offer advice—among other things—on the operating conditions of the banking and financial systems and the relationship between credit institutions and their customers.

eighteenth-century coins. Contrary to England and France, whose coin systems were already unified to some degree, the territory of what would become one German state hosted seven different coin systems.[98] The importance of the simplification of the existing system was obvious. But it was not until after the coming into existence of the second German Reich in 1871 that a single currency was finally introduced.[99]

1.1. The Reichsbank

The Reichsbank was created through the Bank Act of 1875 as a legal person under public law, its initial capital being held by shareholders.[100] The administrative and executive functions of the Reichsbank were conferred upon one organ: the Board of Directors of the Reichsbank (*Reichsbank-Direktorium*). It consisted of a president and other members which were appointed by the emperor (*Kaiser*) for life on recommendation of the Upper House of Parliament (*Bundesrath*).[101] The Bank Act 1875 conferred the managerial power of the Reichsbank on the Reich and thus, the Chancellor of the Reich (*Reichskanzler*) and only under his supervision was the Board of Directors of the Reichsbank in charge of the management.[102] The shareholders, gathered in the General Assembly (*General-versammlung*), took part in the administration.[103] The supervision of the Reichsbank was conferred by the government upon a board of governors, the so-called *Bank-Kuratorium*, consisting of the Chancellor and four additional members.[104] Additionally, the Reichsbank was subject to control by the Court of Auditors (*Rechungshof*) of the German Reich.[105] In legal terms, the Reichsbank was extremely dependent on the government.[106] At the same time it was highly accountable to both the government and the shareholders.

With the introduction of the law concerning the autonomy of the Reichsbank in 1922 the government's power to manage and control the Reichsbank, as introduced in the Bank Act 1875, was, to some extent, removed.[107] The new law constituted an autonomous Act of Parliament only to a limited extent. World

[98] The *Taler* and the *Gulden* were the most common ones.

[99] Verordnung betreffend die Einführung der Reichswährung vom 22. September 1875, RGBl., 303. The *Reichsmark* was introduced on 1 Jan. 1876.

[100] Bankgesetz vom 14. März 1875, RGBl., 177; hereafter referred to as Bank Act 1875; §§ 12, 23 Bank Act 1875. According to a dissenting opinion the Reichsbank constituted a legal person under *private* law; K. Stern, *Das Staatsrecht der Bundesrepublik Deutschland*, Vol. 2 (C.H. Beck, Munich, 1980), § 35 I 2.

[101] Ibid., § 27.

[102] Ibid., §§ 12, 26–7.

[103] Ibid., §§ 30–4.

[104] Ibid., § 12. Three of these members were appointed by the Upper Chamber of Parliament (*Bundesrath*) and one was appointed by the emperor (§ 25).

[105] Ibid., § 29.

[106] E. Wandel, *Die Entstehung der Bank deutscher Länder und die deutsche Währungsreform 1948* (Fritz Knapp Verlag, Frankfurt a.M., 1980), at 78, who suggests that the policies of the Reichsbank were *de facto* governed by (and dependent on) the gold standard.

[107] Gesetz über die Autonomie der Reichsbank vom 26. May 1922, RGBl. II, 135, hereafter referred to as law concerning the autonomy of the Reichsbank of 1922.

War I had left the defeated German Reich subject to the provisions of the peace of Versailles of 1919,[108] which imposed substantial reparation payments upon the German Reich.[109] The post-war economic situation in general, and the reparation payments in particular, increased the demand for means of payment, e.g. credits, by the government. The constant demand for money led to a considerable increase in the amount of money being put into circulation, and fuelled the inflation of the German currency.[110] In this climate of economic—as well as social—decline, some of the victorious states, namely France and Britain, offered a partial moratorium on reparation payments provided that the independence of the Reichsbank from government was enhanced.[111] While leaving the supervision with the government, the law concerning the autonomy of the Reichsbank conferred the task of management of the Reichsbank upon its Board of Directors, thereby removing it from the government. The Board of Directors was no longer subject to the provisions and instructions of the Chancellor. Additionally, the procedure of appointment of the president of the Reichsbank was altered, introducing the participation of the Board of Directors and the General Committee in the form of a right to be heard. The participation of the Reichsbank in the appointment of the Board of Directors was enhanced, as its members were appointed by the president of the Reich (*Reichspräsident*) on the *recommendation* of the Board of Directors.[112] Additionally, the Upper House of Parliament (*Reichsrat*) had to approve the appointees. Hence, the members of the Board of Directors were appointed in a co-operation procedure between the Reichsbank and government. Although the law of 1922 had increased the independence of the Reichsbank, the government kept some of its control and influence.[113]

During the Great Depression and not least as a result of the unrestricted government financing by the Reichsbank during World War I inflation reached record levels. At the height of the crisis, in 1923, the inflation rate reached an astonishing one billion per cent. The government attempted to fight the ruinous inflation with a monetary reform which included the establishment of the so-called *Rentenbank*[114] as the new note-issuing bank, with the *Rentenmarkscheine*[115] as a parallel currency to that issued by the *Reichsbank*.[116]

---

[108] RGBl. 1919, 687.

[109] 132 billion Goldmark, divided in three debenture bonds and payable in US dollars.

[110] D.Marsh, *Die Bundesbank* (C. Bertelsmann, Munich, 1992), 126 *et seq.*, describes this vicious circle in some detail (English version: *The Bundesbank: The Bank that rules Europe* (Mandarin, London, 1993).

[111] During the conference of Cannes in 1922. Ironically, the allies' demand for more independence were not to have a positive influence on the inflation record of the Reichsbank.

[112] § 27 (2) law concerning the autonomy of the Reichsbank.

[113] Marsh, n. 110 above, refers to the influence of the Prussian government in the Upper Chamber of Parliament.

[114] Verordnung über die Errichtung der Deutschen Rentenbank vom 15. Oktober 1923, RGBl. I, 963. It was established by representatives of agricultural, industrial and commercial branches as a legal person under *private* law, § 1.

[115] The new currency was covered through the charge on agricultural land and the commercial businesses. *Supra*, n. 114, § 2.

[116] The *Mark* remained legal tender.

The basic aim of the Bank Act of 1924[117] was to overcome some of the short-comings of the earlier Acts, in particular with regard to unrestricted government financing. The Bank Act 1924 had two major implications. First, it laid the foundation for yet another monetary reform, by replacing the *Rentenmark* with the *Reichsmark*.[118] Secondly, it restructured the internal organisation of the Reichsbank. The main modification, affecting the statutory relationship between the Reichsbank and the government, was implemented in the first sentence of § 1 of the Bank Act 1924. This was set out as if it were a guiding principle: "The Reichsbank is a bank independent from the Reich government". Once more, the development towards a more independent Reichsbank had been influenced from outside Germany, as the allies pressed to remove the influence of the German government, while at the same time enhancing their own influence. The Board of Directors remained the administrator of the Reichsbank. In addition to that, it took on the role of the policy-making body, as for the first time the Bank Act 1924 expressly defined in broad terms the objectives of the Reichsbank. The Board of Directors was charged with the task of implementing the monetary, discount and credit policy of the Bank.[119] The president of the Board of Governors was no longer appointed on recommendation by the Upper Chamber of Parliament but by a so-called General Council (*Generalrat*)[120] which consisted of 14 German and foreign members, for a renewable period of four years.[121] On the Board of Governors the president had a special position, since his vote was decisive in the event of a tie of votes.[122] The independence of the policy board of the Reichsbank in general and the position of its president in particular were narrowed by the right of the General Council to dismiss the president and any other member of the Board of Directors at any time for "important reasons".[123] The Bank Act 1924 fell short of defining this general clause.[124] Apart from its participation in the appointment of the president and the dismissal of members of the Board of Directors of the Reichsbank, the General Council moreover had supervisory powers.[125] Though the Bank Act 1924 introduced a statutory independence from government, the Reichsbank was by no means free from restraining mechanisms. The members of the Board

---

[117] Bankgesetz vom 30. August 1924, RGBl. II, 235, hereafter referred to as the Bank Act 1924.

[118] Chap. I, §§ 1–4 of the Bank Act 1924 on the introduction of the Reichsmark; also Gesetz über die Liquidierung des Umlaufs der Rentenbankscheine vom 30 August 1924, RGBl. II, 252.

[119] *Supra*, n. 117, § 1.

[120] The General Council, with its substantial influence in the appointment and dismissal of the Board of Directors had been newly established by the Bank Act 1924. It had 14 members, including 7 German citizens and always one British, French, Italian, Belgian, American, Dutch and Swiss citizen. The unusual composition was the result of allied demands.

[121] Only one third of the period of service of the other members of the Board of Directors who were generally elected for a renewable period of 12 years, § 12.

[122] § 6 Bank Act 1924.

[123] For the dismissal of an ordinary member the Board, the consent of the president of the Reichsbank was necessary.

[124] § 16 Bank Act 1924.

[125] Ibid., § 18; the Board of Governors (*Bank-Kuratorium*) which had been set up by the Bank Act 1875, was removed.

of Governors were directly accountable to the General Council, which, however, did not resemble a democratically elected body.

1.2. The Reichsbank in the Third Reich

The *Ermächtigungsgesetz* of March 1933 marked the seizure of power of the national socialist regime under Adolf Hitler and the end of parliamentary democracy.[126] What followed was a political process in which all institutions were to be brought in line with government policy. This included the Reichsbank.[127] The statutory independence of the Reichsbank, which had been gradually established with the Bank Acts of 1922 and 1924, was about to be revoked.

The first step was the amendment of the Bank Act 1924 in 1933.[128] The General Council was removed and its role in the appointment and dismissal of the president and other members of the Board of Directors were transferred to the Reich President (*Reichspräsident*). That the general trend of enforced political conformity under the regime of the National Socialist Party (*NSDAP*) with Hitler as its sole policy maker, would also included the Reichsbank became obvious, at the latest, with a second amendment of the Bank Act 1924 in 1937.[129] The amendment followed a speech by Chancellor Hitler in the Lower Chamber of Parliament (*Reichstag*) in January 1933. Rejecting the influence of the allies during the Weimar Republic he declared the unrestricted power of the German Reich over the Reichsbank.[130] To this extent the new § 6 declared:

> "The Bank is administered by the Board of Directors, which is directly subordinate to the *Führer* and Reich Chancellor;"

Thus, the Reichsbank was not only accountable to but furthermore (an external part) of the government.

The process of bringing the Reichsbank in line with the totalitarian regime was completed with a new Bank Act in June 1939, the programmatic preamble to which reflects the conviction at the time.[131] The Reichsbank was renamed

[126] Gesetz zur Behebung der Not von Volk und Reich vom 24. März 1933, RGBl. I, 141, which eliminated the separation of powers between the legislative and the executive by transferring the power upon government to amend legislation outside the constitutional procedure and in contradiction to constitutional provisions.

[127] For a close examination on the role of the private banking sector cf. L. Gall *et al.*, *Die Deutsche Bank 1870–1995* (C.H. Beck, Munich, 1995).

[128] Gesetz zur Änderung des Bankgesetzes vom 27. Oktober 1933, RGBl. II, 827.

[129] Gesetz zur Neuregelung der Verhältnisse der Reichsbank und der Deutschen Reichsbahn vom 10. Februar 1937, RGBl. II, 47.

[130] Foreign influence had previously been a reason for the president of the Reichsbank, Hjalmar H.G. Schacht, to resign in early 1930, only to be re-appointed in March 1933 with the support of Adolf Hitler. Additionally, Schacht became Minister of Finance in 1934.

[131] Gesetz über die Deutsche Reichsbank vom 15 Juni 1993, RGBl. I, 1015, hereafter referred to as the Bank Act 1939. The preamble stated: "Die Deutsche Reichsbank untersteht als deutsche Notenbank der uneingeschränkten Hoheit des Reichs. *Sie dient der Verwirklichung der durch die nationalsozialistische Staatsführung gesetzten Ziele* im Rahmen des ihr anvertrauten

Deutsche Reichsbank. With respect to the internal organisation of the Reichsbank, the Board of Directors had to act in accordance with the instructions of the *Führer.* He also supervised the Bank. On the Board of Directors, the decisions were to be taken by the president of the Board only. Consequently, in order to follow through the principle of full control of the government over the Bank, the president and the other members were elected by the *Führer* and Chancellor of the Reich himself. The latter had the power to determine the period of time the members would serve and to dismiss them at any time without the need for an "important reason".[132] One example is the reaction of the Reich Chancellor, Hitler, following a memorandum in January 1939 signed by all members of the Board of Directors requesting government measures against ruinous inflation. Six of the eight members, including the president and the vice-president of the Reichsbank, were dismissed within weeks.

The Bank Act 1939 was one of many manifestations of the omnipresent *Führerprinzip.* As Marsh describes vividly, the Reichsbank was more than just a victim of political circumstances. Caught up between economic necessities and political collaboration, the Reichsbank played an ambivalent role in the Third Reich, ranging from indirect resistance against to straightforward support for the regime.[133] Its close (statutory) links to government paved the way for its downfall, together with the rest of the German Reich, as defeat and breakdown became inevitable.

1.3. The Bank deutscher Länder *and the* Landeszentralbanken

It was in the early period—"*die Stunde Null*"—of German post-war history that the foundations for an economic success story would be laid. Germany had been divided into different sectors, each sector being controlled and administered by one allied state.[134] From 1945 onwards the United States worked towards the decentralisation of the banking sector and the establishment of State central banks. The American ideas differed considerably from the ideas of German officials, especially on the issue of the supervisory powers of the government over the future State central banks.[135] By 1946, after allied talks on the establishment of a united central bank system for the whole territory of Germany had failed, a final draft of a state central bank law was passed by the American military government and in the following months transformed into state laws

Aufgabenbereiches, insbesondere zur Sicherstellung der deutschen Währung" (emphasis added). The racial policy of the time is to be found as well, e.g. § 11(2) with respect to the descent of the shareholders.

[132] Bank Act 1937, §§ 3, 4.

[133] Marsh, n. 110 above. One sad and horrifying chapter in the history of the Reichsbank in the Third Reich is the storage of jewellery and dental gold which had been robbed from the victims of the regime in the concentration camps of the occupied territories in the east.

[134] The United States, the United Kingdom, France, and the Soviet Union each occupied one zone with the former capital of the German Reich, Berlin, being divided into four separate sectors.

[135] J.M. Dodges, "Central Banking and Banking Supervision", Memorandum of 1 Nov. 1945, as cited in Wandel, n. 106 above, at 50, n. 112.

(*Landesgesetze*) in four German states.[136] The French military government followed the American example and ordered the state governments in its zone to establish State central banks.[137] The British zone of control remained outside this scheme until the UK and the United States finally agreed upon the establishment of the *Bank deutscher Länder* (Bank of German States) in 1948 and State central banks were set up in the four German states of the British zone.[138] The State central banks consisted of a directorate and an administrative council. The directorate, consisting of a president, a vice-president and other members, managed the State central banks. Representatives of industry and commerce, the agricultural sector, employees, the private banks and the state governments made up the administrative council, which was the policy-maker of the State central banks.

In the Soviet-occupied part of Germany the functions of a note-issuing Bank were at first transferred to the newly established, Soviet controlled *Garantie- und Kreditbank* (Guarantee and Credit Bank) which was later replaced by the *Deutsche Notenbank*. So-called issuing and clearing banks (*Emmissions- und Girobanken*) functioned as State central banks in the five Soviet occupied states. Both the *Garantie- und Kreditbank* and thereafter the *Deutsche Notenbank* were strictly centralised.[139]

In March 1948, after vehement debates over the basic structure of a centralising institution between the United States and Great Britain[140], a compromise in the shape of the *Bank deutscher Länder* (BdL) was reached.[141] It was aimed at co-ordinating the State central banks—initially—of these two economic zones.[142] The French military government added its economic zone in June 1948.[143]

The BdL was established as a legal person under public law with its place of business and legal seat in Frankfurt a.M.[144] Its initial capital was not held by shareholders, but by the State central banks according to their total deposits.[145] Though the BdL and the State central banks factually took over the functions of the Reichsbank neither of them can be considered as its legal successor, since it was not until 1961 that the Reichsbank was formally dissolved and liqui-

---

[136] Law no. 60, Military Government Gazette Germany, Issue I, 16 Mar. 1948 (APO 407) (United States Area of Control); Ordinance no. 129, Military Government Gazette Germany, issue no. 27, 991 (British Zone of Control). The four states included Bayern, Württemberg-Baden, Hessen, and Bremen.

[137] State central banks were established in Baden and Rheinland-Pfalz.

[138] Ordinance No. 132, Military Government Gazette Germany , Issue no. 23, 703 (British Zone of Control), establishing State central banks for Niedersachsen, Nordrhein-Westfalen, Schleswig-Holstein and Hamburg. The *Bank deutscher Länder* is hereafter referred to as BdL.

[139] Wandel, n. 106 above, 64–65.

[140] Marsh, n. 110 above, 194 *et seq.*; the Americans preferred the establishment of a "Land Central Bank Commission", which was supposed to co-ordinate and guide the politics of the State central banks, whereas the British preferred a real central bank.

[141] According to Wandel, n. 106 above, 67–8, even the name was subject of disagreement.

[142] N. 141 above.

[143] Verordnung der Militärregierung Nr. 203, Abl. Nr. 250/256, 1912, backdated to Mar. 1948.

[144] Which was part of the United States zone of control at the time.

[145] Art. V(25 a) law establishing the BdL, similar to the Federal Reserve System.

dated.[146] The BdL comprised a Board of Directors (*Zentralbankrat*) and a Board of Managers (*Direktorium*).[147] The Board of Managers was the executive organ of the BdL with the task of executing the policies and decisions of the Board of Directors, and to represent the Bank in judicial proceedings and all other matters.[148] The Board of Directors which consisted of a chairman, the president of the Board of Managers and the presidents of the State central banks was the policy board of the Bank.[149] It had moreover the task of controlling the performance of the Board of Managers which, in executing the BdL's policies, was accountable to the Board of Directors. Article IV (24d) of the law establishing the BdL stated in this respect: "[t]he president of the Board of Managers shall be responsible to the Board of Directors for the execution of all decisions of the Board of Directors and for the general conduct of the business of the Bank". Additionally, the Board of Directors had the right to dismiss any member of the Board of Managers—once again—"for important reasons".[150]

The composition of the Board of Directors, its role as policy-maker and its powers in the control of the Board of Managers were signs of the authority that the State central banks had, putting them on an equal footing with the BdL on the Federal level, making this a real two-tier system. With respect to the relationship between the BdL and the government, the law establishing the BdL allows a twofold assessment. The near coalition of central bank and government, as was the case for the Reichsbank at some stage, was disentangled. Article I(3) of the law establishing the BdL stated: "[e]xcept as otherwise provided herein or by law, the Bank shall not be subject to the instructions of any political body or public non-judicial agency". This provision, however, only referred and applied to German political bodies as the Allies were not about to exclude the BdL from their overall control and supervision of the German economic zones. In determining its policies, the Board of Directors was *de jure* subject to the directions of the Allied Bank Commission, based at the seat of the BdL, which functioned as the supervisory organ of the three western military governments.[151] In order to make the control of the Allied Bank Commission effective, the Bank was obliged to submit to the Allied Bank Commission any reports and information which the Commission required.[152] Cases of misrepresentation and/or false information of the BdL or

[146] Gesetz zur Liquidation der Deutschen Reichsbank und der deutschen Golddiskontbank vom 2. August 1961, BGBl. I, 1165.
[147] These are the official translations used in Law No. 60 of 1948, above. Note that in the context of the Bundesbank different terms are used.
[148] Art. IV(20, 24e–h) law establishing the BdL.
[149] Ibid., Art. IV(20). The chairman was elected by the members of the Board of Directors for a renewable term of three years. During his term of office, the chairman was excluded from membership of the Board of Managers or Board of Directors of any State Central Bank. The chairman held a powerful position on the Board of Directors, as his vote was decisive in the event of a tie in the decision-making process of the Board.
[150] Ibid., Art. IV(24 c). This provision, however, cannot be compared with the somewhat general clause in the case of the Reichsbank, since the conditions had to be stated in detail.
[151] Ibid., Art. II(6).
[152] Ibid., Art. II(7).

State Central Bank by any member of the Board of Directors or Board of Managers could be sanctioned with fines and/or an imprisonment.[153] However, in practice the Allied Banking Commission did not restrict the BdL to a significant extent.[154]

The biggest task which the BdL faced may also be considered its biggest achievement: the monetary reform in the areas occupied by the American, British and French in 1948, thereby replacing the Reichsmark with the *Deutsche Mark*.[155]

The coming into existence of a new German constitution, the Basic Law,[156] which came into force on 24 May 1949, marked the beginning of the end of the BdL, inasmuch as Article 88 of the Basic Law conferred the right to establish a currency- and note-issuing bank as Federal bank upon the Federal government.[157]

An interim law for the amendment of the law establishing the BdL[158] redefined the relationship between the BdL and the Federal government. This interim law was the product of the new democratically elected legislator in a Germany which gradually regained sovereignty. As in many other areas, it marked the passing of control of legislative and executive functions from the allies to the new German Federal state. The interim law removed allied control over the BdL.[159] Instead, the Bank was obliged to observe and, in the framework of its tasks, to support the general economic policy of the Federal government.[160] Moreover, the Federal Ministers of Finance and Economics or their permanent representatives were given the right to participate in the meetings of the Board of Directors. They also had the right to demand meetings of the Board of Directors.[161] In the course of meetings, the members of the Federal government had the right to ask for the suspension of a decision for up to eight days if they raised doubts about the decision's compatibility with the general economic policy of the Federal government.[162] Likewise, the BdL was

---

[153] Law establishing the BdL, Art. VII(35–37).

[154] H. Berger, *Konjunkturpolitik im Wirtschaftswunder, Handlungsspielräume und Verhaltensmuster von Zentralbank und Regierung in den 1950er Jahren* (Diss., Munich, 1995); Marsh, n. 110 above, at 192, who observes that the influence seems to have focused on appointment procedures, as especially the US opposed personnel with a past in the Reichsbank/banking sector in the Third Reich.

[155] For more details cf. e.g. R. Klump (ed.), *40 Jahre Deutsche Mark: die politische und ökonomische Bedeutung der westdeutschen Währungsreform vor 1948* (Steiner Verlag Wiesbaden, Stuttgart, 1989).

[156] Grundgesetz für die Bundesrepublik Deutschland vom 23. Mai 1949, BGBl., 1, as amended; hereafter referred to as the Basic Law.

[157] Cf. Chap. 4 I 1.3. for a detailed evaluation.

[158] Übergangsgesetz zur Änderung des Gesetzes zur Einrichtung der Bank deutscher Länder vom 10. August 1951, BGBl. I, 509; hereafter referred to as interim law 1951.

[159] Art. II(6–7) interim law 1951 removed the Allied Banking Commission.

[160] Ibid., Art. II(6a).

[161] Ibid., Art. II(6b).

[162] Ibid., Art. II(6c); for more details on the application of this mechanism, cf. Chap. 4 V.

obliged to forward any reports and information requested by the Federal government.[163]

Although the German constitution as early as 1949 had conferred upon the Federation the task of setting up a legislative framework for a Federal bank, it took the Federal legislator another eight years until the law governing the Bundesbank was finally brought into force on 1 August 1957.[164] The reason for the delay was to be found in two conflicts. As a competence norm, Article 88 of the Basic Law falls short of stipulating the proper legal basis for the Bundesbank. During the drafting of the BBankG this led to a dispute between the Federal government and the *Länder* about the correct legislative procedure for the establishment of the Bundesbank under Article 88 of the Basic Law ensuring the proper participation of the *Länder*.[165]

In the system of the Basic Law, generally, two different legislative procedures exist, which, to some extent, reveal the Federal structure of the German constitution.[166] The so-called *Einspruchsgesetz*, on the one hand, characterises an Act of the Lower House of Parliament (*Bundestag*), to which the Upper Chamber of Parliament (*Bundesrat*), representing the *Länder* governments, can (only) object.[167] An objection by the Bundesrat can be overruled by the Bundestag in accordance with the procedures laid down in Article 77(4) of the Basic Law, thereby adopting the law against the will of the *Länder*.[168] The so-called *Zustimmungsgesetz*, on the other hand, refers to an act of the Bundestag requiring the consent of the Bundesrat.[169] Unlike in the case of the *Einspruchsgesetz*, the Bundesrat cannot be overruled and thus, without its consent, the Bundestag cannot adopt a law. Except as otherwise provided for by the Basic Law, the normal legislative procedure is considered to be the *Einspruchsgesetz*.[170]

Arguing that Article 88 of the Basic Law does not expressly provide for a *Zustimmungsgesetz*, the Federal government assumed that the consent of the Bundesrat was not required for the adoption of the BBankG. The *Länder*, on the contrary, considered the consent of the Bundesrat mandatory. The dispute on the participatory rights of the *Länder* was more than just an academic question, since the Federal government and the *Länder* had contrary views on the organisational structure of the Bundesbank. The requirement of consent would thus have influenced the drafting of the BBankG considerably. Even though the

[163] Ibid., Art. II(7).
[164] Gesetz über die deutsche Bundesbank vom 26. Juli 1957, BGBl. I, 745, as amended; hereafter referred to as BBankG.
[165] Note that Art. 88 Basic Law confers the task of creating the Bundesbank upon the Federation without explicitly determining the legal basis for this institution. In this context it has sometimes been suggested that the Bundesbank could be established without a formal law. However, the vast majority of publications consider a formal law to be obligatory, cf. Stern, n. 100 above, § 35 II.1., with further references.
[166] Art. 77 Basic Law.
[167] Art. 77(3) Basic Law.
[168] Ibid., Art. 78. Also Chap. 4 V 2.
[169] Art. 77 Basic Law.
[170] Ibid., Art. 77(3).

Federal Constitutional Court has since expressed the view that consent of the Bundesrat is not obligatory, the basic argument still surfaces occasionally, as recent discussions in the context of the restructuring of the BBankG subsequent to German reunification have shown.[171]

The second dispute was closely associated with this conflict of interest between the Federal government and the *Länder*, but related to the organisational structure of the Bundesbank. As has been explained above, Article 88 of the Basic Law confers the task of creating the legislative framework for the Bundesbank upon the Federal legislator. The provision not only falls short of determining the proper legislative procedure, it also falls short of determining the organisational structure with respect to a centralised or decentralised system. This gave rise to intense discussions. The Federal government preferred a one-tier centralised central bank system, whereas the *Länder* were in favour of the existing decentralised system that had been introduced with the BdL and which secured for them a high level of participation and/or influence.[172] But there were also controversies within the Federal government. Dissenting opinions at ministerial level resulted in the presentation of two different drafts in the Bundestag, one by the Ministry of Economics and one by the Ministry of Finance. The so-called Schaeffer-Draft (*Schaeffer-Entwurf*), by the Ministry of Finance, promoted a decentralised Federal system, thereby basically transferring the rights of the Allied Banking Commission to the Federal government, whereas the so-called Erhard-Draft (*Erhard-Entwurf*), by the Minister of Economics, favoured a centralised single tier system, while granting the Bank autonomy from the Federal government.[173] The conflict was finally resolved with the so-called Scharnberg-Compromise (*Scharnberg-Kompromiß*) according to which the State central banks were to be preserved as the main administrations of the Bundesbank in the *Länder*. It also ensured the participation of the State central banks and thus, indirectly, of the *Länder*, in the Bundesbank.[174] Samm refers in this context to an organisational compromise (*Organisationskompromiß*), taking both centralised and decentralised elements into consideration.[175] According

---

[171] BVerfGE 14, 196, at 215; also: F. Klein, "Rechtsgutachten über die Frage, ob das Bundesbankgesetz in der Fassung des Regierungsvorlage vom 18. Oktober 1956 der Zustimmung des Bundesrates bedarf", *WM* (1957), 1074–88; U. Häde, "Das Gesetz zur Änderung von Vorschriften über die Deutsche Bundesbank", *NJW* (1994), 3214–32, 3215 *et seq.*

[172] Note that the influence of the Federal States in the drafting of the BBankG depended to a large extent upon their power in the legislative procedure.

[173] H. Faber, in R. Wassermann (principal publisher), *Kommentar zum Grundgesetz für die Bundesrepublik Deutschland*, Vol. 2, Reihe Alternativkommentare, on Art. 88, cite notation 5. In the legislative procedure, the Bundestag finally forwarded a draft to the Bundesrat which promoted the centralised single tier system.

[174] The compromise was reached in the Conciliation Committee (*Vermittlungsausschuß*) of the Lower and Upper House of Parliament. Cf. also Chap. 4 I.

[175] C.-Th.Samm, "Die Unabhängigkeit der Bundesbank- Verfassungsauftrag oder ordnungspolitische Chance?" in H.J. Hahn (ed.), *Geldverfassung und Ordungspolitik* (Nomos, Baden-Baden, 1989), 143–67, at 151, with further references to the different opinions at the time.

to the new BBankG the State central banks were absorbed by the BdL which in return was taken over by the Bundesbank.[176]

1.4. German Reunification

Finally, German Reunification should be mentioned. In the process of German reunification the Dmark and therefore the Bundesbank in its role as the note-issuing bank of the Federal Republic of Germany, played an important role. After the monetary reform of 1948, once again the Dmark came in at a crucial moment in German post-war history.[177] The Treaty Establishing A Monetary, Economic and Social Union (*Vertrag über die Schaffung einer Währungs-, Wirtschafts- und Sozialunion*) which came into force on 30 June 1990, established monetary union.[178] The monetary system of the German Democratic Republic (GDR) was integrated into that of the Federal Republic of Germany and the Bundesbank extended its activities to the east, thereby replacing the central bank of the GDR, the so-called *Staatsbank*.[179] And as though to reassure everyone that this process would not influence the independent position of the Bundesbank, Article 10 (3) of the Treaty states:

"The Deutsche Bundesbank, *by deploying its instruments on its own responsibility and, pursuant to Section 12 of the Bundesbank Law, independent of instructions from the Governments of the Contracting Parties*, shall regulate the circulation of money and credit supply in the entire currency area with the aim of safeguarding the currency."[180]

Ironically, German reunification also marked one of the rare occasions of open disagreement between the Bundesbank and the Federal government as the former was sceptical about an early monetary union, and in particular opposed the one to one conversion rate advocated by the Federal government and implemented in the Treaty Establishing a Monetary, Economic and Social Union.[181]

---

[176] § 1 BBankG.

[177] With respect to the German monetary union cf. D. Haferkamp, "Die deutsche Währungsunion- bereits Währungsgeschichte?", *DtZ*, vol. 2 no. 6 (1991), 201–20; A. Zöller, *Staatsbank der DDR und Deutsche Bundesbank. Ein Vergleich* (Diss., University Würzburg, 1991), on the *Staatsbank*.

[178] Vertrag zur Schaffung einer Währungs-, Wirtschafts- und Sozialunion vom 10. May 1990, BGBl. II, 518. English translation in (1990) 29 ILM 1108. Cf. in particular Chap. II, Art. 10 of the Treaty.

[179] For more details on the consequences of the monetary union for the structure of the Bundesbank, cf. Chap. 3 III 2.

[180] Emphasis added.

[181] The Bundesbank had advised a two to one conversion rate.

2. Institutional structure

The Bundesbank has its seat in Frankfurt a.M.[182] It constitutes an immediate Federal legal person under public law (*bundesunmittelbare juristische Person des öffentlichen Rechts*).[183] The exact classification of the Bundesbank within the German administrative system, where generally three forms of legal persons, including foundations under public law (*Stiftungen*), public law institutions (*Anstalten*), and public-law corporations (*Körperschaften*), can be distinguished is not undisputed.[184] The Bundesbank has been described as a public law institution (*Anstalt*), but also as an atypical public law institution (*atypische Anstalt*), and an institution *sui generis*.[185] The classification of the Bundesbank as part of the executive branch of government is undisputed. The characterisation of the Bundesbank as an immediate Federal legal person is taken as an argument for the federal, as opposed to *Länder*, ownership of the Bundesbank. Indeed, the capital of the Bundesbank is held by the Federation.[186]

According to § 5 of the BBankG, the Bundesbank consists of three organs, namely the Board of Directors, (*Direktorium*), the State Central Bank Directorates (*Vorstände der Landeszentralbanken*), and the Central Bank Council (*Zentralbankrat*).[187]

2.1. Board of Directors

The Board of Directors is the central executive organ of the Bundesbank. Generally, its objective is to carry out the resolutions (*Beschlüße*) of the Central Bank Council. It guides and administers the Bundesbank to the extent that these tasks have not been assigned to the Directorates of the state central banks.[188] The Board of Directors is—among others—explicitly charged with open mar-

---

[182] § 2 sentence 2 BBankG in the version of 20 Feb. 1991 (*Gesetz zur Änderung des Gesetzes über die Deutsche Bundesbank*, BGBl. I, 481).

[183] Ibid., § 2 sentence 1.

[184] For an overview of the types of legal persons under German public law cf. H.J. Wolff/O. Bachof/R. Stober, *Verwaltungsrecht*(10th edn., C.H. Beck, Munich, 1994), § 34, side notation 6 *et seq.*

[185] Th. Maunz, in Th. Maunz/G. Dürig (eds.), *Grundgesetz: Kommentar*, loose-leaf (7th edn., C.H. Beck, Munich, October 1996), Art. 88, side notation 8; Stern, n. 100 above, § 35 I 4; to the contrary L. Gramlich, "Die deutsche Bundesbank im Verfassungsgefüge des Grundgesetzes", *JuS Lernbogen* 11/88, L 81–88; H.J. Hahn, "Die Deutsche Bundesbank im Verfassungsrecht", *BayVBl.* 1992, Heft 2, 33–37 and Heft 3, 70–4, 70–1, with further references, for whom the Bundesbank is an atypical public law institution; according to D. Uhlenbruck, *Die verfassungsmäßige Unabhängigkeit der Deutschen Bundesbank und ihre Grenzen* (Diss., Cologne, 1967), at 71, the Bundesbank is an institution *sui generis*.

[186] § 2 BBankG.

[187] Note that the order of examination relates to the composition of the different organs, rather than to their functions and importance with regard to monetary policy.

[188] § 7 (1) BBankG, which includes a (non-conclusive) enumeration of the areas of responsibility of the Board of Directors.

ket operations, foreign exchange transactions, and transactions with the Federal government. It represents the Bank judicially and extra-judicially.[189]

The Board of Directors consists of the president, a vice-president, and up to six additional members.[190] The members of the Board are elected for a renewable period of eight years.[191] According to § 9(1) of the BBank charter, the Board of Directors meets on demand normally twice a week on notice of the president of the Bundesbank.[192] In practice these meetings take place on Wednesdays.[193] According to § 9(2) the Board of Directors has a quorum, if half of its members attend the meeting. Since only decisions on the annual accounts require a two-third majority vote, in all other circumstances a simple majority vote has to be considered decisive. Decisions on the internal relocation of functions of the Board of Directors require the attendance of all members of the Board of Directors and, moreover, demand the consent of the President of the Bundesbank.

2.2. State central banks

The existence of State central banks (*Landeszentralbanken*)[194] in essence does not resolve the assessment that the Bundesbank represents a centralised system, albeit with federal structures.[195] This is due to the fact that these institutions merely constitute central offices (*Hauptverwaltungen*), which function as administrative branches of the Bundesbank. In this respect the name State central banks may be misleading as it suggests the existence of autonomous institutions at the level of the *Länder*.[196] At the lowest level, under these central offices local branch offices exist.[197] The tasks of the State central banks in particular include transactions with the Federal states and public authorities in the Federal states, as well as transactions with credit institutions and public authorities to the extent that they do not fall under the authority of the Board of

---

[189] Ibid., § 11 (1).

[190] For a list of the presidents of the Bundesbank since its inception, cf. *Die Bank* (6) 1995, 72 *et seq.*

[191] § 7 (3) BBankG; under special circumstances members may be appointed for a shorter period, but at least two years. For more details on the appointment and dismissal procedures, cf. Chap. 4 IV; also §§ 31 *et seq.* BBankG.

[192] According to § 34 BBankG, in addition to the BBankG, the conduct of the organs of the Bundesbank is governed by a charter (*Satzung*), which the Bundesbank has adopted in accordance with the Federal government. This charter functions as a code of procedure for the different organs of the Bundesbank. It may also only be changed in accordance with the Federal government. Cf. Satzung der Deutschen Bundesbank vom 27. November 1958, BAnz. 1959 Nr.7, hereafter referred to as BBank charter.

[193] This day of the week is deliberately chosen so that matters may be discussed the day before the Central Bank Council meeting.

[194] Occasionally the term "Land central banks" is used instead.

[195] The Federal elements of the Bundesbank will be observed throughout the evaluation of the Bundesbank.

[196] The name is a remainder of the prior system. It is therefore doubtful when Samm, n. 175 above, at 157 refers to a federal structure.

[197] At the time of writing of this book in 1997–8, 167 branches existed.

Directors of the Bundesbank.[198] These transactions are handled through the branch offices of the State central banks.

The term *State* central banks suggests the existence of a central bank in each of the 16 *Länder*. This was in fact the case before the 11 old *Länder* in the course of German reunification were joined by five new *Länder*. The integration of the five new states made a restructuring of the Bundesbank necessary.[199] Instead of creating a new state central bank for each of the five new *Länder*, the structure of the Bundesbank was tightened by creating state-overlapping (*länderüber-greifende*) State central banks, thereby avoiding the enlargement of the decision-making bodies of the Bundesbank.[200] According to § 8(1) of the BBankG the nine State central banks include: Baden-Württemberg; Free State of Bavaria (*Freistaat Bayern*); Berlin and Brandenburg; Free Hanseatic City of Bremen, Lower Saxony and Saxony-Anhalt (*Freie Hansestadt Bremen, Niedersachsen* and *Sachsen-Anhalt*); Free and Hanseatic City of Hamburg, Mecklenburg-Western Pomerania and Schleswig-Holstein (*Freie Hansestadt Hamburg, Mecklenburg-Vorpommern* and *Schleswig-Holstein*); Hesse (*Hessen*); North Rhine-Westphalia (*Nordrhein-Westfalen*); Rhineland-Palatinate and Saarland (*Rheinland-Pfalz* und *Saarland*); and Free States of Saxony and Thuringia (*Freistaat Sachsen* und *Thüringen*).[201]

Each State central bank is headed by a Directorate (*Vorstand*), which is generally composed of a president and a vice-president.[202] The State central bank representing the Free Hanseatic City of Bremen, Lower Saxony and Saxony-Anhalt and the State Central Bank representing the Free and Hanseatic City of Hamburg, Mecklenburg-Western Pomerania and Schleswig-Holstein include an additional member in their Directorates in order to ensure a balanced representation of the individual *Länder* in these state-overlapping banks. All members are appointed for a renewable period of eight years.[203]

Part III (§§ 12–15) of the BBank charter describes the procedures for the internal functioning of the Directorate of the State central banks. The members of the Directorate normally meet twice a week. Decisions are taken by a simple majority vote. In the case of a tie the vote of the President is decisive.[204]

[198] § 8(2) in connection with § 7(1) no. 2 BBankG.

[199] The BBankG was brought into force by the (then still existing) East German legislator cf Gesetz über die Inkraftsetzung von Rechtsvorschriften der Bundesrepublik Deutschland in der DDR vom 21. Juni 1990, GBl. DDR I, 357, § 6.

[200] In order to preserve the balanced representation, the creation of five new State central banks would have made necessary an adjustment of the voting powers in the Central Bank Council, i.e. additional members on the Board of Directors, thereby endangering the effectiveness of the organ; N. Kloten, "Die Anpassung der Struktur an die veränderten staatlichen Gegebenheiten", *Zeitschrift für das gesamte Kreditwesen* (1991), 604–8, with respect to the different models for a restructured Bundesbank.

[201] § 8(1) BBankG. It is unclear whether the state-overlapping central banks moreover represent economically linked areas similar to the districts in the Federal Reserve System.

[202] Ibid., § 8(3).

[203] The appointment and dismissal procedures are examined in detail in Chap. 4 IV.

[204] §§ 13, 14 BBank charter.

Decisions with respect to the internal relocation of the tasks of the State central bank are taken by the Directorate. Such decisions require the consent of the President of the state central bank.

According to § 9 of the BBankG, each State central bank includes an Advisory Board (*Beirat*), which *advises* the president of the State Central Bank in the areas of monetary and credit policy and, more generally, the Directorate on the execution of its tasks.[205] In the view of some the Advisory Boards function as a restraining mechanism channelling the influence of economic and political interest groups from the outside.[206]

2.3. Central Bank Council

The Central Bank Council includes the members of the Board of Directors and the presidents of the State central banks. The Central Bank Council is the policy-making board of the Bundesbank. It determines monetary and credit policy. This includes decisions on the discount and Lombard rate, minimum reserve requirements and the interest rate orientation for open market operations of the Bundesbank. Moreover, the Central Bank Council issues common guidelines for the management and administration, and determines the responsibilities of the Board of Directors and the Directorates of the State central banks. It has the right to issue instructions to the Board of Directors and the Directorates of State central banks.[207]

Decisions are taken in the form of regular meetings. These meetings take place regularly every second Thursday on notice of the President of the Bundesbank.[208] The Central Bank Council is considered to have a quorum if two-thirds of its members take part in the meeting. Decisions are than taken by a simple majority vote.[209] Contrary to the position of the president in the State central bank Directorate, the president of the Bundesbank does not hold a dominant position in the Central Bank Council, since he counts for one vote only. His vote is moreover not decisive in case of a tie. According to § 13(2) of the BBankG, members of the Federal government have the right to take part in the deliberations of the Central Bank Council.[210]

---

[205] Cf. § 9(2) and (4) BBankG on the composition and procedures of appointment.

[206] Samm, n. 175 above, at 153, who characterises the Advisory Boards as part of the decentralised Federal element of the BBank.

[207] § 6(1) BBankG.

[208] Ibid., § 6(3), § 1 BBank charter; further meetings in case of a request by the President or at least three members of the Central Bank Council.

[209] See §§ 1 *et seq*. BBank charter for more details on the procedure of these meetings.

[210] Cf. § 3 BBank charter, according to which other members of the Federal government may also be invited if necessary. For a closer evaluation of the powers of the representatives of the Federal government in the Central Bank Council meetings, cf. Chap. 4 III 1.

3. Tasks

The basic functions of the Bundesbank are already defined in Article 88 of the Basic Law, which refers to a currency- and note-issuing bank. The two major functions of the Bundesbank are therefore to act as a monetary policy-maker and as a note-issuing bank.

3.1. Monetary policy

According to § 3 of the BBankG the Bundesbank regulates the amount of money in circulation and of credit supplied to the economy with the aim of safeguarding the currency. It is supposed to arrange for the handling by banks of domestic and external payments.[211] The principal monetary instruments of the Bundesbank include the refinancing policy, open market operations and the minimum reserve policy.[212]

According to § 15 of the BBankG in order to influence the circulation of the currency and lending the Bundesbank sets the discount and Lombard rates for its own transactions. Under the conditions laid down in § 19 of the BBankG the Bundesbank purchases from and sells to commercial banks bills (of exchange) for a discount rate determined by the Bundesbank. Moreover, the Bundesbank may extend interest-bearing loans to commercial banks in exchange for the pledging of certain types of securities and government-inscribed debts (*Schuldbuchforderungen*).[213] The interest rate for these loans is called the Lombard rate. The Bundesbank has discretion in setting the discount and Lombard rate as statutory limits do not apply.[214]

The extent of open market operations of the Bundesbank is determined by § 21 of the BBankG, according to which the Bundesbank may purchase or sell at market rates bills eligible for rediscount at the Bundesbank, Treasury bills and Treasury discount paper issued by the Federal government or the State governments, bonds and debt register claims, and other bonds officially listed at the stock exchange.

Finally, the Bundesbank is authorised to determine minimum reserve requirements for credit institutions in accordance with § 16 of the BBankG.

Decisions on exchange rate policy remain with the Federal government and thus, decisions on the participation in international organisations and the fixing of the exchange rate parities lay with the latter. As the holder of the national monetary reserves (mainly gold and US dollars) the Bundesbank implements the

---

[211] For more details of the monetary policy objective of the Bundesbank, cf. Chap. 4 II.

[212] For an overview cf. S. Kümpel, "Das währungspolitische Intstrumentarium der Deutschen Bundesbank aus rechtlicher Sicht", *WM*, Sonderbeilage nr. 1/1992.

[213] Art. 19(1) no. 3 BBankG.

[214] With regard to the effect of the discount and Lombard rates for the monetary policy of the Bundesbank, cf. Deutsche Bundesbank, *Die Geldpolitik der Bundesbank* (Frankfurt a.M., 1995), 98 *et seq.*, 105 *et seq.*

exchange rate policy in accordance with the decisions of the Federal government.[215] Since 1979 the Dmark has participated in the Exchange Rate Mechanism (ERM) of the European Monetary System (EMS), with the Bundesbank intervening in the exchange rate markets if necessary to keep currency fluctuations within the narrowly defined margins.

In accordance with the description in Article 88 of the Basic Law the Bundesbank acts as the note-issuing bank.[216]

3.2. Bank of Government

The Bundesbank acts as principal banker to the government. This includes acting as adviser to the Federal government when the latter seeks credit from the money market, making central bank credit accessible, the purchase of debenture bonds (*Schuldverschreibungen*), issuing coins on behalf of the Federal government (the Federal government holds the coining prerogative (*Münzregal*)), holding accounts for Federal government and, to some extent, the *Länder*.

Until 1994 the Bundesbank offered credit facilities to the Federal government, the *Länder* governments, and selected utility funds (*Sondervermögen*), such as the Federal post (*Bundespost*) and the Federal railways (*Bundesbahn*). However, this provision has been erased as a result of the provisions on state financing in the EC Treaty and in particular Article 104 EC.[217]

3.3. Banker's bank

The Bundesbank acts as the lender of last resort to the banking system. Moreover, it offers banking services for the technical realisation of non-cash transactions to private banks and the public sector. For this purpose commercial banks hold accounts at the Bundesbank. It has been pointed out that the Bundesbank also holds the minimum reserves of the commercial banks.

3.4. Banking supervision

The Bundesbank is not directly put in charge of the prudential supervision of the banking system. Rather, prudential supervision is exercised in close cooperation with the Federal Banking Supervisory Office (*Bundesaufsichtsamt für das Kreditwesen*) on the basis of the Banking Act (*Kreditwesengesetz*).[218]

---

[215] Deutsche Bundesbank, n. 214 above, 22 *et seq.*

[216] § 14 BBankG.

[217] Gesetz zur Änderung von Vorschriften über die Deutsche Bundesbank vom 8. Juli 1994, BGBl. I, 1465.

[218] BGBl. 1976 I, 1121, as amended; L. Gleske, "Bundesbank Independence, Organisation and Decision-making", *Central Banking*, vol. 6, no. 1 (1995), 21–8, 21 *et seq.*, on the role of the State central banks and their branch offices; see also Deutsche Bundesbank, *Banking Regulations 2* (Bundesbank, Frankfurt a.M., 1996), 6–15.

IV. DE NEDERLANDSCHE BANK NV[219]

From a legal point of view the Nederlandsche Bank is a good example of a central bank system where the legal position of the central bank may not entirely correspond with the position of the Bank *vis-à-vis* government in reality. On the one hand, in the past the statute of the central bank has not included any reference to the independence of the Nederlandsche Bank and the executive government was believed to retain the ultimate responsibility over monetary policy. On the other hand, as will be observed, in reality the Nederlandsche Bank has conducted monetary policy relatively free from government interventions. From an economic point of view the Nederlandsche Bank may serve as an example of a central bank located in a small and open economy where the internal value of the currency, to a large extent, is defined through the exchange rate limiting the central bank in its choice of monetary policy.

1. Historic development

1.1. Creation and development

The Nederlandsche Bank was set up on the initiative of King Willem I by decision of 25 March 1814 establishing its charter and rules, as a response to the stagnating economy in the Netherlands during and following the French occupation of the Netherlands between 1810 and 1813.[220] The Bank commenced work on 1 April 1814. Initially, the charter of the Bank was valid for a period of 25 years.[221] It was set up as a private company made up of shares (*compagnieschap zonder firma*), the legal forerunner under Dutch law of today's company limited by shares (*Naamloze Vennootschap*).[222] Its initial capital of Fl. 1.5 million was split up into 5,000 shares.[223] Despite its legal nature as a private entity, it becomes clear from the introductory notes to the Royal Charter 1814 that the Nederlandsche Bank was envisaged as a "National Bank initiated by the government".[224] The influence of the Crown, i.e. the Monarch and the government, was reflected in the organisational structure of the Bank. The management and

---

[219] Hereafter referred to as the Nederlandsche Bank.

[220] Besluit van den 25sten Maart 1814, no. 105, houdende het Octrooi en Reglement voor de Nederlandsche Bank, Stb. 1813–14, no. 40; hereafter referred to as Royal Charter 1814.

[221] Art. 1 Royal Charter 1814.

[222] Ibid., Art. 4. It is thus not entirely correct when B.C.J. van Velthoven/A. van Schaik, "De zelfstandigheid van de Nederlandsche Bank inzake het monetaire beleid in historisch, politiek-economisch perspectief" in H.W.J. Bosman/J.C. Brezet, *Sparen en Investeren Geld en Banken* (H.E. Stenfert Kroese B.V., Leiden/Antwerpen, 1987), 366–97, at 369, state: "De Bank verkrijgt bij haar oprichting de status van N.V. . . . "

[223] Arts. 4 and 7 Royal Charter 1814.

[224] Cf. considerations preceding the Royal Charter 1814.

administration of the Bank were handed down to a Governing Board (*directie*) consisting of six directors (*Directeuren*) one of whom was the president of the Bank.[225] The president held a predominant position as, unlike the other five directors, he was employed on a full-time basis. Alongside the Governing Board, a permanent secretary was established. The shareholders of the Bank were represented by the 50 biggest shareholders in the Bank. They appointed by majority of the votes six shareholders, who did not necessarily have to be from among these 50, to become supervisory directors (*Commissarissen*) of the Bank. The task of the Supervisory Directors was to oversee the financial situation of the Bank and in particular to discharge the Governing Board of the Bank at the end of each financial year, and, on advice of the Governing Board, to determine the dividend to be paid to the shareholders.[226] The Crown reserved to itself the right to appoint the president and the secretary without any form of prior consultation for an indefinite period.[227] The other five directors were appointed by the Crown which, however, had to choose from a list compiled by the directors and the Supervisory Directors meeting as a joint body.[228] Initially, the term of office of the directors was 2½ years and could be renewed.[229]

In the beginning, the operations of the Bank included—among others—discounting bills of exchange, trading in precious metals and the holding of current accounts for the receipt of money of the States and all public authorities.[230] Although an explicit legal basis in the Royal Charter 1814 was lacking, the Nederlandsche Bank issued banknotes, albeit that the Bank's operations in this field turned out to be of little success in the beginning.[231] Since the Bank did not have any branches or agencies its activities were mostly restricted to Amsterdam, where it had its seat.[232] In general, it has to be noted that the Bank did not operate very successfully and the general public took little interest in the new bank in the beginning. In fact, by 1816 only 60 per cent of the shares had been distributed in the private sector.[233]

Despite the Crown's original intentions when setting up the Nederlandsche Bank, the government's influence over the Bank was *de facto* relatively limited.[234] The majority of the Governing Board of the Bank was appointed on the initiative of the shareholders and the government had little influence on the

---

[225] Arts. 37–39 Royal Charter 1814.

[226] Ibid., Arts. 53–55.

[227] Ibid., Arts. 49–52.

[228] Ibid., Art. 52.

[229] The term of office derived from the wording of Art. 48 Bank Act 1814, according to which one of the 5 Directors had to resign every 6 months.

[230] Art. 20 Royal Charter 1814.

[231] A.F. Kamp, '*S Konings Oudste Dogter* (De Nederlandsche Bank, Amsterdam, 1968), 11 *et seq.* Several provisions of the Charter imply that the Bank can issue banknotes: Art. 29 *et seq.*

[232] Note, however, that according to Art. 43 Royal Charter 1814 the service was supposed to be extended to other business centres in the Netherlands.

[233] J. de Vries, "De Nederlandsche Bank", in M. Pohl/S. Freitag (eds.), *Handbook on the History of European Banks* (Edward Elgar, Aldershot, 1994), 743–8, at 743.

[234] Reference in H.H. van Wijk, op. cit., Chap. 2, n. 138, above, at 24.

operations of the Bank. In fact, on more than one occasion the Bank refused the Crown recourse to it for means of financing, thereby keeping its distance from government.[235] Part of the reason for the Bank's reluctance to grant loans was the loss of credibility with the general public which resulted from substantial financial backing of the Government.[236] Besides, the somewhat limited economic success of the Bank did not permit the granting of large loans. Despite all this, the Monarch seems to have had an almost affectionate perception of his creation:

> "The Nederlandsche Bank is my oldest daughter, I shall always continue to consider her as such."[237]

1.2. Consolidation

For a period of more than 100 years following its creation the position of the Nederlandsche Bank was consolidated. Apart from a relatively short period of time during the German occupation of the Netherlands during World War II the fundamental structure of the Nederlandsche Bank was preserved until its nationalisation. This is not to say, however, that the Bank was not subject to developments. Indeed, the fact that its privileges were always granted for a limited period of time ensured a regular review of its status both with regard to its tasks and its relationship with government.

After minor changes during the renewal of the royal charter of the Bank in 1838[238] the first major revision of the statute of the Bank took place in 1863. It reflected to a large extent the constitutional developments in the Netherlands in 1848 which—among others—strengthened the role of Parliament (e.g. direct elections, increased powers) and introduced the principle of ministerial accountability.[239] The legal basis of the Nederlandsche Bank was no longer based on a decision by the Crown, but rather on an act of Parliament.[240] The Bank Act 1863 amended the legal status of the Nederlandsche Bank in as much as the latter was transformed into a company limited by shares (*Naamloze Vennootschap* = *NV*).[241] The powers of the government were cut back in some areas, while

---

[235] Van Velthoven/van Schaik, n. 222 above, at 371.

[236] W.F. Duisenberg, "The History of the Nederlandsche Bank; A Guide for Europe?" in *Monetaire geschiedenis als wegwijzer voor de Europese Centrale Bank* (Nederlands Instituut voor het Bank- en Effectenbedrijf/Erasmus Universiteit Rotterdam, 1992), 21–9. When the Bank in 1834 did grant a loan the transactions were made by a figurehead which acted for the Treasury.

[237] Author's translation. Recorded in De Nederlandsche Bank, *Hoedster van de gulden* (4th edn., Amsterdam, 1988), at 4.

[238] Besluit van den 21sten Augustus 1838, waarbij het bestaan der Nederlandsche Bank wordt verlengd en bevestigd, Staatsblad 1838, No. 29; the privileges of the Nederlandsche Bank were prolonged for 25 years until 1864. The capital of the Bank was increased and its operations widened.

[239] K.J. Kraan, "Het Koninkrijk der Nederlanden" in L. Prakke/C.A.J.M. Kortmann (ed.), *Het staatsrecht van der landen der Europese Gemeenschappen* (4th edn., Kluwer, Deventer, 1993), 499–561, 499–500.

[240] Wet van den 22sten December 1863, houdende voorzieningen omtrent de Nederlandsche Bank, Stb. 1863, no. 148; hereafter referred to as the Bank Act 1863.

[241] Art. 3 Bank Act 1838.

strengthened in others. While the Monarch still appointed the president and the secretary on recommendation of the directors and Supervisory Directors, the five other directors were now appointed by those shareholders who were entitled to vote on the basis of nominations on which the directors and the Supervisory Directors agreed in a joint meeting. They were appointed on a rotary basis for a renewable period of five years.[242] For the first time the secretary was considered to be part of the Governing Board of the Bank.[243] The number of Supervisory Directors was raised to a minimum of 15 and they were explicitly charged with the supervision of the Governing Board of the Bank.[244] However, the Act introduced a so-called Royal Commissioner (*Koninklijken commissaris*), to be appointed and dismissed by the Monarch who was charged with overseeing the performance of the Bank on behalf of the government. He had the right to attend any meetings of the shareholders and the Supervisory Directors and could give advice. Although the Royal Commissioner was not admitted to attend the meetings of the Governing Board, the latter, upon request of the former, was obliged to forward complete information on the operations of the Bank.[245] The Governing Board became, moreover, obliged to publish an abridged balance once a week in the government gazette (*Nederlandsche Staatscourant*).[246]

With regard to the tasks of the Bank, the Bank Act 1863 for the first time explicitly authorised the Bank to issue banknotes. Since the Act prohibited other credit institutions from issuing banknotes, the Nederlandsche Bank effectively became the sole note-issuing bank in the Netherlands.[247] However, it was not until 1904 that its banknotes finally had the status of legal tender.[248] With the progressing industrialisation in the second half of the nineteenth century and the growing demand for means of financing as a result, the Bank expanded its activities in the area of discount (*disconteren*) and credit (*belenen*) operations. The Bank gradually established its role as lender of last resort. Moreover, its trading in precious metals effectively made it the holder of the national reserves.[249] The Bank Act 1863 obliged the Bank to expand its services by establishing a branch in Rotterdam and agencies throughout the Netherlands.[250]

[242] Art. 18 subpara. 2 Bank Act 1863.
[243] Compare the wording of Art. 37 Royal Charter 1814 with Art. 17 Bank Act 1863.
[244] Art. 17 sentence 2 Bank Act 1863.
[245] Ibid., Art. 20.
[246] Ibid., Art. 21.
[247] Ibid., Art. 11. It has to be noted, however, that the government reserved to itself the right to issue banknotes (*muntbiljetten*) for some time thereafter: cf. Wet van den 26den April 1852, tot uitgifte van Muntbiljetten, Stb. 1852, no. 90; Wet van den 27den April 1884, houdende nieuwe bepalingen nopens de uitgifte van muntbiljetten, Stb. 1884, no. 98.
[248] Wet van den 31sten December 1903, tot intrekking van den muntbiljetten, Stb. 1903, no. 336.
[249] Van Velthoven/van Schaik, n. 222 above, at 372. Since 1875 the Netherlands participated in the Gold Standard.
[250] Art. 5 Bank Act 1863.

During the preparation of the Bank Act 1888 the relationship between the Nederlandsche Bank and the government became the subject of discussions.[251] First, the legal nature of the Bank was questioned, since it was considered to be a contradiction that the Bank to some extent was observing public interests while at the same time still constituting a (private) company. However, despite proposals for the creation of a state bank (*Rijksbank*) the legal nature of the Bank remained unchanged. Still, the debate carried on until the nationalisation of the Bank. Interestingly, some of the basic arguments put forward today in favour of an independent central can already be found in this early stage in the development of a central bank.[252]

Apart from the debate on the legal nature of the Bank, differences arose between the government and the Bank on the relocation of the annual profits. It was argued that the quasi-monopoly position of the Bank in its areas of operation granted by the State justified that the State received a share in the profits of the Bank. As a result of this the Bank Act 1888 included provisions on profit-sharing.[253] In another area the government extended its grip on the Bank as, upon request of the Minister of Finance, the Bank had to provide the government with an interest-bearing loan.[254] Thereafter, the Bank Act 1903 furnished the government with the right to take out non-interest-bearing loans with the Nederlandsche Bank.[255] However, at the same time the government lost it privilege of issuing notes (*muntbiljetten*).[256]

The Bank Act 1888 amended the internal organisation of the bank to some extent by introducing dismissal procedures for the president, the secretary and the directors. According to this the president and the secretary could be dismissed by the Monarch upon request issued by the Governing Board and the Supervisory Directors in a joint meeting. The Bank Act 1888 did not list any conditions for dismissal. The position of the shareholders *vis-à-vis* the management of the Bank was strengthened in as much as the shareholders authorised to vote had the power to dismiss a Director of the Bank on a recommendation issued by the Governing Board and the Supervisory Directors in a joint meeting.[257] The position of the Royal Commissioner was further strengthened by determining that upon request of the Royal Commissioner the management of the Bank was obliged to forward all information which he required for the proper execution of his task. The Bank Act 1918 broadened the tasks of the Nederlandsche Bank

---

[251] Wet van den 7den Augustus 1888, tot verlening en wijziging van de Nederlandsche Bank verleende octrooi, Stb. 1888, no. 122; hereafter referred to as the Bank Act 1888. It prolonged the status of the Nederlandsche Bank as a bank of issue until 1904.

[252] Van Velthoven/van Schaik, n. 222 above, 374 *et seq.*, with further references.

[253] Art. 10 Bank Act 1888.

[254] Ibid., Art. 7.

[255] Art. 4 Wet van den 31sten December 1903, tot verlenging en wijziging van het aan de Nederlandsche Bank verleende octrooi, Stb. 1903, no. 335; hereafter referred to as the Bank Act 1903.

[256] Wet van den 31sten December 1903, tot intrekking van den muntbiljetten, n. 255 above.

[257] Art. 8 Bank Act 1888.

and also amended the organisational structure to some extent.[258] With regard to the latter the minimum number of directors was reduced to two, whereas the actual number was subject to a decision by the management and the Supervisory Directors in a joint meeting.[259] For the first time the directors had to be employed on a full-time basis. Moreover, an advisory commission (*commissie van advies*) was established consisting of five persons representing the business community to be appointed for a non-renewable term of five years by the shareholders authorised to vote on a recommendation of the Supervisory Board (*raad van commissarissen*).[260] It had to be consulted by the Governing Board on important matters, and the latter became obliged to notify the Supervisory Board of its intentions if it intended to deviate from the advice of the advisory commission. In some respects the advisory commission filled the gap between the Bank and the business community that had opened up as a consequence of abolishing the *non*-executive directors. The Bank Act 1918 also took account of the further development of the operations of the Bank. For example the role of the Nederlandsche Bank as a clearing bank was formally recognised, albeit that the Bank had been active in this area already since 1910.[261]

During the 1930s the tasks of the Bank were broadened further without introducing major institutional changes.[262] The Bank Act 1937 reduced the required number of directors on the Governing Board to one.[263] Moreover, it added an important policy instrument by permitting the Bank to trade in domestic bills of exchange. Finally, from 1940 exchange rate policy was exercised by the Bank on behalf of the government.

On 1 July 1943, after the German Reich had occupied the Netherlands, the Commissioner of the Reich for the occupied Dutch territories *(Reichskommissar für die besetzten niederländischen Gebiete)* replaced the Bank Act 1937 with a regulation which reconstructed the Nederlandsche Bank in its entirety.[264] For a short period the Nederlandsche Bank became a public body (*publiekrechtelijk lichaam/Körperschaft öffentlichen Rechts*) with regulatory

---

[258] Wet van den 25sten Juli 1918, tot verlenging en wijziging van het aan de Nederlandsche Bank verleende octrooi, Stb. II 1918, no. 475; hereafter referred to as the Bank Act 1918.

[259] Art. 11 Bank Act 1918.

[260] Ibid., Art. 13.

[261] Ibid., Art. 4. The first clearing house was set up in Rotterdam in 1910, followed by Amsterdam in 1917 and The Hague in 1920; *cf.* van Wijk, n. 234 above, 44 *et seq.*

[262] E.g. since 1930 the Nederlandsche Bank has participated in the Bank of International Settlement (Stb. II 1930, no. 181). For a detailed examination of the developments cf. A.M. De Jong, *De Wetgeving Nopens de Nederlandsche Bank 1914–1958* (Martinus Nijhoff, The Hague, 1960), 191 *et seq.*

[263] Wet van den 2den Februari 1937, tot verlenging en wijziging van het aan de Nederlandsche Bank verleende octrooi, Stb. I 1937, no. 400 and no. 401; hereafter referred to as Bank Act 1937.

[264] Verordening van den Rijkscommissaris voor het bezette Nederlandsche gebied betreffende De Nederlandsche Bank, No. 58/1943, Verordeningenblad vor het bezette Nederlandsche gebied 1943, 220 (bilingual, including also in a German version), hereafter referred to as Regulation 1943, cf. § 23; For an overview of the changes during the German occupation of the Netherlands cf. J. de Vries, *De Nederlandsche Bank- Geschiedenis Nader Beschouwd* (Martinus Nijhoff, Leiden/Antwerpen, 1992).

powers. Its structure had similarities to that of the Reichsbank in the German Reich at the time. However, despite the imposed new legal structure as a public body the Bank was not nationalised.[265] Complete control over the Bank was guaranteed as it became directly subordinated to the Commissioner of the Reich for the occupied Dutch territories.[266] Internally, the management of the Bank was in principle transferred to the president of the Bank to whom the Governing Board was subordinated.[267] The Supervisory Board and the advisory commission were abolished. De Jong describes the situation during the German occupation drastically:

> "the Nederlandsche Bank [became] inescapably the body through which the ransacking of the country was essentially carried out."[268]

1.3. Nationalisation

Shortly after the liberation of the Netherlands in May 1945 the status of the Nederlandsche Bank under the Bank Act 1937 was re-instated, while at the same time some considerable changes took place extending the influence of the government.[269] The most outstanding change was the right of the Minister of Finance "as far as necessary for the co-ordination of the monetary and financial policies of the government" to give binding instructions to the Nederlandsche Bank.[270] The advisory commission was suspended and a Bank Council (*Bankraad*) was established, consisting of the Royal Commissioner and eight additional members, to be appointed by the Minister of Finance for a period of four years. Made up of representatives of trade and commerce and the scientific community the task of the Bank Council was to advise the Minister of Finance in the exercise of his overriding power.[271] Moreover, the shareholder's appointments to the post of a director of the Bank had to be approved by the Crown.[272] The implications of these changes for the future development of the Nederlandsche Bank became clear from Decision 1945 itself which charged the Minister of Finance with the establishment of an advisory commission further to investigate a strengthening of the "public element" in the statute of the Bank through the transfer from a private towards a public-law or semi-public law ownership of the Bank.[273] By ministerial decree the so-called De Vries Commission (*commissie-De Vries*), was established. Shortly thereafter in

---

[265] However, according to § 8(2) Regulation 1943 certain requirements had to be met by shareholders.

[266] § 1 and § 2(1) Regulation 1943.

[267] Ibid., § 2(2).

[268] Author's translation and brackets added: De Jong, n. 262 above, at 293.

[269] Besluit van 1 October 1945 tot wederinvoering van de Bankwet 1937, Stb. 137, no. 401, hereafter referred to as Decision 1945.

[270] Author's translation. Art. 7 Decision 1945.

[271] Ibid., Art. 6(8).

[272] Ibid., Art. 5.

[273] Ibid., Art. 11.

December 1946 it came to the conclusion that the shares in the capital of the Nederlandsche Bank should be transferred to the State, while leaving intact the legal nature of the Bank as a company limited by shares.[274] The motive behind the commission's advice to uphold the legal nature of the Bank was to maintain the independent status of the Bank. Other ways of nationalisation would have infringed that status. The commission also suggested strengthening the Community element of the Bank, *inter alia*, by including representatives of the different social and economic groups in the Netherlands, and it made suggestions for a strengthening of the government's right to issue instructions to the Bank which had already existed since 1945.[275]

In 1948 the Nederlandsche Bank was nationalised and its shares in capital transferred to the State.[276] The nationalisation of the Bank stood at the end of a development which had its origin in the second half of the nineteenth century. For some observers the conjunction of a private company limited by shares which increasingly dealt with matters of general public concern was a paradox and—as has been observed before—on several occasions led to proposals to replace the Nederlandsche Bank by a state bank or to nationalise it respectively.[277] The Bank Act 1948 came into force on 1 August 1948.[278]

2. Institutional structure

As was the case prior to its nationalisation, the Nederlandsche Bank is a company limited by shares with its registered seat in Amsterdam.[279] Since its nationalisation the State has been the sole shareholder in the capital of the Nederlandsche Bank. The Bank embodies a single-tier structure. It operates a branch office in Rotterdam headed by a Director appointed by the Governing Board of the Bank. The branch is subordinated to the head office.[280] Additionally, the Bank currently features eight agencies located throughout the Netherlands.[281] The regional offices are involved in the circulation of banknotes

[274] Verslag van de Commissie inzake de herziening van het Statuut van De Nederlandsche Bank, Publikatie van de Afdeling Perszaken van het Ministerie van Financiën, The Hague, 1946.

[275] For more details on these and other proposals for the reorganisation of the Nederlandsche Bank by the *Commission de Vries* cf. De Jong, n. 262 above, 366 *et seq.*

[276] Wet van 23 April 1948, houdende verklaring van het algemeen nut van de naasting van de aandelen in het maatschappelijk kapitaal van De Nederlandsche Bank N.V. door de Staat en regeling dier naasting , Stb. II 1948, no. 165; Wet van 23. April 1938, houdende nieuwe bepalingen nopens het Statuut van De Nederlandsche Bank N.V., Stb. II 1948, no. 166, hereafter referred to as the Bank Act 1948.

[277] van Wijk, n. 234 above, at 38 *et seq.*

[278] Koninklijk besluit van 12 juli 1948 Stb. I 1948, no. 291.

[279] Ss. 2(1), 3(1) Bank Act 1948. The authorised capital of the Bank amounts to 20 million guilders, cf. s. 4.

[280] S. 3(2)–(4) Bank Act 1948. Cf. s. 25 on the appointment and removal of all employees of the Bank.

[281] Regional offices are located in Amsterdam, Arnhem, Breda, Drachten, Eindhoven, Hoogeveen, Utrecht and Wassenaar.

and coins and, moreover, provide the head office with information on economic development in the regions.

The Nederlandsche Bank is composed of a Governing Board, a Supervisory Board, a Royal Commissioner and a Bank Council.

2.1. Governing Board

The Governing Board of the Bank (*directie*) consists of a president, a secretary and between two and five executive directors (*directeuren*). The actual number of directors serving on the Board may vary, since it is decided upon by the Governing Board and the Supervisory Board as a joint body.[282] Currently, the Governing Board includes two executive directors.[283] The members of the Governing Board are appointed for a renewable term of seven years.

The Governing Board is in charge of the management of the Bank and the administration of its properties. All policy decisions of the Nederlandsche Bank are taken by the Governing Board. Moreover, the Governing Board is also in charge of appointing and dismissing all employees of the Bank.[284]

In accordance with section 25(2) of the Bank Act 1948 by-laws, drawn up by the joint meeting of the Governing Board and the Supervisory Board, lay down the powers and duties of the Governing Board.[285] Although according to the rules of procedure of the Governing Board, the Governing Board meets every working day, in practice meetings take place once a week on Thursday. The president of the Bank chairs these meetings. In addition to the directors, sub-directors or other employees of the Bank may attend the meetings and can be charged with the recording of minutes.[286] Decisions are taken by a simple majority vote of the members of the Governing Board present at the meeting. In practice decisions are taken by common accord rather than such a formal vote.[287] Only in the case of a tie does the president have a decisive vote. The only exception concerns decisions on a request for a discount loan or the granting of credits where a tie is considered as a rejecting vote.[288]

[282] S. 22(1) and (2) Bank Act 1948.
[283] Ibid., s. 23. For more details of the appointment and dismissal procedures of the members of the Governing Board, cf. Chap. 4 IV.
[284] S. 25 Bank Act 1948.
[285] Reglement van orde van 25 maart 1958 voor de werkzaamheden van der directie van de Nederlandsche Bank N.V., als bedoeld in het tweede lid van article 25 van de Bankwet 1948, here-after referred to as rules of procedure Governing Board.
[286] Ss. 3 and 4 rules of procedure Governing Board.
[287] Ibid., s. 6. The rules of procedure introduce a hierarchical order into the voting procedure, by requiring that the member of the Governing Board with the shortest service begins and that the president of the Bank is the last person to issue his vote. The members of the Governing Board have the possibility to put any dissent with a decision which has been taken by the Governing Board on the record.
[288] Ibid., s. 5.

2.2. *Supervisory Board*

The Supervisory Board (*raad van commissarissen*) consists of 12 members appointed by the Minister of Finance on a rotary basis for a renewable term of four years.[289] It is charged with the supervision of the management of the Bank's affairs and, moreover, approves the annual balance sheet and profit and loss account of the Bank, thereby discharging the Governing Board.[290] This corresponds with the description of the tasks of the Supervisory Board in companies limited by shares given in section 140(2) of the second book of the Dutch Civil Code on legal persons, according to which the Supervisory Board's function is to oversee the conduct of the management and the general course of business. Moreover, members of the Board participate in the Bank Council.

The Board meets at least twice a year, or more often upon request of the president of the Nederlandsche Bank, the chairman of the Board, or five of its members. The Royal Commissioner has the right to participate in these meetings.[291] Decisions are taken by secret ballot only if it concerns persons. Otherwise, decisions are taken orally. The chairman of the Board has a decisive vote in all but personnel matters. In case of a tie personnel matters are decided by drawing lots.

2.3. *Royal Commissioner*

The Royal Commissioner (*Koninklijke Commissaris*) is appointed by the Crown.[292] His task is to monitor the performance of the Bank on behalf of the government. As such he is subject to the instructions of the government.[293] The Royal Commissioner takes part in the meetings of the Supervisory Board and the joint meetings of the Governing Board and the Supervisory Board and, moreover, reviews the balance sheets and the profit and loss account of the Bank. Additionally, he acts as an adviser to the executive government in the person of the Minister of Finance, whom he has to brief on the meetings of the Governing Board he attends, as well the Governing Board of the Bank, subject to prior consultations with the Minister of Finance.[294]

---

[289] For more details of the appointment and dismissal procedures, cf. Chap. 4 IV.

[290] Reglement nopens de taak van de Raad van Commissarissen van De Nederlandsche Bank N.V., als bedoelt in Artikel 29 van de bankwet 1948. For more details of the role of the Supervisory Board, cf. Chap. 4 III 2.

[291] Arts. 3 and 4 Reglement nopens de taak van de Raad van Commissarissen, n. 290 above.

[292] For more details of the appointment and dismissal procedure, cf. Chap. 4 IV. It should be noted that the Royal Commissioner was abolished with the coming into force of the Bank Act 1998.

[293] Koninklijk besluit van 27 oktober 1972, no. 82, tot nadere vaststelling van de instructie van de Koninklijke Commissaris bij De Nederlandsche Bank N.V.

[294] For more details of the significance of the Royal Commissioner, cf. Chap. 4 III 2.

2.4. Bank Council

The Bank Council (*Bankraad*) consists of the Royal Commissioner, four members of the Supervisory Board to be appointed by the same and 12 representatives of different economic and social groupings appointed by the Crown.[295] Additionally, the members of the Governing Board, the Treasurer-General[296] or his alternate, and three representatives named by the Ministers of Economic Affairs, Agriculture, Food and Fisheries, and for Social Affairs and Employment respectively take part in the meetings of the Bank Council in an advisory capacity.[297] The Bank Council is kept informed by the president of the Nederlandsche Bank on the general economic and financial situation and on the policy conduct of the Bank. Until recently, the Minister of Finance, after consulting with the Governing Board, could seek the advice of the Bank Council on principal policy issues, and, more importantly, the Bank Council had the right to make recommendations on its own initiative to the Minister of Finance on such matters.[298] However, these functions of the Bank Council have recently been scratched in connection with an overhaul of the Government Advisory System.[299]

The Bank Council meets at least six times per year under the chairmanship of the Royal Commissioner. Additional meetings can be summoned upon request of the chairman or at least four members of the Bank Council.[300]

3. Tasks

Section 15 of the Bank Act 1948 lists in detail the operations which the Nederlandsche Bank can perform apart from issuing banknotes. In addition to the tasks explicitly listed in the Bank Act 1948, subject to approval by the Crown, after consulting the Bank Council, the Bank can, in the public interest, be charged with other activities, such as the participation in the Bank for International Settlement where the president of the Nederlandsche Bank is a member of the Board of Directors.[301]

---

[295] For more details on the appointment and dismissal procedure, cf. Chap. 4 IV.
[296] The Treasurer-General is a high civil servant in the Ministry of Finance.
[297] S. 33(1) Bank Act 1948.
[298] Ibid., *s.* 33(4) (old version), thereby making use of information gained from contacts with the different economic agents, cf. van Wijk, n. 234 above, at 54.
[299] Wet van 3 juli 1996, houdende opheffing van het adviesstelsel in zaken van algemeen verbindende voorschriften en beleid van het Rijk (Herzieningswet adviesstelsel), Stb. 1996, no. 377.
[300] S. 32(5) Bank Act 1948.
[301] For a detailed list of the additional activities of the Nederlandsche Bank based on s. 21, cf. listing on s. 21 in n. 12 on the Bank Act 1948, as published in De Nederlandsche Bank NV, *Bank Act 1948 and Articles of Association* (1994 edn.).

3.1. Monetary policy

According to section 9(1) of the Bank Act 1948 the Nederlandsche Bank regulates the value of the Dutch guilder with a view to keep it as stable as possible.[302] Due to the small and open character of the Dutch economy the Bank's activities in the area of monetary policy are somewhat limited and focus on the external value of the Guilder, that is the exchange rate regime. The Netherlands participate in the EMS where, in the framework of the ERM, the parity of the Dutch Guilder *vis-à-vis* the other participating currencies has to be kept within predetermined fluctuation margins by the Nederlandsche Bank. The *Dmark* functions as the anchor currency for the Guilder.[303]

It belongs to the traditional tasks of the Nederlandsche Bank as a central bank to have the sole right to issue banknotes and to be charged with the management of their distribution.[304] Moreover, on behalf of the Minister of Finance, the Bank distributes the coins in circulation.[305]

3.2. Government's bank

The Nederlandsche Bank acts as a fiscal agent for the government. It holds the Treasury's accounts and functions as the cashier for the government.[306] All incoming and outgoing payments, such as taxes and social security payments, are handled by the Bank. Until 1993, upon request of the Minister of Finance, the Bank was obliged to grant non-interest-bearing advances to the government to a maximum amount of 150 million guilders on sufficient security of Treasury notes for the temporary strengthening of the Treasury's position.[307] In the light of the newly introduced provisions on EMU into the EC Treaty by the TEU this provision was abolished and an explicit reference to the corresponding provision in the EC Treaty introduced.[308] Section 21a of the Bank Act 1948 states: "[t]he Bank fulfils its tasks in the framework of this law while observing Article 104 of the Treaty establishing the European Community."

3.3. Banker's bank

The commercial banks hold current accounts with the Nederlandsche Bank. The latter grants loans to the former in the form of contingents, specific amount of credit which a bank can take up within a period of three months, and special loans. The size of the contingents and special loans form the primary

---

[302] S. 9(1) Bank Act 1948. For more details on the monetary objective, cf. Chap. 4 II.

[303] J.de Haan, *Financiële markten en instellingen in Nederland* (unpublished, Groningen, 1997, 38 *et seq.*; cf. also Chap. 4 II 1.

[304] Ss. 9(2), 10 *et seq.* Bank Act 1948.

[305] Muntwet 1948, Stb. I 1948, no. 156.

[306] S. 19 Bank Act 1948.

[307] S. 20 Bank Act 1948 was annulled in 1993.

[308] Wet van 9 december 1993, Stb. 1993, no. 676.

instruments for the conduct of the monetary policy of the Nederlandsche Bank. Moreover, the commercial banks are obliged to hold cash reserves with the Nederlandsche Bank. The Nederlandsche Bank also promotes the domestic and foreign money transfer.[309] To this end it provides interbank exchange and settlement systems.[310]

3.4. Banking supervision

In accordance with section 9(3) of the Bank Act 1948 in connection with the Act on the Supervision of the Credit System 1992 (*Wet toezicht kredietwezen*)[311] the Nederlandsche Bank is in charge of the supervision of the credit system. It collects information from the commercial banks on a monthly basis and may enter into further investigations of different aspects of a bank, such as the management of the bank. In the context of prudential supervision the Nederlandsche Bank issues guidelines for the liquidity and solvency of credit institutions and supervises the observance of these guidelines. Only recently the tasks of the Nederlandsche Bank in this area have been extended to include investment firms (*beleggingsinstellingen*) and exchange offices (*wisselkantoren*).[312]

V. THE EUROPEAN SYSTEM OF CENTRAL BANKS AND THE EUROPEAN CENTRAL BANK

The establishment of the ESCB and the ECB constituted the core of what can arguably be considered one of the most, if not *the* most, ambitious projects since the establishment of the European Communities, that is the establishment of an EMU and in particular the introduction of a single European currency. The completion of EMU has emerged as the central integrationist project at a time when some Member States reflect on the desirability of further integration. The EMU will inevitably lead to further harmonisation between the Member States in other areas, such as fiscal policy. The ESCB and the ECB are set to become more than an average of national central banks which participate in the system. The ECB formulates and implements monetary policy for an economic area which, combining both exports and imports, roughly stands for 40 per cent of the world trade turnover.[313] The single currency competes in the global finan-

---

[309] S. 9(2) Bank Act 1948.

[310] For an overview of the role of the Nederlandsche Bank in this area cf. European Monetary Institute, *Payment Systems in the European Union* (Frankfurt a.M., 1996), 391–430.

[311] Wet toezicht kredietwezen, Stb. 1992, no. 722, as amended; hereafter referred to as Act on the Supervision of the Credit System 1992.

[312] Cf. Wet van 27 juni 1990, houdende bepalingen inzake het toezicht op beleggingsinstellingen, Stb. 1990, no. 380, last revision: Wet van 25 september 1996, Stb. 1996, no. 537; Wet van 15 december 1994, houdende bepalingen inzake de wisselkantoren, Stb. 1994, no. 903/904.

[313] This observation is based on numbers from 1995, provided in M. v. Baratta (ed.), *Der Fischer Weltalmanach 1997* (Fischer Taschenbuch Verlag, Frankfurt a.M., 1997).

cial markets alongside with the US Dollar and the Japanese Yen to become one of the major reserve currencies.[314]

1. Historic development

The idea of an Economic and Monetary Union in Europe is not such a recent invention. The Delors Plan and the subsequent implementation of the provisions on EMU in the Treaty on the European Union are rather the realisation of a long lasting project which, in the form of the Werner Plan, already once before had begun to take concrete shape.

1.1. First steps

However, even before that time the co-ordination of economic and monetary policy had been the focus of Community activities. While the original EEC Treaty included provisions on economic policy co-ordination and balance of payments it included hardly any reference to monetary policy, with the exception of Article 104 EEC which called for the establishment of a Monetary Committee comprised of one representative of each central bank and representative of the Treasury of each Member States, as well as two representatives of the Commission.[315] As part of the action programme for the second stage of Customs Union, a committee report in 1962 proposed the establishment of a committee comprised of the governors of the central banks of the Member States in order to exchange information and to consult on monetary matters relating—among others—to credit policies, the adjustment of exchange rates and the use of the International Monetary Fund (IMF) by the Member States.[316] Following these recommendations two years later the Committee of Governors of the Central Banks of the Member States (Committee of Governors) was established,[317] while at the same time strengthening the power of the Monetary Committee provided for by Article 104 EEC.[318] Although the Monetary Committee existed alongside the Committee of Governors it was the latter

[314] Cf. e.g. First European Commission analysis and guidelines on the future role of the Euro in international monetary system, reprinted in Agence Documents no. 2034 of 8 May 1997.

[315] Short overview by J.-V. Louis, in Ch. Gavalda *et al.*, *Dalloz Répertoire de droit Communautaire*, vol. II (Dalloz, Paris, 1992), s. *Monnaie*, 4–5; EEC Council: Rules governing the Monetary Committee of 18 Mar. 1958 ([1958] OJ 17/390).

[316] EC Commission, Action Programme, Oct. 1962, point 132. The IMF had been created under the Bretton Woods Agreement of 1944 in order to manage the exchange rate mechanism also created as part of the Bretton Woods System.

[317] Council Decision 64/300/EEC of 8 May 1965, on co-operation between the Central Banks of the Member States of the European Economic Community (OJ 1206/64). On the creation and evolving role of the Committee of Governors cf. the self-portrait by the Committee of Governors of the Central Banks of the Member States of the European Economic Community, *Annual Report (July 1990–December 1991)* (April 1992), 59 *et seq.*

[318] Council Resolution 64/299/EEC of 8 May 1964 (OJ 1205/64); Declaration of the Heads of Government 64/306/EEC of 8 May 1964 (OJ 1226/64).

which developed into a "centre of European monetary co-operation" over the years.[319] Norton and Walker interpret these early efforts of the Community as the "birth certificate" of EMU.[320] As for the motives behind these efforts, Gros and Thygesen describe the developments in the area of monetary policy matters in the 1960s as the result of fears "that exchange-rate adjustments could disrupt the functioning of the common customs union and the Common Agricultural Policy (CAP)".[321] As both of these areas proved to develop successfully the need for enhanced co-ordination grew.

1.2. The Werner Report and the "Snake"

The Hague Conference of the European Council of 1969 led to the preparation of the so-called Werner Report,[322] named after the Luxembourg Prime Minister and Minister of Finance, Pierre Werner, in 1970. In short, the Werner Report proposed the achievement of an EMU in three stages, the last to be completed by 1980. The final objective set out in the Report was to set up a complete common market, or, in the words of the report, to:

> "[R]ealize an area in which goods and services, peoples and capital will circulate freely and without competitive distortions, without thereby giving rise to structural or regional equilibrium."[323]

The report proposed the creation of a single currency or at least the total convertibility of the European currencies and the creation of fixed exchange rates.[324] More importantly in the present context, it called for the transfer of some authority in the field of monetary and credit policy to the Community level. The report did not make concrete legal and institutional proposals, but rather vaguely suggested "the creation of a centre of decision for economic policy" and the creation of "a Community system of central banks". The report

---

[319] H.J. Hahn, "The European Central Bank: Key to European Monetary Union or Target" (1991) 28 *CML Rev.*, 783–820, at 787. With Council Decision 90/42/EEC (OJ 1990 L78/25), the tasks of the Committee of Governors where extended to include multilateral surveillance of the economies of the Member States with a view to their convergence, and the co-ordination of the Member States monetary policies with the goal of price stability.

[320] J.J.N. Norton/G.A. Walker, *European Monetary Union: An Historical Perspective*, paper presented at the European Monetary Union Special Workshop London, Friday 26 and Saturday 27 Jan. 1996, at 14.

[321] D. Gros/N. Thygesen, op. cit., Chap. 2, n. 9, 10–12.

[322] *Report to the Council and Commission on the Realisation by Stages of Economic and Monetary Union in the Community* of 8 Oct. 1970 (OJ 1970 C136/1), hereafter referred to as Werner Report.

[323] Ibid., at 3.

[324] The divergence with respect to the function of a monetary union became apparent in two main streams, namely the *monetarists*, who saw monetary integration as an instrument to further promote economic and political integration within Europe, as opposed to the *economists*, who wanted the monetary union as the "coronation" of an Europe, which has been integrated both economically and politically beforehand; cf. H. Tietmeyer, "Zur politischen Fundierung des monetären Integrationsprozesses in Europa", in O. Due *et al.* (eds.), *Festschrift für Ulrich Everling*, vol. II (Nomos, Baden-Baden 1995), 1575–84, at 1578.

included an explicit reference to the Federal Reserve System as an example of such a system.[325] An institution on the Community level similar to the Federal Reserve Board was supposed to be established in stage three charged—among others—with taking decisions with respect to monetary policy and in particular the discount rate, banking liquidity, and government financing.[326]

The timetable foresaw the first stage to begin on 1 January 1971 for a period of three years aiming at a closer co-ordination of medium-term economic policies and a closer co-ordination between the Member States' central banks with regard to monetary and credit policies, without a commitment by the participating Member States to enter into any subsequent stage embracing further monetary integration. The creation of the first exchange rate mechanism fell together with the downfall in the early 1970s of the exchange rate system established as part of the Bretton Woods Agreements.[327] In short, the exchange rate mechanism established by the Bretton Woods Agreement was characterised by a system of fixed exchange rates within narrow margins, the fixing of the gold price in US Dollar (gold standard), the convertibility of currencies, and the convertibility between gold and the US Dollar. As a result of inflationary economic policies in the late 1960s the Dollar convertibility had lost credibility. When the United States had cancelled the gold–Dollar convertibility other contracting states stopped purchasing Dollars at the fixed price which resulted in a free floating of the Dollar. In the so-called Smithsonian Agreement of 18 December 1971 the ten leading industrial states agreed upon a mutual realignment of exchange rates which included a Dollar devaluation and new revocable exchange rates with a wider margin of 2.25 per cent.[328] However, these new margins were problematic from the point of view of the participating European currencies since the cross-rates between these currencies could vacillate up to 9 per cent from the central rate.[329] This ran contrary to the aim of a closer link between the currencies of the Member States as defined in the Werner Report. In the Basle Agreement of 10 April 1972 the Member States agreed to restrict the exchange rate margins within the existing exchange rate mechanism between each others' currencies to ±2.5 per cent, while at the same time observing the exchange rate *vis-à-vis* the Dollar as agreed upon in the Smithsonian Agreement. This mechanism, also referred to as "the Snake in the Tunnel"[330] entailed an obligation of unrestricted intervention by the central banks on behalf of the participating Member States' currencies. To this end the central banks supported each other

---

[325] Werner Report, n. 322 above, at 5.

[326] Committee of Governors of the Central Banks of the European Economic Community, *Report on the Questions Posed by the Committee "ad hoc" Chaired by Premier Werner of 1 August 1970* (OJC 136/21, Nov. 1970), at 30.

[327] Cf. Arts. of Agreement of the International Monetary Fund of 22 July 1944; as amended. For a short overview cf. Ch. Gavalda *et al.*, n. 315 above, at 5.

[328] Originally, the margin was 0.75: around the parity, cf. R.Smits, op. cit., Chap. 2, n. 36, 17 *et seq.*

[329] Gros/Thygesen, n. 321 above, at 16.

[330] For a short overview cf. L. Cartou, *Communautés européennes* (10th edn., Dalloz, Paris 1991), 454 *et seq.*; Gros/Thygesen, n. 321 above, 15 *et seq.*

by providing unlimited short-term credits of up to 30 days. However, the grad-ual break-down of the exchange rate mechanism under the Bretton Woods Agreements—among others—due to the exiting from the system of Member States and the continuing weakness of the Dollar, also marked the beginning of the end of the "Snake" arrangement, and, eventually, the project of EMU as foreseen in the Werner report. From the end of March 1973 the currencies remaining in the exchange rate mechanism were free-floated against the Dollar, i.e. the central banks no longer intervened on behalf of the Dollar, while main-taining the exchange rates between their currencies, so-called "block floating". Around the same period, in order to manage the exchange rate mechanism the European Monetary Co-operation Fund (EMCF) was established.[331] The main purpose of the EMCF was to promote the proper functioning of the progressive narrowing of the fluctuation margins between the currencies of the Member States, whenever necessary to intervene in the exchange market on behalf of the currencies of the Member States to ensure that the exchange rates remained within the band, and to reach a settlement between the Member States' central banks leading to a concerted policy on monetary reserves.[332] The EMCF was managed by a Board of Governors comprised of the members of the Committee of Governors of the Member States' central banks, which—among other things—could decide on organisational matters of the Fund.[333] In some respects the EMCF can be considered as a first effort towards the creation of a Community institution for the co-ordination of monetary policy of the partici-pating Member States.[334]

Although the Member States expressed their political will to move towards an Economic and Monetary Union the envisaged timetable could not be met.[335] The second stage on the path towards EMU, which was supposed to commence on 1 January 1974, was postponed. Delaying factors included the slowdown in the economies of some of the Member States, not least as a result of the oil shock.[336] Moreover, the absence of an institutional framework at the Community level, transferring powers to Community institutions for the effec-tive decision-making and operational procedures regarding EMU, hindered

[331] Council Reg. (EEC) 907/73 (OJ 1973 L89/2), which also includes the statute of the EMCF.
[332] Art. 2 Statute EMCF.
[333] Ibid., Arts. 1 and 3.
[334] However, N. Russel-Jones, *1992—The Changing Face of the Financial Services: A Eurostudy Special Report* (Eurostudy, London 1992), at 11, overestimates the role of the EMCF when charac-terising it as "an embryo Central Bank".
[335] During a summit of the Heads of State or Government of the Member States in Paris in Oct. 1972 the participants expressed their political will to move to the second stage of EMU by the begin of 1974, which should than have bee completed by 1980.
[336] P. Coffey, *The European Monetary System—Past, Present and Future* (Martinus Nijhoff Publishers, Dordrecht, 1984), at 13, who describes the final stages of the "Snake" arrangement as "little more than a Deutschmark zone comprising the German, Benelux and Danish currencies". See also European Commission, *Economic and Monetary Union* (Office for Official Publications of the European Communities, Luxembourg 1996), at 6.

effective actions at the Community level. In March 1975, the Majolin Report came to the conclusion that the Werner Plan had failed.[337]

1.3. The European Monetary System (EMS)

Efforts towards an EMU, though on a less ambitious scale, were revitalised in 1977–8 with suggestions for the establishment of the EMS. The plan was finally adopted by the European Council in 1978 and the EMS, with the ERM as its centrepiece, was established and became operational in March 1979.[338] It ceased to exist in the presently described form at the time of the coming into existence of the EMU.[339] The main aim of the EMS is to provide for closer monetary cooperation leading to a zone of monetary stability and in particular to the conquest of inflation, the stabilisation of exchange rates and the convergence of the economic policies of the Member States.[340] The heart of the system is the ERM. Like the "Snake" the ERM sets fluctuation margins for the Member States' currencies against a central rate.[341] Unlike the former exchange rate mechanism, the central rate is not determined by the US Dollar, but rather by the European Currency Unit (ECU), the second important element of the EMS.[342] The ECU is defined as a basket of the currencies of the Member States, that is it is defined as the sum of predetermined amounts of the currencies. Thus, a whole grid of bilateral central parities of the participating currencies exists. The stability of

---

[337] Gros/Thygesen, n. 321 above, at 20.

[338] Resolution of the European Council of 6 and 7 June 1978; Resolution of the European Council on the establishment of the European Monetary System and related matters from 5 Dec. 1978, Bull. EC 7/8–1978; Resolution of the European Council of 12./13 Mar. 1979, Bull. EC 7–1979 point 2; Agreement between the central banks of the Member States of the EEC of 13 Mar. 1979 laying down the operating procedures for the European Monetary System; Council Reg. (EEC) 3180/78 and 3181/78 (OJ 1978 L379/1 and 379/2, amended by Council Reg. (EEC) No 1971/89 (OJ 1989 L189/1). Leading proponents were the president of the European Commission, Roy Jenkins, the German Chancellor, Helmut Schmidt (despite the resistance in the Bundesbank), and the French President, Valéry Giscard-d'Estaing, who presented a proposal for a EMS to the European Council in 1978.

[339] However, a new exchange rate mechanism (ERM II) is set up in stage three of EMU, which then manages the exchange rate relationships between the so-called "Ins" and "Outs", that is to say those States which take part in Monetary Union and those Member States which remain outside for the time being. Cf. Resolution of the European Council on the establishment of an exchange-rate mechanism in the third stage of economic and monetary union Amsterdam of 16 June 1997 (OJ 1997 C236/5).

[340] Cf. Conclusions of the Presidency of the European Council, Brussels, 4 and 5 Dec. 1978. From the wide range of publications on the subject cf. e.g. P. Coffey, "The European Monetary System and Economic and Monetary Union", in P. Coffey (ed.), *Main Economic Policy Areas of the EC—After 1992* (4th edn, Kluwer Academic Publishers, Dordrecht, 1993), 1–29.

[341] For details cf. e.g. S.C.W. Eijffinger, *The Determinations of the Currencies within the European Monetary System*, FEW research memorandum (241), Department of Economics, Tilburg University 1987.

[342] Council Reg. (EEC) 3180/78 (OJ 1978 L379/1), which introduced the ECU as the unit of account of the European Monetary Fund; Council Reg. (EEC) 3181/78 (OJ 1978 L379/2), which empowered the EMCF to issue ECU upon receiving monetary reserves from the Member States, and allowed for the EMCF and the Member States to use the ECU as means of settlement and for transactions among each other. Note that from 1 Jan. 1994, these tasks were taken over by the European Monetary Institute (EMI).

the exchange rates is supposed to be reached through the obligation of the central banks participating in the system to intervene in the foreign-exchange markets if a currency reaches its "ceiling" or "floor" rate as compared to the central rate. The ERM is supplemented by financial mechanisms, not least to support central banks in the managing of their currency and in particular in the case of currency interventions as part of their obligation under the ERM. These borrowing facilities were provided by the EMCF and, with the establishment of the European Monetary Institute (EMI), have been transferred to the latter.[343]

From the start of the EMS until August 1993 the fluctuation margins in the ERM were +/–2.25 per cent or +/–6 per cent respectively[344] from a central rate.[345] Subsequently, after the turmoil of the ERM and the subsequent withdrawal of the British Pound Sterling and the Italian Lira from the mechanism, the margins were widened to +/–15 per cent for all participating Member States' currencies with the exception of the Dmark and the Guilder, which remained within the original margin of +/–2.25 per cent.[346] Since the central rate for each currency could only be changed by mutual agreement of the participating Member States—so-called realignment—the ERM at the time of its establishment resulted in an unknown shift of monetary authority from the national to the European level; exchange-rate policy as an important tool in monetary policy for the national governments was restricted, but not entirely excluded since the exchange rates were not irrevocably fixed.

1.4. From the Single European Act to the Treaty on European Union towards EMU

The adoption of the internal market programme in 1985 and the signing of the Single European Act (SEA) also marked important stages on the path towards EMU. In fact, the completion of the internal market with all its benefits—the abolition of all non-tariff barriers to the free movement of goods, services, people and capital—would be offset to some extent by the transaction costs involved in converting between currencies and the uncertainties involved with unstable exchange rates. The SEA did, however, not include any new provisions on the establishment of an EMU. It did introduce a new Article 102a EEC into the Treaty, recognising the EMS and laying the foundation for further develop-

---

[343] Art. 3 (1) EMI Statute.

[344] For some Member States' currencies the margin was set at +/–6%, e.g. the Lira (1979–90), the Pound Sterling (1990–2).

[345] Until 1987 realignments took place frequently, sometimes 2 or 3 times a year.

[346] F.G. Ozkan/A. Sutherland, *A Model of the ERM Crisis*, CEPR discussion paper no. 879 (Centre for Economic Policy Research, London 1994), with further references; Tietmeyer, n. 324 above, at 1580, observes that these wider margins emphasised the responsibility of each participating Member State for the stability of its currency which in return supports a stable economic foundation necessary for a monetary union.

ment in the field of economic and monetary policy through Treaty amendment.[347]

At the Hanover summit of the European Council in 1988, a study group which, among others, comprised the Governors of the Member States' central banks and which was chaired by Jaques Delors, at the time president of the Commission, was asked to study and propose a concrete programme for the creation of an EMU.[348] The findings of this study group were summarised in the Delors Report, which in general proposed the achievement of an EMU—once more—in three stages, thereby moving from closer economic and monetary co-ordination to a single currency and an ESCB with the ECB as its centrepiece.[349]

The suggestions brought forward in the Delors Report were taken up by the European Council of Madrid in 1989. The first stage, which as decided upon by the Madrid Summit, began on 1 July 1990, set out to complete the internal market, in particular the abolishing of all existing measures restricting capital movements and payments, and to achieve a greater convergence of economic performance through the strengthening of economic and monetary policy co-ordination within the Community's existing legal framework. In this context it was the intention to complete the EMS through the participation of all Member States. However, the turmoil of the ERM, referred to above, has prevented this goal.

With the signing of the Treaty on the European Union (TEU) on 7 February 1992 and its subsequent entry into force on 1 November 1993, together with the Protocols annexed to the TEU, the necessary legal framework for entering stage two and for stage three of EMU were created. In short, this included provisions on a closer co-ordination of the economic policies of the Member States, such as multilateral surveillance and excessive deficit procedures and the prohibition of government financing, and provisions on the establishment of a ESCB and a ECB for a common monetary policy.[350] Moreover, provisions on the transfer to stage three of EMU and in particular the convergence criteria applicable in order to qualify for a participation in stage three of EMU were included.[351]

---

[347] For D. Wyatt/A. Dashwood, *European Community Law* (3rd edn., Sweet & Maxwell, London, 1993), at 662, this provision did not amount to more than "a reminder of the desirability of the convergence of Member States' economic and monetary policies".

[348] Cf. Presidency Conclusions, Hannover European Council, Bull. EC 6–1988, point 3.4.1 (para. 5).

[349] Committee for the Study of Economic and Monetary Union, *Report on Economic and Monetary Union in the European Community* (Office for Official Publications of the European Communities, Luxembourg 1989) (Delors Report). At the outset the Delors Plan foresaw the establishment of a ESCB already in stage two towards EMU: cf. Delors Report, *op. cit.*, No. 57.

[350] Arts. 102a–104c EC on economic policy, and Arts. 105–109 EC on monetary policy.

[351] Arts. 109e–109m EC; for an overview of the convergence criteria cf. H. Kortz, *Die Entscheidung über den Übergang in die Endstufe der Wirtschafts-und Währungsunion*, Diss. (Nomos, Baden-Baden, 1996); A. Emmerich-Fritsch, "Wie verbindlich sind die Konvergenzkriterien?", *EWS*, vol. 7 no. 3 (1996), 77–86.

The second stage on the path towards EMU began on 1 January 1994.[352] Even though taking into account the well-known motivations for the introduction of the provisions on EMU into the EC Treaty, e.g. completion of the internal market, further political integration etc., it may be considered remarkable that the Member States were willing to give up sovereignty over monetary policy and that the central banks which, in the person of their governors, took a decisive role in the drafting of the original proposals in the Delors Report, agreed to give up their powers in favour of an ECB. However, in the light of the fact that the ERM in the past was considered *de facto* as a Dmark block with the Bundesbank effectively determining monetary policy for all the participating Member States, some of the Member States may have simply chosen the lesser of two evils since they would at least be on an equal footing with all participating members on the Governing Council, the monetary policy decision-making organ of the ECB.[353]

For the duration of stage two the EMI, seated at Frankfurt a.M., Germany, was created.[354] The legal basis for the EMI was Article 109f EC on the statute of the EMI.[355] The EMI took over the functions of the Committee of Governors of the central banks of the Member States and of the EMCF, both of which were dissolved.[356] The EMI has generally been referred to as the forerunner of the ECB. However, this description may be misleading, in as much as the EMI did not fulfil the functions commonly associated with a central bank, namely the conduct of monetary policy. Rather, it was charged, first, with the co-ordination of the Member States' monetary policies in stage two and, secondly, with the preparatory work necessary for the establishment of the ESCB and the ECB, including the development of instruments, procedures and strategies necessary for the conduct of a common monetary policy in stage three.[357] For this purpose the EMI had the power to issue statements and to make recommendations on monetary and exchange rate policy matters in the Member States, and it was consulted by the Council on all proposals regarding legislation falling within the dominion of the EMI.[358]

[352] The TEU came into force with some delay due to the difficulties in ratification of the Treaty. This was the case in Germany, which was the last Member State to ratify the Treaty in October 1993, after the Federal Constitutional Court (*Bundesverfassungsgericht*) had ruled that the provisions of the Maastricht Treaty were in accordance with the German constitution (*Grundgesetz*). For more details of this decision, cf. Chap. 4 I 3. The provisions of the EMU were agreed upon at a meeting of the European Council on 9–10 Dec. 1990.

[353] M. Deane/R. Pringle, op. cit., Chap. 2, n. 115, at 332, who describe the behaviour of the central banks at the time of the drawing up of the Delors Report as "close to committing hara-kiri".

[354] The EMI has legal personality according to Arts. 109f(1) EC, 14 EMI Statute. Also Arts. 109e–109m EC with respect to the transitional period, i.e. the second stage towards EMU. The first president was Alexandre Lamfalussy, followed by Willem Frederik Duisenberg, previously governor of the Nederlandsche Bank.

[355] In the following referred to as the EMI Statute. There provisions were introduced by the TEU.

[356] Art. 109f(2) 5th indent EC, Art. 1(3) EMI Statute.

[357] Art. 109f(2) EC. For more details of the tasks of the EMI cf. European Monetary Institute, *Role and Functions of the European Monetary Institute*, February 1996; U. Häde, "Das Europäische Währungsinstitut und die Kommission", *EuZW* (1994), 685–687.

[358] Art. 109f(4) EC. The EMI has published reports on a number of issues, ranging from monetary policy instruments in stage three of EMU to payment systems in the EU.

The EMI was managed by a Council which consisted of a president, appointed by common accord by the Council comprising the heads of State or Government, on the recommendation of the Committee of Governors of the central banks of the Member States and after consulting the EP and the Council, and the presidents of the national central banks.

On 2 May 1998, the Council comprising the Heads of State or Government unanimously decided that 11 Member States fulfilled the convergence criteria set out in the EC Treaty and, thus, for participating in EMU.[359] At the same time the Heads of State or Government also reached a political agreement on the persons to be recommended for appointment to the Executive Board of the ECB.[360] Moreover, on May 2, 1998 it was also decided by the Ministers of Finance of the eleven Member States participating in EMU from the outset that the current bilateral exchange rates in the ERM should form the basis for determining the irrevocable conversion rates to the single currency, the Euro.[361]

Finally, on 25 May 1998, in accordance with Article 109l(1) EC, the governments of the Member States participating in EMU from the outset appointed the members of the Executive Board of the ECB.[362] The appointments took effect on 1 June 1999, which at the same time marked the establishment of the ECB. The EMI was liquidated upon the establishment of the ECB, and the latter has taken over the remaining functions of the former.[363]

From 1 January 1999, in accordance with Article 109c(2) EC, the Economic and Financial Committee (EFC), which replaces the Monetary Committee, comes into existence.[364] To be sure, the EFC is *not* an organ of the ECB or the ESCB. The Commission, the ECB, and the Member States each appoint two members to the EFC.[365] The task of the EFC, on the one hand, is to examine, at least once a year, the situation regarding the movement of capital and the freedom of payments, including all measures relating to capital movements, and to keep under review the monetary and financial situation and the payment

---

[359] Art. 109l EC in the first instance refers to the first procedure under Art. 109j(3) EC, according to which the Council in the composition of the Heads of State or Government no later than 31 Dec. 1996 would set a date for the beginning of the third stage. However, this time-scale proved to be unrealistic. Also Europees Monetair Instituut, *Convergentieverslag* (Frakfurt a.M., Maart 1998).

[360] Cf. also Chap. 4 IV 1.1. on the difficulties involved with the appointment of the first president of the ECB.

[361] According to Art. 109l(4) EC the conversion rate is adopted at the starting date of the third stage, and thus January 1, 1999.

[362] Decision 98/345/EC taken by common accord of the Governments of the Member States adopting the single currency at the level of Heads of State or Government of 26 May 1998 appointing the President, the Vice-President and the other members of the Executive Board of the European Central Bank (OJ 1998 L154/33).

[363] Art. 109l(2) EC. For this reason the main task of the EMI was sometimes referred to ironically as to liquidate itself.

[364] Cf. Proposal for a Council Decision on the detailed provisions concerning the composition of the Economic and Financial Committee (COM/98/0110 final) (OJ 1998 C 125/17).

[365] Interestingly, neither Art. 109c, nor Art. 109k EC excludes Member States with a "derogation". Moreover, Member States which choose not to participate are not excluded from participating.

systems of the Member States with a derogation.[366] The EFC has to report to the Council and the Commission on the results of these examinations. On the other hand, the EFC assists the Council and the Commission by delivering opinions on its own initiative or that of the Council or Commission, and to contribute to the preparation of the works of the Council in the area of the provisions on the free movement of capital and payments and Economic and Monetary Union.[367]

The Treaty of Amsterdam has left the provisions of Title VI of the EC Treaty unchanged. Only the multilateral surveillance and excessive deficit procedures have been concretised and somewhat strengthened through two Council regulations *on the strengthening* of the surveillance and co-ordination of budgetary positions, and on speeding up and clarifying the implementation of the excessive deficit procedure, which are, together with a Resolution of the European Council generally referred to as the Stability and Growth Pact.[368] These regulations were the result of considerable criticism of the existing Treaty provisions, among others from the German side, for lacking the necessary vigour to be effective.[369]

2. Institutional structure

According to Article 106(1) EC, the ESCB is comprised of the ECB and the national central banks. Whereas the ECB has legal personality under Community law[370] and the national central banks under their respective national legal bases, the ESCB itself has no legal personality. Due to its two institutional elements, i.e. the ECB and the national central banks, without further explanation, the ESCB could be interpreted as a two-tier system, since both the ECB and the national central banks incorporate legal personality (different from the Bundesbank, where the State central banks have no legal personality but represent main administrations). This should, however, not result in any delusions with regard to the allocation of powers over monetary policy in the ESCB. Indeed, since the ESCB is governed by the decision-making bodies of the ECB, and the national central banks are obliged to act in accordance with the guidelines and instructions of the ECB, the ESCB may better be viewed as a

---

[366] Art. 109c(2), 2nd indent and (4) EC. Cf. Art. 109k EC on "Member States with a derogation".

[367] Art. 109c(2), 1st and 3rd indent EC. This includes e.g. decisions of the Council to confer upon the ECB tasks in the area of prudential supervision, the amendment of the ESCB Statute under the simplified procedure of Art. 106(5) EC, and decisions with regard to the exchange rate *vis-à-vis* non-Community currencies under Art. 109 EC.

[368] Council Regs.s (EC) 1466/97 and 1467/97 (OJ 1997 L209/1 and 209/6); also: Resolution of the European Council on the Stability and Growth Pact, Amsterdam, 17 June 1997 (OJ 1997 C236/1).

[369] For more details of the legal *and* economic implications cf. F. Amtenbrink/J. de Haan/O. Sleijpen, "The Stability and Growth Pact—Placebo or Panacea?" (I), *EBLR* 8 (1997), 202–10, and (II), *EBLR* 8 (1997), 233–8.

[370] Art. 106(1) EC; Art. 9.1. ESCB Statute goes on to describe in detail the legal status of the ECB in the Member States, e.g. that it should have the right to acquire or dispose of movable and immovable property and should have the capacity to be part of legal proceedings.

single-tier system.[371] In fact, the national central banks function as an executive arm of the ECB, as Article 12.1 of the ESCB Statute states that "to the extent deemed possible and appropriate and without prejudice to the provisions of this Article, the ECB shall have recourse to the national central banks to carry out operations which form part of the tasks of the ESCB".

The ECB has a capital of ECU 5,000 million, which is held by the national central banks of the Member States, including those Member States with a "derogation",[372] according to a key for the capital subscription of the different national central banks described in Article 29 of the ESCB Statute.

The ESCB is managed by the organs of the ECB which include the Governing Council and the Executive Board. Moreover, according to Article 109l(3) EC, a General Council is most likely to exist for some time after entering into the final stage of EMU. Finally, the participating Member States' central banks form an integral part of the ESCB.

2.1. Governing Council

The Governing Council is the policy-making body of the ESCB. It comprises the members of the Executive Board, i.e. the president and vice-president of the ECB and four additional members, and the governors of the Member States without a derogation participating in EMU.[373] The term of office of the Governing Council varies. The members of the Executive Board are appointed for a non-renewable period of eight years, whereas the governors of the national central banks are appointed according to the respective national provisions. However, according to Article 14(2) of the ESCB Statute, the term of office of the governors shall be no less than five years.[374]

In general, the Governing Council is responsible for the adoption of guidelines and for taking the decisions necessary to ensure the performance of the tasks entrusted to the ESCB under the EC Treaty and the ESCB Statute.[375] The Governing Council takes the appropriate decisions relating to key interest rates, intermediate monetary objectives, and the supply of reserves of the national central banks with the ECB.[376] It also issues guidelines for the implementation of

---

[371] Arts. 8 and 14 ESCB Statute; cf. the exemption included in Art. 14.4. ESCB Statute for areas outside the competence of the ESCB. Cf. M.Potacs, "Nationale Zentralbanken in der Wirtschafts- und Währungsunion", *EuR*, vol. 28 no. 1 (1993), 23–40, at 32.

[372] Art. 28 ESCB Statute; Arts. 28 and 29 ESCB Statute generally refers to Member States/national central banks and Member States with a "derogation" are moreover not excluded by the general provisions of Art. 43 ESCB Statute.

[373] Art. 109a(1) EC, Art. 10 ESCB Statute. According to Art. 43.4. ESCB Statute "National central banks", as set out e.g. in Art. 109a (1) EC and Art. 10 ESCB Statute, shall be read as "central banks of Member States without derogation"; Art. 109k EC on Member States with a "derogation". Apart from Greece, which has been considered not to fulfil the convergence criteria, the UK, Denmark and Sweden have decided not to join EMU from the outset.

[374] For more details of the appointment and dismissal procedures, cf. Chap. 4 IV.

[375] Art. 12.1. ESCB Statute.

[376] For more details on the monetary policy objectives, cf. Chap. 4 II 2.

decisions on these policies.[377] According to Article 10(5) of the ESCB Statute, the Governing Council is obliged to meet at least ten times a year. The Governing Council has decided that meetings will take place in the course of a year at regular intervals of two weeks. Apart from the members of the Governing Council, according to 109b(1) EC, the President of the Council and one member of the Commission may participate in these meetings without a right to vote.[378]

Generally, according to Article 10(2) of the ESCB Statute, the Governing Council acts by a simple majority vote with a quorum of at least two-thirds of the members, whereby each member of the Governing Council has one vote. One explanation for the implementation of the principle of "one man, one vote" may be that this was considered to reflect the concept of the independence of the ECB and its officials from the participating Member States to a larger extent than would have been the case in applying a weighting of the votes.[379] Indeed, it has been observed by the Committee of Governors of the Central Banks that "it reflects the consensus that members act on behalf of the System rather than as representatives of the Member States".[380] From this point of view it becomes apparent why the one man, one vote procedure was accepted by the Member States at the time of the drafting of the provision as the political need for a high degree of consensus, which is reflected in the voting procedures of other Community institutions, i.e. the Council, is not necessary in the case of the organs of the ECB. Another reason may be found in the trade-off which exists between the high degree of consensus and the effectiveness of the decision-making process of an organ.[381] Finally, a weighting of votes for monetary policy decisions would have given Germany—among other States—a dominant position within the decision-making body of the ECB. However, as has been pointed out, this would have run counter to the strategy of some Member States of breaking the predominant position of the Bundesbank.

The principle of one man, one vote is disregarded in the case of a tie in the Governing Council. In such an event, the president of the ECB has the casting vote. This power together with the traditionally publicly exposed position of the governor of a central bank gives the president of the ECB an outstanding position inside and outside the Bank. Moreover, decisions with respect to the capital of the ECB,[382] foreign reserve assets,[383] the allocation of monetary income of

[377] Art. 12 ESCB Statute.
[378] For more details cf. Chap. 4 III 1. Cf. also Rules of Procedure of the European Central Bank of 7 July 1998, Arts. 2–5.
[379] J.-V. Louis, "The Project of a European Central Bank" in J. Stuyck (ed.), *Financial and Monetary Integration in the European Economic Community*, General Bank Chair Lectures 1991–2 (Centre for Advanced Legal Studies, Kluwer Law and Taxation Publishers, Deventer-Boston, 1993), 13–28, at 21.
[380] Committee of Governors of Central Banks of the Member States of the European Economic Community, *Annual Report*, n. 317 above, at 51.
[381] R. Cordero, *The Creation of a European Banking System* (Peter Lang Publishing, New York, 1990), at 271, who also emphasises the necessity for voting procedures which ensure quick actions and reactions in the field of monetary policy.
[382] Arts. 28 and 29 ESCB Statute.   [383] Ibid., Arts. 30 and 31.

national central banks,[384] and the allocation of net profits and losses of the ECB,[385] are subject to a weighted voting procedure. This procedure takes into account the national central banks' shares in the subscribed capital of the ECB,[386] and disregards the votes of the participating members of the Executive Board.[387] A decision has been taken if the votes cast in favour represent at least two-thirds of the subscribed capital of the ECB and represent at least half of the shareholders, i.e. Member States. The Governing Council requires a two-thirds majority of the votes cast to decide on the application of operational methods of monetary control in addition to those listed in the ESCB Statute.[388]

2.2. Executive Board

The Executive Board is the managerial board of the ECB.[389] According to Article 109a(2) EC and Article 11 of the ESCB Statute, the Executive Board comprises the president of the ECB, the vice-president and four other members, who are appointed from among persons of recognised standing and professional experience in monetary or banking matters for a non-renewable period of eight years.[390]

Article 12.1 of the ESCB Statute defines the main task of the Executive Board in general terms as implementing the monetary policy in accordance with the guidelines and decisions laid down by the Governing Council, thereby giving the necessary instructions to the national central banks.[391] The Governing Council may also delegate additional powers to the Executive Board.[392] It derives from this that the actual power of the Executive Board depends upon the contents of the guidelines and decisions by the Governing Board, or as Louis puts it: "on the 'political will' of the Governors of the National Central Banks meeting in the Governing Council" and, moreover, "on the requirements of a smooth functioning of the System".[393] A more temporal task of the Executive Board is the preparation of the meetings of the Governing Council.[394]

---

[384] Ibid., Art. 32; cf. also Art. 51.

[385] Ibid., Art. 33.

[386] This is to be expected, since the Member States contribute to these assets to a different extent.

[387] Art. 10.3. ESCB Statute. In one case, that is the simplified amendment procedure under Art. 41 ESCB Statute, a recommendation of the ECB requires a unanimous decision by the Governing Council. This procedure applies—among others—to the definition of the minimum and maximum reserves required from the credit institutions in the Member States.

[388] Art. 20 ESCB Statute.

[389] Ibid., Art. 11.6.

[390] The procedures of appointment and dismissal are examined more closely in Chap. 4 IV.

[391] This provision is complemented by Art. 14.3. ESCB Statute, according to which the national central banks are obliged to act in accordance with the guidelines and instructions of the ECB.

[392] Art. 12.1, sentence 5, ESCB Statute. Cf. also Art. 14 Rules of Procedure of the European Central Bank.

[393] Louis, n. 379 above, at 22.

[394] Art. 12.2. ESCB Statute. According to Art. 20 of the Rules of Procedure of the European Central Bank the Executive Board also selects, appoints and promotes all members of staff of the ECB. Cf. also Art. 11 on the staff of the ECB.

With respect to the decision-making procedure, Article 11.5 of the ESCB Statute states that the Executive Board acts by a simple majority of the votes cast, whereby each of the members present in person during a meeting has one vote. As is the case for the Governing Council, the president of the ECB holds a casting vote in the case of a tie.[395]

2.3. General Council

In accordance with Article 109l(2) EC, the ECB takes over those functions of the EMI which remain to be performed at the time of the liquidation of the EMI.[396] Internally Article 44 of the ESCB Statute confers these functions upon a third decision-making body. The General Council consists of the president and vice-president of the ECB,[397] and the governors of the national central banks.[398] It is chaired by the president of the ECB, who also prepares the meetings. In his absence, the vice-president of the ECB may chair the meetings.[399] The president of the Council and one member of the Commission may attend the meetings of the General Council, however, as is the case for meetings of the Governing Council, without a right to vote.[400] According to the EC Treaty the General Council itself adopts its rules of procedure.[401]

Article 109l(2)–(3) EC identifies the main task of the General Council which is the handling of the Member States with a "derogation", i.e. those Member States which at the time of the Council decision referred to in Article 109j(4) EC, do not fulfil the convergence criteria as defined in Article 109j(1) EC.[402] The responsibilities of the General Council are more closely defined in Article 47 of the ESCB Statute. Apart from those tasks which are basically designed to support the other two organs in their functions, i.e. collection of statistical information and contributions to the reporting activities of the ECB, the more important functions of the General Council refer to its participation in the abrogation of the derogation as specified Article 109kEC and its contribution to the necessary preparations for the determination of an irrevocably fixed exchange rate between the currencies of Member States with a "derogation" and the single currency of the Member States which take part in Monetary Union.[403] It derives

---

[395] Cf. also Arts. 6–8 Rules of Procedure of the European Central Bank.

[396] Art. 109l(2) EC.

[397] Other members of the Executive Board may, however, participate without a right to vote on the relationship between the Governing Council and the General Council, cf. Arts. 12–13 Rules of Procedure of the European Central Bank.

[398] Art. 45 ESCB Statute.

[399] Ibid., Art. 46.   [400] Ibid., Art. 46.2.

[401] Explicit derogation to Art. 12.3. ESCB Statute. Cf. Rules of Procedure of the European Central Bank, Arts. 6–11   [402] Art. 109k EC.

[403] A scenario in which the Governing Council could continue to exist would presuppose that the UK would also decide in the future not to enter into the final stage of EMU, since, according to Art. 9 of the Protocol on certain provisions relating to the United Kingdom of Great Britain and Northern Ireland annexed to the TEU, Arts. 44–48 of the ESCB Statute on the tasks of the General Council in general would apply. The same may be the case if other Member States, e.g. Denmark, decide to remain outside EMU.

from the wording of Article 109l(3) EC that the General Council is not designed as a *permanent* third decision-making body. Rather, the task of the General Council ends when the "derogation" of all Member States have been abrogated.

2.4. National central banks

The national central banks form the second important element of the ESCB. As is the case for the ECB, the national central banks have legal personality, which derives from the respective national legal systems, rather than from Community law. Prior to the creation of the ESCB Statute, the role of the Executive Board in the ECB had for some time been subject of discussion among the Member States' central banks. The prospect of handing over sovereignty in such a sensitive area as monetary policy was bound to meet controversies in more than one area. With respect to the design of the new supranational institution in charge of monetary policy, on the one hand, a strong permanent body was demanded in order to establish the credibility of the new institutional set-up and of the single currency. According to this the ECB needed an explicit mandate for the implementation of monetary policy. On the other hand, it had to be taken into account that a strictly centralised system depriving the national central banks of any role in the future would hardly have been politically acceptable.[404] This discussion amounted to the question whether the ESCB would be set up as a centralised or decentralised system.[405] The provisions on the ESCB and the ECB, which have finally been implemented, clearly have the features of a centralised system, of which the strong position of the Executive Board is only one example. The system however, also has decentralised features, as the national central banks retain their own legal personality and, moreover—more importantly— the ESCB Statute obliges the ECB to have recourse to the national central banks "to the extent deemed possible and appropriate".[406] In this context it should be mentioned that according to Article 9 of the Rules of Procedures of the European Central Bank so-called Committees of the European System of Central Banks (ESCB Committees) are set up, composed of representatives of the ECB and of the national central banks of the participating Member States, to assist in the work of the ESCB. As monetary policy decisions are taken at the level of the ECB, the functions of the national central banks with regard to monetary policy lie in the execution of the decision taken by the ECB. This system has been described as being "clearly in line with the principle of subsidiarity".[407] However, this view either overestimates the position of the national central banks in the ESCB, as it has been described above, or misinterprets the scope of Article 3b EC and the subsidiarity principle, because in as much as monetary

---

[404] Cf. *Vers Un Systeme*, op. cit., Chap. 2, n. 36, 30 *et seq.*

[405] One is reminded of the discussion on the structure of the Bundesbank at the time of its establishment, although the constitutional structure of the country was much clearer, i.e. federal structure.

[406] Art. 12.1, para. 3, ESCB Statute.

[407] "Executive Agencies within the EC: The European Central Bank—a Model?" (1996) 33 *CMLRev.*, 623–31, at 627.

policy is an exclusive competence of the Community, Article 3b EC is not applicable.[408] However, the national central banks may also perform functions *outside* the ESCB in accordance with Article 14.4 of the ESCB Statute to the extent to which the Governing Council does not consider these activities to be interfering with the objectives and tasks of the ESCB.

Although the structure of the national central banks is not prescribed by Community law, a minimum standardisation of the institutional features of the national central banks is anticipated by the EC Treaty and the ESCB Statute. Articles 108 EC and 14.1 of the ESCB Statute may be considered as general clauses preventing diversions between national legislation on central banking and Community law, as they state that "each Member State shall ensure, at the latest at the date of the establishment of the ESCB, that its national legislation, including the statutes of its national central banks, is compatible with this Treaty and this Statute". Moreover, Articles 14.2–14.4 of the ESCB Statute lay down minimum requirements of the institutional set-up of the national central banks, which are designed to ensure a minimum level of independence of the national central banks.[409]

3. Tasks

Articles 105 EC and 3 of the ESCB Statute define the tasks of the ESCB and the ECB, which include the formulation and implementation of monetary policy, the conduct of foreign reserve operations consistent with the decisions of the Council in accordance with Article 109 EC, the holding and managing of the official foreign reserves of the Member States, and the promotion of the smooth operation of the payment systems.[410]

3.1. Monetary policy

According to Articles 105 EC and 3 of the ESCB Statute the primary objective of the ESCB is to maintain price stability, and, without prejudice to this objective, to support the general economic policies of the Community.

The three principal instruments for the implementation of monetary policy foreseen by the ESCB Statute are open market operations, credit operations and the minimum reserve requirements.[411] Both the ECB and the national central banks may operate in the financial markets and conduct credit operations. The

---

[408] See also P.J.G. Kapteyn/P. VerLoren van Themaat/L.A. Geelhoed/C.W.A. Timmermans (eds.), *Inleiding tot het recht van de Europese Gemeenschappen* (5th edn., Kluwer, Deventer, 1995), at 580, who point out that the principle of subsidiarity entails the distribution of competence among different *autonomous* administrative levels, whereas in the case of the ESCB the basic responsibility remains at the central level with the ECB.

[409] For more details cf. Chap. 4.

[410] For a good analysis of the tasks of the ESCB and the ECB cf. R. Smits, "The European Central Bank: Institutional Aspects" (1996) 45 *ICLQ*, 319–42.

[411] Arts. 18 and 19 ESCB Statute. For a detailed analyses cf. Smits, n. 328 above, 264 *et seq.*

operational framework for this is established by the ECB itself.[412] Moreover, the ECB may require credit institutions to hold minimum reserves on accounts with the ECB and the national central banks.[413] The Governing Council of the ECB decides upon the methods of calculation and determination of the required minimum reserves. The Council, acting by a qualified majority either on a proposal of the Commission and after consulting the EP and the ECB or on a recommendation from the ECB and after consulting the EP and the Commission, defines the type of activities of credit institutions which are taken into account when calculating and determining the minimum reserves (referred to as the basis for minimum reserves) and the maximum and minimum amounts which can be demanded.[414]

The ESCB is charged with exchange rate operations in accordance with any exchange rate regime or general guidelines decided upon by the Council.[415]

Finally, the ECB has the exclusive right to authorise the issuing of banknotes within the ESCB. The banknotes can be issued both by the ECB and the national central banks. The Member States retain the right to issue coins. However, the volume is subject to the authorisation by the ECB.[416]

3.2. Services to governments

To a limited extent the ECB and the national central banks can also act as the fiscal agent for Community institutions or bodies, organs or institutions, central governments, local or other public authorities, bodies governed by public law or public undertakings of Member States.[417] However, in accordance with Article 104(1) EC, neither the ECB nor the national central banks are permitted to provide overdraft or any other credit facilities for these entities.[418]

One of the main tasks of the ECB is to act as an adviser both for the Community institutions and the national central banks. The ECB has to be consulted on any proposed Community act as well as on any proposed legislative measures in the Member States, and, moreover, may submit opinions on its own initiative to Community institutions or bodies and national authorities in its field of competence.[419] Finally, the ECB, together with the national central

---

[412] Art. 18.2. ESCB Statute. Cf. European Central Bank, *The Single Monetary Policy in Stage Three: General Documentation on ESCB Monetary Policy Instruments and Procedures* (ECB, Frankfurt a.M., 1998). This report is based on an earlier report by the EMI: European Monetary Institute, *The Single Monetary Policy in Stage Three—Specifications of the Operational Framework*, Frankfurt a.M., Jan. 1997 and Sept. 1997.

[413] Cf. EMI proposal for a draft Council Regulation on minimum reserves, in European Monetary Institute, n. 412 above, 63 *et seq.*

[414] Art. 19.1. ESCB Statute. Note that sanctions are applicable in the case of non-compliance of a national central bank with the minimum reserve requirements.

[415] For more details cf. Chap. 4 II.

[416] Art. 105a EC.

[417] Art. 21.2. ESCB Statute.

[418] Art. 104(1) EC. Note the exception of Art. 104(2) EC, according to which publicly-owned credit institutions are excluded: Art. 21.1. and 3 ESCB Statute.

[419] Art. 105(4) EC in connection with Art. 4 ESCB Statute.

banks, collects the statistical information both from national authorities and economic agents necessary for the fulfilment of the tasks of the ESCB.[420]

3.3. Services to credit institutions

Moreover, the ESCB as a whole, that is both the ECB and the central banks of the participating Member States, is supposed to arrange for the smooth operation of the payment systems, such as electronic transfer of funds, and to provide facilities and, on parts of the ECB, to make regulations to ensure efficient clearing systems.[421] In this context it has been decided to create TARGET, a system aimed at integrating the different payment systems throughout the Member States in order to enhance the conduct of a single monetary policy in EMU.[422] The ECB and the participating Member States' central banks can open accounts for credit institutions and other bodies listed in Article 17 of the ESCB Statute. The ECB also holds and manages the official foreign reserves of the participating Member States[423]

3.4. Prudential supervision

The ECB will have only a very limited role in the area of banking supervision. The basic authority remains with the Member States, as the ESCB only contributes "to the smooth conduct of the policies" which have been decided and are implemented by the Member States. For the time being the ECB will take on a consultative role as it can advise the competent authorities in the Member States on the scope and the implementation of Community legislation relating to the prudential supervision of credit institutions and to the stability of the financial system.[424] The transfer of further tasks in this area to the ECB requires a unanimous decision by the Council, and the consent of the EP and the ECB itself.[425] Interestingly, in the draft statute of the ESCB and the ECB, prudential supervision had been listed as one of the basic tasks of the ESCB, and the ECB was envisaged to take part in "formulation and, co-ordination and execution of policies relating to prudential supervision and the stability of the financial system".[426]

[420] Art. 5 ESCB Statute.
[421] Arts. 105(2), 4th indent EC, and Art. 22 ESCB Statute.
[422] For details of the payment systems *cf*. EMI, *Payment Systems in the European Union* (EMI, Frankfurt a.M., 1996).
[423] Art. 105(2), 2nd indent EC; note the exception in Arts. 105(3) EC, 3.2. ESCB Statute, according to which the Member States' governments may hold "foreign exchange working balances".
[424] Art. 25.1. ESCB Statute.
[425] Art. 105(6) EC.
[426] Committee of Governors of the Central Banks of the Member States of the European Economic Community, "Draft Statute of the European System of Central Banks and of the European Central Bank", *Agence Europe*, nos. 1669 and 1670 of 8 Dec. 1990; Cf. P.B. Kenen, "The European Central Bank and Monetary Policy in Stage Three of EMU", *International Affairs*, vol. 68 no. 3 (1992) 457–74, at 463.

VI. THE RESERVE BANK OF NEW ZEALAND

In recent years the Reserve Bank of New Zealand has been the subject of substantive review mostly in the economic literature, and its new statutory approach to central bank independence has been widely recognised. A large part of the recognition is based upon the economic data coming from New Zealand ever since the institutional changes were introduced by the new government from 1984 onwards. New Zealand has recovered from being one of the worst-performing countries of the Organisation for Economic Co-operation and Development (OECD) to become one of the best-performing OECD countries in terms of inflation.[427] Moreover, New Zealand has made a remarkable economic recovery. But, as will be described below, the fairly new institutional structure of the Reserve Bank is not remarkable merely from the point of view of central bank independence and its potential effects on economic and monetary performance. Parallel to the enhanced statutory independence of the Bank mechanisms of accountability have been introduced which are not only a novelty in the context of the Reserve Bank of New Zealand but also by comparison to other central bank systems.

1. Historic development

1.1. Establishment

The Reserve Bank of New Zealand was established in 1934 on the basis of the Reserve Bank of New Zealand Act.[428] The relatively short existence of the central bank of New Zealand has to be seen against the background of the short history of the state of New Zealand itself. In less than 200 years the country has developed from a British colony to an independent state.[429] The Reserve Bank Act 1933 incorporated the Reserve Bank of New Zealand[430] as a body corporate limited by shares.[431] The Reserve Bank became the sole note-issuing bank in New Zealand.[432] Moreover, according to section 12 of the Reserve Bank Act 1933 the primary duty of the Reserve Bank was "to exercise control, within the

---

[427] M. Lloyd, op. cit., Chap. 2, n. 151.

[428] Reserve Bank of New Zealand Act 1933 of 27 Nov. 1933 (24 Geo. V.); hereafter referred to as Reserve Bank Act 1933.

[429] The Treaty of Waitangi of 6 Feb. 1840, is considered to be the founding document of the nation of New Zealand. In 1947, with the adoption of the Statute of Westminster 1931, the New Zealand Parliament became the sole legislator. The New Zealand Constitution Act 1986 and the New Zealand Bill of Rights Act 1990 are also important constitutional documents. Cf. P.A. Joseph, *Constitutional and Administrative Law in New Zealand* (The Law Book Company Limited, Sydney, 1993), 1 *et seq.*

[430] Hereafter referred to as the Reserve Bank.

[431] The original capital of the Reserve Bank was £500,000 in shares of £5 each and could be held by British citizens with residence in New Zealand: s. 6(1) Reserve Bank Act 1933.

[432] S. 15 Reserve Bank Act 1933.

limits of the powers conferred on it by this Act, over monetary circulation and credit in New Zealand, to the end that the economic welfare of the Dominion may be promoted and maintained". It held the government accounts.[433]

The shareholders of the Bank came together in general meetings where they dealt with such matters as the annual accounts and the report of the managing board, the declaration of annual dividends and the election of directors and of auditors.[434] The Reserve Bank was managed by a Board of Directors, consisting of a governor, a deputy governor and seven other members. According to section 25 of the Reserve Bank Act 1933 the first governor and deputy governor were elected by the Governor-General in Council for a renewable term of office of seven years, whereas all following governors and deputy governors were elected by the Governor-General in Council on recommendation of the Board of Directors.[435] This limited the influence of the government in the appointment of the Board of Directors. The seven other members of the Board of Directors were appointed according to a somewhat complex procedure. Three members, referred to as State Directors, were appointed by the Governor-General in Council for a term of five years. Of the remaining four members, referred to as shareholders' directors, two had to be or to have previously been "actively engaged in primary industry" and the other two "actively engaged in industrial or commercial pursuits". After the appointment of the initial group of shareholders by the Governor-General in Council, the shareholders' directors were thereafter supposed to be elected by the shareholders in the general meeting for a period of five years. The governor and deputy governors had an outstanding position under the Reserve Bank Act 1933 in as much as they were charged with "the permanent control of the administration of the assets and general business of the Bank, with authority to act and to give decisions in all matters which are not by this Act or by the rules of the Bank specifically reserved to the Board or to the general meeting of the shareholders".[436] Moreover, the Secretary of the Treasury functioned as an *ex officio* member on the Board of Directors, albeit without a right to vote.[437]

The Board of Directors was assisted by an executive committee, consisting of the governor, the deputy governor and no fewer than one director "acting as such by direction of the Board or, in the absence of such direction, acting with the concurrence of the governor".[438] The executive committee was explicitly charged with dealing with the discount and credit limits and moreover with any matters as determined by the Board of Directors.

[433] Reserve Bank Act 1933, ss. 21 *et seq.*

[434] Note the enumeration in s. 2, first schedule on the Rules of the Reserve Bank of New Zealand, annexed to the Reserve Bank Act 1933.

[435] S. 25 Bank Act 1933. For more details of the role of the Governor-General in New Zealand, cf. Chap. 4 I 2.

[436] N. 435 above, s. 27.

[437] Ibid., s. 23 (2).

[438] Ibid., s. 34.

The institutional set-up as a private corporation seems unusual in a period when other central banks became increasingly the focal point of government control. At the time of the establishment of the Reserve Bank it was believed that a central bank had to be independent from political interference.[439] One of the observers suggested that "the best method of safeguarding the independence of a Central Bank is to constitute the Central Bank as a private corporation with a capital subscribed by the general public and an independent Board of Directors elected by the shareholders". However, with the participation of the government on the Board of Directors and in the appointment of the State directors the Reserve Bank was far from being insulated from government influence. Besides, the convictions of the early days of the Reserve Bank did not last for long because, as will be described in the following section, two years after the establishment of the Reserve Bank as a private corporation it was nationalised.

1.2. Nationalisation

In 1936, the Reserve Bank was nationalised.[440] The shares in the capital of the Bank were cancelled and the shareholders were reimbursed for the value of their shares either in the form of a cash sum per share or in New Zealand Government stock.[441] The Reserve Bank was placed under the authority of the government. Section 10 of the Reserve Bank Amendment Act 1936 stated:

> "It shall be the general function of the Reserve Bank, within the limits of its powers, to give effect as far as may be to the monetary policy of the Government, as communicated to it from time to time by the Minister of Finance. For this purpose and to the end that the economic and social welfare of New Zealand may be promoted and maintained, the Bank shall regulate and control credit and currency in New Zealand . . . "

The amended Reserve Bank Act provided for overdraft facilities for the Government and, moreover, "any Board or other authority having statutory powers in relation to the marketing of any New Zealand product, for the purpose of financing the purchase and marketing of any such products".[442] With the shareholders being abolished so the distinction between State and shareholders' directors ceased to exist. Instead they were referred to as ordinary members of the Board which were appointed by the Governor-General in Council.[443] The term of office of ordinary directors was not determined albeit that no member was supposed to hold office for a period longer than five years without being re-appointed. The Reserve Bank Amendment Act 1936 abolished the provision according to which the Secretary of the Treasury could attend the meetings, but

---

[439] Account of the evidence presented by Otto Niemeyer in a report presented to the New Zealand House of Representatives in Feb. 1931, para. 9.
[440] Reserve Bank of New Zealand Amendment Act 1936 of 8 Apr. 1936 (1 Edw. VIII.); hereafter referred to as Reserve Bank Amendment Act 1936.
[441] S. 2 Reserve Bank Amendment Act 1936.
[442] Ibid., s. 12.
[443] Ibid., ss. 5 and 7.

not vote on the Board of Directors. The position of the governor and the deputy governor were mainly preserved.

The legal basis of the Reserve Bank was subsequently amended on a number of occasions, each time changing the monetary objectives of the Bank.[444] Prior to the reform in the late 1980s the primary function of the Reserve Bank was to implement the monetary policy of the government.[445] Monetary policy had to be directed to the maintenance and promotion of economic and social welfare "having regard to the desirability of promoting the highest level of production and trade and full employment, and of maintaining a stable internal price level".[446] The Reserve Bank was obliged to provide the government with loans under conditions which were determined by the Minister of Finance. According to the Reserve Bank Act these loans had to serve the purpose of ensuring "the continuing full employment of labour and other resources of any kind".[447] The Minister of Finance was an *ex officio* director of the Bank with voting power. Unlike the governor and the deputy-governor, who were appointed by the Governor-General in Council for a renewable (fixed) term of five years, the seven non-executive directors served "during the pleasure of the Governor-General in Council" and thus could be dismissed by the Governor-General in Council at any time.[448] Besides the general meetings of the directors, discussions took place in the so-called executive committee which consisted of the governor, deputy-governor, and at least one other director.[449]

1.3. Reform

By the late 1980s it was yet again a change of government, and thus a change in policy choices, that subsequently led to fundamental changes of the institutional setting of the Reserve Bank and its relationship with government. Recalling that it was a labour government which nationalised the Reserve Bank, it is interesting to note that it was again a labour government that would bring changes to the Reserve Bank, although, quite to the contrary.[450] In the light of growth rates in New Zealand which were constantly below the average of the OECD countries, low productivity growth, a highly protected economy and a monetary policy that constantly shifted between different objectives and was increasingly dependent upon direct controls via interest rate and exchange controls, the newly-elected government saw the need for an across-the-board re-orientation

[444] For an overview of the amendments from 1964 to 1983, cf. *RS*, vol. 16, 455 *et seq.*

[445] S. 8(1)(d) Reserve Bank of New Zealand Act as amended by the Reserve Bank of New Zealand Amendment Act 1973, reprinted in *RS*, vol. 16, 511.

[446] Reserve Bank of New Zealand Act, s. 8(2).

[447] Ibid., s. 8(4).

[448] Ibid., s. 4. However, the maximum term of office of non-executive directors was 5 years with the possibility of reappointment.

[449] S. 6 Reserve Bank of New Zealand Act, as amended by the Reserve Bank of New Zealand Amendment Act 1977, reprinted in *RS*, vol. 16, 514.

[450] The new Bank of England Act 1998 recently put into place by the new Labour government in the UK may be remembered in this context.

of economic and monetary policy. This involved deregulation in all fields of economic activities, the privatisation or incorporation (independent from government but accountable on a profit or loss basis) of commercial activities by government and the simplification of the tax system. The reforms also included institutional changes for public sector organisations. They were to pursue explicit objectives, making them accountable for the attainment of these objectives. A system of accountability was established whereby the chief executive was given a performance-based contract, while at the same time leaving him with more discretion in managerial and financial matters within a pre-set framework.

In the area of monetary policy, prior to the new legislation, a change in direction could be recorded after 1984. Monetary policy was aimed at reducing inflation in the medium term and the operation of monetary policy through direct controls, such as interest rate and exchange controls, was replaced by operations through marked-based instruments and procedures.[451] In order further to enhance the new anti-inflationary approach of monetary policy, from 1986 onwards the role of the Reserve Bank in the new monetary policy, and especially in what ways the institution could help to increase the credibility of the commitments of the government in the area of monetary policy, became the subject of discussions.[452] The track record on inflation of independent central bank systems, together with the emerging view that central bank independence is a precondition for a sound monetary policy seem to have had a considerable influence on the new institutional design of the Reserve Bank, which was finally introduced by the Reserve Bank of New Zealand Act 1989.[453]

2. Institutional structure

According to section 5(2)–(3) of the Reserve Bank Act 1989, the Bank is a body corporate with perpetual succession and a common seal, and is capable of acquiring, holding and disposing of real and personal property and of suing and being sued. Subject to the provisions of the Reserve Bank Act 1989, the Bank has the rights, powers and privileges of a natural person. The Bank has its seat in the capital of New Zealand, Wellington. The Reserve Bank constitutes a single-tier system. However, it has the right to establish branches and agencies, and to

---

[451] Lloyd, n. 427 above, at 207.

[452] G.E. Wood, "A Pioneer Bank in a Pioneer's Country", *Central Banking*, vol. 5 (1994), 59–74, 63 *et seq.*, who states that the revision was initiated by Roger Douglas, than Minister of Finance in Nov. 1985, who suggested to the Bank to search for more independent ways in which to conduct monetary policy.

[453] Reserve Bank Act 1989 of 20 Dec. 1989, Public No. 157, amended by the Act to amend the Reserve Bank of New Zealand Act 1989 of 8 Aug. 1990, Public No. 96. The Act is referred to as Reserve Bank Act 1989: Lloyd, n. 427 above, and Wood, n. 452 above, on the influence of the theoretical literature. Some see the independence of the central bank also as an important step towards economic independence from Australia with which NZ has close economic ties, among others institutionalised by the Economic Relations Agreement (CER).

appoint agents in New Zealand or elsewhere.[454] Currently, the Bank maintains a branch in Auckland and Christchurch.

The Reserve Bank is run by a governor and deputy governor(s), a Board of Directors, and may also include one or more committees.

2.1. Governor and the deputy governors

The governor and deputy governors hold a dominant position in the structure of the Reserve Bank, since, as will be explained separately in the following section, the Board of Directors does not constitute a decision-making body in the classical sense. The governor is the chief executive of the Bank. Appointed for a renewable term of five years, it is the main duty of the governor to ensure that the Bank carries out the functions imposed on it by the Act.[455] His powers are such that he is authorised, in the performance of those functions, to act in relation to all matters that are not required to be dealt with by the Board of Directors.[456] The governor is supported by one or two deputy governor(s), who is (are) also appointed for a renewable period of five years. In the case of the appointment of two deputy governors, one is designated as deputy chief executive.[457] Currently, the governor is supported by two deputy governors.

The duties and functions of the deputy governors are determined by the governor.[458] In the absence or incapacity of the governor, the deputy chief executive has all the duties, responsibilities and functions of the governor and has the right to exercise his powers.[459] Moreover, the governor can delegate to the deputy chief executive, to the other deputy governors—if existent—or any officer of the Bank any of the governor's functions and powers. The deputy chief executive may be considered superior to the other deputy governor in as much as the governor may delegate to him the power to delegate power to the other deputy governor and any officer of the Bank.[460]

Although formally the governor represents the sole decision-making organ and all policy decisions remain with him, he is supported by the Bank's organisation of departments.[461] With two deputy governors in place, each oversees one half of the departments/sections. Each section is headed by a chief manager who has to report directly to the governor and/or the deputy governors. Discussions are somewhat formalised in a structure of committees which will provide advice on the different policy stances. The Reserve Bank Act 1989 does

---

[454] S. 6 Reserve Bank Act 1989.

[455] S. 40(2) Reserve Bank Act 1989. For a detailed evaluation of the procedure of appointment and dismissal of the governor, cf. Chap. 4 IV.

[456] Ibid., s. 41.

[457] Ibid., ss. 43–44.

[458] Ibid., s. 43(3).

[459] Ibid., s. 47. Cf. s. 48 as regards the procedure in case of a vacancy in office of governor.

[460] Ibid., s. 51.

[461] For details cf. Reserve Bank of New Zealand, *Briefing on the Reserve Bank of New Zealand* (Reserve Bank, Wellington, 1996), fig. 1.

not include any provision on the exercise of the powers of the governor and the deputy governors regarding regular meetings or the like.

2.2. Board of Directors

The Board of Directors consists of seven to ten members. The governor and the deputy governors are *ex officio* members, representing the executive directors of the Board. Additionally between four and seven non-executive directors may be present on the Board.[462] The non-executive directors are appointed for a renewable term of five years. They are banned from employment in the service of the Bank, but may receive fees.[463] Currently, the Board comprises the governor, the two deputy governors and seven non-executive directors. The seven non-executive directors are drawn from different industrial and financial sectors and from the academic community.

In playing a dual role the functions of the Board of Directors distinguish it considerably from organs in other central bank systems bearing a similar name. The Board of Directors does not represent an administrative or executive organ which is in charge of the day-to-day business of the Bank. Its first important function is to recommend the appointment for the post of the governor of the Bank. Hereafter, its second important function lays in the constant review of the performance of the Bank and its governor, the constant review of the Bank's resources, and the submission of advise to the governor.[464]

According to section 60 of the Reserve Bank Act 1989, the Board of Directors meets at least ten times a year. The governor, or in his absence the deputy chief executive, convenes the meetings. Moreover, special meetings are convened upon written request of three or more non-executive directors. The Board of Directors needs a quorum of five directors of whom at least three have to be non-executive directors. Decisions of the Board are taken by a simple majority vote of the members present. The governor, who presides the meetings, has a deliberative and, more importantly, in case of a tie also a casting vote.[465] In the absence of the governor this power is conferred to the deputy chief executive, or, in his absence, to a non-executive director, elected from among the directors present at the meeting.[466]

Anticipating potential conflicts of interests between the functions of the non-executive directors on the Board of Directors and any (business) activities outside the Bank, the Reserve Bank Act 1989 initially obliged the members of the Board of Directors to disclose any interest in a contract or proposed contract with the Bank, or any interest in a contract or proposed contract with the Bank,

---

[462] S. 54 Reserve Bank Act 1989.

[463] Ibid., ss. 54(4) and 63. The fees are determined by the Minister of Finance after considering any recommendation by the Board of Directors.

[464] Ibid., s. 53 Reserve Bank Act 1989. These functions will be evaluated more closely in Chap. 4 III 2.

[465] S. 60(8) Reserve Bank Act 1989.

[466] Ibid., s. 60(4) and (5).

or in the exercise or proposed exercise by the Bank of a power, to the Board Directors, which will consider any such proposals.[467] This provision has been sharpened thereafter to exclude directors from voting in resolutions that relate to such contracts or proposed contracts or the exercise or proposed exercise of powers and, moreover, are not counted for the purpose of determining whether a quorum exists in a particular meeting which deals with such matters.[468]

According to section 62 of the Reserve Bank Act 1989, the Board of Directors is empowered to appoint committees. The Reserve Bank Act 1989 itself does not establish specific committees. The range of functions of these Committees is defined by the functions of the Board of Directors, since the Board can delegate any of its functions and powers, except for the power of delegation, to the committees. The Board moreover has the power to discharge, alter or reconstitute a committee.[469] The committees may embody one or more directors. Currently, three standing committees exist, including a non-executive directors' committee, an audit committee and a registry committee.[470] The non-executive directors' committee assembles when the performance of the governor or his remuneration are subject of discussion. The audit committee monitors the financial management of the Bank and meets about three times a year. Finally, the registry committee functions as an adviser to the governor in matters related to the management of the Banks' commercial registry operations.

3. Tasks

Section 7 of the Reserve Bank Act 1989 states that "the Bank shall act as the central bank for New Zealand". Apart from the conduct of monetary policy, it is the sole issuer of currency in New Zealand, it promotes the maintenance and efficiency of the financial system, is involved in the promotion of banking legislation and payment systems, and offers services to the government and the banking sector at large.

5.1. Monetary policy

The Reserve Bank formulates and implements monetary policy directed to the economic objective of achieving and maintaining price stability.[471] The objective of price stability is closer defined in an agreement between the Bank and the government, referred to as the Policy Target Agreement (PTA).[472] Monetary

[467] Reserve Bank Act 1989, s. 61(1) in its version of 20 Dec. 1989.
[468] Ibid., s. 61(1) in its current version.
[469] Ibid., s. 62(2).
[470] Reserve Bank of New Zealand, n. 461 above, at 9.
[471] S. 8 Reserve Bank Act 1989. For more details of the monetary objective of the Reserve Bank, cf. Chap. 4 II.
[472] For details on the PTA and its role in the democratic accountability of the Reserve Bank cf. Chap. 4 II.

policy is implemented through open market operations in the domestic money market in order to maintain the liquidity of the banking system.

The Reserve Bank carries out the management of foreign reserves on behalf of the government, and, on the basis of a written directive by the government, may intervene in the foreign exchange market on behalf of the latter.[473] However, since 1985 New Zealand has a floating exchange rate as a result of which the value of the New Zealand Dollar is determined by the financial markets.

Moreover, according to section 25 *et seq.* of the Reserve Bank Act 1989, the Reserve Bank has the monopoly over the issue of both banknotes and coins in New Zealand.[474]

3.2. Services to government

Subject to the Public Finance Act 1989,[475] and on the basis of an agreement with the Minister of Finance,[476] the Reserve Bank acts as a banker for the government.[477] The Reserve Bank holds the accounts of the government and pursues government debt operations on behalf of the Treasury. The borrowing requirement of the government has to be covered by the sale of debt instruments to the private sector. The Reserve Bank also acts as an advisor to government in different areas, such as exchange rate matters and matters relating to the operation of the financial system.[478]

3.3. Services related to commercial banks

The Reserve Bank also acts as lender of last resort for the financial system and, moreover, may provide settlement account services for financial services.[479] The Reserve Bank facilitates the inter-bank settlement process. Registered commercial banks hold settlement accounts with the Reserve Bank which are used for the settlement of obligations between the commercial banks, whereby debit balances on an account of a commercial bank at end-of-day are prohibited. The Reserve Bank sets a target for the aggregate balance of these accounts, the so-called *cash target*, and determines the cash received on these funds. This is one of the main instruments for the implementation of monetary policy.[480]

---

[473] Reserve Bank Act 1989, s. 16 *et seq.*
[474] For more details see Reserve Bank of New Zealand, n. 461 above, 55–6.
[475] Reprinted in *RS*, vol. 35, 419.
[476] Known as the Agency Agreement.
[477] S. 34 Reserve Bank Act 1989.
[478] Ibid., ss. 23 and 33.
[479] Ibid., ss. 31–32.
[480] Reserve Bank of New Zealand, *Annual Plan 1997* (Wellington, 1997), at 16.

3.4. Banking supervision

The Reserve Bank registers banks and undertakes prudential supervision of registered banks in a joint effort with the Minister of Finance and the Governor-General in accordance with part V of the Reserve Bank Act 1989, in order to promote the "maintenance of a sound and efficient financial system" and to avoid "significant damage to the financial system that could result from a failure of a registered bank".[481] Moreover, the Bank acts as an adviser to the Minister of Finance. In this context the Bank can require financial institutions to supply relevant information and data related to the business of the specified institution(s).[482]

VII. THE FEDERAL RESERVE SYSTEM

As was observed in relation to the Bundesbank, a comparative study on central banks would be somewhat incomplete without embracing the Fed. Together with the Bundesbank the Fed is recognised as one of the more independent central banks existing today.[483] Not least due to its institutional structure, embracing 12 Federal Reserve Banks throughout the United States and a central body in Washington, DC, the Fed has been discussed as a reference system for the establishment of a central bank for Europe in the early debates.[484] Moreover, the Fed features unique mechanisms of accountability, in particular with regard to its relationship with Congress. Since its creation the democratic accountability of the Fed has always remained a subject for discussions and it remains until the present day a prominent subject-matter of politicians and academics both American and foreign.

---

[481] Ss. 67–156 Reserve Bank Act 1989. For a short overview cf. Memorandum submitted by the Reserve Bank of New Zealand, in Treasury and Civil Service Committee, *The Role of the Bank of England* (House of Commons Paper. Session 1993–4; 98–I, vol.2), Report, together with the proceedings of the Committee. HC Session 1993–4 (HMSO, London, 1993), appendix 17, at 171. Within the Bank this task is relocated to the Banking System Department. For an overview cf. S. Dawe, "The Reserve Bank of New Zealand Act 1989", *Reserve Bank Bulletin*, vol. 53 no. 1 (1990), 26–36, 29 *et seq.*

[482] Ss. 36–38 Reserve Bank Act 1989.

[483] Cf. table 1.

[484] E.g. J.-V. Louis, "Le Federal Reserve System—Rapport sur un mission d'études conduit en septembre 1988" in *Vers Un Système Européen de Banques Centrales*, Rapport du groupe présidé par Jean-Victor Louis (Editions de l'Université de Bruxelles, Brussels, 1989), 269–303.

1. Historic development

1.1. Early efforts

On 23 December 1913 President Woodrow Wilson signed into law the bill creating the Federal Reserve System.[485] It stood at the end of a struggle over the organisation of monetary affairs in the United States that had lasted for more than a century.[486]

The first attempt was the First United States Bank created in 1791, which was chartered to operate for a period of 20 years.[487] The plans for the establishment of a bank which—among others—was designed to regulate the amount of notes issued by the state-chartered banks were met with scepticism. To some the establishment of such an institution by an Act of Congress was potentially unconstitutional since the US Constitution delegated only specific powers upon Congress. Moreover, the application of the general clause of Article I, Section 8, Clause 18, of the US Constitution, allowing Congress "to make all laws which shall be *necessary and proper* for carrying into execution . . . all powers vested by this Constitution in the government of the United States" was considered to create an undesired precedent as regards the power of Congress.[488] The First Bank of the United States existed alongside a small number of state-chartered private banks all of which issued banknotes used in the regions where the respective banks were located. However, resistance to restrictions imposed on these private banks by the First United States Bank, namely regulating the amount of notes which state banks could issue, while at the same time competing in the market place with these banks, led to strong opposition against the renewal of the charter of the Bank. The corresponding bill failed to clear Congress in 1811.[489] The period following the rejection of the First United States Bank is often described as chaotic. The War of 1812[490] marked the beginning of the unrestricted issuing of banknotes and borrowing by the private banks, and, eventually, a decline in value of the notes issued. Additionally, the absence of an institution functioning as the principle banker of the Federal government was felt.

The consequences of the abrogation of the First United States Bank had made even critics of that Bank believe that an institution charged with the control of

---

[485] 38 Stat. 251; hereafter referred to as Federal Reserve Act 1913.

[486] E.g. C.H. Moore, *The Federal Reserve System: A History of the First 75 years* (McFarland & Company, Inc., Publishers, Jefferson, NC, 1990).

[487] Act of 25 Feb. 1791, 1 Stat. 191.

[488] Constitution of the United States of America of 17 Sept. 1787, enacted on 4 Mar. 1789 (hereafter referred to as US Constitution), italics added; E. Flaherty, 1997, *A Brief History of Central Banking in the United States* (online), available from: URL http://odur.let.rug.nl/ (last accessed Jan. 1999); E.C. Mullins, *A Study of the Federal Reserve* (Kasper and Horton, New York, 1952), 5 *et seq.*

[489] The bill renewing the charter failed to pass the House of Representatives and the Senate by one vote each.

[490] The War of 1812, sometimes referred to as "The Second War of Independence", between the United States and Britain lasted from 1812 until 1815.

the nation's money supply was needed. Thus, in 1816, the Second United States Bank was established, once again chartered for a period of 20 years.[491] As had been the case before, the Second United States Bank failed due to strong political resentments. When the charter of the Bank came up for renewal in 1832 the President vetoed the legislation and the Bank ceased to exist with the expiry of its charter in 1836.[492] With the regulatory authority gone once more, the private banking institutions fell back into the practice of unrestricted money creation.[493] The outbreak of the Civil War in 1861 worsened the financial crisis and, in 1863, led to the passing of the National Banking Act.[494] Essentially, the National Banking Act limited the issuing of banknotes to newly established national banks, chartered by the Federal government. However, the new system of national banks also failed to provide a satisfactory currency system. The two foremost problems identified with this failure were the incapability of the existing currency system to expand in order to provide the economy with much needed loans, i.e. inelastic currency, and the insufficient reserve system which often left banks which faced increased withdrawal demands short of funds. This eventually resulted in financial panics and runs on banks, the biggest of which took place in 1907.[495]

1.2. The creation of the Federal Reserve System

The Aldrich-Vreeland Act which passed Congress in 1908, established the so-called National Monetary Commission which was charged with the examination of the existing central bank systems around the world and to report on its findings to Congress. The findings of this Commission, compiled in the so-called Aldrich Plan, suggested the creation of a National Reserve Association.[496] According to this plan the management of the currency would have been centralised considerably by introducing a single-tier structure consisting of a system of autonomous regional reserve banks serving under the control of a central board of directors consisting of commercial bankers. The plan called for a centralised setting of interest rates and power to issue banknotes and for the National Reserve Association to act as the fiscal agent for the Federal government. However, this plan was rejected by those who feared a dominance of commercial bankers. Due to a shift in power to the Democrats after the elections of 1912, the bill never passed Congress.

[491] Act of 10 Apr. 1816 (3 Stat. 266).
[492] President Andrew Jackson generally distrusted banks and favoured the use of coins over banknotes, cf. G. Taylor, *The Federal Reserve System* (Chelsea House Publishers, New York, 1989), at 37.
[493] According to Taylor, Ibid., at 37, an impressive 1.400 private banks were issuing their own banknotes, often without proper reserves to cover withdrawal demands.
[494] 12 Stat. 162; cf. J.W. Hurst, *A Legal History of Money in the United States, 1774–1970* (University of Nebraska Press, Lincoln, 1973), 134 *et seq.*
[495] Moore, n. 486 above, 4–5.
[496] Mullins, n. 488 above, 5 *et seq.*

The legislative proposal for the establishment of a Federal Reserve System which finally did pass Congress had the support of President Wilson and was mainly the work of two men, Representative Carter Glass and H. Parker Willis, an economist.[497] The main aim of the Reserve Bank Act was to establish Federal Reserve Banks, to furnish an elastic currency, to afford means of rediscounting commercial paper and to establish a more effective supervision of banking in the United States.[498] The continental United States were divided into 12 districts.[499] The national banking associations in each of these districts were required to subscribe to the capital stock of the respective Federal Reserve Bank.[500] Otherwise, the membership of state-chartered banks was voluntary. Moreover, it was possible for the public to obtain shares in the Federal Reserve Banks. The Federal Reserve Banks were set up as bodies corporate with the power—among others—to adopt and use a corporate seal, to have succession for a period of 20 years, unless otherwise decided upon by the Congress, to make contracts and to have standing in courts.

The Federal Reserve Act provided for the establishment of a board of directors responsible for the conduct and supervision of each Federal Reserve Bank. The board of directors consisted of nine members appointed for a period of three years. The members of the board of directors were classified into three groups. Three class A directors were representatives of stock-holding banks. The three class B directors had to be actively engaged in commerce, agriculture or "other industrial pursuit" in the respective Federal reserve district at the time of their appointment. The Group A and B directors were nominated by the member banks of the respective Federal reserve district.

The three class C directors were appointed by the Federal Reserve Board. One of the class C directors was designated as the chairman of the board of directors of the respective Federal Reserve Bank and as "Federal reserve agent". The chairman of the Federal Reserve Bank had to make regular reports to the Federal Reserve Board and acted as its official representative for the performance of the functions conferred upon it by the Federal Reserve Act 1913. The Federal Reserve Banks were to set up branch offices within their respective Federal reserve districts which were to be operated by a board of directors under the rules and regulations approved by the Federal Reserve Board.

The Federal Reserve Board, seated in Washington, DC, consisted of seven members (six after 1922), comprising five members to be appointed for a term of ten years by the President "by and with the advice and consent" of the Senate, and the Secretary of the Treasury and the Comptroller of the Currency as *ex officio* members. When making his choice of candidates for nomination to the Federal Reserve Board the President had to have regard to "a fair representation

---

[497] Hurst, n. 494 above, at 206.

[498] Note the first sentence of the preamble to the Federal Reserve Act 1913.

[499] The districts correspond with those still existing today. Cf. Chap. 3VIII 3.

[500] 3% of the subscription of the paid-up capital stock and the surplus of the respective bank; s. 2 Federal Reserve Act 1913.

of the different commercial, industrial and geographical divisions of the country".[501] At least two of the appointees had to have experience in banking and finance. The President had the right to designate one of the five nominees as the governor and one as vice-governor of the Federal Reserve Board.[502]

The Federal Reserve Board was advised by a Federal Advisory Council seated in Washington, DC. It comprised the same number of members as Federal reserve districts. The Council was a concession that had been made to the commercial banks which had demanded a representation of the member banks on the Board of Governors. Each Federal Reserve Bank appointed from its own district one member to this Council. The tasks of the Federal Advisory Council were to advise the Federal Reserve Board on general business conditions, to make oral or written representations concerning matters within the jurisdiction of the Board, to call for information and to make recommendations—among others—on discount rates, rediscount business and note issues.[503] The Federal Advisory Council met at least four times a year. Any decisions were taken by a majority vote of the members.

From the outset the Federal Reserve Act provided for a system of decentralised decision-making. The Federal Reserve Board was charged with the exercising of general supervision over Federal Reserve Banks. The Board had the right "to suspend or remove any officer or director of any Federal Reserve Bank" and even "to suspend, for the violation of any provisions of this Act, the operations of any Federal Reserve Bank, to take possession thereof, administer the same during the period of suspension, and, when deemed advisable to liquidate or reorganize such bank".[504] With regard to monetary policy the Federal Reserve Board was in charge of setting the discount rate and of the supervision and regulation of issuing and retirement of Federal reserve notes through the bureau of the Comptroller of the Currency. In doing so the Board was obliged to make a full report of its activities to the Speaker of the House of Representatives annually. Until the reform of the Federal Reserve Act in 1935 the executive branch of government personified by the Secretary of the Treasury, which chaired the meetings of the Board, had a strong position *vis-à-vis* the Federal Reserve Board. The Federal Reserve Banks, on the other hand, subject to any rules and regulations of the Board had the right to enter into open market operations without prior approval by the Board. They also acted as fiscal agents for the US government.[505] This gave the Federal Reserve Banks a powerful position *vis-à-vis* the Federal Reserve Board.

It was the lack of co-ordination of monetary policy which, step by step, led towards more centralised decision-making in the Fed and a dominance of the

---

[501] Federal Reserve Act 1913, s. 10.
[502] Subsequent to the Banking Act 1935 the governor and vice governor were known as chairman and vice chairman.
[503] S. 12 Federal Reserve Act 1913.
[504] Ibid., *s.* 11(f) and (h).
[505] Ibid., s. 14 and 15.

Federal Reserve Board which had probably not been envisaged by the founders of the Fed.

1.3. The evolution of the Federal Reserve System

In an attempt further to overcome the lack of co-ordination at first, in 1922, the so-called Committee of Governors was created, and shortly thereafter, in 1923, replaced by the Open Market Investment Committee. Both of these committees only constituted forums for discussions of open market operations, since unified decisions were not taken. The Open Market Policy Conference, which was created in 1930, finally had the authority to decide on open market operations binding for all Federal Reserve Banks.[506] Yet, the diversity of interests among the regional Federal Reserve Banks hindered any effective decision-making as the representatives were obliged to act in accordance with the instructions given by the respective Federal Reserve Bank.[507]

The first major reform of the Fed towards the system as it is known today came in 1933 with the Banking Act 1933.[508] The main novelty was the introduction of the Federal Open Market Committee (FOMC) which substituted the Open Market Policy Conference. The FOMC consisted of one representative of each Federal reserve district selected by the respective board of directors of the Federal Reserve Banks. It had the right to make recommendations to the Federal Reserve Board on the conduct of open market operations. However, unlike the provisions which govern the FOMC today, the FOMC could not take binding decisions. Instead, open market operations remained to be adopted by the Federal Reserve Board. Moreover, each Federal Reserve Bank reserved the right not to participate in open market operations. Thus, despite the fact that open market operations were no longer the sole responsibility of the Federal Reserve Banks the latter could still oppose any decisions which did not suit them.

In the atmosphere of economic and social renewal in the New Deal era, President Roosevelt initiated a reform bill which would have further shifted open market operations away from the regional level by vesting the power over open market operations in the Federal Reserve Board and by reducing the role of the Federal Reserve Banks to a participation in an advisory committee which was envisaged to consist of five representatives of the Federal Reserve Banks. By way of removing the Federal Reserve Banks from open market operations the

---

[506] Louis, n. 484 above, at 289.

[507] J. von Hagen, *Monetäre, fiskalische und politische Integration: Das Beispiel der USA*, in *Währungsunion und politische Integration: Historische Erfahrungen und europäische Perspektive*, 9. Wissenschaftliche Kolloquium am 3. November 1995 im Hotel Marriot, Frankfurt am Main, auf Einladung der Deutschen Bundesbank, Bankhistorisches Archiv, Beiheft 30, Fritz Knapp Verlag, Frankfurt a.M., 1996, 35–51, at 48–49. In the meantime in 1922 the Act Amending the Federal Reserve Act (Act of 3 June 1922, Public Law 67–230) altered the institutional structure of the Fed slightly by introducing an additional governor, thereby increasing the number on the Federal Reserve Board to eight. Moreover, the requirement for two of the Presidential appointees on the Federal Reserve Board to be experienced in banking or finance was dropped.

[508] Act of 19 June 1934 (48 Stat. 162).

Roosevelt administration strove to ensure the backing of its economic reforms by the Fed.[509]

The law that finally passed Congress as Banking Act 1935[510] differed substantially from those proposals. The Federal Reserve Board was reduced to seven members and renamed Board of Governors. In what may be considered as a major step towards a more independent Board of Governors, the Secretary of the Treasury and the Comptroller of the Currency were removed from participating as *ex officio* members on the Board.[511] Moreover, the term of office of the members of the Board of Governors was increased to 14 years, and they could only be removed by the President "for cause". Of these seven members the US President appointed two members to act as the chairman and vice chairman of the Board of Governors. Unlike today, the appointment did not require the backing of Congress.

Contrary to the original proposal the FOMC was preserved. However, its composition was changed completely and in a very decisive way. Instead of functioning as a forum for the co-ordination of open market operations for the different regional Federal Reserve Banks with their representatives being bound by the instructions of their respective Bank, the FOMC was transformed into a central decision-making body. The FOMC now included the seven members of the Board of Governors and five representatives of the Federal Reserve Banks selected by the Federal Reserve Bank.[512] The representatives of the Federal Reserve Banks were no longer bound by instructions by the regional Federal Reserve Banks. The FOMC was put in charge of decisions on open market operations to be carried out by the Federal Reserve Banks. Decisions taken by the FOMC were no longer recommendations which could be disregarded.[513] For the first time the Federal Reserve Banks were obliged to act in accordance with the decisions taken by the FOMC. With the introduction of the FOMC the Fed shifted considerably from a regional to a more centralised structure as far as monetary policy decisions were concerned.[514]

The Banking Act 1935 also introduced new reporting requirements. The Board of Governors and the FOMC became obliged to "keep complete records of the action taken by the Board and by the Federal Open Market Committee upon all questions of policy relating to open market operations and shall record therein the votes taken in connection with the determination of open market

[509] W. Patman, "The Federal Reserve System: A Brief For Legal Reform" (1996) 10 *St. Louis University School of Law Journal*, 299–326, reprinted in Joint Economic Committee Congress of the United States, 94th Congress 2nd Session, 3 Jan. 1977, Appendix I, 143–61, at 150.
[510] Act of 23 Aug. 1935 (49 Stat. 684).
[511] Taking effect from Feb. 1936; s. 203(b) Banking Act of 1935 (new s. 10 Federal Reserve Act).
[512] S. 205 Banking Act of 1935. The selection procedures did not differ substantially from those applicable today which will be explained hereafter.
[513] S. 12A(d) introduced by the Banking Act of 1933 was abolished.
[514] Ch. Maskens, *L'Histoire du Fed Peut-Elle Fournir des Enseignements pour une Future Banque Centrale Européenne?*, Documentatieblad Ministerie Van Financiën (Belgium), No. 2, Maart–April 1990, 293–319, at 307.

policies and all reasons underlying the action of the Board and the Committee in each instance".[515]

For a period during and after the two World Wars until 1951 the Fed became subordinated to the Treasury which was firmly in control of setting the goals of monetary policy. In the "Accord" of 1951 between the Treasury and the Fed an understanding was reached that the latter was once again free to conduct monetary policy independently from the executive branch.

The Federal Reserve Reform Act of 1977[516] stood at the end of a decade of intense public discussion on the role and status of the Fed and in particular its accountability *vis-à-vis* the legislative and executive branches of government. A discussion in which Congress took a central role.[517] The Federal Reserve Reform Act 1977 introduced broad guidelines for the implementation of monetary policy.[518] The Board of Governors became obliged to attend hearings before the Banking Committees of both Houses of Congress. Finally, the chairman and vice chairman of the Board of Governors were no longer appointed by the President at his discretion. Instead, the President's selection became subject to the " advice and consent of the Senate".[519]

Finally, the Full Employment and Balanced Growth Act of 1978[520] amended the Employment Act of 1946. It set out to assure that Federal Government policies were committed to full employment, production, and real income, balanced growth, adequate productivity growth, proper attention to national properties, and reasonable price stability.[521] The President became obliged to set forth explicit short-term and medium-term economic goals.[522] Under the Full Employment and Balanced Growth Act the Board of Governors became obliged to transmit to the Congress twice a year a report including projections of the economic development, objectives and plans of the Board and the FOMC with regard to monetary policy and the way in which these objectives and plans are related to the short-term goals of the President.[523]

2. Institutional structure

Despite first impressions, the institutional structure of the Fed is anything but easily defined.[524] On the one hand, the existence of 12 Federal Reserve Banks

[515] S. 203(d) Banking Act of 1935 (new s. 10 (last para.) Federal Reserve Act).
[516] Act of 16 Nov. 1977, 91 Stat. 1387, hereafter referred to as Federal Reserve Reform Act 1977.
[517] For more details of the relationship between Congress and the Fed, cf. Chap. 4 VI 1.
[518] For more details cf. Chap. 4 II 1 on the monetary objectives.
[519] S. 204 Federal Reserve Reform Act 1977 (new s. 10, para. 2 Federal Reserve Act).
[520] Act of 27 Oct. 1978 (92 Stat. 1887); hereafter referred to as Full Employment and Balanced Growth Act.
[521] Preamble to the Full Employment and Balanced Growth Act.
[522] S. 103(a) Full Employment and Balanced Growth Act.
[523] Better known as Humphrey-Hawkins-Procedure, named after the two principle promoters of the bill. N. 522 above, s. 108(a); for more details cf. Chap. 4 VI.
[524] Cf. also Chap. 4 III 2.

which, as will be observed hereafter, are all separate legal entities may promote the impression of a strongly decentralised, i.e. regional, structure. On the other hand, taking into account the role of the Board of Governors of the Fed, and in particular its chairman in the conduct of monetary policy, the System features centralised structures. The Board of Governors of the Fed and Congress seem to agree, although for different reasons, that the Fed has a strong regional basis. The Board of Governors prefers to describe itself as a regional system of Federal Reserve Banks with an administrative centre on the federal level located in Washington, DC. Congress in its criticism of the Fed time and again has pointed out the strong regional basis of the System and—in its view—the strong influence of commercial banks on the Fed and in particular on monetary policy pursued by the FOMC. If the Fed is classified on the basis of where the policy decisions are taken, the scale would be in favour of the central level. In this direction Hasse describes the Fed as "a uniform central bank system with a centralised method of formulating monetary policy".[525] On the other hand, it weighs in favour of the regional level of the System that the application of one monetary policy instrument, that is discount rate policy, is initiated by the Federal Reserve Banks which moreover participate in the meetings of the FOMC which decides on the application of open market operations. The principal organs of the Fed are the Board of Governors, the FOMC, and the Federal Reserve Banks. Additionally, advisory committees exist.

2.1. Board of Governors

The Board of Governors of the Fed consists of seven members appointed by the President on the advice and with the consent of the Senate for a non-renewable term of 14 years.[526] From these seven members two are designated by the President to be the chairman and vice chairman of the Board of Governors for a renewable period of four years.[527] The appointment of the chairman and vice chairman also require the advice and the consent of the Senate

The Chairman of the Board of Governors acts as the executive officer of the Federal Reserve. According to the Internal Administrative Procedures Manual of the Board of Governors he is in charge of the overall management of the Board of Governors in the execution of its objectives, policies, and programmes and the Board can delegate certain administrative responsibilities to him.[528] The chairman is often referred to as a *primus inter pares* because although he does not carry a decisive vote (not even in case of a tie) he takes a dominant position both inside and outside the Board of Governors. This can be explained both

---

[525] R.H. Hasse (ed.), op. cit., Chap. 2, n. 22, at 164.

[526] 12 USC Sec. 241. For more details of the appointment and dismissal procedures of the Board of Governors, cf. Chap. 4 IV.

[527] 12 USC Sec. 242.

[528] Board of Governors of the Federal Reserve System, *Internal Administrative Procedure Manual*, revised version of Feb. 1993.

from the exposed position identified with the chairmanship and the personality of some of the people who have served in that position. Inside the Fed the dominant position of the chairman is founded on his chairmanship of the two decision-making organs, the Board of Governors and the FOMC. This position gives him the chance to include his own perspectives on issues, as he summarises the outcome of the meetings of these two organs.[529] Moreover, due to the fact that he has the largest staff at his disposal he may also have an information advantage over his colleagues. Outside the Fed the chairman is the spokesman of the System. He also represents the most important link to the legislative and executive branches of government. The regular congressional hearings are usually attended by the chairman on behalf of the Board of Governors. It is the chairman who often gives evidence before congressional committees on legislative proposals. Moreover, he has regular contacts with the US President and the Secretary of the Treasury on issues relating to the tasks of the Fed.[530]

The Board of Governors—among others—is in charge of the supervision of the Federal Reserve Banks and financial institutions and the supervision and regulation of the issue of banknotes.[531] With regard to monetary policy the tasks of the Board of Governors may be considered as twofold. First, the Board of Governors is exclusively in charge for two of the three monetary policy instruments utilised by the Fed, that is decisions on the adjustment of the discount rate and the reserve requirements of the member banks. Additionally, as will be discussed below, the members of the Board of Governors take part in the meetings of the FOMC, which decides on open market operations. Internally, the Board's work is carried out by standing committees. At the time of the writing the Board featured five standing committees, covering Federal Reserve Bank Affairs, Economic Affairs, Consumer and Community Affairs and Supervisory and Regulatory Affairs.[532]

The Board of Governors meets at least twice a week at the time of which any matters relating to monetary and credit policies, regulatory and supervisory duties and other questions related to the work of the Board of Governors may become subject of discussions.[533] Decisions are taken by formal vote whereby a simple majority is sufficient to take any decision.

2.2. Federal Open Market Committee

Arguably the most important organ for the formulation of monetary policy in the Fed is the FOMC. The FOMC comprises the members of the Board of Governors of the Fed and five representatives from among the 12 Federal

---

[529] Th. Havrilesky, *The Pressure on American Monetary Policy* (Kluwer Academic Publishers, Boston, 1993), at 4.

[530] For more details cf. Chap. 4 III 2.

[531] 12 USC Sec. 248 with an enumeration of the powers of the Board of Governors.

[532] Each committee consist of a maximum of 3 members selected by the chairman after consulting with the Board of Governors.

[533] Rules of Organization of Board of Governors of the Federal Reserve System, as revised and amended 1 Jan. 1993 (12 CFR 262).

Reserve Banks. These five representatives, who are selected annually on a rotary basis, are required to hold the position of a president or vice president of a Federal Reserve Bank.[534] The Federal Reserve Bank of New York takes a prominent position in the FOMC since its president serves in the FOMC on a permanent basis.[535] At the beginning of each year the FOMC appoints a chairman and vice chairman and elects staff officers to assist the FOMC in the performance of its tasks. Although by law in principle any member of the FOMC can be appointed as chairman or vice chairman it has become an established practice to elect the chairman of the Board of Governors of the Fed chairman and the president of the Federal Reserve Bank of New York vice chairman.

Although only five Federal Reserve Banks are represented in the FOMC with a right to vote on policy decisions, the presidents of the other Federal Reserve Banks have the right to attend the meetings of the FOMC in an advisory capacity.[536] On the one hand, it can be observed that due to the fact that all of the seven members of the Board of Governors participate in the deliberations of the FOMC, the Board and therefore the Federal level, holds the majority of the votes and consequently has the dominant position on the FOMC. This does not, however, convince those observers who have repeatedly argued that the participation of representatives of the 12 Federal Reserve Banks in the meetings of the FOMC gives the regional level *de facto* considerable influence over the monetary policy decisions taken in the FOMC.[537]

The FOMC is in charge of deciding on the application of open market operations undertaken by the Federal Reserve Banks; arguably this is the most important monetary policy instrument.[538] By law the FOMC is required to meet in Washington, DC, at least four times a year and, additionally, at the request of the Board of Governors or at least three members of the FOMC. It has become an established practice for the FOMC to meet eight times a year at intervals of five to eight weeks.[539] The majority of these meetings are devoted to the determination of the monetary policy to be pursued until the following meeting. Moreover, during at least two of these regular meetings long-term monetary policy strategies are decided upon. Decisions are taken by a simple majority vote, and a quorum of at least seven members or their alternates is required for the transaction of business.[540]

[534] 12 USC Sec. 263; cf. also Board of Governors of the Federal Reserve Board, *Federal Open Market Committee Rules*, as amended, effective 1 Jan. 1990.

[535] For more information regarding the appointment and dismissal procedures of the FOMC, cf. Chap. 4 IV.

[536] According to the Board of Governors of the Federal Reserve System, *The Federal Reserve System: Purposes & Functions* (8th edn., Washington, DC, Dec. 1994), at 13: "All the presidents participate in FOMC discussions, contributing to the Committee's assessment of the economy and of policy options . . . ".

[537] For more details cf. Chap. 4 IV 1.

[538] 12 USC Sec. 263(b) and (c), ss. 353–359.

[539] A current FOMC calendar is available (online) from URL http://www.bog.frb.fed.us/FOMC (last accessed Jan. 1999).

[540] S. 272.3. Federal Open Market Committee Rules.

2.3. Federal Reserve Banks

Today, the continental United States are still divided into 12 Federal reserve districts identified by so-called Federal reserve cities, i.e., Boston, New York, Philadelphia, Cleveland, Richmond, Atlanta, Chicago, St. Louis, Minneapolis, Kansas City, Dallas and San Francisco.[541] To each of these districts a Federal Reserve Bank is relocated. Apparently these districts do not correspond with any State borders, nor do the Federal reserve districts necessarily represent the most important economic centres in the United States. Rather, they are a product of economic and political considerations at the time of the establishment of the Federal Reserve System. Each Federal Reserve Bank constitutes a body corporate and as such has legal personality (power to conclude contracts/active and passive standing in court). The share in capital of the Federal Reserve Banks is held by commercial banks, referred to as member banks. Generally, commercial banks in the United States can be divided into two groups: Those that have been Federally chartered, so-called national banks, and those that have been chartered by one of the Federal States—so-called state banks. National banks are obliged under federal law to sign up with the Fed.[542] By contrast, state banks are not required to become members of the Fed.[543] Indeed, the fact that the membership was and is voluntary can function as a counterbalance to the Fed as restrictive regulations imposed on the banks by Congress or the Fed could be opposed by state banks threatening to leave the system.[544] However, there is no evidence that this mechanism has ever materialised.

The state banks are classified into state member banks and state non-member banks. In order to qualify for membership in the System State banks have to satisfy certain requirements set out by the Board of Governors.[545] The shares in capital of the Federal Reserve Banks are effectively held by the member banks of the respective district since the latter, upon acceptance into the Fed, are obliged to subscribe to the capital stock of the Federal Reserve Bank located in the Federal reserve district where the respective bank is located.[546] The Federal Reserve Banks can be distinguished from regular commercial banks in that the stockholders in the capital of the Federal Reserve Banks do not have the rights and privileges of stockholders. Besides, the Federal Reserve Banks do not work

---

[541] According to 12 USC Sec. 222 the Board of Governors is empowered to adjust existing districts or create new districts. Although adjustments have taken place the original 12 districts still exist.

[542] 12 USC Sec. 282.

[543] At the end of 1993, 3.360 national banks and 970 state banks (out of 11.212 commercial banks) were members of the Fed; cf. Board of Governors, n. 536 above, at 14.

[544] Hurst, n. 494 above, 201–2.

[545] 12 USC Sec. 321 *et seq.*

[546] A member bank has to invest 3% of its capital and surplus into the shares in the capital of the respective Federal Reserve Bank. In return, it receives an annual dividend of 6%. This arrangement is a unique feature of the Fed compared to the other central banks observed in this study, since Federal Reserve Banks as fundament of the Fed are neither public institutions (nationalised) nor formally private corporations in which the State holds all shares in the capital of the bank.

on a profit-oriented basis as the net earnings which remain after deduction of shareholder dividends have to be deposited in the surplus fund of the bank from where a large amount is transferred to the Secretary of the Treasury for deposit in the general budget fund of the Treasury.[547]

Each Federal Reserve Bank is conducted under the supervision of a board of directors which administers the affairs of the bank.[548] The board of directors consists of nine members appointed on a rotational basis for a period of three years. Its directors are classified into three categories.[549] Additionally, each Federal Reserve Bank features a president and vice president which are not members of the board of directors. The president functions as the chief executive officer within the Federal Reserve Bank. Most but not all of the 12 Federal Reserve Banks have branches.[550] Like the head office the branches are managed by a board of directors consisting of either five or seven members.[551] Moreover, each Federal Reserve Bank includes several advisory councils.

The Federal Reserve Banks are metaphorically referred to as the "executive arm" of the Fed. As the administrative head the Board of Governors of the Fed relies on the Federal Reserve Banks. They offer services to banks and other depository institutions, such as the function as "lender of last resort", hold the reserve of financial institutions required under the Federal Reserve Act and the Monetary Control Act, act as a fiscal agent to government and perform the examination and supervision of banking institutions. The Federal Reserve Banks also fulfil an important function in examining and reviewing both the national and international economic conditions and provide in particular information on the economic conditions of their respective districts—among others—in the course of FOMC discussions. With regard to monetary policy the Federal Reserve Banks contribute to the System in two ways. First, the point has been made that the presidents of the Federal Reserve Banks participate in the deliberations of the FOMC, albeit that only five of them have a voting power at any given time. The Federal Reserve Bank of New York has an outstanding position among the Federal Reserve Banks as it is in charge of implementing all open market operations decided upon by the FOMC.[552] The day-to-day open market operations are conducted by the manager of the System Open Market Account, a staff of the Federal Reserve Bank of New York designated by the Federal Reserve Bank of New York and approved by the FOMC. This makes some observers believe that the day-to-day open market policy is effectively taken over by the Federal Reserve Bank of New York, since the FOMC meets

[547] 12 USC Sec. 289.
[548] 12 USC Sec. 301.
[549] 12 USC Sec. 302. For further details of the appointment and dismissal procedures of the board of directors of the Federal Reserve Banks, cf. Chap. 4 IV.
[550] S. 3 Federal Reserve Act. For a list of branch offices cf. Board of Governors of the Fed, n. 536 above, 8–9.
[551] Regulation Relating to Branches of Federal Reserve Banks, as amended in 1978.
[552] Louis, n. 484 above, 295–7.

normally only eight times per year.[553] Moreover, the Federal Reserve Banks play an important role in the determination of the discount rates. According to section 14 of the Federal Reserve Act, the Federal Reserve Banks have power "to establish from time to time, subject to review and determination of the Board of Governors of the Fed, rates of discount to be charged by the Federal reserve bank . . . ; but each such bank shall establish such rates every fourteen days, or oftener if deemed necessary by the Board". In practice the board of directors of each Federal Reserve Bank communicates to the Board of Governors every two weeks whether it wants to change the discount rate. The Board of Governors then takes the final decision. Federal reserve officials usually emphasise that the participation of the Federal Reserve Banks amounts to more than making proposals, as they take the initiative for fixing the discount rates.[554] Others see the position of the Federal Reserve Banks as less powerful, describing their actual role as making *recommendations* on the discount rates.[555]

2.4. Advisory bodies

Of the three advisory bodies of the Board of Governors, including the Federal Advisory Council, the Consumer Advisory Council and the Thrift Institutions Advisory Council, only the first—to a limited extent—plays a role in the area of monetary policy.[556]

Seated in Washington, DC, the Federal Advisory Council consists of 12 members who are selected annually by the board of directors of the Federal Reserve Banks. Each member represents one of the 12 Federal reserve districts.[557] The role of the Council is that of an advisor to the Board of Governors of the Fed. The Council takes no part in the management of the Fed. It has the right only to make oral or written observations regarding any subject-matter dealt with by the Board and—in general terms—can make recommendations—among others—with regard to the conduct of monetary policy.[558] However, the practical importance of the Council as an advisor has been described as marginal.[559] The Council is required to meet at least four times a year but may also meet

---

[553] Th. de Saint Phalle, *The Federal Reserve. An Intentional Mystery* (Praeger, New York, 1985), at 98.

[554] Instructive: Office of the Staff Directors for Federal Reserve Bank, Activities Board of Governors of the Fed, *The Role of Directors of the Federal Reserve Banks and Branches in the Functions and Responsibilities of the Fed* (2nd printing, Washington, DC, Feb. 1989), at 14: "[t]hey are expected to establish a rate that in their best judgement is most consistent not only with local credit conditions but with national monetary policy. The rationale underlying the action of a Reserve Bank's board with respect to the discount rate is always the focal point of discussions of the Board of Governors in its review."

[555] E.g. J.M. Berry, "Is the Fed's Power Legitimate?", *Central Banking*, vol. 6 no. 5 (1996), 36–46, at 39.

[556] For a short overview of the other two Advisory Councils cf. Board of Governors, n. 536 above, 14–15.

[557] 12 USC Sec. 261.

[558] 12 USC Sec. 262.

[559] Discussions of officials at the Board of Governors with the author.

upon its own initiative or at the request of the Board of Governors. Decisions are taken by a majority vote. The Council acts more as a link and channel of communication between the Board of Governors on the Federal level and the banking and business community throughout the 12 Federal reserve districts. This explains why the view of the Council frequently reflects the opinions of the big commercial banks.

3. Tasks

The tasks of the Fed include those traditionally associated with a central bank and can be assigned to the areas of monetary policy, services to financial institutions and government and supervision and regulation of financial institutions.

3.1. Monetary policy

According to the Federal Reserve Act, the Board of Governors of the Fed and the FOMC have to promote effectively the goals of maximum employment, stable prices and moderate long-term interest rates.[560] Three instruments are applied by the Fed for the conduct of monetary policy.

Arguably the most important monetary policy instrument are open market operations in the form of the purchasing or selling of government bonds, thereby influencing the amount of money available to banks for loans.

A monetary policy instrument which is less often applied is the discount rate, that is the interest rate which financial institutions are charged when borrowing short-term loans, the so-called "discount window loans", from the Federal Reserve Banks of the district they are located in, thereby influencing the financial institution's borrowing policies.[561] Since the signing into law of the Monetary Control Act of 1980 any financial institution being subjected to the reserve requirements (in connection with the servicing of certain deposits, such as transaction accounts and non-personal time deposits) has the same right of access to the discount window as member banks of the Fed.

Finally, all depository institutions, regardless of their membership of the Federal Reserve System, are subject to reserve requirements.[562] By lowering or raising the percentage of the deposits which the financial institutions have to keep in reserve, either as vault cash or at the Federal Reserve Bank in their district, the Board of Governors can control the amount of money available for loans and thus for money creation. Moreover, changes in reserve requirements

[560] For details on the monetary objectives, cf. Chap. 4 IV 1.

[561] On the type of credits and the borrowing procedures cf. Board of Governors of the Federal Reserve System, n. 536 above, 43 *et seq.*; cf. also Federal Reserve Regulation A on the extension of credit by Federal Reserve Banks. The descriptive phrase originates from the early days of the Fed when bankers would actually appear in person in the Federal Reserve Bank to request a loan at a teller window.

[562] S. 19 Federal Reserve Act.

can indirectly also influence interest rates as these are linked to the availability of bank credits.

Unlike domestic monetary policy, the Treasury is principally responsible for exchange rate policy. The Fed alongside the Treasury's Exchange Stabilisation Fund is authorised by the Treasury to engage in foreign exchange interventions. However, exchange rate interventions are not considered as a primary tool of monetary policy. If conducted, they usually result from informal consultations between the Treasury and the Federal Reserve Board (senior staff level/official staff) and also officials of the Federal Reserve Bank of New York, which acts as an agent for both the Fed and the Treasury's Exchange Stabilisation Fund.

3.2. Services to financial institutions

Generally, the Fed offers services to financial institutions in two ways. First, the Federal Reserve Banks act as "lender of last resort". The availability of "discount windows loans" from the Federal Reserve Banks has a stabilising effect on the financial system as a whole in the case of an acute liquidity crisis of one or more financial institutions. Secondly, the Federal Reserve Banks throughout the 12 Federal reserve districts offer payment system services to financial institutions, such as cheque collection and automated clearing-house services.

Somewhat outside the scope of these services the Federal Reserve Banks also have the task of distributing as well as collecting banknotes and coins. They are authorised to issue banknotes to the extent that they are secured by legally authorised collateral held by the Federal Reserve Banks.[563] Coins are distributed on behalf of the Treasury.

3.3. Government's bank

The Fed acts as the fiscal agent of the United States and provides different services for both the Federal government and its agencies. The Federal Reserve Banks maintain the Treasury's fund account, clear Treasury cheques drawn on that account, conduct nation wide auctions of Treasury securities and issue, service and redeem Treasury securities.[564]

3.4. Banking supervision and regulation

The supervision and regulation of financial institutions in the United States may be considered as the most important task of the Fed apart from conducting monetary policy. The Fed conducts these tasks in a somewhat complex system alongside other institutions charged with the supervision and regulation of certain groups of financial institutions, such as the Office of the Comptroller of the Currency, the Federal Deposit Insurance Corporation, and the Office of Thrift

---

[563] Board of Governors of the Fed, n. 536 above, 95–6.
[564] Ibid., at 108–9.

Supervision, as well as with the several banking agencies in the different Federal states. In short, the Fed examines, inspects and monitors the conditions of member banks and bank holding companies both through on- and off-site examinations.[565]

In its regulatory powers over banks and bank holding companies the Fed relies on authorities granted by Federal laws, including—among others—the Bank Holding Act of 1956, the Bank Merger Act of 1960 and the Change in Bank Control Act of 1978. Acquisitions by bank holding companies and acquisitions by firms which seek to become bank holding companies need prior approval. The same applies to banking mergers when the resulting institution is a state member bank. The Fed also reviews changes in the control of bank holding companies and state member banks.

[565] For more details of the supervisory role of the Fed cf. e.g. M.J.B. Hall, *Banking Regulation and Supervision: A Comparative Study of the UK, USA and Japan* (Edward Elgar, Aldershot, 1993), 49 *et seq.*

4

Evaluating the Democratic Accountability of Central Banks

Having developed criteria for an evaluation of the democratic accountability of central banks, and after having provided a general overview of the central banks included in this study, in this chapter the banks are examined on the basis of these criteria. Where appropriate, the criteria are subdivided into several sections, considering different aspects of a criterion, but, at times, also distinguishing basic differences in the functioning of the central banks. It results from this that the order in which central banks are examined does not remain the same throughout this chapter. Rather, they are put in an order which highlights differences and similarities between the banks with regard to the criteria examined.

I. LEGAL BASIS

In examining the nature of the legal basis of the central banks a distinction can be drawn between central banks which are recognised by the constitution of the country they are located in, and central banks which have been set up by an Act of Parliament. Additionally, the position of the central banks participating in the ESCB is examined.

1. Constitutional recognition of central banks

Generally, three systems may be distinguished: first, central banks which operate in countries with a common law tradition which do not feature a written constitution—this includes in the present context the UK and New Zealand; secondly, central banks which operate in countries with a written constitution, but which are not recognised by that constitution—this is the case for most of the central banks examined; and, finally, central bank systems where such a constitutional recognition exists or is in question. Presently this is the case for the ECB, whereas it is questionable whether this is also the case for the Bundesbank.

1.1. Lack of a written constitution

The Bank of England and the Reserve Bank of New Zealand are placed in constitutional systems which differ fundamentally from those of other central banks. This is due to the fact that the constitutional systems of the UK and New Zealand cannot be identified by one specific written document "which sets out the framework and the principal functions of the organs of government within the state, and declares the principles by which those organs operate".[1]

In the case of the **United Kingdom** the absence of a written constitution does not imply that there is no constitutional system. Rather, the sum of the rules governing the complex and comprehensive system of government incorporated describes the constitutional system of the UK.[2] The supremacy of Parliament may be viewed as the key principle.[3] It follows from this that in the national context Acts of Parliament are the highest source of legal authority (i.e. primary legislation). In fact, many of the early Acts of Parliament, some of which came into existence before the formation of the contemporary UK, make up its constitutional fundament today. Prominent examples include fundamental statutes such as Magna Carta, which spelt out a protest against arbitrary punishment and the right to a fair trial and a just legal system; the Bill of Rights, and the Act of Settlement 1700 which manifested and developed the rights of Parliament *vis-à-vis* the monarch. More recent examples of Acts of Parliament, which add important elements to the constitutional system in the UK include the Parliament Acts 1911 and 1949, the Crown Proceedings Act 1947, and the European Communities Act 1972.[4] Secondary legislation includes acts of ministers and other authorities upon whom Parliament has conferred power, and legislative instruments issued by the Crown under its prerogative powers. Another important source of law, which is categorised as secondary legislation, is *judicial precedent*, that is decisions expounding the common law or interpreting legislation. Other important constitutional rules are outside the scope of legislation or judicial decisions and, thus, of legal rules. Non-legal rules include the political practice and detailed procedures which have been established by the various organs of the government, e.g. law and custom of Parliament.[5] These non-binding rules are summarised by the term *constitutional conventions*.[6]

Although as early as 1781 the Bank of England has been described as "from long habit and usage of many years . . . a part of the Constitution",[7] this does not have the same implications that the constitutional recognition of a central bank in a constitutional system with a written constitution may have. Regardless of whether the Bank of England is recognised by the unwritten constitution in the UK, the principle of the supremacy of Parliament effectively

---

[1] E.C.S. Wade/A.W. Bradley, *Constitutional and Administrative Law* (11th edn., Longman, London and New York, 1993), at 4, with respect to a narrower definition of the phrase *constitution*.

[2] Ibid., refer to a "constitution in its wider sense".

[3] W. Wade/C. Forsyth, *Administrative Law* (7th edn., Clarendon Press, Oxford, 1994), 29 *et seq.*

[4] European Communities Act 1972 (c 68). On the relationship between Community law and Acts of Parliament cf. *R. v. Secretary of State for Transport, ex parte Factortame Ltd.*, [1990] 2 AC 85 and ibid. *(No. 2)* [1991] 1 AC 603.

[5] Wade/Bradley, n. 1 above, at 5, with respect to a broader definition of the phrase *constitution*.

[6] Ibid., 19 *et seq.*, on the origin of this term and the different approaches to a definition.

[7] Lord North, then Prime Minister, as quoted in R. Roberts/D. Kynaston, *op. cit.* Chap. 3, n. 17, Appendix 2.

means that Parliament can change or abolish the Bank of England without any special constitutional requirements which may otherwise be involved when the central bank is recognised in a written constitution.

Like the UK, **New Zealand** does not have one single constitutional document. Given their close historic ties this is hardly surprising. Instead, the constitutional system is made up of a number of written documents, including—among others—the Treaty of Waitangi 1840, the Judicature Act 1908 on the courts, the Legislature Act 1908 on Parliament, the Electoral Act 1993, the State Sector Act 1988, the Constitution Act 1986 and the New Zealand Bill of Rights Act 1990. Additionally, common law and conventions form part of the constitutional system.[8] The Constitutional Act 1986, which gathers together some of the fundamental constitutional provisions on the role of the Sovereign and his representative, the executive government, Parliament and the independence of the judiciary, does not include any provision directly relating to either the Reserve Bank or the functions that are performed by it. Besides, the Constitutional Act 1986 itself is an Act of Parliament and thus, in principle, is not located above the Reserve Bank Act 1989 in the legal hierarchy.

1.2. Lack of a constitutional recognition

In the United States, France and the Netherlands, the respective written constitutions neither explicitly mention the central banks, nor include any general reference to a monetary institution of some sort. Rather, in all three cases the constitutions empower the respective parliaments to establish rules on the establishment of a currency or the monetary system.

In the Constitution of the **United States** the only reference to the tasks of the Fed is to be found in Article I, section 8, clause 5 of the US Constitution, according to which:

> "The Congress shall have power . . . To coin money, regulate the value thereof, and of foreign coin, and fix the standard of weights and measures".[9]

According to Article 1, section 8, clause 18:

> "To make all laws which shall be necessary and proper for carrying into execution the foregoing powers, and all other powers vested by this Constitution in the government of the United States, or any department or office thereof."

Congress has based the Act creating the Fed on Article 1, section 8, of the Constitution. However, this is not to say that this provision was undisputed as the legal basis for the Federal Reserve Act. As has been observed elsewhere, already at the time of the establishment of the First United States Bank

---

[8] With regard to the constitution cf. e.g. E. McLeay, *The Cabinet and Political Power in New Zealand* (Oxford University Press, Auckland, 1995).

[9] J.W. Hurst, *op. cit.*, Chap. 3, n. 494, at 12, on the meaning of this provision.

opponents had argued that this section of the US Constitution delegated specific powers and that for this reason the extension of Article 1, section 8, clause 18, to cover the law at issue would extend the power of Congress undesirably. Since, the power of the Federal government in the area of monetary policy has been upheld by the courts.[10]

Like the US Constitution, in **France** the Constitution of 1958 does not include a specific section or provision on the Banque de France.[11] The only provision relating to the tasks of the Bank is to be found in Article 34(1), number 4 of the Constitution of 1958, according to which "the issue of currency" has to be established by an Act of Parliament.[12] Moreover, since the Banque de France is nationalised, Article 34(2), number 4 of the Constitution of 1958 is generally applicable. This states that "the nationalisation of companies and transfers of company ownership from the public to the private sector" have to be established by an Act of Parliament. These provisions do not amount to a constitutional guarantee of the institution the Banque de France, and certainly not to a constitutional guarantee of a specific institutional set-up, such as a specific degree of independence.[13] Rather, the two constitutional provisions furnish Parliament with legislative authority to regulate the issue of the currency. In fact, as will be observed, the introduction of the Bank Act 1993 has raised questions of constitutional magnitude, since an independent conduct of monetary policy in principle is not compatible with the responsibilities of the executive as foreseen by the Constitution of 1958.[14]

In the **Netherlands** the Dutch constitution[15] also does not include an explicit reference to the institution of a central bank, let alone the Nederlandsche Bank. The only general reference can be found in Chapter 5 of the constitution, on legislation and administration. Here, under the heading *monetary system* Article 106 states:

"The monetary system shall be regulated by Act of Parliament."

Article 106, which was introduced in the course of a constitutional amendment in 1983, may be viewed as the *a posteriori* legal basis for the Bank Act 1948, since

[10] Cf. references in J.W. Hurst, n. 9 above, at 200, n. 259.

[11] Constitution du 4 octobre 1958, as amended. Hereafter referred to as Constitution of 1958.

[12] Art. 34 Constitution of 1958 lists the range of subject-matters which have to be governed by an Act of Parliament, i.e. National Assembly and Senate, cf. definition in Art. 24.

[13] The only possibility seems to be to argue that the Bank as an institution flows from a fundamental principle recognised by the law of the French republic: cf. Ch. Leroy, "Les incidences constitutionnelles de la réforme accordant son indépendance à la Banque de France", *LPA*, no. 85-5 (1994), n. 8, with further references.

[14] Cf. Chap. 4 III 3.

[15] The present Dutch constitution (*Grondwet voor het Koninkrijk der Nederlanden*) has its origin in the Constitution for the Kingdom of the Netherlands of 24 Aug. 1815, Stb. 1815, no. 45. It has since been substantially amended on numerous occasions. It is hereafter referred to as the Dutch constitution: cf. L. Prakke/J.L. De Reede/G.J.M. Van Wissen, *Van Der Pott–Donner: Handboek Van Het Nederlandse Staatsrecht* (13th edn., W.E.J. Tjeenk Willink, Zwolle, 1995), 141 *et seq.*

it did not exist at the time of the drafting of the Bank Act 1948. An assignment for the legislator to establish a specific institution to be charged with performing tasks related to monetary matters cannot be read into this provision. Rather, Article 106 introduces a legal basis for rules relating to the monetary system, thereby restricting the powers of the government in favour of Parliament (*Staten-Generaal*).[16] It is for the legislator to decide on the institutional arrangements in which the monetary system is placed.[17] A constitutional recognition of the Nederlandsche Bank is thus missing.

1.3. Constitutional recognition (?)

Unlike the central bank systems examined above, in **Germany** the Basic Law refers to a "Federal bank" (*Bundesbank*) in Articles 88 and 109(4). The latter provision refers to the federal bank in connection with the budget of the Federation and the Federal states (*Länder*)[18] and thus has little impact on the subject-matter of this work. Article 88 of the Basic Law constitutes an innovation in as much as for the first time in German constitutional history, the central bank is *explicitly* referred to in the constitution.[19] According to Article 88 of the Basic Law:

> "The Federation establishes a currency- and note-issuing bank as Federal bank. In the context of the European Union, its tasks and powers can be transferred to the European Central Bank, which is independent and primarily bound by the purpose of securing stability of prices."[20]

Article 88 of the Basic Law incorporates an obligation to establish a currency- and note-issuing bank as the Federal (i.e. *Bundes*) bank. Therefore, first of all, Article 88 is a competence norm with the Federation as a whole, rather than the *Länder*, as addressee.[21] Besides, it becomes clear from its wording that Article 88 is a constitutional directive, guaranteeing the legal continuity of the institution the *Bundesbank*.[22] Moreover, by referring to a currency- and note-issuing bank Article 88 stipulates and guarantees a minimum of powers of the Bundesbank relating to its functions as a note-issuing and currency bank.[23]

---

[16] Prakke/De Reede/Van Wissen, n. 15 above, at 539.

[17] The following laws are also related to Art. 106: Muntwet 1948; Wet toezicht kreditwezen 1992; Wet wisselkoers van de gulden, Stb. 1978, no. 255; Wet financiële betrekkingen buitenland, Stb. 1980, no. 321.

[18] Hereafter referred to as *Länder*.

[19] K. Stern, op. cit., Chap. 3, n. 100, § 35 1 a. For an overview in English cf. N.G. Foster, *German Legal System & Laws* (2nd edn., Blackstone Press Limited, London, 1996), 140 *et seq.*

[20] Second sentence added by law of 12 Dec. 1993, BGBl. I, 2086.

[21] Stern, n. 19 above; with respect to the consequences for the legislative procedure for the setting up of the Bundesbank. See also Chap. 3 IV.

[22] BVerwGE 41, 334, at 349; E. Bauer, in I. v.Münch/P. Kunig (eds.), *Grundgesetzkommentar*, Vol. 3 (3rd edn., Munich, 1996), Art. 88, side notation no. 4 *et seq.*

[23] D. Coburger, *Die währungspolitischen Befugnisse der Deutschen Bundesbank* (Duncker & Humblot, Berlin, 1988), 39 *et seq.*, refers to a "*verfassungsrechtliche Mindestaustattung*"; Th. Maunz, in Maunz/Dürig (eds.), op. cit., Chap. 3, n. 185, Art. 88, side notation 3, argues that the act of establishment has already taken place in the form of Art. 88 itself.

Without going into great detail, which would exceed the scope of this study, it should nevertheless be observed that theoretical difficulties lie with a precise determination of this guarantee of powers.[24]

More important in the light of this study is the question whether Article 88 of the Basic Law actually guarantees the *independence* of the Bundesbank, as part of its organisational structure. This has been the subject of discussion ever since the coming into existence of the Bundesbank. The issue has implications beyond the scope of Article 88 of the Basic Law, inasmuch as it may influence the degree of democratic accountability of the Bundesbank. If the independence of the Bundesbank is guaranteed by the constitution, a change of the status of the Bundesbank in that respect would require a constitutional amendment. According to Article 79(II) of the Basic Law a constitutional amendment requires a two-thirds majority in the Bundestag and Bundesrat. Consequently, the parliamentary hurdle for changing the legal basis of the Bundesbank would be much higher than would be otherwise the case.[25]

Proponents of a constitutional recognition of the independence of the Bundesbank draw their arguments from traditional methods of interpretation[26] as well as general constitutional considerations. According to one opinion the constitutional guarantee of independence derives from the post-constitutional overall picture (*vorrechtliches Gesamtbild*) in Germany which supposedly offers evidence for a legal tradition of independent monetary institutions.[27] For others the constitutional guarantee derives from the wording and the *ratio legis* of Article 88. According to this opinion, by transferring the functions of a *currency-issuing* bank (*Währungsbank*) to a separate institution, the drafters of Article 88 of the Basic Law have decided to transfer monetary policy to an independent, i.e. free from government instructions, policy-maker.[28] Additionally, the position of Article 88 in the system of the Basic Law has been analysed as guaranteeing the independence of the Bundesbank.[29] In this context, the Bundesbank has been referred to as a constitutional organ (*Verfassungsorgan*).[30]

[24] E.g. H.J. Hahn, *Währungsrecht* (C.H. Beck, Munich, 1995), 258 *et seq.*

[25] On the majority requirements in case of a simple Act of Parliament, cf. Chap. 4 I 2.

[26] Such as *historical*, *literal*, *contextual* and *purposive* interpretation.

[27] This viewpoint has in particular been taken by the German Federal Constitutional Court: BVerfGE 14, at 216.

[28] C.T. Samm, *Die Stellung der Deutschen Bundesbank im Staatsgefüge* (2nd edn., Duncker & Humblot, Berlin, 1971); the same in "Verfassungsgarantierte Bundesbankautonomie", *Zeitschrift für Wirtschafts- und Bankrecht* 1984, Sonderbeilage No. 5/1984.

[29] Samm, *Die Stellung*, n. 28 above, 177 *et seq.*

[30] O.E. Ernst, "Die Stellung der Notenbank im Staatsgefüge", *WM* (1957), 85–93, also in "Das Gesetz über die Deutsche Bundesbank und seine wichtigsten öffentlich-rechtlichen Probleme", *DÖV* (1957), 606–12. However, the majority of writers reject this view, e.g. Bauer, n. 22 above, on Art. 88, side notation 2, with further references. The question is of more than academic value because it basically concerns the question whether the Bundesbank has *locus standi* in court proceedings between administrative bodies (*Organstreitverfahren*), e.g. Bundesbank versus Federal government, in accordance with Art. 93(1), No. 1, Basic Law in conjunction with §§ 13 No. 5 and §§ 63 *et seq.* of the law governing the Federal Constitutional Court (*Bundesverfassungsgerichtsgesetz*). The fact that the legal basis of the Bundesbank does not offer any solutions in case of conflicts between the Bundesbank and e.g. the Federal government, adds to the interest in this question.

Moreover, apart from traditional methods of interpretation, more general constitutional arguments in support of a constitutional foundation of the Bundesbank's independence are advanced. A constitutional guarantee has been justified by the principle of social justice and the welfare state, the so-called *Sozialstaatsprinzip*, arguing that this principle obliges the State to enforce monetary stability, which in return can only be provided for by an independent monetary institution.[31] Some refer to the comprehensive principle of the rule of law (*Rechtsstaatsprinzip*)[32] and—put simply—conclude that an independent monetary institution is necessary in order to provide for a "counterbalancing weight" to unlimited political power.[33]

Yet these arguments in favour of a constitutional guarantee are, with respect, less than wholly convincing. Taking the changeable history of monetary institutions in Germany since 1875 in consideration, arguments in favour of a constitutional guarantee referring to the post-constitutional picture lack any foundation.[34] It has been observed in Chapter 3 that the history of the relationships between previous central banks and government does not provide a uniform picture of independent monetary institutions in Germany.[35] Rather, the assumption is justified that the German history of the relationship between governments and monetary institutions and, thus, of the independence of the central banks, is directly linked to the history of political transformations. The changing political ambitions often initiated changes in the statutory relationship between the central bank and government. Besides, the documents on the drafting of Article 88 do not justify the assumption that the drafters of the constitution thought of Article 88 as foreseeing the independence of the Bundesbank. The same conclusion has to be drawn from an examination of the law governing the Bundesbank which introduces the independence of the Bundesbank in § 12. Apart from the rather obvious observation that there would have been no need for this provision in the first place if the independence of the Bundesbank was guaranteed by the constitution, the legislator obviously presumed that the BBankG, including its independent status laid down in § 12, could be changed by the legislator by a simple majority vote.[36] In order to conclude a constitutional guarantee from the wording of Article 88 (currency- and note-issuing bank), the independent status is apparently assumed to constitute a precondition for a currency bank. However, evidence for the assumption that the objectives of a currency-issuing bank can only be fulfilled by an independent

---

[31] S. Prost, "Die Deutsche Bundesbank im Spannungsbereich anderer unabhängiger Organe und Institutionen" in E. Büschgen (ed.), *Geld, Kapital und Kredit, Festschrift zum siebzigsten Geburtstag von Heinrich Rittershausen* (Pöschel, Stuttgart, 1968), 110–26, 118 *et seq.*

[32] Generally on this principle P. Kunig, *Das Rechtsstaatsprinzip* (Mohr (Siebeck), Tübingen, 1986).

[33] C.-Th.Samm, op. cit., Chap. 3, n. 175, 163 *et seq.*

[34] Also e.g. H. Faber, in R. Wassermann (ed.), op. cit., Chap. 3, n. 173.

[35] Cf. Chap. 3 IV 2 on the historic development of the Reichsbank and the BdL.

[36] Cf. H.J. Hahn, op. cit., Chap. 3, n. 185, at 35, n. 56, with reference to the consultations at the time of the drafting of the BBankG. On the procedure cf. Chap. 4 I 2.

institution is neither to be found in previous German central bank systems, nor in other central bank systems.[37] Faber argues that it is not the formal independence, but rather the political room for manœuvre of an institution which correlates with currency stability, and thus with the objective of a currency-issuing bank. Therefore, transferring those functions to a separate institution does not inevitably call for an independent institution.[38] Arguments deriving from a systematic interpretation of Article 88, such as the fact that the Bundesbank is dealt with in a separate provision, are not convincing. On the contrary, a comparison of Article 88 with Articles 97(1) and 114(2) of the Basic Law, which *expressly* establish the independence of the members of the judiciary and the Court of Auditors, demonstrate that the constitutional legislator has chosen not to implement the independence of the currency- and note-issuing bank in Article 88 of the Basic Law.[39] General constitutional considerations may often be the result of an over-interpretation. According to the vast majority of publications this is in particular the case with respect to arguments deriving from the principle of social justice and the welfare state.[40] Indeed, even though a healthy currency and monetary system is certainly an important element supporting a democracy based on the principle of social justice and the welfare state, the determination of a specific institutional structure of the Bundesbank from this principle, appears to be an exaggerated interpretation of this attribute of the German constitution. Moreover, it is questionable whether the principle of the separation of powers and the reference to the Bundesbank as a necessary "counterbalancing weight" within the system of government can justify a constitutionally independent monetary authority. Indeed, it has been argued that in the system of the Basic Law the removal of parliamentary responsibility and the insulation from government instructions cannot be justified with reference to risks which arise from democratically legitimised organs.[41] Besides, an interpretation of the constitutional independence of the Bundesbank with reference to the principle of the rule of law has to be carefully weighed against other constitutional principles, namely the principle of democracy (*Demokratieprinzip*).[42]

Court decisions dealing with the Bundesbank do not provide a coherent picture. Already in 1956, the Federal Administrative Court (*Bundesverwaltungsgericht*) had observed of the BdL, the forerunner of the Bundesbank, that it held a unique posi-

---

[37] Hahn, n. 24 above, at 261.

[38] Faber, n. 34 above, Art. 88, side notation 24.

[39] Cf. Arts. 97(1) and (2) Basic Law.

[40] E.g. K. v.Bonin, *Zentralbanken zwischen funktioneller Unabhängigkeit und politischer Autonomie*, Diss., Berlin, 1978, n. 283.

[41] BVerwGE 41, 334, at 355, according to which such risks are inherent in a democracy and can only be remedied through a system of checks and balances, and restraints of the three branches of government. See also Chap. 4 III 1.

[42] On this principle see e.g. Th. Maunz/R. Zippelius, *Deutsches Staatsrecht: ein Studienbuch* (29th edn., C.H. Beck, Munich, 1994), § 13. According to Samm, n. 33 above, the transfer of monetary authority to an independent institution is justified in the light of the constitutional structure, which *inter alia* is characterised by a dominance of the principle of the rule of law over the principle of democracy.

tion in the structure of the Federal Republic of Germany with respect to its independence from government.[43] As regards the Bundesbank, the Federal Administrative Court concluded that the independence of the Bundesbank was neither guaranteed nor precluded by the Basic Law.[44] The court took the position that neither the wording, nor the *ratio legis,* nor the legislative history of Article 88 of the Basic Law supported a constitutional guarantee.[45] Despite the fact that this question has never explicitly been placed before the Federal Constitutional Court (*Bundesverfassungsgericht*), a number of observers believe the constitutional guarantee to be implicitly confirmed by the highest German court.[46] In the instant case, the Constitutional Court had to rule on the constitutionality of Allied laws dealing with the transfer of non-commercial payments between West and East Germany. In the course of its reasoning the Constitutional Court referred to the Bundesbank's position *vis-à-vis* government as constitutionally independent. The relevant passage of the court order (*Beschluß*) states:

> "The German Bundesbank, which moreover, *by virtue of its constitution independent position,* is not subject to any supervision by other organs of the executive, is thus in the position of determine itself to a significant extent the criteria on which its practice of approvals is based."[47]

Whether this can be interpreted as an acceptance of the constitutional guarantee by the Constitutional Court is highly questionable. First, the facts of the case did not centre on institutional issues of the Bundesbank. Instead, the court order focused on an area of delegated function of the Bundesbank, for which it is subject to supervision by the Federal government.[48] Thus, as Hahn argues rightly, it seems rather daring to base a constitutional guarantee on this *obiter dictum.*[49] Besides, it is not at all clear whether the court, by referring to a constitutionally independent position, did, in fact, suggest a guarantee of the Bundesbank's independence by the Basic Law. The court may instead have been referring to the BBankG, in particular to § 12, which explicitly establishes the independence of the Bundesbank as the legal basis (constitution) of the Bundesbank. In any event, since the wording of the court order is at least equivocal, it cannot be considered as an unequivocal confirmation of a constitutional guarantee of the institutional structure of the Bundesbank by the Federal Constitutional Court.[50]

[43] BVerwGE 2, 217, at 218.

[44] BVerwGE 41, 334, the court had to decide on the constitutionality of § 16(1) BBankG, which deals with the minimum-reserve policy.

[45] The decision is relevant in some other respects: Chap. II 1.1. with respect to functions of the Bundesbank under Art. 88, and Chap. II 8 with respect to the Bundesbank's role as a regulator.

[46] Samm, Verfassungsgarantierte, n. 28 above, offers an extensive analysis. Faber, n. 34 above, is critical but, nevertheless, seems to interpret the court order as confirming the constitutional independence.

[47] Author's translation. BVerfGE 62, 169, at 183.

[48] Cf. Chap. 4 III 1, on the legal confines of the independence of the Bundesbank.

[49] Hahn, n.24 above, at 263. See to the contrary, Samm, n. 46 above, at 5, according to whom the court deliberately creates a *fait accompli* in order to bring an end to the discussion.

[50] Similar is E. Brandt, *Die währungspolitischen Befugnisse der Bundesregierung,* Diss., Würzburg, 1990.

Like the French constitution, the German Basic Law includes a provision which allows for the transfer of authority in the field of monetary policy to the ESCB. The recently introduced second sentence of Article 88 of the Basic Law narrows the first sentence of Article 88 of the Basic Law inasmuch as it provides a legal basis for the transfer of tasks and powers from the Bundesbank to the ECB.[51] Moreover, it sets conditions for such a transfer, as tasks and powers of the Bundesbank may only be transferred to an ECB which is *independent* and committed to *price stability*.[52] For some the introduction of the second sentence into Article 88 is new evidence of a constitutional recognition of the independence of the Bundesbank, as the reference to an ECB which is independent is thought to be a reflection of the *status quo* of the Bundesbank.[53] To the contrary it can also be argued that the existence of an explicit mention of the ECB underlines the assessment that such constitutional recognition does not exist for the Bundesbank. Instead, the independent status of the Bundesbank is guaranteed by primary Community law since the establishment of the ESCB to the extent to which the Bundesbank fulfils tasks in the framework of the ESCB conferred to it by the ECB.[54]

When observing a constitutional recognition of the **ESCB** and the ECB a fundamental difference from the central banks discussed above can be observed, as the ESCB will not be placed against the background of a national State, but rather of Member States tied together by international agreements, forming a unique system by creating a "new legal order of international law for the benefit of which the states have limited their sovereign rights, and the subject of which comprise not only Member States but also their nationals [who enjoy] rights which become part of their legal heritage".[55] Considering the reasoning of the ECJ according to which the EC Treaty constitutes the "constitutional charter of a Community based on the rule of law",[56] the ECB holds a unique position compared to the other central banks examined in this study in so far as it may be argued that it is explicitly recognised by the constitutional basis of the legal environment it operates in.[57] Articles 4a, 105—109d EC and the ESCB

---

[51] It is questionable whether the creation of a legal basis was necessary: Th. Weikart, "Die Änderung des Bundesbank-Artikels im Grundgesetz mit Hinblick auf den Vertrag von Maastricht", *NVwZ* (1993), 834–41, suggests a *declaratory* meaning. Referring to the scope of the old Art. 24(1) Basic Law, he states that the creation of the second sentence was a political rather than a constitutional necessity.

[52] Weikart, n. 51 above, notes that these conditions create new, legally binding conditions.

[53] E.g. G. Galahn, *Die Deutsche Bundesbank im Prozeß der europäischen Währungsintegration* (Walter de Gruyter, Berlin and New York, 1996), 117 *et seq.*, 192–3, concludes that through the introduction of the second sentence of Art. 88 the independence of the Bundesbank is guaranteed.

[54] E. Benda/W. Maihofer/H.-J. Vogel, *Handbuch des Verfassungsrechts der Bundesrepublik Deutschland* (Walter de Gruyter, Berlin and New York, 1994), at 841–2. Also Chap. 4 I 3.

[55] Case 26/62, *Van Gend en Loos* v. *Nederlandse Administratie der Belastingen* [1963] ECR 1.

[56] Opinion 1/91 [1991] ECR I–6079.

[57] Louis, op. cit., Chap. 3, n. 379, at 17.

Statute thus in primary Community law represent the legal basis of the ECB.[58] According to Article 4a EC:

> "A European System of Central Banks . . . and a European Central Bank . . . shall be established in accordance with the procedures laid down in this Treaty; they shall act within the limit of the powers conferred upon them by this Treaty and by the Statute of the ESCB and of the ECB . . . ".

With Louis it can be observed that it is this implementation in primary Community law that makes up the uniqueness of the legal basis of the ESCB, since in no other legal system has the entire legal basis of the central bank been raised to the constitutional level.[59] By giving the ESCB Statute the rank of primary Community law, a clear priority is given to the preservation of the monetary system, since the provisions are subject to the procedures for the amendment of the Treaty.[60] Article N TEU, which replaced Article 236 EEC, states that:

> "The government of any Member State or the Commission may submit to the Council proposals for the amendment of the Treaties on which the Union is founded. If the Council, after consulting the European Parliament and, where appropriate, the Commission, delivers an opinion in favour of calling a conference of representatives of the governments of the Member States, the conference shall convened by the President of the Council for the purpose of determining by common accord the amendments to be made to those Treaties. *The European Central Bank shall also be consulted in the case of institutional changes in the monetary area. . . .* "[61]

With the exception of the provisions referred to in Article 106(5) EC an amendment of the provisions on the ESCB and the ECB both in the EC Treaty and the ESCB Statute takes place on the intergovernmental level by common accord of the Member States. The right of initiative lies with the Member States and the Commission. The final decision on whether an intergovernmental conference is set up is taken at the level of the representatives of the Member States at ministerial level in the Council and thus requires an "opinion in favour of calling a conference". Decisions on Treaty amendments are taken by "common accord" and thus by unanimity. Remarkably, changing essential portions of the legal basis of the ESCB and the ECB would involve even those Member States which do not take part in the ESCB and the ECB, since Article N does not differentiate between different areas of treaty amendment. Thus, attempts to change the legal

---

[58] Protocols annexed to the TEU, No. 3. Note that protocols annexed to the TEU form an integral part of the EC Treaty and, thus, of primary Community law: Art. 239 EC.

[59] Louis, n. 57 above, at 17.

[60] The only exception is to be found in Art. 106(5) EC, Art. 41 ESCB Statute, according to which a simplified amendment procedure applies for certain provisions, relating among others to the minimum reserve requirements, clearing and payment systems, and external operations. However, this includes neither changes to the institutional structure of the ECB (namely its independent position) nor to the monetary policy objective.

[61] Emphasis added; *Executive Agencies within the EC: The European Central Bank—A Model?*, Editorial Comments, op. cit., Chap. 3, n. 407 at 626, refer to a "constitutional guarantee" of the ECB.

basis could become subject to horse trading, especially by those Member States which, as EMU non-participants, do not have a vital interest in the ESCB. These Member States could make their consent subject to concessions in other areas, effectively blocking a swift amendment of the legal basis. Other policy areas of the Community would inevitably likewise become the subject of discussions. Moreover, a treaty amending primary Community law would require ratification by the Parliaments of the participating Member States. A swift amendment of the legal basis of the ESCB seems therefore unrealistic. In the light of these dangers the possibility of an amendment of the institutional structure of the ESCB hardly has the potential to become an effective mechanism of democratic accountability.

Also unique in the context of the central banks examined in this study is the institutionalised participation of the ECB, which has to be consulted when Treaty provisions on monetary matters are about to be changed. This gives the ECB an influence in the decision of the governments of the Member States to change the constitution of the ESCB and the ECB. Undoubtedly this was meant to strengthen the independent position of the ECB by ensuring that its opinion is heard in the case of changes which relate to the ESCB. Although a consent by the ECB is clearly not required for an amendment of the EC Treaty or the ESCB Statute, the participatory rights of the ECB have to be considered obligatory. Taking into consideration the case law of the ECJ on the mandatory character of participatory rights of Community institutions representing "an essential factor in the constitutional balance intended by the Treaty", disregard of the rights of the ECB under Article N TEU could result in the annulment of the Treaty amendments.[62] It has to be observed, however, that the ECB does not constitute a Community institution in the formal sense, since it has not been added to the list of Community institutions in Article 4 EC, and the provisions on the ESCB and the ECB have not been added to Part V of the EC Treaty on the institutions of the Communities; nevertheless it is clearly a Community organ, as was the Court of Auditors prior to being raised to the status of an institution by the TEU. The significance of the participatory rights of the ECB appears even more notable when examining the role of the EP in the procedure. In fact, the ECB is put on an equal footing with the EP, since the latter also only has a consultative role. This equalising of the participatory rights of the ECB and the EP is remarkable since—unlike the ECB—the EP constitutes the representative assembly through which the citizens of the Member States, although still to a limited extent, take part directly in the exercise of power and as such reflects a "funda-

---

[62] Case 138/79 *SA Roquette Frères* v. *Council* [1980] ECR 3333; Case 70/88 *European Parliament* v. *Council* [1990] ECR 2041, on the institutional balance; Case C–65/93 *European Parliament* v. *Council* [1995] ECR 643, with regards to the limits; Case C–21/94 *European Parliament* v. *Council* [1995] ECR 1827; generally with regard to the choice of the legal basis: Case C–300/89 *Commission* v. *Council* (Titanium Dioxide) [1991] ECR 2867. It has to be noted that the second line of argument on the fundamental democratic principle which the EP reflects on the Community level cannot be applied to the ECB.

mental democratic principle" of the Community.[63] It appears that the ECB is given disproportionate participatory rights compared to the EP. To be sure, the EP does not fulfil the same role in the legal system of the Community as a Parliament in the national context, but it does add to the democratic legitimation of the EU as it constitutes the only Community organ with a direct link to the citizens.

2. Act of Parliament

With the exception of the ECB, the legal basis of all the other central banks examined in this study is found in an Act of Parliament. As a general observation it can be noted that in each system the legislator reserves to itself the right to amend the legal basis of the central bank, thereby changing its institutional structure. In fact, in all cases the legislator could even chose to abolish the existing central bank as a whole. However, where the existence of a note- and currency-issuing bank is prescribed by the constitution, as is the case in Germany, the legislator would be obliged to replace the abolished central bank with another institution. The concrete legislative procedures for amending the legal bases of the central banks differ, depending on the constitutional system they are situated in. All but one country, New Zealand, feature a Parliament consisting of a lower and upper house. In some countries the consent of both houses of Parliament is required to pass a Bill, whereas in other countries the upper chamber can be outvoted by the lower house of Parliament. In principle in the case of all central banks examined in this study the legal basis can be amended by a simple majority vote. However, in some instances qualified majorities are needed to overrule an upper house or the veto of the executive, whereas in some instances the consent of both Houses of Parliament is mandatory. Moreover, the organs which have the right to introduce legislative proposals differ across the different countries.

Since its creation by Parliament, the Bank of England Act 1946 constituted the legal basis of the **Bank of England**. With the Bank of England Act 1998 the newly elected Labour government has introduced a new comprehensive legal basis for the Bank of England, albeit not in order to punish the Bank for certain behaviour, but rather to enhance the credibility of the new government in the market place by granting the Bank operational responsibility for monetary policy.[64] However, the recent developments highlight the power of Parliament to bring about changes to the Bank of England which have considerable institutional implications.

Generally, when considering the creation of legislation in the context of the English legal system a distinction has to be drawn between public and private

---

[63] Case 138/79, n. 62 above.
[64] "Accidental Hero", *Economist*, 21 Sept. 1996, at 42; "Blair's Banker", *The Banker*, June 1997.

Acts. Private Acts are somewhat more limited in their scope as they effectively deal with local matters, such as the granting of powers to local authorities, or personal concern. On the contrary, public Acts are measures which are intended to change the general law, concern the public revenue or the administration of justice or an institution under public law such as the Bank of England.[65] Public Acts may initially be proposed in the form of a Bill by either the executive government, so-called government bills, or by individual members of the House of Commons, so-called Private Members' Bills.[66] The latter may be introduced to the House of Commons on special days and in accordance with ballots determining which MPs may introduce their bills. However, the chances of a Private Member's Bill being adopted without the support of the executive government are slim. This may be inherent in the type of parliamentary democracy to be found in the UK, which is characterised by a dominance of the executive government which usually commands a majority in Parliament. The potentially more successful Government Bills are drafted with ministerial involvement and are decided upon by a committee of the cabinet which is charged with the preliminary approval of these proposals.[67] Sometimes legislative proposals are floated among the public in so-called Green or White Papers beforehand. The Bills are actually drafted by the parliamentary Counsel to the Treasury, specialised lawyers who are charged with legal drafting of Bills on instructions of the government, while consulting governmental departments in the process.[68] A government Bill may be introduced in either the House of Commons or the House of Lords.[69] A Bill generally passes through Parliament after three readings, having been considered either in the House of Commons and thereafter in the House of Lords or *vice versa*. The first reading entails the formal introduction of the Bill into the House of Commons/Lords. The Bill is printed and equipped with an "Explanatory Memorandum". At the second reading the Bill is discussed in general terms without the possibility of amendments.[70] At this stage it is sent to one of the parliamentary standing committees, or at times to a special standing committee, which consider public Bills on a clause-by-clause basis, and which can call upon witnesses and can request evidence. The committee charged with the examination can amend the Bill. Bills of special importance are dealt with in the House of Commons on the Floor in "the Committees of the whole House". In the House of Lords most public Bills are considered on the Floor in the Committees of the whole House.

---

[65] S.H. Bailey/M.J. Gunn, *Smith and Bailey on The Modern English Legal System* (Sweet & Maxwell, London, 1996), 262–3.

[66] Ibid.

[67] Currently this role is fulfilled by the Committee on the Queen's Speeches and Future Legislation; cf. Bailey/Gunn, n. 65 above, at 269.

[68] This interaction often results in the drafting of several versions of the same Bill until it is finally introduced into Parliament.

[69] Note that money bills have to be introduced into the House of Commons. Moreover, politically sensible bills are also usually introduced into the Commons.

[70] Bills entailing costs or financial burdens require a so-called "money-resolution" setting limits for the financial consequences of the respective Bill.

After consideration in the respective committee the Bill is referred back to the House where it originated for further consideration, whereby proposals for amendments are restricted to the contents of the Bill at that stage. This is followed by the third reading. Once the Bill has been decided upon by a simple majority in the House of Commons or Lords it is referred to the other House which in a similar procedure of three readings also has to give its consent with a majority vote. Proposals for amendments by the House considering the Bill secondly require the consent of the House which has agreed to the Bill previously. The British parliamentary system does not foresee special mediating committees as is e.g. the case in Germany. Either both Houses of Parliament agree on the contents of a Bill or the Bill lapses at the end of the parliamentary session.[71] However, any Public Bill which has passed the House of Commons in two successive sessions, on each occasion being rejected by the House of Lords, may obtain the Royal Assent without the consent of the House of Lords. This effectively limits the power of the Upper House of Parliament to block legislation.[72] Bills which have passed both Houses of Parliament also require the Royal Assent to become Acts of Parliament. In practice this is more of a formality, since by constitutional convention the monarch is expected to give his or her assent.

Until recently, the Bank of England Act 1946 could not considered to be a *comprehensive* legal basis setting out the duties and responsibilities of the Bank in any given detail, nor was this Act designed to fulfil this function, since its main aim was to regulate the nationalisation of the Bank. In this context the Act has been described as an "apparently simple Act by which the Treasury merely acquired stock from the Bank's proprietors, made arrangements for the Crown to appoint the governors and Directors, and gave legal support firstly to the ultimate authority of the Treasury over the Bank in matters of policy and secondly to the authority of the Bank over the Banks".[73] Under those circumstances the value of the legal basis as an instrument of democratic accountability was questionable, since a majority of institutional (procedural) settings were based upon *de facto* arrangements between the Bank and the executive government (Treasury), rather than concrete provisions thus limiting the effectiveness of any amendment of the Bank of England Act by Parliament. To be sure, Parliament was not prevented from enacting comprehensive legislation on the Bank of England. However, prior to the recently introduced proposals, Parliament has never made use of this right, not least because the executive government was effectively in charge of the Bank, and the latter could moreover in principle be

---

[71] A parliamentary session lasts about a year and can be best described as a meeting period of Parliament.

[72] Money Bills cannot be blocked. For details of this and other exceptions cf. the short overview in P.S. James, *Introduction to English Law* (Butterworth, London, 1990), 129 *et seq.*

[73] J. Fforde, *The Bank of England and Public Policy 1941–1958* (Cambridge University Press, Cambridge, 1992), at 5, cited after Treasury and Civil Service Committee, *The Role of the Bank of England* (House of Commons Paper. Session 1993–4; 98–I, vol. 1), Report, together with the proceedings of the Committee, HC Session 1993–4 (HMSO, London, 1993), at p. vii.

held accountable by Parliament through the mechanisms of ministerial account-ability. However, the recent changes at the Bank of England, which give the Bank considerable independence of the executive government in the implemen-tation of monetary policy could possibly enhance the importance of Parliament's right to change the legal basis as a mechanism of democratic accountability, since the mechanism of ministerial responsibility effectively runs dry in an area for which the executive government is no longer responsible.

Taking into account the close ties with Britain it is not surprising that, although not identically, the legislative procedure in **New Zealand** has many similarities to that in the UK. Parliament stands for the House of Representatives and the Sovereign, or the Governor-General as his representative, respectively.[74] The Legislative Council which constituted the Upper House of Parliament was abol-ished in 1991. The term of Parliament is three years.[75] The Constitution Act 1989 in broad terms confers legislative competence upon Parliament. Section 15 states that Parliament has full power to make laws.[76] Parliamentary acts are also divided into Public and Private Acts, the former including legislation on the Reserve Bank. Generally bills are also divided into public and Private Members' Bills, while the majority of Bills constitute public Bills introduced by the execu-tive government. Bills receive three readings.[77] In the first reading the Bill is introduced into the House of Representatives by the appropriate minister. Although the Bill is not debated on issues of substance, there is a tendency for debates on the principles of the Bill, which makes its contents public. Unlike in the British parliamentary system, Bills are referred to one of the select commit-tees of the House after the first reading. In the case of a Bill amending the Reserve Bank Act 1989 this would primarily be the Committee for Justice and Law Reform. In the select committee the Bill is discussed and outside advice is collected. At the end the committee reports the Bill together with any proposals for amendments back to the House. In the second reading, a formal debate on the substance of the Bill takes place, whereby all MPs may submit their views. The second reading is followed by a second committee stage, this time in the form of the House of Representatives presiding as a Committee of the whole House. At this stage each separate provision is reviewed, possibly amended, and finally voted on. During the third reading the Bill receives its final farewell. The Bill, as it has resulted from the Committee of the whole House, is discussed in a general debate in the House of Representatives. With the exception of certain sections of the Electoral Act 1993, relating—among others—to the term of Parliament, which requires a 75 per cent majority vote, the House of

---

[74] S. 10 *et seq.* and s. 12 *et seq.* Constitution Act 1986.

[75] Ibid., s. 17.

[76] On the possible limits cf. B.V. Harris, "The Constitutional Base" in H. Gold, *New Zealand Politics in Perspective* (3rd edn., Longman Paul, Auckland, 1992), 56–76, at 61.

[77] On the legislative procedure cf. R.D. Mulholland, *Introduction to the New Zealand Legal System* (8th edn., Butterworths, Wellington, 1995), 101–3.

Representatives can enact, amend or repeal any Act, including the Reserve Bank Act 1989, with a simple majority vote. Like the UK Bills which have passed the House of Representatives New Zealand Bills require the assent of the Sovereign or his representative in New Zealand, the Governor-General.[78]

Since the coming into effect of the Reserve Bank of New Zealand Act 1989, the Act has been amended a number of times, without, however, changing the institutional structure of the Reserve Bank of New Zealand.

In **France** generally legislative action in Parliament is initiated either by one of the two chambers of Parliament, summarised under the expression *proposition de loi*, or the government, so-called *projet de loi*.[79] The applicable legislative procedure according to the Constitution of 1958 depends upon the nature of the legislation. The French constitution differentiates between constitutional amendments, organic laws (*loi organiques*), financial laws and other laws outside the first three categories, which may be considered as simple Acts of Parliament (*loi ordinaires*).[80] The point has been made that the Banque de France is not mentioned in the constitution. Moreover, the Bank Act 1993 does not constitute an organic law, since no reference to that effect is made in the constitution. Finally, the statute of the Bank does not resemble a financial law as described by the constitution.[81] Therefore, the legal basis of the Banque de France is a "simple" Act of Parliament. Bills can be introduced by the executive government, i.e. Prime Minister, or by individual members of the two chambers of the French Parliament, that is the National Assembly (*Assemblée nationale*) and the Senate (*Sénat*).[82] A government or parliamentary Bill is examined successively in both chambers of Parliament. The Bill is forwarded to one or more of the six standing committees or, occasionally, a special committee, of the chamber where it has been introduced.[83] The committee adopts a report

[78] S. 16 Constitution Act 1986. Today, New Zealand is a constitutional monarchy, and the role of the Crown and its personal representative, the Governor-Council, is that of a Head of State, who is separated from the executive in as much as he does not take an active or initiative role in the executive functions of government. It is considered to be a binding convention that the Governor-General in fulfilling his functions always acts on advice of Ministers of the Crown. Moreover, the Governor-General presides over the meetings of the so-called Executive Council, which comprises the Governor-General and all Ministers of the Crown. See also Chap. 4 IV 2.

[79] Art. 39 *et seq*. Constitution of 1958. Note that the legislative power of Parliament is limited to the areas listed in Art. 34. Matters that fall outside these areas fall within the domain of the Government which can issue regulations. This power is known as *règlements autonomes* as opposed to *règlemements d'exécution des lois* which merely supplement parliamentary laws.

[80] Additionally Parliament has to ratify or approve international treaties, cf. Art. 53 Constitution of 1958.

[81] According to Art. 34(5) Constitution of 1958 financial laws in the form of organic laws shall determine the financial resources and obligations of the State.

[82] The members of the National Assembly are elected directly for a term of 5 years, whereas the members of the Senate are elected indirectly in the different regions (*départements*) on a rotational basis for a term of 9 years. Cf. M. Prélot, *Institutions politiques et droit constitutionnel* (11e ed., revue et mise à jour par J. Boulouis, Dalloz, Paris, 1990), 786 *et seq*.

[83] A Bill amending the Bank Act 1993 would be primarily dealt with in the General Assembly by the Finance Committee (*Commission des Finances*), and in the Senate by the Committee for

recommending either the approval, with or without amendments, or rejection of the proposed legislation. Thereafter, the Bill is referred back to the chamber where it originated where the Bill is examined article by article. Amendments may be suggested by both the executive government and members of the respective chamber of Parliament. Once a text has been adopted by one chamber it is transferred to the other, which examines the Bill in a similar procedure. If this chamber makes amendments to the text of the Bill it has to refer the Bill back to the chamber which first examined and possibly amended the original proposal. This intra-parliamentary dialogue in an attempt to reach an identical text is referred to as *navette*. If the two chambers of Parliament cannot agree on an identical text after two readings a joint committee can be convened to adopt a common text. If the joint committee fails, the National Assembly can adopt a text by an absolute majority of its members.[84] Otherwise a simple majority is sufficient.[85] An examination of the adopted text with regard to its constitutionality by the Constitutional Council (*Conseil Constitutionnel*) prior to its promulgation is required only in the case of an organic law and thus not in the case of an amendment of the legal basis of the Banque de France.[86] An amendment of the legal basis of the Bank would therefore ultimately "only" require a simple majority in both chambers of Parliament and, exceptionally, in the case of rejection by the Senate, an absolute majority of the members of the National Assembly. Conversely, a simple majority in the National Assembly could decline such an amendment. Since the implementation of the institutional changes to the Banque de France in 1993, the institutional structure of the Banque de France has not become subject to changes apart from the before mentioned minor amendments to remove the remaining contradictions with the EC Treaty and the ESCB Statute. Indeed, apart from the fact that such changes could run contrary to primary Community law in the context of EMU, the likelihood of any amendment of the statute of the Bank in the national context involving major institutional changes has already previously been questioned.[87]

In the **Netherlands,** as is the case in France, Parliament can choose to amend the legal basis of the Nederlandsche Bank, thereby changing its institutional set-up, or even abolish the Bank completely. The central government is made up of the Crown and the Ministers.[88] The Dutch Parliament consists of two chambers: the 150 members of the second chamber of Parliament are directly elected by the

Economic Affairs and Planning (*Commission des Affaires économiques et du Plan*), and the Finance Committee (*Commission des Finances, du Contrôle budgétaire et des Comptes économiques de la Nation*).

[84]   Art. 46(3) Constitution of 1958.

[85]   Ibid., Arts. 42–45.

[86]   On the role of the Constitutional Council cf. Prélot, n. 82 above, 898 *et seq.*

[87]   Cf. Memorandum submitted by the Banque de France, in Treasury and Civil Service Committee, *The Role of the Bank of England* (House of Commons Paper. Session 1993–4 ; 98–I, vol. 2), Report, together with the proceedings of the Committee, HC Session 1993–4 (HMSO, London, 1993), appendix 5, at 136: "*Une telle hypothèse extrême est très improbable*"

[88]   Art. 41(1) Dutch constitution.

citizens,[89] whereas the first chamber, consisting of 75 representatives, is elected by the provincial councils (*provinciale staten*).[90] The term of both chambers of Parliament is four years. Both the executive government and the second chamber can initiate new legislation. A government Bill is first drafted at the ministerial level before being considered in the Council of Ministers (*ministerraad*) which consists of the Prime Minister (*minister-president*) and the other ministers. Thereafter, with the approval of the Monarch, the proposal is forwarded to the Council of State (*Raad van State*) which has to be consulted on Bills and draft general administrative orders.[91] The Bill is passed on to the second chamber of Parliament which has the right to introduce amendments.[92] At this stage the executive government itself can also introduce amendments. A Bill passes the second chamber with the majority of the votes of the members present, while the quorum for decisions is more than half of the members present at the time.[93] The Bill is forwarded to the first chamber which can only approve or reject it as a whole without having a right to make amendments. Decisions in the first chamber have to be taken by the majority of the votes of the members present, whereby the quorum for decisions is more than half of the members present.[94] Once a Bill has passed both chambers of Parliament it needs to be ratified by the Crown.[95] Bills introduced by the second chamber are basically handled in the same way.[96] The main difference is that the executive government cannot formally influence the contents of the Bill as it is not involved in the parliamentary handling of the Bill.[97]

It results from the above that either on the initiative of the executive government or the second chamber of Parliament, the Bank Act 1948, as the legal basis of the Nederlandsche Bank can be amended or even abolished, if a majority of the members of the second chamber and, thereafter, of the first chamber, vote in

[89] Ibid., Arts. 51–54. The official translation of the constitution refers to "The States General", but in the present context the term Parliament will be applied.

[90] Ibid., Arts. 51–53 and 55. The provincial and municipal councils administer the provinces and municipalities together with the provincial executive (*gedeputeerde staten*) and the King's Commissioner (*Commissaris van de Koning*), cf. Arts. 123 *et seq.* Constitution.

[91] Ibid., Arts. 73 *et seq.* On the functions of the Council of State, including its judicial function, cf. Prakke/De Reede/Van Wissen, n. 15 above, 425 *et seq.*, with further references.

[92] Ibid., Art. 84(1).

[93] Ibid., Art. 67. Generally, Bills pass the second chamber in one reading, including Bills based on Art. 106 of the Constitution. However, in a number of cases and in particular with regard to constitutional amendments special procedures are applicable (two readings/joint session of both chambers).

[94] Ibid., Art. 67.

[95] Ibid., Art. 87(1). This provision does not refer to the Monarch as an individual, but rather to the institution of government consisting of the Monarch and the Ministers. Normally, the Monarch will follow the positions of the Ministers. If a Bill does not pass one of the two chambers it is sent back to the Monarch.

[96] It should be noted in this context however that the second chamber rarely engages in the introduction of new Bills. In most cases Parliament takes the initiative to amend existing legislation: cf. Prakke/De Reede/Van Wissen, n.15 above, at 487.

[97] Note, however, that recently the Ministers have been able take part in discussions in Parliament (aanwijzing voor regelgeving no. 300).

favour of this. It could be concluded from this that, as is the case for other central bank systems, ultimately Parliament can hold the Nederlandsche Bank accountable for its conduct of monetary policy by deciding on an amendment of the legal basis of the Bank with consequences for the power of the Bank in the area of monetary policy (i.e. depriving it of its independent status).

However, the practical value of Parliament's right to change the legal basis of a central bank often stands in clear contrast to practice and it cannot be concluded that Parliament is applying its power as a tool of accountability. There is no record of instances in which Parliament changed the legal basis of the Bank with regard to its position *vis-à-vis* the government in the conduct of monetary policy. This also means that Parliament has not made use of its right in order to sanction the Bank. This may be explained by the institutional set-up of the Nederlandsche Bank. As will be seen hereafter the legislator has chosen a monetary system in which the government remains ultimately responsible for monetary policy. Government rather than the central bank is accountable for monetary policy *vis-à-vis* Parliament. The ministerial responsibility takes the Nederlandsche Bank out of the limelight of parliamentary debates.[98]

In the case of **Germany** apart from the Federal executive government, both chambers of Parliament, that is the Bundestag and the Bundesrat, have the right to initiate legislation.[99] As pointed out above, Article 88 of the Basic Law constitutes a competence norm for the establishment of a currency- and note-issuing bank as a Federal bank. Moreover, Article 73, No.4 of the Basic Law empowers Parliament to pass legislation related to currency, money, and coin related matters, and, on the basis of Article 74, No.11 of the Basic Law, legislation relating to bank and stock exchange matters.

The members of the Bundestag are elected every four years in direct elections. The Bundesrat consists of the representatives of the 16 State governments, and, with election dates at the level of the 16 *Länder* varying, constitutes a permanent body with changing membership. In the case of the Bundestag a minimum of five per cent of the members have to support a legislative proposal in order to be able to introduce it into Parliament.[100] On the part of the Federal executive government, proposals are drafted on the ministerial level and thereafter decided upon by the Cabinet of Ministers chaired by the Federal Chancellor. Governmental legislative proposals cannot be directly introduced into the Bundestag, but first have to be sent to the Bundesrat for comments. It is the Bundesrat which thereafter sends the proposal with or without its own comments to the Bundestag. At the same time the Federal executive government has the opportunity to take into account the comments by the Bundesrat and amend its proposal accordingly, in which case it has to send its amended proposal to the Bundesrat again. The

---

[98] Cf. Chap. 4 III, on the relationship with government and Chap. 4 VI on the relationship with Parliament.

[99] Art. 76(3) Basic Law.

[100] § 10 Rules of Procedure of the *Bundestag* (*Geschäftsordnung Bundestag* = GOBT).

Bundesrat itself may also make a legislative proposal. For this a collective decision of the Bundesrat is required, since individual *Länder* cannot introduce legislative proposals for consideration in the Bundestag. The Bundesrat cannot introduce the proposal into the Bundestag by itself, but has to send it to the Federal executive government, which has to forward it to the Bundestag within six weeks together with a concurring or dissenting opinion.[101] Generally, the Bundestag has the power to decide on draft legislation. The Bundesrat as the Upper House of Parliament participates in the decision-making process to a different extent depending on the nature of the proposed legislation, i.e. *Einspruchs-* or *Zustimmungsgesetz*.[102] Legislation passes the Bundestag after three readings.[103] The first reading deals with the proposal on a general basis. Proposals for amendments are excluded. Rather, the Bundestag decides to send the legislative proposal to one of its standing committees or to drop the proposal. Generally, in addition to the permanent standing committees recognised by the constitution,[104] each electoral term the Bundestag sets up standing committees basically covering the ministries set up under the current government, which—among others—deal with legislative proposals in their respective fields of competence. Often a number of different committees will examine a particular proposal. In the case of a legislative proposal amending the legal basis of the Bundesbank this may include the Finance Committee (*Finanzausschuß*), which is in principle competent for matters relating to monetary policy, the Legal Affairs Committee (*Rechtsausschuß*), the Committee of Economic Affairs (*Wirtschaftsausschuß*), and the Committee on the affairs of the European Union (*Ausschuß für die Angelegenheiten der Europäischen Union*). They examine the proposals in detail and may hold public hearing with expert witnesses and interest groups.[105] Each committee formulates its conclusions in a report to the general assembly, including both the majority and minority views. Thereafter, in a second reading, the Bundestag discusses the provisions of the proposal individually, in the course of which proposals for amendments may be introduced. Finally, at the centre of the third reading stand the discussions on those provisions for which applications for amendments have been introduced. However, quite often the third reading consists only of the voting on the legislative proposal. The Bundestag takes its decisions by a simple majority of the votes that have been issued. The bill is thereafter sent to the Bundesrat which has to decide within three weeks of receiving the decision of the Bundestag whether to agree to the proposal. In case of disagreement the Bundesrat may, with a majority of its members, call for the setting-up of a so-called Conciliation Committee (*Vermittlungsausschuß*), consisting of 11 members of the Bundestag and the

---

[101] Art. 76(3) Basic Law.
[102] Ibid., Art. 77. Cf. Chap. 3 III 1.3. On the different legislative procedures B.-O. Bryde, in H.-P. Schneider/W. Zeh (eds.), *Parlamentsrecht und Parlamentspraxis in der Bundesrepublik Deutschland* (Walter de Gruyter, Berlin and New York, 1989), § 50, 859 *et seq.*
[103] E.g. Th. Maunz, in Maunz/Dürig (eds.), n. 23 above, on Art. 77.
[104] Cf. Chap. 4 VI 2.
[105] § 70 GeschO BT.

Bundesrat.[106] The purpose of the Conciliation Committee is to find political solutions for disagreements between the Bundestag and the Bundesrat on legislative proposals.[107] The Committee can demand amendments of any part of the legislation. If it cannot agree upon a compromise, and thus the Bundesrat maintains its objections to the existing legislative proposal, the Bundestag can pass the legislation without the consent of the Bundesrat, if the proposed legislation is classified as a *Zustimmungsgesetz*.[108] Since, according to most commentators, this is the case for the legal basis of the Bundesbank, the Bundestag can pass legislation on the Bundesbank—if necessary—without the consent of the Bundesrat.[109] If the latter rejects the legislation by a majority of its members, it can be overruled by a majority of the members of the Bundestag. If the Bundesrat has rejected the proposal by a two-thirds majority, the decision can be overruled by a two-thirds majority of the votes cast, but at least a majority of the members of the Bundestag.[110] Therefore, in the case of a disagreement with the Bundesrat on a legislative proposal to amend the legal basis of the Bundesbank a two-thirds majority may be required in the Bundestag to pass the legislative proposal. Thus, while the Bundesrat ultimately cannot block a decision to change the legal basis of the Bundesbank, it can certainly slow down the procedure. This is most likely to happen when the majority in the Bundesrat resembles the opposition in the Bundestag, i.e. when a majority of the executive governments of the Länder, which make up the Bundesrat, are recruited from a political party or parties which is in the minority in the Bundestag.

Since its establishment the legal basis of the Bundesbank has been changed on a number of occasions, in particular, in the context of the German reunification.[111] However, despite some institutional amendments of the legal basis of the Bundesbank, there is no recorded case of Parliament challenging or seriously threatening the legal position of the Bundesbank, especially with regard to its independence, as a result of disagreements with the Bundesbank.[112] Yet, the fact that the institutional structure of the Bundesbank can be changed by a simple Act of Parliament may in itself be a mechanism providing *de facto* democratic accountability. In the past proposals for an alteration of the independent

---

[106] Art. 77(2) Basic Law, § 1 Rules of Procedure Conciliation Committee (*Geschäftsordnung Vermittlungsausschuß* = GeschO VermA). The Bundestag must decide on the draft legislation as proposed by the conciliation committee. Conciliation committees can be initiated by the Bundesrat for both *Einspruchs-* or *Zustimmungsgesetze*. In the case of *Zustimmungsgesetze* such an initiative can also come from the Bundestag and the Federal government. Cf. Bryde, n. 102 above, 875 *et seq.* A similar construction exists on the European level for the Council and the EP in the co-decision procedure under Art. 189b EC.

[107] B. Pieroth, in H.D. Jarras/B. Pieroth, *Grundgesetz für die Bundesrepublik Deutschland* (3rd edn., C.H. Beck, Munich, 1995), on Art. 77.

[108] Cf. Chap. 3 III 1.3.

[109] Art. 42(2) Basic Law.

[110] Ibid., Art. 77(4).

[111] With regard to the amendments in the course of German reunification, cf. Chap. 3 III 2.2.

[112] It remains unclear what O. Hahn, op. cit., Chap 2. n. 45, *Die Währungsbank*, op. cit., 70–1, refers to when suggesting that these amendments are evidence of a certain lack of independence of the Bundesbank. In fact, what is decisive is under what circumstances and what has been changed.

position of the Bundesbank have been opposed by the general public which has backed the Bundesbank. This may be explained by the high reputation which the Bundesbank has in the German public's view.[113] If, therefore, public opinion functions as a guarantor of the *status quo* of the Bundesbank, the latter may have a self-interest in preserving the confidence of the general public by avoiding an excessive use or abuse of its powers.[114] In this respect the influence of the general public against the background of a possible amendment of the legal basis of the Bundesbank, may provide a self-regulating, restraining mechanism.[115]

In the **United States**, according to Article I, section 1 of the US Constitution, all legislative power granted by the constitution is vested in Congress.[116] The Congress consists of two chambers, namely the House of Representatives and the Senate. The members of the House of Representatives are chosen in direct elections from among the 50 Federal states, in proportion to the population in each state, for a renewable term of two years.[117] Presently, the House of Representatives consists of 435 members. Unlike Germany, the second chamber does not consist of government representatives of the different states of the federation. Instead the Senate consists of 100 members, two from each state, elected in direct elections for a renewable term of six years. Every second year one-third of the seats in the Senate is up for renewal.[118] Both chambers of Congress have the right to introduce legislative initiatives.[119] Unlike other constitutional systems where the executive also has the right to initiate legislation, the President of the United States has no such right under the US Constitution, since his power is *de jure* limited to the approval or vetoing of any legislation which has passed both the House of Representatives and the Senate.[120] Generally, legislation can take the form of a Bill, proposing either a public or private matter, or a joint resolution. Although the practical differences between a Bill and a joint resolution

[113] B. Wahlig, "Relations between the Bundesbank and the Federal Government", *Die Bank*, vol. 6 (1995), 52–61, at 56, according to whom the Bundesbank's status of independence is safeguarded by public opinion.

[114] L. Poullain, op cit., Chap. 2, n. 149, at 44.

[115] H.H. v.Arnim, op. cit., Chap. 2, n. 115, at 343, refers to a "selbstregelnden Hemmungsmechanismus"; also instructive is R. Caesar, *Der Handlungsspielraum von Notenbanken* (Nomos, Baden-Baden, 1981), 137 *et seq.*, which refers to a balance between the Federal government/ Parliament and the Bundesbank, as both sides can apply pressure.

[116] With regard to the legislative procedures in Congress cf. e.g. J.Q. Wilson/J.J. DiIulio, Jr., *American Government: Institutions and Policies* (6th edn., Heath, Lexington, Ma/Toronto, 1995), 315 *et seq.*

[117] Art. 1, s. 2 US Constitution.

[118] Ibid., Art. I, s. 3, and 17th Amendment of the US Constitution.

[119] Note, however, that only the House of Representatives can introduce revenue raising Bills: Art. I, s. 7, US Constitution.

[120] Ibid., Art. I, s. 7. However, *de facto* the President can initiate legislation in two ways by either including proposals in his annual "state of the union" report to Congress in accordance with Art. II, s. 3, US Constitution, or by making proposals in the form of so-called "executive communications" usually forwarded in the form of a report to the Speaker of the House of Representatives and the President of the Senate.

are small, the majority of legislative proposals are introduced in the form of a bill.[121] As private Bills by nature address private individuals, a Bill proposing the amendment of the Federal Reserve Act constitutes a public Bill. Bills can only be introduced by one or more members of the House of Representatives or the Senate.[122] After its introduction into either the Senate or the House of Representatives a Bill is then referred to one of the standing, select and/or joint committees, or one of their sub-committees having jurisdiction over the subject-matter of the Bill or any particular part of the Bill.[123] Bills covering different subjects are referred to several committees. Bills proposing the restructuring of the Fed usually fall within the jurisdiction of the Banking Committees of both Houses. Currently, these are the Committee on Banking and Financial Services[124] for the House of Representatives and the Committee on Banking, Housing, and Urban Affairs for the Senate.[125] The respective committees and sub-committees study the proposal—among others—by taking third-party testimony in public hearings and, thereafter, draft the proposal into a final form for reporting to the respective House of Congress. A committee can chose to either endorse a Bill with or without amendments, including a complete new substitute text, reject the proposal, or table it, i.e. not report at all. The Bill, as forwarded by the committee, then is considered on the Senate or House floor where it may become subject to further amendments. Decisions on draft legislation are normally taken by a simple majority vote in both Houses.[126] Once a Bill has passed one House it is referred to the other for consideration. If the Bill passes on this occasion only with amendments it is referred back to the House where it originated. If an agreement on a Bill cannot be reached, a so-called Conference Committee may be set-up, consisting of members of both Houses in order to reach a consensus.[127] Once both Houses of Congress have agreed on the contents of a Bill it is forwarded to the US President who may either explicitly endorse the Bill by signing it and returning it to Congress within ten days, or implicitly by not returning the signed bill and not filing his objections against it

---

[121] E.A. Farnsworth, *An Introduction to the Legal System of the United States* (3rd edn., Oceana Publications, New York, 1996), 61 *et seq.*

[122] Bills are the most common, but not the only, type of congressional action. Other actions include joint resolutions, concurrent resolutions and the simple resolutions: R.B. Dove, 1997, *Enactment of Law* (online), available from URL http://thomas.loc.gov/ (last accessed Jan. 1999).

[123] On the type and role of congressional committees cf. Wilson/DiIulio, Jr., n. 116 above, 309 *et seq.*

[124] For many years known as the Committee on Banking, Finance and Urban Affairs.

[125] The Committees are appointed at the beginning of each Congress. Generally, the proportion of representatives of the Republican Party and Democratic Party correspond with the ratio in the respective house of Congress.

[126] The only exception is a Bill which has been vetoed by the President which then required a two-third majority in both Houses.

[127] Sometimes referred to as the "Third House of Congress". Unlike the so-called Joint Committees of Congress, the members of Conference Committee vote separately according to their membership of the House of Representatives and the Senate. In each case a simple majority is required.

within that period.[128] In both cases the bill finally becomes law. The President's powerful position in the US constitutional system in part derives from his right to veto legislation.[129] If the President objects to the contents of the Bill, it is referred back to the House of Congress where it originated which may then choose to reconsider the contents of the Bill and/or pass the Bill with a two-thirds majority vote. If the Bill passes both Houses with a two-thirds majority it becomes law regardless of the Presidential veto. The President can only veto a Bill in full, since he does not have a line-item veto, which would allow him to reject only certain provisions of a Bill. Summarising, Congress can amend and theoretically even abolish the Fed by changing or abolishing its legal basis, the Federal Reserve Act. For this a simple majority (or in the case of a Presidential veto a two-thirds majority) in both Houses of Congress is required.

In contrast to what can be observed for other central bank systems, the Federal Reserve Act has been substantially amended on a number of occasions, affecting the institutional structure of the Fed and its relationship with Congress and the executive government. Major examples include the Banking Act of 1933 and even more so 1935, as well as the Federal Reserve Reform Act of 1977 and the Full Employment and Balanced Growth Act of 1978. However, compared to the number of proposals introduced in Congress in particular in the course of the last three decades the actual number of amendments implemented is modest.[130] Yet, in a number of instances Congress may have pushed the Fed in complying with congressional wishes by threatening to amend the Federal Reserve Act.[131]

3. A constitutional recognition of Member States' central banks in the ESCB?

It has been observed so far that, except in the case of the ECB, constitutional protection of the institutional structure is lacking in the case of all central banks examined in this study. However, with the establishment of an ESCB the question arises whether such constitutional recognition derives from the EC Treaty and the ESCB Statute. At the centre of the obligations under Community law stands Article 107 EC and the independence of the national central banks from national and Community organs in the exercise of powers and the carrying out of duties in the framework of the ESCB. Article 108 EC obliges the Member States at the latest at the time of the establishment of the ESCB to amend *and* to

---

[128] Art. 1 s. 7, US Constitution.

[129] Unlike the old dispute in German constitutional law, with regard to the extent of the right of examination of the *Bundespräsident* when signing bills into law, the US President can veto legislation for any reason, including substantive issues.

[130] Congressional action will be discussed in more detail in Chap. 4 VI.

[131] This is suggested by M.A. Akhtar/H. Howe, "The Political Independence of U.S. Monetary Policy", *BNL Quarterly Review* 178 (1991), 343–89, at 354; Th. Havrilesky, op. cit., Chap 3, n. 529, 81 *et seq.* finds that threat influences monetary policy. Congressional action will be discussed in more detail in Chap. 4 VI 1.

maintain their national central bank statutes in compliance with the EC Treaty and the ESCB Statute.[132] In general this affects any provisions having an impact on the institutional, personal, functional and financial independence of the national central banks. The effect on the participating central banks will be highlighted throughout the examination of the other criteria hereafter. With regard to the legal basis it may be observed that once the statutes of a national central bank have been brought into line with the EC Treaty and the ESCB Statute, the national legislator is effectively barred from changing the legal basis of the national central bank in any way which would run contrary to the EC Treaty and the ESCB Statute. In short, the legal status of the national central banks is safeguarded by primary Community law to the extent that the banks fulfil ESCB-related tasks. Thus national parliaments effectively lose their most drastic mechanism for holding the central bank accountable in the area of monetary policy. Arnim has argued for the Bundesbank that the mechanism of checks and balances which is provided, on the one hand, by the credibility of the Bundesbank among the German population and, on the other hand, by Parliament's power to change the legal basis, would not be available in case of a constitutional guarantee of independence of the Bundesbank either through an interpretation or amendment of the German constitution.[133] With the independence being safeguarded by primary Community law the Bundesbank, or for that matter any other participating national central bank, no longer requires public confidence in order to prevent the legislator from amending the *status quo* of its independence. Although it would be somewhat exaggerated to argue that the self-regulating and restraining mechanism establishing a form of democratic accountability to the general public is abandoned with the establishment of an ESCB through the recognition of the ECB in primary Community law, it seems at least doubtful to what extent a similar mechanism will develop with regard to the ECB. The position of the citizens of the EU *vis-à-vis* the ECB is not set to be much different from that *vis-à-vis* the existing Community institutions. However, it has already been observed that a true European identity among the citizens of the EU is still lacking, as national issues prevail.[134]

In the case of three of the four Member States whose central banks are examined in this study, that is France, Germany and the Netherlands, this transfer of legislative power from the national to the Community level is backed by constitutional provisions.[135] In at least two of the three countries the TEU became the subject of critical review during the ratification procedures. In the case of France a change of the Constitution of 1958 became necessary in order to ratify the

---

[132] According to Art. 109 e(4) EC: "During the second stage, each Member State shall, as appropriate, start the process leading to the independence of its central bank, in accordance with Art. 108". Note that Art. 109k EC on Member States with a derogation does not exclude Arts. 107 and 108 EC for those Member States.

[133] H.H. v. Arnim, n. 115 above, at 341.

[134] Cf. Chap. 2 II 1.

[135] It has been observed that the UK has negotiated a separate Protocol on EMU annexed to the TEU.

provisions on EMU, and in particular the transfer of authority for monetary policy. The reason for this is to be found in the first ruling of the Constitutional Council on the TEU.[136] The Constitutional Council found that the restriction of national sovereignty as a result of the adoption of obligations in order to establish or develop a permanent international organisation which constitutes a legal entity and which has decision-making competence transferred to it by the contracting States, was admissible subject to *reciprocity*, that is to say that the other participating States restrict their sovereignty to an equivalent extent.[137] The Constitutional Council pointed out that constitutional amendments were needed where international treaties included provisions which violated the constitution or affected substantial conditions for the practice of national sovereignty. With regard to the provisions on EMU included in the TEU, the court stated that the goal of EMU was to be pursued by a common monetary and exchange-rate policy, thereby stripping the Member States of central competence in the execution of their national sovereignty, which, in the case of France, could not be justified under the existing Constitution.[138] The Constitutional Council concluded that the French ratification law implementing the TEU could only be approved after an amendment of the Constitution of 1958.[139] As a result of this ruling the Constitution was amended, thereby introducing the new Article 88.[140] In a follow-up decision the Constitutional Council indirectly approved of the constitutional amendments by concluding that the TEU did not (i.e. no longer) include any provisions which were in contradiction with the (amended) constitution.

As with France, the Law on Accession to the TEU was the object of judicial review in Germany by the Federal Constitutional Court in the context of two constitutional complaints (*Verfassungsbeschwerden*).[141] In the only constitutional complaint which was considered admissible, the petitioner claimed an infringement of rights under Article 38 of the Basic Law, which guarantees and protects the right of every citizen to a democratically legitimated representation in the Bundestag and protects the right to participate in the exercise of public

---

[136] Décision no. 92–308 DC of 9 Apr. 1992, RUDH 1992, 336; Décision no. 92–312 DC of 2 Sept. 1992, RUDH 1992, 341; Décision no. 92–313 of 23 Sept. 1992, RUDH 1992, 344.

[137] This requirement derives from para. 15 of the preamble of the constitution of 27 Oct. 1946 which is still applicable.

[138] Décision no. 92–308 DC, n. 136 above. The court also examined the provisions introduced by the TEU on Union citizenship and the entry and movement of third-country nationals in the single market (immigration) and came to the conclusion that Art. 8b(1) EC on the electoral rights of EU citizens in local elections and Art. 100c(3) EC on Council decisions on visa requirements for third-country nationals were unconstitutional. Cf. K. Highet/G. Kahale III/J.B. Kokott, "French Case Note", *AJIL*, vol. 86 (1992), 824–82.

[139] Décision no. 92–308 DC, n. 136 above. E.g. F. Luchaire, "L'Union Européenne et la Constitution", prèmiere partie, *RDP* (1992), 589–616 and P. Oliver, "The French Constitution and the Treaty of Maastricht" (1994) 43 *ICLQ*, 1–25.

[140] Loi constitutionnelle no. 92–554 du 25 juin 1992, Art.5. Cf. Chap. 4 III 1.

[141] BVerfGE 89, 155, Arts. 93(1) no. 4a Basic Law and 90(1) Federal Constitutional Court Act (*Bundesverfassungsgerichtsgesetz*) list the conditions for a constitutional complaint.

authority.[142] The petitioner saw his constitutional right under Article 38 of the Basic Law substantially diminished, since with the Law of Accession the Bundestag would effectively assign essential powers to organs of the European Communities, and, furthermore, under Article F(3) TEU agree to powers which could establish a residual power (*Kompetenz-Kompetenz*) in favour of the EU. As a result of this the German population would no longer participate in the exercise of public authority, since with the broadening of the Community competence the public authority would no longer effectively be exercised by the elected representatives of the entire German people in the Bundestag. It was in particular argued that this was also the case for the provisions on EMU, since the decision on entering into stage three of EMU was already taken with the ratification of the TEU, and thus a consent by the Bundestag and the Bundesrat prior to entering stage three of EMU is irrelevant in Treaty terms. The plaintiffs stated that "in the monetary union monetary policy will be withdrawn from any parliamentary influence and other democratic legitimation".[143]

The court recognised it as a "substantive component" of the democratic principle that the carrying-out of state functions and the exercise of public authority derive from the people of the State and that those charged with exercising this authority are "fundamentally answerable to the people".[144] However, the court emphasised the openness of the German constitution towards participation of Germany in an international legal community and considered the acceptance of the binding effect of decisions taken in the fora of such an international legal community as compatible with this general choice for integration expressed in the Basic Law. Furthermore, it was argued that it is in the nature of a supranational organisation which is granted sovereign rights that democratic legitimation cannot be provided in the same form as within a unified and closed constitutional order, since the national Parliament, and thus the people in the Member States, lose influence as the decisions no longer depend on the will of one Member State alone. In the opinion of the Federal Constitutional Court the democratic legitimation of the EU in the first place derives through the feedback of the actions of the European institutions into the parliaments of the Member States which have to ratify the treaties incorporating the transfer of sovereign power:

> "In the law assenting to accession to a community of states resides the democratic legitimation, both of the existence of the community of states itself and its powers to take majority decisions which are binding on the Member States."[145]

---

[142] Other claims, namely those arguing that monetary union would infringe the petitioner's constitutional rights under Arts. 12 and 14 Basic Law (right to choose an occupation/property) were considered inadmissible by the court. Also see the court order of 31 Mar. 1998—2 BvR 1877/97 and 2 BvR 50/98, where the Federal Constitutional Court dismisses two constitutional complaints in connection with the introduction of the single currency.
[143] B 1(b), of the decision.
[144] Ibid., C.I.2.
[145] Ibid., C.I.2(a)–(b).

In Germany the conferring of sovereign power in accordance with Articles 23 and 24 of the Basic Law requires a prior legislative resolution.[146] Thus, with the national Parliament playing a crucial part in the democratic legitimation of the EU, the court concluded, it would also have to decide on membership of the EU, as well as its continuation and development. However, a law which did not define "with adequate certainty" the powers which are transferred and the "intended programme of integration", would amount to a general authorisation which is incompatible with Article 38 of the Basic Law, and the right to participate in the exercise of public authority. With regard to monetary union the court concluded that the provisions of the TEU give legal certainty, and despite the fact that the development of the monetary union was not foreseeable with regard to its specific stages toward economic significance, the participating Member States and the timetable, the court concluded that the challenged Law on Accession fulfilled the requirements of parliamentary responsibility. Interestingly in this context, the court observed that the German Parliament reserved the right to make its own assessment of the decision by the Federal government to enter into stage three of EMU.[147] These remarks by the court have sometimes been criticised for recognising a right of the Bundestag to take a final decision whether to enter into stage three of EMU.[148] Yet a somewhat more restricted reading of both the German and English version of the court's ruling suggests that the court merely meant to point out that Parliament still has the ability to influence the further integration of the European legal order by influencing the Federal government in its (voting) behaviour in the Council in the context of Article 109j(3) and (4) EC.[149] This reading is enhanced by the otherwise questionable remark of the court that "the time for the commencement of the third stage of economic and monetary union must be seen as a target rather than as a legally enforceable date".[150]

With a view towards Article 88, sentence 2 of the Basic Law the court found that "the obligation of the European Central Bank ECB to aim at securing price stability . . . also satisfies a separate constitutional obligation of the Federal

---

[146] In short, Art. 24 Basic Law allows for the transfer of sovereignty to intergovernmental institutions, and in particular collective security systems, e.g. NATO, whereas Art. 23 Basic Law regulates the transfer of sovereign powers to the EU and in particular the participation of the different constitutional organs at the national level.

[147] C II 2 d 2) (3), of the decision. Note also the resolution of the Bundestag on Economic and Monetary Union, BTDrucks. 12/3906, in which the Bundestag emphasises that a decision by the Federal government in the Council for entering stage three of EMU requires its affirmative vote.

[148] A. Weber, "Die Wirtschafts- und Währungsunion nach dem Maastricht-Urteil des BVerfG", *JZ*, vol. 49 no. 2 (1994), 53–60, at 57.

[149] II 2 d 2) (5), of the decision: "the Treaty open the way to a further integration of the European legal Community by stages, which at every further step is subject either to already foreseeable conditions for the Parliament *or to a further assent from the Federal Government which may be influenced by parliamentary means*" (emphasis added).

[150] C II 2 d 2) (1), of the decision. This assessment of the court has been rightly criticised for overlooking the irreversibility of the process of EMU as stated in the EC Treaty. See e.g. E. Bauer, n. 22 above, on Art. 88, side notation 24.

Republic of Germany as a Member State of the European Community".[151] Interestingly, in the view of the court this constitutional obligation within the national context also has consequences for the Community as a whole:

"the EC is a community under the rule of law and under Art. 5 of the EEC Treaty the principle of loyal cooperation is applicable to it."[152]

This reasoning has been criticised by Pernice, who observes that the obligation of the ESCB to pursue a policy of stability derives from an explicit reference in the Treaty, and thus not from the general principle of loyal co-operation of Article 5 and, furthermore, not because this may be a precondition for the transfer of sovereignty in the constitution of one Member State.[153] Moreover, he points out rightly that the danger of such a line of reasoning is that the German definition of stability could become a European yardstick, something which is neither agreed upon in the TEU nor in line with the structure of the Communities.[154]

The German Federal Constitutional Court recognises the potential conflict between the transfer of power over monetary policy to an independent ECB and the (German) principle of democracy:

"The possibility for influence by the Bundestag, and therefore by the electorate, on the exercise of sovereign powers of European institutions have no doubt almost been taken away completely insofar as the European Central Bank has been made independent vis-à-vis the European Community and the Member States (Art. 107, EC Treaty). An essential political area, where the maintenance of the value of the currency supports individual freedom, and the money supply determines public finances and the political spheres dependent thereon, has been excluded from the regulatory power of sovereign authorities, and also—excluding treaty amendment—from the lawgiver's control of areas of responsibility and means of action. Placing most of the tasks of monetary policy on an autonomous basis in the hands of an independent central bank releases the exercise of sovereign powers of the state from direct national or supranational parliamentary responsibility, in order to withdraw monetary matters from the reach of interest groups and holders of political office concerned about re-elections."[155]

Yet, the court considered this restriction of democratic legitimation to be compatible with the Basic Law. It referred in particular to the second sentence added to Article 88 of the Basic Law:

"The will of the legislature, therefore, in amending the Constitution is clearly to create a constitutional basis for the monetary union as provided for in the Union Treaty,

[151] C II.2. d) (2), of the decision.
[152] Ibid.
[153] I. Pernice, "Das Ende der währungspolitischen Souveränität Deutschlands und das Maastricht-Urteil des BVerfG" in Due *et al.* (eds.), op. cit., Chap. 3, n. 324, Vol. I, 1057–70, at 1064.
[154] Such a tendency has emerged in the public discussions on the interpretation of the convergence criteria for the entering of stage three of EMU laid down in Arts. 109j in connection with 104c EC.
[155] C II. 3 a), of the decision.

but restricting the granting of independent powers and institutions to that case. This modification of the democratic principle for protecting the confidence placed in the value of a currency is acceptable because it takes account of the special characteristic—in the German legal context tested and proven, in scientific terms as well—that an independent central bank is a better guarantor of currency value, and thus of a general economic basis for state budgetary policy and for private planning and transactions in the exercise of the laws of economic freedom, than sovereign bodies which in their possibilities and means of action are essentially dependent on the supply and value of the currency and rely on the short-term consent of political forces. To that extent the placing of monetary policy on an independent footing within the sovereign jurisdiction of a European Central Bank, which is not transferable to other political areas, satisfies the constitutional requirements whereunder the principle of democracy may be modified."[156]

One is reminded of the economic discussion on central bank independence and, indeed, the court justifies the independence of the ECB and the loss, or—in the court's own words—modification, of democratic principles by observing that an independent central bank is a necessary prerequisite not only for the state but also for the private individual. In the opinion of the court this seems to outweigh the concerns raised in connection with the principle of democracy, reflected— among others—by Article 38 of the Basic Law.[157] However, considering the somewhat inconclusive international theoretical and empirical evidence on central bank independence, it is not entirely convincing when the court observes almost by the side that in the German case this was "tested and proven, in scientific terms".[158] The court has evaluated the independence of the ECB against the background of the Bundesbank which enjoys a considerable amount of independence within the German constitutional system.[159] Besides, the reasoning of the Federal Constitutional Court is questionable to the extent that it justifies the removal of monetary policy from the legislator with the existence of an escape clause in the form of an amendment of the EC Treaty. In fact, the escape clause may not amount to much once the ESCB is in place. Even in the case of Treaty amendment the German legislator could not simply give his assent to an amendment of important parts of the ESCB and the ECB because, as the court points out itself, in accordance with the second sentence of Article 88 of the Basic Law the independence of the ECB, as well as price stability as its primary objective, is a constitutional precondition for the transfer of sovereignty in the area of monetary policy. Thus, it would not be possible for the German Parliament to ratify a treaty amending primary Community law in accordance with the

---

[156] Ibid.

[157] M. Herdegen, "Maastricht and the German Constitutional Court: Constitutional Restraint for an 'Ever Closer Union'" (1994) 31 *CMLRev.*, 235–49, at 246 *et seq.*

[158] T. Koopmans, op. cit., Chap. 2, n. 91, at 249, himself at the time Advocate General of the Dutch Supreme Court, refers in this context to judicial prose, and questions why a court opinion on economic terms is supposed to be more important than the opinion of the majority of Parliament or the Finance Minister.

[159] Weber, n. 148 above, at 59.

procedure under Article N TEU thereby changing the institutional structure of the ECB with regard to its independent position without changing the German constitution first. With the introduction of the second sentence of Article 88 the German legislator has effectively restricted itself with regard to the type of institution to which sovereignty over monetary policy may be transferred.[160] This would also mean that any attempt by the other Member States to alter the structure of the ECB in that respect would have to be considered as a violation of the conditions under which the transfer of authority to the ECB is considered compatible with the principle of democracy under the German Basic Law.

In the Netherlands no special provision has been introduced into the Dutch Constitution for the transfer of authority over monetary policy to the Community level. Indeed, the TEU, including the provisions on the establishing of a ESCB, has been ratified with remarkably little resistance in the Netherlands. Generally, Articles 90–95 of the Dutch Constitution govern the applicability of supranational legal rules in the Dutch legal order. According to Article 92, legislative, executive and judicial powers may be conferred on international institutions by or pursuant to a treaty. Binding provisions of treaties and of resolutions by international institutions become binding in the Netherlands upon publication, and statutory regulations in force in the Netherlands are inapplicable if their application is in conflict with binding provisions of treaties.[161] According to Article 91 of the Dutch Constitution international treaties are regularly binding in the Netherlands only upon approval by Parliament.[162] Decisions are normally taken by a simple majority vote in Parliament. However, if any provision of a treaty is in conflict with the Constitution or may lead to such a conflict a majority of at least two-thirds of the votes cast in each chamber of Parliament is required for approval.[163] This makes the Dutch Constitution very accessible for the influence of supranational law, since treaty provisions which are in contradiction to the Constitution are not *per se* unconstitutional as they can be approved by Parliament without constitutional amendments. At the time of the ratification of the TEU there was some argument whether a two-thirds majority was required to pass the provisions—among others—related to EMU, since, as has been observed, Article 106 of the Dutch Constitution transfers legislative competence with regard to the monetary systems onto Parliament, whereas by means of the TEU sovereign power is transferred to the European level.[164] This view has been contested with refer-

---

[160] In this respect it may be somewhat inaccurate to say that the independence of the Bundesbank is guaranteed by the second sentence of Art. 88 Basic Law. Rather, the independence of the Bundesbank is guaranteed by the EC Treaty and the ESCB Statute in the framework of the ESCB to which the tasks and powers of the Bundesbank may be transferred.

[161] Arts. 93 and 94 Dutch Constitution.

[162] Exceptions to this rule have to be defined in an Act of Parliament; cf. Rijkswet van 7 juli 1994, Stb. 542, houdende regeling betreffende de goedkeuring en bekendmaking van verdragen en de bekendmaking van besluiten van volkenrechtelijke organisaties.

[163] Art. 91(3) Dutch Constitution.

[164] A.W. Heringa, "Het verdrag van Maastricht in strijd met de Grondwet", *NJB* (1992), 749–52.

ence to the genesis of Article 106. It has been argued that at the time of the drafting of Article 106 the government was of the opinion that a transfer of authority with regard to the monetary system by means of a treaty would not be considered unconstitutional in the light of Article 106.[165] Moreover, the constitutional endowment of Parliament with regulatory powers does not mean that these task cannot be fulfilled by means of an international treaty.[166] It may also be observed that Parliament effectively makes use of its power to regulate the monetary system in accordance with Article 106 by ratifying the provisions on EMU included in the TEU. In any event, despite some discussion, the executive government and a majority of Parliament considered a simple majority vote to be sufficient to adopt the TEU. The reason that the TEU met little resistance in Parliament was the widespread belief that the ratification Bill would pass Parliament with a large majority anyway.[167] Moreover, the Council of State (*Raad van State*), a constitutionally recognised advisory body[168] which has to be consulted by Parliament on Bills (*wetsvoorstellen*), draft general administrative orders (*ontwerpen van algemene maatregelen van bestuur*) and proposals for the approval of treaties (*goedkeuring van verdragen*), did not find the TEU to be in contradiction to the Dutch Constitution, and in particular Article 106.[169] This consensus on the constitutionality of the TEU seems remarkable in the light of the difficulties which the ratification of the TEU faced in other Member States, and may in fact be evidence of the "Open Constitution" to be found in the Netherlands.[170] Article 108 EC which recognises the independent status of the national central banks participating in EMU is directly applicable in the Netherlands. Therefore, starting from stage three at least the independent position of the Nederlandsche Bank is recognised, and for that matter guaranteed, by primary Community law.

Considered by itself the inability of national parliaments to change the legal basis of their central banks in particular with regard to their independent position may not have such a great impact on the democratic accountability of the national central banks. The reason for this is that the decision-making power of the national central banks with regard to monetary policy is transferred to the ECB, thus to a large extent removing the responsibilities of the national central

[165] Cf. M.C. Burkens/B.P. Vermeulen, "Maastricht in strijd met de Grondwet? reactie 1", *NJB* (1992), 861–2; C.A.J.M. Kortman, *Constitutioneel Recht* (2nd edn., Kluwer, Deventer, 1994), at 189.

[166] J.G. Brouwer, "Wijkt het Unie-Verdrag van Maastricht af van de Grondwet of van het Statuut?", *NJB* (1992), 1045–19, at 1048, with further references.

[167] A. den Hartog, "The Netherlands and the Ratification of the Maastricht Treaty" in S.F. Laursen/S. Vanhoonacken, *The Ratification of the Maastricht Treaty—Issues, Sebates and Future Implications* (European Institute of Public Administration, Martinus Nijhoff Publishers, Maastricht, 1994), 213–25.

[168] Art. 73(1) Dutch Constitution.

[169] Advies Raad Van State, Tweede Kamer, Vergaderjaar 1991–2, 22647 (R1437), A, 1 *et seq.*, 46 *et seq.*

[170] A term used by L.F.M. Besselink, "An Open Constitution and European Integration: The Kingdom of the Netherlands", *SEW*, vol. 44 no. 6 (1996), 192–206.

banks in this area. The emphasis shifts from the national to the European level, and the question arises whether the loss of this mechanism of democratic accountability is effectively compensated for by the EC Treaty and the ESCB Statute. Yet, as has been pointed, out apart from a few minor exceptions, an amendment of the legal basis of the ESCB and the ECB would require an amendment of the EC Treaty itself which requires the common accord of all Member States.

II. MONETARY OBJECTIVES

It has been observed that the existence of a clear monetary objective can enhance central bank accountability inasmuch as it may form an important precondition for the evaluation of its performance.[171] Under the EC Treaty and ESCB Statute the legal bases of Member States' central banks participating in the ESCB have to reflect unambiguously the primary objective of the ESCB, i.e. price stability.

The monetary objectives of the central banks included in this study are defined to a different degree. Generally, three groups of central banks emerge from an examination of the respective central bank statutes. A first group of central bank statutes features a monetary objective which is either vague or consists of a number of objectives. This group is referred to as central banks with an indistinct monetary objective. The second group of central banks features a single monetary objective or a clear hierarchy between different objectives. These banks may be summarised as central banks with a primary monetary objective. Finally, the third group of central banks features a statute which not only defines a primary monetary objective, but also demands the determination of specific numeric targets for reaching the objective. This group is referred to as central banks featuring a quantified monetary objective.

1. Central banks with an indistinct monetary objective

Of the seven central bank systems examined in this study three may be considered to include broad monetary objectives in their legal basis. This amounts in some instances to poorly defined objectives and/or the inclusion of more than one objective without establishing a hierarchy between them. In either instance the central banks are left with a large degree of discretion to define the vague monetary objective.

The **Fed** may be considered as a central bank system incorporating an indistinct monetary objective, featuring both multiply and unquantified objectives. According to section 2A(1), sentence 1 of the Federal Reserve Act:

---

[171] Cf. Chap. 2 II.2.2.2.

"The Board of Governors of the Fed and the Federal Open Market Committee shall *maintain long run growth of the monetary and credit aggregates* commensurate with the economy's long run potential to increase production, so as to promote effectively the *goals of maximum employment, stable prices, and moderate long-interest rates.*"[172]

In principle the monetary policy objectives of maximum employment, stable prices and moderate long-term interest rates have to be considered on equal terms since neither the Federal Reserve Act nor any other law provides for any hierarchy.[173] However, multiple objectives can conflict with each other and in order to strike an even balance between them judgements have to be made by the institution charged with the implementation of such objectives.[174] In its *Strategic Framework 1997–2002* the Board of Governor states:

"The fundamental mission of the Federal Reserve System is to foster the stability, integrity, and efficiency of the nation's monetary, financial, and payment systems so as to promote macroeconomic performance."

With regard to monetary policy this includes:

"To formulate and conduct monetary policy toward the achievement of maximum sustainable long-term growth; price stability fosters that goal."[175]

The Federal Reserve Act does not include many guidelines for the implementation of the monetary policy objectives and, indeed, the Fed has taken different approaches to the implementation of monetary policy over time.[176] According to section 2A(1), sentences 2 and 3:

"the Board of Governors of the Fed shall transmit to the Congress, not later than February 20 and July 20 of each year, independent written reports setting forth . . . (2) the objectives and plans of the Board of Governors and the Federal Open Market Committee with respect to the ranges of growth or diminution of the monetary and credit aggregates for the calendar year during which the report is transmitted, taking account of past and prospective developments in employment, unemployment, production, investment, real income, productivity, international trade and payments, and prices; and (3) the relationship of the aforesaid objectives and plans to the short-term goals set forth in the most recent Economic Report of the President . . . and to any short-term goals approved by the Congress. In addition, as a part of its report on July 20 of each year, the Board of Governors shall include a statement of its objectives and plans with respect to the ranges of growth or diminution of the monetary and credit aggregates for the calendar year following the year in which the report is submitted. . . . "

[172] Also 12 USC Sec. 225a. Emphasis added.
[173] Akhtar/Howe, n. 131 above, 351–2.
[174] This is recognised by the Fed itself: Board of Governors of the Federal Reserve System, op. cit., Chap. 3, n. 536, 17–18.
[175] Cf. Board of Governors of the Federal Reserve System, *Strategic Framework 1997–2002*, Washington, DC, Dec. 1996, at 1.
[176] Cf. Remarks by Chairman A. Greenspan at the 15th Anniversary Conference of the Center for Economic Policy Research at the Stanford University, Stanford, Cal., 5 Sept. 1997; Th. de Saint Phalle, op. cit., Chap. 3, n. 553, 87 *et seq.*

The introduction of these reporting requirements by the Full Employment and Balanced Growth Act of 1978[177] stood at the end of a long struggle between Congress and the Fed, which began in the mid 1960s, over the introduction of more meaningful guidelines for the conduct of monetary policy by the Fed in order to enable Congress to conduct more effective oversight of the Fed, and at times also in an attempt to commit the Fed to a certain operational approach to monetary policy implementation.[178] As will be seen, this struggle continues today. In the original Act of 1913 the only reference to the objective of the Fed was to be found in the preamble according to which the Federal Reserve Act was: "to provide for the establishment of Federal reserve banks, to furnish an elastic currency . . . ".[179] The Employment Act of 1946 obliged the Federal government "to use all practical means ... to promote maximum employment, production and purchasing power".[180] The Fed took on these objectives at the time. With House Concurrent Resolution 133 Congress required the Board of Governors to consult Congress at semi-annual hearings before the Committee on Banking, Housing and Urban Affairs of the Senate and the Committee on Banking, Currency and Housing of the House of Representatives (since replaced by the Committee on Banking and Financial Services) about the Board of Governors' and the Federal Open Market Committee's objectives and plans with respect to the ranges of growth or diminution of monetary and credit aggregates in the ensuing 12 months.[181] The Fed complied despite the fact that the Concurrent Resolution hardly constituted a legally binding obligation. However, the semi-annual reports on the objective and plans turned out to be largely ineffective as a congressional tool to hold the Fed accountable for its past performances since the Fed was free to determine and adjust its targets.[182] Still, as Kettl observes "for the first time Congress had voted to require Fed officials to testify regularly and publicly on past policies and future plans".[183] The

---

[177] Act at 27 Oct. 1978; 92 Stat. 1887.

[178] For an overview until the Full Employment and Balanced Growth Act of 1978, cf. R.E. Weintraub, "Congressional Supervision of Monetary Policy", *Journal of Monetary Economics* 4 (1978), 341–62.

[179] This description is still to be found in the preamble of the Federal Reserve Act today.

[180] Act of 20 Feb. 1946; 60 Stat. 23.

[181] H.Con.Res. 133 of 24 Mar. 1975. It also directed the Board of Governors of the Federal Reserve System and the Federal Open Market Committee to pursue policies in the first half of 1975 so as to encourage lower long-term interest rates and expansion in monetary and credit aggregates and to maintain long run growth of monetary and credit aggregates. See also S.Con.Res. 18 of 12 Feb. 1975.

[182] The practice of announcements of the objectives and plans of the Board of Governors and FOMC with regard to the ranges of growth or diminution of monetary and credit aggregates in congressional hearings turned out to be of little success from the point of view of Congress since the Fed did not commit itself to concrete monetary targets, but rather reported on the projections of a broad range of targets (monetary aggregates M1–M5) for the following 12 months. In fact, the Fed interpreted House Concurrent Resolution 133 to the effect that new projections for the following 12 months were introduced for each hearing, thereby being able to correct any departures from the earlier targets (so-called "base rolling").

[183] D.F. Kettl, *Leadership at the FED* (Yale University Press, New Haven and London, 1986), at 146.

Federal Reserve Reform Act of 1977 codified the practice established under House Concurrent Resolution 133 into the Federal Reserve Act by introducing a new section 2 A with the telling title "General policy: Congressional Review". However, in its enacted form, the Federal Reserve Reform Act of 1977 failed to remedy the shortcomings of the arrangements under Resolution 133, namely to require the Fed to commit itself to a set of monetary targets. The Full Employment and Balanced Growth Act of 1978 extended the reporting requirements by obliging the Board of Governors to put its objectives and plans with respect to the ranges of growth or diminution of the monetary and credit aggregates into perspective to the Economic Report of the President and, furthermore, any short-term goals set by Congress. In addition to reporting its objectives and plans for the year in which the report was submitted the Board of Governors became obliged to report once a year on its objectives and plans for the year following the report.

Despite the enhanced reporting requirements of the Board of Governors under the Federal Reserve Act, and the fact that, ever since, the Fed has not been able constantly to adjust its own projections, it is still free to determine its own targets. As a recent Memorandum by the chairman of the Board of Governors observes:

> "Neither the Act nor any other law specifies particular numerical targets for economic growth, unemployment, inflation, money supply growth, or interest rates."[184]

Moreover, the Board of Governors is not irrevocably committed to the targets it sets, since section 2A(1), sentence 6, provides for an "escape route":

> "Nothing in this Act shall be interpreted to require that the objectives and plans with respect to the ranges of growth or diminution of the monetary and credit aggregates disclosed in the reports submitted under this section be achieved if the Board of Governors and the Federal Open Market Committee determine that they cannot or should not be achieved because of changing conditions: *Provided*, that in the subsequent consultations with, and reports to, the aforesaid Committees of the Congress pursuant to this section, the Board of Governors shall include an explanation of the reasons for any revisions to or deviations from such objectives and plans."

It may be argued that this provision stands in the way of any clear commitment of the Board of Governors and/or the FOMC with regard to the conduct of monetary policy. Both the Board of Governors and the FOMC have discretionary power to decide whether their own objectives and plans can and should be achieved under the existing conditions. The Federal Reserve Act does not specify in any way the circumstances in which such a deviation from the self-proclaimed targets would be justified.[185] Even if the Board of Governors has to

---

[184] Memorandum submitted by the United States Federal Reserve System, in Treasury and Civil Service Committee, *The Role of the Bank of England* (House of Commons Paper. Session 1993–4; 98–I, vol. 2), Report, together with the proceedings of the Committee, HC Session 1993–4 (HMSO, London, 1993), app. 20.

[185] Different e.g. from the Reserve Bank of New Zealand; cf. Chap. 4 II 3.

justify its deviation from the objectives and plans in reports to and consultations with the congressional Banking Committees it may not actually stop the Fed from changing its own objectives and plans in due course because it can always exculpate itself by stating the reasons for doing so. The Federal Reserve Act falls short of providing for a sufficient yardstick which the Congress can apply in order to judge whether the Fed's action was justified. Adding to the difficulties of the broadly defined monetary objectives of the Fed are recently raised doubts about the usefulness of the only guidelines for the implementation of monetary policy which the Federal Reserve Act does provide.[186] Besides, it seems that Congress has shown little interest in the past in the announcement of these targets.[187]

Despite numerous proposals over the years both in Congress and in academic circles to change the Federal Reserve Act in order more closely to define the monetary objective or to reduce it to a single objective, nothing has changed.[188] Even the Fed seems to be in favour of a single monetary policy objective.[189] The key to an answer to the question why no such reforms has ever passed Congress may lay in the relationship between Congress and the Fed.[190]

The monetary objective of the **Nederlandsche Bank** is similarly broadly defined as that of the Fed. According to section 9(1) of the Bank Act 1948:

> "It shall be the duty of the Bank to regulate the value of the Netherlands monetary unit in such a manner as will be most conducive to the nation's prosperity and welfare, and in doing so seek to keep the value as stable as possible."

The formulation of the statutory objective of the Nederlandsche Bank in section 9(1) of the Bank Act 1948 emerges as somewhat vague. By only referring to the "value of the Netherlands monetary unit" the provision falls short of distinguishing between the internal and the external value of the currency, that is between price stability and the exchange-rate. Furthermore, section 9(1) does not offer any concrete guidelines for the conduct of the monetary objective,

---

[186] E.g. testimony of Alan Greenspan, Chairman, Federal Reserve Board, 22 July 1997 (pursuant to the Full Employment and Balanced Growth Act of 1978). The limited practical implications of these aggregates for the monetary policy pursued by the Fed was confirmed by Fed officials.

[187] This view was taken by Fed officials. For more details on the relationship between Congress and the Fed; cf. Chap. 4 VI 1.

[188] For a overview of the congressional activities in this field in the period 1979–1990 cf. Akhtar/Howe, n. 131 above. More recent examples of Bills introduced in Congress include S.1266 of 22 Sept. 1995 and HR 1498 of 29 Sept. 1995 both of which propose to oblige the Board of Governors of the Federal Reserve System to focus on price stability in establishing monetary policy to ensure the stable, long-term purchasing power of the currency.

[189] E.g. Statement by J.L. Jordan, President of the Federal Reserve Bank of Cleveland before the Committee on Banking, Finance and Urban Affairs, US House of Representatives, 19 Oct. 1993, reprinted in *Federal Reserve Bulletin*, vol. 79 no. 12 (Dec. 1993), 1110–20, at 1119, stating that "the Congress could best contribute to a classification of the FOMC's policy direction . . . [by specifying] . . . an ultimate goal of achieving the highest sustainable rate of real economic growth through the maintenance of purchasing power stability".

[190] For more details cf. Chap. 4 VI.

except for stating that the Bank must pursue the objective "in such a manner as will be most conducive to the *nation's prosperity and welfare*",[191] while attempting "to keep the value as stable as possible". It emerges from the explanatory statements to the draft Bank Act 1948 (*memorie van toelichting*) that it was in fact the intention of the legislator at the time of the drafting of the Bank Act 1948 to formulate the monetary objective of the Nederlandsche Bank in an open manner. While referring to the diverging theories on the directions of monetary policy, the reference to the "nation's prosperity and welfare" was thought to constitute the only feasible guideline for the Bank at the time. In this context the explanatory statements leave no doubt about who was envisaged to be in charge of defining this guideline. It was explained that the openness of the monetary objective did not amount to a permit for the Nederlandsche Bank to determine monetary policy, but rather that the decision on concrete measures in the area of monetary policy was the responsibility of the executive government, and that this consideration was reflected in the right of the Minister of Finance to issue directions to the Bank under section 26 of the Bank Act 1948.[192] In modern terms the Bank was supposed to have instrumental, but not goal, independence with the government retaining full responsibility for the formulation of monetary policy.[193] Section 9(1) of the Bank Act 1948 has been identified as one of the foundations of the independence of the Nederlandsche Bank. It has been argued that the last half sentence of section 9(1), i.e. "and in doing so seek to keep the value as stable as possible", is essential, as it provides the Bank with its own policy responsibility (*beleidsverantwoordelijkheid*) which forms the basis of the independence of the Nederlandsche Bank.[194]

The monetary objective of the Nederlandsche Bank becomes anything but clear from the Bank Act 1948. The relationship between the reference to the "nation's prosperity and welfare" and the stability of the monetary unit is ambiguous, to say the least. It could even be concluded that the wording of section 9(1) supports the view that the stable value of the monetary unit is not the primary goal in itself, but rather is supposed to be observed in the course of regulating the monetary unit "in such a manner as will be most conducive to the nation's prosperity and welfare". In other words it could be stated that the prosperity and welfare of the nation rather than price stability are the underlying objectives of the Nederlandsche Bank.

What appears to be a rather vague objective in theory is commonly interpreted as being directed towards the management of both the internal and external value of the Dutch Guilder. Since the Netherlands is a relatively small and open economy more weight lies on exchange rate stabilisation (so-called *kleine monetaire beleid*). The Bank is not entirely free in its conduct of the

---

[191] Emphasis added.

[192] Cf. A.M. De Jong, op. cit., Chap. 3, n. 262, 409 *et seq.*; also Chap. 4 V 3.

[193] On the terminology cf. Chap. 2 I.

[194] W. Eizenga, "Uit de Bibliotheek—Geschiedenis van de Nederlandsche Bank", *Bank- en Effectenbedrijf*, vol. 44 no. 3 (1995), 16–18, at 18.

exchange rate. In fact, on the basis of the Dutch Guilder Exchange Rate Act 1978 (*Wet inzake de wisselkoers van de gulden*) the decision regarding participation in exchange rate arrangements and parity changes lies effectively with the Minister of Finance, having received the consent of the Council of Ministers and having consulted the Governing Board of the Nederlandsche Bank.[195] Decisions have to be forwarded to both chambers of Parliament together with the opinion of the Nederlandsche Bank. The decision is published in the two Dutch Government Gazettes (Nederlands Staatsblad and Nederlandse Staatscourant). Under the Dutch Guilder Exchange Rate Act 1978 the Nederlandsche Bank is also obliged to provide the Minister of Finance with the information necessary for the determination of the exchange rate regime.[196] The responsibility of the executive government for the exchange rate policy may result in conflicts with the Nederlandsche Bank. In 1983 an open conflict arose with regard to the devaluation of 2 per cent of the Dutch Guilder *vis-à-vis* the Dmark. The Nederlandsche Bank openly advised against it, but the Minister of Finance decided against the Bank. As has been pointed out, the Netherlands participate in the EMS and the ERM as its centrepiece since 1979. Here, the normal fluctuation margins between the participating Member States' currencies in relation to the central rate (ECU) have to be observed.[197] At the same time, since 1983, the Nederlandsche Bank has pursued a stable exchange rate of the Dutch Guilder *vis-à-vis* the German Dmark on the basis of the good track record of German inflation performance and the importance of Germany as a trading partner. For this reason the actual margins between the Guilder and the Dmark are kept well within those provided for by the ERM. The Nederlandsche Bank does not consider currency interventions to be the ideal instrument for exchange rate stabilisation, as frequent interventions are considered to cause uncertainties in the financial markets. It is for this reason that the interest rate on the money market (*geldmarktrente*) is considered to be the more important instrument for the management of the exchange rate. The external stability of the Guilder is achieved by raising or lowering the interest rate when the Guilder exchange rate comes under pressure or becomes very strong, thereby influencing foreign investment in the Dutch currency. Since the Guilder is linked to the Dmark, the Nederlandsche Bank orientates itself strongly towards the decisions on the key interest rates of the Bundesbank, arguably with little margin for real autonomous decisions. Until recently, the Nederlandsche Bank also targeted the internal value of the Guilder (so-called *grote monetaire beleid*) indirectly through intermediate monetary targets in the form of the growth rate of the money aggregate. In this context the Act on the Supervision of the Credit System provides the Nederlandsche Bank with the instruments for a monetary supervision of the commercial banks with regard to the possibility of the latter to render credit facilities.

[195]   Wet van 25 mei 1978, Stb. 332, inzake de wisselkoersen van de gulden, s. 2.
[196]   Ibid., s. 5.
[197]   Cf. Chap. 3 V 1.3.

In summary, the Bank Act 1948 does not provide the Nederlandsche Bank with a clear monetary objective. Although section 9(1) is effectively interpreted as referring to the stabilisation of the internal and external value of the Dutch Guilder, this falls short of providing a clear yardstick for the evaluation of the conduct of monetary policy by the Bank. First, because it derives from the genesis of section 9(1) of the Bank Act 1948 that the interpretation of the monetary objective of the Bank applied today is not imperative.[198] In the context of qualification for the ESCB the European Monetary Institute has observed that the statute of the Nederlandsche Bank "does not unambiguously reflect the primacy of maintaining price stability".[199] In the new Bank Act 1998 it has been replaced by the explicit objective to maintain price stability.[200]

Like the Nederlandsche Bank the monetary objective of the **Bundesbank** does not become entirely clear from its legal basis. According to § 3 BBankG:

> "The Deutsche Bundesbank shall regulate the amount of money in circulation and of credit supplied to the economy, using the monetary powers conferred on it by this act with the aim of *safeguarding the currency*, and shall arrange for the handling by banks of money of domestic and external payments."[201]

The scope of this provision in particular with respect to the interpretation of the term "to safeguard the currency" is far from clear. It has been argued that § 3 has to be interpreted to the effect that the task of the Bundesbank is to guide or at least influence money growth in such a way that creditory and monetary causes of undesired development of prices which has its effects in inflation or deflation are prevented or removed.[202] Simply put, the majority opinion interprets the monetary objective of the Bundesbank with maintaining the value of the currency, i.e. price stability.[203] It may be argued that the recently introduced second sentence of Article 88 of the Basic Law which expressly makes price stability as the primary monetary objective a precondition for the transfer of authority over monetary policy to an ESCB and an ECB confirms this interpretation, as this reference may be taken as a hint that price stability is also

---

[198] In this context H.H. van Wijk, op. cit., Chap. 2, n. 138, at 57, points out that the currency can be stabilised using different yardsticks.

[199] European Monetary Institute, *Progress Towards Convergence 1996* (EMI Frankfurt a.M., 1996), at 132.

[200] Cf. s. 2 Bank Act 1998.

[201] Translation provided by E. Grabitz, "The Deutsche Bundesbank, Answers to the Questionnaire on Key functions and Legal Structure of Central Banks and Banking Supervision Authorities" in *Vers un Systeme Europeen de Banques Centrales*, Rapport du groupe présidé par Jean-Victor Louis (Editions de l'Université de Bruxelles, Brussels, 1989), 161–70, emphasis added.

[202] J. Siebelt, *Der juristische Verhaltensspielraum der Zentralbanken* (Nomos, Baden-Baden, 1988), at 158, with further references.

[203] Hahn, n. 36 above, 36 *et seq.*; also Deutsche Bundesbank, op. cit., Chap. 3, n. 214, at 24, which refers to "overall price level stability" (*Preisniveaustabilität*). According to R. Schmidt, "Grundlagen und Grenzen der Unabhängigkeit der Deutschen Bundesbank", in E. v.Caemmerer *et al.* (eds.), *Festschrift für Pan J. Zapos*, Vol. II (Ch. Katsikalis Verlag, Athens, 1973), 655–80, at 661, the term "to safeguard the currency" includes the internal and external value of the currency.

considered to be the pre-eminent monetary objective in the national context. This view is also somewhat backed by the remarks of the German Federal Constitutional Court in the *Brunner* decision observed above.[204] The BBankG does not define the monetary objective of the Bundesbank in any detail. In particular the monetary objective stated in § 3 BBankG cannot be interpreted to exclude any inflation above zero per cent, or even to set upper limits for inflation.[205] Moreover, no other rules in the form of guidelines or agreements between the Bundesbank and the Federal government exist. Fischer criticises the broadness of the monetary policy objective by arguing that the danger of such an objective is that there might be "little to prevent [the central bank] from pursuing a socially excessive anti-inflationary policy".[206] The Bundesbank itself applies intermediate targets. Since 1974 for each year intermediate targets for the growth of central bank money, and from 1988 growth in M3, have been announced.[207] The discretion which the Bundesbank allows itself in meeting these targets is considerable, not least due to the fact that since 1979 a target range rather than a point target is employed.[208] It each year it also announces whether it aims for the upper or lower half of the target range. Indeed, as Mishkin and Posen observe, for the Bundesbank itself situations are foreseeable "where it would consciously allow deviations from the announced target path to occur in order to support other economic objectives".[209] If one considers the monetary target of the Bundesbank as the best way to judge the performance of the Bundesbank, as Maier and de Haan do, the track record of the Bank is astonishingly bad, as the bank hit its targets only about 50 per cent of the time.[210] Indeed, the method of determining the target growth rate for M3 may also provide evidence that the Bundesbank favours flexibility over a clear commitment. Rather than publishing an estimate for the growth of long run production, the Bank estimates the *potential* for growth in the course of the forthcoming year. Moreover, the Bank uses a "medium-term price assumption" in order to take

---

[204] Cf. Chap. 4 I 3.

[205] L. Gramlich, *Bundesbankgesetz Währungsgesetz Münzgesetz* (Carl Heymanns Verlag KG, Cologne, 1988), § 3, side notation 17.

[206] S. Fischer, op. cit., Chap. 2, n. 39, at 293. R. Vaubel, "Eine Public-Choice-Analyse der Deutschen Bundesbank und ihre Implikationen für die Europäische Wirtschaftsunion" in D. Duwendag/J. Siebke (eds.), *Europa vor dem Eintritt in die Wirtschafts- und Währungsunion* (Duncker & Humblot, Berlin, 1993), 28 *et seq.*, criticises the absence of any rule providing an incentive to attain a target, and which imposes sanctions in case that the target is missed.

[207] With regard to the main differences cf. F.S. Mishkin/A. Posen, op. cit., Chap. 2, n. 159, at 23. M3 is made up of notes and coins in currency in circulation, sight deposits, time deposits, time deposits of less than 4 years, and savings deposits at statutory notice.

[208] It is therefore not entirely correct when Schmidt, n. 203 above, at 676, observes that the Bundesbank cannot become active with regard to its monetary objective since it is determined by the legislator. For 1997 the target range announced by the Bundesbank was between 3 and 6% of M3, for 1998 it was 5%.

[209] Mishkin/Posen, n. 207 above, at 24.

[210] P.Maier/J.de Haan, "How Independent is the Bundesbank Really?" a survey, forthcoming in: J. De Haan (ed.), *50 Years of Bundesbank: Lessons for the ECB* (Routledge, London), who emphasise that this is a sign that the Bundesbank *de facto* takes other economic variables into account in the course of the year.

inflation into account. The problems in the light of the democratic accountability of the Bundesbank involved with this is that the Bank leaves itself much space for finding justifications for short-term economic performance. Besides, the fact that the Bundesbank explains and justifies the self-determined intermediate targets to the general public does not by itself ensure the democratic accountability of the Bundesbank.

It has been pointed out that "to safeguard the currency" refers both to the internal and external value of the currency. However, the Bundesbank is restricted in the framework of any exchange rate systems in which Germany participates. This is the case with the EMS in which Germany participates since the establishment of the system in 1979. In the framework of the ERM the Bundesbank is obliged to intervene in foreign exchange markets in accordance with the parities agreed upon by the Federal government and the foreign governments participating in the exchange rate mechanism. In as much as the Federal government has the right to realign the exchange rate parities in such an exchange rate system it sets conditions for the monetary policy of the Bundesbank with regard to the external value of the currency.[211] Yet, since the Dmark can be considered as the anchor currency in the EMS, the Bundesbank is hardly restrained by this right of the executive government. Only where such an exchange rate system does not exist, that is with regard to free floating currencies, does the Bundesbank conduct foreign exchange operations aiming at stabilising the value of the currency free from government regulation.[212]

Apart from the fact that the monetary objective "to secure the currency" is far from self-explanatory, it is, moreover, not the sole objective of the Bundesbank since according to § 12 sentence 1 of the BBankG:

> "*Without prejudice to the performance of its functions*, the Deutsche Bundesbank shall be required to support the general economic policy of the Federal government."[213]

In principle the economic policies of the Federal government are defined by the four macroeconomic goals (*gesamtwirtschaftliche Ziele*), which are introduced by Article 109 II of the Basic Law and § 1 of the Act of 1967 on stability and economic expansion (*Stabilitätsgesetz*).[214] Apart from price stability they also include the goals of a high rate of employment, foreign trade equilibrium, and steady and adequate economic growth. In the light of a possible conflict of goals between the Bundesbank's independence from government with respect to monetary policies, on the one hand, and the obligation to support government economic policies, on the other hand, the question arises to what extent § 12 of the

---

[211] Galahn, n. 53 above, at 193, argues that this power of the executive government may not infringe the function of the Bundesbank as a currency bank as stated in Art. 88, sentence 1, Basic Law.

[212] Deutsche Bundesbank, n. 203 above, at 26.

[213] English translation as provided in L.W. Gormley/J. de Haan, op. cit., Chap. 2, n. 106; emphasis added. For more details of the second sentence of § 12 cf. Chap. 4 III.

[214] Gesetz zur Förderung der Stabilität und des Wachstums der Wirtschaft of 8 June 1967, BGBl. I, 582.

BBankG provides for a hierarchy between the obligation of the Bundesbank to support the Federal government and its functional independence. By stating that the Bundesbank is required to support the Federal government *without* prejudice to its functions § 12, sentence 1, of the BBankG establishes such a hierarchy. The functions of the Bundesbank are laid down in § 3 of the BBankG and, as has been observed, are effectively interpreted as maintaining price stability.[215] Thus, the Bundesbank may support the economic policy of the Federal government only if it does not conflict with the objective of price stability. To this end it has been argued that the Bundesbank's obligation to support government policies ends where the Bank cannot at the same time fulfil its obligations under § 3 of the BBankG.[216] Similarly, it has been argued that the emphasis of § 3 of the BBankG on the protection of the currency is supposed to rule out any dominance by the other macro-economic goals.[217] Thus, while the primary goal of the Bundesbank is to safeguard the currency, it does have to give consideration to the economic policies of the Federal government in accordance with the goals set out in § 1 of the Act of 1967 on stability and economic expansion. Without guidelines the Bundesbank has considerable discretion in determining to what extent it considers supporting the Federal government compatible with its tasks. Mechanisms in the case of a conflict between the Bundesbank and the Federal government on the interpretation of the tasks of the former or its obligation under § 1 of the Act of 1967 on stability and economic expansion are not foreseen. The lack of such a mechanism has been described as a concise choice of the drafters of the BBankG, leaving it to Parliament to settle a conflict through an amendment of the legal basis of the Bundesbank.[218]

Nevertheless, the somewhat vague description of the monetary objective of the Bundesbank, together with the obligation of the Bundesbank to support the economic policies of the Federal government, have also led some to believe that "to safeguard the currency", or effectively price stability, may not even be the primary objective of the Bundesbank. Price stability does not take precedence over the other economic goals but rather the Bundesbank has to strike a balance between the different goals.[219] In this context it has been argued that the Bundesbank is subject to the provision of §13 III of the Act of 1967 on stability and economic expansion, according to which the immediate Federal (*bundesunmittelbar*) public-law corporations (*Körperschaften*), public law institutions (*Anstalten*), and foundations under public law (*Stiftungen*) have to observe the goals of § 1 of the Act of 1967 on stability and economic expansion. Others view

---

[215] Critical are J.v. Spindler/W. Becker/O.-E. Starke, *Die Deutsche Bundesbank* (4th edn., Verlag W. Kohlhammer, Stuttgart, 1973), § 12, 258–9.

[216] L. Gramlich, op. cit., Chap. 3, n. 185, at L 83.

[217] E.g. Th. Werres, "The Deutsche Bundesbank and its relationship with the Federal Government", in *Europe's Economy in the 1990s* (AGENOR Research Unit's European Research Project on Autonomy Phase I, 1989–90, Vol. II, Brussels, 1989), at 13.

[218] D. Uhlenbruck, op. cit., Chap. 3, n. 185, 67 *et seq.*

[219] W. Frotscher, *Wirtschaftsverfassungs- und Wirtschaftsverwaltungsrecht* (C.H. Beck, Munich, 1988), at 70, with further references.

the independence of the Bundesbank as being principally limited in its scope, since it is the task of the Federal government to decide which of the four goals listed in § 1 of the Act of 1967 on stability and economic expansion takes precedence, whereas the independence of the Bundesbank is limited to the implementation of that goal with the instruments at its proposal. Faber refers to a plan-limited autonomy (*plangebundenen Autonomie*).[220] However, both systematic and historical arguments are put forward against this opinion and in favour of the view that the objective of the Bundesbank is directed towards the regulation of the amount of money in circulation, as stated in § 3 of the BBankG, and thus not at the macro-economic equilibrium (*gesamtwirtschaftliches Gleichgewicht*).[221] It can be in particular observed that § 13 III of the Act of 1967 on stability and economic expansion does not introduce an unconditional obligation for immediate Federal legal persons under public law to observe the economic goals set out in § 1 of the Act of 1967 on stability and economic expansion, but rather states that these institutions have to observe these goals in the framework of their tasks.[222] An interpretation to the contrary would also run contrary to § 12 of the BBankG.[223]

It should be noted that as at 1 January 1999, a new provision on the monetary policy objective of the Bundesbank has applied, stating that the Bundesbank forms an integral part of the ESCB and that it fulfils its tasks primarily with the goal to safeguard price stability.[224]

2. Central banks with a primary monetary objective

In the case of the Banque de France and the ECB, the Bank Act 1993 and the EC Treaty and the ESCB Statute, respectively, introduce multiple objectives, but at the same time establish a hierarchy between them. In both cases the primary monetary objective explicitly refers to price stability. However, the legal bases of both banks fail to quantify this objective. Moreover, the primary monetary objective is stated in clear terms. In both cases price stability.

In the case of **France**, according to Article 1(1) of the Bank Act 1993:

"The Bank shall formulate and implement monetary policy with the aim of ensuring price stability. It shall carry out these duties within the framework of the Government's overall economic policy."

This is a clear departure from the regime of the Bank Act 1973, according to which the role of the Bank, as regards monetary policy, was that of an executive

---

[220] H. Faber, *Wirtschaftsplanung und Bundesbankautonomie* (Nomos, Baden-Baden, 1969); H.-J. Arndt, "Von der politischen zur plangebundenen Autonomie" in D. Duwendag (ed.), *Macht und Ohnmacht der Bundesbank* (Athenäum Verlag, Frankfurt a.M., 1973), 15–35. This view has some points in common with the distinction between goal and instrument independence.
[221] Siebelt, n. 202 above, 159–60.
[222] v.Spindler/Becker/Starke, n. 215 above, § 12, at 258.
[223] S. Kümpel, op. cit., Chap. 3, n. 212, at 3. For details on the independence cf. Chap. 4 III.
[224] Cf. revised § 3 BBankG.

organ of the executive government, as the former was constrained to prepare and take part in the implementation of monetary policy that had been decided by the latter with the help of the National Credit Council.[225] In order to provide for an institutional framework for the independent conduct of monetary policy by the Bank, the CPM has been introduced by the Bank Act 1993.[226] Article 7(1) states:

> "The Monetary Policy Council shall be responsible for formulating monetary policy. It shall monitor changes in the money supply and its counterparts."

The objective of price stability is not closer defined in the Bank Act 1993 or any other law. Instead, the Bank itself quantifies the objective of price stability in the framework of the Annual Report, which, by law, has to examine the prospect for monetary policy.[227] In its presentation of the "monetary policy targets for 1998" the Bank states:

> "1. The ultimate objective of monetary policy is, as required by legislation, price stability. *The objective of the Monetary Policy Council is to ensure that the increase in prices, as measured by the consumer price index, does not exceed 2% in 1998 and in the medium term.*
> 2. To meet this ultimate goal, the Banque de France uses two intermediate objectives, one of which is external and the other internal . . . "[228]

A direct targeting of the monetary objective of price stability does not take place. Instead, the final objective is targeted through a number of intermediate monetary policy objectives, including a stable external value of the currency, i.e. the exchange rate, and an internal growth target for the money aggregate.[229] The Banque de France follows the objective of a stable external value of the Franc. Since 1979, the French Franc has participated in the ERM and as part of that mechanism it is the task of the Banque de France to maintain the value of the Franc against the other currencies within the margins of +/−15 per cent from the central rate. Since 1983 France has followed a policy of *franc fort*, whereby the Franc is kept in close margins to the Dmark. Yet, somewhat conflicting with this first intermediate objective, the Bank also maintains that it monitors the money supply trends with a view to prevent excessive growth of money assets

---

[225] Art. 4 Bank Act 1973; J. Bouvier, op. cit., Chap. 3, n. 49, 95 *et seq*. Created under the Banking Act 1984 (Arts. 24 *et seq*.) the Conseil National du Crédit constitutes a consultative body which comprises representatives of different economic groups appointed by the Minister of Economic Affairs and Finances.

[226] G.Iacono, "Le nouveau statut de la Banque de France, une étape vers l'union économique et monétaire", *Recueil Dalloz Sirey* no. 12 (1994), 89–92, at 92, which states that the independence of the Banque de France materialises in the provisions on the CPM.

[227] Cf. Chap. 4 VII 2.

[228] Banque de France, *Monetary Policy Guidelines for 1998* (online), available from URL http://www.banque-france.fr/us/actu/1.htm (last accessed Oct. 1998), emphasis added.

[229] M. Redon/D. Besnard, *La Banque de France* (3e edn., série Que Sais-Je, Presses Universitaires De France, Paris, 1996), 61 *et seq*.

which are positively correlated to inflation.[230] The monetary policy targets for 1998 state in this respect:

> "growth of the money supply will continue to be assessed on the basis of a 5% target compatible with price inflation of no more than 2% and non-inflationary real GDP growth of about 2.5%, which should be exceeded in 1998 in view of the potential for growth to catch up in the medium term."

Whether the self-imposed quantification of the monetary objective, i.e. price inflation of 2 per cent or less, amounts to a legally binding provision is doubtful. But this is not to say that the monetary guidelines cannot in principle function as a yardstick for the evaluation of the performance of the Banque de France by Parliament. Moreover, a certain stringency of the announced targets could derive from the expectations which are created with the general public and in particular the financial markets. A drastic deviation from the guidelines could result in a loss of credibility of the Bank. On the contrary it may be argued that with the discretion it has in determining the inflation target in the first place, the Bank has enough opportunities to ensure it sets a target which leaves enough room for manœuvre. From within the Banque de France the view has been expressed that the target is neither legally binding nor otherwise fixed. Moreover, it could even be argued that the Bank Act 1993 does not give absolute priority to price stability as the result but rather the orientation towards the objective, since Article 1(1), sentence 1 of the Bank Act 1993 refers to implementation "with the aim of ensuring price stability".

It is also questionable whether the reference to the overall economic policy of the government in Article 1(1), sentence 2 of the Bank Act 1993 can be interpreted as additional objectives. Compared to other central bank statutes this provision does not appear at first sight to be exceptional. It has been observed, for instance, that the legal basis of the Bundesbank refers to the general economic policies of the government in the context of the objectives of the Bank. In fact, in the opinion of Duprat Article 1(1), sentence 2, does not amount to more than a reflection of Article 12 of the BBankG.[231] However, a closer examination reveals an important difference. Article 1(1) of the Bank Act 1993 does not provide for a hierarchy of the different incentives, thereby giving price stability priority over the economic policy of the government. This may also be highlighted by a comparison of the wording of Article 1(1) of the Bank Act 1993 with that of § 12, sentence 1 of the BBankG, according to which the Bundesbank is to observe the general economic policies of the Community *without prejudice* to the performance of its functions, in other words only if the monetary policy objective of the Bank is not endangered. On the contrary, Article 1(11) of the Bank Act 1993 states that the Bank carries out it duties on the basis of ("*within*

---

[230] In the case of capital mobility a targeting of both the exchange rate and the money growth is difficult to envisage, since exchange rate operations influence the money stock.

[231] J.-P. Duprat, L'Indépendance de la Banque de France: Aspects Constitutionnels et Européens (Suite et Fin), L.P.A., n. 49, 4–11, at 10.

202 Evaluating the Democratic Accountability of Central Banks

the framework of") the government overall economic policies. Furthermore, the genesis of Article 1(1), sentence 2, gives rise to the view that the provision was in fact intended to restrict the Bank in the conduct of monetary policy, and as such was politically motivated. Against the background of the Constitution of 1958 and the prerogative of the government in the field of economic policy, the provision was included in the Bank Act with a view to averting a possible over-ruling of the rules on the independent conduct of monetary policy by the Constitutional Council.[232] However, it may be recalled that in its ruling on the Bank Act 1993 the Constitutional Council held that Article 1(1), sentence 2 of the Bank Act 1993 in fact did not ensure government authority in the field of eco-nomic policy as required by the constitution at the time of the ruling.[233] The court argued that any restriction of the independent conduct of monetary pol-icy by the Bank is in effect neutralised by Article 1(2) of the Bank Act 1993 on the independent status of the organs of the Bank.[234] Although, subsequently, with the coming into effect of Article 88 of the Constitution of 1958, the ruling of the Constitutional Council on the unconstitutionality of the transfer of pow-ers in the field of monetary policy to the Bank has become obsolete, the inter-pretation of Article 1(1), sentence 2 of the Bank Act 1993 remains valid. This correlates with the opinion of the Banque de France itself, which has made it clear that it does not understand the reference to the economic policy of the gov-ernment as a restriction of its independence in the field of monetary policy.[235] Still, the Constitutional Council has merely provided a negative definition of Article 1(1), sentence 2, that is to say what it does not constitute, while falling short of spelling out its significance. One—narrow—interpretation may be that the intention behind the reference to the government's overall economic policy is to emphasise the indivisibility of monetary and economic policy, and to facil-itate a process of communication between the Bank and the Government. If the view is taken that the reference to Article 1(1), sentence 2, does not restrict the Bank in the independent formulation and implementation of monetary policy, the reference to the economic policy of the government may only be interpreted as a secondary objective. As such it is not defined by the Bank Act 1993, but rather is determined by the government in accordance with Article 20 of the Constitution of 1958. Nevertheless it seemed unlikely that Article 1(1), sentence 2 of the Bank Act 1993 could remain in effect once France entered stage three of EMU, as a rigid interpretation demanding the subordination of monetary pol-icy under the general economic policy of the government would undoubtedly stand in the way of Articles 107 and 108 EC and the requirement of the func-tional independence of the national central banks.[236]

---

[232] J.-P. Duprat, "L'Indépendance de la Banque de France: Aspects Constitutionnels et Européens (1ère Partie)", *LPA* no. 47 (1994), 4–10, at 8.

[233] Décision no. 93–324 DC; P. Collas, op. cit., Chap. 3, n. 36, 596 *et seq.*

[234] For more details of Art. 1(2) Bank Act 1993 cf. Chap. 4 III.

[235] Banque de France, op. cit., Chap. 3, n. 67, at 6.

[236] Cf. European Monetary Institute, n. 199 above, 98 *et seq.*

With regard to exchange rate policy Article 2(1) of the Bank Act 1993 confers the power to determine the exchange rate regime and the parity of the French Franc upon the government. On behalf of the executive government, the Minister of Economic Affairs and Finances determines the guidelines of exchange rate policy on the basis of which the Bank implements the concrete rules for the exchange rates. As can be observed in the context of other central bank systems, the government retains the power in the field of exchange rates.

In the revised statute of the Bank, applicable from 1 January 1999, the objective is described as complying with the objectives conferred upon the ESCB by the EC Treaty and within this framework, and without prejudice to the primary objective of price stability, to support the general economic policy of the (French) Government.[237]

As with the Banque de France, the primary objective of the **ECB** is to maintain price stability. Article 105(1), sentence 1, EC states to this end:

"The primary objective of the ESCB is to maintain price stability."[238]

This objective can be found as a guiding principle in provisions on EMU throughout the EC Treaty and the Protocols. It is referred to—indirectly—in the general provision of Article 2 EC on the tasks of the Community, where reference is made to "non-inflationary growth". In Article 3a(2) EC on the tasks of the Community in the EMU price stability is defined as the primary objective for a single monetary and exchange-rate policy in the EU and Article 3a(3) EC defines "stable prices" as one of the "guiding principles" in the activities of the Member States and the Community. Moreover, the achievement of a high degree of price stability is one of the four major convergence criteria implemented in Article 109j(1) EC, which the Member States have to fulfil in order to participate in stage three of EMU. Despite the fact that the legal basis of the ECB, unlike that of the Bundesbank, unambiguously declares price stability to be the primary objective, the mandate of the ESCB has already been criticised for being too vague to make the ECB adequately accountable for its conduct of monetary policy.[239] Indeed, neither the EC Treaty nor the ESCB Statute quantifies the monetary objective of the ECB through the introduction of an inflation target or target range, nor is the determination of such targets through the Council, or in an agreement with the ECB, foreseen. It is left to the Governing Council of the ECB to decide on the operational framework for monetary policy. Already in 1997, the EMI had published two reports outlining the operational aspects of the ESCB's monetary policy and in particular the instruments and procedures applied by the ECB.[240] With regard to monetary policy strategies the first report of the EMI outlines the available options. Two of the

---

[237] Art. 1(1) and (2) Banque de France Act 1998.
[238] Cf. also Art. 2 ESCB Statute.
[239] I. Harden, op. cit., Chap. 2, n. 89, at 14; Ch. Goodhart, op. cit., Chap. 2, n. 155, at 4.
[240] European Monetary Institute, op. cit., Chap. 3, n. 412.

key elements of a monetary policy strategy of the ECB referred to in the report are:

> — "the public announcement of a quantified definition of the final objective of price stability in order to enhance the transparency and credibility of the ESCB's strategy;"
> —"the public announcement of a specific target (or targets) against which the performance of the ESCB can be assessed on an ongoing basis by the general public, thereby enhancing accountability . . . "[241]

The EMI emphasises in its report that "[T]he strategy has to enable the ESCB to meet its final objective over the medium term, thereby providing an anchor for inflation expectations, but nevertheless providing the ESCB with some discretion in response to short-term deviations from the target".[242] Both monetary targeting, an approach e.g. taken by the Bundesbank, and direct inflation targeting, an approach e.g. taken by the Bank of England, have been identified as strategies which may in principle be adopted by the ECB. In October 1998 the Governing Council of the ECB agreed that price stability is defined as a year-on-year increase in the so-called Harmonised Index of Consumer Prices (HICP) for the Euro area of below 2%, whereby price stability is to be maintained over the medium term, thereby leaving room for temporary distortions triggered by short-term factors.

The second sentence of Article 105(1) EC and of Article 2 of the ESCB Statute provide for what effectively amounts to a secondary objectives of the ESCB and the ECB.[243] According to the identical wording of the two provisions:

> "[W]ithout prejudice to the objective of price stability, it [the ESCB] shall support the general economic policies in the Community with a view to contribute to the achievement of the objectives of the Community as laid down in Article 2 of this Treaty. The ESCB shall act in accordance with the principle of an open market economy with free competition, favouring an efficient allocation of resources, and in compliance with the principles set out in Article 3a of this Treaty."[244]

The objectives of the Community defined in Article 2 EC include—*inter alia*— the "promotion throughout the Community of a harmonious and balanced development of economic activities, sustainable and non-inflationary growth respecting the environment, a high degree of convergence of economic performance, a high level of employment and of social protection, the raising of standard of living and quality of life, and economic and social cohesion and

[241] European Monetary Institute, at 10 and Annex 2.

[242] Ibid., at 7. Cf. also W.F. Duisenberg, The ESCB's stability-oriented monetary policy strategy, speech held on 7 Dec. 1998 in Paris, available from URL http:\\www.ecb.int.key/sp981207en.htm [last accessed Jan. 1999].

[243] Gormley/de Haan, n. 213 above, at 101, on the one hand emphasise that no objective other than price stability is expressly stated, while shortly thereafter stating that "these additional objectives *can be seen* as secondary" (emphasis added). Although it may be true in a *literal* sense that the EC Treaty does not embody secondary objectives, since both the Treaty and the ESCB Statute refer only to a primary objective, there cannot be any misunderstanding about the nature of these additional aims as objectives in a *technical* sense.

[244] Cf. P.B. Kenen, op. cit., Chap. 3, n. 426, 457 *et seq.*, n. 12, who points out the small, but important differences between the Treaty text and the Committee of Governors draft with regard to the scope of economic policy.

solidarity among Member States". Finally, the second sentence of Article 105(1) EC sets out underlying principles which the ECB ought to observe. In Article 3a EC on the activities of the Member States and the Community for the purposes of Article 2 EC, emphasis is once more placed on the principle of an open market economy with free competition. The motive behind the inclusion of these guiding principles may be to ensure that the conduct of monetary policy by the ECB does not disturb the common market both economically and financially.[245] Analogous to the legal basis of the Bundesbank, but even more clearly, the second sentence of Article 105(1) EC introduces a clear hierarchy between the objective of price stability and the general economic policies of the Communities. Yet certain powers of the Council in the field of exchange rate policy foreseen by the EC Treaty have been described as having the potential of running contrary to the primary objective of the ECB, and may *de facto* outweigh the primary objective of price stability. According to the second sentence of Article 109(1) EC:

> "[T]he Council may, acting unanimously on a recommendation from the ECB or from the Commission, and *after consulting the ECB in an endeavour to reach a consensus consistent with the objective of price stability*, after consulting the European Parliament, in accordance with the procedure in paragraph 3 for determining the arrangements, *conclude formal agreements on an exchange rate system for the ECU in relation to non-Community currencies.*"[246]

Additionally, according to Article 109(1), 3rd sentence, EC:

> "[T]he Council may, acting by a qualified majority on a recommendation from the ECB or from the Commission, and *after consulting the ECB in an endeavour to reach a consensus consistent with the objective of price stability, adopt, adjust or abandon the central rates of the ECU within the exchange rate system.*"[247]

From the wording of these two provisions it becomes clear that the Council can decide to establish an exchange rate mechanism and/or to adopt, adjust or abandon the central rates of the Euro in such an exchange rate system, even though such measures may *not* be consistent with the objective of price stability, as long as the Council has "endeavoured to reach a consensus".[248] Article 109(1) EC leaves it to the discretion of the Council to decide what it considers to be sufficient endeavours in a concrete case. Therefore, a situation becomes conceivable in which a measure by the Council proves to be an *actus contrarius* to the efforts of the ECB to maintain price stability and thus, to run counter to dominating objective of EMU. The ECB has only a right to be consulted. It does not derive from the wording that its

---

[245] Louis, n. 57 above, at 18.

[246] Emphasis added. For Dehousse, in V. Constantinesco/R. Kovar/R. Simon, *Traité sur l'Union Européenne (signé à Maastricht le 7 février 1992): commentaire article par article* (Economica, Paris, 1995), on Art. 109 EC, the reference in the EC Treaty to both the internal and external exchange rates amounts to a fundamental contradiction with the primary objective of the ESCB.

[247] Emphasis added.

[248] This provision is similarly vague in other official languages: "*en vue de parvenir à un consensus compatible avec l'objectif de la stabilité des prix.*"; "*in dem Bemühen, zu einem mit dem Ziel der Preisstabilität im Einklang stehenden Konsens zu gelangen.*"

consent is needed. Indeed, Article 109(1) EC with respect to the role of the ECB is vague, since the word "consulting" seems to refer to a scenario where the ECB gives only an advice, whereas the expression "to reach a consensus" by itself seems to imply that a conforming advice of the ECB is needed.[249] It has to be presumed, however, that the ECB cannot object to the Council's decisions, even if they are contrary to its primary objective. Interestingly, while the Council can formulate general orientations for exchange rate policy in relation to non-Community currencies in the absence of an exchange rate mechanism, i.e. in a world of floating exchange rates, these general orientations—unlike the above mentioned actions in the field of exchange rate policy—may not infringe the primary objective to maintain price stability.[250] Thus, actions by the Council have to take fully into account the primary objective of the ECB.[251]

With respect to the independence of the ECB, it may be argued that the powers of the Council under Article 109(1) EC have a restrictive effect on the ECB in the field of monetary policy.[252] It is generally within the discretion of the ECB to decide whether to intervene on foreign exchange markets. Thus, where the Council takes decisions relating to the exchange rate market by adopting, adjusting or abandoning the central rates of the Euro within the exchange rate system, the exchange rate management is taken away from the ECB. This has consequences for the conduct of monetary policy as well, since interventions on foreign exchange markets can affect the money supply.[253] Consequently, it could be argued that where the Council makes use of its rights reserved under Article 109(1) EC thereby—to some extent—modelling monetary policy, the ECB is restricted in the independent performance of its basic task, that is to define and implement the monetary policy of the Community based on the objective of price stability.[254] However, both a theoretical and a practical argument can be brought against this argument. First, from the practical point of view it may be observed that this restriction would only become relevant if the Council were to decide on participation in a fixed exchange-rate system, similar to the Bretton Woods System, including one or more currencies of countries outside the EU. The prospect of such a development, for the time being, is rather small. Yet, where such an exchange rate system does not exist, the Council may only formulate "general guidelines for exchange-rate policy *vis-à-vis* non-Member States' currencies" in a way which does not infringe the primary objec-

---

[249] Dehousse, n. 246 above, on Art. 109 EC.

[250] Art. 109(2) EC.

[251] Sceptical are M. Deane/R. Pringle, op. cit., Chap. 2, n. 115, at 334, who wonder who will judge whether the general orientations are in line with the primary objective.

[252] Cf. Goodhart, n. 239 above, at 5, on the relationship between exchange rate policy and monetary policy states that the arrangements with respect to the external financial relationships and the requirement of the ECB to hold inflation down is "simply inconsistent".

[253] Kenen, n. 244 above, at 466.

[254] Cf. Art. 105(2) EC, Art. 3 ESCB Statute on the basic tasks of the ECB; Art. 17 *et seq.* ESCB Statute on the monetary functions and operations of the ESCB and the ECB. Dehousse, n. 246 above, on Art. 109 EC finds that "le premier problème posé par la politique de change tient à sa compatibilité avec l'indépendance du SEBC".

tive of the ESCB.[255] From a more theoretical point of view it may be observed that the argument that Article 109(1) EC may result in the restriction of the independence of the ECB is only tenable to the extent to which monetary policy is an *exclusive competence* of the ESCB and the ECB. According to Article 105(2) EC, and Article 3(1) of the Statute, it shall be a basic task of the ESCB to define and implement monetary policy of the Community. At the same time it is to conduct foreign exchange operations consistent with the provision of Article 109 EC. It derives from this wording of Article 105(2) EC and Article 3.1 of the ESCB Statute that competence in the field of exchange rate policy is twofold. Whereas the Council has competence under Article 109 EC to determine the general guidelines of exchange rate operations, through either the conclusion of formal agreements or the formulation of general orientations for exchange rate policy, the ESCB and the ECB have competence to execute exchange rate operations within those margins. It becomes clear from this that whereas the task "to define and implement the monetary policy of the Community" refers to the *internal* monetary policy of the Community, "foreign exchange rate operations" refer to the *external* monetary policy of the Community. Therefore, in the field of external monetary policy, the power of the ESCB and the ECB is limited in scope.[256] It is up to the Council to define the broad guidelines of the external monetary policy. Consequently, it could be argued that Article 109(1) EC does not result in the restriction of the functional independence of the ECB, since the ESCB and the ECB have no competence in the determination of the broad guidelines of the external monetary policy. In fact, their only involvement is their right to be consulted. However, such a conclusion would only be defensible if the exclusive competence of the Council under Article 109 EC were of no consequence for the functioning of the ECB in the framework of its exclusive competence. On the one hand, the competence of the Council to adopt, adjust or abandon the Euro central rates has consequences for the internal monetary policy, since, as has been observed elsewhere, actions by the Council under Article 109 EC have consequences for the primary objective of price stability. If the maintenance of price stability is recognised as the primary objective of the monetary policy of the Community, the Council intervenes in the internal monetary policy, which is within the exclusive competence of the ESCB and the ECB, when taking actions in accordance with Article 109 EC which are not consistent with the objective of price stability.

3. Central banks with a statutorily quantified monetary objective

The legal basis of the Reserve Bank of New Zealand includes a single monetary objective which is furthermore quantified through a formal agreement between

---

[255] Art. 109(2) EC.

[256] P.J.G. Kapteyn/P. VerLoren van Themaat/L.A. Geelhoed/C.W.A. Timmermans (eds.), op. cit., Chap. 3, n. 408, at 586, point out that Art. 109(1) sentence 2, EC constituted a compromise between the somewhat contradictory approaches to monetary policy of Germany and France with regard to state interventions at the time of the drafting of the TEU.

the New Zealand Minister of Finance and the governor of the Reserve Bank. Since 1992 in the UK a system of government-announced inflation targets had been in operation. Not least against the background of the institutional arrangements at the Reserve Bank of New Zealand, with the new Bank of England Act 1998 a single monetary objective, which is quantified by the executive government, has been introduced for the Bank of England.

The monetary objective of the **Reserve Bank of New Zealand** is defined by several elements foreseen by the Reserve Bank Act 1989, including in the first place the monetary objective, but also the Policy Target Agreement. Section 8 of the Reserve Bank Act 1989 describes the primary function of the Bank:

> "The primary function of the Bank is to formulate and implement monetary policy directed to the economic objective of achieving price stability and maintaining stability in the general level of prices."

It could therefore be concluded that the Reserve Bank Act 1989 includes a single objective for the Reserve Bank, that is to achieve and maintain price stability. However, this view could be challenged. According to section 10 of the Reserve Bank Act 1989, in formulating and implementing monetary policy, the Bank has to have regard to the efficiency and soundness of the financial system, and, furthermore, has to consult with, and give advice to, the Government and such persons or organisations as the Bank considers can assist it to achieve maintain the economic objective of monetary policy.[257] By obliging the Bank to have regard to the financial system, the existence of a link between monetary stability and financial stability is recognised. The Bank has to prevent instability and inefficiency in the financial markets in its conduct of monetary policy, especially when choosing the monetary instruments.[258] Moreover, the Bank is obliged to initiate discussions outside the Bank with both the government and other organisations. It has been suggested that the existence of section 10 together with the provisions on the Bank's function as lender of last resort possibly conflict with the explicit objective of price stability, since extensive interventions by the Bank on the grounds of financial stability could undermine price stability. On the one hand, it could be argued that section 8 of the Reserve Bank Act 1989 explicitly points to price stability as the underlying objective of monetary policy, and the fact that the Bank shall have regard to the financial system in the formulation and implementation of monetary policy does not devalue that objective. In other words, considerations apart from the objective of price stability can only be taken into account in the formulation and implementation of monetary policy, if they do not conflict with the underlying objective. Seen from this point of view, section 10 of the Reserve Bank Act 1989 does not formulate objectives, but rather factors which have to be taken into account when pursuing the single objective. On the contrary, section 13 of the Reserve Bank Act 1989 states that, except as provided in sections 9–12, nothing in that Act or in any other legisla-

---

[257] S. 10 Reserve Bank Act 1989.
[258] A. Fischer, op. cit., Chap. 2, n. 184, at 37.

tion, whether passed before or after the commencement of the Reserve Bank Act 1989, limits or affects the obligation of the Bank to carry out its primary function, i.e. implementing monetary policy directed to price stability. Consequently, as an *argumentum e contrario* it may be stated that the Bank's obligations under section 10 are not *per se* subordinated to the primary function of the Bank. However, this interpretation would ignore the point that it also results from section 13 that functions of the Bank which are outside the scope of sections 9–12 may not limit or affect the Bank's primary function. Thus, for example, a conflict between the Bank's function as a lender of last resort and its primary function would have to be resolved in favour of the latter. Although section 10 of the Reserve Bank Act 1989 does not amount to a secondary objective, it should be recognised that serious disturbances in the financial sector could result in circumstances in which the Bank would have to consider whether the primary objective under section 8 of the Reserve Bank Act 1989 should be promoted at the expense of a major financial crisis, which could—in the long run—result in pressure on the level of inflation and thus, on the objective of price stability.

The motives behind the selection of the current monetary objective in many respects resemble the general observations on monetary objective as a criterion of democratic accountability in Chapter 2. Lloyd observes that, by referring to price stability, the legislator has taken account of the view that monetary policy is ultimately responsible for inflation in the long run, while recognising that output in terms of growth and employment cannot benefit from a lax position on monetary policy in the long run.[259] Moreover, the single objective reflects the conviction that monetary policy cannot be directed towards—possibly conflicting—multiple objectives. The previous Reserve Bank Act 1964 may be a good example of such multiple monetary objectives. It states that monetary policy "shall be directed towards the maintenance and promotion of economic and social welfare, having regard to the desirability of promoting the highest level of productivity and trade, and full employment, and of maintaining a stable internal price level".[260] The concept of a primary and secondary monetary objective has been rejected for the Reserve Bank on grounds that even a combination of primary and secondary, i.e. subsidiary, objectives would in practice have resulted in two equally weighted objectives, since the Bank would be judged on the basis of the pursuit of both objectives, thereby leaving no choice but to pay equal attention to both objectives; thus *de facto* facing multiple objectives.[261] However, such a conclusion assumes that the interrelationship between the primary—prevailing—objective and the subsidiary objective is not acknowledged and that the Bank's performance is evaluated without taking into account the priorities which the Bank has to follow. Whereas such an undifferentiated evaluation may prevail in parts of the general public and the financial markets, the

---

[259] M. Lloyd, op. cit., Chap. 2, n. 151, at 209; also G.F. Wood, op. cit., Chap. 3, n. 452, at 64.
[260] S. 8(2) Reserve Bank Act 1964.
[261] Lloyd, op. cit., Chap. 2, n. 151 above, at 209.

institution charged with the evaluation of the performance, and thus of holding the Reserve Bank accountable, may pay more attention to this interrelationship, in particular since the Bank is likely to emphasise the clear priority which is given to price stability in the Reserve Bank Act 1989.

In formulating and implementing monetary policy the Bank is not only restricted by the clear statutory objective, but in addition to that by so-called *policy targets*.[262] Unlike other systems, in which much of the definition of the broadly formulated monetary objective(s) is left to the central banks, the Reserve Bank Act 1989 requires the quantification of the monetary objective by calling for the establishment of policy targets. According to section 9 of the Reserve Bank Act 1989:

> "The Minister [of Finance] shall, before appointing, or re-appointing, any person as Governor, fix, in agreement with that person, policy targets for the carrying out by the Bank of its function during that person's term of office, or next term of office, as governor."[263]

The Minister of Finance and the governor may review or alter policy targets and may substitute new policy targets for previously fixed targets. The policy targets are laid down by agreement between the Minister of Finance and the governor of the Reserve Bank. This agreement, which is recorded in writing, is commonly referred to as the Policy Target Agreement (PTA) and is in principle concluded for the term of office of the governor of the Reserve Bank. The PTA is a separate agreement which does not form part of the agreement on the conditions of employment. Nevertheless, as will be seen hereafter, in some respects the PTA is closely related to the employment of the governor. The Reserve Bank Act 1989 does not predetermine the contents of the PTA. The actual influence of the governor in the negotiations of the PTA is difficult to assess, since information on this sensitive issue cannot be obtained. However, even within the Bank there seems to be an understanding that ultimately the governor of the Bank has to give way to the political will of the democratically elected government as regards the contents of the PTA. If he cannot accept responsibility for the transformation of the political will, he is considered to be unfit for the post. The Reserve Bank Act 1989 does not set a specific strategy for the targeting of price stability which then has to be defined in the PTA. In other words, the targets defined in the PTA do not necessarily have to be related to inflation targets.[264] Since the establishment of the new procedure, three PTAs have been in place, the fourth, agreement was signed on 15 December 1997.[265] Generally, the PTA

---

[262] With regard to the rationale of this approach see e.g. D.J. Archer, "The New Zealand Approach to Rules and Discretion in Monetary Policy", *Journal of Monetary Economics*, vol. 39 (1997), 3–15.

[263] Brackets added.

[264] Fischer, n. 258 above, 37 *et seq.*, who points out that alternatively a money or exchange rate target could be introduced.

[265] Cf. Reserve Bank of New Zealand Policy Targets Agreement of 15 Dec. 1997, No. 2a. reprinted in App. 1. The first PTA was signed on 2 Mar. 1990, followed by the second on 16 Dec. 1992, and the third on 16 Dec. 1996.

includes provisions on the price stability target, the measurement of price stability, the deviations from the targets and the re-negotiation and implementation of targets. From the outset the PTA states in clause 1 that:

> "the Reserve Bank shall formulate and implement monetary policy with the intention of maintaining a stable general level of prices, so that monetary policy can make its maximum contribution to sustainable economic growth employment and development opportunities within the New Zealand economy."

It is interesting to note in this context that, unlike the first and second PTAs, the third and also the fourth PTA define goals to the contribution of which monetary policy should be orientated. By doing so the current government makes clear that it does not understand price stability as a goal of monetary policy in itself, but, rather, as a promoter of sustainable economic growth employment and development opportunities. This shows that the content of the PTA is by no means fixed and renewal more than a formality. A change in government may well result in the drafting of a new PTA reflecting the change in government and any shifts on policy stands that result from that.

The PTA defines the objective of price stability under section 8 of the Reserve Bank Act 1989 as the formulation and implementation of monetary policy with the intention of maintaining "a stable general level of prices". So in order to measure the achievement of the monetary objective the PTA introduces two yardsticks: the "stable general level of prices" is determined by the measurement of a range of price indices; the general price stability target is defined in terms of an *All Groups Consumer Price Index Excluding Credit Services* (CPIX). On the basis of the latter yardstick, the objective of price stability is furnished with a target range. Clause 2(b) of the most recent PTA states that:

> "For the purpose of this agreement, the policy target shall be 12-monthly increases in the CPIX of between 0 and 3 per cent."

The target range has been subject to changes since the PTA has been first agreed upon. During the time of the first and second PTAs a margin of 0–2 per cent was considered consistent with price stability.[266] As would be the case for any normal contractual agreement, it is the duty of the signatory, here the governor of the Bank, to fulfil his obligations under the agreement. Section 11 of the Reserve Bank Act 1989 makes clear that:

> "It is the duty of the Governor to ensure that the actions of the Bank in implementing monetary policy are consistent with the policy targets fixed under section 9 of this Act."

The governor is personally responsible for the implementation of the PTA. The performance of the Bank, and more particularly of the governor himself, is judged on the basis of the deviation of the CPIX inflation rate from the specified

---

[266] Note also that with the recent PTA the previously targeted Consumer Price Index (CPI) has been abolished in favour of the CPIX.

target. In fact, as will be seen, the governor is held accountable in that he can be removed from office if he is considered not to have fulfilled his duties under section 11 of the Reserve Bank Act 1989, e.g. if the CPIX has not stayed within the 0–3 per cent range over the specified time.[267] Somewhat devaluing the existence of these arrangements is the fact that the Reserve Bank Act 1989 and the PTA leave the definition of the key to the evaluation of the performance of the governor, that is the measure of inflation (i.e. headline or underlying inflation), to the Bank.[268]

The PTA not only quantifies the monetary objective by setting out a specific monetary target range for which the governor is responsible, but also specifies the circumstances under which a deviation from the targets may be justified. It acknowledges a range of possible price shocks which lie outside the sphere of influence of the Reserve Bank arising from external forces, government policy changes or even natural crises. Rather than providing an exclusive list the PTA provides examples of possible shocks, such as shifts in the aggregate price level as a result of exceptional movements in the prices of commodities traded in the world markets, changes in indirect taxation, significant government policy changes directly affecting prices, or a natural disaster affecting a major part of the economy.[269] By specifying—to some extent—the circumstances under which a deviation from the targets can be admissible, rather than leaving it to a general description, the accountability of the governor is much more closely defined. This has two effects. On the one hand, the governor cannot exculpate himself for his own bad performance by reference to some obscure general exemption clause, which would almost certainly be subject to a great deal of interpretation. On the other hand, the governor will not be held accountable for outcomes which he could not influence. In this context it is interesting to note that the PTA recognises "significant government policy changes" as one source of price shocks which are outside the influence of monetary policy. It becomes much more difficult for the government to use the Reserve Bank, personified in the governor, as a "scapegoat" for its own shortcomings. Monetary policy becomes more transparent by pointing out interactions between government policy and monetary policy, not only for those who are directly involved in holding the Bank accountable, but also the general public. But the exemption clause provided for by the PTA may also provide a balance between price stability and other real economic goals in the face of supply shocks.[270]

To be sure, the PTA does not feature some sort of automatism, according to which the governor of the Reserve Bank is no longer responsible for the outcome

---

[267] Cf. Chap. 4 IV, on the appointment and dismissal procedures. At the time of the drafting of the Reserve Bank Act 1989 it was even considered to provide the governor of the Bank with an extra incentive to achieve the targets, by offering a bonus payment: cf. C.E. Walsh, op. cit., Chap. 2, n. 157, at 151.

[268] Mishkin/Posen, n. 207 above, at 38.

[269] Clause 3(a) PTA.

[270] Mishkin/Posen, n. 207 above, 38 *et seq.*, who comment that the Reserve Bank is not as single-minded as believed by some.

of such shocks on monetary policy. In fact the contrary happens to be the case. The PTA states in clause 4(b):

> "It is acknowledged that, on occasions, there will be inflation outcomes outside the target range. On those occasions, or when such occasions are projected, the Bank shall explain in Policy Statements made under section 15 of the Act why such outcomes have occurred, or are projected, and what measures it has taken, or proposes to take, to ensure that inflation comes back within that range."

Moreover, the PTA states clearly that in the case of a crisis it is the duty of the Bank generally to react "in a manner which prevents general inflationary pressures emerging".[271] The Bank and, thus, ultimately the governor is charged with the burden of proof with regard to any price shocks, in as much as the Bank has to justify the deviation of the CPIX inflation rate from the target and is thereafter accountable for the handling of the crisis.

Apart from price shocks, the availability or effectiveness of monetary policy instruments may also have a negative influence on the conduct of monetary policy and, thus, on the achievement of the targets. In such a case the PTA holds a certain degree of flexibility by offering the opportunity to renegotiate the targets set in the PTA, if the governor considers that changes are needed. New policy targets are then set in an agreement between the Minister of Finance and the governor of the Reserve Bank.

In addition, by quantifying the monetary objective of price stability with an explicit target range, the PTA offers general guidelines for the Bank in the conduct of monetary policy. The current PTA states in clause 4(d) that:

> "The Bank shall be fully accountable for its judgements and actions in implementing monetary policy."

The approach taken by the Reserve Bank Act 1989 has since been taken up in the UK. With the Bank of England Act 1998 for the first time in history an explicit and quantified monetary objective has been introduced for the **Bank of England,** which—at the same time—has gained operational responsibility for monetary policy. According to section 11 of the Act:

> "In relation to monetary policy, the objectives of the Bank of England shall be
> (a) to maintain price stability
> (b) subject to that, to support the economic policy of Her Majesty's Government, including its objectives for growth and employment."

The Bank of England therefore pursues a primary and secondary objective, whereby the primary objective of price stability takes precedence over the secondary objective to support the economic policy of the government. Until recently, under the arrangements provided for by the Bank of England Act 1946, an explicit monetary policy objective did not exist. The lack of a concrete objective may actually have fallen within the logic of a central bank system, which to

---

[271] Clause 3(b) PTA.

a large extent was dependent on the government. It has been observed that there is a "logical difficulty" in specifying independent policy goals for a non-independent agency.[272] The executive government rather than the Bank of England was in charge of formulating and implementing monetary policy, in the form of setting the interest rate. The Bank supported the government's objectives, rather than pursuing its own preferences. In the course of restoring its counter-inflationary credibility, subsequent to the withdrawal of the Pound Sterling from the ERM in 1992, the executive government reviewed its monetary framework. As a result of this a system of targeting emerged.[273] Basically, the Treasury set a target range between 1–4 per cent range for underlying inflation over the medium term, whereby the trajectory was a downward path.[274] A target range for inflation of 2 per cent or less was envisaged in the long term.[275] The inflation target was updated thereafter in June 1995 to aim at an underlying inflation rate of 2.5 per cent or less.[276] The existence of inflation targets cannot be equated with the existence of a clear monetary objective. Rather, existing monetary targets may be interpreted as a reflection of underlying objectives.[277] To this end the described practice of government announced inflation targets has been characterised as "a system of "voluntary" self-imposed price-discipline".[278]

While introducing an explicit monetary policy objective for the Bank of England, the new legislation also aims at formalising the former practice of inflation targeting. Section 12(1) of the Bank of England Act 1998 states in this respect:

"The Treasury may by notice in written to the Bank specify for the purpose of section 11—
  (a) what price stability is to be taken to consist of, or
  (b) what the economic policy of her Majesty's government to be taken to be."

The Treasury is charged with defining price stability, whereby under the Bank of England Act 1998 the executive government is in principle not restricted to introducing inflation targets. Likewise, a money or exchange rate target could

[272] Fischer, n. 206 above, at 265.
[273] A.G. Haldane, *Rules, Discretion and the United Kingdom's New Monetary Framework*, Working paper Series no. 40 (Bank of England, London, 1995).
[274] In Oct. 1992, at the time of the establishment of the inflation target, Chancellor of the Exchequer Lamont made it clear that the lower part of the 1–4% range should be reached by the end of the Parliament of the time.
[275] A. Bowen, "British Experience with Inflation Targetry", in L. Leiderman/L.E.O. Svensson, op. cit., Chap. 2, n. 184, 53–68, 55 *et seq.*
[276] Underlying inflation is measured by the annual change in the retail price index excluding mortage interest payments (RPIX).
[277] Roll Report, op. cit., Chap. 2, n. 1, 22–23.
[278] F. Vibert, "Memorandum Submitted to the Treasury and Civil Service Select Committee", in Treasury and Civil Service Committee, *The Role of the Bank of England* (House of Commons Paper. Session 1993–4 ; 98–I, vol. 2), Report, together with the proceedings of the Committee, HC Session 1993–4 (HMSO, London, 1993), app. 29, 213–19, at 216.

be introduced. Currently, the target is 2.5 per cent for retail price inflation, excluding mortgage interest payments (RPIX).[279] As such it is a point target rather than a target range, as had earlier been the case. Under the Bank of England Act 1998 the targets have to be confirmed in the annual Budget statement of the Chancellor of the Exchequer. Moreover, the Treasury has to publish its announcement, and, moreover, deposit a copy of it in the library of the House of Commons.[280] Apart from quantifying the monetary policy objective of the Bank of England, the executive government also has to announce what its own economic policy will be. In this respect it may be argued that the executive government is not only committing the Bank of England to certain values, but by outlining its plans also commits itself. Parliament does not play any role in defining the statutory monetary policy objective of the Bank of England. In its report on the role of the Bank of England, the Treasury and Civil Service Committee had suggested that the targets should result from an agreement between the executive government and the Bank, like the arrangements in New Zealand, and, furthermore, that the targets should be set out in an Order by the Chancellor of the Exchequer, which should be subject to an affirmative resolution procedure in the House of Commons.[281] The new legislation foresees the participation neither of the Bank nor of the House of Commons. Despite the fact that the participation of Parliament in setting the targets would have introduced an additional element of *ex ante* democratic accountability, it can be concluded that, by charging the Bank of England with operational responsibility for monetary policy while at the same time introducing a clear monetary objective which is furthermore quantified by the government announcement of targets, democratic accountability for the conduct of monetary policy is enhanced. The previous system with the executive government principally in charge of monetary policy has been criticised for not allowing for clear parliamentary accountability, since the Bank did not have the final responsibility for monetary policy decisions, and the Chancellor of the Exchequer defended monetary policy only as part of the general parliamentary accountability for the management of the economy.[282] Under the new arrangements there is a clear division of labour, with the executive government defining price stability and the Bank of England implementing monetary policy independently with the aim of achieving this quantified monetary policy objective. Adding to this evaluation is the fact that under the current arrangements the governor of the Bank is required to explain any deviation which exceeds 1 per cent either side of the target in an open letter to the Chancellor of the Exchequer. This includes spelling out the reasons for the deviation, the expected duration of that deviation and any actions which have been taken to remedy the situation.[283] Interestingly the Bank of England

---

[279] Announced on 12 June 1997.
[280] S. 12(3) Bank of England Act 1998.
[281] Treasury and Civil Service Committee, n. 73 above, Vol. I, at xxi.
[282] Ibid.
[283] P. Rodgers, op. cit., Chap. 3, n. 31, at 243.

Act 1998 does not include any provisions to formalise this *de facto* mechanism of accountability of the governor of the Bank to the executive government. In this context it would have been desirable to give it a concrete legal form which could then also have spelled out the consequences of such a deviation from the quantified monetary policy objective.

III. THE RELATIONSHIP WITH THE EXECUTIVE BRANCH OF GOVERNMENT

When examining the relationship with the executive branch of government, generally a distinction can be drawn for the central banks included in this study on the basis of whether an explicit reference to the independence exists in the legal basis of the bank. Where such a provision exists it forms the basis for the relationship foremost, but not exclusively, with the executive government.

Under the EC Treaty and the ESCB Statute there is no formal mechanism which provides third parties with the possibility of influencing the final decision of a central bank; indeed there is an express prohibition on the ECB seeking or accepting instructions expressed in Article 107 EC and repeated in Article 7 of the ESCB Statute. Some of the central banks examined in this study include provisions allowing for members of government to participate in meetings of the monetary policy board of the central bank and, *vice versa*, for central bank representatives to participate in government meetings. In so far as these provisions do not go beyond what is foreseen in case of the ECB they do not appear to be in contradiction with primary Community law.[284]

1. Central bank statutes with an explicit reference to independence

Where the legal basis establishes explicitly the independence of the central bank the relationship between the former and the executive government is basically determined by such a provision, while additional provisions may allow for some level of co-operation between the two. This is the case for the Bundesbank, the Banque de France, and the ECB. Interestingly, the Bundesbank has been the blueprint for the respective provision for the ECB, and the new statutory independence of the Banque de France has been modelled against the background of Articles 107 and 108 EC on the independent status of the ECB and the national central banks.[285]

The relationship between the **Bundesbank** and the Federal government is characterised by the independence of the Bundesbank *vis-à-vis* the Federal government enshrined in its legal basis. The most prominent provision describing

---

[284] European Monetary Institute, n. 199 above, at 101: "The crucial issue is whether a national institution has any formal mechanism at its disposal to ensure that its views influence the final decision". Note, however, the changes at the Banque de France, Bundesbank and Nederlandsche Bank.

[285] Cf. Chap. 3 II.

the relationship between the Bundesbank and the Federal government is to be found in § 12, sentence 2 of the BBankG:

> "Without prejudice to the performance of its functions, the Deutsche Bundesbank shall be required to support the general economic policy of the Federal government. *In exercising the powers conferred upon it by this Act, it shall be independent of instructions from the government.*"[286]

The structure of § 12 of the BBankG is unusual since the independence of the Bundesbank, as introduced in the second sentence, appears to be an add-on to the obligation to support the economic policy of the Federal government introduced in the first sentence.[287] A closer look, however, reveals that the independence is already recognised to some extent in the first sentence, which restricts the obligation to support the Federal government to areas of general economic policy, which do not interfere with the performance of the Bundesbank's functions. Nevertheless, the second sentence of § 12 is at least of equivalent importance, as it guarantees the independence of the Bundesbank on a broader scale, that is to say with respect to *any* of its functions.

Since its establishment there has always been a discussion on the legitimisation and the limits of the special position of the Bundesbank as part of the executive power. For those who advocate the existence of a constitutional independence of the Bundesbank the legitimation derives directly from Article 88 of the Basic Law.[288] For those rejecting such constitutional recognition the question has long since been whether the independent position of the Bundesbank as stated in § 12, sentence 2 of the BBankG is constitutional.[289]

The basic argument presented against the constitutionality of this provision is the prohibition of so-called ministerial or government free areas which originates from the principle of democracy deriving from Articles 20(1) and 28(1) of the Basic Law[290]. Under the Basic Law any exercise of state power requires democratic legitimation. Thus, in principle any institution with executive powers has to be subject to the control and orders of the executive government, which in return is accountable to the Bundestag, in accordance with the parliamentary principle.[291] Sub-governments (*Nebenregierungen*) are considered to be incompatible with the principles of a parliamentary democracy. Yet, § 12, sentence 2 of the BBankG states that the Bundesbank is independent of instructions from the Federal government. Against the background of this provision,

---

[286] English translation as provided in Gormley/de Haan, n. 213 above.

[287] Cf. Chap. 4 II 1; Schmidt, n. 203 above, at 672, states that the structure of § 12 is faulty, as the two sentences should be in reverse order.

[288] Cf. references in Chap. 4 I 1.

[289] It should be noted in this context that the question of the constitutionality of the independent position of the Bundesbank, although undoubtedly linked, has to be separated from the issue, observed in Chap. 4 I 1.3., whether the independence of the Bundesbank is guaranteed by the Constitution.

[290] For an overview cf. W. Müller, "Ministerialfreie Räume", *JuS*, vol. 25 no. 7 (1985), 497–508.

[291] Maunz, n. 23 above, on Art. 88, side notation 18, with further references.

the Bundesbank has been characterised as something like a sub-government.[292] Besides, § 12, sentence 2 of the BBankG is not the only provision in the BBankG which safeguards independence. According to § 29 of the BBankG, the two main organs of the Bundesbank, the Central Bank Council and the Board of Directors, have the status of supreme federal authorities (*oberste Bundesbehörden*) with the consequence that these organs enjoy the highest ranking in the administrative structure, and as such are on an equal footing with the Federal ministries and cannot be subject to the instructions of a minister.[293] Finally, § 2 of the BBankG, according to which "the German Bundesbank is a legal person under public law, directly dependent on the Federation", has been interpreted as safeguarding the institutional independence of the Bundesbank, giving it a unique position within the German legal system.[294]

Ministerial or government-free areas are at the same time Parliament-free areas in as much as a minister cannot be held responsible by Parliament for an area in which he cannot give any instructions.[295] In this context von Bonin argues that the self-restraint of Parliament from control of *superior* executive tasks is not possible. Considering the management of monetary policy as one of the most central governmental tasks in connection with the economic policies, he draws the conclusion that a statutory provision which would give the Bundesbank *unrestrained* political autonomy *vis-à-vis* the executive government and Parliament is not compatible with the Basic Law.[296] Ehrenberg takes a clear stand on the position of the Bundesbank, arguing that anybody taking parliamentary democracy serious should have reservations against furnishing an independent "committee of state officials" such extensive and parliamentary uncontrolled powers.[297]

Despite these reservations against the constitutionality of the independent position of the Bundesbank, the majority of observers consider the current position of the Bundesbank to be constitutional. It is recognised that in a parliamentary democracy an institution exercising executive powers cannot be independent to the extent that it is not subject to direct or indirect parliamentary accountability, and thus institutions under public law which are not subject to the orders of the Federal government are considered to break through the parliamentary principle laid down in Articles 65, 67 and 68 of the Basic Law. It is, moreover, undisputed that the Bundesbank exercises executive functions.[298] However, according to the majority view this restriction of the parliamentary

---

[292] v. Arnim, n. 115 above, at 341.
[293] Samm, n. 33 above, at 149. The state central banks have only the status of Federal authorities.
[294] Werres, n. 217 above, at 4, with further references.
[295] Müller, n. 290 above, at 498; Schmidt, n. 203 above, at 678 is sceptical.
[296] v. Bonin, n. 40 above, at 170, also referring to BVerfGE 9, 268, 282 *et seq.*
[297] H. Ehrenberg, *Zwischen Marx und Markt* (Societäts-Verlag, Frankfurt a.M., 1973), at 33.
[298] E.g. Benda *et al*, n. 54 above, § 18, side notation 88, who refer to the Bundesbank as a sort of governmental organ without having the formal status of a constitutional organ.

principle is backed by a specific constitutional admissibility.[299] This admissibility is thought to be provided by Article 88 of the Basic Law itself.[300] It is argued that the drafters of Article 88 did not mean to exclude the establishment of an independent Bundesbank, and, moreover, that they and, thereafter, the drafters of the BBankG considered the stability of the currency as a doctrine of the highest priority from a national point of view. If this doctrine is interpreted as an order of constitutional magnitude, the legislator has discretion with regard to the establishment of an institution which best fulfils this prerogative.[301] However, it seems questionable when Maunz attempts constitutionally to justify the independence of the Bundesbank with a comparison with the independence of the Federal Audit Office (*Bundesrechnungshof*) or the right of self-regulation of the Communes in the Federal states, since the provisions on both of these institutions refer *explicitly* to independence and right of self-regulation respectively.[302] Such an explicit reference is missing in the case of Article 88 of the Basic Law and the Bundesbank. It has also been argued that the Bundesbank is not completely removed from Parliament, since the independence of the Bundesbank does not include Parliament in its function as legislator as, according to Article 20(3) of the Basic Law, the executive is bound by law and justice.[303] Indeed it is pointed out that at the time of the establishment of the Bundesbank the legislator did realise the dilemma between the desired independence of the Bundesbank from Federal government and the principle of parliamentary accountability, and that the intention was to solve the conflict, on the one hand, by removing the Bank from direct government influence in the form of the chancellor's power to decide on government policies (*Richtlinienkompetenz*) and the Federal ministers' supervisory power (*Fach- oder Dienstaufsicht*), while, on the other hand, giving Parliament the power to change the statute of the Bundesbank.[304] Ladeur observes that by means of the statutory independence of the Bundesbank parliamentary scrutiny is not meant to be excluded, but rather fixed on a long-term perspective, whereby frustration of expectations with regard to the successful conduct of monetary policy, as well as functioning self-controls by the Bundesbank, can lead to institutional changes.[305] Besides, it may be argued that

---

[299] Bauer n. 22 above, Art. 88, side notation no. 22, who refers to other examples of independent institutions, such as the Federal Insurance Institution for Salaried Employees (*Bundesversicherungsanstalt für Angestellte*) and the public broadcasting corporations (*Rundfunkanstalten*).

[300] E.g. Benda *et al.* (eds.), n. 54 above, § 18, side notation 86 *et seq.*, with further references.

[301] Coburger, n. 23 above, 33 *et seq.*

[302] E.g. Müller, n. 290 above, at 498, with further references, who argues that the indirect state administration (*mittelbare Selbstverwaltung*), such as the self-regulation of the Communes, falls outside the scope of the concept of ministerial-free areas.

[303] E.g. D. Studt, *Rechtsfragen der europäischen Zentralbank* (Dunker & Humblot, Berlin, 1993), at 89. In this context it is often emphasised that despite its independent position the Bundesbank is in principle not excluded from judicial review.

[304] Hahn, n. 36 above, at 35, who refers to the discussions in the parliamentary committee at the time, reprinted in BTDrucks. 2/3603, at 5.

[305] K.-H. Ladeur, "Die Autonomie der Bundesbank- ein Beispiel für die institutionelle Verarbeitung von Ungewißheitsentscheidungen", *Staatswissenschaften und Staatspraxis* 3 (1992), 486–508, at 500.

the Bundesbank is not even completely removed from the executive, since the relationship between the former and the Bundesbank is characterised by manifold dependencies, such as the appointment procedures and the co-operation procedures under § 13 of the BBankG.[306] Yet, it is questionable whether the democratic legitimation of the Bundesbank derives from the will of the democratically elected Parliament to establish the Bundesbank as an independent institution within the executive branch of government. Indeed, the independent position of the Bundesbank has been described as self-restraint by Parliament.[307] Generally, in the German constitutional order an Act of Parliament does not rank above the Constitution and thus has to be compatible with the same.[308] Thus, there are limits to the extent to which Parliament can exercise self-restraint through the creation of laws without violating basic democratic principles of the German constitution.

Several courts have considered the question of the constitutionality of the Bundesbank in passing, thereby implicitly accepting the independent position of the Bundesbank. It has been observed that the Federal Administrative Court has concluded that the Basic Law neither guaranteed nor excluded the independence of the Bundesbank, and the German Federal Constitutional Court has at least confirmed the constitutionality of the independent position of the Bundesbank *vis-à-vis* the executive by referring to "its constitutional independent position".[309] Finally, in its decision on the constitutionality of the Law of Accession to the TEU the German Federal Constitutional Court justifies the transfer of authority over monetary policy to the ECB by observing that an independent central bank is a better guarantor of currency.[310] Although at the time of the coming into existence of the ESCB, Parliament's right to change the BBankG is considerably restricted, the German Federal Constitutional Court seems to have accepted this restriction on the principle of democracy which goes further than what is already presently the case for the Bundesbank. To be sure, the independence of the Bundesbank is not limitless. In fact, according to the wording of § 12, sentence 2 of the BBankG the independence of the Bundesbank is limited to the competence conferred upon it by the BBankG (*Eigenzuständigkeit*). As an *argumentum e contrario* it can be concluded from this that the Bundesbank is subject to supervision by the Federal government for all other areas of its activities.[311] This includes in particular the exchange rate policy where determined

---

[306] v. Bonin, n. 40 above, who, despite his basic criticism, finds provisions which restrict the autonomy of the Bundesbank *vis-à-vis* the Federal government and the Bundestag.

[307] v. Arnim, n. 115 above, at 342; Samm, n. 33 above, 148 *et seq.*, with further references, is critical.

[308] This argument is applied by R.H. Kaiser, *Bundesbankautonomie—Möglichkeiten und Grenzen einer unabhängigen Politik* (Rita G. Fischer Verlag, Frankfurt a.M., 1980), at 66.

[309] BVerfGE 62, 169, at 183.

[310] Cf. Chap. 4 I 3.

[311] Cf. H.P. Bull, in R. Wasserman (principal editor), *Kommentar zum Grundgesetz für die Bundesrepublik Deutschland*, Vol. 2 (Reihe Alternativkommentare, Luchterhand, Neuwied, 1989), on Art. 86 Basic Law.

by the Federal government, but also such tasks which are established by other laws, such as the External Economic Relations Act (*Außenwirtschaftsgesetz*).[312]

As indicated earlier, although the BBankG explicitly refers to the independence of the Bundesbank from the Federal government, it is also characterised by a number of provisions governing the relationship between the two. The obligation to support the general economic policies of the Federal government, as stated in § 12, sentence 1 of the BBankG, has already been observed in the context of the monetary objective of the Bundesbank.[313] Moreover, § 13 of the BBankG provides for co-operation between the Bundesbank and the Federal government in order to enable co-ordination in the areas of economic and monetary policies.[314] According to § 13(1):

> "The Deutsche Bundesbank has to advise the Federal government on issues of essential interest for monetary policy, and to inform the Federal government upon request."

Generally, the Bundesbank is free to provide economic and legal advice on its own initiative but, upon request by the Federal government, the former is obliged to provide the relevant information which it has been asked for. Since the obligation to provide information is limited to issues of *substantial* monetary importance, the Bundesbank is not required to inform the Federal government on just any monetary issue. Exactly what issues have to be considered substantial remains unclear.[315] This provision has been identified as another element of the independent status of the Bundesbank since it functions as a restraining mechanism limiting the influence of the Federal government.[316] Neither § 13 nor any other provision of the BBankG includes rules in case of a conflict between the Bundesbank and Federal government.[317] Should the Bundesbank consider a certain issue to be outside the scope of co-operation, i.e. not of substantial monetary importance, the Federal government could hardly enforce its right to information. This, however, is believed to have been the intention of the legislator at the time of the drafting of the BBankG, in order to force the parties to solve any conflicts that may arise by means of co-operation rather than unilateral enforcement.[318] Ultimately only the legislator could solve such a conflict by amending the BBankG.

---

[312] In fact, the Bundesbank is sometimes characterised as being *partially* independent, since its independence is limited to the internal monetary policy; cf. Brandt, n. 50 above, 13 *et. seq.*

[313] Cf. Chap. 4 II.

[314] v.Spindler/Becker/Starke, n. 215 above, § 13, at 271.

[315] E.g. recently the Federal government asked the Bundesbank to comment on the fulfilment of the convergence criteria in accordance with Art. 109j EC: cf. Deutsche Bundesbank, *Stellungnahme des Zentralbankrates zur Konvergenzlage in der Europäischen Union im Hinblick auf die dritte Stufe der Wirtschafts- und Währungsunion*, Frankfurt a.M., 26 Mar. 1998.

[316] v.Spindler/Becker/Starke, n. 215 above, § 13, who fall short of explaining in what respects the obligation to supply information can have a negative influence on the level of independence of the Bundesbank.

[317] For Ehrenberg, n. 297 above, at 33, this is problematic from the point of view of parliamentary democracy.

[318] Kaiser, n. 308 above, at 45; § 13(2) sentence 2 BBankG, which, to some extent, represents an exception to this concept, will be discussed later.

On the one hand, the obligation to provide information may enhance the transparency of monetary policy which in turn could form an element of democratic accountability for the Bundesbank. However, the value of § 13(1) of the BBankG as an element of accountability is diminished by the fact that this provision creates a scheme of co-operation rather than providing for means of accountability *vis-à-vis* the Federal government. This is due to the fact that the obligation to inform may be considered vague and limited both with respect to its scope and its enforceability. Indeed, this observation may not only be limited to § 13(1), as an examination of § 13(2) of the BBankG reveals. That provision deals with the participation of the members of the Federal government in the deliberations of the Central Bank Council and states that:

> "The members of the Federal government have the right to attend meetings of the Central Bank Council. They have no voting rights but can make proposals."

Provisions on the procedures of Central Bank Council meetings which could reveal the actual level of influence cannot be found in the BBankG. Such provisions are included in the BBank charter. According to § 3 of the BBank charter, the Federal Ministers for Economics and Finances are invited to every meeting of the Central Bank Council generally by the process of receiving of the Central Bank Council's agenda for the meeting. In practice, the ministers will also receive the preparatory documents for the meeting.[319] Usually, one of the two ministers attends the meetings which determine the annual money growth rates. Other members of the Federal government are only invited if a specific subject on the agenda makes their appearance necessary.

Although the actual influence of the Federal government is difficult to assess, the legal framework puts clear limits on what is legally permissible, as the members of the Federal government can only make contributions which are not binding for the Central Bank Council and, moreover, as they have no voting right at all.[320] Indeed, it has been suggested that the ministers in practice will be reluctant to make formal proposals which could provoke undesired reactions by the central bankers, since the latter may interpret the ministers' action as an attempt to limit the independence of the Bundesbank.[321] The mere fact that the Federal government is represented in these meetings does not directly enhance either the accountability of the Bundesbank *vis-à-vis* Federal government nor the control of the Bundesbank by the Federal government. As the influence of the Federal government is limited in this respect so is Parliament's ability to hold the relevant member of the Federal government accountable for his/her conduct in these meetings. However, as will be seen in the course of the examination of override mechanisms, the Federal government may not be completely powerless.[322]

---

[319] Wahlig, n. 113 above, at 57.
[320] With regard to the right to ask for a deferral of a decision in accordance with § 13(2), sentence 3, BBankG, cf. Chap. 4 V.
[321] Werres, n. 217 above, at 7.
[322] Cf. Chap. 4 V 2.

With § 13(3) a further element of co-operation is incorporated into the BBankG:

> "The Federal government ought to [*soll*] invite the President of the Deutsche Bundesbank to its consultations on matters related to monetary policy."

Article 13(3) of the BBankG may be considered as the counterpart to § 13(1) of the BBankG and the Federal government's right to participate in meetings of the Central Bank Council. Whether § 13(3) of the BBankG constitutes an obligation cannot be determined from its wording. However, contrary to the obligation of the Bundesbank in § 13(1) of the BBankG, the obligation of the Federal government to consult the president of the Bundesbank is at least not limited to issues of *substantial* monetary importance. In any event, § 13(3) leaves the decision which issues are considered to be of monetary importance and thus, the decision on when the president of the Bundesbank may participate in meetings of the Federal government (so-called *Kabinettssitzungen*) at the discretion of the Federal government.[323] As is the case with § 13(1) of the BBankG, § 13(3) does not include rules applicable in case of a conflict. Apart from being invited to meetings of the Federal government, the Bundesbank takes part in meetings of Economic Policy Council (*Konjunkturrat*) and the Financial Planing Council (*Finanzplanungsrat*) of the Federal government.[324]

From the examination of § 13(1) and (3) it could be concluded that the relationship between the Bundesbank and the Federal government is best characterised by co-operation instead of confrontation. Yet, the regular contacts between the Minister of Finance and the members of the Board of Directors of the Bundesbank do not amount to any form of co-ordination of fiscal and monetary policy. Suggestions for the establishment of a co-ordinating organ have generally been rejected.[325] The lack of any provisions for the resolution of a conflict between the Federal government and the Bundesbank does not mean that such conflicts cannot arise, but rather that they do not necessarily become known to the general public, leaving transparency veiled. In fact, there seems to be a general understanding that differences are not dragged into the public arena.[326] In this respect the recent openly fought dispute between the executive government and the Bundesbank over the revaluation of the gold reserves may be viewed as exceptional. It also demonstrates that in cases where the interactions between the Federal government and the Bundesbank become public not only the behaviour of the Bundesbank, but also that of the Federal government,

---

[323] Siebelt, n. 202 above, at 181, states that ultimately the President would have to call upon an administrative court which would have to decide whether the participation of the President of the Bundesbank was necessary.

[324] Cf. § 18 Act of 1967 on stability and economic expansion (*Stabilitätsgesetz*), § 51 law on basic budgetary rules (*Haushaltsgrundsätzegesetz*).

[325] v.Spindler/Becker/Starke, n. 215 above, at 255; Kaiser, n. 308 above, 64 *et seq.*, with further references, is critical.

[326] Werres, n. 321 above, at 9 and 39 *et seq.*, who describes the conflicts between the Bundesbank and the Federal government in the early 1980s.

can become the subject of parliamentary debates and concrete criticism. Although it may be said that numerous contacts on different levels between the Bundesbank and the Federal government function as a mechanism which *de facto* restrains the independence of the Bundesbank, the lack of any provisions for the resolution of a conflict may result in such cases being fought out in the twilight of unofficial contacts, whereby it becomes difficult, if not impossible, to hold the parties concerned accountable.

As at 1 January 1999, a revised version of Article 12 of the BBankG applies. The unusual structure of Article 12, observed above, is revised, as the first sentence of Article 12 emphasises the independence of the Bundesbank of the Federal government in carrying out its tasks. Thereafter, the second sentence states that the Bundesbank supports the general economic policy of the Federal government to the extent to which this does not infringe the tasks of the Bank in the ESCB. The parts of Article 13 of the BBankG presently discussed remain unchanged.[327]

As with the legal basis of the Bundesbank, the Bank Act 1993 enshrines the independence of the **Banque de France** in the field of monetary policy. Basically three provisions are at the centre of the relationship between the Bank and the Government in the field of monetary policy. Article 1(2) of the Bank Act 1993 determines:

> "The Banque de France, represented by its Governor, Deputy Governors or any member of the Monetary Policy Council, shall neither seek nor accept instructions from the government or any other person in the performance of his duties."

Article 1(2) cements the independence of the Bank in the conduct of monetary policy. It rules out government interventions in the form of instructions either on its own initiative or upon request of the CPM itself. The provision supplies evidence of the ambitions of the creators of the Bank Act 1993 to anticipate the statutory requirements under the EC Treaty and the ESCB Statute. It resembles Article 107 EC on the prohibition of instructions from Community and/or government bodies in the context of the ESCB. Furthermore, it has been pointed out that the reference to the government's overall economic policy in Article 1(1), sentence 2 of the Bank Act 1993 does not restrict the Banque de France in pursuing the monetary objective of price stability independently nor does it furnish the executive government with a right to issue general guidelines for the conduct of monetary policy.[328]

As in the case of the Bundesbank, the independent position of the Banque de France has raised questions of constitutional magnitude. The occasion for these concerns to become public was the introduction of the Bank Act 1993. A group of senators and deputies of the National Assembly called upon the Constitutional Council to pronounce on the proposal, claiming the Bank Act

---

[327] Cf. Chap. 4 V 2, with regard to the limited override mechanism of the Bundesbank.
[328] Cf. Chap. 4 II 2.

1993 was incompatible with the Constitution of 1958.[329] The plaintiffs argued that the transfer of power to the Banque de France to formulate and implement monetary policy, and in particular Articles 1, 3, 7, 8, 9, 10 and 35 of the proposed law constituted an infringement of Article 20(1) of the Constitution of 1958 according to which:

"[T]he Government shall determine and direct the policy of the nation."

It was also alleged to infringe Article 21(1) of the Constitution of 1958, according to which:

"[T]he Prime Minister shall direct the operation of the government."

The plaintiffs were furthermore of the opinion that the proposed provisions did not respect the principle of national sovereignty and deprived Parliament of its competences. Reference was made *inter alia* to Article 34 of the Constitution of 1958 according to which Parliament passes laws on the rules concerning the issue of currency (fourth indent of Article 34).[330] The Constitutional Council considered the wording of Article 1(1) of the Bank Act 1993 to be unconstitutional in so far as it stated that the Banque de France was in charge of formulating monetary policy with the aim of ensuring price stability. The Council argued that the provision effectively deprived government of its competence to determine and conduct monetary policy as an "essential element" of the economic policies of the government.[331] Moreover, the transfer of power over monetary policy to the Banque de France was considered to deprive the Prime Minister to some extent of his constitutional function of directing the operation of the government.[332] The Constitutional Council did not consider the second sentence of Article 1(1) of the Bank Act 1993, which explicitly stated that the Bank is to "carry out these duties *within the framework of the Government's overall economic judgment*", to be an efficient provision to ensure the government's authority over monetary policy. It found evidence for this observation in Article 1(2) of the Bank Act 1993 which explicitly prohibited government instructions to the Bank. Consequently Article 1(2) was also ruled to be unconstitutional. Moreover, the same applied to Article 7(1) of the Bank Act of August 1993 in so far as it stated that the Monetary Policy Council would be "responsible for formulating monetary policy". Concerning the complaint of the deputies of the National Assembly, the Constitutional Council stated that it was within the

---

[329] Décision no. 93–324 DC, JORF 1993, at 11014. According to Art. 61(2) Constitution of 1958 the Constitutional Council can also review the constitutionality of Acts of Parliament upon request by the President of the Republic, the Prime Minister, the President of the National Assembly or 60 of its members, or the President of the Senate or 60 of its members. Art. 61(2) amounts to a preventive normative control, since provisions which are declared unconstitutional may be neither promulgated nor implemented.

[330] The plaintiff also relied on Art. 3 of the *Déclaration des droits de l'homme et du citoyen* and on Arts. 2 and 3 Constitution of 1958.

[331] The following words in Art. 1(1) were considered to be unconstitutional: "*defini et . . . dans le but d'assurer la stabilité des prix*".

[332] Décision no. 93–324 DC, at 11015.

competence of Parliament to decide to transfer to the Banque de France the functions referred to in the relevant provisions of the contested law.

The Council observed, contrary to the plaintiff's argument, that Article 88 of the Constitution of 1958 in principle did constitute a sufficient legal basis for the transfer of power necessary for the establishment of an EMU, and that the provisions of the new Bank Act 1993 were merely anticipating the amendments of the legal basis of the Banque de France necessary at the time of the establishment of the ESCB. Article 88(1) states:

> "The Republic shall participate in the European Communities and the European Union, constituted by States that have freely chosen, by virtue of the treaties that have instituted those bodies, to exercise some of their powers in common."

More explicitly, Article 88(2) states:

> "On the condition of reciprocity, and according to the procedure laid down in the Treaty on European Union signed on 7 February 1992, France shall agree to transfer powers necessary for the establishment of the European economic and monetary union. . . . "

Although, while recognising that Article 88(2) in principle justified a transfer of monetary authority to the extent foreseen by the Bank Act 1993, the Constitutional Council considered this provision to be inapplicable on grounds of a lack of *reciprocity* since the TEU had not yet been ratified by all Member States.[333] In doing so it followed another argument of the plaintiffs which had claimed that a constitutional review of the contested provisions would have to exclude Article 88(2). The Constitutional Council reviewed the Bank Act 1993 on the basis of the constitutional situation prior to the introduction of Article 88 and took up its line of argumentation developed in the first of its decisions on the TEU. It argued that the Constitution of 1958 without prior amendment did not permit the removal of power over monetary policy from the (national) government.[334] On 31 December 1993, after the coming into effect of the TEU, a second Bank Act reinstated the provisions which had been considered unconstitutional.[335] Still, it seems questionable whether the newly introduced Article 88 of the Constitution of 1958, which is considered to justify the independent status of the Banque de France actually solves the discrepancies between the independent conduct of monetary policy, as foreseen by the Bank Act 1993, and the overall responsibility of government for the policies of the nation, as foreseen by Article 20 of the Constitution of 1958, since the wording of Article 88(2) can also be interpreted to the effect that it only allows for the transfer of powers to a

---

[333] Décision no 92–308 DC, JORF at 11015.

[334] Cf. Chap. 4 I 3.

[335] Loi no. 93–1444 du 31 décembre 1993 portant diverses disposistions relatives à la Banque de France, à l'assurance, au crédit et aux marchés financiers, JORF 1994, 231 *et seq.*; also décret no. 93–1278 du 3 décembre 1993 sur la Banque de France, JORF 1993, 16854 *et seq.*, hereafter referred to as décret 1993.

European institution in the context of EMU.[336] Indeed, this inconsistency in the Constitution of 1958 has led to proposals to introduce a separate Article on the Banque de France into the Constitution, similar to the provisions on the Audit Office (*Cour des comptes*).[337]

While ensuring the independence of the Banque de France, the Bank Act 1993 also provides for co-operation with the executive government. Both the Prime Minister and the Minister of Economic Affairs and Finances have the right to attend the deliberations of the CPM. According to Article 9(3) of the Bank Act 1993:

> "The Prime Minister and the Minister of Economic Affairs and Finances may attend meetings of the Monetary Policy Council, but may not vote. They submit proposals for consideration by the Council."

According to Article 9(4) of the Bank Act 1993 the Minister of Economic Affairs and Finance may be represented by a person specifically nominated and especially empowered to do so, in case the minister is unable to attend. Currently, the minister is represented by the Head of the Treasury at the Ministry of Economic Affairs and Finances who, at the same time, is appointed as the Censor in the General Council. Thus the Censor is *de facto* present at the deliberations of the CPM, be it in the role of the representative of the minister. The Prime Minister and Minister of Economic Affairs and Finances do not have a voting right. The provision is similar to that applicable to the Bundesbank, but more definite in some respects, since it specifies the members of government which may attend the meetings. Unlike the situation in Germany, the governor and/or deputy governors of the Banque de France do not have the right to take part in the deliberations of the Council of Ministers on issues relating to monetary policy. Nevertheless, government participation has been viewed as a guarantee of a good relationship between the government and the monetary authority and has even been interpreted as one important element of democratic accountability.[338]

The role of the Censor is not limited to representing the government ministers. He is a permanent member of the Banque de France, and the Bank Act 1993 has preserved the historically developed role of the Censor to some extent. According to Article 12(5) of the Bank Act 1993:

> "A Censor, or his alternate, appointed by the Minister of Economic Affairs and Finance, shall attend the meetings of the General Council. He may submit proposed decisions for the consideration of the Council."[339]

Unlike the Bank Act 1973, Article 12(5) of the Bank Act 1993 outlines the functions of the Censor in the General Council to a greater extent. The Censor may

---

[336] Leroy, n. 13 above, 5 *et seq.* is critical.

[337] Duprat, n. 231 above, at 10.

[338] Cf. e.g. remarks made by the Governor of the Banque de France J.C. Trichet, reported in "Trichet outlines vision of 'open and democratic' central bank", *Financial Times*, 8–9 Jan. 1994.

[339] Note that the Bank Act 1993 does not specify the term of office of the Censor.

submit proposed decisions for the consideration of the General Council. This
correlates with the role of the Prime Minister and the Minister of Economic
Affairs and Finance in meetings of the CPM. However, in contrast to the representatives of the government on the CPM the Censor also plays a decisive role in
the decision-making process of the General Council. According to Article 12(6):

> "Decisions adopted by the General Council shall be final, *unless* any objection is
> lodged by the Censor or his alternate."[340]

It derives as an *argumentum e contrario* from this provision that despite the fact
that the Censor does not have a formal right to vote, the General Council *de
facto* cannot take an effective decision without his consent, since his veto stands
in the way of a "final decision". The fate of a decision which has been objected
to by the Censor is unclear. The previous statute of the Bank, which already
included the Censor's right of veto, was more descriptive in this respect, as
Article 16(3) of the Bank Act 1973 indicated:

> "The decision shall be final, unless any objection is lodged by the Censor. *In the latter
> case the governor brings about a new consideration in due course.*"[341]

Taking into consideration the similarities with regard to the role of the Censor
between the Bank Act 1993 and the Bank Act 1973 it has to be assumed that
decisions of the General Council do not formally come into effect until either
the Censor has withdrawn his objection or a different decision is taken by the
General Council, which is not being objected to by the Censor. Although the
Censor cannot force a certain decision upon the General Council, the latter cannot bypass the former. In effect, the procedure calls for co-operation between
the General Council and the Censor. As an appointee of the Minister of
Economic Affairs and Finance, the Censor is at times referred to as an agent or
representative of the Minister of Economic Affairs and Finance, thereby indicating the interdependence between the Censor and the government.[342] In contrast to the members of the CPM and the General Council, the Censor is not
insulated from government influence. Article 1(2) of the Bank Act 1993 on the
independence of the Banque de France does not apply to the position of the
Censor, since he is a member neither of the CPM, nor of the General Council,
whose meetings he "only" attends as an outsider. The government's choice of
Censors may provide evidence for the close links between the Censor and the
governor. Currently, the Head of the Treasury at the Ministry of Economic
Affairs and Finances has been appointed Censor.[343] To be sure, the influence of
the Censor and thus, ultimately, that of government is limited to the range of
decisions which the General Council is authorised to take. This includes deci-

[340] Emphasis added.
[341] Emphasis added.
[342] J.-P. Duprat, op. cit., Chap. 3, n. 62, at 144, refers to the Censor as "an emanation of the executive".
[343] As at 12 Oct. 1995, cf. Banque de France, *Annual Report 1995*, (Direction générale des Études,
Banque de France, 1996), at 170.

sions on operational matters concerning the conduct of the Bank's activities. This does not include, however, decisions directly effecting the formulation and/or implementation of monetary policy.[344] Indeed, the existence of the Censor has been identified as one of the reasons for the maintenance of the General Council alongside the CPM, albeit that almost the same persons are present in both organs.[345] The separation of functions made it possible to limit the influence of the Censor to administrative matters, while retaining the conduct of monetary policy free from government influence.

In the revised statute of the Banque de France the provision referring to the independence of the CPM has been slightly amended, linking independence to the performance of the tasks arising from the participation of the Bank in the ESCB.[346] The role of the Censor is preserved. The revised statute of the Bank makes it clear that the General Council, in which the Censor takes part, decides on issues related to the conduct of the Banque de France's activities other than those deriving from the tasks of the ESCB.[347]

The third central bank for which an entire provision describes the independence is the **ESCB** and the ECB. According to Article 107 EC:

> "When exercising the powers and carrying out the tasks and duties conferred upon them by this Treaty and the Statute of the ESCB, neither the ECB, nor a national central bank, nor any member of its decision-making bodies shall seek or take instructions from Community institutions or bodies, from any government of a Member State or from any other body. The Community institutions and bodies and the governments of the Member States undertake to respect this principle and not to seek to influence the members of the decision-making bodies of the ECB or of the national central banks in the performance of their tasks."[348]

Neither the EC Treaty nor the ESCB Statute defines what actions are actually regarded as "influencing" the decision-making bodies. Article 157(2) EC on the composition of the Commission and the obligation of its members, which includes a similar provision on the independence of the members of the Commission, may provide some orientation in this respect.[349] The members of the Executive Board, as well as the national central bank governors, are neither allowed to seek instructions, nor do they have to act in accordance with any instructions from either Community institutions or any other bodies, e.g. the Council in the composition of the Ministers of Economics and Finance

---

[344] Cf. Art. 11(2), which expressly excludes the responsibilities set out in Art. 1 Bank Act 1993.
[345] Duprat, n. 231 above, at 7, according to whom the primary reason is the participation of a representative of the staff of the Bank in the General Council.
[346] Cf. Art. 1(3) Banque de France Act 1998.
[347] Ibid., Art. 11(2).
[348] Also Art. 7 ESCB Statute.
[349] Cf. J. Cloos/G. Reinesch/D. Vignes/J. Weyland, *Le Traité De Maastricht: genèse, analyse, commentaires* (2nd edn., Emile Bruylant, Brussels, 1994), at 259; H. Schmitt von Sydow, in H. v.d.Groeben/J. Thiesing/C.-D. Ehlermann, *Kommentar zum EWG-Vertrag* (4th edn., Nomos, Baden-Baden, 1991), vol. III, on Art. 157 EC.

(ECOFIN), or from any government of a Member State.[350] However, unlike Article 157(2) EC, Article 107 also prohibits the influencing of the members of the Governing Council and Executive Board of the ECB and the respective decision-making bodies in the national central banks by Community institutions as well as bodies and governments of the Member States. On the one end of the scale, this must include any action falling short of a formal instruction. However, according to the wording this should theoretically also include any attempts to convince central bank officials of certain positions.[351] Yet, this interpretation would be in contradiction to the participatory rights of the President of the Council and a representative of the Commission in the meetings of the Governing Council, and the reporting requirements of the ECB to the EP.[352] It has to be interpreted from the *ratio legis* of the provision granting participatory rights that they have the right not only to state their opinions, but also to try and convince the Governing Council of its view.[353] Anything else would not only be unrealistic in practice, but would also render the participation utterly meaningless.

As with the Bundesbank and the Banque de France, the EC Treaty foresees mechanisms for co-ordination between the ECB and the Council. According to Article 109b(1) EC, the President of the Council and one member of the Commission may participate in the meetings of the Governing Council without a right to vote. With regard to the President of the Council, the member of the ECOFIN Council representing the Member State which holds the Presidency will participate. Neither the EC Treaty, nor the ESCB Statute specifies the member of the Commission who is supposed to take part, but it seems likely that the representative of the Commission will be related to the Directorate-General entrusted with economic and monetary matters, while the President of the Commission may participate occasionally.[354] On the European level the participation of a representative of the Commission had its predecessor in the participation of a representative of the Commission in meetings of the Committee of Governors.[355] The fact that the President of the Council is also given a right to participate shows the importance which the Member States assembled in the Council assign to the Governing Council of the ECB, which takes decisions on monetary policy which are binding for all participating Member States.

---

[350] The words "Community . . . bodies" have been implemented notably with a view to the European Council; cf. Cloos/Reinesch/Vignes/Weyland, n. 349 above, at 259.

[351] On the contrary, since Art. 157(2) does not include any reference to outside influence, Member States may try to convince Commissioners of their particular views. Cf. Schmitt von Sydow, n. 349 above, on Art. 157, side notation 25.

[352] With regard to the reporting requirements cf. Chap. 4 VI 1.

[353] R. Stadler, *Der rechtliche Handlungsspielraum des Europäischen Systems der Zentralbanken* (Nomos, Baden-Baden, 1996), 123–4.

[354] Under the current organisational structure of the Commission this would be Directorate-General II on Economic and Financial Affairs.

[355] Council Decision 64/300 [1963–4] OJ Spec. Ed., amended by Council Decision 90/142 ([1990] OJ L78/25). According to Art. 2, subpara. 2, the Commission was invited to send a member as a representatives to meetings of the Committee. The Commission could even request an emergency meeting: Art. 4.

It has been suggested that the participation of the President of the Council and a member of the Commission enhances the transparency of the ECB.[356] Yet, while this may be the case from the point of view of the Council and the Commission this is not necessarily the case from the point of view of the general public.

The counterpart to the participation of the Council and the Commission in the meetings of the Governing Council is the right of the president of the ECB to take part in meetings of the EU Council, when the latter is discussing matters relating to the objectives and tasks of the ESCB.[357] However, his influence in the decision-making process of the Council can only be informal in nature, since the EC Treaty does not give him a voting right. A general right of the Council to ask the president and/or other members of the Executive Board of the ECB to report to the Council like that to the EP has not been included in the EC Treaty and the ESCB Statute.[358] However, the president of the ECB does have to present the Annual Report on the activities of the ESCB and the monetary policy of the past and current year to the Council.[359]

2. Central bank statutes without an explicit reference to independence

In the case of the Fed, the Nederlandsche Bank, the Reserve Bank of New Zealand and the Bank of England, the legal basis does not include a provision explicitly referring to the independence of the respective central bank. However, as will be seen later, it cannot be automatically concluded from this that such central banks are under the control of the executive government, or for that matter more accountable. Rather, the relationship between the central bank and the executive government emerges from a summary of different provisions and *de facto* arrangements which have to be observed in order to evaluate the demo-cratic accountability of the central bank.

Although the **Fed** is commonly referred to as one of the more independent central banks, the Federal Reserve Act does not include a provision explicitly referring to the independence of the Fed *vis-à-vis* the executive government. Not least due to this lack of a clear rule, a large number of studies examine the rela-tionship between the Fed and the executive branch. The relations between the US President and the Board of Governors, and in particular its chairman, pre-dominate in the discussions. Here, the debate mostly boils down to the question whether and to what extent the President has any influence over the Fed or, as it is often put, can put pressure on monetary policy, and, on the contrary, how

---

[356] Committee of Governors of the Central Banks of the Member States of the European Economic Community, *Annual Report* (July 1990–Dec. 1991), Apr. 1992, at 52.

[357] Art. 109b(2) EC.

[358] This has been one of the suggestions in the Delors Report; cf. Committee for the Study of Economic and Monetary Union, op. cit., Chap. 3, n. 349, at 22.

[359] Art. 109b(3) EC.

much influence the Fed exercises over the President. A similar approach is also taken to study the relationship between the Treasury and the Fed.

The legal nature of the Fed and its relationship with the executive are not easily determined. On the one hand, the Fed relies on a network of 12 regional Federal Reserve Banks all of which constitute bodies corporate with separate legal personalities owned by commercial banks which hold shares in their capital. On the other hand, the Federal Reserve Banks can be clearly distinguished from (private) commercial banks since the former do not work on a profit-oriented basis. Therefore, the Fed combines public with private elements. On the one hand, the Fed has been created by Congress and is supervised by a Board of Governors. Despite its classification as an independent administrative agency,[360] the latter in effect belongs to the executive branch of government. Moreover, the salary of the Chairman of the Board of Governors of the Fed is linked to those of government employees and is listed—among others— together with the Deputy Secretary of the Treasury and the Chairman of the Council of Economic Advisors.[361] Besides, like government agencies, the Board of Governors has issued rules of organisation.[362] On the other hand, the budget of the Fed is excluded from the appropriation process in Congress, and the executive branch is not represented on the Board of Governors.[363] It becomes clear from this description that the Fed cannot be described as independent of government. Conversely, the Fed cannot be assigned to the executive branch either. It remains situated somewhere between these two branches of government.[364] In short, the Fed may be characterised as a regional system of Federal Reserve Banks which combines private with public elements and which is independent within rather than of government.

Despite the powerful position of the US President under the US Constitution as the holder of the executive power neither the Federal Reserve Act nor any other law makes the Board of Governors, FOMC or the board of directors of the Federal Reserve Banks directly accountable to the former. This may be highlighted by the fact that the objectives and plans of the Fed by law do not have to be in line with the economic goals of the President.[365] It is this detachment of the

---

[360] With regard to the main differences between executive department agencies and independent administrative agencies, cf. D.L. Carper *et al.*, *Understanding the Law* (2nd edn., West Law Publishing Company, Minn./St. Paul, 1995), 194 *et seq.*

[361] Cf. 5 USC Sec. 5313.

[362] According to 5 USC Sec. 552 each "agency" has to make public information—among others— its rules of procedure. S. 551 of Title 5 of the United States Code defines "agency" as "each authority of the Government of the United States, whether or not it is within or subject to review by another agency".

[363] Cf. Chap.s 4 IV and 4 VIII.

[364] "A pretty queer duck" was the description used by Wright Patman, member of the House of Representatives and the most famous critic of the Fed at his time. Recorded in W. Greider, op. cit., Chap. 2, n. 175, at 49–50. Outside the area of monetary policy and in particular with regard to its regulatory tasks the Fed can be classified as an Independent Regulatory Authority, see M. Englert, *Der Handlungsspielraum der amerikanischen Bundesbank im Regierungssytem* (Schäuble Verlag, Rheinfelden, 1988), 39 *et seq.*, with further references.

[365] With regard to the reporting requirements under s. 2A(1) Federal Reserve Act, cf. Chap. 4 II 1.

Fed from the head of the executive which forms an important cornerstone in the evaluation of the Fed as an independent central bank. However, it should not be concluded from this that the role of the President is confined to that of an observer on the side-lines. Rather, the relationship is defined by a number of formal and informal arrangements which provide anything but a clear picture. First, arguably the most direct impact that the President has on the Fed is his power to appoint the members of the Board of Governors, including the chairman and vice chairman, which also stands for a majority of the members in the FOMC.[366] Secondly, although not foreseen in the Federal Reserve Act, the chairman of the Fed and the President come together in occasional consultations and the former advises the latter on issues relating to economic and monetary policy.[367] The actual relationship between the President and the chairman of the Fed depends to a large degree on the personalities of the two principal actors. In some instances the chairman is reported to have had close relations to the President.[368] Finally, the Board of Governors has strong links with the US President's Council of Economic Advisors ("the President's men") with meetings taking place every two weeks at the Board of Governors.[369]

Some studies indicate that the US President exercises a considerable influence over monetary policy conducted by the Fed. [370] Others take a more sceptical view of the actual influence of the President. Newton, for instance, argues that the Fed in the end pursues the policies it favours, according to the motto "[t]he president proposes, the Fed disposes", and draws the conclusion that "the control of the Federal Reserve policy apparatus is vested in what is in fact a self-perpetuating oligarchy".[371] Closest to the truth may be the view that the relationship between the President and the chairman of the Board of Governors is determined by the interdependence of the two for the performance of their tasks in the area of economic policy. Kettl finds four reasons for this interdependence which has grown over time: the growing recognition of the interdependence of

---

[366] For details of the procedure and the limitations of this power, cf. Chap. 4 IV 1.

[367] J.M. Berry, op. cit., Chap. 3, n. 555, at 45: "there is a decided circumspection in the discussions of monetary policy and interest rates, some participants say. No one wants to be seen trying to tell the Fed what to do".

[368] One such example has been the relationship between President Nixon and chairman Burns who had previously advised the President on the Council of Economic Advisors. In contrast, the relations between President Reagan and chairman Volker are reported to have been poor: cf. Kettl, n. 183 above, 193 *et seq.*

[369] M. Feldstein, "The Council for Economic Advisors and Economic Advising in the United States", *The Economic Journal*, vol. 102 (1992), 1223–34, refers to an informal body, the so-called "Troika", for the discussion of economic issues consisting of the Secretary of the Treasury, the chairman of the Council of Economic Advisors, the Director of the Office for Management and Budget, and, occasionally, the chairman of the Board of Governors.

[370] M.C. Mung/B.E. Roberts, "The Federal Reserve and its Institutional Environment: A Review" in Th. Mayer (ed.), *The political economy of American monetary policy* (Cambridge University Press, Cambridge, 1990), 83–98; also J. de Haan/L.W. Gormley, "Independence and Accountability of the European Central Bank" in M. Andenas/L.W. Gormley/C. Hadjiemmanuil/I. Harden (eds.), op. cit., Chap. 1, n. 5, 331–53, 344 *et seq.*, with an overview ofr the different studies examining the presidential influence on the Fed.

[371] M. Newton, *The FED* (Times Books, New York, 1983), at 123 and 128 *et seq.*

monetary and fiscal policy; government spending had proven to be no longer pursuable as an economic policy tool; increased public awareness with regard to presidential performance with regard to the economy ("expect the president to deliver"), and the internationalisation of economic issues.[372] According to this view the President cannot pursue economic policy successfully without the support of the Fed, and the Fed cannot operate without credibility/public confidence. Pierce refers to an "unholy alliance" between the Fed and the elected politicians. Kane describes the monetary policy-making as a series of games between the Fed and politicians which, when carried into the open, includes what he refers to as "Fed-bashing", where elected politicians blame the monetary policy of the Fed for the state of the economy and distance themselves from unpopular monetary policies.[373] Suggestions have been made to strengthen the role of the President *vis-à-vis* the Fed. On a number of occasions legislative proposals were introduced in the Senate or the House of Representatives to strengthen his role *vis-à-vis* the Board of Governors by having the term of the chairman of the Board of Governors coincide with that of the President and, more generally, to shorten the terms of the members of the Board of Governors.[374] It has also been suggested that the Board of Governors should be enlarged by two members to include nine governors.

With regard to the relationship between the Fed and the Treasury the Federal Reserve Act does not foresee any formal relationship. Neither the chairman nor any other part of the Fed is in any way subordinated to the Treasury.[375] The only instance in which the Treasury may take precedence over the Board of Governors is the case of a conflict of jurisdiction between the Secretary of the Treasury and the Board of Governors or the federal reserve agent.[376] The Secretary of the Treasury and the chairman of the Fed meet regularly, usually once a week, to discuss monetary policy issues. On a lower level regular contacts exist between the under-secretary for monetary affairs of the Treasury and members of the Board of Governors, as well as other Fed and Treasury officials. With regard to the actual influence of the Treasury *vis-à-vis* the Fed Havrilesky observes what he refers to as politically-inspired monetary activism by the administration. He detects a statistically significant relationship between signalling from the Treasury and monetary policy pursued by the Fed. Similar influence of the President or the Council of Economic Advisors has not been found.[377] On the contrary, Newton is critical of the actual influence of the Treasury on the monetary policy pursued by the Fed. Observing that between

---

[372] Kettl, n. 183 above, at 194.

[373] J.L. Pierce, "The Federal Reserve as a Political Power", in Mayer (ed.), n. 370 above, 151–164, at 152; E.J. Kane, "Bureaucratic Self-interest as an Obstacle to Monetary Reform", in Mayer (ed.), n. 370 above, 283–98.

[374] Cf. Chap. 4 IV 1.

[375] Note, however, that in matters relating to external monetary policy the Fed only acts as an agent for the Treasury which is responsible for the exchange rate regime: cf. Chap. 3 VII 3.

[376] S. 10(6) Federal Reserve Act.

[377] Havrilesky, n. 131 above, at 16.

1945 and 1980 the important position of Under Secretary for Monetary Affairs in the Treasury was held by figures who had close links to the Federal Reserve Banks and, having worked for them previously, for its philosophies, he refers to a "happy little game of musical chairs".[378] With regard to the Department of the Treasury it has been recommended that the Secretary of the Treasury should be made an *ex officio* member of the Board of Governors again, or that the Secretary of the Treasury and/or the Chairman of the Council of Economic Advisors should be members of the FOMC.[379] Under the original Federal Reserve Act of 1913 the Secretary of the Treasury and the Comptroller of the Currency were *ex officio* members on the Board of Governors. A less stringent suggestion has been to introduce *formal* consultations in a forum consisting of the members of the FOMC on the one side and the Secretary of the Treasury, the Director of the Office of Management and Budget and the chairman of the Council of Economic Advisors.[380] The question which needs to be addressed with regard to all of these suggestions is whether the proposed changes would enhance the co-ordination between the President and the Fed to the advantage of the democratic accountability of the Fed or whether they would only provide the executive branch with more influence over monetary policy with all the attendant apparent dangers. The advantages for the democratic accountability of the Fed are at least not apparent. The reason for this is that the executive branch is more independent of Parliament, i.e. Congress, than is the case in some of the other countries examined in this study. The concept of ministerial accountability on which the British parliamentary system is based to a large extent, but which also exists in other countries, such as Germany or the Netherlands, does not exist as such in the US constitutional system. Therefore, enhanced power of the executive branch over the Fed also does not result in more influence of Congress.

Like the Federal Reserve Act, the Bank Act 1948 does not include a specific provision on the independence of the **Nederlandsche Bank**. Nevertheless, the Nederlandsche Bank is generally considered to incorporate a large degree of independence *vis-à-vis* government in the conduct of monetary policy. This *de facto* independence is the result of an addition of different provisions of the Bank Act 1948, in particular Section 9(1) of the Bank Act 1948 on the monetary objective of the Bank.[381]

Neither the Minister of Finance nor any other member of the government has the right to participate in the meetings of the Governing Board of the Bank. However, this is not to say that the government is not at all present in the Nederlandsche Bank. Although not a member of the executive government

---

[378] Newton, n. 371 above, 121 *et seq.*

[379] Over the years there have been numerous proposals in Congress: cf. Akhtar/Howe, n. 131 above, with an overview.

[380] H.R. 2917 (103rd Congress).

[381] Cf. Chap. 4 II 1.

236 *Evaluating the Democratic Accountability of Central Banks*

himself, the Royal Commissioner oversees the affairs of the Bank on behalf of the government. As such he receives his instructions by a Royal decision.[382] The Royal Commissioner does not take part in any capacity in the meetings of the Governing Board of the Bank and thus in the monetary policy decisions of the Nederlandsche Bank. However, he has the right to request any information from the Governing Board "which he may deem necessary for the proper performance of his supervisory duties".[383] Whether this would in practice also include the otherwise confidential minutes of the meetings of the Governing Board remains unclear. The Royal Commissioner also plays an important role in the yearly discharging of the Governing Board, as he reviews the legality of the annual accounts.[384] He has the right to take part in the meetings of shareholders, i.e. the Council of Ministers representing executive government, and the joint meetings of the Governing Board and the Supervisory Board in an advisory capacity. The participatory rights of the Royal Commissioner are limited to the subject areas dealt with by the meeting of the shareholders and the joint meeting the Governing Council and the Supervisory Board. Accordingly, the Royal Commissioner can advise the Council of Ministers/Minister of Finance, representing the State as the sole shareholder, on the appointment of the Supervisory Board (section 27(2) of the Bank Act 1948), and can advise the joint meeting of the Governing Board and the Supervisory Board on the drafting of rules and regulations referred to in the Bank Act 1948 (sections 8, 18(2), 22(2), 29), the recommendation lists drawn up for the appointment of the members of the Governing Board and the Supervisory Board (section 23), the nomination of Alternate Directors (section 24) and, finally, the proposal for the suspension or dismissal of a member of the Governing Board (section 23(4)). The Royal Commissioner is also an *ex officio* member of the Bank Council and chairs its meetings.

The Bank Council may be considered as an important cornerstone in the relationship of the Nederlandsche Bank not only with the government, but also *vis-à-vis* trade and industry. This becomes evident from the mixed representation in the Bank Council resulting from a somewhat complex appointment procedure explained in detail in the section on appointment and dismissal procedures. This results in a representation of different, sometimes potentially contrary, interests on the Bank Council, such as for instance between representatives of employers and employees. The Bank Council is designed to offer a forum for discussion on the position and the tasks of the Nederlandsche Bank. The report on economic and financial developments and the monetary policy pursued by the Governing Board, which is presented by the president of the Bank at the beginning of each meeting, provides the Bank Council with first-hand information on the situation of the Bank.[385] Moreover, upon request of one or more of its members, the Bank

---

[382] Koninklijk besluit van 27 oktober 1972 (no. 82).
[383] S. 30(3) Bank Act 1948.
[384] For more details, cf. Chap. 4 VIII.
[385] S. 33(2) Bank Act 1948.

Council may discuss any subject related to the position and/or tasks of the Bank. In this respect its chequered composition, including the Governing Board, the Royal Commissioner, members of the Supervisory Board, representatives of trade and industry, the Treasurer-General and the Governing Board, can ensure a large platform for discussion of the role of the Bank. Indeed, the motive behind having a Bank Council was to strengthen the "community element" in the legal basis of the Nederlandsche Bank and to create what nowadays is commonly referred to as a think-tank.[386] Until recently, the Bank Council also had a role as an advisor to the Minister of Finance. It could be called upon by the Minister of Finance, after having consulted the Governing Board, to give advice on the principles of the Bank's policy. *Vice versa* the Bank Council itself could take the initiative to advise the Minister of Finance on such principles. It has been observed that these functions of the Bank Council have recently been terminated as part of an overhaul of the Government Advisory System.[387]

Within the narrow margins set by the Bank Act 1948, arguably the most crucial function of the Bank Council is related to the application of the override mechanism under section 26(1) of the Bank Act 1948. In order to issue instructions under that provision the Minister of Finance has to consult the Bank Council. This function has not been removed from the Bank Council. Since section 26 has never been put to use, no track record exists of the behaviour of the Bank Council in this context. A potential conflict of interest for some members of the Bank Council with regard to the advisory role under section 26 is anticipated by limiting the participatory rights of the Governing Board, the Treasurer-General and the three representatives, named by the Ministers of Economic Affairs, Agriculture, Food and Fisheries, and for Social Affairs respectively to an advisory capacity on the Bank Council.[388] This means that they could not take part in a formal decision on a recommendation given to the Minister of Finance, thereby possibly influencing the direction of the recommendation to the Minister of Finance in favour of the Bank or the Government. Although an explicit reference in the Bank Act 1948 is lacking, it becomes apparent from the explanatory statements to the draft law (*memorie van toelichting*) that the Bank Council is also supposed to advise the Governing Board itself. Until recently, due to the ambivalent division of labour, i.e. adviser to government *and* Governing Board of the Bank, the position of the Bank Council has been described as somewhere between the Minister of Finance and the Governing Board of the Nederlandsche Bank.[389]

Yet the relationship between the government and the Bank is not limited to the contact points in the Bank, i.e. presence or representation of the government

[386] de Jong, n. 192 above, 509 *et seq.*
[387] Cf. Chap. 3 IV.
[388] It should be noted that the Treasurer-General is a civil servant in the Ministry of Finance, rather than a member of the government.
[389] de Jong, n. 192 above, at 513–14, with references to parliamentary discussions during the drafting of the Bank Act 1948.

in the Nederlandsche Bank. Although the members of government are excluded from participation in the deliberations of the Governing Board, the president of the Nederlandsche Bank can attend the meetings of the Council of Economic Affairs, one of the sub-committees of the Council of Ministers. The sub-committees have the right to invite experts in an *advisory* capacity.[390] Consequently, the president of the Nederlandsche Bank does not take part in the decisions of the Council of Ministers or its sub-committees. Moreover, the president of the Nederlandsche Bank is a member of the government's main advisory board, the so-called Social and Economic Council (*Sociaal-economische raad*) which offers advice on all social and economic matters and under specific circumstances may have regulatory power conferred by law.[391] These somewhat formal contacts are rounded off by traditional weekly luncheons attended by the president of the Nederlandsche Bank, the Minister of Finance and the Treasurer-General. During these meetings current economic, financial and monetary topics are discussed.[392] Moreover, there are regular contacts between the staff of the Nederlandsche Bank and the Ministry of Finance.

Under the provisions of the Bank Act 1998, a reference to the independence of the Nederlandsche Bank in carrying out the tasks in the ESCB is included. According to this the Bank may only ask for or receive instructions from the ECB.[393] The institution of the Royal Commissioner is abolished.[394] The Bank Council is also restructured—among others—taking into account that the function of the Royal Commissioner and the override mechanism are abolished.[395] However, the president of the Bank will remain obliged to report to the Bank Council and to discuss the policies of the Nederlandsche Bank.[396]

The Reserve Bank Act 1989 does not formally recognise the independence of the **Reserve Bank of New Zealand** either. Rather, its independence derives from an overall assessment of the statutory provisions as implying that the Bank is independent from executive government in the implementation of monetary policy, and thus has instrument independence. At the centre of the relationship between the Reserve Bank and the executive government stands the PTA agreed upon between the governor of the Bank and the Minister of Finance, which, together with the monetary objective, defines the goals of monetary policy. In the light of the fact that in the absence of a monetary policy board the governor himself is in charge of monetary policy decisions it is not surprising that the Reserve Bank

---

[390] Art. 23 Reglement van orde voor de ministerraad.

[391] The Social and Economic Council has been established by law: Wet op de bedrijfsorganisatie, Stb. 1950, no. 22; for details cf. Prakke/De Reede/Van Wissen (eds.), n. 15 above, 682–3, with further references.

[392] Cf. A. Vondeling, *Nasmaak en voorproef* (Uitgeverij De Arbeiderspers, Amsterdam, 1968), at 164, recalling his time as a Minister of Finance.

[393] Cf. s. 3(3) Bank Act 1998.

[394] Cf. Memorie Van Toelichting, Tweede Kamer, Vergaderjaar 1997–8, 25 719, nr. 1–3, at 12.

[395] Cf. s. 15 Bank Act 1998. See also Chap. 4 V 3.

[396] S. 15(5) Bank Act 1998.

Act 1989 does not foresee participation of the Minister of Finance or other members of the executive government in the meetings of a monetary policy board which does not exist. In theory no provision of the Reserve Bank Act 1989 prohibits the government from influencing the governor in the conduct of his duties. It is the governor who is responsible for the conduct of monetary policy and ultimately he has to decide what policy decisions he can justify. Yet, the transfer of responsibility may prevent a governor from falling victim to extended influence from outside, since he may be reluctant to follow third-party preferences for which he is ultimately held accountable.

The Board of Directors takes a prominent role in the accountability of the Reserve Bank. Indeed, it has been referred to as "the eyes and ears of government".[397] It is positioned outside the executive structure of the Bank, in as much as it does not take part in the decision-making processes. It plays a dual role. First, it takes part in the appointment of the governor.[398] Apart from that, the primary function of the Board of Directors may be compared with that of an internal controller, charged with the review of the performance of the governor and the institution at large from within the Bank. Section 53 of the Reserve Bank Act 1989 explains the duties of the Board in some detail and obliges the Board to keep under constant review all aspects of the performance of the Bank. This includes its performance in carrying out its functions as such, the performance of the governor in discharging his responsibilities, and whether the governor secures the Bank's achievement of the policy targets fixed in the PTA.[399] Moreover, the Board reviews whether the policy statements of the Bank are consistent with the primary functions under section 8(1) of the Reserve Bank Act 1989, i.e. price stability, and the PTA.[400] The Board of Directors also acts as an adviser to the governor on any matter relating to the performance of the Bank's functions and the exercise of its powers.[401] In addition to identifying the areas of responsibilities which the Board of Directors reviews, section 53(3) of the Reserve Bank Act 1989 also defines in some detail the areas in which misconduct by the governor will result in further actions by the Board. These are mostly based upon the areas of review mentioned above, but also include reasons to be found in the person of the governor himself. The Board reviews whether a governor is unable to carry out the responsibilities of office or has been guilty of misconduct. The Board of Directors also considers whether a governor has contradicted the conditions of his employment while holding office by pursuing any (business) interests outside the Reserve Bank.[402] The Board does not have the authority to impose sanctions. It notes the breach of duties and thereafter offers its written advice to the Minister of Finance. More importantly, the Board can

---

[397] An expression which has surfaced during discussions during a visit to the Reserve Bank of New Zealand.
[398] For more details of the appointment and dismissal procedures, cf. Chap. 4 IV.
[399] S. 53(1)(a)–(c) Reserve Bank Act 1989.
[400] Ibid., s. 53(1)(d).
[401] Ibid., s. 53(2).
[402] Ibid., s. 53(3)(f)–(g).

recommend to the Minister of Finance that the governor be removed from office.[403] A decision of the Board to recommend a removal of the governor is taken by a simple majority vote. Since a quorum of five members, of whom three have to be non-executive directors, is needed, it should in principle be ensured that the governor cannot block a decision to recommend a removal with the help of his two deputy governors, thereby avoiding his responsibility. Even in case of a tie, the governor could not make use of his decisive vote to his advantage, since section 61(2) of the Reserve Bank Act 1989 states that a director, i.e. including governor and deputy governor(s), is not entitled to vote or be counted in a quorum present at a meeting in which the exercise or proposed exercise of a power is considered in which the respective director has an interest.[404] Moreover, section 60(9) of the Reserve Bank Act 1989 ensures that the governor and his two deputy governors cannot take advantage of a possible deadlock due to a tie in a situation in which only three non-executive directors are present at a meeting of the Board, since in such a case the deputy governor who is not Deputy Chief Executive is not entitled to vote. In practice questions concerning the performance of the governor or his remuneration will be discussed in the forum of the non-executive committee and, thus, without the participation of the governor and/or deputy governors.[405] The non-executive committee also meets the Minister of Finance for discussions twice a year.

Summing up, it is an important function of the Board of Directors to act as an agent of the Minister of Finance in keeping the governor's and Bank's performance under constant review. Although the Board does not have the power autonomously to sanction any actions of the governor it can issue recommendations to the Minister of Finance to remove the governor from office.

Until recently the **Bank of England** did not enjoy statutory independence from the executive government, since the Bank of England Act 1946 included no provision on the independence of the Bank and/or its officials. On the contrary, section 4(1)–(2) of the Bank of England Act 1946 stated:

> "(1) The Treasury may from time to time give such directions to the Bank as, after consulting with the Governor of the Bank, they think necessary in the public interest.
>
> (2) *Subject to any such directions*, the affairs of the Bank shall be managed by the court of directors . . . ".[406]

Nevertheless, in the view of some the Bank of England enjoyed a considerable degree of independence, albeit *within* rather than *from* government, inasmuch as it could freely express its views to the executive government.[407] Prior to the recent institutional changes a development towards more independence for the

---

[403] Reserve Bank Act 1989, s. 53(3)(g).
[404] The same applies where a contract or proposed contract is considered.
[405] On the committees of the Board of Directors, cf. Chap. 3 VI 2.2.
[406] Emphasis added.
[407] M. Moran, "Monetary Policy and the Machinery of Government", *PA*, vol. 59 (1981), 47–61.

Bank of England in the implementation of monetary policy could be detected. Initially, during monthly meetings with the governors of the Bank, the Chancellor of the Exchequer decided on the adjustments of interest rates and, moreover, on the timing of the implementation of any adjustments. The Bank of England was eventually given some room for discretion in so far as it could decide itself on the timing of the implementation of the changes to the interest rate, although the Bank could not postpone that decision endlessly, thereby subverting the Treasury's intentions behind the decisions to change the interest rate. The clear implication of this arrangement was that the Chancellor's decision had to be put into force before the next monthly meeting between Chancellor and governor. Despite this apparent domination of the executive government, the Bank nevertheless may have had an influence on interest rate decisions by the Chancellor of the Exchequer. A Chancellor who intended to change interest rates against the explicit advice of the Bank ran the risk of losing credibility because his action could be interpreted as evidence of a lack of commitment to the government's announced monetary policy. This arguably increased the pressure on the executive government at least seriously to take account of the views of the Bank.

The Bank of England Act 1998 does not include a provision explicitly granting the Bank independence of the executive government either. Instead, it is a combination of provisions which in effect give the Bank of England instrument independence with regard to monetary policy. To this end, monetary policy has been exempted from directions by the Treasury.[408] Within the framework set by the monetary policy objective, as quantified by the Treasury, the MPC has responsibility within the Bank for formulating monetary policy.[409]

Although close contacts between the Treasury and the Bank can be assumed to continue, the new legislation does not foresee any institutionalised contacts between the Bank and the executive government with regard to monetary policy decisions. The Act introduces a right for a representative of the Treasury to participate and speak at any meeting of the MPC. A voting right is not foreseen.[410] Equally, provisions introducing the participation of the governor or other representatives of the Bank in cabinet or other meetings of the executive government do not exist.

Like the Board of Directors at the Reserve Bank of New Zealand, the Court of Directors of the Bank of England takes on the function of keeping under review the Bank's performance in relation to its objectives and strategy. Thereafter, it also reviews the extent to which the Bank's financial management objectives have been met. Moreover it keeps under review the internal financial controls of the Bank. The MPC is required to submit a monthly report on its activities to the Court of Directors.[411] These functions have been delegated to

---

[408] S. 10 Bank of England Act 1998.
[409] Ibid., s. 13(1).
[410] Ibid., sched. 3, para. 13.
[411] Ibid., sched. 3, para. 14.

the sub-committee of the Court of Directors.[412] The Court of Directors has to report on the performance of these functions to the Chancellor of the Exchequer once a year.[413] The assessment that the court of directors functions as a check on the Bank on behalf of the executive government may also be highlighted by the fact that the members of the Court of Directors are appointed by the executive government.

IV. APPOINTMENT AND DISMISSAL PROCEDURES

With regard to appointment procedures, a number of general observations emerge from the examination of the central banks included in this study. While in most instances the executive government is charged with the appointment of central bank officials, in a number of instances other institutions, including Parliament, take part in the procedures. In some instances this may be a reflection of the federal structures of a bank. In other instances it may reflect the strong position of Parliament. Thereafter, differences in the terms of office and, even more importantly, with regard to the possibility of reappointments can be detected. Generally, many differences emerge from the different institutional designs of the central banks. For dismissal procedures a general distinction between dismissal for misconduct and performance-based dismissal can be made.

1. Appointment and reappointment

In the case of all central banks examined in this study the (re-)appointment procedures are in the hands of the executive government. Nevertheless, a number of considerable differences exist, in particular with regard to the participation of Parliament. Another main difference which can be observed concerns the possibility of the reappointment of central bank officials.

According to Article 14.2 of the ESCB Statute, the statutes of the participating national central banks have to provide for a minimum term of office of five years for the governors. The national legislator is in principle not prohibited from providing for shorter terms for the other members of the monetary policy board or the managerial board of the central bank.[414]

---

[412] Bank of England Act 1998, s. 1(3).

[413] Ibid., s. 4. Cf. also Chap. 4 VIII 1.

[414] A different view is taken by the German federal government, which has made it clear in the explaining memorandum to the draft legislation for the amendment of the legal basis of the Bundesbank in the light of the ESCB that this must be the case for all members of the monetary policy board of the Bundesbank, i.e. Central Bank Council. Cf. BTDrucks. 13/7728 of 21 May 1997.

1.1. *Appointment procedures with parliamentary participation*

In the case of the Fed, the Banque de France, and the ECB, Parliament participates to a different degree in the appointment procedures.

Arguably the most extensive participation of a Parliament in the appointment
procedures is to be found for the **Fed** with regard to the Board of Governors.
The seven members of the Board of Governors are appointed by the President
"by and with the advice and consent of" the Senate for a non-renewable term of
14 years.[415] From these seven members the President appoints the chairman and
vice chairman of the Board of Governors for a renewable term of four years.[416]
Since the Federal Reserve Reform Act of 1977 these appointments also require
the consent of the Senate.[417] The consent of the Senate is more than just a rub-
ber stamp, as it conducts its own screening of the candidates in hearings before
the Committee on Banking, Housing, and Urban Affairs, where Presidential
nominees are questioned in detail.[418] Due to his outstanding role on the Board
of Governors the Senate takes special interest in the appointment of the chairman of the Board of Governors. After the Committee has reported its findings
regarding a nominee the full Senate decides by simple majority.[419] Although the
Senate has yet to reject a Presidential appointment to the Board of Governors it
should not be concluded from this that Congress in all instances agrees with the
presidential choices. Rather, disagreements between the President and the
Senate over a nomination are communicated early on in the process and differences are resolved prior to a formal vote in the Senate. The delay in appointments caused by the "confirmation" process in the Senate is also utilised to test
public perception of the candidates. It has been suggested that this power of
the Senate to reject appointments to the Board of Governors makes the Fed
more responsive to the Senate Banking Committee during the semi-annual
hearings.[420]

---

[415] S. 10.1 Federal Reserve Act. Members who are appointed to serve for the unexpired portion
of a term may be re-elected. Within the executive branch of government there is an established
administrative procedure for the nominations to the Board of Governors and the Treasury usually
takes the lead in these proposals.

[416] The term of office of the chairman and vice chairman is not linked to his 14-year term as a
member of the Board of Governors. Nevertheless, when a new chairman is appointed by tradition
his predecessor resigns from the Board of Governors to give the President the opportunity to appoint
a new member to the Board of Governors; cf. Akhtar/Howe, n. 131 above, at 346.

[417] The participation of the Senate in the appointment procedure has its basis in Art. II, s. 2, cl. 2
US Constitution, according to which the US President nominates and, by and with the advice of the
Senate, appoints ambassadors, other public ministers and consuls, judges of the Supreme Court, and
all other officers of the United States. For a critical assessment of the situation before 1977: *Making
the Fed More Accountable*, opening statements by Henry S. Reuss, Chairman of the House
Committee on Banking, Finance and Urban Affairs, for hearings on HR 8094, a bill to promote the
accountability of the Fed, 10.00 a.m., Monday 18 July 1977.

[418] R.H. Hasse (ed.), op. cit., Chap. 2, n. 22, at 166, sees the President's right of nomination limited by "the need to obtain the Senate's consent".

[419] Cf. s. 10(5) Federal Reserve Act on the appointments during the recess of the Senate.

[420] Havrilesky, n. 131 above, at 238. Cf. Chap. 4 VI 1.

244 *Evaluating the Democratic Accountability of Central Banks*

The Federal Reserve Act includes a number of grounds of disqualification which apply to members of the Board of Governors. First, in order to prevent any conflict of interests, members of the Board are prohibited from holding the position of an officer or director of any Federal Reserve Bank or commercial bank, banking institution, trust company, and, moreover, may not hold any stock in a commercial bank, banking institution or trust company.[421] Moreover, members of the House of Representatives and the Senate are barred from becoming members of the Board of Governors or a director or officer of a Federal Reserve Bank.[422]

The 14-year terms of the members of the Board of Governors have been the subject of criticism for some time. The basic argument is that the long terms place the Board "beyond the reach of the President and the administration".[423] Indeed, it is noteworthy that only federal judges and the comptroller general of the United States, who directs the General Accounting Office (GAO), serve longer terms.[424] The terms of office of the governors are staggered in such a way that the post of one member of the Board comes up for replacement every two years. Thus in theory each US President can make two appointments to the Board during a four-year term of office. Moreover, the President also has the opportunity to appoint the chairman and vice chairman of the Board of Governors during his term of office, since they only serve four-year terms. However, this may only be the case towards the end of the Presidential term. Therefore, the President may have no other choice than to tolerate and work together with a Board of Governors in the formulation of which he may have had little influence. Different suggestions have been made to change this situation. With regard to the position of the chairman it has been proposed to let his term of office coincide with that of the US President, thereby giving each President the opportunity to appoint a chairman (with the co-operation of the Senate) at the beginning of his term of office.[425] On the more general issue of the 14-year terms of office, it has been suggested that the presidential grip on the appointment of the governors should be strengthened by shortening the terms; suggestions have varied from 12 down to three years.[426] Whether the implementation of such proposals would effectively add to the accountability of the Fed is questionable. The long terms of the governors seem to exist on paper rather than in reality. Most members do not serve a full term of 14 years on the Board, either due to their advanced age or due to the fact that they move

[421] S. 10(4) Federal Reserve Act.

[422] Ibid., s. 4(13).

[423] W. Patman, op. cit., Chap. 3, n. 509, at 150.

[424] Federal judges are appointed "during good behaviour", often, if ironically , referred to as "for life", and the comptroller general serves for a term of 15 years.

[425] Cf. e.g. HR 12934, A bill to promote the independence and accountability for the Fed, 31 Mar. 1976; HR 4009, A bill to modernize the Fed, 28 Sept. 1983; recently: HR 2917, A bill to reform the Fed, 6 Aug. 1993.

[426] For a recent example cf. HJRes.554 of 24 Sept. 1992, which proposed *inter alia* to limit the terms of the members of the Board of Governors to 7 years.

on to more profitable occupations before their term of office expires.[427] Consequently, a President may have the opportunity to appoint more than two governors during his four-year term of office. Moreover, although shorter terms may provide the President and the Senate of the day with at least some increased influence over the composition of the Board of Governors, it would not necessarily increase the accountability of the governors *vis-à-vis* the Executive and Congress.[428] The reason for this is that the term of the members of the Board of Governors is non-renewable and a performance-based dismissal is excluded. The key to judging the performance of the members of the Board of Governors and for holding them accountable thereafter would be the possibility of reappointing members.[429] The President could consider the Board of Governors' conduct of monetary policy in relation to his own economic goals and the Senate could hold the members accountable for their pursuit of the broad objectives set out in the Federal Reserve Act. It seems that shorter terms without the possibility of reappointments would only increase the influence, in particular, of the President and, thus, decrease the independence of the Fed *vis-à-vis* the executive without balancing this with increased accountability. Thus, shorter terms of office may only work in favour of a more accountable Board of Governors if its members can be re-appointed.

Proposals for attaching the term of the chairman of the Board of Governors to that of the US President do not face this shortcoming, since chairmen can be and regularly are re-appointed. Yet, this does not necessarily mean that such proposals would lead to a more accountable chairman of the Board of Governors. First, in practice the President may not always face a true choice between re-electing or replacing the chairman because he may find himself trapped in a situation where the replacement of a chairman would send undesired signals to the financial markets.[430] As a result of this he may find himself left with no alternative but to stick to his predecessor's choice and re-appoint the chairman. In such instances coinciding of terms is of no practical value because the chairman would be reappointed notwithstanding the fact that the President and/or the Senate may be dissatisfied with his or her performance.[431] Secondly, even if a President were to make use of his power to appoint a new chairman at the beginning of his term, the question remains whether in reality this would lead to more accountability of the chairman (and the Board of Governors) for the conduct of monetary policy or rather only more government

---

[427] According to Akhtar/Howe, n. 131 above, at 362, the average term of office of a governor on the Board of Governors has been less than 5 years.

[428] *Ex ante* and *ex post* accountability, cf. Chap. 2 II 2.

[429] The other option would be to introduce performance-based dismissals, in which case the length of the term becomes irrelevant.

[430] This is reported to have been the case with regard to the reappointment of the Reagan appointee, Alan Greenspan, as Chairman of the Board of Governors by George Bush in 1991. Cf. G. Brüggemann, "Wenn Greenspan redet, hält die Welt die Luft an", *Die Welt*, 24 July 1997.

[431] One could even argue that linking the terms worsens this potential dilemma since a newly elected President, who has yet to establish himself, may find it even more difficult effectively to remove such a prominent figure as the chairman of the Board of Governors.

influence over monetary policy. The President may abuse his power by making the reappointment of the chairman subject to concessions by the latter. The same holds true for the reappointment of the other members of the Board of Governors. This could put restrictions on the independent conduct of monetary policy without any benefits in terms of democratic accountability.

The FOMC is formed of the members of the Board of Governors and five additional members to be chosen from among the presidents or vice presidents of the 12 Federal Reserve Banks. As only fewer than half of the Federal reserve districts are represented on the FOMC with a voting right at any one time, four of the five mandates rotate among the Federal reserve districts on an annual basis. The fifth appointment is reserved to the Federal Reserve district of New York which, by itself, has the right to elect one member annually. The Federal reserve districts are divided into four groups each of which will elect one president or vice president from among themselves to serve on the FOMC for one year. In the voting procedure each Federal Reserve Bank, i.e. its board of directors, has one vote. The first group consist of the Federal Reserve Banks of Boston, Philadelphia and Richmond. The second group consist of the Federal Reserve Banks of Cleveland and Chicago. The third group consist of the Federal Reserve Banks of Atlanta, Dallas and St. Louis, and the fourth group consist of the Federal Reserve Banks of Minneapolis, Kansas City and San Francisco.[432] The president of the Federal Reserve Bank of New York is an *ex officio* member of the FOMC given the important role which the Federal Reserve Bank of New York plays in the implementation of open-market policies.

The president and a first vice president of each of the Federal Reserve Banks are appointed for a term of five years by the board of directors of each Bank, subject to the approval by the Board of Governors.[433] To be sure, the president and vice president are not members of the board of directors of the respective Federal Reserve Bank.

The nine members of the board of directors of the Federal Reserve Banks are chosen according to a diversified and somewhat complex procedure, thereby taking into account the different groups they represent. Class A and B directors are voted into office for a term of three years on a rotational basis by the shareholders of the respective Federal Reserve Bank, i.e. the member banks.[434] Each member bank nominates one candidate for each class A and B position and forwards the two names to the chairman of the Federal Reserve Bank of its district. Thereafter, a list consisting of all the nominated candidates, in each case indicating the nominator(s), is distributed by the chairman to the member banks within 15 days of its completion. Each member bank designates an electoral delegate from within the bank who will indicate on the list his first, second and "other choices" for the post of the class A and class B director and will return

---

[432] 12 USC Sec. 263(a).

[433] The board of directors moreover elects annually one member of the Federal Advisory Council: s. 12 Federal Reserve Act.

[434] S. 4 Federal Reserve Act.

the list to the Chairman of the Federal Reserve Bank within 15 days. If a candidate receives the majority of all votes cast in the column for first choice for either class A or B directors he is considered to be elected. Otherwise, the votes cast for the candidates in the second column and, if necessary, in the third column are added until one candidate has the majority of the votes and the highest number of combined votes.[435] The class C directors, from among whom the chairman and vice chairman of each Federal Reserve Bank are chosen, are appointed by the Board of Governors.[436]

Since the Federal Reserve Act does not state otherwise it can be assumed that in principle directors are eligible for indefinite reappointment. However, in practice class C directors generally do not serve for more than two terms in that capacity or more than seven years on the board of directors of a Federal Reserve Bank. Generally, the same practice is maintained for the class A and B directors selected by the member banks.[437]

With regard to qualifications, class A directors represent solely the stockholding companies.[438] Class B and C directors are elected to represent the public. In doing so "due but not exclusive consideration" ought to be paid to the interests of agriculture, commerce, industry, services, labour and consumers.[439] The enumeration of interests which is to be considered when selecting the class B and C directors does not amount to an occupational requirement for the candidates. This would probably even be contrary to the Federal Reserve Act, according to which the class B and C directors are precisely not to represent private interests. Nor is this enumeration final, as class B and C directors tend to have diverse backgrounds including some which are not mentioned in the Federal Reserve Act, e.g. non-profit-making organisations, and academics.[440] Class C directors must have been residents of the Federal Reserve District for which they are appointed for at least two years. The designated chairman moreover has to be a person of "tested banking experience".[441] No similar provision exists for any of the other directors including the class A and B directors. With regard to the selection of all three classes of directors it is prohibited to discriminate on the basis of race, creed, colour, sex or national origin.[442] Senators or members of the House of Representatives are *expressis verbis* excluded from holding the position of a director or even officer of a Federal Reserve Bank, and class B and C directors may not be officers, directors or employees of any bank.[443] Additionally, stockholders are excluded from becoming class C

---

[435] Ibid., s. 4(16).

[436] Ibid., s. 4(20). Critical on this power of the Board of Governors and a tendency to block appointments of Fed critics is Newton, n. 371 above, at 127.

[437] Office of the Staff Director, op. cit., Chap. 3, n. 554, 4–5.

[438] S. 4(10) Federal Reserve Act.

[439] Ibid., s. 4(11).

[440] Office of the Staff Director, n. 437 above, at 3.

[441] S. 4(20) Federal Reserve Act.

[442] This provision has been introduced by the Federal Reserve Reform Act of 1977 following criticism of an under-representation of minorities.

[443] This includes bank holding companies.

directors.[444] Internally, the Board of Governors pursues a policy which pro-hibits directors and officers of Federal Reserve Banks and their branches "from active and public participation in, and association with, a political party, parti-san political candidate, or partisan political activity at the national, state, or local level". Moreover, a *Guide to Conduct for Directors of Federal Reserve Banks and Branches of Federal Reserve Banks*, issued by the Board of Governors lays out in detail—among others—potential sources of conflict of interest.[445]

For some the participation of the Federal Reserve Bank presidents in the FOMC promotes the spread of information throughout the system.[446] Others view the role of the Federal Reserve Bank presidents on the FOMC somewhat more critically. In fact, criticism of the Fed has centred on the composition of the FOMC. The argument goes as follows: by including the presidents of the Federal Reserve Banks on the FOMC officials who have been effectively selected by private individuals take part in the decision-making process of the most important monetary policy organ of the Fed.[447] In short, unelected and unac-countable individuals take part in the decision-making process with regard to monetary policy (public versus private control over monetary policy). This may be concluded from the observation that the president and first vice president of each Federal Reserve Bank are appointed by the board of directors of the respec-tive bank for a five-year term, and that these appointments are only subject to approval by the Board of Governors. Indeed, it has been argued that it is in prin-ciple possible that a majority of Federal Reserve Banks in favour of a certain measure as regards the discount rate can put pressure on the Board of Governors. Taking into account the legal nature of the Federal Reserve Banks as private entities (commercial banks are the shareholders) this would then amount to a legally private institution telling the Board of Governors what to do.[448] In favour of the view that such a danger is not preposterous is the fact that, unlike the majority of the members of the Federal Reserve Bank's board of directors, the president and vice president are at least not required by law to rep-resent the public.

One prominent proposal for change has been to introduce new appointment procedures for the Federal Reserve Bank presidents by making them presiden-tial nominees requiring the consent of the Senate.[449] Another suggestion has been to replace the Federal Reserve Bank presidents on the FOMC by five mem-bers selected by the Federal Advisory Council, appointed by the President by

---

[444] 12 USC Sec. 303.

[445] For details cf. Office of the Staff Directors, n. 437 above, 7 *et seq.*

[446] C.R. Whittlesey, "Power and Influence in the Federal Reserve System", *Economica* 30 (1963), 30–43, at 37, who finds that personal contacts in the FOMC "promote friendly relations and high morale".

[447] A.J. Clifford, *The Independence of the Federal Reserve System* (University of Pennsylvania Press, Philadelphia, 1965), at 31.

[448] Berry, n. 367 above, at 45.

[449] Cf. compilation by Akhtar/Howe, n. 131 above; more recently HR 888 (104th Congress), A bill to promote accountability and the public interest in the operation of the Fed, and for other purposes, 10 Feb. 1995, introduced by Representative Gonzales.

and with the advice and consent of the Senate.[450] Yet more recommendations sought to abolish the FOMC as a whole and to transfer the authority over open-market operations onto the Board of Governors[451] or to establish a Federal Advisory Committee to advise the Board of Governors of the Federal Reserve System on the conduct of open-market operations.[452] None of these proposals has materialised.

Supporters of the existing system maintain that presidents of the Federal Reserve Banks owe their position not entirely to private bankers, since their nomination has to be approved by the Board of Governors. Moreover, the situation in the FOMC is such that the Board of Governors and thus Presidential appointees are in the majority in the Committee, thereby limiting the supposed private influence.[453] It is also argued that the participation of the Federal Reserve Banks on the FOMC is thought to reflect the overall structure of the Fed (regional system) and provide a link to the private sector.[454] Furthermore, attempts to challenge the constitutionality of the current arrangements in court have failed.[455]

At the **Banque de France,** Parliament also plays a role in the appointment procedure. Interestingly, the governor and deputy governor are excluded from this, as a somewhat diverse appointment procedure applies to the CPM. According to Article 13(7) of the Bank Act 1993:

"The Governor and the two Deputy Governors shall be appointed by an order made in the Council of Ministers for a six-year term of office, which may be renewed once. The age limit for holding these offices shall be sixty-five."

Despite their membership of the CPM the governor and deputy governors of the Bank are appointed in a different way from the other members of the CPM. More importantly, only the governor and the deputy governors can be re-appointed for *one* additional term. The fact that, unlike the rest of the members of the CPM, Parliament, the Economic and Social Council and the CPM are not assigned any role in the appointment of the governor and deputy governors shows that the drafters of the new statute of the Bank were well aware of the outstanding position of the governor in the management of the Bank. The selection of candidates and the final decision on their appointment has been firmly placed with the executive government, where it had been under the previous statute.[456] The limitation of the duration of office to a six-year term is a novelty

[450] E.g. HR 2917 (103rd Congress).
[451] Patman, n. 423 above, 144 *et seq.*. For a Congressional bill cf. e.g. HR 7001 (96th Congress).
[452] E.g. HR 11 (93rd Congress).
[453] This has also been maintained by Fed officials, e.g. Statement by A.F. Burns before the Committee on Banking, Currency and Housing, House of Representatives, 9 Apr. 1976.
[454] J.-V. Louis, op. cit., Chap. 3, n. 484, at 292; Office of the Staff Directors, n. 437 above, 12 *et seq.*
[455] *Reuss v. Balles,* and *Riegel v. Federal Open Market Committee,* Chap. 1, n. 9 above.
[456] Art. 10 Bank Act 1973.

in as much as that period was not fixed under the Bank Act 1973.[457] In principle, the six-year term with the option of a single reappointment gives the executive government the ability to review the performance of the governor and deputy governors at somewhat shorter intervals with the option of re-appointing or replacing them. Apart from the age limit, no provisions exist on the qualification of the governor and deputy governors. As members of the CPM the same restrictions as regards additional occupations and the holding of elected offices apply to the governor and deputy governors.[458]

Apart from the governor and the deputy governors, the six members of the CPM are appointed in rotation whereby the terms of office of one-third of the members come up for renewal every three years.[459] Unlike the governor and deputy governor the other members of the CPM serve nine-year terms which are non-renewable.[460] This has been interpreted as evidence for the independent status of these members of the CPM.[461] However, at the same time it may diminish the value of the participation of Parliament and the Economic and Social Council in the appointment procedure in as much as it cannot hold a member of the CPM *ex post* accountable for his performance by not proposing him for re-election, thereby sanctioning his conduct.

The appointment of the six members of the CPM involves a diversified pro-cedure which, in some respect, is quite different from that of the other central banks examined in this study. Two months before the regular end of a term of office or immediately after the extraordinary dismissal of a member of the CPM, the Minister for Economic Affairs and Finances asks the President of the Senate, the President of the National Assembly and the President of the Economic and Social Council (*Conseil économique et social*) to provide a list of names com-prising *three times* the number of posts up for renewal. According to Article 8(3) this list is drawn up by mutual consent. However, the statutory provisions antic-ipate that such consent, which, all things considered, has to be a political one, may not always materialise. In such an event the list is drawn up in equal parts

---

[457] Art. 10 Bank Act 1973. In practice a *lettre séparée* fixed the duration of office of the governor to a period of five years. However, this practice had not been always followed, cf. M. Lombard, op. cit., Chap. 3, n. 65, at 493.

[458] Art. 10 I(2) Bank Act 1993. According to Art. 10 I(4) Bank Act 1993 the governor and deputy governors are barred from engaging in any professional occupation without the authorisation of the CPM for period of 3 years—as opposed to one year for the other members of the CPM—after relin-quishing office for other reasons than dismissal for serious misconduct. They continue to receive their remuneration for that period. However, they may hold an elected office or become member of the government.

[459] Art. 8 Bank Act 1993 and Art. 1 decree 1993. Note the similarities to the French Senate the members of which are also elected for a term of 9 years, one-third of whom are renewed every three years. The first CPM has been appointed by an Order in Council on 27 Jan. 1994, JORF (1994), 464.

[460] Cf. Art. 8(6) Bank Act 1993. The only exception to this rule is the case where a member of the CPM has only served out the remainder of the term of office of another member who had been replaced in accordance with Art. 8(4) Bank Act 1993, he is eligible for re-appointment if his term of office has not exceeded 3 years.

[461] Cf. Duprat, n. 342 above, 145, who refers to remarks made by M. Alphandéry, Débuts Sénat, 2 July 1993, JORF (1993), 2063.

by the three groups involved. This way each group has the opportunity to present its preferred choice of candidates for the list. As regards the professional qualification of candidates Article 8(3) of the Bank Act 1993 states that:

> "The names on the list shall be chosen from among persons of recognised standing and professional experience in monetary, financial and economic matters."

Upon establishment the list is forwarded by the President of the Senate to the governor of the Bank, who introduces the list of candidates to the CPM for considerations. Within five days of the transfer of the list to the Bank the CPM has to forward an advice on the proposals to the Presidents of the Senate, the National Assembly and the Economic and Social Council. Thereafter, the list, supplemented by the advice of the Bank, is forwarded by the President of the Senate to the Minister for Economics Affair and Finance. Based on this list the members of the CPM are appointed by an Order in the Council of Ministers.[462] Neither the list of candidates nor the position of the Banque de France with regard to that list is published.[463]

The rather complex procedure of nomination of the candidates for the CPM seems to ensure the participation of a broad social spectrum. Notably the participation of the National Assembly, but also the equal participation of the Economic and Social Council which comprises the main social and economic interests, may be viewed as a remarkable feature. The fact that the Economic and Social Council has a right of nomination demonstrates the outstanding role attributed to the CPM, since the constitutionally foreseen role of the Economic and Social Council is to act as an adviser to the government on problems of an economic or social nature and, furthermore, government or parliamentary bills, or ordinances and decrees of an economic or social character.[464] However, the participation of the different (interest) groups could potentially function as a counterbalance to the executive government.[465] The argument goes as follows: the government has to choose the names from the list with which it is presented, whether it approves of the candidates or not. Acting by mutual consent the different groups could draw up a list of candidates which leaves the government no choice but to appoint one or more candidates of which it disapproves. However, taking into account the diversity of the different participating groups, such mutual consent is difficult to achieve. Consequently, it is more probable that three different sets of candidates will be presented.[466] Under such circumstances the democratic element does not carry very far, since the government can pick and choose from the final list of candidates, which will usually include a number of candidates which are (more) acceptable to the government. Indeed, the

---

[462] Art. 8(1) Bank Act 1993.
[463] Art. 1 I(4) decree 1993.
[464] Arts. 69 and 70 Constitution of 1958.
[465] In this direction see Collas, n. 233 above, at 594.
[466] Cf. e.g. "Banque de France: choix final le 3 janvier" in *Le Monde*, 12 Dec. 1996.

dominant role of the executive government in the appointment procedure has been described as anti-democratic.[467]

During their term of office the members of the CPM are barred from any other public or private professional occupation regardless of whether it is remunerated.[468] The only exception is membership of the Economic and Social Council (*Conseil économique et social*) as well as—subject to an authorisation by the CPM—teaching activities and participation in international organisations.[469] The fact that the members of the CPM may participate in the Economic and Social Council strengthens their position in the selection of candidates for the CPM, since both the CPM and the Economic and Social Council are involved in the selection procedure.

Article 10(3) of the Bank Act 1993 explicitly excludes the maintenance of an elected office. Thus, members of both chambers of Parliament are excluded. Members of the executive government are not covered by this restriction, since they are not elected by Parliament but rather appointed by the President of the French Republic and, moreover, are explicitly barred from holding a parliamentary mandate.[470] Nevertheless, members of the government are effectively excluded from the appointment to the CPM as, according to Article 23(1) of the Constitution of 1958, they may not "hold an office at national level in business, professional trade or trade union organisation, or any public employment or professional activity". Consequently, membership of the Prime Minister or any of the government ministers of the CPM would be unconstitutional. Besides, it would seem that the prohibition of a public professional occupation for members of the CPM and, more generally, Article 1(2) on the independence of the members of the CPM from government instructions would exclude such a participation. Civil servants are not *per se* excluded from becoming successful candidates. However, they are detached from their respective posts for the duration of their membership of the CPM and may not be selected for discretionary promotion in their original post. The intention is to ensure the independence of the appointee during his stay on the CPM by assuring that he is neither pressured nor corrupted into certain policy stands.

The representative of the staff[471] of the Banque de France is elected by the officials of the Bank according to the procedure specified in Articles 13 and 14 of the decree 1993 in one secret ballot.[472] The candidate with the most votes is elected. The organisation and surveillance of the election is overlooked by a specially set-up electoral committee, the so-called *Commission supérieure de l'élection*.[473] The representative is elected for a term of office of six years and is

---

[467] Iacono, n. 226 above, at 92, according to whom the Financial Commission made concrete proposals to counterbalance this procedure by enhancing parliamentary control.

[468] This has already been the case under the Bank Act 1973, cf. Art. 11.

[469] Art. 10(3) Bank Act 1993.

[470] Art. 23(1) Constitution of 1958.

[471] Cf. Part 5 Bank Act 1993.

[472] Art. 12 decree 1993.

[473] For details cf. Arts. 18 *et seq.* decree 1993.

eligible for re-election.[474] During his term of office the representative of the staff may not fulfil other functions linked to the representation of the staff within the Bank, and his mandate ends in the case of discharge from his functions as Bank official.[475] The Censor is appointed by the Minister of Economic Affairs and Finance. Neither the Bank Act 1993 nor the decree 1993 contains any additional provisions on the appointment and/or dismissal of the Censor.[476] No specific professional qualifications are required, nor are certain groups, such as elected officials or civil servants, excluded or restricted. The term of office of the Censor, as well as the procedure for his dismissal remain open.

The appointment procedures and in particular the role of Parliament, remain unchanged in the revised statute of the Bank applicable in stage three of EMU.

The **ECB** also belongs in this first group of central banks, since the EP has a role in the appointment of the Executive Board, albeit a very limited one. Generally, the appointment of the organs of the ECB involve the European level as well as the level of the Member States. According to Articles 109a(2) EC and 11.2 of the ESCB Statute the members of the Executive Board are appointed by common accord of the governments of the Member States *without* a derogation at the level of the Heads of State or Government on a recommendation from the Council, which has to consult the EP and the Governing Council of the ECB beforehand.[477] The appointment procedure reflects the importance which has been assigned to the ECB by the drafters of these provisions, since even for the appointment of the Commission only a common accord of the governments of the Member States, and thus not necessarily of the Heads of State or Government, is required.[478]

As far as the EP is concerned, the Council proposal on the appointment of a member of the Executive Board is handled by the standing committee in the EP charged with monetary affairs. Presently, this is the Committee on Economic and Monetary Affairs and Industrial Policy and its sub-committee on monetary affairs.[479] The committee, having considered the proposal, finally presents a report on its findings to the plenary session, thereby recommending either acceptance or rejection of the proposal. The plenary session will deal with the proposal in one reading and by a simple majority vote adopt or reject the candidate.[480] The opinion of the EP, to whatever extent it may differ from the Council's proposal, is not binding on the Council. In principle, the EP can only delay the appointment of a member of the Executive Board.[481] The EC Treaty and the ESCB Statute do

---

[474] Art. 12(1) Bank Act 1993.

[475] Cf. Art. 15 decree 1993 on the requirements of the staff member; Art. 16.

[476] Art. 13 Bank Act 1973 is similar.

[477] Since not all Member States participate, P. Brentford, op. cit., Chap. 2, n. 191, at 84, questions whether a true *European* central bank will be created.

[478] Cf. Art. 158(2) EC.

[479] Cf. Chapter XVII rules of procedure EP ([1997] OJ L049/1).

[480] Rule 58–59 rules of procedure EP.

[481] Generally, on the limits of delays by the EP cf. Case C–65/93 *European Parliament* v. *Council* [1995] ECR I 643. See case note by T. Heukels in (1995) 32 *CML Rev.*, 1420–6.

not reach as far as the Federal Reserve Act in making an appointment subject to parliamentary consent. Such a power was proposed by the EP at the time of the drawing up of the respective provisions in the form of the co-decision procedure.[482] Louis remarks in this context that the opportunity has been missed to increase "the democratic legitimacy of the ECB" which would have "given a greater weight to the institutional dialogue between Parliament and Central Bank".[483] Nevertheless, the participation of the EP in the appointment of ECB officials is quite remarkable, considering that a similar participation of the national parliaments is missing, at least in case of three of the four European national central banks examined in this study. It will depend upon the EP to what extent it makes use of its right under the consultation procedures. Since the EP committee does not deal with a legislative proposal as such, the usual areas of examination, such as the verification of the chosen legal basis, the examination whether the proposal respects the principle of subsidiarity, and the fundamental rights of citizens, seem of little practical relevance. Rather, discussions similar to those taking place in the Banking Committees of the US Congress are likely to prevail. In fact, according to the rules of procedure of the EP, standing committees can organise hearings of experts and, moreover, may in principle invite any person to attend and speak at a meeting.[484] Thus in principle the candidates for ECB posts, and in particular those for the post of the president and vice president, can be invited to attend and speak at the committee meeting. To be sure, under the existing provisions an appearance cannot be considered obligatory, and the candidates do not necessarily need to have the incentive to appear, since their confirmation by the EP is not required. Yet, the EP could certainly become a factor in the forming of public opinion on the candidates, albeit that it remains to be seen whether the role of the EP amounts to "a vote of confirmation in which Parliament enjoys a virtual right of veto".[485] The hearings which have taken place at the time of the first appointment of the members of the Executive Board, whom were questioned in public hearings before the competent standing committee of the EP, give an indication for the EP's approach to these appointments.[486]

---

[482] Resolution of the European Parliament on Economic and Monetary Union of 10 Oct. 1990 ([1990] OJ C149/66), Art. 10.

[483] J.-V. Louis, "Economic and Monetary Union (European Central Bank)" in T.M.C. Asser Instituut, *The Treaty on European Union—Suggestions for Revisions*, Conference Reader (Stichting T.M.C. Asser Instituut, The Hague, 1995), 247–57, at 252.

[484] According to rule 151(3), sentence 2, rules of procedures EP, by special decision, any person may be invited.

[485] This is suggested by F. Jacobs/R. Corbett/M. Shackleton, *The European Parliament* (3rd edn., Cartermill Publishing, London, 1995), 250–1. Cf. also C. Randzio-Plath, "Democratic Accountability of the European Central Bank", *Central Banking*, vol. 8 no. 3 (1997/8), 22–5.

[486] On 13 May 1998, a majority of the EP voted in favour of the candidates. Cf. transcripts of the hearings involving the questioning of the candidates available from URL http://www.eurparl.eu.int (last accessed Oct. 1998). Also see the Resolution embodying the opinion of the European Parliament on the proposal for the appointment of the President of the European Monetary Institute (A.Lamfalussy) of 6 Dec. 1993 ([1996] OJ C329/131); Resolution embodying Parliament's opinion on the appointment of the President of the European Monetary Institute (Willem Duisenberg) of 16 Dec. 1996 ([1996] OJ C380/55).

Apart from the EP, according to Articles 109a(2) EC and 11(2) of the ESCB Statute, the Governing Council of the ECB, of which the members participate in the Executive Board, and the governors of the national central banks, also have to be consulted on the proposal of the Council in the composition of the Heads of State or Government.

With regard to the qualification of the candidates, the members of the Executive Board fulfil their duties on a full-time basis as a result of which members may not engage in any occupation without the prior consent of the Governing Council.[487] Moreover, they have to be nationals of a Member State without a "derogation".[488]

The members of the Executive Board, including the president of the ECB, are appointed for a term of eight years. In this context it may be recalled that the appointment of the first president of the ECB became a political issue. In November 1997, at a time when it appeared that the Dutch candidate, Willem Duisenberg, was set to become the first president, the French government proposed Jean-Claude Trichet, governor of the Banque de France as its candidate for the first presidency. Only after considerable efforts and what seems like a gentlemen's agreement according to which Duisenberg would not serve a full term in office, did the France government agree to the appointment of the Dutch candidate.[489] Yet, this compromise that the first term of office should be split between the two candidates is questionable. While the president of the ECB in principle has the right to resign, it contradicts the *ratio legis* when the long tenures intended by the drafters of the statute of the ESCB and ECB would be deliberately shortened on the basis of such an informal agreement. The grimness of the exchanges between the Netherlands and France on this issue highlights that the appointment in particular of the president of the ECB is far from shielded from political considerations. Indeed, neither in the case of the Dutch nor the French candidate has the personal integrity or the professional qualifications been doubted. Apart from what can be assigned to national prestige, one is left with the impression that some Member States associate a political influence with the presidency of the ECB which the drafters of the statute have meant to forestall.

This is also underlined by the fact that the reappointment of members of the Executive Board is excluded.[490] Contrary to the existing arrangements, the EP had suggested a *renewable* term of five years.[491] Within the margins described above, the possibility of the renewal of the term would have given the EP and in particular the competent committee the chance to question the candidate on his past performance, although, ultimately the EP could not have held the candidate

---

[487] Art. 11.1. ESCB Statute; see too R. Smits, op. cit., Chap. 2, n. 36, at 501.
[488] Arts. 109 a(b) and 109 k(3) EC.
[489] "Ein Kompromiß bei der Amtszeit Duisenbergs macht den Weg frei für die Wirtschafts- und Währungsunion", *Frankfurter Allgemeine Zeitung*, 4 May 1998.
[490] Cf. wording of Art. 109a(2)(b) sentence 2, EC and Art. 11(2) Statute.
[491] Resolution of the European Parliament on Economic and Monetary Union of 10 Oct. 1990, Art. 10.

accountable, since its consent would be no more required than in the case of a new appointment. A comparison to the members of the Commission, which are appointed for four-year terms and are eligible for reappointment, shows how much emphasis has been put on the insulation of the members of the Executive Board from political influence.[492] Since the Governing Council of the ECB comprises the members of the Executive Board *and* the governors of the national central banks without a "derogation", the respective rules on the appointment of the national central bank governors apply. The only exception in this respect is Article 14.2 of the ESCB Statute, according to which the national central bank statutes have to provide for a term of office of the governor of no less than five years. Other restrictions on Member States' freedom to regulate the procedure of appointments of the governors of the national central banks could derive from the general provision of Article 14(1) of the Statute, according to which the Member States have to ensure that their national legislation, including the statutes of their central banks, is compatible with the EC Treaty and the ESCB Statute. Since the EC Treaty and the ESCB Statute do not state anything to the contrary, it has to be assumed that Community law does not stand in the way of a provision in a national central bank statute allowing for the possibility of a reappointment of the governor. This results in a situation where some of the governors of the national central banks participating in the Governing Council may be re-appointed, whereas others, like the members of the Executive Board, are excluded from a second term in office. Those governors who may be re-appointed are likely not only to be judged by the appointing body in relation to past performance of the respective national central bank, but also in the light of that of the ECB.

1.2. Appointment without parliamentary participation

In the case of the other four central banks, the Bundesbank, the Bank of England, the Nederlandsche Bank and the Reserve Bank of New Zealand, the legal basis does not provide for participation by Parliament in the appointment of central bank officials.

The fact that the **Bundesbank** is the result of an organisational compromise between the Federal government and the *Länder* at the time of its drafting becomes most obvious while examining the procedures of the appointment of organs of the Bundesbank.[493] The different procedures of appointment can be relocated according to the different organs of the Bundesbank and the different levels of the decision-making, i.e. Federal or State level.

The members of the Board of Directors are appointed on the Federal level by the Federal President (*Bundespräsident*), as the Head of State, on a (binding) recommendation of the Federal government which is obliged to hear the Central

---

[492]   Cf. Art. 158(1), subpara. 2 EC.
[493]   Cf. Chap. 3 III 1.

Bank Council.[494] The Federal government is not bound by the opinion of the Central Bank Council.

For the members of the Directorate of the State central banks two different procedures of appointment apply. The presidents of State central banks are appointed by the President of the Federal Republic of Germany on the recommendation of the Bundesrat.[495] The Bundesrat makes its recommendation in accordance with recommendations forwarded by the executive governments of the *Länder*, after hearing the Central Bank Council. It is therefore somewhat misleading to state with reference to the Bundesrat that Parliament takes part in the appointment of some of the presidents of the State central banks participating in the Central Bank Council, as this implies that someone other than the *Länder* executive governments decide on the appointments.[496] Much more so than in the case of the Board of Directors of the Bundesbank, the appointment of the State central bank presidents is subject to party political considerations. In fact, Vaubel argues that the presidents of the State central banks are almost always sympathetic to the ruling party which elected them.[497] Where State central banks are set up for the area of more than one Federal state, the participating states have to agree upon one recommendation. The BBankG falls short of providing any solution if the participating *Länder* cannot decide on one candidate. It has to be presumed that in such a case the Bundesrat has to make the final decision.[498] The influence of the Federal government in the appointment of the presidents of the State central banks is marginal. However, it is not totally excluded, since acts of the Federal President, including the appointment of the members of the Board of Directors and the presidents of the State central banks, have to be countersigned by a member of the executive government before they become valid. Moreover, the appointment of the members of the Board of Directors is based on a contractual agreement between the appointee and the Board. The contract has to be approved by the Federal government.[499]

The vice-president and any additional member of the Directorate of the State Central Bank are appointed by the president of the Board of Directors of the Bundesbank on recommendation of the Central Bank Council.[500] Thus, the vice-president and the additional member of the State Central Bank are removed from any direct influence from both the Federal and the State governments. Whether and to what extent the Federal or State government(s) can indirectly influence the appointment of the vice-president and any additional members

[494] § 7(3) BBankG.
[495] Ibid., § 7(3), sentences 1 and 2.
[496] E.g. R.M. Lastra, op. cit., Chap. 2, n. 65, at 484, who states that the presidents of the State central banks are nominated by the Bundesrat, which she translates without any further explanation with Parliament.
[497] Vaubel, n. 206 above, 51 *et seq.*, which includes an index of the political composition of the Central Bank Council.
[498] U. Häde, "Das Gesetz zur Änderung von Vorschriften über die Deutsche Bundesbank", *NJW* (1994), 3214–32, at 3216.
[499] § 7(4) and § 8(5) BBankG.
[500] § 8(3), sentence 3 BBankG.

depends upon the personal behaviour of the members of the Central Bank Council and the Board of Directors, i.e. whether and to what extent they take the position of government into consideration.

Finally, the members of the Advisory Boards of the State central banks are appointed by the President of the Bundesbank for a period of three years on recommendation of the State government for the area in which the State Central Bank operates after having heard the Directorate of the State central bank.[501]

Both the members of the Board of Directors of the Bundesbank and directors of the State central banks are subject to a legal relationship under public law (*öffentlich-rechtliches Amtsverhältnis*). With regard to the qualifications of the candidates, both for the Board of Directors and the State central bank directorates, the legal basis of the Bundesbank states only that they have to have special professional competence without, however, requiring a specific professional/academic background. Some conclude from this that practical qualifications are more important than party political considerations, and that in practice a balance of the political party spectrum on the Central Bank Council is ensured.[502] However, it has been pointed out that empirical evidence seems to suggest the opposite.[503]

Both the members of the Board of Directors and the presidents of the State central banks are appointed for a term of eight years. Exceptionally, the term of office may be shorter but has to be at least two years.[504] The BBankG does not list the conditions under which a shorter term may be applied. Besides, this provision has to be considered incompatible with the EC Treaty and ESCB Statute, and in particular Article 14.2 of the ESCB Statute, according to which the minimum term of office has to be five years. Since the BBankG does not state otherwise it has to be assumed that both the members of the Board of Directors, including the president of the Bundesbank, and the members of the Directorates of the State central banks can be re-appointed.[505]

The composition of the Central Bank Council, i.e. members of the Board of Directors and presidents of the State central banks, ensures the broad participation of Federal and State governments not only in the appointment of the managerial board of the Bundesbank and the State central banks but also of the monetary policy board, that is the Central Bank Council. In this respect the Bundesbank includes Federal elements despite its characterisation in general as a centralised system. It is this broad participation which may be identified as an important factor in the legitimation of the independent position of the Bundesbank. In particular the composition of the Central Bank Council comprising both the Board of Directors on the central level and the presidents of the

---

[501] § 8(3), sentence 3 BBankG, § 9(3), § 17 BBank charter, on the appointment of representatives.
[502] Werres, n. 217 above, at 12.
[503] Vaubel, n. 206 above.
[504] § 7(3), sentence 2, and § 8(4), sentence 4 BBankG.
[505] This takes regularly place, e.g. Helmut Schlesinger has been on the Board of Directors of the Bundesbank from 1972–93, serving as the president of the bank from 1991. Cf. *Die Bank*, vol. 6 (1995), 72 *et seq.*, with a list of all the Presidents of the Bundesbank.

State central banks can be associated with a system of separation of powers and checks and balances within the Bank.[506] Indeed, this representation may be one reason why the Bundesbank has been able to defend its independent position and has not become subject of heavy public criticism.[507] However, one may be sceptical about whether these arrangements can actually offset the lack of parliamentary control and the independence from executive government in the case of the Bundesbank, as Kloten seems to suggest.[508] On the one hand, it has been observed that the (re-)appointment procedures are merely one element of democratic accountability. On the other hand, it is also questionable whether they actually provide the democratically elected executive government with discretion with regard to the (re-)appointment, since the opinion of the Central Bank Council, which has to be heard on the appointments of all those participating in the Central Bank Council, cannot easily be ignored by the Federal government without possibly provoking an open conflict with the Bank. In such a conflict both the bank and the executive government could lose credibility.

In the case of the **Nederlandsche Bank**[509], according to section 23 of the Bank Act 1948, the president and the secretary are appointed by the Crown for a term of seven years. Both can be re-appointed.[510] For each appointment a recommendation list comprising two nominees is drawn up by a joint meeting of the Governing Board and the Supervisory Board which is thereafter submitted to the Crown by the Governing Board. In practice the decision on the appointments is taken in the Council of Ministers upon the initiative of the Minister of Finance. According to section 4 l of the rules of procedure of the Council of Ministers (*reglement van orde voor de Ministerraad*) the latter is generally in charge of issuing proposals for those appointments and dismissals for which a royal decision is necessary.[511] This includes the president and secretary of the Nederlandsche Bank. The Council of Ministers has full discretion with respect to its decision and is not bound by the recommendation list, as section 23(1), last sentence of the Bank Act 1948 states only that "the Crown shall pay regard to this recommendation list *as it thinks fit*".[512] However, it has become an established practice to give preference to the first name on the recommendation list.[513]

---

[506] Hahn, n. 24 above, at 238.
[507] E. Kennedy, *The Bundesbank* (Pinter Publishers, London, 1991), at 21. However, as has been pointed out, arguably the more important reason is the commitment of the German public to the Dmark and the culture of stability cultivated by the Bundesbank, both of which have their roots in the experiences with hyperinflation in the German history.
[508] N. Kloten, op. cit., Chap. 3, n. 200.
[509] Note the new appointment procedures under the Bank Act 1998, Ss. 12 and 13 Bank Act 1998.
[510] S. 23(1) and (3) Bank Act 1948.
[511] Besluit van 2 maart 1994, houdende vaststelling van een reglement van orde voor de minister-raad, Stb. 1994, no. 203; hereafter referred to as rules of procedure Council of Ministers.
[512] Emphasis added.
[513] van Wijk, n. 198 above, at 53.

The two directors are also appointed for a seven-year term in a similar fashion from a list containing three names. Unlike the appointment procedure of the president and secretary, section 23(2) sets a time limit of three weeks from the date of the nomination for the appointment of a director. If an appointment has not been made within the specified period a second list containing three names is drawn up. Thereafter, if the second list does not result in an appointment either, according to section 23(2) the Crown "shall make provision for the appointment". This effectively means that the Council of Ministers can make its own choice, if it cannot agree to choose a name from the list. This also means that the government cannot appoint a person apart from those listed, before it has failed to appoint a nominee from one of the two lists. As with the appointment of the president and secretary, it has become an established practice to give preference to one of the nominees on the first recommendation list.[514] The directors can be reappointed for an unlimited number of terms.[515]

Interestingly, the Bank Act 1948 does not include any provisions on the qualification and disqualification of the candidates for the post of president, secretary and executive directors of the Bank.[516] In this context the question arises whether in principle members of Parliament or the executive government could be appointed. The Dutch constitution does not contain any provisions on the incompatibility of a membership of Parliament or government with any other professional activities. According to Article 57 of the Dutch constitution no one may be a member of both chambers of Parliament and a member of Parliament may not be a minister, State Secretary, member of the General Chamber of Audit (*Algemene Rekenkamer*), member of the Supreme Court (*Hoge Raad*) or Procurator General or Advocate General at the Supreme Court.[517] The law on the incompatibility of public offices with the membership of the Dutch Parliament and EP (*Wet incompatibiliteiten Staten-Generaal en Europees Parlement*), which is based on Article 57, does not contain any restrictions either.[518] The same applies to the rules of procedure of the first and second chamber of Parliament (*Reglement van Orde van de Eerste/Tweede Kamer der Staten-Generaal*). However, in practice the view is taken that a membership of Parliament or executive government is considered to be incompatible.

The 12 members of the Supervisory Board are appointed by the Minister of Finance by rotation for a renewable term of four years from a list of three names for each vacancy drawn up by the Supervisory Board and the Bank Council in a joint meeting. According to the wording of section 27(2) of the Bank Act 1948 the members are appointed by "the shareholders". However, since the State is the only shareholder in the capital of the Bank, it is the government which is

---

[514] van Wijk, n. 198 above, at 53.
[515] S. 23(3) Bank Act 1948.
[516] Vondeling, n. 392 above, 164 *et seq.*, describes what he considered to be the necessary qualifications of a President of the Nederlandsche Bank at the time when he was the Minister of Finance.
[517] Art. 57(2) Dutch constitution.
[518] Wet incompatibiliteiten Staten-Generaal en Europees Parlement, Stb. 1994, no. 295.

effectively in charge of the appointments.[519] The Bank Act 1948 does not include any provisions on the qualifications of the members of the Supervisory Board. However, as a legal person under private law the provisions on companies limited by shares (NV) of the second book of the Dutch Civil Code on legal persons are generally applicable if not explicitly excluded by the Bank Act 1948. Therefore, persons employed by the Nederlandsche Bank and administrators or persons employed by a labour union which is involved in the establishment of the working conditions for the personnel of the Bank are excluded from membership. In practice the Supervisory Board consists of representatives of different social groups, including for example company chairmen, industrialists, and leaders of regional and local government, but also members of the Royal family.

The Royal Commissioner is appointed and dismissed by the Crown, i.e. Government represented by the Minister of Finance. The Bank Act 1948 does not specify the term of office, the qualifications of the Royal Commissioner and the conditions for his dismissal. It can be explained from the function of the Royal Commissioner as an agent of the government that the latter has full discretion over the appointment and dismissal of the former. As already noted, the institution of the Royal Commissioner has been abolished at the time of the establishment of the ESCB.[520]

The Bank Council comprises the Royal Commissioner as an *ex officio* member and four members of the Supervisory Board appointed by the latter. Additionally, the Bank Council includes 12 members who are appointed by the Crown by rotation for a renewable term of four years.[521] Each year three of these 12 members retire. The 12 outside members are chosen by a diversified procedure. Generally, the appointments are made on the basis of a list of two names for each appointment. According to section 31(1)(c) of the Bank Act 1948 this list is drawn up by a number of bodies or institutions which are specified in a Royal Decree, including—among others—several labour unions and trade associations, as well as monetary and banking experts.[522] According to section 32(2) of the Bank Act 1948 commercial (including transport), industrial and agricultural interests shall be represented by two members each, and labour and financial interests outside those groups by three members each. Apart from that, the Bank Act 1948 does not include any provisions on the qualifications of these 12 members. Unlike other organs, the Bank Council is deliberately not insulated from government and private interests, as its purpose is to provide a forum for

---

[519] This is not contrary to s. 158(2) of the second book of the Dutch Civil Code, according to which the members of the Supervisory Board of a large company limited by shares are appointed by the Supervisory Board itself, since under the conditions stated in s. 158(12) the statutes of the company limited by shares may provide that one or more members are appointed by the government.

[520] Cf. Chap. 4 III 2.

[521] Art. 32 Bank Act 1948.

[522] For a list of the participating organisations cf. Besluit van 14 februari 1948 tot uitvoering van artikel 32, tweede lid, van de Bankwet 1948, Stb. 37.

discussions for the different social groups. In fact, this role of the Bank Council could even gain importance in the future, with the ESCB and the ECB having— to a large degree—taken over the functions of the Nederlandsche Bank in the area of monetary policy. The Bank Council could function as a forum for discussion on the conduct of monetary policy. These discussions may determine/influence the standpoint of the Nederlandsche Bank in the Governing Council of the ECB. Yet, such discussions would have to be considered incompatible with primary Community law to the extent that they potentially influence the decisions of the Governing Board of the Nederlandsche Bank.

In the case of the **Bank of England**, in accordance with the new arrangements under the Bank of England Act 1998, the governor, deputy governors, and the 16 additional directors of the Court of Directors are appointed by "Her Majesty", i.e. the Crown.[523] In practice, the Crown will make its appointments on the recommendation of the executive government. The new legislation does not provide for Parliament to participate in the appointment procedure, despite the proposal by the Treasury Committee of the House of Commons, which had recommended that the appointment of the members of the MPC be subject to confirmation by Parliament.[524] In any event, the committee has made clear that it intends to instigate hearings and make reports to Parliament on appointees.[525]

Members of the executive government, persons serving in a government department in respect of which remuneration is funded by Parliament, and servants of the Bank are disqualified from appointment to the Court of Directors.[526] Consequently, members of the House of Commons, Ministers of the Crown and civil servants are precluded from obtaining an office on the Court of Directors.[527] In his letter to the governor of the Bank of England outlining the new monetary policy framework, the Chancellor of the Exchequer has underlined that the Court of Directors is supposed to be "representative of the whole of the United Kingdom" and that the non-executive members are supposed to be appointed for their expertise and will be drawn widely from industry, commerce and finance.[528]

The term of office of the members of the Court of Directors differs. The governor and deputy governors, as executive directors, serve five-year terms. The 16

---

[523] S. 1(2) Bank of England Act 1998.

[524] "MPs seek veto on Brown's appointments", *The Independent*, 5 Sept. 1997. First Report from the Select Committee on Treasury, *Accountability of the Bank of England*, Session 1997–8, HC 282, consideration 47.

[525] Third Report from the Select Committee on Treasury, *Confirmation Hearings*, Session 1997–8, HC 571.

[526] Sched. 1, para. 5, Bank of England Act 1998. A similar provision was included in the Bank of England Act 1946. Note that the 4 members serving on the MPC which are appointed by the Chancellor of the Exchequer are also excluded, since they are considered to be servants of the Bank: sched. 3, para. 4(1).

[527] This does not, however, *per se* exclude members of Parliament.

[528] Letter of the Chancellor of the Exchequer Gordon Brown to the governor of the Bank of England, 6 May 1997, reprinted in *Bank of England Quarterly Bulletin*, vol. 37 no. 3 (1997), 244–5. Interestingly, the Bank of England Act 1998 does not include any reference to this.

non-executive directors serve three-year terms by rotation.[529] Unlike the arrangements under the Bank of England Act 1946, none of the 16 additional members of the Court of Directors is appointed on a full-time basis.[530]

The six members who make up the MPC, together with the governor and the two deputy governors, are appointed according to different procedures. Two members are appointed by the governor of the Bank of England after consulting with the Chancellor of the Exchequer. The other four members are appointed by the Chancellor of the Exchequer without any participation by the Bank. The participation of the governor in the appointment of two of the six members may be explained by the outstanding position which these two members have on the MPC. One member is put in charge of executive responsibilities for monetary policy analysis, and the other of monetary policy operations. This makes close co-operation between the governor and those two members necessary. All six members of the MPC, other than the governor and deputy governors, are appointed by rotation for a term of three years. The only positive reference to the qualification of the candidates relates to the four members appointed by the Chancellor of the Exchequer, who have to have "knowledge or experience which is likely to be relevant to the Committee's functions".[531] With regard to disqualification of candidates rules similar to those set out above relating to the Court of Directors apply. Under the new arrangements a provision is inserted in the House of Commons Disqualification Act 1975 according to which the six places of the MPC, other than the governor and deputy governors, will be regarded as offices disqualifying holders for the membership in the House of Commons.[532] A similar provision does not exist for the members of the court of directors, including the governor and deputy governors of the Bank.

All of the members of the Court of Directors and the MPC, including the governors and the two deputy governors, may be reappointed, or appointed to any other office on the Court of Directors. Due to a lack of any contradictory provision it has to be concluded that the members of the Court of Directors and the MPC may be re-appointed for an unlimited number of terms.[533]

Considering that the **Reserve Bank of New Zealand** is often applied as an example for a new approach to democratic accountability, it may be somewhat surprising for some that Parliament does not play any role in the appointment procedures. The governor is appointed by the Minister of Finance on the recommendation of the Board of Directors of the Bank for a renewable term of five years.[534] Although the Minister is not obliged to appoint the person recommended by the Board of Directors, he cannot appoint a person who has not been

---

[529] Bank of England Act 1998, sched. 1, para. 1. The term of office has been shortened, since under the Bank of England Act 1946 the 16 additional members served for a term of four years.

[530] Previously, four of the 16 directors were allowed to work on a full-time basis.

[531] S. 13(4) Bank of England Act 1998.

[532] Ibid., sched. 3, para.15.

[533] This can be interpreted from sched. 1, para. 6. and sched. 3, para. 6 Bank of England Act 1998.

[534] S. 40(1) Reserve Bank Act 1989.

recommended either. Consequently, as each side has a right of veto, neither side can impose a candidate upon the other. A consensus has to be reached between the executive government and the Board of Directors of the Bank. This arrangement is unique in the context of the central banks examined in this study. The potential for conflicts may be less manifest, however, than may at first seem, since the composition of the Board of Directors is effectively in the hands of the Minister of Finance, and thus his choice of candidates can prevent conflicts deriving from opposite opinions.

The deputy governors are appointed by the Board of Directors on the recommendation of the governor of the Bank for a renewable term of five years.[535] Here, also each side has a veto. The influence of the executive government on the choice of deputy governors is very limited as the former can only hope that the Board of Directors takes into account its preferences.

Section 46 of the Reserve Bank Act 1989 lists in considerable detail the conditions for the disqualification of a candidate for appointment or reappointment as governor or deputy governor. Apart from personal characteristics, such as age (no older than 70), the existence of a criminal record or a mental illness, or a bad track record in business, the Reserve Bank Act 1989 above all excludes two groups of potential candidates: members of Parliament and members of a government department. By excluding members of Parliament from becoming governor or deputy governor, section 46(1)(a) of the Reserve Bank Act 1989 effectively excludes not only any participation of the legislature in the running of the Reserve Bank, but moreover implicitly excludes the members of government, in as much as they are all required to be members of Parliament.[536] Moreover, the heads of the government departments, that is the Chief Executives, the members of a senior executive service and employees of a government department appointed under the State Sector Act 1988 are prohibited from holding the position of governor or deputy governor. Upon appointment the conditions of employment for the governor and deputy governors are determined. In the case of the governor this is done by an agreement between the Minister of Finance and the governor after consulting the Board of Directors.[537] The agreement has to be consistent with the Bank's functions and the governor's functions related to those.[538] Consequently, the Minister of Finance could not have the governor sign an agreement which would effectively subordinate the latter to the former. The agreement has to be tabled at the first meeting of the Board of Directors after its conclusion. In a similar way the conditions of employment are determined by the Board of Directors for the designated deputy governors.[539] Unlike the agreement between the Minister of Finance and the governor, the conditions of employment of the deputy governors have to

[535] S. 40(1) Reserve Bank Act 1989, s. 43.
[536] S. 6 Constitution Act 1986.
[537] S. 42(2) Reserve Bank Act 1989.
[538] Ibid., s. 42(3).
[539] Ibid., s. 44(2).

specify the grounds on which the governor may recommend that a deputy governor be removed from office by the Board of Directors.

The members of the Board of Directors are appointed by the Minister of Finance for a renewable term of office of five years. The Reserve Bank Act 1989 specifies in its section 56 considerations which the Minister of Finance has to take into account when making his choice. The Minister has to have regard to the professional qualifications of the candidates, that is to say their knowledge, skills and experiences.[540] The Reserve Bank Act 1989 also anticipates potential conflicts of interests arising as a result of the recruitment of non-executive directors from outside the Bank. Section 56(b) of the Reserve Bank Act 1989 obliges the Minister of Finance to take into account "the likelihood of any conflict between the interests of the Bank and any interests which that person has or represents". Controversies with regard to the role of non-executive directors, such as have in the past arisen in the case of the Bank of England, are defused. Moreover, by explicitly obliging the Minister of Finance to take account of potential conflicts of interest, he becomes accountable for his choice of candidates and any entanglements between public and private interests that may result from that.

In addition to the abovementioned conditions the Reserve Bank Act 1989 includes a detailed list of disqualifications for non-executive directors.[541]

2. Dismissal

With regard to the dismissal of central bank officials, the spectrum of arrangements existing for the central banks examined in this work ranges from central bank statutes which include no, or an incomplete, dismissal procedure to adequately defined procedures which are limited in their scope as they do not include performance-based dismissal, and, finally, dismissal procedures which allow for performance-based dismissal of the governor of the bank.

With regard to the ESCB, unlike the appointment procedures the conditions for the dismissal of the governors of the national central banks who make up the Governing Council of the ECB have been specified in detail in Article 14(2) EC: "[a] Governor may be relieved from his office only if he no longer fulfils the conditions required for the performance of his duties or if he has been guilty of serious misconduct". Thus in accordance with primary Community law any grounds for dismissal other than those for serious misconduct have to be considered inadmissible. Since Article 14.2 of the ESCB Statute refers only to the governors of the national central banks, the other members of the decision-making organs of the national central banks could in principle be subjected to other conditions for dismissal. Yet, it may be argued that in the logic of the EC

---

[540] Ibid., s. 56(a).
[541] Ibid., s. 58.

Treaty and the ESCB Statute, at least for the deputy governor of a central bank, who may at times represent the governor at a particular meeting of the Governing Council of the ECB, the same strict conditions for dismissal must be applicable.

2.1. Lack of explicit provisions on dismissal

In the case of the **Bundesbank**, the legal basis does not include any provisions on the dismissal of the members of the Board of Directors. Nevertheless, the majority opinion accepts a right of dismissal. As with the appointment procedures, the Federal government and the Bundesrat are considered to be competent. Yet, the legal justification and extent of such a right of dismissal are far from resolved. In the centre of these discussions stands the potential conflict between a right of dismissal and the independent position of the Bundesbank *vis-à-vis* the Federal government as laid down in § 12, sentence 2 of the BBankG. The right of dismissal has been explained by analogy with the law on stock companies (*Aktiengesetz*), the right of cancellation of the contracts of the members of the Board of Directors and the presidents of the State central banks by analogy with the laws on the judiciary, and by an analogy with political appointees.[542] One main difference between these various approaches lies in the conditions under which dismissal is permitted. Thus, proponents of an analogy with the law on stock companies argue that dismissal is permitted in the case of a loss of trust on the part of the Federal government in the monetary policy pursued by the members of the Central Bank Council.[543] According to another opinion a right of dismissal is possible because the contract between the members of the Central Bank Council and the Bundesbank may include provisions on cancellation of the contract for important reasons and, therefore, dismissal for imperative reasons must be feasible.[544] With reference to the legal relationship under public law of the central bank officials, an analogy with the legal position of the Federal Ministers, who serve at the discretion of the Federal Chancellor, and political appointees, who can be retired at any time without stating reasons, has been drawn. While recognising that the members of the Central Bank Council of the Bundesbank have a special position *vis-à-vis* the Federal government, it is argued that the possibility of dismissal for important reasons, including political ones, compensate for the independence of the Bundesbank.[545] However, the majority of writers tends to prioritise the independence of the Bundesbank. In this context it is argued by analogy with the law on the judiciary that dismissal

---

[542] For an overview cf. Hahn, n. 24 above, 242 *et seq.*, with further references.

[543] v.Spindler/Beck/Starke, n. 215 above, § 7, side notation 4. Dismissal is excluded when it is based on evidently unobjective reasons.

[544] O.-E. Starke, "Das Gesetz über die Deutsche Bundesbank und seine wichtigsten öffentlich-rechtlichen Probleme", *DÖV* (1957), 606–12, at 612; Gramlich, n. 205 above, § 7, side notation 21, is critical and argues that removal is possible only in the case of inability to undertake the duty or for important reasons.

[545] v.Bonin, n. 40 above, 185–6.

is only possible in the case of grave violations of official duty, but not for reasons which derive from the tasks for which the central bank officials are not constrained by any (mandatory) instructions.[546] Since there are no examples of dismissal of members of the Central Bank Council, it can only be assumed that in such an event the option, according to which dismissal is only possible in the case of gross violations of official duties, like the existing provisions in the statutes of other central banks, would prevail. This view may also be considered consistent with the EC Treaty and the ESCB Statute on the dismissal of members of the Executive Board.

Interestingly the revised legal basis of the Bundesbank, applicable from 1 January 1999, still does not include any explicit reference to dismissal procedures. A clarification of the legal basis in this area would have been desirable.

2.2. Ambiguous provisions on dismissal

Unlike the statute of the Bundesbank, the legal bases of the Nederlandsche Bank and the Fed include provisions on dismissal. However, in both cases the conditions for dismissal are largely undetermined.

In accordance with section 23(4) of the Bank Act 1948 any member of the Governing Board of the **Nederlandsche Bank**, including the president, can be dismissed *or* suspended from office by the Crown on the proposal of the Governing Board and the Supervisory Board meeting as a joint body. In the case of suspension a recommendation to fill up the vacancy temporarily has to be made by the initiators. The Bank Act 1948 does not make the suspension or dismissal of a member of the Governing Board subject to any conditions. Therefore, the Council of Ministers, which in practice will be in charge of suspension or dismissal, enjoys a large degree of discretion, as according to the wording of section 23(5) the Crown is not bound by the recommendation of the Governing Board and the Supervisory Board. However, in one exceptional case, the Bank Act 1948 does dictate the dismissal of a member of the Governing Board: if a member of the Governing Board refuses or deliberately fails to comply with any directions issued by the Minister of Finance in accordance with section 26 of the Bank Act 1948, the former may be removed by the Crown, acting on the advice of the Council of State, and under the conditions laid down in sections 23(5) and 26.[547] However, since section 26 has never been applied there have been no removals from office on grounds of non-compliance either.[548]

The fact that the Bank Act 1948, apart from that one exception, does not define the conditions for dismissal of the members of the Governing Board is remarkable. From the point of view of the (legal) independence of the Bank this

---

[546] Siebelt, n. 202 above, at 177.

[547] Cf. Chap. V 3.

[548] The only reported dismissal was linked to a death in office. It has been observed that this provision has been abolished together with the override mechanism at the beginning of stage three of EMU.

observation has a negative impact since, at least formally, the government has a large degree of discretion which it could in principle apply to put pressure on the Bank.[549] From the point of view of the accountability of the Bank it could be interpreted as having positive indications, as any member who is thought not to perform his or her tasks can be suspended or even dismissed. With the existence of such an authority the government can in principle be held accountable in Parliament for its decision either to use or discard this power in a given circumstance. However, any potential mechanism of accountability is weakened by the fact that the decision of the Minister of Finance to suspend or dismiss requires a prior recommendation of the Governing Board and the Supervisory Board meeting as a joint body. A situation in which the Governing Board would recommend the dismissal of one of its own members, e.g. the president, on grounds of bad performance is hardly realistic. Besides, the absence of clear rules on the application of the dismissal procedures runs the danger of an improper application of the mechanism by the executive government.

The Bank Act 1948 does not contain any provisions on the dismissal of the members of the Supervisory Board, but as a company limited by shares the Nederlandsche Bank in this respect is subject to the rules generally applicable to companies limited by shares.[550] Finally, the Royal Commissioner serves at the pleasure of the Crown and as such can be dismissed by the executive government, represented by the Minister of Finance, at any time.

Section 23 of the Bank Act 1948 has been abolished with the Bank Act 1998. Instead, the dismissal of a member of the Governing Board is only admissible in the case of serious misconduct or personal incapability.[551]

In the case of the **Fed**, as with the Nederlandsche Bank, the Federal Reserve Act falls somewhat short of providing the exact conditions for dismissal. With regard to the dismissal of members of the Board of Governors section 10(2) of the Federal Reserve Act[552] states:

> "each member shall hold office for a term of fourteen years . . . unless sooner *moved for cause* by the President".

Section 10 includes the only, somewhat concealed, reference in the Federal Reserve Act to the dismissal of the members of the Board of Governors. However, it does not include any details of the conditions for dismissal. By requiring a "cause" at least a distinction is made from those Presidential appointees which serve "at the President's pleasure", as is the case for most of the heads of the executive agencies.[553] The exact circumstance in which dismissal will be per-

---

[549] A non-legal approach to central bank independence would take into account whether the dismissal procedure has actually been applied, cf. Chap. 2 I 2.2.

[550] Cf. Ss. 152 *et seq.*, book 2 of the Dutch Civil Code.

[551] Cf. s. 12(3) Bank Act 1998.

[552] Also 12 USC Sec. 242.

[553] In *Humphrey's Executor* v. *United States*, a case involving the attempted removal of the head of another administrative agency, the Federal Trade Commission, by the US President, the US

missible remains unclear. Practical examples are lacking, since this provision has never been applied. Although the wording of section 10(2) of the Federal Reserve Act does not exclude a member of the Board of Governors, and in particular its chairman, being dismissed as a result of an unsatisfactory monetary policy performance, but at the same time also for political reasons, most observers conclude that a dismissal would only be acceptable in cases of serious misconduct by a member of the Board of Governors.[554] Thus the members of the Board of Governors enjoy tenure akin to that of Federal judges. Interestingly, unlike in the case of appointment, the consent of the Senate is not required for dismissal.

The Federal Reserve Act does not include any detailed provisions on the dismissal of members of the board of directors of the Federal Reserve Banks. Section 11(f) only states that:

"The Board of Governors of the Federal Reserve system shall be authorized and empowered: . . . To suspend or remove any officer or director of any Federal reserve bank, *the cause of such removal* to be forthwith communicated in writing by the Board of Governors of the Fed to the removed officer or director and to said bank."[555]

The question arises under what circumstances the Board of Governors can suspend or dismiss an officer and, more importantly, director of a Federal Reserve Bank. On the one hand it could be concluded that the decision is left to the discretion of the Board of Governors.[556] On the other hand, the language of this provision assumes the need for a cause of which the removed officer or director and the respective Federal Reserve Bank have to be informed.

2.3. Dismissal for serious misconduct

The legal basis of the Bank of England, the Banque de France and the ECB include clearly defined conditions for dismissal.

At the **Bank of England** generally, any member of the Court of Directors, including the governor, may be removed by the Bank with the consent of the Chancellor of the Exchequer in the case of absence from meetings of the Court for more than three months without the consent of the court, bankruptcy or the like, or in case of inability or unfitness to discharge the functions of a

---

Supreme Court held: "When Congress provides for the appointment of officers whose functions, like those of the Federal Trade Commissioners, are of legislative and judicial quality, rather than executive, and limits the grounds upon which they may be removed from office, the President has no constitutional power to remove them for reasons other than those so specified": 295 US 602 (1935).

[554] This is the definition usually applied by Fed officials. Louis, n. 454 above, at 272, refers to "incompetence, neglect of duty or malfeasance in office". However, Hasse (ed.), n. 418 above, at 165, even seems to question whether members of the Board of Governors can be dismissed at all when stating that "it is a moot legal point whether and, if so, under what conditions the Chairman and the other members of the BoG can be dismissed by state authorities".

[555] Emphasis added.

[556] Louis, n. 454 above, at 299, seems to hint at this view when pointing to the directors of the branch offices who serve at the pleasure of the Board of Governors.

member.[557] The six members of the MPC may be dismissed on the same grounds. The only difference is that the dismissal is delegated to the sub-committee of the Court of Directors consisting of the 16 directors of the Bank.[558] The first two grounds of dismissal appear to be particularly associated with the non-executive directors on the Court who may also be involved in commercial activities outside the Bank. Dismissal on grounds other than those described, and in particular dismissal on grounds of past performance, is excluded. Indeed, formally the Chancellor of the Exchequer does not even have a right to initiate the dismissal of members of the Court, since, as with the Nederlandsche Bank, this initiative has to come from within the Bank, and the Chancellor of the Exchequer may only reject or declare his consent.

Although in the case of the **Banque de France** the executive government still appoints the governor and deputy governors, the Bank Act 1993 has removed the government's power to remove the governor and/or deputy-governors at its discretion at any time.[559] Consequently, the government cannot easily dispose of a governor it finds unacceptable. However, apart from preventing politically motivated dismissals this also prevents the government in the short term from holding the governor and deputy governors accountable for their performance. In the long run the executive government can decide not to re-appoint a governor and/or deputy governor(s) who do not meet its expectations.

With regard to the dismissal of the members of the CPM Article 10 I(2) of the Bank Act 1993 states

> "A member may be removed before his term of office expires only if he is no longer capable of performing his duties or if he is guilty of serious misconduct. Any such removal shall require a reasoned opinion from the Monetary Policy Council acting on a majority vote of its members excluding the person concerned."

This provision has implications both for the independence and the accountability of the Bank. First, it explicitly lists the reasons for the early retirement of a member of the CPM. A member of the policy decision-making body of the Bank cannot be removed for any reasons other than those listed.[560] This ensures the independence of the members of the CPM, who cannot be dismissed subject to the discretion of government or Parliament. However, this also rules out dismissal on grounds of an unsatisfactory performance record. By locating the power of dismissal outside the government, Article 10 I(2) ensures that dismissals are not utilised for the application of political pressure on to the monetary policy board of the Bank. This may be considered one of the corner-stones of the independence of the Bank. However, by putting the CPM itself in charge,

---

[557] Sched. 1, para. 8 Bank of England Act 1998.

[558] Ibid., s. 3 and sched. 3, para. 9.

[559] Cf. questionnaire on key functions and legal structure of central banks and banking supervisory authorities, in *Vers un Système Européen de Banques Centrales*, Rapport du groupe présidé par Jean-Victor Louis (Editions de l'Université de Bruxelles, Brussels, 1989), at 204.

[560] Collas, n. 233 above, describes the terms of office as quasi-irrevocable.

the already limited value of the ground of dismissal for serious misconduct for the democratic accountability of the members of the CPM is further diminished. Neither the government nor Parliament has the power to dismiss, and it seems questionable whether even the extent of accountability provided for by Article 10 I(2) will be effectively enforced given the fact that this requires an initiative of the CPM itself.

The Censor owes his position to the Minister of Economic Affairs and Finances and he remains in this position at the discretion of the government. The Censor is fully accountable to the executive government which can dispose of him at any time.

As is the case for the (re-)appointment of the officials of the **ECB**, the dismissal of the members of the Executive Board and the Governing Council involve different procedures. With regard to the dismissal of members of the Executive Board, Article 11.4 of the ESCB Statute states that:

> "If a member of the Executive Board no longer fulfils the conditions required for the performance of his duty or if he has been guilty of serious misconduct, the Court of Justice may, on application by the Governing Council or the Executive Board, compulsorily retire him."

Upon examination this provision may be regarded as problematic in two respects, namely the participants in the dismissal of members of the Executive Board and the preconditions for dismissal. The dismissal of a member of the Executive Board has to be initiated either by Executive Board itself or by the Governing Council, which also includes the members of the Executive Board. Evaluated from the point of view of accountability this amounts to a mechanism of self-control. A similar arrangement has already been observed for the Nederlandsche Bank, the Bank of England and the Banque de France. Only if the Executive Board itself—though presumably excluding the member at issue— and, in the case of the Governing Council and the governors of the national central banks, consider a member of the Executive Board to be no longer fit for the performance of his tasks or guilty of serious misconduct is a procedure for its dismissal triggered. Neither the Council of the EU in its composition of the Heads of State or Government, nor the EP, both of which take part in the procedure of appointment of the Executive Board, plays any role in its dismissal. But interestingly, and quite uniquely in the light of the other central banks examined in this book, the judiciary in the form of the ECJ takes part in the procedure for the dismissal of the members of the Executive Board. On the European level the participation of the ECJ has its precursor in Article 160 EC on the compulsory retirement of members of the Commission by the ECJ. With regard to the motivation of dismissal the ESCB Statute fails to define the circumstances in which it may be concluded that a member of the Executive Board no longer fulfils the conditions required for the performance of the duties or has committed a serious misconduct. Here, an analogy to the interpretation of similar provisions in the statutes of national central banks seems appropriate. According to this view, dismissal is possible only in the case of a serious illness or punishable behaviour.[561] Moreover, similar arrangements already exist for the members of the Commission. They may in principle only be dismissed, i.e. compulsorily retired, by the ECJ on the application of the Council or the Commission itself, if no longer fulfilling the conditions for the performance of their duties or in the case of serious misconduct.[562] In this context it has been argued that serious misconduct does not necessarily require punishable behaviour, but may also be based on failure to comply with the duty to co-operate and the duty of loyalty.[563] The right of review by the ECJ is limited to the verification of the existence of the pre-conditions for retirement, and in particular the question whether particular behaviour is to be interpreted as *serious* misconduct. Despite the restricted possibility of dismissals, in principle it is also possible that a member of the Executive Board, and in particular the president of the ECB, would him/herself decide to resign, e.g. as a result of public pressure, or insurmountable disagreement within the Executive Board, or with the governments of the Member States.

It has been observed that the national central bank governors may also only be dismissed under the same conditions under which the members of the Executive Board may be dismissed. A decision to this effect may be referred to the Court of Justice by the governor concerned or the Governing Council on grounds of infringement of Community law, or the respective national law relating to the application of the dismissal procedure. Such proceedings have to be instituted within two months of the publication of the decision, or of its notification to the plaintiff or, in the absence thereof, of the day on which it came to the knowledge to the latter, as the case may be. At first sight, the role of the ECJ in the dismissal of the governors may seem surprising, taking into consideration that the governors of the national central banks, unlike the members of the Executive Board, are not appointed on the European level, but rather according to the respective national provisions.[564] However, the role of the ECJ can be explained with the underlying concept to be found repeatedly in the context of the provisions on the ESCB, that is to say the independence of the system as a whole. The drafters of the TEU wanted to ensure that the position of governors of the national central bank represented on the monetary policy board of the ECB does not at any given time become the subject of political preferences of the

---

[561] Stadler, n. 353 above, 149–50.

[562] Art. 160 EC. The only reported case of the compulsory retirement of a member of the Commission took place in May 1976 when a Commissioner suffered a stroke: cf. Dec. 76/619 [1976] OJ L201/31; K.P.E. Lasok, *The European Court of Justice—Practice and Procedures* (2nd edn., Butterworths, London, 1994), at 572.

[563] W. Hummer, in E. Grabitz/M. Hilf (eds.), *Kommentar zur Europäischen Union* (C.H. Beck, Munich, 1988), Art. 160.

[564] J.A. Usher, *The Law of Money and Financial Services in the European Community* (Clarendon Press, Oxford, 1996), at 174, refers to "a unique example of a national official becoming subject to Community jurisdiction".

national governments, and that a governor cannot be persuaded towards a more government friendly position on the Governing Council of the ECB by threatening to dismiss him. On the contrary, it may be argued that the existence of this procedure may also have justified the introduction of a performance-based dismissal, as judicial review would have ensured the existence of the conditions for such dismissal, and thus excluded the abuse of this procedure by politically motivated dismissal.[565]

2.4. Performance-based dismissal

The legal basis of the **Reserve Bank of New Zealand** arguably contains the most precise provisions on dismissal of central bank officials compared to the other central banks examined in this study. Besides, and more importantly, the provisions include performance linked dismissal. This is unique in the context of the central banks examined in this study.

Generally, a distinction must be drawn between the governor of the Bank and other members of the Board of Directors. The governor can be dismissed by the Governor-General by Order in Council on recommendation of the Minister of Finance.[566] The Governor-General has no discretion but is obliged to act in accordance with the recommendation of the Minister of Finance. The grounds on which the Minister of Finance can recommend dismissal of the governor are listed in detail in section 49(2) of the Reserve Bank Act 1989. This includes first of all the "traditional" grounds to be found in central bank statutes, such as inability to carry out the office and serious misconduct. However, unlike other central bank systems, the Reserve Bank Act 1989 foresees additional performance-related grounds for dismissal. According to Article 49(2) they include among others:

"(a) That the Bank is not adequately carrying out its functions; or
(b) That the Governor has not adequately discharged the responsibilities of office; or
(c) That the Governor has obstructed, hindered, or prevented the Board from discharging its responsibilities under this Act; or
(d) That the performance of the Governor in ensuring that the Bank achieves the policy targets . . . has been inadequate; or
(f) That a policy statement . . . is inconsistent in a material respect with the Bank's primary function or any policy target fixed . . . ; or
(g) That the resources of the Bank have not been properly or effectively managed . . . "

It is interesting to note that the Minister of Finance is not obliged to act on a recommendation of the Board of Directors in accordance with section 53(3) of the Reserve Bank Act 1989. Therefore, the Minister constitutes a separate level charged with the review of the Governor's performance. In the judgment of this performance it is conceivable that the Minister of Finance and the Board of

[565] Cf. Chap. 5 III.
[566] S. 49(1) Reserve Bank Act 1989.

Governors may come to different conclusions as regards the necessity for dismissal of the governor. But in the end the decision is a matter for the Minister.

A deputy governor can be removed from office according to the same procedure as the governor, if the Minister of Finance finds that the deputy governor has been guilty of misconduct, acted against the conditions of his employment, is unable or has failed to perform the duties as a member of the Board of Directors or has obstructed, hindered, or prevented the governor from discharging his responsibilities. Moreover, according to section 45 of the Reserve Bank Act 1989, the governor has the right to recommend the removal of a deputy governor on grounds which have to be pre-determined and specified in the conditions of employment of the deputy governor concerned. On the basis of such a recommendation the Board of Directors may remove a deputy governor from office. From the wording of this provision, i.e. "may", it has to be concluded that the Board of Directors retains a discretion as regards the decision to remove a deputy governor. It cannot be determined from the statutory provisions whether this discretion is limited to the review of the validity of the grounds for dismissal. However, taking into account the strong position of the governor within the Bank and his overall responsibility of the conduct of the Bank, it seems reasonable to assume that this is in fact the case. The ratio of this provision is to give the governor the power to dispose of an immediate subordinate if he or she does not act in accordance with the conditions of employment, that is to say does not fulfil his or her function satisfactorily.

Non-executive directors can be removed from office by the Governor-General through an Order in Council on the advice of the Minister of Finance.[567] The Minister may advise the Governor-General to dismiss a non-executive director, if the former is convinced that the non-executive director in question is unable, or has failed, to perform the duties of a member of the Board of Directors, or has been guilty of misconduct, or has obstructed, hindered or prevented the governor from discharging his responsibilities.[568] It is questionable under what circumstances the Board of Directors or individual non-executive directors would be considered to have obstructed, hindered or prevented the governor from discharging his responsibilities. The task of the Board to monitor the Governor's performance includes the inherent danger that the governor in a given case may be obstructed by these activities to some extent. Taking into account that the Minister of Finance takes the final decision whether to dismiss a non-executive director on these grounds it could be argued that this limits the independent review of the governor's and, generally, the Bank's performance by the Board of Directors to some extent.

---

[567] S. 49(1) Reserve Bank Act 1989, s. 59(1).
[568] Ibid., s. 59(2).

V. OVERRIDE MECHANISM

For the central banks examined in this book generally three different arrangements can be observed, including the lack of any override mechanism, the existence of a limited override mechanism, that is to say the executive government one way or the other can intervene in the decision-making procedure of the monetary policy board without overriding decisions of the latter or taking over the conduct of monetary policy, and, finally, the presence of a full override mechanism.

In the case of the Member States' central banks participating in the ESCB the existence of override mechanisms in the respective legal bases is considered to be incompatible with the EC Treaty and the ESCB Statute. This includes legal constructions providing third parties with a right to give instructions, to approve, suspend or defer decisions, or to censor decisions on legal grounds.[569]

1. Central bank systems precluding an override mechanism

Three of the seven central banks examined in this study, the Fed, the Banque de France, and the ECB, do not include any type of override mechanism, as defined in Chapter 2.[570]

For the **Fed** the Federal Reserve Act does not include any provision which would give the President or any other part of the executive the power to override decisions of the Board of Governors or the FOMC. Ultimately, the only override mechanism is the power by Congress to amend the Federal Reserve Act as described above.

Similarly, in case of the **Banque de France**, the Bank Act 1993 does not foresee any provisions which would give the Prime Minister, the Minister of Economic Affairs and Finances or their alternate a right to override, suspend or veto any decision by the CPM on issues relating to monetary policy. It has been observed that the powers of the Censor are effectively restricted to the functions of the General Council, where the latter *de facto* cannot take a decision without the consent of the former.[571] The power of the Censor is thus limited to matters decided upon by the General Council, i.e. decisions on the management of the Bank which are *not* related to the formulation and implementation of monetary policy.

The same assessment applies to the **ECB**, since neither the EC Treaty nor the ESCB Statute contains any provisions which would enable the Council or any other Community institution to override the ECB with regard to monetary policy.[572] It has been observed that the President of the Council and one

---

[569] European Monetary Institute, n. 199 above, 98 *et seq.*
[570] Cf. Chap. 2 II 2.2.
[571] Cf. Chap. 4 III.
[572] Cf. Chap. 4 II, on the powers of the Council with regard to exchange rate policy.

member of the Commission may take part in the meetings of the Governing Council. However, this does not include a right to take part in the voting.[573] Moreover, neither the EC Treaty nor the ESCB Statute contains any provision which would enable the President of the Council and/or the representative of the Commission formally to block, postpone or overrule decisions of the Governing Council. The introduction of such an override mechanism had been suggested by various circles during the drafting of the provisions on the ESCB and the ECB. Like the limited override applicable to the Bundesbank, the EP had proposed to give the President of the Council, or a person authorised by him or her, a right to postpone the deliberations of the Governing Council on subjects of great importance for the economic and monetary policy of the Community for a period of up to one week, whereas a similar French proposal foresaw the same possibility, but for a period of up to two weeks.[574] But the introduction of an override mechanism of any kind was apparently considered incompatible with the envisaged independent status of the ESCB and ECB.

2. The limited override mechanism of the Bundesbank

The legal basis of the Bundesbank does not include an override mechanism in the classical sense that the executive government can overrule a decision by the central bank, or override the statutory monetary policy objective by issuing directions. It has been observed that the relationship between the Bundesbank and the executive government is characterised by co-operation rather than confrontation. Sanctions in the case of a conflict between the Bundesbank and the Federal government are not provided for. In this context, the presence and contents of the third sentence of § 13(2) of the BBankG represent something of a stranger, as they envisage a difference of views. They confer upon the members of the Federal government the power to suspend the decision-making of the Central Bank Council for a period of up to two weeks. The nature of the decisions which can be temporarily blocked is defined through the powers of the Central Bank Council, that is to say by the nature of the decisions which the Central Bank Council can take and thus, by definition, includes monetary policy decisions.[575] In order to evaluate this override mechanism with respect to its effectiveness as a means of accountability, first, the procedure for its application, who precisely can suspend the decision-making and how, needs to be

---

[573] Art. 109b(1) para. 1, EC.

[574] Resolution of the European Parliament on Economic and Monetary Union, Art. 6, 3rd para.; Art. 4.3 of the French government draft of a Treaty on Economic and Monetary Union of 25 Jan. 1991, reprinted in German language in H. Kägenau/W. Wetter, *Europäische Wirtschafts- und Währungsunion—Vom Werner Plan zum Vertrag von Maastricht* (Nomos, Baden-Baden, 1993), 342 *et seq.*; cf. also the CEPREM proposal for Treaty Art. 17, 3rd para., in *Vers un Système Européen De Banques Centrales*, Rapport du groupe présidé par Jean-Victor Louis (Editions de l'Université de Bruxelles, Brussels, 1989), at 47.

[575] For a description of Central Bank Council functions, cf. Chap. 3 III 2–3.

examined. § 13(2) of the BBankG only limits the period of the application of the override mechanism to only two weeks. It is clear that decision-making cannot be blocked beyond two weeks with respect to the same issue, and decision-making remains with the Central Bank Council. Thus, the Federal government does not take over the functions of the Central Bank Council, thereby establishing itself as the monetary authority, and § 13(2) does not contain a genuine right of veto.[576] § 13(2) cannot be considered to be a full override mechanism, but rather a provisional override mechanism, which forces the Central Bank Council to reconsider its position on a certain monetary issue. Moreover, it gives the Federal government time to try to persuade the Bundesbank of its view. In this sense it does not fall completely outside the scheme of co-operation: persuasion rather than confrontation. The influence of the Federal government happens in the run-up to the final decision, and its actual level of effectiveness depends upon co-operation with the Bundesbank. Neither the BBankG nor the charter of the Bundesbank contains any provisions on the procedure of its application. Besides, an application of the override mechanisms of § 13(2) of the BBankG has never been officially recorded.[577] However, experiences in the 1950s with the BdL, the forerunner of the Bundesbank, suggest that the Federal government may nevertheless have made use of this provision in the past. In fact, it may be the case that interventions by the Federal government following the communication of potential decisions to be taken by the Board of Directors have in practice been interpreted by the Central Bank Council as a government application of the override mechanism, and have *de facto* resulted in the postponement of decisions to a later meeting. Berger describes a concrete example for this phenomenon, dating back to 1956.[578] The BdL had communicated an intended increase of the discount rate to the Federal government, which in return intervened, informally asking the BdL in telephone conversations to postpone the decision. The BdL effectively interpreted these informal requests as an exercise of the rights of the Federal government under § 6(2) of the interim law for the amendment of the law establishing the BdL.[579] This became clear when shortly thereafter a formal request for the postponing of the decision on the raising of the discount rate was rejected by the BdL, whereby the latter emphasised that the one-time right under § 6(2) had already been exercised, and that the decision had already been postponed once as a result of that. It is in principle possible that similar incidents have occurred in which the Bundesbank has *de facto* interpreted interventions by the Federal government in consultations as an application of § 13(2) of the BBankG and postponed decisions. However, if the Central Bank Council has postponed decisions in the past as the result of an

---

[576] v.Spindler/Becker/Starke, n. 215 above, § 13, at 272.

[577] It is thus not quite clear to what Lastra, n. 496 above, at 495, n. 88, is referring when she states that "the Government's temporary blocking power . . . has only been *used on a few occasions*" (emphasis added).

[578] For details cf. H. Berger, op. cit., Chap. 3, n. 154, at 62, 253 *et seq*.

[579] Cf. Chap. 3 III 1.3.

interpretation of interventions by the Federal government as an implicit request to postpone a decision, even in the framework of the limited effect it has, it may be of little value for the democratic accountability of the Bundesbank. First, it remains completely unclear under what circumstances the provision will be applied. Consequently, the Federal government cannot easily be held accountable for its behaviour by Parliament. The lack of transparency in the procedures works against the democratic accountability of the Bank.[580] Moreover, it has been argued by some that the limited scope of the existing override mechanism fails to recognise the connections between monetary and economic policy, and that experience shows that the Federal government will *de facto* override the Bundesbank in the case of severe economic shocks anyway, with the only difference that this does not take place in a transparent manner.[581]

If the common opinion that § 13(2) has never been applied is accepted, it may yet be premature to conclude that the provision is of no practical relevance at all, and as a matter of fact resembles hardly more than a paper tiger. Kennedy suggests that the non-application of the override mechanism "intensifies the threat to use it". A practical example from the history of the Bundesbank, highlighting this point, is an incident in 1961, when the Bundesbank abandoned its publicly-stated position on the revaluation of the Dmark and voted in favour of government policy after an implied threat by the Federal government to make use of its right under § 13(2) of the BBankG. On the contrary, the Federal government may be reluctant to apply formally the override mechanism, thereby openly admitting a conflict between the government and the guardian of the Dmark.[582]

Regardless of the effectiveness of §13(2) of the BBankG as an override mechanism, it has to be considered incompatible with the EC Treaty and the ESCB Statute and thus the relevant sentence has been eradicated from the statute of the Bundesbank applicable in stage three of EMU.

3. Central bank systems incorporating a full override mechanism

The legal bases of the Nederlandsche Bank, the Reserve Bank of New Zealand and the Bank of England include provisions according to which the executive government can issue directions on the conduct of monetary policy to the respective bank. One of the main differences between these override mechanisms that emerges is the extent to which the decision to apply the override mechanism is subject to review.

---

[580] Cf. Chap. 4 VII 1, on transparency in the decision-making procedures of the Bundesbank.

[581] Vibert, n. 278 above, at 215, with reference to the dispute between the Federal government and the Bundesbank during the German reunification.

[582] On the eve of the 1972 Federal elections in a disagreement between the president of the Bundesbank, Karl Klasen, and the Minister of Economics, Karl Schiller, over the revaluation of the DM, the Federal government eventually turned against its own Minister and voted in favour of the Bundesbank policy.

In the legal basis of the **Reserve Bank of New Zealand** the override mechanism is included in section 12(1)–(2) of the Reserve Bank Act 1989:

> "(1) The Governor-General may, from time to time, by Order in Council, on the advice of the Minister, direct the Bank to formulate, and implement monetary policy for any economic objective, other than the economic objective specified in section 8 of this Act, for such period not exceeding 12 months as shall be specified in the order.
>
> (2) Notwithstanding anything in section 8 of this Act, the Bank shall formulate and implement monetary policy in accordance with any economic objective specified in an Order in Council in force under subsection (1) of this section."

Unlike some central bank systems, the override mechanism is not directly vested in the executive government. As will be seen, however, this should not lead to the conclusion that government is not in control. The wording of section 12(1) may be misleading in as much as it states that the Governor-General acts on the *advice* of the Minister of Finance. It would be a misjudgement to conclude from this that the government is only consulted, whereas the decision is taken by the Governor-General. Instead, as is the case for the dismissal procedures, the Governor-General is obliged by convention to act in accordance with the instructions given by the executive government.[583] Hence, *de facto* the government, represented by the Minister of Finance, decides to issue an Order in Council.[584] The role of Governor-General is effectively limited to the signing (into law) of the Order in Council which will give directions to the Bank in accordance with section 12. The Order in Council takes the legal form of a regulation.

Section 12 of the Reserve Bank Act 1989 does not provide for an override mechanism that vests a right in government to issue instructions as such. Rather, government has the option to override the economic objective implemented in section 8(1) of the Reserve Bank Act 1989, i.e. price stability, by introducing an alternative economic objective.[585] The Bank remains in charge of the formulation and implementation of monetary policy, albeit for a new objective. The period of duration of the Order in Council has to be specified in the order itself and may not exceed 12 months. However, according to section 12(3) of the Reserve Bank Act 1989, the period of application can be prolonged each time for up to 12 months by a new Order in Council. Interestingly, section 12(3) does not specify a limit for the prolongation of the order. Thus, the override mechanisms could in principle be renewed for an indefinite number of times.[586]

The Reserve Bank Act 1989 recognises the potential conflicts that may arise between the Bank's obligation to formulate and implement monetary policy in

---

[583] Subjects at issue in the Executive Council have previously been extensively discussed in the Cabinet.

[584] A quorum in the Executive Council requires the presence of the Governor-General and two ministers or, in the absence of the Governor-General, of three ministers.

[585] Therefore G.E. Wood, op. cit., Chap. 3, n. 452, at 64, is mistaken when stating that "the PTA can be overridden by Government". Instead, the PTA is altered as a result of the new economic objective.

[586] The observation by O.U. Wood, n. 585 above, at 64, that the override mechanism can last for a maximum of one year is only correct in as far as thereafter a prolongation becomes necessary.

accordance with the economic policy determined by the Minister of Finance and the obligations arising under the PTA. According to section 12(7)(a), the policy targets cease to have effect if an Order in Council is issued. However, the Minister of Finance and the governor of the Bank are also obliged to fix new policy targets for the period of time that the order under section 12(1) or 12(3) of the Reserve Bank Act 1989 remains in place.[587] By obliging the Minister of Finance and the governor of the Bank, within 30 days of the making of the Order, to formulate new policy targets for the time being, the Reserve Bank Act 1989 ensures the accountability of the Bank during the application of the directions, since a clear yardstick for the judgement of the performance of the Bank remains in place. Moreover, a new policy target has to be fixed in accordance with the economic objective specified in the Reserve Bank Act 1989 within 30 days of the cessation of the Order in Council.[588] However, it seems to be a small loophole in this procedure that if an Order in Council were to be in force for less than 30 days, the Bank could end up formulating and implementing monetary policy without a properly adjusted policy target in place. The same would be the case for the period following the cessation or revocation of an Order in Council until a new PTA was in place. Any judgement of the performance of the Bank for that period of time would then solely rely on the economic policy specified in the Order in Council. The more broadly that economic policy is formulated the harder it will become to hold the Bank accountable for a specific policy outcome.

The application of the override mechanism under section 12 of the Reserve Bank Act 1989 is transparent in as much as the Minister of Finance is obliged to publish a copy of the order in the Gazette and must lay a copy before the House of Representatives.[589] It is not clear from the statutory provisions whether the Order in Council has to state the reasons on which it is based, thereby revealing the motivation for overturning the economic objective of price stability. Interestingly, the override mechanism does not foresee the review of the decisions of the executive government to apply the override, either in the form of a right of appeal of the Reserve Bank or an affirmation procedure before the House of Representatives. To be sure, this does not exclude Parliament passing a judgment on the decision by the executive government in the framework of ministerial responsibility. Besides, the threat of losing credibility in the financial markets may put pressure on the executive government not to apply section 12 too hastily. This may not even be necessary in all instances, since the government has the right to initiate changes to the PTA. Yet, given the existence of an explicit override mechanism, the executive government should in principle be prohibited from making use of this power in a way that may result in the evasion of the application of the override mechanism in accordance with the procedural requirements under section 12 of the Reserve Bank Act 1989.

[587] S. 12(7)(b)(i) Reserve Bank Act 1989.
[588] Ibid., s. 12(7)(b)(ii) and (8).
[589] Ibid., s. 12(6): "as soon as practicable".

Both economic and political reasons have been identified for the introduction of the current override mechanism into the Reserve Bank Act 1989. From an economic point of view, the introduction of an override mechanism explicitly and openly defining the government's limited powers to interfere with the economic objective of the Reserve Bank Act 1989 may enhance the credibility of monetary policy to some extent in as much as the government's influenced is channelled, institutionalised and dragged into the open. From a political point of view, Lloyd notes that the Reserve Bank Act 1989 recognises that monetary policy is ultimately the responsibility of government, rather than that of "unelected officials", i.e. central bankers.[590] More important from the point of view of accountability may, however, be the observation that by providing a statutory override mechanism, the government's influence is dragged into the limelight of publicity, rather than taking place unofficially and behind closed doors, leaving the outside observer in doubt about the actual decision-making process. The mechanism is formalised to an extent that its application under normal circumstances will not result in the loss of accountability. Hitherto, section 12 of the Reserve Bank Act 1989 has not been applied. Indeed, such a move has to be regarded as a last resort for government, since it would expose the government's abandoning of the explicit monetary objective of price stability. Such a move could result in a loss of credibility in the markets. From this point of view it seems unlikely that the executive government could renew the override mechanism once it has been applied, since it would be assumed that the government has abandoned the objective of price stability once and for all.

Unlike the Reserve Bank of New Zealand, for the **Nederlandsche Bank** section 26 of the Bank Act 1948 not only incorporates an explicit override mechanism, but also provides for a defence for the Bank in case of application:

> "(1) Our Minister [of Finance] may, after consulting with the Bank Council, give such directions to the Governing Board as he thinks necessary for the Bank's policy to be properly co-ordinated with the Government's monetary and financial policies. Except as provided in the subsection (2) below, the Governing Board shall comply with such directions.
>
> (2) If the Governing Board has any objections to the directions as referred to in subsection (1) above, it may communicate the said objections to Us [the Crown] in writing within three days after receiving the directions. We shall decide whether or not the directions are to be complied with."[591]

Section 26 presents itself as a strong override mechanism. Subject to prior consultation of the Bank Council, the Minister of Finance has full discretion to issue any directions he deems necessary, as section 26 does not make the application of the override mechanism subject to any additional conditions. Section 26(1) neither defines the scope of the directions, nor does it set a time-limit for their

---

[590] Lloyd, n. 259 above, at 211.
[591] Cf. also n. 610 below with regard to the Bank Act 1998.

application. The somewhat broad wording of section 26 became the subject of criticism during discussions of the Bank Act 1948 in Parliament. However, proposals to define the Minister's right under section 26 in more concrete terms did not materialise.[592] Section 26 also provides the only explicit provision in the Bank Act 1948 which makes the Governing Board directly accountable for its performance. Section 23(5) states:

> "Any member of the Governing Board who refuses or deliberately fails to comply with any directions referred to in section 26 . . . may be removed from office by Us [the Crown], acting with the advice of the Council of State."

This provision gives the executive government a powerful tool for the enforcement of the override mechanism, as a member of the Governing Board, including the president of the Bank, can be dismissed if he or she does not comply with the directions of the executive government. But the Governing Board of the Bank is not entirely left defenceless against an application of section 26, as it can complain in writing to the Crown within three days after the directions have been issued to the Bank.[593] The Crown will then decide whether the directions have to be followed. By referring only to the Crown, and thus in this case executive government, the Bank Act 1948 itself does not explicitly preclude the Minister of Finance from participating in the decision on the complaint by the Bank. However, according to § 2, Article 4, of the rules of procedure of the Council of Ministers, such decisions on objections of the Governing Board of the Bank are discussed and decided upon in the forum provided for by the Council of Ministers. Where the Council of Ministers decides that the directions have to be followed, the decision, including the reasons for the dismissal of the objection of the Governing Board, together with the Governing Board's objections, must be published in the Dutch Government Gazette (*Nederlandse Staatscourant*), unless such a step is "contrary to the national interest".[594] It is interesting to note in this context that section 26 does not include any obligation to publish the consultations of the Bank Council as well. Nevertheless, the obligation of the executive government to publish its motives for rejecting the Governing Board's objections, together with the objection itself and the decision by the Council of Ministers, can be considered as an important counterweight to the power of the executive government under section 26 of the Bank Act 1948. A dispute between the Bank and the executive government becomes public and the decision of the Council of Ministers to override the Bank is bound to become the subject of parliamentary and public scrutiny. Parliament may decide in a given case to support the view of the Nederlandsche Bank which could even result in a vote of no-confidence against the executive government of the day. Moreover, making the dispute known openly can work to the advantage or dis-

---

[592] De Jong, n. 192 above, 487 *et seq.*
[593] S. 26(2) Bank Act 1948.
[594] Ibid., S. 26(4).

advantage of both parties in the dispute, as public opinion makes up its own mind as to whom is to blame.

The override mechanism is generally considered to be a reflection of the constitutional principle of ministerial responsibility primarily embedded in Article 42(2) of the Dutch Constitution.[595] Section 26 effectively puts the Minister of Finance in charge of any decision taken by the Nederlandsche Bank. He can either issue directions to the Bank, or by not issuing any directions, implicitly approve the policy of the Bank.[596] The Minister's right to issue directions has been considered as a necessary correlation to section 9 of the Bank Act 1948, which formulates in broad terms the monetary objective of the Nederlandsche Bank, thereby leaving much room for the formulation of concrete measures, a task for which the executive government is believed to be ultimately responsible.[597] At the time of the drafting of the Bank Act 1948 it was the intention to give the monetary and financial policies of the executive government priority over the policies of the Nederlandsche Bank.[598] With regard to the right of appeal it becomes clear from the explanatory statements to the draft Bank Act 1948 (*memorie van toelichting*) that the existence of this right was intended to ensure the degree of independence from executive government which was considered to be necessary for a proper functioning of the Bank.[599]

Section 26 has not been put to the test in the five decades of the existence of the Bank Act 1948.[600] In fact, from the very beginning this provision was intended to constitute an *ultimum remedium* in the case of a clash of interests of the executive government with the Bank which could not be otherwise resolved through consultations.[601] Indeed, any application of this instrument would have sent out clear, but undesired, signals to the financial markets and the public at large that a major disagreement on the conduct of monetary policy existed between the executive government and the Nederlandsche Bank. Another explanation of why the override mechanism has never been applied is the lack of any substantial potential for conflicts between the executive government and the Bank in the area of monetary policy: for the Netherlands, as a small and open economy, exchange rate policy plays a predominant role, and with participation

---

[595] M.W. Holtrop, *De Functie van de centrale bank*, AO–Reeks Boekje No. 1162, at 8; J.L.S.M. Hillen, *Bank-, munt- en nationale schuldwetgeving: voorzien van aantekeningen en alfabetisch register* (Nederlandse staatswetten: editie Schuurman & Jordens ; 143–I) (W.E.J. Tjeenk Willink, Zwolle, 1993).

[596] S.C.W. Eijffinger, *Het Monetaire Beleid Van De Nederlandsche Bank*, Serie Researchmemorandum, Vrije Universiteit Ekonomische Fakulteit Amsterdam, 1993–19, at 4; E. Schokker, op. cit., Chap. 2, n. 107, at 42.

[597] *Bijl. Hand* II, 1946–7, no. 488, 5, at 11–12.

[598] De Jong, n. 192 above, at 486.

[599] *Bijl. Hand.* II, 1946–7, no. 488, 5, at 14.

[600] J. Zijlstra, *Per Slot van rekening: memoires* (Contact, Amsterdam, 1992), 215–16, refers to a conflict between the executive government and the Nederlandsche Bank in 1977, when the Cabinet Den Uyl (1974–1977) seriously considered applying s. 26, after the Nederlandsche Bank had introduced credit restrictions.

[601] W. Eizenga, "Zelfstandigheid van centrale banken", *Bank- en Effectenbedrijf*, vol. 43 no. 9 (1994), 20–5, at 23.

in exchange rate mechanisms, monetary policy is decided on a national level only to a limited extent, thereby rendering potential conflicts otiose.[602] To some extent the non-application of the override mechanism may also be explained by the culture in the relationship between the Bank and the executive government, which has established itself over time and which cannot be fully apprehended from the statutory arrangements only.[603]

The override mechanism of section 26(1) of the Bank Act 1948 has implications for accountability to, as well as the independence of, the Nederlandsche Bank from executive government. The Bank is fully accountable to the executive government which can override the former by issuing directions at any time. Democratic accountability is established by way of the principle of ministerial responsibility in Parliament.[604] The fact that section 26 has never been put to use does not necessarily mean that it is ineffectual as an instrument of accountability, since it arguably has a psychological effect on the relationship between the Nederlandsche Bank and the executive government. Whether the non-application of section 26 is evidence of the Bank's recognition of the executive government's supreme responsibility over monetary policy is questionable. The majority of observations on the Nederlandsche Bank establish that the non-application of section 26 is proof of the *de facto* independent status of the Bank.[605] On the contrary, some interpret section 26 as a *"stok achter de deur"* (a stick behind the back) in order to force the Bank to comply with the preferences of the Minister of Finance.[606] Yet one step further, while taking into consideration the public-choice literature on central bank independence, it has been argued that the non-application of the override mechanism is merely a proof of the *de facto* self-imposed subordination of the Nederlandsche Bank to the policies of the executive government.[607] The right of objection under section 26, which restricts the uncontrolled application of the override mechanism by the executive government, supports the independent position of the Bank, while at the same time holding the executive government accountable. In this context it has been observed that the purpose of the right of objection is to place the Bank on the same level as the Minister of Finance with regard to monetary policy, rather than to subordinate it.[608] Holtrop, a former President of the Nederlandsche Bank, summarises the discussion on the relationship between the executive government and the Bank as follows:

[602] Memorandum submitted by the Netherlands Central Bank, in Treasury and Civil Service Committee, *The Role of the Bank of England* (House of Commons Paper. Session 1993–4 ; 98–I, vol. 2), Report, together with the proceedings of the Committee, HC Session 1993–4 (HMSO, London, 1993), App. 10, at 148.

[603] W.F. Duisenberg, op. cit., Chap. 3, n. 236, at 24.

[604] De Vries, n. 236 above, at 745, concludes that the override mechanism "benefits a democratic system".

[605] E.g. Memorandum submitted by the Netherlands Central Bank, n. 602 above, 148.

[606] J.Th. Degenkamp, *Inleiding Economisch Recht* (2nd edn., Samsom H.D.Tjeenk Willink, Alphen aan den Rijn, 1989), at 230.

[607] B.C.J. van Velthoven/A. van Schaik, op. cit., Chap. 3, n. 222, 386 *et seq.*, with further references.

[608] De Jong, n. 192 above, at 494.

"On the ship state there is but one captain and that is the government. But the legislator, in his wisdom, has prescribed that in the difficult waters of monetary policy the government makes use of services of a pilot. The pilot is the Nederlandsche Bank. An experienced captain trusts his pilot. But as any seaman knows, even if the pilot is aboard and in charge of navigating, the captain bears the final responsibility."[609]

Section 26 of the Bank Act 1948 has been considered incompatible with the EC Treaty and the ESCB Statute and thus has been abolished by the new Bank Act 1998. As already observed, this also includes section 23 of the Bank Act 1948 on the dismissal of members of the Governing Board on grounds of non-compliance with directions.[610]

In the case of the **Bank of England**, with the transfer of operational responsibility over monetary policy from the Treasury to the newly established Monetary Policy Committee, an explicit override mechanism as a counterweight has been introduced in the Bank of England Act 1998.[611] Rather than providing for a right of the Bank to object to an application, the override mechanism is subject to parliamentary affirmation. The Act, referring to the "Treasury's reserve powers", states in section 19(1) and (2):

"(1) The Treasury, after consultation with the Governor of the Bank, may by order give the Bank directions with respect to monetary policy *if they are satisfied that the directions are required in the public interest and by extreme economic circumstances.*

(2) An order under this section may include such consequential modifications of the provisions of this Part relating to the Monetary Policy Committee as the Treasury thinks fit."[612]

Section 19 allows the Treasury to override the monetary policy objective of the Bank by issuing directions on interest rates to the MPC, and, furthermore, even modifying the provisions relating to the MPC. However, it places a number of restraints on this power. First, extreme economic circumstances must prevail and it must also be required by the public interest. A closer definition of these conditions is missing however. Secondly, the application of the override mechanism requires subordinate legislation by the executive government which needs to be approved by Parliament to be effective beyond a maximum period of 28 days as section 9(3) and (4) of the Bank of England Act 1998 provides:

"(3) A statutory instrument containing an order under this section shall be laid before Parliament after being made.

(4) Unless an order under this is *approved by resolution of each House of Parliament before the end of the period of 28 days* beginning with the day on which it is made, it shall cease to have effect at the end of that period."[613]

---

[609] Holtrop, n. 595 above, at 8. Author's translation.
[610] Tweede Kamer, Vergaderjaar 1997–8, no. 2., Art. 22.
[611] For the situation under the Bank of England Act 1946, cf. Chap. 4 II 2.
[612] Emphasis added.
[613] Emphasis added.

In order for such a resolution to pass through Parliament, approval by a simple majority in both House is required.[614] As such, the requirement of parliamentary approval may be interpreted as an extension of the principle of ministerial accountability, since the decision of the Chancellor of the Exchequer to apply the override mechanism becomes subject to parliamentary scrutiny. Nevertheless, parliamentary scrutiny and any criticism resulting from that are likely to be limited to the opposition and have little chance of resulting in a rejection of the order of the Treasury to the Bank of England, since the ruling party will usually hold a majority in Parliament. Yet, the procedure will provide for transparency, and the public perception is likely not to be completely disregarded by the executive government in its decision to make use of its "reserve power". This may in particular be the case for left-wing governments which have to fight off the reputation of being less inflation-adverse. But the proposed legislation will also put a limit to the period of application of the (approved) override mechanism, since it ceases to have effect after three months from the day of its application.[615] The legislation does not include any reference to a promulgation of the override mechanism, but it has to be assumed that in principle the Treasury is not excluded from issuing a new order, which once again has to be approved by Parliament. Moreover, this in principle does not exclude the Treasury issuing an order which is only intended to be in effect for a period below the threshold of 28 days.

Despite the fact that one of the reasons for the institutional changes of the Bank of England may have been to bring the Bank closer in line with the requirements under the EC Treaty and the ESCB Statute in case the UK eventually should decide to join EMU, the newly established override mechanism would have to be considered incompatible with primary Community law, like previously the provisions existing for the Bundesbank and Nederlandsche Bank.

VI. RELATIONSHIP WITH PARLIAMENT

With regard to the relationship between the central bank and the legislative branch of government a pattern emerges from the examination of the central banks included in this study. A number of central bank statutes include an explicit reference to the relationship between the central bank and Parliament, or such a relationship has developed *de facto* over time. In the present context these central banks are referred to as central banks with an institutionalised relationship with Parliament. Arguably the most prominent example for such an institutionalised relationship between a central bank and Parliament is the Fed. To a somewhat more limited extent this is also the case for the Banque de France, the

---

[614] Generally, positive and negative resolutions exist, whereby in the case of the former an order does not come into force until it has been approved by Parliament, and, in the case of the latter, an order remains in force unless a resolution of Parliament to the contrary is adopted.

[615] S. 19(6) Bank of England Act 1998.

ECB, the Reserve Bank of New Zealand and the Bank of England, under the new arrangements. Other central bank statutes are characterised by the lack of any provisions relating to Parliament. Here, the relationship between the central bank and Parliament has to be determined with the help of general rules. This is generally the case for the Bundesbank and the Nederlandsche Bank.

With regard to the relationship between the national central banks and the national parliaments it has to be observed that any arrangements infringing the independent position of the national central banks as prescribed by Article 108 EC have to be considered incompatible with the EC Treaty and the ESCB Statute.

1. Institutionalised relationship between the central bank and Parliament

In a number of instances the legal basis of central banks provides for explicit provisions on the relationship between the central bank and Parliament. Provisions on reporting requirements prevail.

The **Fed** arguably constitutes the prime example of a central bank which has a close relationship with Parliament. The relationship between the Fed, and the Board of Governors, and Congress is usually to be found at the centre of any discussion of the democratic accountability, not only of the Fed. The relationship between the Fed and Congress can best be examined in three parts or stages, including the reporting requirements under the Federal Reserve Act, the legislative activities of Congress, and an assessment of the role of Congress in the democratic accountability of the Fed. It has already been observed in the context of the monetary objective of the Fed that the Board of Governors of the Fed is obliged to transmit to the Congress, not later than 20 February and 20 July of each year, independently written reports.[616]

The semi-annual report of the Board of Governors introduced by the Full Employment and Balanced Growth Act of 1978 consists of a statement prepared by the chairman of the Board of Governors and approved by the latter (sometimes referred to as testimony), and a separate report, prepared by the Board of Governors' staff, including analysis of recent financial and economic developments, as well as an outlook on monetary policy and the economy. The report is forwarded to the President of the Senate and the Speaker of the House of Representatives. In the House of Representatives the report is dealt with by the Committee on Banking and Financial Services or its sub-committee on domestic and international monetary policy respectively, and in the Senate by the Committee on Banking, Housing, and Urban Affairs. Both Committees have the task of evaluating both the testimony and the report and reporting back to its respective body on its findings as regards the intended policies of the Fed.

[616] 12 USC Sec. 225s. For the wording cf. Chap. 4 II 1.

Alternately, the chairman of the Board of Governors appears first before the Senate or the House Banking Committee followed shortly thereafter by the other Committee. Committee hearings will usually begin with a presentation of any statements which have been prepared by members of the Committee. Thereafter, the chairman of the Board of Governors presents a prepared statement. The remaining part of the hearing is reserved for questions by the members of the Committee. Usually, each member is granted five minutes in question time, with hearings usually lasting a total of between two and three hours. Since these hearings take place on a regular basis with the chairman of the Fed providing testimony on monetary policy and due to the TV coverage of the event, this so-called Humphrey-Hawkins-Procedure has gained publicity over the years. Members of Congress are eager to be seen acting in the interest of their constituencies.[617] This will especially be the case in periods before elections, and taking into account the short two-year terms of the members of the House of Representatives this is almost always the case. Besides, certain groups of the general public and in particular the financial market participants also show much interest in these hearings in anticipation of announcements of policy changes by the chairman of the Fed. However, this considerable interest in the appearances of the chairman of the Fed may also in some respects limit what can be expected from these public hearings in terms of insights into the monetary policy pursued by the Fed. The experience with turmoil in the financial markets subsequent to remarks by the chairman during such appearances have resulted in a cautious approach to these hearings. As one observer put it: "[h]e's got three hours to blow smoke".[618] Although the Humphrey-Hawkins-Procedure undoubtedly provides for the most important hearings, Fed officials have numerous other appearances before congressional committees in the course of a year on a whole range of subject-matters.[619]

As has been observed elsewhere, the Federal Reserve Act has undergone major changes with the Banking Acts of 1933 and 1935 and the Federal Reserve Reform Act of 1977. In particular the third of these three amendments has introduced provisions into the Federal Reserve Act which today form the central elements of the democratic accountability of the Fed. The actual number of amendments to the Federal Reserve Act in its more than 80-year history has been minor. Still, the number of proposals and the extent of overhaul of the Fed suggested by them is noteworthy. Indeed, considering some of the other central bank systems included in this study, the number of bills introduced into Congress, often with the express intention of enhancing its accountability, is remarkable. Since the late 1960s the number of bills introduced into Congress

---

[617] However, J.M. Berry, "Kid Gloves for Greenspan", *Central Banking*, vol. 7 no. 3 (1996–7), 30–5, finds that the members of Congress take a "kid glove approach" in the discussions with the chairman of the Fed.

[618] Cited in ibid., at 30.

[619] A current list of appearances can be found on the homepage of the Board of Governors: see App. 3.

has increased considerably. Akhtar and Howe have analysed the activities of Congress for the period of five consecutive Congresses between 1979 and 1990, thereby assembling 200 congressional proposals, which include more than 300 recommendations for changes of the institutional structure of the Fed.[620] The actual number of recommendations derives from the classification of the proposals which fall into five categories: policy targets or mandate; accountability to the political process; influencing of the president and the administration; democratising the Federal Reserve; and public and private elements in the FOMC. The findings are summarised in Table 2. To be sure, not every bill

Table 2: Legislativ proposals to restructure the Fed 1979–90[621]

	Policy Targets or Mandate	Accountability to the Political Process	Influence of the President and the Administration	Democratising the Federal Reserve	Public and Private Elements in the FOMC	Total
Board of Governors (Chairman)	25[622]	46 [623] [624] [625] (12)	53[626] (32)	27[627]	2[628]	153 (44)
Reserve Banks	16[629]	32[630]		16		64
FOMC	76	36	14[631]	11[632]	17[633]	154
Total	117	114	67	54	19	307[634]

Source: Akhtar/Howe (1991)

[620] Akhtar/Howe, n. 131 above.

[621] Akhtar/Howe, n. 131 above. Since 1990 the number of proposals has dropped. An inquiry for the period covering the 102nd to the 104th Congress (1991–6) using the Library of Congress online database has produced 23 proposals in the form of bills originating in the Senate or the House of Representatives.

[622] 11 proposals to redeem US currency in gold in both places.

[623] 13 proposals to bring the Fed budget under congressional appropriations, 14 proposals to have the GAO audit Fed activities, and 4 proposals to repeal the Federal Reserve Act counted in both places.

[624] One proposal to add *ex officio* Governors counted in both places.

[625] Two proposals to expand the Board to 9 members counted in three places.

[626] Cf. n. 625.

[627] Cf. n. 624.

[628] Cf. n. 625.

[629] Cf. n. 622.

[630] Cf. n. 623.

[631] 14 proposals to add the Secretary of the Treasury and/or Chairman of the CEA to the FOMC counted in both places.

[632] Two proposals to include all Reserve Bank presidents on the FOMC and one proposal to remove Reserve Bank presidents from the FOMC counted in both places.

[633] Cf. nn. 631 and 632.

[634] Row and column totals add up to 307, exceeding the total number of proposals by the 60 proposals double counted and the two proposals triple counted.

introduced in Congress in the period covered was of equal importance. Thus, in order to measure their importance, Akhtar and Howe observe the number of sponsors that a bill had and the extent to which the bill has been dealt with in Congress. Another indicator of the seriousness of a bill may be the extent to which the bill reflected the public discussion at the time.

Apart from introducing bills and joint resolutions for the overhaul of the Fed, both in the Senate and the House of Representatives, concurrent and simple resolutions are introduced which either call for the amendment of the Federal Reserve Act or seek to direct the Fed, and in particular the FOMC, to pursue monetary policy in a certain direction. Such resolutions fall into a category of congressional activities which arguably do not amount to genuine legislative proposals.[635] Whereas bills and joint resolutions take on the character of legislation once adopted by both the Senate and the House, concurrent and simple resolutions generally do not.[636] Nevertheless, concurrent and simple resolutions have undoubtedly important implications as they may function as an indicator for the relationship between the Fed and Congress, and in particular any disagreements between the two, as was for example the case when two resolutions of the House of Representatives called for the impeachment of the chairman of the Board of Governors, at the time Paul Volker, and the members of the FOMC.[637] And although concurrent and simple resolutions cannot be considered as genuine legislative proposals they may indicate future actions of the Congress to restructure the Fed.

Two questions arise in connection with the legislative activities of Congress. First, how can the active involvement of Congress with monetary policy and the Fed be explained, taking into account the inactivity of other parliaments in relation to other central bank systems? Furthermore, why is it that the vast majority of proposals to restructure the Fed fails to gain the necessary support in Congress to be enacted?

The legislative activities of Congress with regard to the Fed cannot be attributed to a single factor only. One explanation may be found in the distinct political system of the United States. For one thing, the division between the executive and the legislature is larger than in parliamentary democracies in which the other central bank systems examined in this study are situated. It is not inherent in the US political system either that the executive branch of government governs with a majority in Congress, or that the majority in both

---

[635] See otherwise Akhtar/Howe, n. 131 above, 377 *et seq.*, who include concurrent and simple resolutions in their table on the legislative proposals to change the structure of the Fed. On the legislative procedure cf. also Chap. 4 I 2.

[636] Instead, concurrent resolutions agreed to by both the Senate and the House may be considered as a general expression of the will of the Congress, whereas simple resolutions passed by either the Senate or the House alone express the will of the respective institution.

[637] Cf. H.Res. 31 and 32 (98th Congress) sponsored by Representative Gonzales, resemble two unsuccessful attempts to initiate impeachment procedures against the chairman of the Fed and all members of the FOMC.

Houses is controlled by the same political party.[638] The reason for this is the fact that the US President, in whom all executive power is vested, is not elected or appointed by Congress, but through a system of State electors.[639] Consequently, the executive branch of government is somewhat more removed from the legislative branch than is the case in other parliamentary systems, where the executive usually holds a majority in Parliament. Yet another particularity of the US constitutional system, explaining the number of proposals to restructure the Fed, is the fact that individual members of the Senate or the House of Representatives can introduce legislative proposals in their respective body. An obligation for a minimum number of sponsors for the introduction of a Bill, as has been observed e.g. for Germany, thereby filtering out legislative proposals without a minimum consensus, does not exist. Indeed, in a large number of cases Bills introduced into the Senate or the House are sponsored by one member only.

In the past, the Banking Committees of both Houses of Congress have played a crucial role in the relationship between Congress and the Fed, having produced some of the best-known critics of the Fed. Representative Wright Patman, Democrat, who at some stage chaired the House Banking Committee, was known well beyond the insider circles of Capitol Hill to take a critical and sometimes even aggressive approach to the Fed, and is still cited today in connection with issues relating to the democratic accountability of the Fed. He himself introduced numerous proposals for the restructuring of the System. It may be considered symptomatic for the activities of members of Congress with regard to the Fed in general that none of them was ever enacted. He found worthy successors in members of Congress like Representative Henry B. Reuss, Democrat, who became chairman of the House Banking Committee, and, for the Senate William Proxmire, chairman of the Senate Banking Committee.[640] The regular appearances of members of the Board of Governors before the Banking Committees, first as a result of House Concurrent Resolution 133, and thereafter under the new provisions introduced by the Full Employment and Balanced Growth Act of 1978, has institutionalised and, as a result of that intensified, the congressional handling of the Fed. But the congressional activities cannot only be explained by the particularities of the United States constitutional/political system. At times it has also been a reaction to the Fed's approach to monetary policy. Kettl has observed the increase in congressional bills related to the Fed for the period of 1951 and 1983 and concludes that "congressional concern has been the greatest when interest rates have been highest", and that "there is nothing like a sudden increase in interest rates to bring the Fed sharply to the public—and thereby to the congressional—eye."[641] This congressional

---

[638] L.G. Sager, "The Sources and Limits of Legal Authority" in A.B. Morris, *Fundamentals of American Law* (Oxford University Press, Oxford, 1996), 27–56, at 43.

[639] Art. II, s. 1, US Constitution.

[640] In more recent years, Representative Gonzales has made himself a name for scrutinising the role of the Fed closely.

[641] Kettl, n. 183 above, at 162 *et seq.*

focusing on interest rates is confirmed by the numerous resolutions stating the concern either of the Senate or the House over the approach of the Fed to interest rates, or explicitly asking the FOMC to adopt and pursue certain monetary policies.[642]

Yet, despite these congressional activities, the actual number of amendments of the legal basis of the Fed has been minimal and none of the overhauls proposed since 1979 has passed Congress to be implemented in the Federal Reserve Act. The short answer to the question that results from this analysis is that none of the concrete proposals ever had the support of the majority of both Houses of Congress. In some instances the short legislative period of two years of the House of Representatives may have resulted in a certain discontinuity. A more precise explanation may be that despite the vast number of proposals the majority in Congress has never fundamentally disagreed with the monetary policy conducted by the Fed. This supposes a broad consensus in both Houses of Congress in favour of the present institutional structure of the Fed.[643] A less flattering conclusion may be that Congress has failed to hold the Fed effectively accountable. One explanation for this may be that Congress does not have the ability to conduct efficient supervision. Roberts argues that Congress does not take the oversight of monetary policy seriously as a result of a lack of knowledge and understanding of the issues involved.[644] While recognising that the Humphrey-Hawkins-Procedure has improved congressional oversight of monetary policy, he criticises the legislation for not enabling Congress to make an "objective, analytical evaluation of the Federal Reserve's monetary policy plans and objectives".[645] In the same context Weintraub calls into doubt the efficiency of congressional supervision on the basis of the monetary objective of the Fed provided for by section 2 A of the Federal Reserve Act, which provides for multiple objectives and which gives the Fed the freedom to set targets for a multiplicity of aggregates.[646] This is confirmed by the evaluation of the monetary objective of the Fed in this study.[647] The lack of a clear yardstick for the evaluation of the performance of the Fed in the area of monetary policy may not be the only obstacle which Congress faces in holding the Fed accountable for its conduct of monetary policy, since the allocation of decision-making powers within the Fed may well add to this problem. The formulation and implementation of monetary policy are shared by three organs within the Fed, namely the Board of Governors, the FOMC and the Federal Reserve Banks. Decisions on

---

[642] An inquiry of the Library of Congress online database for the period covering the 103rd and 104th Congress has revealed 5 such resolutions, including one House Joint Resolution, 2 Senate Resolutions, and two House Resolutions.

[643] Louis, n. 454 above, at 276. Berry, n. 367 above, at 46, refers to a "political acceptance" of the role which the Fed plays in stabilising the American economy.

[644] S.M. Roberts, "Congressional Oversight of Monetary Policy", *Journal of Monetary Economics*, vol. 4 (1978), 543–56.

[645] Ibid., 548.

[646] Weintraub, n. 178 above, 341–62.

[647] Cf. Chap. 4 II 1.

reserve requirements are the domain of the Board of Governors, whereas open-market operations are decided upon by the FOMC. However, the implementation is left to the Federal Reserve Banks and foremost to the Federal Reserve Bank of New York. Finally, interest rate changes are initiated by the Federal Reserve Banks but the final decision is taken by the Board of Governors. This complex intertwining of different organs in the decision-making process can make it rather difficult for an outsider to assign responsibilities for monetary policy decisions to a certain organ, let alone to specific individuals.[648]

More recent studies take a quite different approach to explaining the behaviour of Congress *vis-à-vis* the Fed. It is argued that Congress has little to gain from holding the Fed effectively accountable. Indeed, the weak spot in the democratic accountability of the Fed to Congress may have its basis in the very nature of Congress as a body consisting of *elected* representatives whose first concern is to be re-elected. Kane argues that "defects in control policy and reporting survive, not because of policy-makers' ignorance or ineptitude, but because these defects serve policy-makers' political and bureaucratic interests".[649] Politicians may have an interest in turning the Fed into a "scapegoat" for their own shortcomings by having the benefit of blaming the bad state of the economy on an institution whose decisions they arguably cannot influence.[650] Elected representatives also take the opportunity to leave difficult political choices which involve a trade-off between different economic aggregates, such as low inflation, economic growth and full employment, to the Fed.[651] Evidence for this argument may be found in the observation made above that much of the congressional attention to the Fed is focused on changes in the interest rates; an approach which may have its roots in the constitutional system of the United States itself.[652] It may be concluded from this that it would not seem to be in the self-interest of politicians to make the Fed more accountable because it would at the same time undermine their position *vis-à-vis* the electorate in claiming that the Fed pursues monetary policy insulated from elected politicians. But it may, moreover, also not be in the interest of the Fed which, to some extent, seems to accept the role of the "scapegoat", because more meaningful congressional oversight would decrease its independent position *vis-à-vis* the executive branch. When it is argued that the Fed is not being held effectively accountable,

---

[648] See also Clifford, n. 447 above, at 34. This problem is enhanced by the disclosure polices of the Board of Governors and the FOMC; cf. Chap. 4 VII.

[649] N. Beck, "Congress and the Fed: Why the Dog does not Bark in the Night", in Th. Mayer (ed.), n. 370 above, 131–50, 133 *et seq.*, with further references; J.L. Pierce, "The Myth of Congressional Supervision of Monetary Policy", *Journal of Monetary Economics* 4 (1978), 363–70, at 364, who argues that Congress "has salved its conscience" by passing Concurrent Resolution 133 and thereafter the Humphrey-Hawkins-Act "but it has showed little interest in providing meaningful oversight over monetary policy".

[650] Generally critical on the delegation practices of the Congress is D.Schoenbrod, *Power without Responsibility: How Congress Abuses the People Through Delegation* (Yale University Press, New Heaven and London, 1993).

[651] Kettl, n. 183 above, at 165.

[652] Ibid., at 197.

this assumption can only be made from the fact that Congress has failed to influence the Fed, notably in the way it conducts monetary policy, or because, since 1979, Congress has never gone further than passing concurrent and simple resolutions and thus has not made use of its power to amend the Federal Reserve Act. Whereas the latter observation is a matter of fact, the former is not entirely uncontested as some studies do find that congressional oversight influences the Fed in its conduct of monetary policy.[653] However, even where present, congressional influence does not necessarily result in the democratic accountability of the Fed. Indeed, it may be argued that it decreases democratic accountability to the extent to which this influence is part of the above observed relationship between Congress and the Fed. If this relationship is compared with a game, both players can only lose in the event of a strengthening of the mechanism of democratic accountability. Congress loses because it may appear less convincing in blaming the Fed, and the Fed loses because its ability in implementing monetary policy in accordance to its own preferences will be decreased.

On the contrary, it cannot be denied that the institutionalised dialogue between Congress and the Fed, together with Congress's power to amend the legal basis of the Fed, has provided Congress with the tools necessary for making the Fed democratically accountable. Whether Congress makes effective use of this tool may not always be ensured. However, this is a problem of the effectiveness of Congress rather than of a lack of a mechanism for congressional accountability of the Fed. Moreover, the institutionalised relationship enhances the transparency of the conduct of monetary policy by the Fed. This means, on the one hand, that Fed officials can provide the System with the kind of publicity it needs to secure support for its views. On the other hand, with monetary policy being dragged into the limelight, monetary policy formulation of the Fed becomes subject to closer public scrutiny. It is difficult to envisage the Fed pursuing a monetary policy for a long time which is unpopular with the President and/or Congress and the public at large.

While granting the **Banque de France** independence with regard to the formulation and implementation of monetary policy, Chapter IV of the Bank Act 1993, under the telling heading, "Report to the President of the Republic/ Accountability to Parliament", introduced a provision on the relationship between the Bank and parliament. According to Article 19 of the Bank Act 1993

"(1) At least once a year, the Governor of the Banque de France addresses a report on the Bank's activities and on monetary policy and the prospects for it to the President of the Republic and to Parliament.

(2) The Governor of the Banque de France is heard at the request of the Finance Committees of the two Chambers, and may request to be heard by them.

[653] Havrilesky, n. 131 above, at 20, who finds that the Humphrey-Hawkins-Procedure by the Senate Banking Committee has a statistically significant effect on the Federal Fund Rate. Cf. also K.B. Grier, "Congressional Influence on U.S. Monetary Policy", *Journal of Monetary Economics*, vol. 28 (1991), 201–20, who develops a model of congressional influence on the Fed.

(3) The accounts of the Banque de France and the report of the statutory auditors shall be forwarded to the Finance Committees of the National Assembly and of the Senate."

The reporting requirements of the Banque de France *vis-à-vis* both chambers of Parliament may be viewed as the counterpart to the creation of the CPM and the fact that the Bank is formulating and implementing monetary policy independently. From the wording of Article 19(2) of the Bank Act 1993 it has to be concluded that the governor of the Bank is in fact obliged to appear upon request of one or both of the Finance Committees. In principle apart from the governor of the Bank no other member of the CPM is heard by the Finance Committees, and experience has shown that hitherto the governor has always appeared before the committees himself.[654] This corresponds with the view that the CPM constitutes a collegial organ in which the governor takes a predominant position as the representative of the Banque de France.[655] In practice it is not unusual for one of the Finance Committees to request the governor to appear before it. A more recent example from October 1997 was triggered by the raising of the interest rates by the Banque de France following similar adjustments by the Bundesbank.[656] Interestingly, this example also highlights differences of opinion between the Banque de France and Parliament on the nature of these appearances. Initially the Finance Committee had "summoned" the Bank to appear before it. Only after the committee had rephrased its request into an "invitation" did the governor agree.[657] What is remarkable is that the Banque de France itself does not seem to interpret the duties under Article 19 of the Bank Act 1993 as obligations *vis-à-vis* Parliament. In a recent questionnaire submitted to the British Treasury and Civil Service the Banque de France summarises Article 19 only to come to the conclusion: "*Ces trois éléments ne permettent pas d'établir une responsabilité de la Banque centrale devant Parlement. Toutefois, celui-ci ne peut ni déterminer, ni influencer la politique monétaire qu'elle entend suivre*".[658] While it seems that the wording of Article 19(2) of the Bank Act 1993 in the French language version suggests that the governor has to appear upon request,[659] the latter does not have an enforceable right to appear before one or both of the committees upon his or her own request. Proposals during the preparatory works for the Bank Act 1993 to institute a stricter parliamentary control of the CPM along the lines of the accountability of the FOMC of the Fed did not find their way into the Bank Act 1993. These strict reporting requirements were believed to be necessary in order to provide for a counterbalance to the appointment procedures of the CPM

---

[654] The respective committees are the *Commission des Finances* of the National Assembly, and the *Commission des Finances, du Contrôle Budgétaire et des Comptes Economique* of the Senate.
[655] Duprat, n. 231 above, n. 72.
[656] Reported in Financial Times, 5 Nov. 1997.
[657] Ibid.
[658] Memorandum submitted by the Banque de France, n. 87 above, at 138.
[659] On the other hand, the English language version of the recent Banque de France Act 1998 also suggests the lack of such an obligation.

which were considered anti-democratic.[660] According to this view, the governor of the Banque de France would have been heard by the Financial Committees of both chambers of the Parliament at least once a year. This would have institutionalised parliamentary control to a greater extent, as the appearance of the governor would not have been limited to requests by these Committees. On the contrary, it is interesting to note in this context that for some even the procedure finally adopted was considered too far reaching. Proposals were made to make an appearance of the governor before Parliament subject to the approval of the Minister for Economic Affairs and Finances.[661]

The revised statute of the Banque de France emphasises that the reporting requirements are subject to the provisions of Article 107 EC and the confidentiality rules of the ECB.[662]

The reporting requirements for the **ECB** differ from those applicable to the Banque de France foremost with regard to their stringency. According to Article 109b(3) EC:

> "The ECB shall address an annual report on the activities of the ESCB and on the monetary policies of both the previous and the current year to the European Parliament, the Council, the Commission, and also to the European Council. The president of the ECB shall present this report to the Council and the European Parliament which may hold a general debate on that basis.
>
> The President of the ECB and other members of the Executive Board may, at the request of the European Parliament or on their own initiative, be heard by the competent Committees of the European Parliament."

Generally, Article 109b(3) concerns two different procedures. First, the president has to present an annual report to the EP, which has to include details on the monetary policy which has been pursued by the ECB. Although not explicitly stated it can be assumed that the nature of these presentations will be oral before the relevant Committee of the EP, but possibly also before the plenary session.[663] On the basis of the wording of Article 109b(3), sentence 1, EC it seems that in this context a general debate of the EP is limited to the contents of the annual report ("general debate *on that basis*"). However, it is difficult to envisage the EP restricting itself in this respect.

Additionally, the second sentence of Article 109b(3) EC introduces a procedure for members of the Executive Board to appear before the EP on their own initiative, or at the request of the EP. Contrary to the presentation of the annual report, it cannot be concluded from the wording of that provision ("*may . . . be heard*") that the additional appearances before the EP constitute an obliga-

---

[660] Cf. reference made by Iacono, n. 226 above, at 92.
[661] Duprat, n. 231 above, at 9
[662] Cf. Art. 19(2) Banque de France Act 1998.
[663] de Haan/Gormley, n. 370 above, at 343.

tion.[664] Indeed, the wording of Article 109b(3) EC differs from the original proposal of the EP which had suggested that the president of the ECB should appear before relevant committees of the EP on a regular basis (at least) every six months.[665] The EP has confirmed its initial approach to these hearings in its rules of procedure. According to Rule 39 on statements by the European Central Bank:

> "The President of the European Central Bank and other Executive Board Members may be invited to attend a meeting of the committee responsible to make a statement and answer questions. The President of the Bank *shall attend such meetings twice a year.* He may be invited to attend additional meetings if circumstances justify it in the opinion of the committee responsible confirmed by the Conference of Presidents."[666]

It can be observed that the wording of this provision is more stringent than that of the corresponding provision in the EC Treaty. While the intention of the EP to hold the ECB accountable becomes clear from this provision, it does not introduce an obligation for the members of the Executive Board to appear before the committee, since the wording of the second sentence of Article 109b(3) EC may be considered decisive on this point. Against the background of these observations it seems problematic to draw a parallel to the Humphrey-Hawkins-Procedure of the Fed, where the governor is obliged to appear before the congressional Banking Committees on a regular basis.[667] According to Louis the reporting requirements should not be underestimated as means of an "institutionalised opportunity for dialogue" as they could help to avoid an isolation of the ECB and the development of exclusive relationships with the Executive.[668] Yet, much will depend on the approach taken by the EP in making use of appearances of the president and other members of the Executive Board as a means of holding the ECB accountable.[669] The relative inactivity of some national parliaments does not necessarily give rise to optimism, but the EP may be an exceptional case, as it is still eager to establish a distinct role for itself *vis-à-vis* the Council and the Commission. It has been observed in the context of the appointment procedures that in the past the EP has already shown a

---

[664] I. Harden, "The European Central Bank and the national central banks in Economic and Monetary Union" in K. Gretschmann (ed.), *Economic and Monetary Union: Implications for National Policy-makers* (European Institute of Public Administration, Maastricht, 1993), 149–76, at 161, who points out rightly that the Executive Board of the ECB cannot insist on being heard and the EP cannot compel the former to appear.

[665] Resolution of the European Parliament on Economic and Monetary Union of 10 Oct. 1990 ([1990] OJ C284/62), Art. 13, 4th para., according to which the president should have been heard every six months *or* at the time when the EP considers it to be feasible.

[666] Emphasis added.

[667] E.g. J.-J. Rey, op. cit., Chap. 2, n. 42, at 157.

[668] Louis, n. 57 above, at 24; see also J.-V. Louis, *Economic and Monetary Union*, n. 483 above, at 252, who concludes that the institutional co-operation (Art. 109b EC) and the reporting requirements should not be modified.

[669] The limits of evidence by members of the Executive Board are described in Art. 10.4 ESCB Statute, and in any case exclude the disclosure of the proceedings of meetings of the Governing Council since the Governing Council can only decide to make the outcomes of its deliberations public.

298 *Evaluating the Democratic Accountability of Central Banks*

considerable interest in the appointment of the presidents of the EMI, and, on a more general basis, in the institutional arrangements in the final stage of EMU.[670] Moreover, despite the lack of an obligation, it is difficult to envisage a situation in which members of the Executive Board would refuse to appear before the EP, as this would potentially damage their public reputation and may even raise doubts about the independent position of the ECB on a large scale. It seems that the ECB will put every effort into achieving the degree of public support that has saved the Bundesbank in the past from changes to its independent position.[671] However, the EP is likely to hold a weaker position than a national Parliament, in as much as the former does not hold the ultimate sanction, that is to change the legal basis of the ECB.

One important implication of the second sentence of Article 109(3) EC, which may easily be overlooked, is that the explicit reference to the members of the Executive Board implicitly excludes the appearance of the governors of the national central banks before the EP. Indeed, with 11 central bank governors— as of now—participating in the Governing Council of the ECB, a majority of the members of the monetary policy board of the ECB are excluded, or indeed exempt, from appearances before the EP. This is especially interesting, since the key monetary policy decisions are taken by a majority vote in the Governing Council. Although, given the efforts for consensus in monetary policy decisions on monetary policy boards of central banks, this will arguably seldom be the case, in principle a situation is foreseeable where the members of the Executive Board (six members) have been outvoted, e.g. on the issue of raising the interest rate, and nevertheless are the only ones that may be questioned by the EP on this decision. The reason for the exclusion of the national central bank governors from appearances before the EP may be that, unlike the members of the Executive Board, they are not appointed at the European level by the Council, but rather by the governments of the Member States. The accountability of the national governors is therefore left to the national sphere. However, it is questionable whether and to what extent the national central bank governors become subjected to similar procedures at the national level. Regardless of whether the national laws foresee parliamentary hearings in the first place, such hearings would effectively be limited to an exchange of information. First, the collegiate structure of the Governing Council poses a problem for the accountability of the national central bank governors at the national level similar to that in the relationship between a national Parliament and the representative of the national government participating in the Council. It becomes difficult to pinpoint responsibilities unless decisions are taken unanimously. In the case of the

---

[670] On the role of the EP in the appointment procedures of the presidents of the EMI, cf. Chap. 4 IV 1.

[671] D.G. Mayes, *Accountability for the Central Bank in Europe*, paper prepared for the 11th Lothian Conference (A Central Bank for Europe), 19 Nov. 1997, Whitehall Place, London, at 2, prognosticates that the ECB is likely to make the hearings "showpiece demonstrations of the care and professionalism it is using in achieving the goals set out for it". Cf. also Hearing at the European Parliament's Sub-Committee on Monetary Affairs on 18 January 1999, Introductory statement delivered by Dr. William F. Duisenberg, President of the European Central Bank.

Council of the European Union the number of areas where unanimous decisions are taken have decreased steadily, not least with the TEU. In the case of the Governing Council of the ECB unanimous decisions are only required exceptionally.[672] Holding the governor of a national central bank personally responsible for the collegiate decisions taken in the Governing Council of the ECB, and thus effectively holding him accountable also on behalf of all other members, is hardly possible. This is in particular the case if the proceedings of the meetings are not disclosed.[673] Besides, serious attempts to hold the governor accountable could be considered incompatible with the EC Treaty and the ESCB Statute to the extent that this could be interpreted as infringing the institutional independence of the national central bank. Monetary policy is no longer the responsibility of the national central banks, and any dealing with monetary policy by the national Parliament beyond the provision of information and the exchange of views could be interpreted as an "interference with the independence of the members of the decision-making bodies of the NCB's [national central banks]", or an infringement of "the ECB's competence and accountability at the Community level as well as the special status of a governor in his or her capacity as a member of the decision-making bodies".[674] This definitely excludes any form of sanctions at the national level. It has already been observed that primary Community law restricts the dismissal of the governors of the national central banks for reasons other than those applicable to the Executive Board, and moreover gives them a right to appeal to the ECJ.

Another instrument at the disposal of the EP, which may be applied in some cases, is the right to set up temporary Committees of Inquiry pursuant to the request of a quarter of the MEPs, in order to investigate alleged contraventions or maladministration in the implementation of Community law.[675] Although the EP cannot dismiss or address a vote of confidence against the members of the Executive Board of the ECB, the recently highly publicised rebuke by a majority of the EP of the Commission in the handling of the BSE crisis shows that EP could have some means of dealing with the conduct of the ECB.[676]

Finally, it should be observed that any role which a national Parliament may play in holding the executive government accountable for its behaviour *vis-à-vis* the central bank is basically ruled out for the EP. This is due not only to the fact that the Council and the Commission *de jure* have very limited means of influencing the conduct of monetary policy by the ECB, but moreover to the institutional structure of the EU as such, where the EP does not fulfil to the same extent

---

[672] Cf. Chap. 3V 2.

[673] Cf. Chap. 4 VII 2.

[674] European Monetary Institute, n. 199 above, at 101. Brackets added.

[675] Art. 138c EC.

[676] The role of the Commission became subject of an investigation by the *Temporary Committee instructed to monitor the action taken on the recommendations made concerning BSE (bovine spongiform encephalopathy) (Apr.–Nov. 1997)*, cf. *Final consolidated report to the temporary committee of the European Parliament on the follow-up of recommendations on BSE* (COM/97/509 Final).

the control functions *vis-à-vis* the executive branch commonly to be found in national States.

Under the Bank of England Act 1946 the role of Parliament in holding the **Bank of England** accountable was very limited.[677] Indeed, apart from the possibility of changing the legal basis of the Bank, Parliament did not have any formal means by which to hold the Bank accountable. Not surprisingly the Bank of England Act 1946 does not include any provisions in this respect, not least because monetary policy was effectively in the hands of the Treasury. Consequently, accountability for monetary policy was focused on the relationship between the executive government and Parliament. The Chancellor of the Exchequer was responsible *vis-à-vis* Parliament for the conduct of monetary policy as part of his general responsibility for the management of the economy. In this respect the old provisions on the powers of the Treasury over the Bank in the Bank of England Act 1946 not only functioned as a legal basis for the government to control the activities of the Bank, but they also enabled Parliament to hold the Treasury accountable for its conduct of monetary policy.[678] Yet, it has been observed that the overall responsibility for the economy blurred the accountability of the executive government for monetary policy. Despite the absence of any formal relationship between the Bank and Parliament, in the past the competent select committee of the House of Commons has monitored the role of the Bank of England *inter alia* with regard to monetary policy.[679] This may be best highlighted with the 1993 report by the Treasury Select Committee on *The Role of the Bank of England* which contained extensive evidence provided by specialists in the field both from inside and outside the UK, in particular on aspects of central bank independence and accountability.[680] A considerable number of the proposals which resulted from this report for institutional changes, together with the findings of the Roll Report, have since been adopted in the Bank of England Act 1998. Regardless of the lack of any corresponding provisions in the Bank of England Act 1946, it has been established practice for some time that the governor, together with other members of the Board of Directors and senior staff, appear before the competent standing committee to answer questions—*inter alia* monetary policy related matters, such as the development of interest rates.[681]

---

[677] D.E. Fair, op. cit., Chap. 2, n. 74, at 8.

[678] T. Daintith, "The Functions of Law in the Field of Short-Term Economic Policy", *LQR*, vol. 92 (1976), 62–78, at 69.

[679] On the role of select committees see e.g. Wade/Bradley, n. 1 above, at 221. The Bank of England fell within the scope of the Select Committee of Nationalised Industries until the latter was dismantled in 1979. Subsequently, the Treasury and Civil Service Committee became competent. Currently, the competent standing committee is the Treasury Select Committee.

[680] Treasury and Civil Service Committee, n. 73 above; a recent example outside the area of monetary policy where the Bank of England has been criticised for its role in banking supervision is the First Report from the Treasury Select Committee, *Barings and International Regulation*, Session 1996–7, HC 65, which investigates the collapse of the merchant bank Barings.

[681] For an account of one of those meetings cf. N. Courtis, "Mr. George goes to Westminster", *Central Banking*, vol. 7, no. 3 (1996–7), 24–9, at 24, who refers to an atmosphere during these hearings which "manages to combine inquisition with informality".

In his letter of May 1997 to the governor of the Bank of England, outlining the new monetary policy framework, the Chancellor of the Exchequer made it clear that the Bank of England is expected to give evidence to the Treasury Select Committee of the House of Commons "on an enhanced basis".[682] Interestingly in this respect, the Bank of England Act 1998 does not include any provision which would oblige members of the MPC, and in particular the governor, to appear before Parliament. The only reference to a reporting requirement included in the Act is an obligation of the court of directors to issue a report at the end of the financial year, which includes a review of the Bank's performance, including that in the field of monetary policy. This report has to be presented to the Chancellor of the Exchequer, who in return has to forward a copy to the House of Commons, which may hold a debate on the annual report.[683] To the extent that the governor and other officials of the Bank of England will continue to appear before the competent select committee of the House of Commons, it may be argued that *de facto* an institutional relationship exists. Under the new arrangements the importance of these hearings increases, since the Bank of England itself is in charge of implementing monetary policy in accordance with the monetary objective as defined by the inflation target. It emerges from the recently published report on the accountability of the Bank of England that the Treasury Select Committee envisages for itself, and Parliament in general, a strong role in the accountability of the Bank of England in the future.[684] The report examines in particular ways in which the committee should judge the performance of the Bank of England in achieving the monetary policy objective as defined by the inflation target. While considering that the committee should not only rely on the Bank's inflation projections set out in the quarterly inflation reports, but should also take into account outside forecasts, the report concludes:

> "Indeed we believe that the focus for our inquiries should not lie exclusively in using the Inflation Report to examine the Bank's recent and planned monetary stance but that a degree of *past accountability* is also called for. Once the arrangements are established, we will be examining the inflation outturn in relation to the inflation target. *If inflation deviates substantially from the target, we will seek a comprehensive explanation from the Bank.*"[685]

The report concludes that in particular two of the select committee's sessions should be dedicated to the inflation reports of the Bank, following each November and May publication. It is envisaged that the governor and two members of the MPC represent the bank on these occasions. It has been observed that under the new arrangements the governor of the Bank is expected to explain in a letter to the Chancellor any deviation of more than one percentage point above or

---

[682] Letter of the Chancellor of the Exchequer, Gordon Brown, n. 528 above, s. six.

[683] Cf. Chap. 4 VII 2.

[684] First Report from the Select Committee on Treasury, n. 524 above.

[685] *Supra*, n. 684, consideration 20. With regard to the quarterly inflation reports cf. Chap. 4 VII 2.

below the point target, and the Treasury Select Committee has made it clear that it expects to receive a copy of that letter from the governor, and that it would call upon the governor to explain the deviation from the target before the committee.[686] As has been the case before, the standing committee itself has no tools at its disposal to sanction the behaviour of the Bank, but its findings stated in a report to the House of Commons may become the subject of plenary debates, possibly resulting in actions by the House of Commons. Under the new arrangements the latter not only has the power to amend the legal basis of the Bank, but has a say in the application of the "reserve powers" of the Treasury. Therefore, officials at the Bank of England may have an incentive to ensure parliamentary support for their views.

Since responsibility for monetary policy has been divided between the Bank of England and the executive government, the latter also remains accountable to Parliament, namely for the setting of the monetary policy targets and its definition of monetary policy.[687] The House of Commons has different means of examining government activities. Its select committees can examine the whole range of government activities, in the course of which they may hear witnesses and appoint specialist advisers. In its recent report the Treasury Select Committee emphasised that it will continue to examine the broader aspects of monetary policy, and intends to ask the Chancellor to give evidence on the inflation target and in the case of an application of the override mechanism.[688] However, under existing rules a Minister in principle cannot be obliged to appear. Parliamentary questions, adjournment debates and regular debates in the House of Commons are the more basic ways of examining government activities. In principle, where Parliament out-votes the government on a major issue or where a majority of the House of Commons approves a vote of censure, the executive government is obliged to seek a dissolution of Parliament, since no government is supposed to remain in power without a majority in the House of Commons. However, there have been occasions where a government has "survived" such defeats in the House of Commons.[689] Moreover, the limits or, one may say, shortcomings of the system of ministerial accountability in the British context, in particular with regard to access to information, have only recently been highlighted by the Scott Report and the subsequent publications which have evoked a discussion on the effectiveness of ministerial accountability.[690]

Taking into account the common evaluation of the **Reserve Bank of New Zealand,** its legal basis includes surprisingly little on the relationship of the

---

[686] Ibid., considerations 32 *et seq.*

[687] Cf. Chap. 4 II 3.

[688] *Supra*, n. 684, consideration 62.

[689] Sometimes a government may be defeated on a major issue but still win a subsequent vote of confidence. Thus the members of the party may send a signal to the government without actually bringing it down.

[690] Sir R. Scott, "Ministerial Accountability", [1996] *PL*, 410–26; Ch. Foster, "Reflections on the True Significance of the Scott Report for Government Accountability", *PA*, vol. 74 (1996), 567–92.

Bank with Parliament. In fact, the Reserve Bank Act does not include any provision on the appearance of the governor or other officials of the Bank before Parliament, or any of its committees.[691]

In accordance with section 15 of the Reserve Bank Act the Bank is obliged to publish half-yearly policy statements for the purpose of reviewing the implementation of monetary policy in the preceding period and to reflect on the ways in which the goal of price stability can be achieved in the future, which have to be delivered to the Minister of Finance and moreover published.[692] These reports have to be tabled in the House of Representatives and before any parliamentary committee responsible for the overall review of financial management in government departments and other public bodies.[693] Despite the absence of any corresponding provision in the legal basis of the Reserve Bank in practice the routine has been established that the governor of the Bank is cross-examined on each of these policy statements by the Select Committee for Finance and Expenditure (SCFE). The SCFE holds formal hearings, usually four times a year, following the publication of a monetary policy statement or an economic forecast.[694] During these meetings the governor will usually present a prepared statement, and he and other officials of the Bank are questioned on the contents of the monetary policy statements by the members of the committee. It appears that these meetings have gained importance since the coming into existence of the Reserve Bank Act 1989 together with the higher profile of the Bank and increased public awareness. The discussions have been described as "intense".[695] Arguably the most powerful tool of Parliament for holding the Reserve Bank accountable exists with regard to the Bank's expenditure. It is based on an agreement between the Minister of Finance and the Bank which requires the ratification by the House of Representatives.[696] So far there is no reported case in which Parliament has refused to ratify such an agreement. However, it has been observed so far that the fact that a certain mechanism has not been applied does not necessarily mean that it does not function as a mechanism for holding the central bank accountable. Rather, a central bank which is aware of the existence of such a mechanism may have the incentive to ensure that the institution in charge of applying the mechanism is not provoked into doing so.

Apart from the policy statements the House of Representatives receives a copy of the Annual Report of the Reserve Bank and in the case of an application of the override mechanism by the Minister of Finance a copy of the Order in Council. On both occasions the performance of the Bank and/or the Minister of Finance may become the subject of parliamentary debates.

---

[691] As with the British system select committees may initiate inquiries and review government policies, as well as summon witnesses; cf. A. Mitchell, "The New Zealand Way of Committee Power", *Parliamentary Affairs*, vol. 46 no. 1 (1993), 91–100.

[692] For more details of these reports cf. Chap. 4 VII 2.

[693] S. 15(3)(a) Reserve Bank Act 1989.

[694] Cf. Chap. 4 VII.

[695] This has been the outcome of discussions during a visit to the Reserve Bank of New Zealand.

[696] For details cf. Chap. 4 VIII.

2. Central banks without an institutionalised relationship with Parliament

In the context of the central banks examined so far with regard to their relationship with Parliament the Bundesbank and the Nederlandsche Bank stand out from the rest. Both central bank systems are characterised by a lack of any statutory provisions in the legal bases describing the relationship with Parliament, and such things as regular appearances of central bank officials before Parliament.

The legal basis of the **Bundesbank** does not contain any provisions on the relationship between the Bundesbank and the Bundestag. Indeed, the Bundesbank is not obliged to forward any reports to the Bundestag, nor is the president or any other official of the Bundesbank obliged to appear before Parliament. Generally, the Bundestag can discuss Bundesbank matters in the course of its sessions and may make resolutions.[697] The Basic Law prescribes the existence of four standing committees, of which only the Committee on the affairs of the European Union may in practice deal with monetary and banking matters in connection with EMU.[698] These and other standing committees, set up for the term of a Parliament, deal with legislative proposals in their respective fields of competence, but may also on their own initiative deal with other matters falling within the scope of their jurisdiction.[699] The committees can ask the competent minister, but may also invite expert witnesses, and even representatives of interest groups, to appear before them. The president of the Bundesbank has been invited to attend committee meetings in the past to provide evidence on a whole range of subjects, but not on a regular basis, and not explicitly to review the performance of the Bundesbank with regard to monetary policy. Besides, committee meetings are usually not open to the public, which decreases the transparency which may be assigned to such hearings.[700] Under the current committee structure the Finance Committee is in principle competent for matters relating to monetary policy, but subjects relating to the Bundesbank may also be dealt with by a number of standing committees, such as the Legal Affairs Committee and the Committee of Economic Affairs. In principle the Bundesbank could also come under the scrutiny of a parliamentary investigat-

[697] Art. 42 Basic Law, §§ 19 *et seq.* Rules of procedure of the German Bundestag (Geschäftsordnung des Deutschen Bundestages of 2 July 1980).
[698] The other prescribed committees are the Foreign Affairs Committee (*Ausschuß für auswärtige Angelegenheiten*), the Defence Committee (*Ausschuß für Verteidigung*), and the Committee on Public Petitions (*Petitionsausschuß*), cf. Arts. 45, 45a, and 45c Basic Law.
[699] Cf. P. Badura, *Staatsrecht-System. Erläuterungen des Grundgesetzes für die Bundesrepublik Deutschland* (2nd edn., C.H. Beck, Munich, 1996), 405 *et seq.*
[700] One example of a public hearing was the hearing on the Commission Green Paper on the practical arrangements for the introduction of the single currency (COM(95)333 final), staged by the Finance Committee. Both the president of the Bundesbank, Hans Tietmeyer, and the president of the EMI, Alexandre Lamfalussy, were invited. Cf. *Finanzen: Ist-Daten von 1997 sollen entscheidend sein. Waigel, Tietmeyer und Lamfalussy skizzierten ihre Vorstellungen zur Einführung der Europawährung*, Deutscher Bundestag WIB Heft 22/6.12.1995.

ing committee (*Untersuchungsausschuß*).[701] The right of investigation of such parliamentary committees is not unrestricted. They have no right to intervene in the current affairs of an organ of the executive, and thus, for example, may not issue recommendations on monetary policy to the Bundesbank, as is sometimes the case for the Fed.[702] Unlike for example in the US constitutional system, the establishment of a permanent investigating committee or standing banking committee in the Bundestag would actually have to be considered unconstitutional in the German context, as this would infringe the doctrine of the separation of powers.[703] In principle the Bundestag can also discuss matters related to monetary policy in plenary session (in connection with parliamentary debates on financial affairs, the budget and taxes), but such discussions do not take place on a regular basis. One such occasion has recently been the parliamentary debate on the legislative proposal by the executive government concerning the revaluation of the gold reserves of the Bundesbank, a plan which had been publicly opposed by the Bundesbank.[704] The Bundesbank was supported in this conflict by the opposition in the Bundestag, as well as large parts of the general public. The executive government was more or less left with no other choice but to abandon its plan.[705] In some ways this dispute may also serve as a good example of the powerful position which the Bundesbank has in Germany, having *de facto* influence on the type of legislative proposals which the executive government may introduce.

Taking into consideration that the legal basis of the Bundesbank does not provide for the case of a conflict between the Bundesbank and the Federal government, Parliament's right to amend the legal basis is often referred to as a last recourse for the settlement of conflicts.[706]

In principle the executive government, and in particular the Minister of Finance himself, could be held accountable before for its approach to the Bundesbank. Thus, for example, minor and major interpellations could be addressed to the Federal government both on the latter's relationship with the Bundesbank, and generally on matters related to monetary policy, to which the Federal government would be obliged to reply.[707] Yet, the Federal government can only be held accountable by Parliament to the extent to which it has an influence on the Bundesbank.[708] This could in principle be the case with regard to the Federal government's right to postpone a decision of the Central Bank Council.

---

[701] Art. 44 Basic Law.

[702] C.Degenhart, *Staatsrecht I* (11th edn., C.F. Müller Verlag, Heidelberg, 1995), side notation 390 *et seq.*

[703] Siebelt, n. 202 above, at 187.

[704] Cf. Erklärung von Bundesbankpräsident Prof. Dr. Tietmeyer vom 1. Juni 1997.

[705] Cf. Protocol of the plenary session of the Bundestag (*BT-Plenarprotokoll*) 13/177 of 4 June 1997, 15893D–15897A; "Waigel Backs Down on Gold", *Financial Times*, 4 June 1997.

[706] Cf. above Chap. 4 I 2.

[707] §§ 105 and 110 GeschOBT; v.Bonin, n. 40 above, at 189, with reference to a concrete example of a minor interpellation by a number of MPs.

[708] Cf. also Chap. 4 III 1, on the relationship between the Bundesbank and the Federal government.

Where the Federal government does not make use of this power it may be assumed that it generally agrees with the monetary policy pursued by the Bundesbank, and Parliament could take this implied agreement as an opportunity to criticise the monetary policy of the Bundesbank and the lack of action by the Federal government. However, there is no evidence that Parliament made extensive use of this power to hold the executive government accountable for its approach to the Bundesbank. In general it may be observed that as long as the Bundesbank can meet the expectations of the German public to safeguard the stability of the Dmark, parliamentary criticism of the Bundesbank will remain the exception. The transfer of authority over monetary policy to the ECB will make such criticism of the Bundesbank even more unlikely in the future. However, this is not to say that the ECB could not become the subject of criticism in Germany, given that it does not meet the public expectations, not least defined by the past performance of the Bundesbank.

In the **Netherlands**, as with the legal basis of the Bundesbank, there is not a single reference to Parliament in the Bank Act 1948. The statute of the Bank does not include any obligation of the Governing Board or any other organ or representative of the Bank to appear before either chamber of Parliament or any parliamentary committees respectively. This lack of any *direct* accountability of the Nederlandsche Bank to Parliament has its origin in the government's overall responsibility for monetary policy which is reflected in the government's right to issue directions to the Bank under section 26 of the Bank Act 1948. Thus, an individual minister, such as the Minister of Finance and/or the government as a whole (individual and collective ministerial responsibility), rather than the Nederlandsche Bank, is answerable to Parliament. For this reason occasional proposals of members of Parliament to introduce regular meetings between the Finance Committee and the Governing Board of the Nederlandsche Bank have been rejected in the past.[709] Central bank officials do not appear before Parliament on any regular basis, although they might give evidence in their field of expertise in the course of a parliamentary inquiry.[710] In this context it has been observed that the Nederlandsche Bank has a less exposed position in the political system than a central bank which may be considered more independent, because its legal basis does not include a provision giving the executive government the right to issue directions.[711] Vondeling, a former Minister of Finance, recalls having put at one time the somewhat rhetorical question to the president of the Nederlandsche Bank:

[709] R.J. Schotsman, *De Parlementaire Behandeling van het Monetaire Beleid In Nederland Sinds 1863*, Doctorate thesis, University of Brabant, 1987, 340–1, who also refers to occasional informal discussions between the Finance Committee and the Governing Board of the Nederlandsche Bank.

[710] E. Nierop/J. van der Veer/R. Smits, "De Nederlandsche Bank" in *Vers un Système Européen de Banques Centrales*, Rapport du groupe présidé par Jean-Victor Louis (Editions de l'Université de Bruxelles, Brussels, 1989), 233–47, at 246; Memorandum submitted by the Netherlands Central Bank, n. 602 above, at 149.

[711] Schotsman, n. 709 above, at 349.

"do you now that a secret Constitutional provision exists, stating: The president of the Nederlandsche Bank is immune, the Minister of Finance is responsible?"[712]

However, officials of the Bank may be called upon in connection with a parliamentary inquiry in accordance with Article 70 of the Dutch constitution (*enquêterecht*), according to which the two chambers of Parliament jointly or separately have the right to initiate an inquiry into any subject through a select committee or an *ad hoc* committee.[713] The committee charged with the inquiry can oblige witnesses and expert witnesses to appear and testify. Thus, in principle the Nederlandsche Bank and its conduct of monetary policy could become the subject of such an inquiry and members of the Governing Board and/or other central bank officials could be called upon to appear before the committee. However, the practical value of the so-called *enquêterecht* as a parliamentary tool to hold the central bank accountable is very limited. First, the establishment of a parliamentary inquiry requires a majority vote in either chamber of Parliament or in a joint session, respectively, with at least half of the total number of members present in each case. Despite repeated efforts to amend the procedure a "minority right of inquiry" has never been introduced.[714] Therefore, since the political parties in power will usually command a majority in both Houses of Parliament, the certain co-operation of at least parts of the executive government, i.e. a coalition partner, will be required to stage an inquiry involving the Nederlandsche Bank. By supporting the initiation of an inquiry into the Nederlandsche Bank the government would effectively vote for an inquiry into its own conduct, since the latter is considered to be ultimately responsible for monetary policy. Besides, parliamentary practice shows that the *enquêterecht* is not a commonly used instrument. Since its establishment in 1850 fewer than 20 inquiries have taken place, and none was related to the Nederlandsche Bank.[715] Apart from the *enquêterecht*, Parliament's prospect of reviewing the conduct of monetary policy is somewhat limited. Both chambers of Parliament have standing committees for each ministerial department and thus—among others—for financial affairs (*vaste commissie voor Financiën*) and economic affairs (*vaste commissie voor Economische Zaken*). Moreover, *ad hoc* committees can be set up for special subjects.[716] Moreover, Parliament can request information (Article 68 of the Dutch Constitution) from, and make interpellations, pose questions orally, or in writing, and introduce motions to a minister. But in addition to the fact that Parliament's grip on the Nederlandsche Bank is somewhat limited, evidence exists to support the view that Parliament

---

[712] Author's translation cited in Vondeling, n. 392 above, at 150.

[713] The parliamentary inquiry is governed by a separate law: Wet Parlementaire Enquête, Stb. 1991, no. 416. Moreover, detailed provisions are included in the rules of procedure of both chambers of Parliament: Reglement van Orde van de Eerste Kamer der Staten-Generaal, ss. 128–138; Reglement van Orde van de Tweede Kamer der Staten-Generaal, ss. 140–150.

[714] On the efforts to introduce such a right cf. Prakke/De Reede/Van Wissen, n. 15 above, 549–50.

[715] For a list of the subjects of the inquiries cf. Prakke/De Reede/Van Wissen, n. 15 above, 547–8.

[716] Reglement van Orde van de Eerste Kamer der Staten-Generaal, s. 32; Reglement van Orde van de Tweede Kamer der Staten-Generaal, ss. 16 and 18.

takes rather limited interest in monetary policy in the first place. The reasons for this parliamentary abstinence may originate in the special position of the Nederlandsche Bank. Schotsman argues that the Nederlandsche Bank conducts monetary policy at some distance from the political arena due to the objective approach to monetary policy. Moreover, in his view the Bank holds a special position *vis-à-vis* the executive government and both chambers of Parliament in so far as it is "primarily responsible for the instruments of the monetary policy", whereas a conflict between the Governing Board of the Bank and Parliament would not be "in the interest of the country".[717] Finally, Schotsman refers to the discretion with which monetary matters are discussed in Parliament. He summarises the relationship between the Nederlandsche Bank and Parliament in as follows:

> "It is our conclusion that the relationship between the Staten-Generaal and the DNB [De Nederlandsche Bank] is characterised by remarkable continuity. In the 120 years covered by us, parliamentary activities in the field of monetary policy have been marked by calmness and harmony, that is to say that Parliament normally has not been directly involved with monetary policy. The behaviour of the Staten-Generaal towards the Bank was characterised by a great deal of self-restraint on the part of both chambers of the Staten-Generaal to discuss monetary policy with the Minister [of Finance]. The Staten-Generaal paid little attention to monetary policy."[718]

In some respects ministerial responsibility functions as a filter between Parliament and the central bank. Parliament is restricted to putting pressure on the government and the Minister of Finance in particular to issue directions to the Bank under section 26 of the Bank Act 1948, which forms the backbone of this relationship.

As has been observed, the override mechanism ceases to exist under the Bank Act 1998. Interestingly, the new statute of the Bank for the first time includes an explicit reference to Parliament.[719] According to this, while observing his independence, the president of the Nederlandsche Bank, upon request by the Parliament or upon his own initiative, may be heard by the competent committee of Parliament with regard to the tasks and actions relating to objective of the Nederlandsche Bank to maintain price stability. Against this background, the Staten-Generaal has made it clear that it expects the president of the Nederlandsche Bank to appear before Parliament upon request, as the president of the ECB appears before the EP. The difficulties with this approach have already been cited above. Nevertheless, this development is remarkable in as much as the role of a national parliament *vis-à-vis* a national central bank is increased at a time at which authority over monetary policy is transferred to the ESCB and the ECB.

---

[717] Schotsman, n. 709 above, at 349.
[718] Author's translation: ibid., at 349.
[719] Cf. s. 19 Bank Act 1998.

With regard to the transparency of the central banks examined in this study generally a differentiation can be made between transparency in the decision-making procedures of the central banks with regard to monetary policy and, moreover, any publications or other means to enhance the transparency of the conduct of monetary policy by the central bank.

1. Transparency in the decision-making procedures of the central banks

Considerable differences exist between the various central banks with regard to the publication of minutes of the meetings of the monetary policy board. The arrangements range from the absence of any form of disclosure of the meetings to the extensive publication of the decisions and minutes. With regard to the central banks participating in the ESCB any provisions which could infringe the tasks that are assigned to them in the framework of the ESCB have to be considered incompatible with the EC Treaty and the ESCB Statute. This includes an infringement of the confidentiality rule of the ECB, e.g. the publication of details of the meetings of the Governing Board of the ECB by national central banks which, under the EC Treaty or due to a decision of the Governing Board, are exempted from publication.

In the case of the Nederlandsche Bank, the Banque de France and the Reserve Bank of New Zealand no minutes of the proceedings of the monetary policy boards are published.

The meetings of the Governing Board of the **Nederlandsche Bank** are attended by its members, and are open to staff members. However, they are not open to the public. The Bank Act 1948 does not include any provisions on the publication of the minutes of the meetings of the Governing Board.[720] Nevertheless, minutes of the meetings of the Governing Board are kept, which reflect the views of the participants expressed during the meetings and the decisions. However, they are not published, nor are they made available to the public. Decisions on interest rate adjustments are published—among other places on the Internet.

The **Reserve Bank of New Zealand** likewise does not publish any minutes. However, the reason for this is to be found in the institutional structure of the Bank, according to which monetary policy decisions are effectively taken by the governor himself, rather than by a collegiate body. Consequently no minutes of the meetings of such a body can exist. Monetary policy decisions of the governor are made public—among other places on the Internet.

---

[720] The law on the public accessibility of government documents (Wet van 31 october 1991, Stb. 703, houdende regelen betreffende de openbaarheid van bestuur; as amended) does not apply.

Apart from this, transparency does play an important role in the New Zealand model of central banking and may actually be considered as one of its functional bases. For the area of monetary policy this is expressly stated in point 4(c) of the current PTA:

> "The bank shall implement monetary policy in a sustainable, consistent *and transparent* manner."[721]

This broadly formulated duty is reflected by the Reserve Bank Act 1989. On a broader scale, the main feature of transparency of the Reserve Bank is the clear monetary objective set out in section 8 of the Reserve Bank Act 1989 and quantified by the PTA. It is moreover reflected in the clear and unequivocal override mechanism provided for by section 12 of the Reserve Bank Act 1989.

In the past the **Banque de France** has also not published minutes of the meetings of the CPM. The deliberations of the CPM are recorded in minutes which are kept in a special registry. The minutes of each meeting have to be approved by the CPM at its next meeting.[722] It is left to the CPM to decide whether and subject to what conditions the minutes of its meetings are made public.[723] During the first press conference of the Banque de France, operating under the new Bank Act 1993, the governor of the Bank was in favour of the delayed publication of the minutes, including the votes, of past meetings of the CPM.[724] The deliberations of the General Council are likewise recorded in minutes in a special registry.[725] The minutes are forwarded to the members of the General Council and the Censor, and have to be approved at the following meeting of the General Council. Unlike in the case of the CPM no statutory provisions exist on the publications of these meetings.

According to Article 40 of decree 1993 the decisions of the CPM and the General Council are published in the official journal of the French Republic (*Journal officiel de la République française*). Moreover, legal acts adopted by the CPM or the General Council can be published on the initiative of the adopter.

According to § 7(1) of the BBank charter, minutes of the **Bundesbank**'s Central Bank Council meetings, recording the negotiations and decisions, are kept. The form of these minutes has evolved over time from literal minutes to a summary of the meetings.[726] The contents of these minutes have to be approved by the members of the Governing Council. This does not include the members of the Federal government who participate in the Central Bank Council meetings, since they are not members of the Central Bank Council. Neither the BBankG nor the charter of the Bundesbank includes any provisions on the publication of

---

[721] Emphasis added.
[722] Art. 3(1) decree 1993.
[723] Ibid., Art. 3(2).
[724] n. 338 above,
[725] Art. 10 decree 1993.
[726] Cf. D. Marsh, op. cit., Chap. 3, n. 110.

these minutes. Generally, copies of these minutes are sent to every member of the Central Bank Council, and in some instances to government agencies. Other than that, the minutes remain secret for 30 years. Since the minutes are kept secret for a long time, and even thereafter are only made available to the public in the form of summaries, they seem to be of little value for transparency in the decision-making procedure of the Bank. Discussions which may have taken place, and any differences of opinion between the members of the Central Bank Council and the representatives of the executive government, are of little more than historical interest, but in any case cannot become the basis for making the central bank and the executive government accountable for their approach to monetary policy in an effective way.

With regard to the publication of the decisions, according to § 33 of the BBankG, decisions on interest and discount rates, as well as minimum reserve requirements have to be published in the German Government Gazette (*Bundesanzeiger*). Moreover, the Internet home page of the Bundesbank indicates the current discount and Lombard rates.

Apart from the obligations of the Board of Governors of the **Fed** under the Humphrey-Hawkins-Procedure, and any additional appearances before Congress, the extent to which monetary policy is conducted in a transparent manner is determined by different factors. In the first place the transparency in the decision-making process of the Board of Governors and the FOMC, the two principal policy-formulating organs of the Fed should be noted. According to section 10(10) of the Federal Reserve Act the Board of Governors has to keep a complete record of all actions taken by the Board and the FOMC "upon all questions of policy relating to open-market operations and shall record therein the votes taken in connection with the determination of open-market policies and the reasons underlying the action taken by the Board and the Committee in each instance". The Board of Governors is moreover obliged to keep a similar record with respect to all questions of policy decided by the Board. This includes decisions on reserve requirements and discount rates for the area of monetary policy. These records have to be included in the Annual Report to Congress which will usually include a summary of the actions of the Board of Governors on discount rates, including details of the Board votes, and the minutes of the meetings of the FOMC.[727]

The Federal Reserve Act does not establish any further obligations for the Board of Governors and the FOMC to make public minutes of its meetings and/or decisions taken during such meetings. However, the Board of Governors publishes the edited transcript of the minutes of its meetings roughly quarterly.[728] Moreover, immediately after each meeting the Board makes a public

---

[727] Cf. Board of Governors of the Federal Reserve Board, *83rd Annual Report 1996* (Fed, Washington, DC, 1997), 87 *et seq.*, and 101 *et seq.*

[728] For Berry, n. 367 above, at 44, considers the minutes of the Board of Governors "still a far cry from those of the FOMC".

announcement of the decisions it has taken. As a government agency the Board
of Governors is subject to the provisions of the Government in the Sunshine Act
of 1976,[729] and accordingly the Board of Governors' Rules Regarding Public
Observation of Meetings provide for about half of the meetings of the Board of
Governors to be open to the general public. However, this does not include
deliberations on monetary policy issues. Under the Government in the Sunshine
Act the disclosure of information which is likely to lead to significant financial
speculation in currencies, securities or commodities, or significantly endangers
the stability of any financial institution, can be exempted from the obligation to
disclose. The same applies to the disclosure of information which is likely to
frustrate significantly the implementation of a proposed action.[730] Meetings of
the FOMC are permanently closed to the public, since they deal solely with
monetary policy issues which fall within the exemption under the Government
in the Sunshine Act. The FOMC publishes its deliberations on open-market
operations in three ways. First, since early 1994, the FOMC has released short
statements immediately after each meeting announcing policy decisions taken
during the meeting.[731] Moreover, after each meeting the FOMC publishes the
approved minutes of the previous meeting.[732] The minutes include a summary
of the discussions during the meeting, however, without identifying the views
taken by individual members (e.g. "A few Members argued . . . ").[733] Committee
votes on actions are listed, including the names of the members in favour and
against a particular action. Finally, the FOMC publishes *edited* transcripts of its
meetings, which are electronically recorded, with a five-year delay. Behind the
current practice of publications of the FOMC lay years of heated debate
between the supporters of more public disclosure of the decision-making
process of the Board of Governors and the FOMC, namely members of
Congress, and the opponents of such changes, namely the Board of Governors
of the Fed. Before 1976 the FOMC had recorded the meetings and published a
so-called memorandum of understanding with a five-year lag.[734] Moreover,
decisions of the FOMC were released with a 90-day delay.[735] This practice was
challenged in *Merrill* v. *Federal Open Market Committee et al.*[736] under the
newly enacted Freedom of Information Act of 1986[737] and as a result the FOMC

---

[729] Public Law 94–409, 90 Stat. 1241; cf. W.Gellhorn *et al.*, *Administrative Law* (8th edn., The
Foundation Press, Mineola, NY, 1987), 780 *et seq.*

[730] 5 USC. § 552b(c)(9)(A) and (B); cf. also *A.G. Becker Inc.* v. *Board of Governors of Federal
Reserve System*, 502 F Supp. 378, with regard to meetings discussing both exempted and non-
exempted material.

[731] In Feb. 1995 the Fed announced that it would make the practice permanent.

[732] Before 1994 this publication was referred to as "policy records" since they were less detailed.
The members have to agree that the minutes accurately reflect the meeting.

[733] However, it is commonly said that the minutes reflect the "contents and flavour" of these
meetings.

[734] Memoranda were kept from 1936 but not published until 1965.

[735] As a result of congressional pressure the FOMC reduced the waiting period to 45 days from
1975 onwards.

[736] 413 F Supp. 494 (1976). On the unsuccessful appeal, see 565 F 2d. (1977).

[737] Public Law 99–570.

started to publish policy records of the previous meeting after each meeting. However, instead of publishing the memoranda more speedily the FOMC abandoned them.[738] This was in principle lawful since by law the FOMC was not obliged to keep such records in the first place. As Kettl observes: "[t]he Fed could not be forced [under the Freedom of Information Act] to release minutes that did not exist".[739] It seems that this is a negative example of a Fed which dodged further public disclosure, and draws attention to the ambivalent position of the Fed as regards public disclosure at the time.

Until today, the Fed's approach to public disclosure has been subjected to criticism. It is argued that the classic defence of the Fed against public disclosure, according to which this would have a negative impact on the economy as it would make certain monetary policy instruments largely ineffective, is "exaggerated" and, in fact, that more disclosure would have economic advantages.[740] For others the Fed's secrecy "enhances the mystique" of the central bank.[741] Alongside proposals for institutional reforms of the Fed, there have been numerous proposals to strengthen the transparency of the Fed through enhanced public disclosure. Such proposals have included those to oblige the FOMC to publish unedited transcripts of proceedings immediately after each meeting (more accountability *vis-à-vis* general public versus protection against overreactions and financial market speculates). A more recent proposal by Representative Gonzales, which did not materialise, included enhanced transparency in the FOMC meetings (public meetings/videotaping etc.) and the immediate publications of decisions on open market operations.[742]

In its report on the accountability of the **Bank of England**, the Treasury Committee of the House of Commons has emphasised that the Bank should be held accountable not only to Parliament, but to the public at large.[743] Since 1993, the minutes of the monthly meetings of the Chancellor of the Exchequer and the governor of the Bank of England had been published. In the minutes the discussions between the Chancellor and the governor and their positions on issues, in particular with regard to the interest rate, became visible, as well as the decision finally taken by the Chancellor. Thus either agreement or, at times, disagreement on monetary policy issues between the executive government and the

---

[738] Berry, n. 367 above, at 44.

[739] Kettl, n. 183 above, at 153 and 159.

[740] R.D. Erb, "Introduction and Summary" in R.D. Erb (ed.), *Federal Reserve Policies and Public Disclosure* (American Enterprise Institute for Public Policy Research, Washington, 1978), 2–12, at 12.

[741] Greider, n. 364 above, at 54.

[742] Cf. HR 28 (103rd Congress)—*A bill to promote accountability, diversity, and the public interest in the operation of the Federal Reserve System and for other purposes.* Cf. also the statements by different Fed officials on these proposals before the Banking Committee, reprinted in Federal Reserve Bulletin, vol. 79 no. 12 (Dec. 1993), 1100 *et seq.*, in which such proposals were rejected.

[743] First Report from the Select Committee on Treasury, n. 524 above, consideration 13.

Bank became apparent.[744] Both the Chancellor and the governor have some-times been judged in retrospective on their (different) opinions on economic developments, against the background of actual economic developments.

With the establishment of the MPC, which is in charge of operational decisions on monetary policy, new reporting requirements, enhancing the transparency of the Bank, have been introduced. The MPC keeps minutes of its meetings which are published no later than six weeks after the respective meeting. The Bank of England Act 1998 includes an obligation to publish these minutes.[745] According to this, the minutes include the voting preferences of the members of the MPC taking part in a particular meeting. However, one exception exists, that is the publication of the minutes of meetings relating to decisions to intervene in the financial markets. The reason for this is explained in the legislation itself, as only those minutes on decisions may be exempted from publication for which the MPC has decided that publication of a decision to intervene would be likely to impede or frustrate the achievement of the intervention's purpose.[746] Thus, if an early publication could result in a reaction in the financial market which could counteract the proposed measure by the MPC, the latter may decide to keep the minutes of these meetings from publication. However, minutes of such meetings have to be published eventually, that is within six weeks of the publication of the statement about the decision to intervene.[747] The published minutes include an overview of the discussions that have taken place during the meeting, whereby the language is in general terms not revealing of the views of individual members referred to by name. This is followed by a summary and the policy conclusions. Different opinions/assessments are restated without identifying the individual members supporting one or the other view. The minutes list the members who participated in the particular meeting of the MPC, and, moreover, whether a representative of the Treasury took part. However, it is noteworthy that not only the decisions which have been taken, but also the voting preferences are published.[748] A summary of economic data, which have become the basis for the assessments of the MPC, is annexed to the minutes.

With regard to the publications of the monetary policy decisions prior to the publication of the minutes, the new legislation foresees the publication of the decisions "as soon as practical after each meeting".[749] Codifying existing practice, decisions on intervening in financial markets are excluded from this rule in as much as such an immediate publication by the MPC is thought to run counter to the purpose of such interventions. However, as soon as that danger has

---

[744] For an example of such disagreement cf. *Minutes of the Monthly Monetary Meeting of 5 June 1996*, where the Bank, in its demand to leave the interest rates unchanged, was basically overruled by the Chancellor of the Exchequer.

[745] S. 15(1) Bank of England Act 1998.

[746] Ibid., s. 15(2).

[747] Ibid., s. 15(3).

[748] Cf. also Chap. 5, n. 7.

[749] S. 14(11) Bank of England Act 1998.

ceased to exist the MPC has to make public what decisions have been taken and when they have been taken.[750]

The provisions on the publication of the decisions and the minutes of the MPC enhance transparency in the conduct of monetary policy by the Bank of England. The provisions on an exceptional longer delay in publication of decisions on interventions and minutes relating to meetings where such decisions have been taken are remarkable compared to what can be observed for other central banks, in as much as they ensure that these exceptions are limited to cases where such a publication could dilute the effect of the measure. It needs to be observed whether and to what extent the Bank may use this provision in a way which may decrease transparency, since, after all, it is for the Bank to decide when such exceptional circumstances exist. In any event, under the Bank Act 1998 it becomes possible to judge *ex post* whether the conditions for a delay of a publication existed at the time of the decision.

Unlike the Bank of England, for the **ECB** neither the EC Treaty nor the ESCB Statute includes any explicit provision regarding minutes of the meetings of the Governing Council, or, for that matter, the Executive Board. Thus it could be argued that it is basically for the Governing Council to decide whether and to what extent it keeps and, thereafter, publishes minutes of its meetings. The provision which may give some guidance in this respect is Article 10.4 of the ESCB Statute:

> "[T]he proceedings of the meetings shall be confidential. The Governing Council of the ECB may decide to publish the results of its deliberations."

The scope of this provision is not very clear. Apparently, Article 10.4 of the ESCB Statute excludes the meetings of the Governing Council taking place in public, or members of the public being granted access to these meetings. However, it is questionable whether and to what extent the reference to the confidentiality of the meetings also excludes the subsequent publication of such deliberations in the form of minutes of the meetings, in particular, since the provision states that the ECB may (only) decide to publish the outcomes of its meetings. Indeed, it is not clear either whether the latter is a reference only to the publication of the decisions that have been taken in such meetings, or also to some kind of summary of the subject-matter discussed in the meeting. It seems, that at least the publication of full minutes or transcripts of the deliberations within a reasonable period of time would run counter to the ratio of Article 10.4, sentence 1 of the ESCB Statute, which intends to ensure not only open discussions on monetary policy among the members of the Governing Council, but arguably thereafter also the effective implementation of monetary policy measures. Thus, even if the ECB will have an incentive to make debates in the

---

[750] Ibid., s. 14(2)–(5).

Governing Council public in order to establish its credibility,[751] there may be limits to the extent to which these minutes could state details of the meetings of the Governing Council, and in particular any differences of opinion between different members of the Governing Council and the motives behind it.[752] Besides, not everybody seems to be convinced of the positive effect of a publication of minutes by the ECB. The first president of the ECB himself has raised doubts about the practicability of the publication of minutes of the Governing Board.[753] The obligation to keep secret the proceedings of the meetings may in practice result in the decision-making process and especially any diverse views within the Governing Council being kept from public scrutiny. The Governing Council of the ECB presents itself as a collective organ, which takes collective decisions, rather than a collection of individual and diverse views on monetary policy, which result one way or another in decisions.

As has been indicated, the reference to the results of the deliberations in Article 14.4, sentence 2 of the ESCB Statute also means that the Governing Council has discretion with regard to the decision to publish decisions which have been taken in those meetings.[754]

2. Transparency through publicity

The transparency of the central banks examined is not only defined by the extent to which they publish minutes. Other publications, and in particular regular reports on the past conduct and future development of monetary policy may not only enhance the understanding of monetary policy or the amount of information available, but can function as a yardstick for holding the central bank accountable. It is with regard to these reports that differences exist between the various central banks. Otherwise all central banks publish an annual report, and provide for other regular and occasional publications. It can be observed for all the central banks included in this study that they make use of the new information technology: they all maintain a homepage on the Internet where they publish general information on there structure and tasks, but also regular reports, speeches, and press releases.[755]

---

[751] As suggested by Mayes, n. 671 above, at 2.

[752] This approach to transparency on the European level can also be observed for the Commission. Its minutes are not published. In any event only the discussions are recorded without any details of the voting behaviour or any particular views expressed in the meetings.

[753] Such doubts have been reportedly raised by Willem Duisenberg, cf. "Dutch Resist 'Deal' on Bank Job", *Financial Times*, 31 Jan./1 Feb. 1998. Cf. also Art. 23.1. Rules of Procedure of the European Central Bank, according to which the proceedings of the decision-making bodies of the ECB and of any committee or group established by them shall be confidential unless the Governing Council authorises the President to make the outcome of their deliberations public. However, it can be concluded from Art. 5.2. of the Rules of Procedure that minutes of the proceedings of the Governing Council are kept.

[754] Cf also Art. 34.2. ESCB Statute.

[755] App. 3 includes a list of the central banks on the Internet.

The legal basis of the **Bundesbank** includes relatively little on regular publications, and no explicit reference to a monetary policy or inflation report. According to § 18 of the BBankG the Bank may publish monetary and banking statistics, and the Bundesbank does so on a weekly basis in the form of a return showing its assets and liabilities.[756] Apart from that the Bundesbank publishes an Annual Report.[757] The Annual Report commences with a foreword by the president. It thereafter examines in detail—among others—the economic development in Germany, including details of economic and monetary trends, the policies pursued by the Bundesbank, as well as its operations. This includes records of domestic and external monetary policy measures, as well as explanations for specific monetary policy measures.[758] Moreover, the development of the intermediate target applied by the Bundesbank is documented in detail, whereby the report sets out to explain and justify existing (upward) deviations from the target.[759] It also explains the targeting strategy for the following year, thereby introducing a specific intermediate target range for money growth with a time horizon of one year.[760] However, the Annual Report does not include any explicit forecasts.

Despite the absence of a legal requirement, the Bundesbank publishes a Monthly Report (*Monatsbericht*).[761] It includes—among others—details of monetary development in the period subsequent to the last report. The conduct of monetary policy by the Bundesbank is explained and justified. The Monthly Report includes an overview of the development of inflation and the monetary aggregate (M3) which the Bundesbank uses as an intermediate target.[762] While the reports include details of the past performance of the Bundesbank, they do not include any projections on future developments. Rather, at times considerations of a general nature on the *expected* increase in prices ("*Preissteigerungs-erwartungen*") can be found. In this context Mishkin and Posen have observed that "the Bundesbank makes itself accountable on the basis of its explanations for past performance, but it does not leave itself open to be evaluated as a forecaster".[763] Vaubel explains the absence of explicit forecasts with the "prestige motive" according to which the Bundesbank prefers not to publish forecasts rather than to lose its prestige in the case of false forecasts.[764]

---

[756] For details of the scope of these statistics from a legal point of view cf. Gramlich, n. 205 above, § 18.

[757] With the Annual Report the Board of Directors of the Bundesbank fulfils its obligation under § 26(3), sentence 3, BBankG to publish an annual statement of accounts, which is included in the Annual Report. Cf. Chap. 4 VIII 1.

[758] Cf. Deutsche Bundesbank, *Annual Report 1996* (DBB, Frankfurt a.M., 1997), 56 *et seq.*

[759] Ibid., 69 *et seq.*

[760] Ibid., at 73. Note that against the background of the begin of the third stage of EMU on 1 Jan. 1999, in the *Annual Report 1996*, n. 758 above, the time horizon was increased to two years, in order to cover the period until EMU.

[761] Interestingly, the Bundesbank refers in this context to a publication in response to § 18 BBankG. However, the Monthly Report goes beyond what may be considered monetary and banking statistics.

[762] Cf. Chap. 4 II 1.

[763] Mishkin/Posen, n. 207 above, at 25, refer to a "depersonalisation" of monetary policy.

[764] Vaubel, n. 206 above, 26 *et seq.*

The Bundesbank issues press releases and publishes public speeches by its president and other members of the Central Bank Council and the Board of Directors.

Like the Bundesbank, the **Fed** does not publish regular monetary policy or inflation reports as such either. The Board of Governors oversees a number of regular publications. In accordance with section 10(6) of the Federal Reserve Act[765] the Board of Governors forwards to Congress an Annual Report which includes an overview of the monetary policy and the US economy for the year concerned, records of policy actions by the Board of Governors and the minutes of the meetings of the FOMC, as well as the financial statements of the Board of Governors. The Annual Report does not include details of the approach to monetary policy in the forthcoming year, nor does it include reflections on future developments of economic aggregates. However, it should be recalled in this context that the Board of Governors is obliged to forward a report on its objectives and plans with regard to the development of the monetary and credit aggregates twice a year.[766]

On behalf of the Fed, the Board of Governors also publishes balance sheets on a weekly basis. Together with the minutes of the FOMC the weekly balance sheets have been described as the essence of the transparency of the Fed since open-market operations and monetary policy at large become open. The Board of Governors also publishes a monthly *Federal Reserve Bulletin* which discusses economic and monetary trends and developments, reprints evidence given by Fed officials before Congress, and includes the minutes of the meetings of the FOMC. However, it does not include any forecasts. This is completed by publications of the result of research (e.g. working paper series) of the staff of the Board of Governors.

Moreover, each Federal Reserve Bank has its own series of publications ranging from monthly bulletins to research papers. The chairman and the other members of the Board of Governors make regular public appearances which are often used to explain the viewpoint of the Fed on certain issues and occasionally are even used to publicly justify certain monetary policy decisions.[767]

The legal basis of the **Nederlandsche Bank** includes little on the reporting requirements of the Bank. Apart from the annual accounts, the only explicit reference is to be found in the obligation to publish weekly summary balance sheets (*verkorte balans*) in one of the two Dutch Government Gazettes, i.e. the

---

[765] The Board of Governors of the Fed shall make annually full report of its operations to the speaker of the House of Representatives who prints the report for the information of Congress.

[766] Cf. Chap. 4 II 1.

[767] E.g. Remarks by A. Greenspan, Chairman of the Federal Reserve System, at the 1997 Haskins Partners Dinner of the Stern School of Business, New York University, NY, 8 May 1997, on the approach to monetary policy.

Nederlandse Staatscourant.[768] Apart from this, the Nederlandsche Bank publishes an annual report.[769] This begins with a general report (*algemene verslag*) by the president, followed by, *inter alia*, an overview of the development of the Dutch economy, as well as the development of monetary policy. Indeed, the annual report, and notably the introductory part by the president, has been regarded as the primary source of justification of the Nederlandsche Bank of its performance.[770] Since Dutch monetary policy is directed at a close link between the Guilder and the Dmark, the Nederlandsche Bank no longer targets money growth.[771] The report does not include any projections on the future development of economic aggregates.

Although not mentioned in the legal basis, the Nederlandsche Bank also publishes quarterly bulletins (*Kwartaalbericht*), which include reprints of speeches and articles on a number of different subjects, but also an overview of current economic and monetary developments. This includes details of the development of inflation, as well as economic and monetary trends, and in particular the development of the Dmark compared to the Guilder.[772] The quarterly reports do not include any forecasts of the development of economic aggregates.

Finally, the Bank also publishes staff papers, speeches and press releases, which can be viewed on the homepage of the Nederlandsche Bank.[773]

For the **ECB**, generally Article 15 of the ESCB Statute describes the reporting requirements. This includes the presentation of an annual report on the activities of the ESCB and the monetary policy of the past and current years. From the wording of Articles 109b(3) EC and 15.3 of the ESCB Statute it cannot be concluded that this report has to include projections on the future development of monetary policy. Furthermore, the ECB has to publish a report on the activities of the ESCB at least on a quarterly basis.[774] The EC Treaty and ESCB Statute are silent on the scope of these reports. Whereas it is likely that these will explain in detail past monetary policy, the ECB could take an approach similar to that of the Bundesbank in avoiding forecasts.[775]

Finally, the ECB is obliged to publish weekly consolidated financial statements of the ESCB.[776] All of these reports have to be made to interested third parties free of charge.[777] Since the ECB will constitute a complete new

---

[768] S. 35 Bank Act 1948. On the contents of the summary balance sheet cf. Besluit van 19 mei 1988, houdende goedkeuring van de vorm van de verkorte balans van De Nederlandsche Bank NV, Staatscourant 1988, no. 88.

[769] The obligation to publish an annual report is not to be found in the Bank Act 1948 itself, but rather derives from its status as a company limited by shares (NV).

[770] van Velthoven/van Schaik, n. 607 above, at 391.

[771] Cf. Nederlandsche Bank, *Jaarverslag 1996* (Kluwer, Deventer, 1997). See also Chap. 4 II 1.

[772] Cf. e.g. De Nederlandsche Bank, *Kwartaalbericht September 1997* (Kluwer, Deventer, 1997).

[773] Cf. App. 3.

[774] Art. 15.1. ESCB Statute. Cf. also Art. 16 Rules of Procedure of the European Central Bank.

[775] See otherwise European Monetary Institute, n. 199 above; cf. also Chap. 4 II 2.

[776] Art. 15.2. ESCB Statute.

[777] Ibid., Art. 15.4.

institution with no prior reputation, it is likely to have the incentive to seek to establish its credibility, first, in the financial markets, but also with the public at large. It is thus likely to take a pro-active approach in general to transparency in its conduct of monetary policy, and in particular with regard to any publications which explain its stance on monetary policy issues. Despite this probability, it would have been desirable to ensure the transparency of the ECB through the introduction of more detailed provisions on the content of the quarterly reports in the ESCB Statute in order to ensure that they can function as a yardstick to hold the ECB accountable for its conduct of monetary policy, rather than leaving this choice to the ECB itself.

The reporting requirements of the **Banque de France** may be considered somewhat more meaningful than those of the central banks examined as far as their usefulness for holding the Bank accountable is concerned. According to Article 19(1) of the Bank Act 1993:

> "At least once a year, the Governor of the Banque de France shall address a report on the Bank's activities and on monetary policy *and the prospects for it* to the President of the Republic and to Parliament."[778]

The interesting feature of this provision establishing the obligation to draw up an annual report is that it is explicitly stated that this report has to include forecasts for monetary policy. In the past the Bank has fulfilled this obligation by forwarding an annual report to the President of the Republic and both chambers of Parliament which bears the initials of the governor and includes an introductory letter by him. The annual report is made public. It includes projections about the international environment and economic developments in France in the previous year, France's balance of payments, the financial and foreign exchange markets, the banking and financial system, the payment system and the development of monetary policy in the past and the future. With regard to the future development of monetary policy, it has been observed that the annual report includes monetary guidelines which the CPM intends to observe during the following year.[779] Article 34 of the Bank Act 1993 obliges the Bank to publish weekly statements on its financial position in the official journal of the French Republic (JORF). Moreover, on its own initiative the Bank publishes weekly and quarterly bulletins, which analyse the monetary situation and the economic environment in France and abroad, and monetary statistics on a weekly, monthly and annual basis. Finally, the Bank promotes irregular publications on a wide range of subjects, including monetary policy issues to banking supervision.[780] The Bank also regularly issues press releases on matters it finds appropriate to make public, such as monetary guidelines.

---

[778] Emphasis added.

[779] Cf. Banque de France, n. 343 above, 58–9; cf. Chap. 4 II 2.

[780] For more details see the (annual) publication catalogue issued by the information service of the Banque de France.

The Reserve Bank of New Zealand and the Bank of England stand out from the central banks already discussed, in as much as both banks are obliged by law to publish reports on the development of monetary policy on a regular basis. The transparency of the **Reserve Bank of New Zealand** with regard to the day-to-day conduct of monetary policy is promoted by a wide range of publications, including the Monetary Policy Statement, the Annual Report, the Reserve Bank Bulletin, economic forecasts, weekly statistical releases and other publications. Together with regular public appearances of officials of the Reserve Bank before the House of Representatives and elsewhere, communication with the elected representatives, the markets and the public at large is enhanced. It should be noted in this context that the Reserve Bank of New Zealand has joined the growing number of central banks which make use of the new information technology. The Bank features its own homepage on the Internet which includes general information on the Reserve Bank as well as the periodically published reports.

Arguably the most important regular publication is the Monetary Policy Statement (MPS). In accordance with section 15(1)–(1A) of the Reserve Bank Act 1989 the Bank is obliged to deliver a policy statement every six months.[781] The statement includes a review and assessment of the implementation of monetary policy in the period subsequent to the previous statement and a statement including the Bank's proposal for the implementation of monetary policy with the goal of achieving price stability for the next five years.[782] This includes forecasts for "headline" and "underlying" inflation. Finally, the Bank has to specify and explain the policies and means by which it intends to achieve the policy targets fixed in the PTA.[783] The MPS has to be signed by the governor, thereby creating personal liability of the governor for the authenticity of the contents of the monetary policy statement. However, the MPS is not only published by the Reserve Bank, but, as has been pointed out, also has to be presented to the Minister of Finance and, more importantly, tabled in Parliament.[784]

But the MPS is not the only regular publication of the Reserve Bank of New Zealand. According to section 163 of the Reserve Bank Act 1989, within three months after the end of each financial year the Bank has to deliver an annual report on the operations of the Bank during the financial year.[785] This report includes a statement by the governor, and detailed statements of services performance of the Bank, including among others monetary policy formulation, market operations, financial system oversight, currency operations, foreign reserves management and banking services. The annual report also includes the Bank's balance sheet. The annual report is referred to the House of Representatives and its Select Committee for Finance and Expenditure (SCFE) where it may be subject to debate.[786]

[781] Reserve Bank Act 1989 as amended by the Act to amended the Reserve Bank of New Zealand Act 1989 of 8 Aug. 1990.
[782] S. 15(2)(c)–(d) Reserve Bank Act 1989.
[783] Ibid., s. 15(2)(a)–(b).
[784] Cf. Chap. 4 VI 1.
[785] S. 163(1)(a) Reserve Bank Act 1989.
[786] Ibid., s. 163(3). Cf. Chap. 4 VI 1.

The Reserve Bank also publishes a so-called annual plan which explains the Bank's functions and organisational structure, but also its activities in the current financial year, in particular with regard to monetary policy.[787] The annual plan also includes strategies with regard to performance monitoring and control, and for a proper communication with the public. Of the central banks examined in this study, the Reserve Bank of New Zealand is the only central bank which publishes such a general outline of the activities in the year ahead and financial resources involved. It certainly adds another element to the transparency of monetary policy and the activities of the Reserve Bank of New Zealand, in particular taking into account the accessible style in which the information have been prepared for this publication.

Although not explicitly foreseen in the Reserve Bank Act 1989, the half-year monetary policy statements have been supplemented by quarterly economic forecasts, which include the whole range of the economy and thus not only the inflation figures. The economic forecasts were published at alternate intervals with the monetary policy statements. However, the Reserve Bank of New Zealand has decided to stop this publication; the last forecasts were published in March 1998. Since, the publication of the Monetary Policy Statements, which also include the contents of these economic forecasts, has been stepped up, to be issued at quarterly intervals.[788]

Finally, the Bank publishes weekly statistical releases, and a quarterly bulletin, which includes background articles, usually written by staff of the Bank, and reprints of speeches—among others—by the Governor of the Bank.[789]

Like the Reserve Bank of New Zealand, the **Bank of England** produces a monetary policy report in the form of the so-called inflation report, which not only assesses the past developments but includes an outlook on the development of inflation. Already since February 1993, in connection with the newly established inflation targets, the Bank of England has published a quarterly inflation report which reveals the current inflation and the prospects of inflation over the following 18–24 months. The publication of these reports was based on an informal agreement between the Chancellor of the Exchequer and the Bank. In the beginning the inflation report had to be approved by the Treasury prior to its publication, but in September 1993 the Chancellor announced that the inflation reports no longer required the approval of the Treasury.[790] However, the

---

[787] A current version of the Annual Plan can be obtained (online) from URL http://www.rbnz.govt.nz/ (last accessed Jan. 1999).

[788] The decision has been justified with the equal importance which is given the MPS and the economic forecasts by the financial markets, and the confusion which the publication of two different documents seems to have caused with parts of the public and the media.

[789] Much of it is to be found on the homepage of the Reserve Bank of New Zealand: cf. App. 3.

[790] It seems that the credibility of the inflation reports and, more specifically, the Bank's estimates on the prospect of inflation, were diminished by the fact that the draft of the inflation report had to be approved by the Treasury. In fact, the mistrust of the markets may have been justified to some extent, since the Treasury has been known to introduce changes to the contents of the inflation reports.

Treasury did not give up its influence over the contents of the inflation reports completely, since the Bank was obliged to inform the Treasury of its views expressed in the report prior to publication. The Bank of England Act 1998 has formalised the practice of publishing inflation reports. According to section 18 of the Act, the Bank is obliged to prepare and publish a report including a review of monetary policy decisions published by the Bank normally for the previous three months, an assessment of the developments in inflation in the UK economy for that period, as well as an indication of the expected approach to meeting the Bank's monetary objectives.[791]

The quarterly inflation reports by the Bank of England function as a guideline for the performance of, or even as an intermediate target for the Bank. First, the current progress of the Bank with regard to the inflation target previously set by the government can be judged on the basis of the data on inflation presented in the inflation report. To put it bluntly, "[t]he Report is a watchdog".[792] Moreover, the Bank's own estimate of inflation over the succeeding 18–24 months may add a short- or medium-term objective to the existing inflation target in the sense that the Bank's performance will not only be judged on the basis of the pre-set inflation target, but its own estimates will also be taken into account. Therefore, even if the Bank has reached the inflation target, it may nevertheless be subject to criticism with regard to its performance, if the Bank has failed to meet its estimates on the development of inflation for the six-month period up to the next inflation report. However, this also harbours the danger that the Bank might produce estimates which it is certain to reach. Furthermore, if it is postulated that the failure to meet the previously stated estimates for inflation results in a loss of credibility of the Bank, the estimates become something similar to objectives/goals, which the Bank tries to pursue in order to meet the self-imposed performance targets. The inflation report may also reflect the level of commitment of the Bank to the inflation target.

The Bank also publishes a quarterly bulletin, which includes a summary of monetary operations, and also articles and speeches by leading Bank officials on economic and financial topics.[793] It has been observed that under the new arrangements the Court of Directors has to forward a report on its activities on an annual basis to the Chancellor of the Exchequer, which includes a report on the activities of the MPC.[794] Other publications include speeches by the governor and the deputy governors, as well as working papers and consultative papers.

---

[791] The Treasury and the MPC may agree to have the report cover a different period of time.

[792] R. Pennant-Rea, "The Bank of England: Yesterday, Today, Tomorrow", in R. Roberts/D. Kynaston (eds.), *The Bank of England* (Clarendon Press, Oxford, 1995), 217–24.

[793] Prior to the introduction of the inflation report, it included a general economic commentary and assessment.

[794] Cf. Chap. 4 III 2.

When examining the budgetary position of the seven central banks examined in this study it can be observed that in not one single case does the budget of a central bank form part of the general government budget which is subject to parliamentary approval. The central banks are financially completely self-sufficient, as they finance themselves through operations in the financial markets. Despite the fact that the banks have to produce annual accounts which, one way or another, become subject to review by auditors and/or a Court of Auditors or the like, in the overall assessment the banks have a large degree of budgetary independence. The Reserve Bank of New Zealand may be considered as an exception in this respect, since the New Zealand legislator has chosen to make the central bank budget subject to an agreement with the executive government, thereby limiting the budgetary independence of the Bank.

In accordance with the EC Treaty and the statute of the ESCB and ECB the legal bases of the Member States' central banks participating in the ESCB must ensure that executive governments and/or the legislatures do not have any influence on the determination of the budget of the central bank or the distribution of profits to the extent that this could impede the proper functioning of the ESCB-related tasks. Moreover, it should be observed that with regard to ESCB-related tasks the accounts of the national central banks also become subject to a separate audit on the European level.[795]

1. Budgetary independence

The Fed, the Bank of England, the Nederlandsche Bank, and the ECB all stand for a large degree of budgetary independence. This is primarily marked by the fact that the central banks finance themselves through their own operations. Their financial resources do not form part of the general budget of the government and thus do not become subject to a parliamentary appropriation procedure. Another characteristic of these central banks is the restricted role, if any, which Court of Auditors or the like, charged with the general task of reviewing the spending of public money, plays in the review of the finances of the banks.

In the case of the **Fed** the net earnings of the Federal Reserve Banks, that is the earnings remaining after the deduction of necessary expenses, the payment of the annual dividend to stockholders and a small deposit to the surplus fund, are transferred to the Secretary of the Treasury for deposit in the general fund of the Treasury.[796] Until 1921 the Fed was subject to the audit by the Department of

---

[795] With regard to potential conflicts between the national and European audits cf. Smits, n. 487 above, 1997, at 168.

[796] Sec. 7(a) and (b) Federal Reserve Act (12 USC Sec. 290). The income of the Fed is mainly requisitioned through interest on US government securities acquired through open-market operations,

the Treasury. Thereafter, the task was taken over by the General Audit Office (GAO). The Banking Act of 1933 ended the audit by the GAO by confirming what had previously already been the principle, that is that the funds of the Fed did not represent "Government funds or appropriated money" and as such were not subject to the congressional appropriation process.[797] In the period thereafter, until 1952, the System was audited by teams from the Federal Reserve Banks. Since then, this has been done by outside private accounting firms which also prepare the reports. The Federal Banking Agency Accounting Act of 1978[798] subjects the Board of Governors, as well as the Federal Reserve Banks and their branches to audits by the General Accounting Office (GAO). However, a significant exemption is made with regard to the conduct of monetary policy. According to 12 USC Section 714(b):

> "Audits of the Federal Reserve Board and Federal reserve banks [by the Comptroller General] may not include—
> (1) transactions for or with a foreign central bank, government of a foreign country, or non-private international financing organisation;
> (2) *deliberations, decisions, or actions on monetary policy matters*, including discount window operations, reserves of member banks, securities credit, interest on deposits, and open-market operations;
> (3) transactions made under the direction of the Federal Open Market Committee; or
> (4) a part of a discussion or communication among or between members of the Board of Governors and officers and employees of the Fed related to clauses (1)–(3) of this subsection."[799]

This provision is often the starting point for proposals for institutional changes. The most far-reaching proposal has been to extend the audit of the GAO to include the monetary operations of the Fed.[800] The difficulty involved with these proposals is to agree on the extent of audit of the monetary policy operations by the GAO. Referring to discussions by the Comptroller General, head of the GAO, Smale points out differences between financial and performance-based audits.[801] Unlike financial audits, performance-based audits include an assessment not only of the situation but also the efficiency and economy of an organisation ("economy and efficiency audits") and, moreover, a review of the compliance of the organisation with legislation/programmes ("program audits"). The main fear of the opponents of an extended audit by the GOA is

discount rates, that is the interest earned from lending to commercial banks, and fees for services to commercial banks, interest on investment in foreign currency investments: cf. Board of Governors of the Federal Reserve System, n. 174 above, at 12.

[797] The Federal Reserve Banks have to forward their budgets to the Board of Governors for approval.

[798] Public Law 95–320.

[799] Italics added.

[800] Kettl, n. 183 above, 153 *et seq.*

[801] P. Smale, *Audits of the Federal Reserve System: Past, Present and Proposed*, CRS Report for Congress, 24 Jan. 1995 (Congressional Research Service, Library of Congress, Washington, DC, 1995).

that such an audit would not only relate to financial aspects, i.e. expenses for the conduct of monetary policy, but would also involve a general evaluation of the performance of the Board of Governors and the FOMC with regard to monetary policy and that this would deprive the Fed of its independent position; an argument which can equally be applied for other central banks.

The Fed does not publish detailed financial statements, but only summary statements as part of the Annual Report to Congress. While Fed officials will acknowledge the importance of these reports, as they display the results which the Fed has produced over the previous year, it also seems to be the general feeling that Congress does not show much interest in these reports compared to the semi-annual hearings. However, the Fed's operations do become subject to congressional hearings with Fed officials giving evidence.[802]

The fact that the budget of the Fed is not subject to congressional approval over the years has led to a number of congressional bills which have sought to change this situation by making the budget of the Fed subject to the general appropriation process of Congress.[803]

The budget of the **Bank of England** does not form part of the general government budget either, and thus is not subject to parliamentary approval. With regard to the allocation of the profits of the Bank, under the Bank of England Act 1998 the previously existing provisions have been amended to the effect that, as a rule, 25 per cent of the net profits (the profits stated in the audited accounts for the respective year less the amount of the tax charge) have to be paid to the Treasury.[804]

As has been the case under the Bank of England Act 1946, the new legislation generally puts the Court of Directors in charge of the financial affairs of the Bank. Internally, the sub-committee of the Board of Directors is in charge of keeping under review the internal financial controls of the Bank. It has to ensure the proper conduct of financial affairs, and has to monitor whether and to what extent the Board of Directors' financial management strategies have been implemented.[805] The Board of Directors has to make a report to the Chancellor of the Exchequer on its activities after the end of each financial year.[806] This report has to include a copy of the statement of accounts, which consists of a balance sheet and a profit and loss account for each financial year.[807] The Bank of England has to appoint one or more external auditors, who audit the accounts of the Bank and the statement of accounts, and issue a report on their findings. A copy of

---

[802] Cf. e.g. Testimony of Chairman Alan Greenspan Before the Committee on Banking, Housing, and Urban Affairs, US Senate, 26 July 1996, on the efficiency of the management of the Federal Reserve System.

[803] E.g. S.2417 (97th Congress); HR 2795 (101st Congress). For details see Smale, n. 801 above, 6 *et seq.*

[804] S. 8 Bank of England Act 1998.

[805] Ibid., ss. 2(2) and (4), and 3.

[806] Ibid., s. 4. Cf. also Chap. 4 III.

[807] Ibid., s. 7.

these reports, together with the statement of accounts, has to be sent to the Chancellor of the Exchequer, who may require the Bank in writing to publish any additional information.[808] Moreover, a copy of the reports and the statements is included in the Court of Directors' yearly report on its activities to the Chancellor of the Exchequer, which is forwarded by the latter to Parliament.[809] However, Parliament does not play any formal role in discharging the Bank. Moreover, an audit of the Bank's account by the Comptroller and Auditor General, who is not only charged with the appropriation of public funds, but also reviews the accounts of all Government departments and a large number of other public bodies, does not take place.[810]

In the case of the **Nederlandsche Bank**[811] a maximum of 20 per cent of the annual profits is paid into the general reserve fund of the Bank, which covers any losses sustained on the authorised capital of the Bank.[812] The remaining profits are transferred to the State.[813] The Supervisory Board plays a central role in the adoption of the annual accounts. According to section 28(1) of the Bank Act 1948 the Supervisory Board discharges the Governing Board by approving the balance sheet and the annual accounts. In accordance with section 139 of book 2 of the Dutch Civil Code, the members of the Governing Board are in principle liable for any damages arising from misleading information in the annual report, the annual accounts or interim data made public.[814] If the Supervisory Board has objections to the forwarded balance sheet and/or annual accounts it has to inform the Governing Board. If the Supervisory Board and the Governing Board cannot settle their differences, an expert committee consisting of five members is set up which subsequently is authorised to make the changes it regards necessary.[815] The balance sheet and the annual accounts as amended by this committee are thereafter approved by the Supervisory Board. Similarly, the Royal Commissioner can raise objections to the annual accounts, if he is of the opinion that they are incompatible with the Bank Act 1948 or the statute of the Bank.[816] If the differences with the Bank cannot be resolved, the problem is referred to a special panel of three arbitrators to be appointed equally by the

---

[808] Ibid., s. 7(3) and (9) on the applicability of the Companies Act to the Bank in preparing the profit and loss accounts.

[809] Ibid., s. 4(2)(b).

[810] The Bank of England is not listed among the bodies the accounts of which are audited. Cf. list of audited accounts (online) at URL http://www.open.gov.uk/nao/acs_aud.htm#intro (last accessed Jan. 1999).

[811] Note the new provisions (s. 18 *et seq.*) under the Bank Act 1998.

[812] Cf. s. 5 Bank Act 1948 on the reserve funds.

[813] S. 36 Bank Act 1948.

[814] As a company limited by shares the Nederlandsche Bank is in principle subject to the provisions on the annual accounts (annual balance sheet and profit and loss accounts) and the annual report laid down in book 2 of the Dutch Civil Code. However, s. 28a Bank Act 1948 excludes a number of provisions.

[815] S. 28(2) Bank Act 1948. The Supervisory Board and the Governing Board each select 2 members, and the fifth member is chosen by the 4 members.

[816] Ibid., s. 31(1).

Minister of Finance, the Governing Board and the president of the District Court of Amsterdam (*Rechtbank te Amsterdam*).

The Court of Audit (*Algemene Rekenkamer*) is in principle charged with the auditing of public companies whose issued share capital is owned by the State. It can examine the annual accounts, any reports reviewing the annual accounts and other documents, and can demand additional information from the respective minister, as well as from the company at issue. Although it has been observed that the state is the sole stockholder in the Nederlandsche Bank, according to section 59 of the Government Accounts Act (*Comptabiliteitswet*),[817] special provisions apply to the Nederlandsche Bank. The Court of Auditors cannot directly request documents or additional information from the Nederlandsche Bank, but rather this takes place through the Minister of Finance. Moreover, the Court of Auditors may only request documents concerning the annual accounts and any reports on these accounts.[818] The Nederlandsche Bank is exempt from specific investigations by the Court of Auditors.[819] This excludes in any event the review of the performance of the Bank in the area of monetary policy.

The General Council of the **Banque de France** plays a dominant role in the administration of the budget.[820] It decides on the allocation of the Bank's own funds by putting up a budget for expenditure and a statement on the anticipated profits for the financial year.[821] The proposal is reviewed by the members of the General Council as well as the Censor and his representative at least two months before the meeting of the General Council which addresses the budget.

According to Article 11(4) of the Bank Act 1993 the General Council draws up the balance sheet and accounts and proposes the appropriation of net profit and the dividend to be paid to the State.[822] At the end of each financial year the governor closes the annual accounts and establishes a report which describes the current situation of the Bank and its activities during the financial year. The General Council meets within four months of the end of the financial year to consider and discusses the annual accounts of the past financial year which are presented by the governor. The annual accounts of the Bank, including the balance sheet and the annual results, which have to be forwarded to the Finance Committees of both chambers of Parliament, are included in the Annual Report of the Bank.

---

[817] Wet van 8 december 1976, Stb. 671, as amended.

[818] S. 59(4) Government Accounts Act.

[819] Ibid., S. 59(3).

[820] Its financial resources derive from the performance of the Bank's main functions, that is the conduct of monetary policy and holding of the foreign exchange reserves and, moreover, from non-monetary related income, such as commercial banking operations and other operating income: cf. *Annual Report, 1995*, Direction générale des Études, Banques de France, Paris, 1996..

[821] Art. 11(4) Bank Act 1993; Art. 25 decree 1993.

[822] Arts. 27–28 decree 1993; also Arts. 29–32 decree 1993 on the accounting rules applying to the Banque de France.

In accordance with Article 11(5) of the Bank Act 1993 in conjunction with Article 33(3) of decree 1993, the General Council, on the recommendation of the governor, appoints two statutory auditors (*Commissaires aux Comptes*). The statutory auditors review the annual accounts of the Bank, whether they are regular and genuine and whether they provide a faithful picture of the operational results of the last financial year. The General Council also reviews the financial situation as at the end of the financial year. The auditors are invited to attend the meeting of the General Council at which the accounts have to be approved, and they present their findings.[823] It should be recalled in this context that according to Article 19(3) of the Bank Act 1993 the annual accounts and the report of the statutory auditors have to be forwarded to the financial committees of both chambers of Parliament. The auditor's report may be considered as a publication referring to the Bank, although it is not published by the Bank itself and is not included in the annual report.

Since the Banque de France resembles a public entity with the capital owned by the State, its accounts are subject to review by the Audit Office (*Cour des comptes*) which assists Parliament and the executive government in supervising the implementation of financial laws by reviewing the budgets and accounts of public entities.[824]

Apart from a minor part which functions *inter alia* as statutory savings, the majority of the profits of the **Bundesbank** have to be forwarded to the Federal government.[825] The Bundesbank has been exempted in important respects from the Federal Budget Order (*Bundeshaushaltsordnung*) which is generally applicable to immediate Federal legal persons under public law.[826] This includes in particular any participatory rights of the executive government in the budget of the Bundesbank.[827] According to § 26 of the BBankG the Board of Directors has to produce an annual statement of accounts (*Jahresabschluß*) for its performances as private banker in accordance with the principles of sound accounting practices.[828] The annual accounts are included in the annual report of the Bank. The Central Bank Council appoints, in agreement with the Federal Court of Auditors (*Bundesrechnungshof*), one or more certified accountants (*Wirtschaftsprüfer*) who examine the annual statement of accounts by the Board of Directors. The audit report by the certified accountants represents the basis for the examination by the Federal Court of Auditors (*Bundesrechnungshof*).[829] The Court of

---

[823] Art. 11(5) Bank Act 1993.

[824] For details e.g. C. Debbasch/J.-C. Ricci, *Contentieux administratif* (6th edn., Dalloz, Paris, 1994), 182 *et seq.*

[825] § 27 BBankG. The Bundesbank finances itself *inter alia* from the receipts from fees for the lending to domestic credit institutions.

[826] Cf. § 112 II *Bundeshaushaltsordnung*.

[827] Gramlich, n. 205 above, 190 *et seq.*; Brandt, n. 50 above, 22 *et seq.*

[828] The financial year of the Bundesbank corresponds with the calendar year.

[829] Cf Gesetz über den Bundesrechnungshof vom 11. Juli 1985, BGBl. I 1145; also Bundeshaushaltsordnung vom 19. August 1969, BGBl. III 63–1, §§ 105 *et seq.* on Federal legal persons under public law (*bundesunmittelbare juristische Personen des öffentlichen Rechts*).

Auditors may not only review the audit report, but may also itself undertake its own audit.[830] Yet, as with what has been observed for the Fed, according to the majority opinion it may not review the monetary policy decisions of the Bundesbank.[831] Outside the area of monetary policy decisions, the Bundesbank has been heavily criticised in the past by the Federal Court of Auditors for its financial behaviour.[832] The audit report together with the statements by the Federal Court of Auditors are then reported to the Minister of Finance. A direct presentation in Parliament is not foreseen. Moreover, in principle neither the government nor the Federal Court of Auditors has any particular means of forcing the Bundesbank to remedy certain behaviour.

The revised versions of §§ 26 and 27 of the BBankG, applicable in stage three of EMU, take into account the participation of the Bundesbank in the ECB with regard to the contents of the annual accounts and the profit distribution.

Like the above-mentioned central banks, primary Community law does not foresee any role of the EP in the determination of the budget of the **ECB**.[833] Apart from a certain percentage reserved for the general reserve fund of the ECB, the net profits of the ECB are distributed among the participating national central banks, representing the shareholders of the ECB, in accordance with the shares they hold in the ECB.[834] With regard to the accountability for the financial affairs of the ESCB, Article 26(2) of the ESCB Statute determines that:

> "The annual accounts of the ECB shall be drawn up by the Executive Board, in accordance with the principles established by the Governing Council and shall thereafter be published."

The accounts of the ECB *and* the national central banks are audited by external auditors appointed upon recommendation of the Governing Council of the ECB subject to the approval of the Council. In doing so the external auditors have full power to examine all books and accounts of the ECB and national central banks and obtain full information about their transactions.[835] Whether, apart from the annual accounts itself, the findings of the external auditors are published in a report does not become clear from the EC Treaty or the ESCB Statute.

Generally, the European Court of Auditors, charged with the examination of the accounts of revenue and expenditure of all bodies set up by the Community, is also competent for the ECB. However, under Article 27.2 of the ESCB Statute in connection with the second sentence of Article 188c(1) EC, this examination

---

[830] Gramlich, n. 205 above.

[831] v.Spindler/Becker/Starke. n. 215 above, § 26, Anm. 4.

[832] E.g. BTDrucks. 11/5383, 16 Oct. 1989, 120–5.

[833] The ECB will finance itself *inter alia* from the investments of the official reserves of the Member States, cf. R. Smits, n. 487 above, op. cit., 1997, at 167.

[834] Art. 33.1. ESCB Statute. Eventual losses are offset *inter alia* against the general reserve fund. With regard to the net profits which the national central banks make in the conduct of ESCB-related tasks; cf. Art. 32 ESCB Statute.

[835] Art. 27.1. ESCB Statute.

is restricted to the operational efficiency of the management of the ECB, and thus explicitly excludes a review of the efficiency of monetary policy operations. Although not explicitly foreseen, it is unclear why operational efficiency should not also become the subject of discussions in the EP on the basis of the annual accounts. The presentation of the annual report by the president of the ECB could be one occasion for such debate.

With regard to the national central banks Article 26.4 of the ESCB Statute orders the Governing Board of the ECB to establish rules which will standard-ise the accounting and reporting of operations undertaken by the national central banks.

2. Limited budgetary independence

The Reserve Bank of New Zealand stands out from the rest of the central banks presently examined in so far as Parliament plays a role in the setting up of the budget. Despite the fact that, like other central banks, the Reserve Bank finances itself through its own operations,[836] it is not *per se* free in its financial manage-ment. The basis of the expenditure of the Bank is an agreement between the Minister of Finance and the governor of the Reserve Bank. Moreover, the Bank has to publish extensive financial statements. Finally, the Bank's performance is reviewed by auditors.

According to section 159 of the Reserve Bank Act, the Minister of Finance and the governor enter into a so-called funding agreement. Unlike with the PTA, the House of Representatives plays an active role in the conclusion of the Funding Agreement. Pursuant to section 161 of the Reserve Bank Act 1989 the Minister of Finance has to lay each Funding Agreement before the House of Representatives. The House of Representatives does not have the power to introduce changes to the Agreement, but can deny its ratification. This effec-tively gives the House of Representatives a right of veto, since the Funding Agreement does not become effective unless ratified by a resolution of the House.[837]

The funding agreement consists of a written document similar to the PTA, which specifies the total expenditure to be incurred by the Bank in applying its income.[838] It also specifies the areas of expenditure which are supposed to be covered by this amount.[839] Generally, for each financial year a funding agree-ment applies, whereby one funding agreement covers a period comprising five

---

[836] Mainly from returns on investments funded by the issue of currency in circulation and by the Bank's equity base.

[837] S. 161(2) Reserve Bank Act 1989.

[838] Cf. App. 2.

[839] According to s. 3 of the 1995 Funding Agreement the Bank is self-funding in the areas of for-eign exchange dealings, settlement banking and government banking. Excluded therefore is expen-diture in connection with registry services under ss. 67 *et seq.* Reserve Bank Act 1989.

consecutive financial years.[840] By concluding an agreement for such a period the financial position of the Bank is ensured, thereby removing it from unanticipated changes by the government. Not only the Bank, but also the government, is committed to the financial plan. The objective of the funding agreement is to specify the amount of income of the Bank to be used to cover the non-commercial operating expenditure incurred by the Bank in each financial year.[841] As with the PTA the funding agreement specifies the circumstances that may justify a deviation from the agreed limits for expenditure. First, if the inflation target agreed upon in the PTA is amended, the limits for expenditure are adjusted in order to reflect any change between Bank's new and old path of inflation.[842] Secondly, changes in the nature or extent of the work undertaken by the Bank in respect of any of its functions and activities covered by the funding agreement lead to the re-determination of the levels of expenditure.[843] Moreover, the funding agreement can be suspended and exchanged for a new funding agreement by mutual agreement of the Minister of Finance and the governor of the Reserve Bank.[844]

The provisions on the funding agreement in the Reserve Bank Act 1989 are consistent with the broader public sector reform in New Zealand of which financial efficiency and accountability were important aspects.[845] It safeguards the financial position of the Bank, while ensuring that the Bank's financial incentives are not inconsistent with the Bank's overall economic objective according to the Reserve Bank Act 1989. The Reserve Bank itself emphasises that the funding agreement is designed to provide for accountability of the taxpayers' resources.[846] It is for this reason that the House of Representatives effectively has a right of veto in the case of a new funding agreement.

As is the case for the PTA, the funding agreement provides for structured accountability. It sets a clear yardstick against which the performance of the Bank can be judged. In doing so it adds to the transparency of the Bank as a whole. Moreover, by obliging the governor to sign the agreement, a specific person, charged with the performance of the Bank in accordance with the contents of the funding agreement, is identified.

In addition to the reports and publications of the Reserve Bank, the Bank is obliged to deliver to the Minister of Finance audited financial statements for each financial year. For this purpose one or more auditors are appointed by the Minister of Finance for a renewable term of office of two years.[847] The auditor's

---

[840] S. 159(2). The first Funding Agreement was signed on 17 Apr. 1991 and has since been replaced by the current Funding Agreement signed on 30 June 1995.

[841] Cf. s. 159(1) which specifies the areas of functions.

[842] S. 4(a) of the 1995 Funding Agreement.

[843] Ibid., s. 4(b).

[844] S. 159(3) Reserve Bank Act 1989; s. 4(c) of the 1995 funding agreement.

[845] Lloyd, n. 259 above, at 217.

[846] Reserve Bank of New Zealand, *An Introductory Guide* (Online), available from URL http://www.rbnz.govt.nz/ (last accessed Jan. 1999), s. 1, part 3.

[847] S. 166 Reserve Bank Act 1989. Under the Public Finance Act 1989, the audit is exercised by the Audit Office, or any other auditor appointed pursuant to any Act. The latter is the case for the Reserve Bank of New Zealand.

report on those financial statements and a statement of the projected income and expenditure for the next financial year also have to be forwarded to the Minister of Finance.[848] Section 164 of the Reserve Bank Act 1989 lists in detail the required contents of the financial statements. Alongside the financial statements, the Bank has to publish a management statement which comprises a statement of the management's responsibilities for the preparation of the annual financial statements and the judgements used in them, as well as a statement of its responsibility for establishing and maintaining a system of internal control designed to provide reasonable assurance regarding the integrity and reliability of financial reporting.[849] Moreover, the management statement has to include an explicit statement that, in the opinion of the management, the financial statements "fairly reflect the financial position of the Bank".[850]

Finally, the Minister of Finance has the right to appoint one or more persons to be the auditor or auditors of the Bank for a renewable period of up to two years.[851] The Reserve Bank Act 1989 does not specify the functions of the auditors.

[848] Ibid., s. 163(1)(b)–(d).
[849] Ibid., s. 165(1) and (2)(a)–(b).
[850] Ibid., s. 165(2)(c). These practices correspond with the requirements for financial statements of Crown agencies under the Public Finance Act 1989, cf. ss. 42 *et seq.*
[851] Ibid., s. 166.

5

Democratic Accountability—
Quo Vadis?

Having examined the structure of the central banks against the background of the chosen criteria, the final chapter focuses on the position of the concept of democratic accountability for central banks today. In a first step, a summarising look is taken at the degree of democratic accountability of the existing central bank systems included in this study. Instead of restating every detail of the different aspects of democratic accountability of each bank, the main lines of democratic accountability are traced, thereby gradually drawing a model of an accountable central bank. A fresh approach is considered in explaining democratic accountability by integrating the criteria which were developed in Chapter 2 into a broader approach to democratic accountability. Indeed, observing the concept of democratic accountability for central banks from a certain distance, a distinction emerges between criteria which amount to preconditions for democratic accountability and those which may be considered as instruments applied in exercising democratic accountability. This basic classification does not constitute a rigid system, as an element constituting a condition may also itself provide an instrument for holding the central bank accountable. Not least against the background of this evaluation, the institutional arrangements of the ECB are examined in conclusion with regard to possible institutional changes which have the potential to enhance its democratic accountability. Thereafter, this chapter will turn to the question whether and to what extent an index for the democratic accountability of central banks, similar to those for central bank independence, can be established. The chapter is finally rounded off by returning to the point of departure of this book in Chapter 2, and the relationship between central bank independence and democratic accountability.

I. CONDITIONS FOR DEMOCRATIC ACCOUNTABILITY

Parliament's right to change the legal basis, as well as the executive government's right to dismiss or not to re-appoint central bank officials, or to override the central bank, may be considered as instruments of democratic accountability. Yet, the effectiveness of these mechanisms of democratic accountability relies upon the existence of certain preconditions. The application of all of these instruments stands at the end of a decision-making process in which those institutions in charge of these instruments have to evaluate the past performance of the central bank. This assessment forms the platform on which a decision to apply any of the described instruments of democratic accountability is taken. Two elements may be considered as the supportive pillars of this platform: a yardstick is required in order to measure the performance of the bank, and an arena must exist which enables the review of the performance of the central bank.

1. Introducing a yardstick

First of all, a yardstick is needed for the body charged with holding the bank accountable in order to determine whether the central bank has satisfactorily discharged its duties. Where such a yardstick is missing, an assessment of the central bank performance as such may not take place, or is based on variables in the form of political or other indeterminate considerations. Both the monetary policy objective of a central bank and its projections on monetary policy and quantified intermediate targets can form the basis for such a yardstick.

1.1. Monetary policy objectives

Basically, the legal basis of every central bank examined in this study includes a provision which can form the basis of a yardstick, in the form of the monetary policy objective of the bank. However, this is not to say that all or even a majority of the central bank systems examined provide for an efficient yardstick to hold the bank accountable. Indeed, it has been observed that the monetary policy objectives range from broadly defined to quantified objectives. Broadly defined objectives may be considered the least useful in terms of providing a yardstick for the evaluation of the performance of the central bank. These objectives are characterised by a lack of clarity and/or the existence of multiple monetary objectives. Moreover, the legal basis of the central bank does not define the monetary policy objective in detail by introducing policy targets which the bank has to follow in order to achieve the monetary objectives. The central bank not only has to decide whether and when to apply the monetary policy instruments, but moreover has to define the monetary objective and decide on the approach it takes in achieving this objective. In economic terms such a central bank is described as having both instrument and goal independence. The same applies to central bank statutes which provide for a single monetary objective, e.g. price stability, or a clear hierarchy between several objectives, e.g. price stability and general economic policies, without however quantifying the monetary objective, e.g. price stability = 0–2 per cent inflation. Where a central bank has both instrument and goal independence, the body charged with holding the central bank accountable is not provided with an effective statutory yardstick for evaluatinge the performance of the bank, and thus for holding the bank accountable for its conduct of monetary policy. For this, not only must the legal basis of the bank provide for an unambiguous single, or at least, primary, monetary objective, but the objective should also be quantified. Whether the monetary policy objective is directed towards price stability or another economic aggregate is secondary from the point of view of democratic accountability, as long as it is quantifiable in a way that allows for the formulation of a point target or target range. To be sure, while it should not be left to the central bank to decide upon the monetary policy objective, the bank should be free to decide on the strategy for reaching the quantified objective. This includes not only the application of monetary policy instruments, but, moreover, the decision on intermediate targets e.g. in the form of growth rates.

Of the central bank systems examined, all but the Reserve Bank of New Zealand, and, recently, the Bank of England, lack a clear statutorily defined yardstick for holding the bank accountable. The Federal Reserve Act includes multiple objectives which are *de jure* of equal importance. It is left to the Board of Governors to interpret these objectives. The Federal Reserve Act also fails to provide sufficient guidelines for their implementation. The obligation of the Board of Governors to report to the Congress the objectives and plans of the Board of Governors and the FOMC with regard to the ranges of growth or diminution of the money and credit aggregates for the current and forthcoming year cannot substitute for a quantified objective. Besides, the Federal Reserve Act provides for an "escape clause" which allows the Fed to amend or deviate from the self-proclaimed targets by explaining the reasons to Congress. This diminishes the usefulness of the procedure under section 2A(1) of the Act as a yardstick for an *ex post* evaluation of the performance of the Fed by Congress. The monetary objective of the Nederlandsche Bank is likewise broadly defined. The monetary policy objective is the result of an interpretation by the Nederlandsche Bank rather than concrete provisions in the legal basis. Indeed, it derives from the genesis of the relevant provision that the interpretation of the monetary objective of the Bank applied today is not imperative.[1] In the case of the Bundesbank, at least according to the majority authors referred to, a hierarchy between the primary objective to safeguard the currency and the secondary objective to support the general economic policy of the Federal government exists. But it is open to interpretation what the primary objective stands for. Even if the majority view that the monetary objective effectively amounts to observing price stability is accepted, the legal basis does not provide for any definition of that objective. This is left to the Bundesbank.[2]

Unlike those of the central banks discussed above, the legal basis of the Banque de France not only provides for a clear hierarchy between the primary and secondary monetary objective, but moreover unambiguously defines the primary monetary objective, i.e. price stability. Yet, even here it is left to the

---

[1] Cf. Chap. 4 II 1.
[2] Chap. 4 II 1.

Banque de France to quantify the monetary objective. However, unlike in the case of the Fed and the Bundesbank, this is at least done by the Banque de France itself.

While it is in principle not ruled out that a quantification of the monetary policy target which has been decided upon by the central bank can function as a yardstick for the evaluation of its performance, this arrangement has a number of shortcomings.[3] Principally, it may be observed that it does not properly describe a principal–agent relationship when the agent defines the yardstick by which his performance is judged. Besides, it is questionable to what extent these self-announced quantifications amount to concrete rules, in particular in the light of potential deviations. The disadvantages associated with self-proclaimed quantifications can be avoided by choosing a firmer basis for quantification of the monetary policy objective. This can be done in the legal basis of the central bank, by an executive government announcement, or alternatively by applying the contract approach, the latter quantifying the monetary policy objective in an agreement between the government and the central bank. Since it is the central bank which in the end has to meet the quantified monetary objective in implementing monetary policy, it may enhance its commitment to define the monetary objective in the form of a target range in an agreement with the executive government. This latter approach is taken in the case of the Reserve Bank of New Zealand via a single monetary objective which is quantified in the form of a target range for inflation in the Policy Target Agreement between the executive government and the governor of the Bank, and which moreover fixes the conditions in which an exceptional deviation from this target is admitted. The performance of the bank can and in practice is judged on the basis of this target range, as any deviation from the target puts the governor of the bank under immediate pressure to justify the performance of the bank. The role of Parliament is limited to the *ex post* judgement of the performance of the Bank against the monetary policy objective as specified in the PTA, since it does not participate in the conclusion of the PTA. However, in the light of the occasional criticism of this, it is presently submitted that this statutory set-up merely reflects the common approach that monetary policy ultimately forms part of economic policy, for which the executive government is responsible. Thus, the quantification of the monetary policy objective falls within the responsibility of the executive government which is responsible *vis-à-vis* Parliament. The recently introduced institutional changes at the Bank of England, in many respects similar to the arrangements in New Zealand, also reflect this approach. The monetary policy objective of price stability is defined by the Treasury, which is obliged to announce policy targets on an annual basis. In the case of the Bank of England it can be argued that the transfer of operational responsibility over monetary policy to the Bank enhances the overall accountability for monetary policy in the UK, because a clear division of labour is introduced with the

---

[3] Cf. Chap. 2 II 2.2.2.

Treasury setting the inflation targets and the Bank being responsible for achieving these targets. However, unlike the legal basis of the Reserve Bank of New Zealand, the Bank of England Act 1998 does not define the circumstances under which a deviation from the targets is considered exceptional. Yet, by defining the situations in which a deviation from this target is considered exceptional, and hence justified, it is recognised that circumstances can arise which lie outside the responsibility or influence of the central bank, while at the same time the possibility of conflicts between the central bank and Parliament and/or the executive government over the justifiability of a deviation from the target are limited. The Bank of England Act 1998 also does not state the consequences of an unexceptional deviation. Yet it is the latter which forms a basic instrument of democratic accountability.[4]

The central bank should not itself be in charge of measuring progress in meeting the quantified monetary policy objective. Otherwise the central bank may find room for manoeuvre with regard to the interpretation of the economic data, possibly concealing its own shortcomings. This approach has been the subject of critical comments in relation to the Reserve Bank of New Zealand.

In the case of both the Reserve Bank of New Zealand and the Bank of England, not only are the banks committed to meeting the monetary policy objective as quantified, but, moreover, the respective executive governments have to spell out what their economic policy amounts to. In the case of the Reserve Bank of New Zealand this is included in the PTA, whereas in the case of the Bank of England the Treasury has to make a corresponding announcement at the time of the announcement of the annual inflation target. Such a government announcement of its economic policies is of particular value where a central bank statute calls for the supporting of the economic policy of the government as a secondary objective. The government announcement may give some guidelines as to what such an obligation may embrace. Although not quantified as the monetary policy objective, the economic policy of the government has to be defined to some extent. This also includes a commitment of the executive government. It becomes more easily recognisable when the latter is pursuing an economic policy contrary to its prior announcements.

Although the self-proclaimed intermediate targets of the Bundesbank cannot substitute a quantified monetary objective, they could in principle be applied to make the Bundesbank, and for that matter any other central bank pronouncing such targets, at least accountable for its self-proclaimed targets. Yet, at least in the case of Germany, experience in the past has been that there seems to be little interest in these intermediate targets as a means of performance-evaluation, and thus accountability, despite a rather mixed track-record of the Bundesbank in meeting these targets.

---

[4] Cf. Chap. 5 II.

1.2. Monetary policy projections

It has emerged from the examination in Chapter 4 that for some central banks another yardstick for judging the bank's performance with regard to monetary policy exists in the form of regular reports on monetary policy. To the extent to which these reports include details of past performance they may add to transparency in the conduct of monetary policy, as information is provided which can be used in evaluating the performance of the bank. These reports may also include projections as to future development of monetary policy in the form of forecasts by the bank with regard to the final monetary policy objective, or the intermediate targets. Such forecasts, estimations or projections not only indicate the bank's strategies in implementing monetary policy, but over time may themselves become a yardstick by which to measure the bank's performance in retrospect, with regard to both the achievement of the policy target and the bank's analytical abilities. In order to ensure that the central bank publishes its forecasts a corresponding provision should be included in the legal basis. If this is left to the discretion of the central bank, it may not have the incentive to make itself subject to additional judgement. In the case of New Zealand, the Reserve Bank publishes forecasts for "headline" and "underlying" inflation, and moreover explains its strategies in achieving the policy target as defined in the PTA. The inflation reports published by the Bank of the England equally include estimates of inflation. On the contrary, the Bundesbank does not explicitly publish forecasts, but, as has been observed, it does publish its intermediate targets.

2. Creating an arena

When referring to an arena as one of the prerequisites of democratic accountability this phrase is to be understood in a broad sense, including not only concrete fora in which monetary policy may become the subject of discussions, but also an environment which supports opinion-forming on the performance of the central bank. The latter point is a reference to the transparency with which a central bank conducts monetary policy.

2.1. Transparency

Information may be considered as the key to the evaluation of central bank performance. Yet, without transparency, information on the performance of the bank is difficult to come by. The central bank has to be committed to conducting monetary policy in a transparent manner. Generally, a trend towards a more transparent conduct of central banks can be detected. The exploding development in the area of computerisation can be considered an important factor in this development. Often these developments have been initiated by the central banks themselves. This may be explained by the "survival instinct" of the banks, which realise that public acceptance and credibility of their independent status may be the best insulation against executive or legislative intervention. Indeed, central bank credibility is the heading under which such measures are often discussed not only by central bankers. The difficulty with this approach is that conditions of democratic accountability are determined by those who are supposed to be held accountable. It is for this reason that it has been submitted above that it should not be left to the central bank to decide on the particulars of this transparency.

Transparency, first, stands for the openness of the decision-making process of a central bank and, thereafter, for the degree to which it explains its conduct in regular publications. Generally, it has to be recognised that the importance of the publication of minutes varies between central bank systems, depending on their institutional structure. Where monetary policy decisions are the sole responsibility of the governor of a central bank, minutes as such become superfluous, since no deliberations on monetary policy decisions take place. Thus, it is not surprising that in the case of the Reserve Bank of New Zealand, with the governor of the Reserve Bank of New Zealand being personally responsible for the conduct of monetary policy, no monetary policy board exists, and consequently no minutes of such meetings are published. In the case of such personalised responsibility for monetary policy the publication of an explanatory memorandum, stating the reasons for the decisions which have been taken, could be an alternative. On the contrary, where monetary policy decisions are conferred upon a collegiate organ within the bank, minutes may reveal the different views within the decision-making organ, as well as the motives behind monetary policy decisions. The insights deriving from such minutes flow into the evaluation of the performance of the central bank.

Despite the fact that all central banks consider transparency to be an important policy, in none of the systems presently examined are monetary policy decisions taken in the open. Not only the general public, but in a number of instances any third persons, are excluded from attending the meetings of the monetary policy board. Moreover, none of the central bank statutes provides for the immediate disclosure of the minutes of such meetings. Even the decisions taken at those meetings are not published in all instances. As has been observed, this is usually explained by the circumstance that public deliberations or the immediate disclosure of these deliberations may frustrate the effective implementation of monetary policy measures decided upon in these meetings. This indicates a basic conflict between full disclosure and an effective discharge by the central bank of its functions with regard to monetary policy. It is submitted that this potential conflict cannot be easily resolved in favour of disclosure and thus transparency. Indeed, it has to be recognised that while full disclosure would enhance transparency, the latter is not a goal in itself, but rather is meant to add to democratic accountability, which in return is supposed to secure the proper discharge by the central bank of its functions. Yet, where full disclosure has the potential of hindering the bank in the proper conduct of monetary policy, transparency, and for that matter democratic accountability, misses its objective. Besides, from the point of view of keeping the central bank accountable for monetary policy, a moderate time-lag between the taking of decisions and their publication together with the deliberations has little negative impact. What is decisive is that the minutes are made public within a period of time after which it still appears possible, and where there is still a basic interest, to hold the central bank accountable for its approach to monetary policy. Thus, Greenspan was in principle correct to observe that "in a democratic society all public policy making should be in the open, except when such a forum impedes the primary function assigned to an institution".[5] Thus, only those matters of policymaking remain closed which are essential for pursuing monetary policy with the goal of achieving the objective(s). To this end explicit rules have to be provided for in the legal basis of a central bank laying down the conditions under which minutes and decisions may be withheld. Besides, it should be ensured that this exempted information is published as soon as the circumstances justifying the withholding of the information no longer prevail. The Bank of England Act 1998 sets a positive example in this respect, as it governs such conditions profoundly.[6] It should in any event not be left to the central bank to decide whether and to what extent, and under what conditions, it publishes its minutes and decisions. Yet, this is the approach which has been observed for the Banque de France, where the legal basis leaves it to the discretion of the bank to decide on the publication of the minutes. The legal basis of the Nederlandsche Bank does not refer to minutes at all, and although minutes are reportedly kept, they are not published. But even if published, minutes have to reflect accurately the discussions on the monetary policy board, including voting behaviour, in order to be meaningful. The significance of voting behaviour can be determined from the recent events at the Bank of England, where the minutes of the MPC revealed open disagreement among its members on the question of an adjustment of the interest rate.[7] Revealing such differences of opinions in retrospect not only assists in judging the performance of the bank, and even individual central bank officials, with regard to the adequacy of their assessments, but also educates a larger audience in understanding monetary policy as a sequence of judgements based on more or less reliable economic data, rather than an exact science. The motives for monetary policy decisions need to become apparent, and contrary views among the members of the monetary policy board should be reflected in these minutes. Accordingly, not in all cases does the publication of minutes add anything to the accountability of the central bank. In the case of the Bundesbank the legislator has also left it to the Bundesbank to decide whether to publish minutes of the meetings of the Central Bank Council. Thus, the fact that the

---

[5] A. Greenspan, *Statement before the Committee on banking, Finance, and Urban Affairs*, US House of Representatives, 13 Oct. 1993, 1100–7, at 1005.

[6] Cf. Chap. 4 VII 1.

[7] Bank of England, *Minutes of the Monetary Policy Committee Meeting 7 and 8 January 1998*, available from: URL http://www.bankofengland.co.uk/mpcmtg.htm#ann (last accessed Oct. 1998).

Bundesbank publishes these minutes only after 30 years results in these minutes being of little practical value for transparency in the decision-making procedure of the Bank. In the case of the Fed, and more recently also the Bank of England, a different approach is taken. While in the case of the Bank of England minutes of the meetings of the MPC are published after the next meetings, and thus after four weeks, in the case of the Fed a diverse approach is taken. The minutes of the meetings of the FOMC are published after the following meeting (after five to eight weeks), whereas the minutes of the meetings of the Board of Governors are only published about quarterly. Interestingly, from the different approaches to the publication of minutes the conclusion may be drawn that the argument for secrecy does not seem to carry the same weight in all central bank systems.

Openness in the decision-making process of a central bank is only one, albeit very important, aspect of transparency. All of the central banks included in this study produce an impressive list of regular publications, occasional research and staff papers, speeches by central banks officials, and even take advantage of the new information technologies by publishing on the Internet. Yet, the number of publications tell little about their quality and usefulness as a basis for holding the central bank accountable for its conduct of monetary policy. What is decisive is whether and to what extent a central bank explains its conduct of monetary policy in regular reports, in addition to the annual report which each bank publishes. The annual report can add to, but not replace, such regular reports, by including reflections on the past performance of the bank and details of the future strategies for monetary policy. The introductory statements to the annual reports, which are usually reserved for the governors of the central banks, give the latter the opportunity to explain and possibly justify the performance of the bank. It has been observed for a number of central banks examined in this study that their legal bases in principle do not oblige the central banks to publish such regular reports on monetary policy. Nevertheless, all of them publish reports on a regular basis. But it should be observed that the content of these reports varies.[8] In order to ensure a minimum standard, the legal basis of a central bank should not only generally determine the publication of reports on a regular basis, but moreover define the minimum contents of such publications. Along the lines of the New Zealand model this should include reflections on the implementation of monetary policy, as well as the bank's plans with regard to the implementation of monetary policy in the future. Moreover, the bank should be obliged to specify and explain in these reports the strategies which it pursues in meeting the policy targets.

Finally, the point has been made that the whole structure of a central bank may also influence transparency. The clarity of the legal basis, e.g. with regard to the monetary objective, and the complexity of the decision-making processes within the bank are important factors influencing the level of the overall transparency of a bank. The more straightforward the provisions governing the cen-

---

[8] Cf. Chap. 4 VII 2.

tral bank, and the simpler its institutional structure, the more accessible the decision-making processes within the central bank may become for outsiders, and the easier it is to judge its performance. This is not so much a problem for centralised central bank systems as for decentralised systems. Of the central banks examined, arguably the prime example of such a bank is the Fed, with its somewhat complex decision-making structure.

Transparency not only serves the executive government and Parliament in judging the performance of the bank, but also influences the general public's perception of the central bank. Openness *vis-à-vis* the general public itself can become an important precondition for the democratic accountability of the central bank. Indeed, if an independent central bank has gained public confidence, a legislator planning to change crucial central bank provisions may feel unable to do so in the light of public opposition. On the contrary, a bank which does not have that public support may become subject to changes by a legislator which has come under public pressure to amend the legal basis of the central bank. Therefore, the central bank and the legislator are accountable to the general public for their actions, and loss of confidence of either of the two may lead to support of the other. Most central banks seem to be quite aware of this point and try to ensure public support.

2.2. Institutionalised contacts

The legal basis of a central bank should provide for institutionalised contacts between the bank and Parliament and the executive government. While the transparent conduct of monetary policy supports both Parliament and the executive government in its decision-making process about the performance of the bank, institutionalised contacts support the overall transparency of monetary policy. The executive government and Parliament have the opportunity to review the performance of the central bank with regard to monetary policy on a regular basis, while the central bank at the same time can explain and justify its conduct. These contacts have to be foreseen in the legal basis of the central bank, and thus institutionalised, in order to form the basis for the regular and ongoing accountability of the central bank *vis-à-vis* Parliament and/or the executive government.

The role of Parliament in holding the central bank accountable can be viewed as a constant reminder of the fact that a central bank in principle exercises monetary policy on behalf of the democratically elected Parliament which, at least in the national context, has delegated—but not abrogated—these powers.[9] However, in the case of both the Bundesbank and the Nederlandsche Bank the legal bases do not include any reference to Parliament, nor do central bank officials appear before Parliament on a *regular* basis.[10] Moreover, little evidence is

[9] Cf. Chap. 4 III 2.2.
[10] It has been observed that this changes under the Bank Act 1998 for the Nederlandsche Bank.

to be found of a strong involvement of Parliament with monetary policy and the central bank. The reasons for this lack of a direct relationship between Parliament and the central bank differ somewhat between the two countries, and have their foundation in the institutional structure of the banks as well as the peculiarities of the respective constitutional systems. In the case of the Bundesbank the subsidiary role of Parliament is considered to be a direct consequence of the statutory independence of the bank. On the contrary, in the Netherlands, the lack of any institutional relationship between the Nederlandsche Bank and Parliament has been a consequence of the consideration that in principle the Minister of Finance, and thus the executive government, is responsible for monetary policy *vis-à-vis* Parliament. Another explanation, valid for both central bank systems, is the general consensus which exists in the two countries with regard to the way in which the respective banks conduct monetary policy.

In the case of the Banque de France, the Reserve Bank of New Zealand and the Bank of England, the governors of the central banks do appear before parliamentary committees. Yet, for the Reserve Bank of New Zealand and the Bank of England this is due to the powerful position of parliamentary committees in the respective parliamentary system, rather than from concrete provisions in the legal bases of the banks. And while the governor of the Banque de France does appear before the Financial Committees of Parliament, and the statute of the Banque de France does refer to such appearances, there seems to be some disagreement between the bank and Parliament on whether the governor is actually obliged to appear.[11] Yet, the fact that proposals for the introduction of a stricter regime for reporting requirements were not considered may provide evidence for the assumption that an institutionalisation through appearances in regular intervals was deliberately left outside the statute of the Banque de France.

Indeed, of the central bank Acts examined in this study only the Federal Reserve Act follows through such a concept of statutorily-prescribed regular appearances before the Banking Committees of both Houses of Congress. Indeed, the Humphrey-Hawkins-Procedure arguably is the prime example of statutory provisions creating a forum in which Parliament can review the performance of the central bank at regular intervals. Over time these hearings have developed into an important event in the calendar, both for the members of Congress and the chairman and other members of the Board of Governors of the Federal Reserve System. Much of the interest which the Congress presently takes in the Fed and monetary policy in general can be attributed to the existence of these regular hearings. The point is that through the statutory obligation for regular hearings the contacts between Congress and the Fed have been institutionalised. As a result the Fed becomes obliged to explain and at times defend its conduct of monetary policy. At the same time Congress is required to deal with monetary policy and the performance of the Fed on a regular basis.

---

[11] Cf. Chap. 4 VI 1.

The decision in principle to review the performance of the central bank should be left to the discretion neither of the central bank nor of Parliament. However, this is the case where regular appearances are not obligatory, and where the central bank has discretion with regard to the question whether it appears and/or Parliament has discretion with regard to the question in principle whether it initiates such hearings by inviting the central bank officials. To be sure, parliamentary involvement with monetary policy does not necessarily require the appearance of central bank officials before parliamentary committees. It is also in principle possible to insert the executive government between Parliament and the central bank, such as is the case in the Netherlands. Where the executive government is ultimately responsible for monetary policy, the competent minister takes the place of the central bank officials in as much as the former should be obliged to explain himself at regular intervals before Parliament. However, this requires that the executive government holds instruments to hold the central bank accountable for its conduct of monetary policy, e.g. in the form of an override mechanism. Otherwise in practice nobody would be accountable for monetary policy because the central bank would not be directly accountable to Parliament, and the Minister could hardly be held accountable for the performance of monetary policy by a central bank over which he has no authority. While it is recognised that this system reflects the particular institutional structure of the Nederlandsche Bank, and the constitutional structure of the Netherlands, it may be questionable whether this system is to be preferred over direct accountability of the central bank to Parliament. First, it may be argued that the threat of political influence on monetary policy is greater in a system where the minister mediates the accountability for monetary policy between Parliament and the central bank. The minister can only be held accountable by Parliament to the extent to which he can have a guiding influence on monetary policy. For the rest neither the minister nor the central bank is accountable. On the contrary, direct contacts between Parliament and the central bank in the form of parliamentary hearings include a wide spectrum of political views including all parties represented in Parliament. Moreover, as has been observed for the Bank of England, the accountability for monetary policy may be diminished where it forms part of the overall economic policy for which a minister is responsible to Parliament. To be sure, a system of ministerial responsibility for monetary policy is unworkable in constitutional systems where the executive government is not directly answerable to Parliament, such as in the United States.

Institutionalised contacts between the central bank and the executive government are equally important. To the extent to which the latter is in charge of instruments for holding the bank accountable it too needs to review the performance of the bank. Informal contacts entail a higher risk of political pressure on the central bank to pursue polices other than those determined in the legal basis and the policy target. This not only conflicts with the independent position which a central bank may have, but moreover runs contrary to keeping the bank accountable for following the quantified monetary policy objective. It was observed that the relationship between the central bank and the executive government is to a large extent defined through the existence or absence of an explicit reference to the independence of the central bank in its legal basis. Where the emphasis has been placed on expressing the independent status of the central banks, provisions on the type and extent of co-operation between the central bank and the executive government also exist, whereas central bank legislation without such a provision also includes fewer details on the relationship between the central bank and the executive government. It could be argued that this makes sense since in the case of a statutorily independent central bank it is important to define the existing relationship between the bank and the executive government in detail. However, this view is flawed in as much as it implies that central banks without a separate provision on independence are by definition less independent from executive government, and thus do not require to the same extent provisions regulating the relationship with the executive government. Indeed, laws governing the positions of central banks, such as the Fed, which are commonly considered to enjoy a high degree of independence do not include an explicit reference to that independence in their legal basis. However, it cannot be concluded from the lack of relevant provisions in the legal basis of a central bank that the executive government is completely excluded from any dialogue with the central bank. Rather, such dialogues take place on an informal basis. Yet, these informal and discrete contacts may also be considered to carry with them a high danger of political influence on the bank. In as much as central bank systems with statutory independence also define the relationship between the central bank and the executive government they are to be favoured over central bank systems without an explicit reference to independence, but also without any reference to the relationship with government. This conclusion suggests that an explicit statutory reference to the independent position of the central bank may also indirectly have a positive influence with regard to the conditions of democratic accountability.

II. INSTRUMENTS OF DEMOCRATIC ACCOUNTABILITY

The conditions for democratic accountability have to be complemented by concrete instruments to hold the central bank democratically accountable. In the course of this study a number of instruments have emerged. The distribution of these instruments between the executive government and Parliament provides for the *democratic* element in keeping the central bank accountable. Moreover, they may also provide for a certain degree of checks and balances between the two branches, as often the executive government is accountable to Parliament.

1. Threat of change—the constraining effect of the legal basis

The legal basis is both a mechanism of *ex ante* and *ex post* democratic account-ability. In as much as Parliament has passed the respective legislation creating the central bank it has exercised *ex ante* accountability. Yet, this unique demo-cratic legitimisation cannot function as a mechanism for holding the central bank accountable for its performance of monetary policy, nor does it legitimise the removal of a central bank from mechanisms of democratic accountability. However, in as much as Parliament can amend the legislation it has once passed, it arguably possesses the most drastic instrument for holding the central bank accountable. It can decide to change the institutional structure of the central bank, thereby restricting its independent position and/or changing its tasks. In the case of all of the six national central banks included in this study, the legal basis is an Act of Parliament, and thus the latter reserves the right to change the legal basis of the central bank. In all but one case Parliament could even decide to abolish the central bank altogether. The Bundesbank is an exception in this respect, in as much as Article 88 of the Basic Law instructs the legislator to establish a Federal bank as currency- and note-issuing bank. In a number of instances the legal bases of central banks have been amended recently by their respective parliaments, bringing about considerable changes to the institutional structure of the banks. This has been the case for the Reserve Bank of New Zealand, the Banque de France and the Bank of England, the development in all of these cases having gone in the direction of more independence from govern-ment.

It is somewhat surprising that despite the emphasis on independence in some central bank systems, such as the Bundesbank and the Fed, the hurdle for amending the statute of the central bank appears to be relatively low at first sight. In the case of all six central bank systems, generally, a simple majority vote in Parliament is sufficient. Yet, a closer look reveals the diversity in the leg-islative procedures applicable in the different constitutional systems. On the one hand, a difference between single- and dual-chamber parliamentary systems can be observed. In parliamentary systems with two chambers the procedure for amending the legal basis is more complex. First, two chambers rather than one will examine the legislative proposal. Secondly, if the second chamber does not agree with the first chamber, the hurdles for the legislation to be adopted are higher. In the UK the House of Lords can only delay the signing into law of a bill which has the support of the House of Commons for two successive sessions of Parliament before the Bill can receive the Royal Assent, bypassing the House of Lords. In France (absolute majority), and Germany (either majority of the mem-bers or two-thirds majority), the upper chambers can be overruled by qualified majorities. Only in the Netherlands is a consent of both Houses mandatory for legislation to pass through Parliament. The United States may be considered an exception in as much as Bills which have passed both Houses of Congress may be vetoed by the US President as the head of the executive. In such a case both Houses of Congress have to pass the Bill with a two-thirds majority in order for the Bill to become law despite the Presidential veto. Of the national central banks examined in this study only in the case of the Reserve Bank of New Zealand does an amendment become law with a simple majority in the House of Representatives. The differences in the legislative procedures are of more than just academic interest, since in the case of some constitutional systems, including Germany, and the United States, at times one of the parliamentary chambers is dominated by the executive government, while the other is dominated by the opposition. In the case of the United States, moreover, the head of the executive may be a member of the political party which forms the minority in one or both Houses of Congress, as is presently the case with the Clinton administration. Moreover, differences may exist with regard to the organs authorised to introduce legislative proposals, and the conditions under which they may be introduced.

Although in all six national systems examined parliament holds the basic power to hold the central bank accountable for its past performance by changing the legal basis of the bank, no concrete evidence was offered in Chapter 4 that any of the parliaments has made use of this power to sanction certain past behaviour or performance of a national central bank. Moreover, little could be reported on parliamentary activities in the area of monetary policy. The only exception in this respect is the Fed, where Congress, although not meaning it as a punishment, at some stage has actually opted for an amendment of the Federal Reserve Act to strengthen the democratic accountability of the Fed. It has emerged from the examination of the different central banks that the reasons for the general absence of parliamentary activity differ, in some instances resulting from the institutional structure of the central bank, while in other instances political, or even social, reasons apply. Until recently, the Bank of England had neither goal nor instrument independence with regard to the conduct of monetary policy, as the Chancellor of the Exchequer was firmly in charge of monetary policy decisions, with the Bank basically fulfilling an advisory role. It may thus be argued that the accountability for monetary policy focused on the executive government rather than the Bank of England. Despite this *de jure* clear designation of responsibility for monetary policy to the executive government, in practice monetary policy was but one aspect of the overall responsibility of the executive government for the economy. Besides, in exercising its function as an adviser to the Chancellor of the Exchequer the actual influence of the Bank of England might have been more than that which can be concluded by observing the institutional arrangements. There may have existed a grey zone in which the Bank had *de facto* influence on monetary policy decisions, while at the same time the executive government was officially responsible for the conduct of monetary policy. In the case of the Nederlandsche Bank, the institutional structure of the Bank corresponds with the basic understanding that it is the executive government which is ultimately accountable to

Parliament for monetary policy. Thus, ministerial, rather than central bank accountability applies. In some cases, namely those of the Bundesbank and the Nederlandsche Bank, a broad parliamentary consensus can be observed for the position and performance of the respective central banks. Yet in the case of the Fed such consensus does not become apparent, bearing in mind the extensive discussions and legislative proposals to change just about any institutional aspect of the Fed. The simple answer may be that despite all this a majority still approves of the position of the Fed and its past performance. A somewhat more complex explanation entails understanding the relationship between the Fed and Congress as a dynamic one in which the latter uses its power to hold the Fed accountable, primarily, to ensure public support, while the former outwardly accepts is responsibility *vis-à-vis* Congress to ensure its own independent position.[12]

Since the establishment of the ESCB and the ECB the parliaments of the participating countries are restricted in their power to hold the central banks accountable via changes in their legal bases. The restriction is the extent to which the EC Treaty determines the legal set-up of the national central bank, by stating that the national central bank statutes have to be in accordance with the EC Treaty and the ESCB Statute.[13] The EC Treaty and the ESCB Statute determine the basic institutional structure of the national central banks with regard to their independent position. An amendment of a national central bank statute by the national legislator contrary to this basic structure would amount to a breach of primary Community law and could result in infringement proceedings against the respective Member State in accordance with Article 169 EC, initiated by the Commission, and possibly also another Member State (Article 170 EC). Thus it may be argued that an important element of *ex post* democratic accountability of the central bank *vis-à-vis* Parliament vanishes as a collateral to central bank independence. However, it may be observed that in as far as monetary policy is concerned, this instrument would in any event not be of much use for national parliaments once monetary policy decisions were decided upon by the ECB rather than independently by the national central banks, because in the Governing Council each central bank governor has only one vote in monetary policy decisions. The emphasis shifts from the national to the European level, and focuses on the ECB, and the question is whether here a similar mechanism exists.[14]

2. Collegiate principle v. personal responsibility—the (re-)appointment and dismissal of decision-makers

The dismissal, but also the (re-)appointment of central bank officials charged with making monetary policy decisions can function as an instrument of

[12] Cf. Chap. 4VI 1.
[13] Art. 108 EC.
[14] Cf. Chap. 5 III 1.

democratic accountability. It has become clear from the examination of the six national central bank systems that in all cases the executive government is basically in charge of appointing the members of the different organs of the central bank, namely the policy and managerial boards. But the appointment procedure is of only limited value as an instrument of accountability. Although it can be regarded as an expression of the democratic nature of the appointment procedures, which in return may function as part of a democratic legitimation of the central bank and its decision-makers, it adds little to the evaluation of the past performance of the central bank. In all central bank systems appointments of central bank officials in the final analysis are political and usually reflect both the structure of the central bank and the country it is situated in. This can in particular be observed for central bank systems with a structure which entails elements of decentralisation, situated in a federally organised state, such as the Bundesbank, and the Fed. Only in two cases does Parliament play a role in the appointment procedures at all. In France, the members of the CPM, other than the governor and deputy governor, are appointed on the basis of a list of names which is drawn up with the participation of the National Assembly, the Senate and the Economic and Social Council. Yet, even here the democratic element may not carry very far, since the executive government can still choose from a list comprising three times the number of names compared to the positions to be filled. Besides, arguably the two most important positions at the Banque de France, the appointment of the governor and deputy governors, have been excluded from this procedure, leaving it entirely to the executive government to decide. The US Senate has a more powerful position in this respect. Rather than only taking part in the selection of candidates, the Presidential appointments to the Board of Governors and the nomination of the chairman and vice-chairman of the Board require the consent of the Senate. It has been observed that this amounts to more than a formality as candidates, and in particular the future chairman and vice chairman, may face substantial questioning by the Banking Committees. In the UK the proposals for the new Bank of England Act 1998 in the context of granting the Bank of England operational independence for monetary policy included proposals to involve Parliament in the appointment procedures. In the final version of the Act such a right has not been included however. In Germany and the Netherlands, Parliament does not play any role in the appointment of central bank officials. It should be noted in this context that the participation of the Bundesrat in the appointment of the presidents of the state central banks, which also participate in the Central Bank Council of the Bundesbank, does not amount to genuine parliamentary participation, as sometimes suggested, in the sense that the State executive governments put forward the recommendations for the appointments. Interestingly, even in the case of the Reserve Bank of New Zealand, often considered as a prime example of a more democratic approach to central banking, the House of Representatives does not participate in the appointment procedures.

From the point of view of democratic accountability, the term of office of the central bank officials is important in as much as it determines the period of time in which certain political appointments are in charge of monetary policy. In the national context the difficulty with long terms of office is that a newly elected government may have the incentive to change the political appointments of the former government. Yet, it is precisely for this reason that proponents of central bank independence are in favour of long terms which do not coincide with government elections. However, with the monetary policy objective clearly stated in the legal basis and moreover quantified, there may be little to be gained in substance with regard to political influence for a new government with new appointments. Instead, the policy target approach could be followed through and the possibility for the executive government either to announce or negotiate a new policy target could be opened. Though, while this approach seems to work in the case of the Reserve Bank of New Zealand where differences in the PTA for different governments could be observed, it is questionable whether such an approach could work in countries with a history of executive governments resigning prior to the end of their term of office, such as has been the case in the past in Italy.

While the appointment procedure itself is of limited value as an instrument of democratic accountability, the possibility of the reappointment of central bank officials can be an instrument for holding the latter accountable for their behaviour, and for passing judgement on the performance of the bank in the area of monetary policy. Different approaches to the reappointment of central bank officials have been observed. In some instances the members of the monetary policy board can be reappointed for an unlimited number of terms, as is the case in the United Kingdom, Germany, the Netherlands, and New Zealand. In other countries only the governor and deputy governor may be reappointed once, as is the case in France, or certain members of the monetary policy board are excluded from reappointment, such as is the case for the Fed. Generally, the possibility of reappointment offers the opportunity to pass judgement on the past performance of the central bank official concerned. On the contrary, this may also provide politicians with the opportunity of influencing or even putting pressure on central bank officials to consider their demands. Thus do democratic accountability and central bank independence for once contradict each other? It has been observed above that political pressure does not necessarily result in more democratic accountability. Yet, whether the possibility of reappointment automatically leads to government-conforming central bankers is questionable. The fact that the members of the Board of Directors of the Bundesbank, who as *ex officio* members of the Central Bank Council take part in monetary policy decisions, often serve a number of terms, certainly has not damaged its reputation as an independent central bank.[15]

Another solution could be to make the reappointment subject to conditions along the lines of the dismissal procedures of the Reserve Bank of New Zealand.

---

[15] Cf. Chap. 4 IV 1.

This would embrace making the reappointment of central bank officials subject to their performance in meeting the monetary objective of the bank, whereby the criteria would have to be laid down in detail in order to exclude an abuse of the procedure. However, this approach has its limits. It requires the transfer of responsibility for monetary policy decisions onto a single central bank official, most likely in the person of the governor of the bank, who is personally responsible for achieving the monetary policy objective. The decision to reappoint the governor could then be based on his track-record. Yet, where monetary policy decisions are taken in collegiate form it would be difficult to introduce such a performance-based reappointment, since the individual performances of members of the monetary policy board are difficult, if not impossible, to judge.[16] However, passing judgement on the monetary policy board as a whole will be difficult to achieve, since the central bank officials usually serve staggered terms in order to safeguard the personal continuity of the bank. The suggested solution is to assign responsibility for monetary policy to the governor of the bank, but this proposal may only be a realistic option in centralised central bank systems. More decentralised central bank systems are often characterised by diverse representation on the monetary policy board, at times reflecting the constitutional structure of the country in which the central bank is located. This has for example been observed for the Bundesbank. This point is sometimes overlooked by those proposing to make the governor of the central bank accountable for the achievement of the quantified monetary policy objective.

Even more than the possibility of reappointments, the dismissal of central bank officials can be an instrument of democratic accountability. All but one of the central banks examined feature similar arrangements for the dismissal of central bank officials, according to which a dismissal is only legitimate in the case of the inability of a central bank official to perform his or her duties, or serious misconduct. In no instance is serious misconduct interpreted as including the failure to discharge functions properly in accordance with the statutory objectives of the central bank, and thus in terms of bad performance. Rather, serious misconduct is understood in terms of fraudulent behaviour.[17] In the case of some of the central bank statutes presently examined even this restricted right of dismissal results from statutory interpretations rather than concrete provisions in the legal basis of the bank. The statute of the Bundesbank does not include any provision on dismissal at all, whereas in the case of the Fed the Federal Reserve Act, somewhat vaguely, demands the existence of "cause". The threat of dismissal is largely ineffective as an instrument of democratic accountability to the extent that dismissal on grounds of past performance of central

---

[16] R. Chote, "Victims of 'Groupthinking' ", *Financial Times*, 7 Sept. 1998.

[17] Taking into account the powerful position which central bank officials hold, one may even wonder whether it is acceptable to exclude a dismissal for slight misconduct. Sometimes people fall on their own sword, after revelations of a personal nature, as happened when the deputy governor of the Bank of England, Rupert Pennant-Rea resigned.

bank officials is excluded.[18] This is even more the case when the initiative for dismissal has to come from within the bank, as is the case for the Nederlandsche Bank and the Bank of England. In the case of the Nederlandsche Bank actually the same body from which a member may be dismissed has to propose such a dismissal.[19]

The Reserve Bank of New Zealand constitutes an exception in this context in as much as its legal basis allows for a performance-based replacement of the governor, namely if the performance of the latter with regard to meeting monetary policy targets is considered "inadequate". The Reserve Bank itself summarises this in the following: "[t]he focus of power on a single individual acts to reinforce accountability, by making clear the 'ownership' of decisions and actions and by preventing diffusion of responsibility".[20] Yet, it has been pointed out that the relevant provisions of the Reserve Bank Act 1989 are not entirely unequivocal, as they leave the executive government with a certain amount of discretion in the decision to dismiss the governor. It cannot be concluded from the Reserve Bank Act 1989 that the performance of the governor is automatically considered inadequate if the Bank has not met the inflation target. This is confirmed by actual events. For example, when it was determined that underlying inflation in New Zealand for the year ending March 1996 had exceeded the target range of 0–2 per cent, the executive government demanded an explanation, which thereafter was provided in writing by the governor, but the governor was not discharged.[21] The discretion which the executive government possesses leaves room for the decision to apply the procedure, but also to abstain from applying it, depending on what might be politically opportune. There is even the possibility of horse-trading whereby the executive government leaves the governor in office in return for taking the government's wishes into consideration in implementing monetary policy. Excluding this risk demands the introduction of an automatic process whereby the governor of the bank is dismissed where certain conditions exist, such as an unexceptional deviation from the policy target. In this context, additionally, it can be observed that the legal basis of the Reserve Bank does not provide for any kind of review of the decision of the executive government to apply the mechanism.

In the light of the overall positive assessment of the arrangements at the Reserve Bank of New Zealand, the question arises whether this system of performance-based dismissal could equally be introduced for other central banks. As with the proposals for performance-based reappointment, performance-based dismissal in practice would only be possible in central banks with a clear

---

[18] The dismissal of central bank officials of the Nederlandsche Bank for failure to comply with the directions of the Minister of Finance in applying the override mechanism are presently not considered as dismissal based on the past performance with regard to monetary policy objective of the Bank.

[19] Cf. Chap. 4 IV 2.

[20] Reserve Bank of New Zealand, op. cit., Chap. 3, n. 461, at 8.

[21] Cf. Federal Reserve Bank of San Francisco, *Accountability in Practice: Recent Monetary Policy in New Zealand*, FRBSF Economic Letter No. 96–25; 9 Sept. 1996.

hierarchy, where the governor is ultimately responsible for monetary policy, as is the case in New Zealand. Where monetary policy decisions are taken in collegiate form it becomes impractical to introduce such performance-based dismissal, because the monetary policy board would have to be replaced as a whole, as the option of dismissing a certain group within the monetary policy board which has made up the majority in past key monetary policy decisions is somewhat unrealistic. However, this excludes the application of such a mechanism for any central bank system incorporating Federal structures, or otherwise featuring a monetary policy board in which the governor of the bank does not have a decisive vote. A step in the right direction could be to link the failure to meet the quantified monetary policy objective to concrete sanctions for the central bankers in the form of a cut in salaries.[22]

3. The stick behind the back—the override mechanism

The existence of an override mechanism can be regarded as an important instrument of democratic accountability. This is the case not only in the sense that the central bank may be overridden in case of sub-optimal performance, and thus a means of sanctioning, but also in the sense that with the executive government in charge of this instrument the overall responsibility of the latter for economic policy is recognised.[23] Moreover, in countries where the executive government is thought to be ultimately responsible for monetary policy, the existence of an override mechanism can build the required bridge between the conduct of monetary policy by the central bank and the overall responsibility of the executive government *vis-à-vis* Parliament. The existence of an override mechanism has emerged as one of the criteria in which substantial differences exist between the different central banks. Despite the different forms of override mechanisms observed in Chapter 2, in the course of Chapter 4 only two types of override mechanisms have surfaced. The limited override mechanism of the Bundesbank and the full override mechanisms of the Nederlandsche Bank, the Reserve Bank of New Zealand and the Bank of England. The fundamental difference between these two forms of override mechanisms is that in the case of the former, the central bank continues to formulate and implement monetary policy in accordance with the monetary policy objective stated in the legal basis, as the executive government can only delay the taking of any particular decision for a period of two weeks, and thus for the period between two meetings of the Central Bank Council of the Bundesbank. The executive government can neither overrule a decision by the Central Bank Council, nor can it force the latter to implement certain policies. It can only negotiate some additional time to try to convince the

---

[22] E.g. S. Fischer, op. cit., Chap. 2, n. 39, at 293. In the UK if a motion is carried in the House of Commons that the salary of a Minister be reduced by one penny, the Minister has to resign.

[23] Cf. Chap. 2 II 2.2.5.

central bankers of its views. From this point of view it may be described as a provisional override mechanism, whereby the word *override* tends to overstate the magnitude of the mechanism. Moreover, the lack of transparency of the override mechanism may be highlighted by the fact that, despite the official line that the override has never been applied, doubts have been raised about the accuracy of this statement. The override mechanisms to be found for the Nederlandsche Bank, the Reserve Bank of New Zealand and also the Bank of England, reach further, not only in this respect. The executive government can direct the Bank to implement monetary policy for objectives other than those set out in the legal basis of the Bank. In fact, the best form of an override mechanism may constitute a combination of the approaches taken in the statutes of the three different central banks.

First, the application of the override mechanism should not be unconditional. The legal basis of the central bank should lay down in detail the conditions under which an application of the override mechanism is admissible, e.g. by defining the exceptional economic circumstances in which the central bank may be overridden. To be sure, the application will have to be decided on a case-by-case basis, but the discretion of the executive government should be limited to predetermined exceptional circumstances.[24] In this respect the Bank of England Act 1998 points in the right direction by referring to "public interest" and "extreme economic circumstances" as conditions, but in its current form it falls short of providing any details of how to interpret these indefinite terms. The legal basis of the Nederlandsche Bank, and also that of the Reserve Bank of New Zealand, includes no provision in this respect. However, in the case of the Reserve Bank of New Zealand the legal basis otherwise restricts the executive government in its application of the override mechanism by extending the working of the PTA. The Minister of Finance and the governor of the Reserve Bank have to fix a new policy target in accordance with the government-prescribed economic objective. In a way these arrangements hold accountable both the executive government in applying the override mechanism, and the central bank in performing monetary policy in conformity with government directions. The executive government has to define what its overriding policy is, while at the same time the Reserve Bank remains fully accountable for its performance. Interestingly, the application of the override mechanism for the Reserve Bank of New Zealand is not limited.[25] In the case of the Bank of England, the "reserve powers" of the Treasury foreseen in the Bank of England Act 1998 may be applied for a maximum period of three months before ceasing to have effect. It has been observed that it is not ruled out in principle that the Treasury may issue a new order, which, however, once again has to be approved by Parliament. The override mechanism applicable for the Nederlandsche Bank is even more liberal as no time-limit applies in the first place.

[24] However, P. Brentford, op. cit., Chap. 2, n. 191, at 108, suggests that the government may choose not to make use of mechanism for sake of political considerations, such as elections.
[25] Cf. Chap. 4 V 3.

Generally, the application of the override mechanism should be limited in time from the outset. It is suggested that the period of its application should be bound to the duration of the exceptional circumstances which have given rise to the application of the mechanism in the first place.

Apart from making the application subject to certain conditions, the decision to apply the override should also be subject to review. This can basically be achieved in two ways. First, following the approach taken in the Bank of England Act 1998, the executive government's decision to apply the override could be made subject to approval by Parliament. However, the restricting effect of such parliamentary consent may be limited in parliamentary democracies where the executive government usually reflects the majorities in Parliament. In such a case parliamentary consent alone cannot ensure that the override mechanism is not used for political ends. Another approach is to give the central bank a right to appeal against the application of the override mechanism. While the legal basis of the Nederlandsche Bank may be considered weak with regard to the definition of the conditions and timing for an application of the override mechanism, it does include one unique feature not to be found in the other central bank systems, by granting the monetary policy board of the bank the right to appeal against a decision by the Minister of Finance to override the bank. Interestingly, the same executive government which, in the person of the Minister of Finance, has decided to apply the override mechanism in the first place, thereafter, in the composition of the Council of Ministers, also decides on the validity of the objection by the Bank. Thus, the instrument amounts to a reconsideration, rather than a real appeal. However, since the Council of Ministers is obliged to publish a decision overturning the bank's objection, together with the objection itself, in the Dutch Government Gazette, it can at least be assumed that it would give the objection of the bank, together with the initial decision to apply the override mechanism, considerable (second) thought. This also implies that Parliament is likely to discuss the matter with possible consequences for the Minister of Finance or the Cabinet if Parliament supports the Bank's objections.

Despite the theoretical evidence supporting the view that an effective override mechanism can add to democratic accountability of a central bank, empirical evidence seems less convincing at first sight. Neither in the case of the Nederlandsche Bank, nor the Reserve Bank of New Zealand has the override mechanism been used in the past. Even whether the limited override mechanism for the Bundesbank has been applied is questionable, although evidence has been presented suggesting an application in the past.[26] The question arises whether this is a sign that there have not been any serious conflicts between the central bank and the executive government, or, on the contrary, that the override mechanism is not properly applied in holding the central bank accountable.

---

[26] Chap. 4 V 3.

Neither of these two explanations by itself may be considered satisfactory. Rather, the point of departure for a comprehensive understanding must be that in all of these systems, and thus not only the Nederlandsche Bank, the application of the override mechanism is considered as an *ultimum remedium*, a last resort.[27] This is not least the view of the general public which would consider an application as a sign of a major conflict between the executive government and the central bank, potentially having a destabilising effect on the economy. Executive governments may thus be very reluctant to apply the override mechanism.

Yet the central bank too has an incentive to avoid being overridden by the executive government, since this potentially also damages its own credibility, in particular as an independent monetary authority, in the financial markets, and moreover with the general public, which may begin to question the role of the bank. The override mechanism functions as a "stick behind the back" in the hands of the executive government, which provides the central bank with some motivation for behaving in a manner which will prevent it from being overridden. This "stick" comes in different sizes for different central bank systems, since the postponement of a particular decision on monetary policy to the following meeting is certainly less severe than the issue of directions by the executive government. The experiences in the central bank systems examined in this study suggest that the existence of an override mechanism may make its application superfluous. On a broader scale it may be concluded that the override mechanism holds the relationship between the executive government and the bank in the balance, since both sides may only lose by its application. At the same time, with the introduction of an override mechanism the executive government becomes responsible to Parliament for its decision to apply or not to apply the mechanism, which implies the acceptance by the former of the monetary policy as conducted by the central bank.

It has been observed that primary Community law excludes the existence of any kind of override mechanism for the national central banks participating in the ESCB. Since monetary policy decisions are taken by the ECB, this mechanism would be of limited value in the national context anyway. However, this is not to say that such a mechanism could not be of similar importance in the European context. This point is further developed in the final assessment of the ESCB and ECB.

4. Checking where the money goes—budgetary accountability

Budgetary accountability is a subject area sometimes neglected in reflections on the democratic accountability of central banks. Yet, where central banks constitute institutions under public law, or institutions in which the state is the sole

---

[27]   This expression has been coined for the Nederlandsche Bank: cf. Chap. 4 V 3.

shareholder, the money spent by the central bank in performing monetary policy, as well as any profits it makes, may be considered as part of the national wealth. Indeed, in some instances the annual profits of the central bank have become a substantial item in the government budget, whereby unexpectedly high profits are readily accepted to polish up the tight government budget. To hold the central bank responsible for its financial conduct is thus an important element of democratic accountability.

In the course of this study two main issues have emerged with regard to budgetary accountability. The first issue is related to the fact that in the case of none of the central banks examined in this study is the budget of the central bank made up of taxpayers' money. Central banks are financially self-supporting in as much as they finance their expenses from profits from operations—mainly—in the financial markets. As a result the central banks do not receive money out of the government budget. Since the budget of the central bank does not form part of the general budget of the government it is not subject to parliamentary approval. It may therefore be concluded that in the case of the central bank Parliament is deprived of what may very well be described as one of the areas in which Parliament has the most influence, budgetary control. Parliamentary approval of the central bank budget as a means of *ex ante* democratic accountability, but also as a means to sanction the bank *ex post* for past performance, is thus excluded.

It may be observed that the power to appropriate budget is essentially the power to control, and in essence it is this knowledge which makes proponents of central bank independence believe that parliamentary control over the central bank budget is bound to result in a decline of independence for the central bank and, subsequently, in a sub-optimal monetary policy.[28] Yet, the arrangements at the Reserve Bank of New Zealand may offer an approach which can reconcile the seemingly incompatible concepts of budgetary accountability and central bank independence. With the funding agreement a contract approach similar to the PTA has been chosen. Although Parliament cannot determine the contents of the agreement which is concluded between the Minister of Finance and the governor of the bank, it can actually veto the coming into effect of the agreement. Since the budget of the bank remains outside the parliamentary appropriation process, and, furthermore, the funding agreement covers a period of five financial years, the financial position of the bank is secured, once the funding agreement is signed, removing it from unanticipated changes by the government.

The second issue arising in the context of budgetary accountability relates to the *ex post* budgetary democratic accountability of the central bank and the question of whether and to what extent the financial operations of the central banks can be audited by a court of auditors or an institution fulfilling that function. A full audit may be regarded as potentially conflicting with the indepen-

---

[28] The economic case for central bank independence has been observed in Chap. 2 I.

dence of the central bank, similar to an application of the parliamentary appropriation process, in as much as such an audit includes a review of monetary policy decisions with financial implications. It is thus not surprising that the *ex post* budgetary accountability, first, focuses on a review of the annual accounts and balance sheets by independent auditors, and, thereafter, if applicable, by a court of auditors, with monetary policy decisions and the like explicitly or implicitly being excluded. The former is for example the case for the Fed. The latter is the case for the Bundesbank, where such a restriction is interpreted from its legal basis. It is presently argued that an enhanced audit by the court of auditors is not required in order to ensure the budgetary accountability of a central bank. First of all, it should be the executive government and Parliament in the first place who hold the central bank accountable for its conduct of monetary policy, rather than an independent organ which has been charged with a very specific task, not at all related to passing judgement on policy choices. Moreover, in so far as the operations of the bank with regard to monetary policy have financial implications, the abovementioned funding agreement could function as a yardstick. Indeed, having a funding agreement which specifies the expenses for the different areas of operation makes it superfluous to introduce a review of financial aspects of monetary policy decisions. Instead, the actual expenses can be reviewed against the background of that agreement.

III. THE *STATUS QUO* AND FUTURE OF THE DEMOCRATIC ACCOUNTABILITY OF THE ECB

What has emerged from the foregoing discussion is something like a blueprint for the democratic accountability of central banks, embracing both instruments and pre-conditions required for an effective democratic accountability. The first question which arises is how the democratic accountability of the ESCB and the ECB is to be evaluated against the background of this blueprint. Have the lessons, which could arguably be learned from experiences with the existing central bank systems, influenced the institutional structure of the ECB with regard to its democratic accountability? To the extent that this has not been the case, how could changes of the legal basis enhance the democratic accountability of the ECB?

1. The subsidiary role of democratic accountability

Compared with the importance which has been assigned to the independence of the ECB, the concept of democratic accountability plays a subsidiary role in the institutional structure of the ECB.

The legal basis of the ESCB does not introduce a clear yardstick for judging the performance of the ECB with regard to monetary policy. Although the EC Treaty and the ESCB Statute unambiguously declare price stability to be the primary monetary policy objective, a quantification of that objective is missing. With a statutory or contractually agreed point target or target range missing, it is the ECB itself which, to some extent, decides upon the yardstick which will be applied in measuring its performance. The ECB not only implements monetary policy with the instruments at its disposal, but moreover quantifies the monetary policy objective. It has instrument and, to some extent, goal independence. To be sure, an inflation rate of 5 per cent would definitely be considered to be inconsistent with the monetary objective of price stability as formulated by primary Community law. But it is not so clear, for example, whether 3 per cent inflation is consistent or inconsistent with this objective.

The EC Treaty and the ESCB Statute in its present form are weak, both with regard to transparency and institutionalised contacts. It has repeatedly been emphasised by the different parties involved in the preparation of EMU, and notably by the Commission and the EMI, that the ECB will operate in a transparent manner. The EMI describes transparency as one of the guiding principles, by which "the process of setting targets and making decisions on the basis of the strategy must be clear to the public".[29] Yet, it stands out that the legal basis does not contain any provisions on the publication or even maintenance of minutes of the meetings of the Governing Council of the ECB. Indeed, while it becomes clear from the Rules of Procedure of the European Central Bank that minutes of the meetings of the Governing Council are kept, it has been observed that the same Rules of Procedure explicitly forbid the publication of the proceedings of the decision-making bodies of the ECB. Thus, Art. 10.4. of the ECB Statute has been effectively interpreted by the Governing Council to exclude the publication of minutes on a regular basis, as only the outcomes of the deliberations may be made public by the president of the ECB if authorised by the Governing Council. However, this certainly excludes the publication of details of the discussions and the voting-behaviour in the Governing Council. While regular press conferences following the meetings of the Governing Council may reveal some information on the proceedings, they cannot function as an effective substitute for the publication of minutes. It has been observed in this context that the publication could be anything from a summary of the deliberations to the publication of the decisions which resulted from the confidential deliberations. The legal basis foresees the publication of reports on the activities of the ESCB on at least a quarterly basis. Whether and to what extent they will include details of the past performance and projections on the future development of monetary policy and/or self-proclaimed targets for monetary policy is left to the ECB to decide, as the EC Treaty and ESCB Statute do not include any details on the contents of these reports. Despite the announcements that the ECB will conduct monetary policy in a transparent way, doubts may be voiced whether the ECB will have the same incentive to ensure general public support, and not only that of the financial markets as a national central bank. The ECB operates some-

---

[29] European Monetary Institute, op. cit., Chap. 3, n. 412.

what more remotely from the general public than a national central bank, as a true European general public, beyond the somewhat static concept of European citizenship, has yet to emerge. This decreases the threat of an amendment to the legal basis as a result of a loss of public support.

Although the EC Treaty and the ESCB Statute establish an institutionalised relationship between the ECB, the EP and the Council, this relationship is rather weak. This is not least the result of the great emphasis which has been placed on insulating the organs of the ECB from political pressure by both Community and Member States' institutions and bodies. Article 107 EC emerges as the cornerstone of the institutional set-up of the ECB. The participation of the president of the Council and a member of the Commission in the meetings of the Governing Council may provide a forum in which discussions can take place and which may assist the Council and the Commission in gaining the information required for judging the performance of the ECB. The same may be observed for the right of the president of the ECB to participate in Council meetings. These contacts may not, however, necessarily enhance the transparency of monetary policy beyond the sphere of the Council and the Commission.

It can be positively noted that, unlike its prototype, the Bundesbank, the ECB features an institutionalised relationship with the EP. Yet the provisions on the reporting requirements to the EP lack stringency. Apart from the presentation of an annual report by the president of the ECB to the EP, the EC Treaty does not provide for hearings on a regular basis. In fact, *de jure* neither the president nor any other member of the Executive Board is obliged to appear before the EP at all. While it is unlikely that the president of the ECB under normal circumstances would refuse to appear upon request, the lack of a clear obligation certainly puts him in a stronger position *vis-à-vis* the EP. The EP is given the role of a supplicant, rather than an authority. Besides, the observed lack of substantial backing of the EP by the people also means that the authority which a national parliament may gain beyond statutory provisions from public support, adding weight to a parliamentary request to appear, has yet to be gained by the EP. Direct elections alone do not as yet seem to provide that public support (particular in view of the low turnouts in many Member States). Moreover, with the national central bank governors, the majority of members of the Governing Council have been excluded from appearances before the EP. It has been observed that this cannot be justified with reference to the accountability of the national central bank governors at the national level because they can hardly be made personally responsible for the collegiate decisions on monetary policy at the Community level in the Governing Council of the ECB, even if some national parliaments may show more interest in monetary policy issues in the future.[30] What is more, any such attempts could be interpreted to infringe the personal independence of the governor of the national central bank, and thus incompatible with the EC Treaty and the ESCB Statute.

---

[30] Evidence for this increased interest by national parliaments may be e.g. the new statutory relationship between the Nederlandsche Bank and the Dutch parliament.

Corresponding with the weak prerequisites, primary Community law does not provide for sufficient instruments to hold the ECB democratically accountable. The unique position which the ECB holds even among the most independent of central banks is due to the fact that its entire legal basis has been enshrined in primary Community law. A change of the institutional structure requires a change of primary Community law itself. The restraining effect which the threat of an amendment of the legal basis can have on the behaviour of a central bank is virtually non-existent in the case of the ECB, as the probability of such a Treaty amendment is remote. With this, the legal basis of the ECB is more insulated from changes than is the case for any other of the central banks examined in this study. In none of these countries would unanimity be required to change the legal basis, even if a legal basis was considered to form part of the constitution. What is more, Article N TEU gives the ECB a right to be consulted in the case of such a Treaty amendment. This shows the powerful position which has been granted to the ECB in the Community structure and which is unique in comparison to even the most independent central banks included in this study. Indeed, the ECB has been elevated to the same level with the EP in as much as the latter does not play a more substantial role in the Treaty amendment procedure. As with the ECB, the EP only has to be consulted. In fact, the national parliaments will play a greater role in changing the institutional structure of the ECB than the EP, in as much as treaty amendments have to be ratified by all the Member States in order to enter into force.[31]

The appointment and dismissal procedures do not add substantially to the democratic accountability of the ECB. The nature of the Governing Council, comprising the Executive Board of the ECB and the national central bank governors, results in diverse appointment procedures. Notably the possibility of reappointments of the national central bank governors stands out. Moreover, contrary to a number of proposals prior to the establishment of the TEU, the EP has not been given any substantial role in the appointment of the members of the Executive Board similar to that of the US Senate in the appointment of the members Board of Governors of the Fed. The EP cannot block appointments.[32] Nevertheless, it has to be acknowledged that the participation of the EP in the appointment of the Executive Board of the ECB does not fall behind the existing arrangements, at least in the case of the four European national central bank systems included in this study, since parliamentary participation can only be observed for the Banque de France.

With regard to dismissal procedures, the legal basis of the ECB more or less reflects the existing provisions or practice, at least of almost all of the national central bank systems examined in this study, in as much as performance-based dismissal is not foreseen. Indeed, not only does primary Community law exclude dismissal for reasons other than inability to perform duties and serious

---

[31] Art. N(1), para. 3 TEU.

[32] See the recent report by the EP: Committee on Economic and Monetary Affairs and Industrial Policy, *Report on democratic accountability in the 3rd phase of EMU*, Doc. A4–0110/98.

misconduct of the members of the Executive Board of the ECB, but also of the governors of the participating national central banks. Primary Community law insulates national central bank governors from dismissal on grounds which are considered incompatible with the provisions on the ESCB by giving them a right to appeal to the ECJ, thereby removing any remaining discretion at the national level to remove a governor. On the contrary, the eight-year term of office of the members of the Executive Board of the ECB cannot be considered excessive compared to other central banks. Indeed, it is only just over half as long as that of the members of the Board of Governors of the Fed. Besides, even longer terms would not have the same restricting effect on the Council. Whereas a newly-elected national government may have the incentive to replace the central bank officials appointed by the former government, this incentive does not exist to the same degree for the Council of Ministers because the latter is not elected or appointed at once at regular intervals, and its members are appointed or elected according to different procedures under national law at different intervals.

The EC Treaty and ESCB Statute do not provide for an override mechanism *vis-à-vis* the ECB. Corresponding proposals from different sides have been discarded against the background of ensuring the independence of the ESCB and the ECB from government instructions along the lines of Article 107 EC.[33]

Finally, with regard to the budget of the ECB, arrangements similar to those found for the national central banks exist. The ECB is financially independent in as much as its budget does not form part of the Community budget. This may be more significant than in the national context, since much of the power of the EP derives from its role in the determination of the non-compulsory expenditure of the Communities.[34] The Court of Auditors in principle reviews the annual accounts of the ECB together with the reports of the external auditors, but the efficiency of monetary policy as such is excluded from this review.[35]

2. A new approach for a democratically accountable ECB

It has become apparent by now that the EC Treaty and the ESCB Statute fall short of providing the conditions and instruments required in principle to hold the ECB democratically accountable. Smits proposes that the existing provisions on accountability should be "stretched to their limits by a combination of the ECB endeavouring to be transparent and give account and the political bodies, notably the European Parliament, monitoring closely, with interest and insight, the conduct of central banking activities".[36] Yet this may not be sufficient to ensure the necessary degree of democratic accountability. While

---

[33] Cf. Chap. 4 V 1.

[34] On the role of the EP in budgetary procedures see e.g. P.J.G. Kapteyn/P. VerLoren van Themaat/ L.A. Geelhoed/C.W.A. Timmermans(eds.), op. cit., Chap. 3, n. 408, 213 *et seq.*

[35] Cf. Chap. 4 VIII 1.

[36] R. Smits, op. cit., Chap. 2, n. 36, at 176.

the existing arrangements should indeed be applied in an effective way, this approach has its limits where primary Community law excludes certain mechanisms. Besides, much depends upon the degree of self-commitment which the ECB is willing to make, rather than on concrete legal rules. For some, legislative steps to ensure accountability are superfluous, as the ECB has the incentive to make "extensive pre-commitments" to this end.[37] But it seems at least questionable whether the incentive is to safeguard a democratic coupling-back of the independent central bank to the general public, or rather the credibility in, and reassurance of the financial markets. While the latter is undoubtedly vital from the point of view of the proper functioning of the ESCB, it cannot be put on an equal footing with democratic accountability. Besides, leaving it to the central bank to decide what it considers to be the appropriate amount of accountability can hardly be considered satisfactory.

Submitting that the democratic accountability of the ECB is not sufficiently provided for calls for concrete proposals to improve matters. During the Intergovernmental Conference (IGC) revision of provisions on EMU, including those on the ESCB, was excluded from discussions and, thus, those provisions were not revised in the Treaty of Amsterdam of June 1997. It is recognised that such a change of the institutional structure of the ECB subsequent to its establishment will raise a certain degree of uncertainty in financial markets, and it should have been introduced before the establishment of the ECB. However, since this has not taken place, it is submitted that a change of the legal basis should be considered in the future, thereby strengthening the democratic accountability of the ESCB and the ECB.[38]

2.1. Improving the foundation

With regard to preconditions for democratic accountability, the legal basis of the ECB could be enhanced, introducing a clear yardstick for monetary policy and enhancing the arena in which the performance of the ECB is reviewed. Although the legal basis provides the ECB with the primary objective of price stability, it would be desirable to quantify the monetary policy objective of the ECB. Contrary to what is sometimes suggested, it should not be left to the ECB to define its objective. One suggestion could be to put the ECOFIN Council, the members of which are democratically legitimised through the respective Member States, in charge of defining the monetary policy objective in the form of a point target or a target range for inflation. However, more in line with the position of the ECB envisaged in primary Community law would be to define price stability in an agreement between the Council and the ECB. The contract approach could be a compromise between the independent position of the ECB and the need for enhanced democratic accountability. It would emphasise the

---

[37] Central Banking, "Interview with Jean-Jacques Rey", *Central Banking*, vol. 7 no. 1 (1996), 29–36; D.G. Mayes, op. cit., Chap. 4, n. 671, at 3.

[38] Perhaps at the time of the next accessions.

independent status of the ECB in primary Community law in the conduct of monetary policy by securing it a say in the formulation of monetary policy. The ECB would have instrument independence, but would have to agree upon the goals with the representatives of the Member States' governments gathered in the Council, who are at least to some extent accountable to their respective national parliaments.[39] These agreements would be reached for a fixed period of time, such as five years. In order to ensure the operation of the ECB under fixed policy targets at all times, initially the Council would decide upon the first policy target. Thereafter, the point target or target range would be negotiated between the ECB and the Council, the previous quantified objective remaining in place until a new one has been agreed upon. The conditions under which deviation from the quantified monetary policy objective is allowed should be fixed because otherwise even if the ECB could not decide on the goals of monetary policy, it would still remain undetermined whether and under what circumstances deviation from the quantified objective would be acceptable. In such a case the ECB would still retain a large amount of discretion in explaining a deviation as exceptional.

In order to enhance transparency in the conduct of monetary policy, the publication of the minutes of the Governing Board should be made mandatory. In this respect Article 10.4 of the ESCB Statute should be amended to oblige the Governing Board to publish minutes of its meetings following the next meeting. It has been recognised that public deliberations or full transcripts of the deliberations in those meetings may decrease the performance of a central bank in implementing monetary policy. But rather than not publishing any minutes at all, or leaving it for the bank to decide what information is published, explicit provisions should be introduced on the type of sensitive information which may be excluded from publication. At the same time it should be ensured that the minutes accurately reflect the discussions on the monetary policy board, including voting behaviour.[40] Different, possibly contrary, views expressed during the meetings, as well as the motives for monetary policy decisions, should become apparent. The report on the activities of the ESCB which the ECB is obliged to publish at least quarterly should amount to an inflation report. Together with the introduction of policy targets the ECB should become obliged to include details of past performance and projections on the future development of monetary policy. It is expected that the ECB will in fact do so, but under the EC Treaty and the ESCB Statute presently there is no obligation to do so.

The preconditions for the democratic accountability of the ECB can also be enhanced with regard to the role of the EP. This may be particularly desirable, as in the context of the other central bank systems examined in this work some evidence suggests that an institutionalised relationship between the central bank

---

[39] The difficulties in making the Ministers participating in the Council responsible *vis-à-vis* their respective national Parliaments have been highlighted in Chap. 2 II 1.

[40] W.H. Buiter, *Britain and EMU*, July 1998, emphasises that the confidentiality of the votes destroys any vestige of individual accountability of ECB board members.

and Parliament is a precondition for the latter to become seriously interested in the behaviour of the former. The presentation of annual reports and irregular appearances upon request seem hardly appropriate in this respect. Article 109b(3) EC should be enhanced, by obliging the president and the other members of the Executive Board to appear before the EP upon request of the latter. However, an institutionalisation of the relationship would require an additional step, making appearances at regular intervals before the Committee on Economic and Monetary Affairs and Industrial Policy or its sub-committee on monetary affairs, respectively, a statutory obligation. Such appearances could be linked to the publication of the inflation reports, but in any case should take place at least twice a year. There is no reason why these regular appearances should not also include the national central bank governors participating in the Governing Council. Although they are appointed at the level of Member States according to national procedures, to the extent that they fulfil ESCB-related tasks and participate in the Governing Council of the ECB, the national central bank governors may be considered as ECB rather than national central bank officials.[41] Indeed, despite the fact that they are not appointed at the European level, the EC Treaty itself puts them on an equal footing with their colleagues of the Executive Board with regard to the conditions for dismissal and the right to appeal to the ECJ. Obliging national central bank governors to appear before the EP together with their colleagues from the Executive Board of the ECB would fill the gap between the limited extent to which the central bank governors can be held accountable at the national level and the absence of any provisions in Community law. On the contrary, suggestions that the members of the Executive Board of the ECB should also be required to appear at hearings before the national parliaments are not convincing.[42] Apart from the practical problems involved in appearing before up to 15 or more national parliaments, it would be a unique case of EC officials having to explain their course of action in national parliaments. This may be compared to imposing an obligation on Commissioners to appear in hearings before national parliaments.[43] While enhanced reporting requirements can strengthen the role of the EP *vis-à-vis* the ECB, the basic hurdle remains, as a strong role of the EP in holding the ECB accountable would require that it has instruments at its disposal to take, or at least initiate, action against the ECB having reached the conclusion that measures had to be taken.

[41] See otherwise L.B. Smaghi, *The Democratic Accountability of the European Central Bank* (EMI, Frankfurt a.M., May 1998), at 16, who finds it "peculiar to request the NCB's Governors to be accountable" to the EP.

[42] This has been suggested e.g. by L. Calmfors, "An Accountable Bank", *Financial Times*, 23 February 1998.

[43] To be sure, Commissioners and senior officials of the Commission have voluntarily appeared before committees of national parliaments, such as the UK House of Lords Select Committee on the European Communities, to explain and discuss various matters, but not to account for the institution or its policies.

2.2. *Strengthening the instruments*

Maybe the most basic question which arises is whether the legal basis of the ECB has to be as insulated from changes as foreseen by requiring an application of the procedure under Article N TEU, and all the difficulties associated with that.[44] First, under Article N all Member States, including those not participating in the ESCB, take part in the discussions. Secondly, not least due to the non-participating Member States, discussions would almost certainly not be limited to the amendment of the institutional structure of the ECB. Finally, Treaty amendment is a time-consuming procedure, taking into account the necessary ratification procedures in the Member States. Under these circumstances an amendment of the legal basis of the ECB may be a very unattractive option in the eyes of the Member States participating in EMU, and thus unlikely to be a priority concern. It is submitted that uncoupling the decision to change the institutional structure of the ECB from the momentous decision to enter into Treaty amendment negotiations under Article N TEU should be considered. Since it is hardly realistic to transfer the legal basis into secondary Community law, this would require the introduction of a simplified Treaty amendment procedure. This would not be such a new approach in Community law. The Treaty establishing the European Coal and Steel Community (ECSC) allows within certain limits a simplified amendment of the Treaty.[45] In the EC Treaty, the second subparagraph of Article 104c (14)EC, introduced by the TEU, provides that the Council, acting unanimously on a proposal from the Commission and after consulting the European Parliament and the ECB (EMI), can adopt "the appropriate provisions" to replace the Protocol on the excessive deficit procedure.[46] Since the Protocols annexed to the EC Treaty form an integral part thereof and are thus of primary Community law, the second subparagraph of Article 104c(14) EC provides for a simplified form of Treaty amendment which falls outside the scope of the generally applicable Article N TEU.[47] Against the background of these examples, a provision could be introduced into the EC Treaty stating that the Council, in the composition of the Member States participating in the ESCB and ECB, acting unanimously on a proposal from the Commission and after consulting the EP, can amend the provisions of the EC Treaty and the ESCB Statute annexed to the Treaty. This would not restrict the independence of the ECB any more than is the case for other evidently independent central banks, such as the Bundesbank and the Fed, whose legal bases can be changed by the national legislator even without the requirement of unanimity. Yet, it

---

[44] Cf. Chap. 4 I 1.3.

[45] Art. 95, subparas. 3 and 4, ECSC.

[46] On the basis of this provision Council Regulation 1467/97 ([1997] OJ L209/6) on speeding up and clarifying the implementation of the excessive deficit procedure, which form part of the Stability and Growth Pact has been created. Cf. F. Amtenbrink/J. de Haan/O. Sleijpen, op. cit., Chap. 3, n. 369, 233 *et seq.*

[47] Art. 239 EC. Cf. J. Cloos/G. Reinesch/D. Vignes/J. Weyland, op. cit., Chap. 4, n. 349, at 250.

would give the participating Member States the opportunity, if desired, to reconsider the institutional structure, as well as the objectives and tasks of the ESCB and the ECB, without opening Pandora's Box of Treaty amendment entirely. Removing some of the obstacles to an amendment of the legal basis of the ECB could result in a restraining effect on the ECB similar to that observed for the national central banks. What makes this proposal potentially controversial is the fact that the Member States effectively would have to transfer more power to the Community level because, with the dropping of the need for a ratification by the Member States, the national parliaments would no longer take part in an amendment of Treaty provisions relating to the ESCB and the ECB.[48]

The role of the EP in an amendment of the legal basis can in any event only be limited, as long as the legal basis of the ECB constitutes primary Community law. Under the present Community structure it is difficult to envisage that the EP will be given any more participatory rights in this respect, let alone make an amendment subject to approval by the EP, similar to the co-decision procedure under Article 189b EC for the adoption of secondary Community law. This would require a reform of the Community institutions as a whole, developing the EP more into the direction of a true legislative branch. In other words, enhancing the role of the EP in this area would be embedded in the much broader context of a deeper political integration and a further democratisation of the EU. For the time being it has to be recognised that the EP will not play the same central role in the amendment of the legal basis of the ECB as national parliaments do both with regard to the legal basis of the national central banks and the ECB.[49]

With regard to the appointment and dismissal procedures, improvements may be possible in two areas. First, the participatory rights of the EP fall short of the type of mandatory participation to be found for the Fed, despite the fact that such a right was discussed at the time of the establishment of the rules on the ESCB. In fact, making the appointment of members of the Executive Board of the ECB subject to the consent of the EP would not be such a novelty. In the case of the appointment of the members of the Commission, not only does the EP have to be consulted on the nominations for the presidency of the Commission, but it also has to approve the Commission in its personal composition.[50] The European Environmental Agency is an example of an executive

---

[48] Cf. J. Pipkorn, op. cit., Chap. 2, n. 124, at 280, who suggests that Art. 104c(14) subpara. 14, EC may only be justifiable due to its limited scope, relating to a Protocol with a technical content, rather than "the 'constitutional' level of treaty provisions which need the ratification of twelve parliaments before any changes can be made".

[49] M. Deane/R. Pringle, op. cit., Chap. 2, n. 115, at 335, who point out that the EP does not possess the same ultimate sanction as the national legislators, that is the power to amend the legal basis of the central bank. To the contrary R.M. Lastra, op. cit., Chap. 2, n. 65, at 499, states that the Maastricht Treaty strengthens the role of the EP, thus diminishing any existing democratic deficit of the ESCB.

[50] Art. 158(2) EC. However, the efficiency of this procedures has been questioned, e.g. B. Boyce, op. cit., Chap. 2, n. 101, at 469, criticises the approval procedure as "purely voluntary exercise which creates but an illusion of democratic accountability".

agency where the EP has been given a substantial role in the appointment procedures, since it has the right to designate two of the members serving on the
management board.[51] Putting the EP on an equal footing with the Council in the
appointment of central bank officials could to some extent provide a counterweight to the independent position of the ECB. The argument that such participation by the EP would politicise the appointment procedures and possibly
endanger the independent position of the ECB is not convincing. First, it can be
argued that the participation of various bodies in the appointment procedure
may actually reduce the chances of political manipulation. Besides, placed in the
hands of the Council, the appointment of the Executive Board is a political decision in any event. The political exchanges between France and the Netherlands
on the candidate for the first presidency of the ECB support this evaluation.[52]
The participation of the representatives of the peoples of the Member States
would undoubtedly add to the democratic legitimation of the ECB. However,
although enhancing the *ex ante* accountability of the ECB, it does little in terms
of keeping the ECB accountable *ex post* for its performance of monetary policy.

It is questionable whether the role of the EP could be more substantial in this
respect too if the possibility of reappointment of the members of the Executive
Board were introduced. The possibility of reappointment is for example given
for the members of the Commission, which are often compared with the officials
of the ECB, with regard to their personal independence.[53] It would also put the
members of the Executive Board on an equal footing with the governors of a
number of national central bank which can be reappointed. It has yet to be
shown that the members of the Executive Board would be more vulnerable to
political pressure in the case of the possibility of reappointments than the
national central bank governors. The example of the Bundesbank has been mentioned.[54] However, this has been learned from experience, and the Bundesbank
has earned this reputation over time, something which could not be built into
the legal basis of the ECB. The drafters of the legal basis of the ECB feared that
the possibility of reappointments would be regarded as impairing the personnel
independence of the new central bank. However, other problems linked to a
reappointment may be more substantial. Introducing a kind of automatism to
the reappointment by linking it to the performance of the Executive Board
would involve, as already mentioned, the problem of how to judge the performance of an individual member of a collegiate organ in which all decisions are
taken by majority, such as is the case for the Governing Council with regard to
monetary policy. Here, making reappointment subject to performance would
only be feasible if the terms of all members of the Executive Board were up for

[51] Council Regulation (EEC) 1210/90 on the establishment of the European Environment Agency
and the European Environment Information and Observation Network ([1990] OJ L120/1), Art. 8.
The other members are one representative of each Member State and two representatives of the
Commission.
[52] Cf. Chap. 4 IV 1.
[53] Art. 158(1) EC, second sentence.
[54] Cf. Chap. 5 II 2.

renewal at the same time, e.g. as is the case with the members of the Commission. However, this may cause problems in the management of the ECB, since this would result in discontinuity, which was meant to be avoided by the staggered terms. Besides, even if all members of the Executive Board could be reappointed at once, they would still only account for less than half of the members with a voting right on the monetary policy board of the ECB, i.e. Governing Council. A similar observation can be made with regard to the dismissal procedure. The introduction of performance-based reappointment and dismissal, along the lines of the New Zealand model, would require a change of the institutional structure of the ESCB, vesting the final responsibility for monetary policy decisions in the president of the ECB. Yet, despite the fact that the national central banks' governors are by law as independent as the members of the Executive Board, the Member States would view such a concentration of power in one person, appointed by the Council, as a step towards more centralisation resulting in the loss of what influence remains for them in appointing the national central bank governors participating in the Governing Council of the ECB.

Another rather controversial suggestion in the eyes of proponents of an independent ECB, which is advocated in the light of this study, is the introduction of an override mechanism. With an override mechanism it would be acknowledged that the danger of an independent central bank pursuing a deflationary monetary policy is as realistic as that of a dependent central bank pursuing an inflationary policy. Currently, with the primary monetary policy objective of price stability and the independence being implemented in primary Community law, effective safety measures have only been taken in the case of the latter. Moreover, as has been observed, the existence of such a mechanism would recognise that ultimately a democratically legitimised government has to have responsibility for economic policies. In the case of the ECB, this role would be fulfilled by the Council comprising the governments of the Member States.[55] Even the legal basis of the Bundesbank, on which the ECB has been modelled, recognises this, albeit to a limited extent. The introduction of an override mechanism vested in the Council could also defuse some of the criticism of the independent position of the ECB and the lack of an economic government as a counterweight to the ECB, especially voiced in France.

The ECOFIN Council, in the composition of the Member States participating in ESCB, could decide by a unanimous decision to give directions to the ECB to pursue monetary policy for an economic objective other than price stability. The application of this override mechanism should be linked to a number of conditions which effectively ensure that the independence of the ECB in conducting monetary policy is maintained as far as possible, while at the same time restricting the Council in the unconditional application of the override mechanism.

---

[55] See also L.W. Gormley, *Europäische Währungsunion und Demokratieprinzip*, Zentrum für Europäisches Wirtschaftsrecht, Vorträge und Berichte, No. 90, 1997, at XV.

First, the conditions for the application of the override mechanism should be laid down in detail. The Bank of England Act 1998 includes examples of the types of circumstances which could make the application of the override mechanism in principle acceptable. A certain amount of discretion in the hands of the Council will be inevitable in this context. The decision by the Council should become subject to review. For this, the provisions on judicial review by the ECJ already existing in the EC Treaty could be applied. Thus, in principle a Council decision to apply the override mechanism could become the subject of an annulment procedure under Article 173 EC in an action brought by the ECB for the purpose of protecting its prerogative, i.e. its independence in the conduct of monetary policy. It may be that such an action would have to be automatically expedited by the Court. Another proposal, which would have to be introduced together with the override mechanism, would be to make the application of the override mechanism subject to parliamentary consent or approval. This would strengthen the position of the EP *vis-à-vis* both the Council and the ECB, as well as the democratic element in the override mechanism. However, the approval of the EP subsequent to the application of the override mechanism, similar to the procedure foreseen in the Bank of England Act 1998, may have its disadvantages on the European level because where the EP finds that the application of the mechanism was not justified under the given circumstances, it has no means of holding the Council accountable for its behaviour. The requirement of consent by the EP prior to the application of the override mechanism does not have this disadvantage, as the Council can be prevented from applying the mechanism in the first place.[56] Following the New Zealand model, for the time of the application of the override mechanism a new point target or target range should be defined according to the same procedure suggested earlier. This will ensure that the Council commits itself to a specific economic policy which the ECB has to implement, rather than issue some vague instructions. The requirement for the quantification of the new objective of the bank would arguably also restrain the Council with regard to the type of economic objective it could instruct the ECB to pursue, since the economic objective would have to be quantifiable. At the same time the new policy target ensures the continuing existence of a yardstick for judging the performance of the ECB in pursuing that new objective. Finally, the period of application of the override mechanism should be limited, either by a statutory fixed maximum duration, or by linking the duration of the override to the existence of the conditions which have lead to the application of the override.

Finally, the budgetary accountability of the ECB could be enhanced by introducing a budgetary agreement along the lines of the New Zealand model, on the one hand ensuring the existence of clear guidelines for the relocation of financial resources in the ECB, while on the other hand ensuring the financial independence of the ECB.

---

[56] A strict time frame would have to be introduced for the participation of the EP in order to ensure that the override mechanism can be applied within a reasonable time.

3. Conclusions

The designing of the ECB from scratch offered the opportunity to take a new approach to central banking by aiming not only for an independent, but also democratically accountable central bank. While Briault, Haldane, and King find that "over the last few years many central banks have made significant strides towards greater accountability and independence",[57] it has been shown that in the case of the ECB this development has been mainly limited to independence. The legal basis of the ESCB and the ECB has been drawn up against the background of the theoretical and empirical evidence on the benefits of central bank independence. Similar weight has not been given to considerations of the democratic accountability of central banks. Instead, the concepts of independence and accountability seem to have been regarded as somewhat contradictory.[58] In particular the example of the Bundesbank and its insulation from government has been considered worth following, not least due to the good track-record of the Bundesbank in formulating and implementing monetary policy. However, the historical, political and legal settings which form the bedrock, indeed the democratic legitimation, of the Bundesbank have not and could not possibly have been reproduced under artificial conditions in the TEU. Especially in the case of Germany, central bank independence has its roots in something more settled than the reasonableness of, and dedication to the modern economic arguments brought forward in favour of central bank independence. It is the actual and increasingly learned experience of the German people with government abuse of monetary policy and the resulting hyperinflation, which has made the powerful independent position of the Bundesbank acceptable in the German constitutional system for the last 40 years. This is confirmed by observing the diverse approaches to monetary policy to be found in other countries, with a less dramatic historic background, which feature a less stringent central bank regime. The Netherlands, until 1993 the Banque de France and until recently the Bank of England, are examples in this respect. Even in the case of the Fed, Congress and parts of the general public have always remained sceptical about the independence of the central bank. Public acceptance to some extent legitimises the position of a central bank, and a loss of public support can call into question the independent position of a central bank. However, these mechanisms which lie outside the legal provisions governing a central bank cannot be prescribed for a central bank. They have to grow. Indeed, central bank independence itself is not a static concept. In the case of some central banks it has developed as a practice rather than a legal concept. And even in countries with an explicit reference in the statute of the central bank independence has been modulated in practice in accordance with public acceptance and has relied on public acceptance.

[57]   C.B. Briault/A.G. Haldane/M.A. King, op. cit., Chap. 2, n. 108, at 7.
[58]   Cf. Chap. 2 III and Chap. 5 V, below.

It has become apparent that there are limits to the extent to which the ECB can be made democratically accountable both under its present institutional structure, e.g. collegiate decisions, and the constitutional structure of the Communities as a whole. Thus, where the EP cannot be regarded as a true legislative branch in other Community policy areas, it cannot be expected to play such a role with regard to the ECB either. The so-called "democratic deficit" of the Communities extends to the ESCB. In this respect, the extent to which the improvement of the democratic accountability of the ECB requires institutional reforms of the EU forms part of the more general question of how to reduce the "democratic deficit" on the European level.[59] It emerges from this that it is indeed misleading to point towards EMU and the ESCB for further integration in as much as changes which the ESCB itself requires in order to be democratically accountable cannot be substituted for changes in the EU as a whole.[60]

Despite these shortcomings in the institutional structure of the EU itself, it is important to realise that the institutional choices which have been made with regard to the ECB were indeed choices and not compulsory, albeit that this may be the impression sometimes given by the defenders of the *status quo*. Believing in the necessity for the exclusion of any possibility of government abuse of monetary policy, the drafters of the TEU have not only *de jure* insulated the ECB from any influence at the level of the Communities and Member States, but, in some respects, also effectively insulated the ECB from becoming democratically accountable. Suggestions have been made to remedy these shortcomings to the extent possible under the present structure. It should in any event not be left to the ECB to provide a sufficient degree of democratic accountability, as occasionally suggested. Although it may be considered over-suspicious to conceive that sub-optimal arrangements of accountability are inescapably the result, it has to be acknowledged that the interest which the ECB has in giving account of its actions is based on grounds other than the interest of the general public in holding the central bank accountable. Indeed, credibility in the financial markets may not be the first concern of an electorate which, through its representatives, has delegated the power over monetary policy to an institution which is independent of the executive government. Public commitments by those in charge of monetary policy in the future are not always backed by concrete legal obligations in the EC Treaty and the ESCB Statute. Indeed, they disguise the fact that the legal arrangements for the democratic accountability of the ECB are not sufficient. Remarks such as that by the president of the Bundesbank, Hans Tietmeyer, stating that "every member of the ECB Governing Council has a

---

[59] Cf. Chap. 2 II 1.1.

[60] F. Capie/Ch. Goodhart/N. Schnadt, "The Development of Central Banking" in F. Capie *et al.*, at 61, point out that the development with regard to EMU is somewhat different from the previous examples in history, where monetary union followed political unification. Also F. Amtenbrink, Wirtschafts-und Währungs-union-Schlünel oder Hindermis zur Integration?, Verbraucher und Recht 12 (1998), 393–94.

personal responsibility for the sustainable stability of the Euro in the whole Monetary Union", amount to little more than mere pledges.[61]

With the transfer of monetary authority from the national to the European level, the existing mechanisms of democratic accountability have to be replaced by mechanisms on the European level. Yet, to the extent to which the democratic accountability of the ECB has been considered insufficient, the transfer of responsibility for monetary policy may diminish the degree of democratic accountability previously found in the Member States.

The example of the ESCB highlights how the transfer of authority over a certain policy area to a supranational institution can result in the loss of mechanisms of democratic accountability at the national level without the existence of sufficient substitutes. However, it could be argued that this is merely a conscious choice of national states and in particular the national parliaments which have ratified the TEU. Yet in the time and age of globalisation of the financial markets the question arises whether monetary policy can be effectively decided upon and controlled by any one institution, be it of the magnitude of the ESCB comprising 15 or more national economies.[62] An observer of events may at times get the impression that central banks react to financial market developments rather than themselves set the tone with respect to monetary policy. This may be inevitable in a world of unrestricted capital mobility, yet it adds a new dimension to the discussion of democratic accountability, as the true source of decisions becomes increasingly difficult to locate. While this question goes beyond the scope of this study, it is submitted that this may be the starting point for further research.

IV. TOWARDS AN INDEX FOR DEMOCRATIC ACCOUNTABILITY

Examining different systems with regard to their advantages and disadvantages for certain institutional aspects almost inevitably comes to the point where the question arises how the different systems rank against each other. As has been observed, a vast number of studies focus on such indexing of central banks for the aspect of central bank independence. It was not until recently that similar attempts were made for the accountability of central banks. Briault, Haldane, and King were the first to produce such an index on the basis of four criteria of accountability.[63] They come to the conclusion that the New Zealand model,

---

[61] Author's translation; reported in "Tietmeyer: EZB-Mitglieder persönlich verantwortlich", *Der Tagesspiegel*, 28 Nov. 1997.

[62] See e.g. R. Cox, "Democracy in Hard Times: Economic Globalization and the Limits to Liberal Democracy" in A. McGrew (ed.), *The Transformation of Democracy? Globalization and Territorial Democracy* (Polity Press, Cambridge, 1997), 49–71; J.C. Lerda, "Globalization and Loss of Autonomy by the Fiscal, Banking and Monetary Authorities", *CEPA Review*, no. 58 (Apr. 1996), 65–78; A. Fazio, "Role and Independence of Central Banks" in P. Downes/R. Vaez-Zadeh (eds.), *The Evolving Role of Central Banks* (Central Banking Department, International Monetary Fund, Washington, DC, 1991), 121–39, at 137.

[63] C.B. Briault/A.G. Haldane/M.A. King, n 57 above, at 7. Their set of criteria includes the external monitoring by Parliament, publication of the minutes of meetings on monetary policy, publica-

somewhat surprisingly, alongside the Bank of England, provides for the highest degree of accountability.[64] The ECB was not included in this index. Using a somewhat broader set of criteria, de Haan, Amtenbrink, and Eijffinger have also developed an index of central bank accountability, which not only takes into account recent developments in the legal bases of the banks, but moreover includes the ECB.[65] The index has been drawn up against the background of three groups of questions referring to what is considered in that context as the three main features of democratic accountability:

— The decisions about the final objectives of monetary policy: this embraces the first four aspects, the questions whether the central bank law stipulates the objective of monetary policy (1), and thereafter clearly prioritises (2), defines (3), and quantifies (4) the objectives.
— Transparency of actual monetary policy: the next three aspects cover the issues whether the bank publishes an inflation or monetary policy report (5), makes public the minutes of the meetings of the monetary policy board within a reasonable time (6), and explains publicly to what extent it has been able to reach the quantified objective (7).
— Who bears final responsibility for monetary policy: six aspects make up this last group of questions, namely monitoring of the central bank by Parliament (8), a right of government (or Parliament) to give instructions (9), the existence of a review as part of the procedure to apply the override mechanism (10), a right of the central bank to appeal against the application of the override mechanism (11), a parliamentary right to change the legal basis of the bank by a simple majority vote (12), and whether the legal basis of the bank foresees a performance-based dismissal (13).

In constructing the indicator the number of positive answers have simply been added up. The result is reflected by Total. The index includes 16 central bank systems, including the seven systems examined in the present study. It is shown by this index that the ECB has a low degree of democratic accountability. The assessment of the Bank of England, which is based on the proposed new legislation, shows that the envisaged reforms provide for a high degree of accountability of the Bank. In fact the envisaged arrangements provide for a higher degree of democratic accountability than is the case for the Reserve Bank of New Zealand.

tion of inflation or monetary policy reports and the existence of an override mechanism to be applied "in case of certain shocks".

[64] It does not become clear on the basis of which legal and non-legal arrangements the rating of the Bank of England has been based, but it certainly could not have taken account of the changes under the Bank of England Act 1998.

[65] J. de Haan/F. Amtenbrink/S.C.W. Eijffinger, *Accountability of Central Banks: Aspects and Quantifications*, 1998, Center for Economic Research, Discussion paper, no. 9854, Tilburg University, May 1998. As the index compares the ECB with the existing central bank systems, it does not include the amendments of the legal bases of the banks participating in the ESCB in order to bring them in line with the EC Treaty.

Table 3: An indicator for central bank accountability

ASPECTS	AUS	B	CAN	DK	F	FRG	I	JAP	NL	NZ	ESP	SWED	CH	UK	US	EU
1.	*	–	*	*	*	*	–	*	*	*	*	–	*	*	*	*
2.	–	–	–	–	*	*	–	–	–	*	*	–	–	*	–	*
3.	–	–	–	–	*	–	–	–	–	*	*	–	–	*	–	*
4.	–	–	–	*	–	–	–	–	–	*	–	–	–	*	–	–
Subtotal	1	0	1	1	3	2	0	1	1	4	3	0	1	4	1	3
5.	–	–	*	–	–	–	–	–	–	*	*	*	–	*	*	–
6.	*	–	–	–	–	–	–	–	–	–	–	–	–	*	*	–
7.	*	–	*	*	*	–	*	*	–	*	*	*	–	*	*	*
Subtotal.	1	0	2	1	1	0	1	1	0	2	2	2	0	3	3	1
8.	*	–	*	*	*	–	*	*	–	*a	*	*	–	*a	*	–b
9.	*	*	*	–	–	–	–	*	*	*	–	*	–	*	–	–
10.	*	–	–	–	–	–	*	*	*	–	–	–	–	*	–	–
11.	*	*	–	–	–	–	–	–	*	–	–	–	–	–	–	–
12.	*	*	*	*	*	*	*	–	*	*	*	*	*	*	*	–
13.	–	–	–	–	–	–	–	–	–	*	–	–	–	–	–	–
Subtotal	5	3	4	2	2	1	3	4	4	4	2	3	1	4	2	0
Total	7	3	7	4	6	3	4	6	5	10	7	5	2	11	6	4

Source: de Haan/Amtenbrink/Eijffinger (1998)

Note: The indicator for central bank accountability is constructed by simply adding the number of positive answers (*) on the aspects with respect to decisions about the ultimate objectives of monetary policy (1–4), the transparency of actual monetary policy (5–7) and the final responsibility for monetary policy (8–13).

a By constitutional convention.
b Apart from the presentation of the Annual Report by the President of the ECB, Art. 109b(3), and in particular its third sentence, does not introduce a legal obligation to appear before the European Parliament at regular intervals. On the contrary, Art. 39 of the current rules of procedure of the EP foresees that the President of the ECB will attend hearings twice a year. Practice may develop.

Generally, the pitfall of such indices is that they have a tendency to generalise. An index provides a kind of chart, suggesting both winners and losers in terms of democratic accountability. Yet explaining complex institutional structures in the tight corset of an indicator may have its limitations. Regardless of how detailed the set of criteria on which the index is based may be, they will hardly ever reflect all the relevant aspects which explain the degree of democratic accountability of a central bank. The constitutional background against which a central bank is situated forms the foundation for the need for the democratic accountability of a central bank. It sets the goalposts for the degree of democratic accountability necessary. Moreover, the balance between different mechanisms of democratic accountability, which together make up the degree of accountability, remains largely outside the scope of such an index. A weighing of criteria could only take place on a case-by-case basis, but not on a criterion-by-criterion basis. Where an index is solely based on statutory provisions, historic and social developments in a country influencing the actual degree of democratic accountability are ignored. Yet, how does one weigh such additional elements against each other and, moreover, between different constitutional systems?

To some extent these observations provide a negative answer to the question whether an ideal central bank in terms of democratic accountability exists. From the institutional arrangements examined in this study, a model of a democratically accountable central bank may emerge, but this model cannot be arbitrarily imposed on any country and central bank system. Placed against the legal, political, economic, and social background to be found in a particular country, one or the other feature, in theory considered to be ideal in terms of democratic accountability, turns out to be ineffective or indeed inapplicable. These findings point back to Chapter 2, where it has been observed that a general definition of democratic accountability is difficult to formulate. Proposals for strengthening the democratic accountability of central banks can only be forwarded on a case-by-case basis. Benjamin Barber has observed in a somewhat broader context that:

> "The belief in the universality of democratic forms rests largely on the myth that democracy is no more than certain formal political arrangements that can be plopped down like a tent more or less on any soil anywhere in the world: the myth that it is a used car to be handed over from generation to generation, an old reliable heap, that, with a few new parts, a little accommodation to climate and conditions, can be driven anywhere. History suggests, however, that democracy is not an automotive universal, a blueprint to be followed regardless of conditions. It cannot be imposed top down. It grows bottom up, and anyone hoping to design survivable democratic institutions needs first to understand the landscape and topology on which their structures are to be erected."[66]

---

[66] B.R. Barber, "Three Challenges to Reinventing Democracy" in P. Hirst/S. Khilnani, *Reinventing Democracy* (Blackwell Publishers, Oxford, 1996), 144–56, at 146.

V. CENTRAL BANK INDEPENDENCE
AND DEMOCRATIC ACCOUNTABILITY REVISITED

The study started out by observing the well-established discussion on central bank independence, and it will close with some final observations on the relationship between central bank independence and democratic accountability.[67]

From a legal point of view it emerges from this study that promoters of an independent central bank should not *per se* consider every mechanism of accountability as an infringement of the position of the bank. It has been pointed out that certain mechanisms can promote the independent position and the accountability of the central bank at the same time. One example is the quantification of the monetary policy objectives of a central bank. The relationship between central bank independence and democratic accountability is not only characterised by a trade-off between the two principles, and a democratically accountable central bank is not simply a bank which has been stripped of its independence.[68] The dilemma between the economic rationale for central bank independence and the legal need for mechanisms of democratic accountability does not exist to the extent often suggested. The relationship between the two may be described as mutual dependency rather than as dominance of one over the other.

What is more, recent studies by economists recognise that the relationship between central bank independence and accountability is more complex than that one restricts the other. Eijffinger and de Haan conclude that a trade-off between central bank independence and accountability exists only in the short run, since "a central bank that continuously conducts policy that lacks broad political support will sooner or later be overridden".[69] Thereafter, Nolan and Schaling, defining accountability as a mechanism whereby an agent's actions are made apparent to the principal, have come to the conclusion that "accountability makes economic sense", and, indeed, that accountability may serve as a partial substitute for central bank independence.[70] The ratio behind this argument is that if economic agents are uncertain of the bank's actions their expectations of inflation are higher than they otherwise would be, and that it is generally likely that inflation expectations are higher than would otherwise be the case. It is thought that the way to reduce these inflation expectations is to increase the accountability and/or the degree of independence of a central bank. For Nolan and Schaling "for a given target level of inflation the optimal degree of central bank accountability is higher, the lower is the degree of central bank indepen-

---

[67] Cf. also Chap. 2 III.
[68] Sometimes narrowed down to the formula central bank accountability = central bank independence – 1.
[69] S.C.W. Eijffinger/J. de Haan, op. cit., Chap. 2, n. 8, at 54.
[70] C. Nolan/E. Schaling, *Monetary Policy Uncertainty and Central Bank Accountability*, Bank of England Working Paper Series no. 54, Oct. 1996, at 28.

dence".[71] Examining these findings, de Haan observes that a negative relationship between central bank accountability and independence, which is based on a comparison of the degree of accountability with the degree of independence of a central bank, does not show up when using indices for independence different from those used by Nolan and Schaling.[72]

The rather new approach to explaining the relationship between (democratic) accountability and central bank independence also involves risks, as it resembles many of the characteristics of the discussion on central bank independence, which centres on the institutional structure for an optimal monetary policy. The relationship between economic aggregates and central bank independence stands at the centre of the discussions dominated by economists. A similar development has already taken place for the subject of democratic accountability. Democratic accountability becomes a pre-condition of optimal monetary policy or, indirectly, legitimises central bank independence which in return promotes "optimal outcomes". The subject-matter of democratic accountability runs the danger of having many of the characteristics of a book-keeping exercise. Lawyers tend to surrender in the face of seemingly complex macroeconomic models.

It needs to be considered carefully in which areas and to what extent a central bank requires independence to fulfil its statutorily prescribed objectives. Writing out a blank cheque in the form of complete insulation from outside influence is as inadequate as considering the subordination of monetary policy under the executive government as a solution to the problem of democratic accountability. There are certain limits to what monetary policy can achieve, and realising those constraints is as essential as realising that a central bank has to be democratically accountable to be independent. It cannot be denied that institutional choices in favour of democratic accountability inevitably affect the position of the central bank *vis-à-vis* the executive and legislative branch. Yet, one of the lessons of this study is that living in a democratic system may bear inevitable costs. A stable monetary regime is a valuable asset, but it is to be carefully weighed against basic principles such as that of democracy. Economists observe the costs of democratic accountability for central bank independence and thus economic output. On the contrary, the costs of independent central banks for a democracy could also be calculated. Somewhat overstated, the question may be asked how much authority a society may transfer to independent institutions for the sake of an optimal monetary policy regime, thereby excluding itself from the making of alternative choices, and still consider itself to be democratic. Monetary policy is not a goal in itself, but rather serves the public interest. It makes sense to remove monetary policy from short-term political considerations, but at the end of the day it is the electorate which must have the

---

[71] Ibid., at 5.
[72] J. de Haan, op. cit., Chap. 2, n. 143, 417 *et seq.*

basic choice between different alternatives. To the extent to which this choice may result in a sub-optimal monetary policy, this may be considered as one of the "costs of democracy".[73]

[73] A term used by W.R. Keech, *Economic Politics: The Costs of Democracy* (Cambridge University Press, Cambridge, 1995).

APPENDIX 1

This agreement between the Treasurer and the Governor of the Reserve Bank of New Zealand (the Bank) is made under sections 9(1) and 9(4) of the Reserve Bank of New Zealand Act 1989 (the Act) and shall apply for the balance of the Governor's present term and for his next five year term, expiring on 31 August 2003. It replaces that signed on 10 December 1996.

In terms of section 9 of the Act, the Treasurer and the Governor agree as follows:

1. Price stability
Consistent with section 8 of the Act and with the provisions of this agreement, the Bank shall formulate and implement monetary policy with the intention of maintaining a stable general level of prices, so that monetary policy can make its maximum contribution to sustainable economic growth, employment and development opportunities within the New Zealand economy.

2. Policy target
a) In pursuing the objective of a stable general level of prices, the Bank shall monitor prices as measured by a range of price indices. The price stability target will be defined in terms of the All Groups Consumers Price Index excluding Credit Services (CPIX), as published by Statistics New Zealand.
b) For the purpose of this agreement, the policy target shall be 12-monthly increases in the CPIX of between 0 and 3 per cent.
c) Notwithstanding clause 2(a), the Treasurer and the Governor may agree to use an alternative index of consumer price inflation following the implementation of the changes to the calculation of consumer prices proposed by the Government Statistician to take effect during 1999.

3. Unusual events
a) There is a range of events that can have a significant temporary impact on inflation as measured by the CPIX, and mask the underlying trend in prices which is the proper focus of monetary policy. These events may even lead to inflation outcomes outside the target range. Such disturbances include, for example, shifts in the aggregate price level as a result of exceptional movements in the prices of commodities traded in world markets, changes in indirect taxes, significant government policy changes that directly affect prices, or a natural disaster affecting a major part of the economy.

b) When disturbances of the kind described in clause 3(a) arise, the Bank shall react in a manner which prevents general inflationary pressures emerging.

4. Implementation and accountability

a) The Bank shall constantly and diligently strive to meet the policy target established by this agreement.

b) It is acknowledged that, on occasions, there will be inflation outcomes outside the target range. On those occasions, or when such occasions are projected, the Bank shall explain in Policy Statements made under section 15 of the Act why such outcomes have occurred, or are projected to occur, and what measures it has taken, or proposes to take, to ensure that inflation comes back within that range.

c) The Bank shall implement monetary policy in a sustainable, consistent and transparent manner.

d) The Bank shall be fully accountable for its judgments and actions in implementing monetary policy.

Signed

Hon Winston Peters   Donald T. Brash
Treasurer   Governor Reserve Bank of New Zealand

Dated at Wellington, this 15th day of December 1997

APPENDIX 2

FUNDING AGREEMENT

1) This is an Agreement between the Minister of Finance and the Governor of the Reserve Bank pursuant to section 159 of the Reserve Bank Act 1989. It supersedes and replaces the Agreement signed on 17 April 1991.

2) It is hereby agreed that the amount of the Bank's income to be applied in meeting the expenditure of the Bank needed to carry out the functions and to exercise the powers specified in section 159 shall be:

$38,000,000   for each of the years commencing 1 July 1995 and 1 July 1996,
$39,000,000   for the year commencing 1 July 1997, and
$40,000,000   for each of the years commencing 1 July 1998 and 1 July 1999.

3) It is agreed, under section 159(1)(f), to include within this limit expenditure on foreign exchange dealings, settlement banking and government banking as defined in Part II sections 16, 32 and 34 of the Act.

4) It is further agreed that—
(a) if the policy target for inflation agreed by the Minister and the Governor in terms of section 9 of the Act of 0 to 2 per cent per annum is reviewed and a new policy target substituted, the agreed level of Bank expenditure as specified above will be adjusted to reflect any difference between the Bank's new and old path for inflation:
(b) if there is any material change in the nature or extent of the work undertaken by the Bank in respect of any of the functions or activities covered by this Agreement, the Minister and Governor will redetermine the levels of expenditure set out in 2 above to reflect such changes:
(c) this Agreement may be suspended and renegotiated at any time by mutual agreement between the Minister and the Governor but any such renegotiation will require ratification by Parliament.

Signed

Bill Birch   Donald T. Brash
Minister of Finance   Governor of the Reserve Bank

30 June 1995

APPENDIX 3

Central Banks on the Internet

Bibliography

BOOKS AND ARTICLES

AKHTAR, M.A./HOWE, H., "The Political Independence of U.S. Monetary Policy", *BNL Quarterly Review* 178 (1991), 343–89.

ALESINA, A., "Macroeconomics and Politics", in S. Fischer (ed.), *NBER Macroeconomic Annual 1988* (MIT Press, Cambridge, Ma, 1989), 17–52.

—— "Politics and Business Cycles in Industrial Countries", *Economic Policy*, no. 8 (1989), 55–98.

——/GRILLI, V., "The European Central Bank: Reshaping Monetary Politics in Europe", in M.B. Canzoneri/V. Grilli/P.R. Masson (eds.), *Establishing a Central Bank: Issues in Europe and Lessons from the US* (Cambridge University Press, Cambridge, 1992), 49–77.

——/SUMMERS, L.H., "Central Bank Independence and Macroeconomic Performance: Some Comparative Evidence", *Journal of Money, Credit and Banking*, vol. 25, no. 2 (1993), 151–62.

AMTENBRINK, F., "Anmerkungen zur demokratischen Kontrolle von Zentralbanken in der Europäischen Währungsunion", in *Europäische Integration- Schon eine "Union des Rechts"? Zwischen Erfolgsbilanz und Balanceverlust*, Almanach junger Wissenschaftler, Hans-Martin-Schleyer-Stiftung, V. Kongreß "Junge Juristen und Wirtschaft", Essen, 29.–31. May 1996, 16–17.

—— "Wirtschafts-und Währungs-union-Schlünel oder Hindemis zur Integration?", *Verbraucher und Recht* 12 (1998) 393–4.

——/HAAN, J. DE/SLEIJPEN, O., "The Stability and Growth Pact—Placebo or Panacea? (I)," *EBLR* 8 (1997), 202–10, (II), *EBLR* 8 (1997), 233–8.

ARCHER, D.J., "The New Zealand Approach to Rules and Discretion in Monetary Policy", *Journal of Monetary Economics*, vol. 39 (1997), 3–15.

ARNIM, H.H. V., *Staatslehre der Bundesrepublik Deutschland* (Verlag Franz Vahlen, Munich, 1984).

ARNDT, H.-J., Von der politischen zur plangebundenen Autonomie", in D. Duwendag (ed.), *Macht und Ohnmacht der Bundesbank* (Athenäum Verlag, Frankfurt a.M., 1973), 15–35.

BADURA, P., *Staatsrecht-System. Erläuterungen des Grundgesetzes für die Bundesrepublik Deutschland* (2nd edn., C.H. Beck, Munich, 1996).

BAILEY, S.H./GUNN, M.J., *Smith and Bailey on The Modern English Legal System* (Sweet & Maxwell, London, 1996).

BANK OF ENGLAND, *The Value of Money* (online), available from: URL http://www.bankofengland.co.uk/value.htm (last accessed Oct. 1998).

BANQUE DE FRANCE, *History, Organization, Role* (Banque de France, Paris, 1995).

BARATTA, M.v. (ed.), *Der Fischer Weltalmanach 1997* (Fischer Taschenbuch Verlag, Frankfurt a.M., 1997).

BARBER, R.B., "Three Challenges to Reinventing Democracy", in P. Hirst/S. Khilnani (eds.), *Reinventing Democracy* (Blackwell Publishers, Oxford, 1996), 144–56.

BARNETT, A., "The Creation of Democracy", in P. Hirst/S. Khilnani, *Reinventing Democracy* (Blackwell Publishers, Oxford, 1996), 157–74.

BARRO, R./GORDON, D., "Rules, Discretion and Reputation in a Model of Monetary Policy", *Journal of Monetary Economics*, vol. 12 (1983), 101–21.

BEAUFORT WIJNHOLDS, J.A.H. DE, *Van kapiteins, loodsen en rechters: de wereldwijde beweging naar centrale bank autonomie* (Inaugurele rede, Groningen, 1992).

BEAUFORT WIJNHOLDS, J.O. DE/HOOGDUIN, L.H., *Central bank Autonomy: Policy Issues*, in J.O. de Beaufort Wijnholds/S.C.W. Eijffinger/L.H. Hoogduin (eds.), *A Framework for Monetary Stability* (Kluwer Academic Publishers, Dordrecht, 1994), 75–95.

BECK, N., "Congress and the Fed: Why the Dog does not Bark in the Night", in Th. Mayer (ed.), *The Political Economy of American Monetary Policy* (Cambridge University Press, Cambridge, 1990), 131–50.

BENDA, E./MAIHOFER, W./VOGEL, H.-J., *Handbuch des Verfassungsrechts der Bundesrepublik Deutschland* (Walter de Gruyter, Berlin and New York, 1994).

BERGER, H., *Konjunkturpolitik im Wirtschaftswunder, Handlungsspielräume und Verhaltensmuster von Zentralbank und Regierung in den 1950er Jahren*, Diss., Munich, 1995.

BERRY, J.M., "Is the Fed's Power Legitimate?", *Central Banking*, vol. 6 no. 4 (1996), 36–46.

—— "Kid gloves for Greenspan", *Central Banking*, vol. 7 no. 3 (1996–7), 30–5.

BESLEY, T./CASE, A., *Does Electoral Accountability Affect Economic Policy Choices? Evidence From Gubernatorial Term Limits*, National Bureau Of Economic Research Inc., Working Paper no. 4575, Cambridge, 1993.

BESNARD, D./REDON, M., *La monnaie: politique et institutions* (2e édition, Dunod, Paris, 1987).

BESSELINK, L.F.M., "An Open Constitution and European Integration: The Kingdom of the Netherlands", *SEW*, vol. 44 no. 6 (1996), 192–206.

BIARD, H., *Le Nouveau Statut de la Banque de France*, thesis, Université de Paris, 1937.

BOARD OF GOVERNORS OF THE FEDERAL RESERVE SYSTEM, *The Federal Reserve System: Purposes & Functions* (8th edn., Washington, DC, Dec. 1994).

BÖCKENFÖRDE, E.W., "Demokratie als Verfassungsprinzip", in I. Isensee/P. Kirchhof (eds.), *Handbuch des Staatsrechts*, vol. I (F. Müller Juristischer Verlag, Heidelberg, 1987).

BONIN, K.v., *Zentralbanken zwischen funktioneller Unabhängigkeit und politischer Autonomie*, Diss., Berlin, 1978.

BOUVIER, J., "The Banque de France and the State from 1805 to the Present Day", in G. Toniolo (ed.), *Central Banks' Independence in Historical Perspective* (Walter de Gruyter, Berlin and New York, 1988), 73–103.

BOWEN, A., "British Experience with Inflation Targetry", in L. Leiderman/L.E.O. Svensson (eds.), *Inflation Targets* (CEPR, London, 1995), 53–68.

BOYCE, B., "The Democratic Deficit of the European Communities", *Parliamentary Affairs*, vol. 46, no. 4, 458–77.

BRANDT, E., *Die währungspolitischen Befugnisse der Bundesregierung*, Diss., Würzburg, 1990.

BRENTFORD, P., "Constitutional Aspects of the Independence of the European Central Bank" (1998) 47 *ICLQ* 75–116.

BRIAULT, B.C./HALDANE, A.G./KING, M.A., *Independence and Accountability*, Bank of England Working Paper Series no. 49 (Bank of England, London, 1996).

BROUWER, J.G., "Wijkt het Unie-Verdrag van Maastricht af van de Grondwet of van het Statuut?", *NJB* (1992), 1045–9.

BRYDE, B.-O., in H.P. Schneider/W. Zeh (eds.), *Parlamentsrecht und Parlamentspraxis in der Bundesrepublik Deutschland* (Walter de Gruyter, Berlin and New York, 1989).

BUITER, W.H., *Britain and EMU*, mimeo (University of Cambridge, July 1998).

BURDEKIN, R.C.K./WIHLBORG, C/ WILLET, T.D., "A Monetary Constitution Case for an Independent European Central Bank", *World Economy*, vol. 15 no. 2 (1992), 231–49.

BURKENS, M.C./VERMEULEN, B.P., "Maastricht in strijd met de Grondwet? reactie 1", *Nederlandse Juristenblad*, vol. 67 no. 27 (1992), 861–2.

CAESAR, R., "Die Unabhängigkeit der Notenbank im demokratischen Staat", *Zeitschrift für Politik*, vol. 27, no. 4 (1980), 347–77.

——*Der Handlungsspielraum von Notenbanken* (Nomos, Baden-Baden, 1981).

CAIRNCROSS, A., "The Bank of England: Relationship with the Government, the Civil Service, and Parliament", in G. Toniolo (ed.), *Central Bank's Independence in Historical Perspective* (Walter de Gruyter, Berlin and New York, 1988), 39–72.

CAPIE, F./GOODHART, CH./SCHNADT, N., "The Development of Central Banking", in F. Capie *et al.*, *The Future of Central Banking* (Cambridge University Press, Cambridge, 1994), 1–231.

CARPER, D.L. *et al.*, *Understanding the Law* (2nd edn., West Law Publishing Company, Minn./St.Paul, 1995).

CARTOU, L., *Communautés européennes* (10th edn., Dalloz, Paris, 1991).

CENTRAL BANKING, "Interview with Jean-Jacques Rey", *Central Banking*, vol. 7 no. 1 (1996), 29–36.

CHRISTIANSEN, T., "Gemeinsinn und Europäische Integration. Strategien zu Optimierung von Demokratie- und Integrationszielen", in W. Steffani/U. Thaysen, *Demokratie in Europa: Zur Rolle der Parlamente*, ZParl Sonderband 1/95 (Westdeutscher Verlag, Opladen, 1995), 51–64.

CLIFFORD, A.J., *The Independence of the Federal Reserve System* (University of Pennsylvania Press, Philadelphia, 1965).

CLOOS, J./REINESCH, G./VIGNES, D./WEYLAND, J., *Le Traite de Maastricht: genèse, analyse, commentaires* (2nd edn., Emile Bruylant, Brussels, 1994).

COBURGER, D., *Die währungspolitischen Befugnisse der Deutschen Bundesbank* (Duncker & Humblot, Berlin, 1988).

——"Mindestreserve- und Diskontpolitik der deutschen Bundesbank aus rechtlicher Sicht", *WM* (1989), 1005–8.

COFFEY, P., "The European Monetary System and Economic and Monetary Union", in P. Coffey (ed.), *Main Economic Policy Areas of the EC—After 1992* (4th edn., Kluwer Academic Publishers, Dordrecht, 1993), 1–29.

——*The European Monetary System—Past, Present and Future* (Martinus Nijhoff Publishers, Dordrecht, 1984).

COLLAS, P., "Le 'Dépeçage' de l'administration- un nouveau pas: la tentive d'autonomiser la Banque de France", *RRJ*, 1994–2, 557–98.

CONGDON, T., "Memorandum submitted to the Treasury and Civil Service Select Committee", in Treasury and Civil Service Committee, *The Role of the Bank of England* (House of Commons Paper. Session 1993–4; 98–I, vol. 2), Report, together with the proceedings of the Committee. HC Session 1993–4 (HMSO, London 1993), app. 25.

CONSTANTINESCO, V./KOVAR, R./SIMON, R., *Traité sur l'Union Européenne (signé a Maastricht le 7 fevrier 1992): commentaire article par article* (Economica, Paris, 1995).

CORDERO, R., *The Creation of a European Banking System* (Peter Lang Publishing, New York, 1990).

COTTRELL, P.L., "Bank of England", in M. Pohl/S. Freitag (eds.), *Handbook on the History of European Banks* (Edward Elgar, Aldershot, 1994), 1190–2.

COURTIS, N., "Mr. George goes to Westminster", *Central Banking*, vol. 8 no. 3 (1997), 24–9.

COX, R., "Democracy in Hard Times: Economic Globalization and the Limits to Liberal Democracy", in A. McGrew (ed.), *The Transformation of Democracy? Globalization and Territorial Democracy* (Polity Press, Cambridge, 1997), 49–71.

CROW, J.W., *Monetary Policy, and the Responsibilities and Accountability of Central Banks*, The Gerhard de Kock Memorial Lecture at the University of Pretoria, Bank of Canada, Ottawa, 1993.

CUKIERMAN, A., *Central Bank Strategy, Credibility, and Independence* (MIT Press, Cambridge, 1992).

——/WEBB, S.B./NEYAPTI, B., "Measuring the Independence of Central Banks and Its Effects on Policy Outcomes", *The World Economic Review*, vol. 6, no. 3 (1992), 353–98.

DAINTITH, T., "The Functions of Law in the Field of Short-Term Economic Policy" (1976) 92 *LQR*, 62–78.

—— "Between Domestic Democracy and an Alien Rule of Law? Some Thoughts on the 'Independence' of the Bank of England" [1995] *PL*, 141–55 (reprinted in M. Andenas/L. Gormley/C. Hadjiemmanuil/I. Harden, I. (eds.), *European Economic and Monetary Union: The Institutional Framework* (Kluwer Law International, London, 1997), 357–72.

DAWE, S., "The Reserve Bank of New Zealand Act 1989", *Reserve Bank Bulletin*, vol. 53, no. 1, 1990, 29–36.

DAY, P./KLEIN, R., *Accountabilities: Five Public Services* (Tavistock Publications, London/NY, 1987).

DE JONG, A.M., *De Wetgeving Nopens de Nederlandsche Bank 1914–1958* (Martinus Nijhoff, The Hague, 1960).

DEANE, M./PRINGLE, R., *The Central Banks* (Viking, London, 1993).

DEBBASCH, C./RICCI, J.-C., *Contentieux administratif* (6th edn., Dalloz, Paris, 1994).

DEBELLE, G./FISCHER, S., *How Independent Should a Central Bank Be?*, CEPR conference paper no. 392, Stanford, 1994.

DEGENHART, C., *Staatsrecht I* (11th edn., C.F. Müller Verlag, Heidelberg, 1995).

DEGENKAMP, J.TH., *Inleiding Economisch Recht* (2nd edn., Samsom H.D. Tjeenk Willink, Alphen aan den Rijn, 1989).

DEUTSCHE BUNDESBANK, *Die Geldpolitik der Bundesbank* (DBB, Frankfurt a.M., 1995).

DHORDAIN, R./CLODONG, O., *Les Banques Centrales* (deuxième tirage, Les Éditions d'Organisation, Paris, 1994).

DISCH, W., *Die geldpolitische Konzeption der Banque de France und der Deutschen Bundesbank* (Centaurus-Verlagsgesellschaft, Pfaffenweiler, 1995).

DONNER, J.P.H., "De derde pijler en de Amsterdamse doolhof", *SEW*, vol. 45, no. 10 (1997), 370–7.

DOVE, R.B., 1997, *Enactment of Law* (online), available from: URL http://thomas.loc.gov/ (last accessed Jan. 1999).

DUFAUR, M., *La Nouvelle Organisation de la Banque de France*, Diss., Université de Toulouse 1937.

DUISENBERG, W.F., "The History of the Nederlandsche Bank; A Guide for Europe?", in *Monetaire geschiedenis als wegwijzer voor de Europese Centrale Bank* (Erasmus Universiteit, Rotterdam; Nederlands Instituut voor het Bank- en Effectenbedrijf, Amsterdam, 1992), 21–9.

—— "The ESCB's stability-oriented monetary policy strategy speech", held on 7 Dec. 1998 in Paris, URL http:\\www.ecb.int.key/sp981207en.htm [last accessed Jan. 1999].

DUNSIRE, A., *Control in Bureaucracy: The Execution Process* (Martin Robertson, London, 1967).

DUPRAT, J.-P., "L'Indépendance de la Banque de France: Aspects Constitutionnels et Européens (1ère Partie)", LPA, no. 47 (1994), 4–10, (*Suite et Fin*), LPA, no. 49, 4–11.

—— "The Independence of the Banque de France: Constitutional and European Aspects" [1995] *PL*, 133–49.

DUVERGIER, J.B., *Collection Complète des Lois, Décrets d'Intérêt Général* (Tome Trente-Sixième, Recueil Sirey, Paris, 1936).

—— *Collection Complète des Lois, Décrets d'Intérét Général* (Recueil Sirey, Paris, 1945).

—— *Collection Complète des Lois, Décrets, Ordonnances, Réglements, et Avis du Conseil-D'État* (Tome Douzième, Paris, 1826).

EHRENBERG, H., *Zwischen Marx und Markt* (Societäts-Verlag, Frankfurt a.M., 1973).

EIJFFINGER, S.C.W., *The Determinations of the Currencies within the European Monetary System*, FEW research memorandum (241), Department of Economics, Tilburg University, 1987.

—— *Het Monetaire Beleid van de Nederlandsche Bank*, Serie Researchmemorandum, Vrije Universiteit Ekonomische Fakulteit Amsterdam, 1993.

——/SCHALING, E., *Central Bank Independence: Criteria and Indices*, Department of Economics Research Memorandum, FEW 584, University of Tilburg, March 1992.

——/—— *The Ultimate Determinants of Central Bank Independence*, Center for Economic Research Discussion Paper, no. 9505, Tilburg University, January 1995.

——/—— "Central Bank Independence in Another Eleven Countries", *BNL Quarterly Review*, vol. 192 (1995), 39–83.

——/HAAN, J. DE, *The Political Economy of Central-Bank Independence*, Special Papers in Economics no. 19, International Finance Section, Department of Economics, Princeton University, Princeton, NJ, 1996.

——/SCHALING, E./HOEBERICHTS, M., *Central Bank Independence: A Sensitivity Analysis*, Center for Economic Research Discussion Paper, no. 9710, Tilburg University, 1997.

EINHORN, B./KALDOR, M./KAVAN, Z., *Citizenship and Democratic Control in Contemporary Europe* (Edward Elgar, Cheltenham/Brookfield, 1996).

EIZENGA, W., "Uit de bibliotheek—geschiedenis van de Nederlandsche Bank", *Bank- en Effectenbedrijf*, vol. 44 no. 3 (1995), 16–18.

—— "Zelfstandigheid van centrale banken: Duitsland koploper", *Bank- en Effectenbedrijf*, vol. 43 no. 9 (1994), 20–5.

EMMERICH-FRITSCH, A., "Wie verbindlich sind die Konvergenzkriterien?", *EWS*, vol. 7, no. 3 (1996), 77–86.

ENGLERT, M., *Der Handlungsspielraum der amerikanischen Bundesbank im Regierungssytem* (Schäuble Verlag, Rheinfelden, 1988).

ERB, R.D., "Introduction and Summary", in R.D. Erb (ed.), *Federal Reserve Policies and Public Disclosure* (American Enterprise Institute for Public Policy Research, Washington, DC, 1978), 2–12.

ERICHSEN, H.-U. (ed.), *Allgemeines Verwaltungsrecht* (10th edn., Walter de Gruyter, Berlin and New York, 1995).

ERNST, O.E., "Das Gesetz über die Deutsche Bundesbank und seine wichtigsten öffentlich-rechtlichen Probleme", *DÖV* (1957), 606–12.

—— "Die Stellung der Notenbank im Staatsgefüge", *WM* 1957, 85–93.

ESCHWEILER, B./BORDO, M.D., *Rules, Discretion, and Central Bank Independence: The German Experience 1880–1989*, NBER Working Paper Series, no. 5597, National Bureau of Economic Research, Cambridge, Ma, 1993.

EUFRUN, B., *La Banque de France* (Berger-Levrault, Paris, 1995).

FABER, H., *Wirtschaftsplanung und Bundesbankautonomie* (Nomos, Baden-Baden, 1969).

FAIR, D.E., *Relationship Between Central Bank and Government in the Determination of Monetary Policy* (Société Universitaire Européenne de Recherches Financiéres (SUERF), 1980).

FARNSWORTH, E.A., *An Introduction to the Legal System of the United States* (3rd edn., Oceana Publications, New York, 1996).

FAZIO, A., "Role and Independence of Central Banks", in P. Downes/R. Vaez-Zadeh (eds.), *The Evolving Role of Central Banks* (Central Banking Department, International Monetary Fund, Washington, 1991), 121–39.

FEATHERSTONE, K., "Jean Monnet and the 'Democratic Deficit' in the European Union", *JCMS*, vol. 32 (1994), 149–70.

FEDERAL RESERVE BANK OF SAN FRANCISCO, *Accountability in Practice: Recent Monetary Policy in New Zealand*, FRBSF Economic Letter no. 96–25, 9 Sept. 1996.

FELDSTEIN, M., "The Council for Economic Advisors and Economic Advising in the United States", *The Economic Journal*, vol. 102 (1992), 1223–34.

FFORDE, J., *The Bank of England and Public Policy 1941–1958* (Cambridge University Press, Cambridge, 1992).

FISCHER, A., "New Zealand's Experience with Inflation Targets", in L. Leiderman/ L.E.O. Svensso (eds.) *Inflation Targets* (CEPR, London, 1995), 32–52.

FISCHER, S., "The Role of Macroeconomic Factors in Growth", *Journal of Monetary Economics*, vol. 32 (1993), 485–512.

—— "Modern Central Banking", in F. Capie *et al.*, *The Future of Central Banking* (Cambridge University Press, Cambridge, 1994), 262–308.

FLAHERTY, E., 1997, *A Brief History of Central Banking in the United States* (online), available from: URL http://odur.let.rug.nl/ (last accessed Oct. 1998).

FOSTER, CH., "Reflections on the True Significance of the Scott Report for Government Accountability", *PA*, vol. 74 (1996), 567–92.

FOSTER, N.G., *German Legal System & Laws* (2nd edn., Blackstone, London, 1996).

FROTSCHER, W., *Wirtschaftsverfassungs- und Wirtschaftsverwaltungsrecht* (C.H. Beck, Munich, 1988).

GALAHN, G., *Die Deutsche Bundesbank im Prozeß der europäischen Währungs- integration* (Walter de Gruyter, Berlin and New York, 1996).

GALL, L. *et al.*, *Die Deutsche Bank 1870–1995* (C.H. Beck, Munich, 1995).

GATES, S./HILL, J., "Democratic Accountability and Governmental Innovation in the Use of Nonprofit Organisations", *Political Studies Review*, vol. 14 no. 1/2 (1995), 137–48.

GAVALDA, CH./KOVAR, R./BÉCAM, J./BERNARD, A., *DALLOZ Répertoire de Droit Communautaire*, vol. II (Dalloz, Paris, 1992).

GELLHORN, W. *et al.*, *Administrative Law* (8th edn., The Foundation Press, Mineola, NY, 1987).

GEORGE, E./PENNANT-REA, R., "Minutes of Evidence", in Treasury and Civil Service Committee, *The Role of the Bank of England* (House of Commons Paper. Session 1993–4; 98–I, vol. 2), Report, together with the proceedings of the Committee. HC Session 1993–4 (HMSO, London, 1993), 22–37.

GLESKE, L., "Bundesbank Independence, Organisation and Decision-making", *Central Banking*, vol. 6 no. 1 (1995), 21–8.

GOODHART, CH., "Minutes of Evidence", in Treasury and Civil Service Committee, *The Role of the Bank of England* (House of Commons Paper. Session 1993–4; 98–I, vol. 2), Report, together with the proceedings of the Committee, HC Session 1993–4 (HMSO, London, 1993), 1–10.

—— *The Central Bank and the Financial System* (Macmillan, London, 1995).

GORMLEY, L.W., "Europäische Währungsunion und Demokratieprinzip", Zentrum für Europäisches Wirtschaftsrecht, Vorträge und Berichte, no. 90, 1997.

——/HAAN, J. DE, "The Democratic Deficit of the European Central Bank" (1996) 21 *ELRev.*, 95–112.

GRABITZ, E., "The Deutsche Bundesbank, Answers to the Questionnaire on Key Functions and Legal Structure of Central Banks and Banking Supervision Authorities", in J.-V. Louis (ed.), *Vers un Système Européen de Banques Centrales* (Editions de l'Université de Bruxelles, Brussels, 1989), 161–70.

——/HILF, M. (eds.), *Kommentar zur Europäischen Union* (loose-leaf, since 1984, C.H. Beck, Munich, 1988).

GRAMLICH, L., *Bundesbankgesetz Währungsgesetz Münzgesetz* (Carl Heymanns Verlag KG, Cologne, 1988).

—— "Die Deutsche Bundesbank im Verfassungsgefüge des Grundgesetzes", *JuS-Lernbogen* 11/1988, L 81–L 88.

GREIDER, W., *Secrets of the Temple* (Simon and Schuster, New York, 1987).

GRIER, G.B., "Congressional Influence on U.S. Monetary Policy", *Journal of Monetary Economics*, vol. 28 (1991), 20120.

GRILLI, V./MASCIANDARO, D./TABELLINI, G., "Political and Monetary Institutions and Public Financial Policies in the Industrial World", *Economic Policy*, no. 13 (1991), 162–212.

GRIMM, D.G., "Braucht Europa eine Verfassung?", *JZ*, vol. 50 no. 12 (1994), 581–91.

GROEBEN, H.V.D./THIESING, J./EHLERMANN, C.-D. (eds.), *Kommentar zum EWG-Vertrag* (4th edn., Nomos, Baden-Baden, 1991, 5th edn. in the course of publication, 1987–98), vol. 3.

GROS, D./THYGESEN, N., *European Monetary Integration* (Longman, London, 1992).

HAAN, J.DE, *Financiële markten en instellingen in Nederland* (Groningen, 1997).

—— "The European Central Bank: Independence, Accountability and Strategy: A Review", *Public Choice*, vol. 93 (1997), 395–426.

——/EIJFFINGER, S., *De politieke economie van centrale bank onafhankelijkheid* (Wolters-Noordhoff, Groningen, 1994).

——/GORMLEY, L.W., "Independence and Accountability of the European Central Bank", in M. Andenas/L. Gormley/C. Hadjiemmanuil/I. Harden (eds.), *European*

Economic and Monetary Union: The Institutional Framework (Kluwer Law International, London, 1997), 331–53.

——/KOOI, W., "What Really Matters: Conservativeness or Independence?", *BNL Quarterly Review*, no. 200 (1997), 23–38.

HAAN, J.DE/AMTENBRINK, F./EIJFFINGER, S.C.W., *Accountability of Central Banks: Aspects and Quantifications*, Center for Economic Research, Discussion paper, no. 9854, Tilburg University, May 1998.

HÄDE, U., "Das Europäische Währungsinstitut und die Kommission", *EuZW* (1994), 685–7.

—— "Das Gesetz zur Änderung von Vorschriften über die Deutsche Bundesbank", *NJW* (1994), 3214–32.

HAFERKAMP, D., "Die deutsche Währungsunion- bereits Währungsgeschichte?", *DtZ*, vol. 2 no. 6 (1991), 201–20.

HAGEN, J. VON, *Monetäre, fiskalische und politische Integration: Das Beispiel der USA*, in *Währungsunion und politische Integration: Historische Erfahrungen und europäische Perspektive*, 9. Wissenschaftliche Kolloquium am 3. November 1995 im Hotel Marriot, Frankfurt am Main, auf Einladung der Deutschen Bundesbank, Bankhistorisches Archiv, Beiheft 30 (Fritz Knapp Verlag, Frankfurt a.M., 1996), 35–51.

HAHN, H.J., "Die Deutsche Bundesbank im Verfassungsrecht", *BayVBl.*, no. 2 and no. 3 (1982), 33–7 and 70–5.

—— *Währungsrecht* (C.H. Beck, Munich, 1990).

—— "The European Central Bank: Key to European Monetary Union or Target" (1991) 28 *CMLRev.*, 783–820.

——/HÄDE, U., "Europa im Wartestand: Bemerkungen zur Währungsunion", in O. Due *et al.* (eds.), *Festschrift für Ulrich Everling*, Vol. I (Nomos, Baden-Baden, 1995), 381–98.

HAHN, O., *Die Währungsbank: Behörde, Unternehmen, Autorität* (Erich Schmidt Verlag, Berlin, 1993).

HALDANE, A.G., *Rules, Discretion and the United Kingdom's New Monetary Framework*, Working Paper Series no. 40, Bank of England, London, 1995.

HALL, M.J.B., *Banking Regulation and Supervision: A Comparative Study of the UK, USA and Japan* (Edward Elgar, Aldershot, 1993).

HARDEN, I., "The European Central Bank and the National Central Banks in Economic and Monetary Union", in K. Gretschmann (ed.), *Economic and Monetary Union: Implications for National Policy-makers* (European Institute of Public Administration, Maastricht, 1993), 149–76.

—— "Democracy and the European Union", in P. Hirst/S. Khilnani (eds), *Reinventing Democracy* (Blackwell Publishers, Oxford, 1996).

Harris, B.V., "The Constitutional Base", in H. Gold, *New Zealand Politics in Perspective* (3rd edn., Longman Paul, Auckland, 1992), 56–76.

HARTOG, A. DEN, "The Netherlands and the Ratification of the Maastricht Treaty", in S.F. Laursen/S. Vanhoonacken, *The Ratifiaction of the Maastricht Treaty—Issues, Debates and Future Implications* (European Institute of Public Administration, Martinus Nijhoff Publishers, Maastricht, 1994), 213–25.

HASSE, R.H. (ed.), *The European Central Bank: Perspectives for a Further Development of the European Monetary System* (Bertelsmann Foundation Publishers, Gütersloh, 1990).

HAVRILESKY, TH., *The Pressure on American Monetary Policy* (Kluwer Academic Publishers, Boston, 1993).

HEALEY, N./LEVINE, P./ PEARLMAN, J., *The Political Economy of a European Central Bank*, conference paper, 2nd ECSA-World Conference: Federalism, Subsidiarity and Democracy in the European Union, Brussels, 5–6 May 1994, Working Group II.

HENNESSY, E., "The Governors, Directors and Management of the Bank of England", in R. Roberts/D. Kynaston (eds.), *The Bank of England—Money, Power and Influence 1694–1994* (Clarendon Press, Oxford, 1995), 185–216.

HERDEGEN, M., "Maastricht and the German Constitutional Court: Constitutional Restraint for an 'Ever Closer Union' " (1994) 31 *CMLRev.*, 235–49.

HERINGA, A.W., "Het verdrag van Maastricht in strijd met de Grondwet", *NJB* (1992), 749–52.

HEUKELS, T., case note on *European Parliament* v. *Council, Case C–65/93 [1995] ECR I 643* (1995) 32 *CMLRev.*, 1420–6.

HEYLEN, F./POECK, A. VAN, "Central Bank Independence: Only Part of the Inflation Story", *De Economist*, vol. 144 (1996), 45–61.

HIGHET, K./KAHALE III, G./KOKOTT, J.B., "French Case Note", *AJIL*, vol. 86 (1992), 824–82.

HILLEN, J.L.S.M., *Bank-, munt- en nationale schuldwetgeving: voorzien van aantekeningen en alfabetisch register* (Nederlandse staatswetten: editie Schuurman & Jordens; 143–I) (W.E.J. Tjeenk Willink, Zwolle, 1993).

HIRST, P., *Representative Democracy and Its Limits* (Polity Press, Oxford, 1990).

—— "Democracy and Civil Society", in P. Hirst/S. Khilnani (eds.), *Reinventing Democracy* (Blackwell Publishers, Oxford, 1996), 97–116.

HOLMES, P., "From the Single European Act to Maastricht: The Creation of the European Union", in B. Einhorn/M. Kaldor/Z. Kavan, *Citizenship and Democratic Control in Contemporary Europe* (Edward Elgar, Cheltenham/Brookfield, 1996), 54–68.

HOLTROP, M.W., "De Functie van de centrale bank", *AO–Reeks Boekje* No. 1162.

HOOD, C., "Concepts of Control over Public Bureaucracies: 'Comptrol' and 'Interpolable Balance' ", in F.X. Kaufmann (ed.), *The Public Sector* (Walter de Gruyter, Berlin and New York, 1991), 347–66.

HOPPE, H.-D., *Der Rechtsschutz gegen Akte der Währungspolitik*, Diss., Würzburg, 1994.

HUBER, P.M., "Die Rolle des Demokratieprinips im europäischen Integrationsprozeß", *Staatswissenschaft und Staatspraxis* (3) 1992, 349–79.

HURST, J.W., *A Legal History of Money in the United States, 1774–1970* (University of Nebraska Press, Lincoln, Neb., 1973).

IACONO, G., "Le nouveau statut de la Banque de France, une étape vers l'union économique et monétaire", *Recueil Dalloz Sirey*, no. 12 (1994), 89–92.

JACOBS, F., CORBETT, R/SHACKLETON, M., *The European Parliament* (3rd edn., Cartermill Publishing, London, 1995).

JAMES, P.S., *Introduction to English Law* (Butterworth, London, 1990).

JARRAS, H.D./PIEROTH, B., *Grundgesetz für die Bundesrepublik Deutschland* (Commentary, 3rd edn., C.H. Beck, Munich, 1995).

JOHNSON, C., "Memorandum submitted to the Treasury and Civil Service Select Committee", in Treasury and Civil Service Committee, *The Role of the Bank of England* (House of Commons Paper. Session 1993–4; 98–I, vol. 2), Report, together with the proceedings of the Committee. HC Session 1993–4 (HMSO, London, 1993), app. 22.

JORDAN, J.L., "Statement by the President of the Federal Reserve Bank of Cleveland before the Committee on Banking, Finance. and Urban Affairs", US House of Representatives, 19 Oct. 1993, reprinted in *Federal Reserve Bulletin*, vol. 79 no. 12, Dec. 1993, 1110–20.

JOSEPH, P.A., *Constitutional and Administrative Law in New Zealand* (The Law Book Company Limited, Sidney, 1993).

KÄGENAU, H./WETTER, W., *Europäische Wirtschafts- und Währungsunion—Vom Werner Plan zum Vertrag von Maastricht* (Nomos, Baden-Baden, 1993).

KAISER, R.H., *Bundesbankautonomie—Möglichkeiten und Grenzen einer unabhängigen Politik* (Rita G. Fischer Verlag, Frankfurt a.M., 1980).

KAMP, A.F., *'S Konings Oudste Dogter* (De Nederlandsche Bank, Amsterdam, 1968).

KANE, E.J., "Bureaucratic Self-interest as an Obstacle to Monetary Reform", in Th. Mayer (ed.), *The Political Economy of American Monetary Policy* (Cambridge University Press, Cambridge, 1990), 283–98.

KAPTEYN, P.J.G./VERLOREN VAN THEMMAT, P./GEELHOED, L.A./TIMMERMANS, C.W.A. (eds.), *Inleiding tot het recht van de Europese Gemeenschappen* (5th edn., Kluwer, Deventer, 1995).

KEECH, W. R., *Economic Politics:The Costs of Democracy* (Cambridge University Press, Cambridge, 1995).

KENEN, P.B., "The European Central Bank and the Monetary Policy in Stage Three of EMU", *International Affairs*, vol. 68 no. 3 (1992), 457–74.

KENNEDY, E., *The Bundesbank* (Pinter Publishers, London, 1991).

KETTL, D.F., *Leadership at the FED* (Yale University Press, New Haven, Conn., and London, 1986).

KLEIN, F., "Rechtsgutachten über die Frage, ob das Bundesbankgesetz in der Fassung des Regierungsvorlage vom 18. Oktober 1956 der Zustimmung des Bundesrates bedarf", *WM* (1957), 1074–88.

KLOTEN, N., "Die Anpassung der Struktur an die veränderten staatlichen Gegebenheiten", *Zeitschrift für das gesamte Kreditwesen* (1991), 604–8.

KLUMP, R. (ed.), *40 Jahre Deutsche Mark: die politische und oekonomische Bedeutung der westdeutschen Währungsreform vor 1948* (Steiner Verlag Wiesbaden, Stuttgart, 1989).

KOCH, H., *L'histoire de la Banque de France et de la monnaie sous la IV République* (Dunod, Paris, 1983).

KOOPMANS, T., "Rechter, D-mark en democratie: het Bundesverfassungsgericht en de Europese Unie", *NJB* (1994), 245–51.

KORTMAN, C.A.J.M., *Constitutioneel Recht* (2nd edn., Kluwer, Deventer, 1994).

KORTZ, H., *Die Entscheidung über den Übergang in die Endstufe der Wirtschafts- und Währungsunion*, Diss. (Nomos, Baden-Baden, 1996).

KRAAN, K.J., "Het Koninkrijk der Nederlanden", in L. Prakke/C.A.J.M. Kortmann (eds.), *Het staatsrecht van der landen der Europese Gemeenschappen* (4th edn., Kluwer, Deventer, 1993), 499–561.

KREDIETBANK, "La banque centrale idéale—I", *Kredietbank-Bulletin hebdomadaire*, vol. 48 no. 26 (1993), 1–6, —II, *Kredietbank-Bulletin hebdomadaire*, vol. 48 no. 27 (1993), 1–5.

KÜMPEL, S., "Das währungspolitische Instrumentarium der Deutschen Bundesbank aus rechtlicher Sicht", *WM* (1992), Sonderbeilage no. 1/1992.

KUNIG, Ph., *Das Rechtsstaatsprinzip* (Mohr (Siebeck), Tübingen, 1986).

KYDLAND, F./PRESCOTT, E., "Rules rather than Discretion The Inconsistency of Optimal Plans", *Journal of Political Economy*, vol. 85 no. 3 (1977), 473–91.

LADEUR, K.-H., "Die Autonomie der Bundesbank- ein Beispiel für die institutionelle Verarbeitung von Ungewißheitsentscheidungen", *Staatswissenschaften und Staatspraxis* 3 (1992), 486–508.

LASOK, K.P.E., *The European Court of Justice—Practice and Procedures* (2nd edn., Butterworths, London, 1994).

LASTRA, R.M., "The Independence of the European Central Bank", *Harvard International Law Journal*, vol. 33 (1992), 475–519.

—— "European Monetary Union and Central Bank Independence", in M. Andenas/L. Gormley/C. Hadjiemmanuil/I. Harden (eds.), *European Economic and Monetary Union: The Institutional Framework* (Kluwer Law International, London, 1997), 289–329.

LERDA, J.C., "Globalization and Loss of Autonomy by the Fiscal, Banking and Monetary Authorities", *CEPA Review*, no. 58 (April 1996), 65–78.

LEROY, CH., "Les incidences constitutionnelles de la réforme accordant son indépendance à la Banque de France", LPA, no. 85–5 (1994), 5–10.

LEVAGGI, R., "Accountability and the Internal Market", *Financial Accountability & Management*, vol. 11 no. 4 (1995), 283–96.

LIPPI, F., *Central Bank Independence and Credibility*, Tinbergen Institute Research Series (Erasmus University Rotterdam, 1997).

LLOYD, M., "The New Zealand Approach to Central Bank Autonomy", *Reserve Bank Bulletin*, vol. 55 (1992), 203–20.

LOMBARD, M., "Le nouveau statut de la Banque de France", *L'Actualité juridique—Droit administratif*, 20 juillet/20 août 1994, 491–5.

LOUIS, J.-V., "Le Federal Reserve System—Rapport sur une mission d'études conduite en septembre 1988", in *Vers Un Systeme Européen de Banques Centrales*, Rapport du groupe présidé par Jean-Victor Louis (Editions de l'Université de Bruxelles, Brussels, 1989), 269–303.

—— "The Project of a European Central Bank", in J. Stuyck (ed.), *Financial and Monetary Integration in the European Economic Community*, Generale Bank Chair Lectures 1991–1992, Centre for Advanced Legal Studies (Kluwer Law and Taxation Publishers, Deventer-Boston, 1993), 13–28.

—— "Economic and Monetary Union (European Central Bank)", in T.M.C. Asser Instituut, *The Treaty on European Union—Suggestions for revisions*, Conference Reader (Stichting T.M.C. Asser Instituut, The Hague, 1995), 247–57.

LÖWENTHAL, P., "De l'autonomie des autorités monétaires", *Réflets perspectives de la vie économique*, vol. 30 no. 3, 161–9.

LUCHAIRE, F, "L'Union Européenne et la Constitution", première partie, RDP (1992), 589–616.

MAIER, P./HAAN, J. DE, "How Independent is the Bundesbank Really?" A survey, forthcoming in: J. De Haan (ed.), *50 years of Bundesbank: Lessons for the ECB* (Routledge, London).

MAJONE, G., *Independence vs. Accountability? Non-Majoritarian Institutions and Democratic Government in Europe*, EUI Working Paper SPS No. 94/3 (European University Institute, Florence, 1993).

MANKIW, N.G. *Macroeconomics* (3rd edn., Worth Publishers, New York, 1997).

MARSH, D., *The Bundesbank: The Bank that Rules Europe* (Mandarin, London, 1993).

—— *Die Bundesbank- Geschäfte mit der Macht* (2nd edn., C. Bertelsmann, Goldmann Verlag, Munich, 1995).

MASKENS, CH., *L'Histoire du Fed Peut-Elle Fournir des Enseignements pour une Future*

Banque Centrale Europeenne?, Documentatieblad Ministerie Van Financiën (Belgium), no. 2 (Maart–April 1990), 293–319.

MASSON, P.R./TAYLOR, M.P., "Fiscal Policy within Common Currency Areas", *JCMS*, vol. 31 (1993), 29–44.

MAUNZ, TH./DÜRIG, G. (eds.), *Grundgesetz: Kommentar* (loose-leaf, 7th edn., C.H. Beck, Munich, October 1996).

——/ZIPPELIUS, R., *Deutsches Staatsrecht: ein Studienbuch* (29th edn., C.H. Beck, Munich, 1994).

MAYES, D.G., *Accountability for the Central Bank in Europe*, conference paper prepared for the 11th Lothian Conference (A Central Bank for Europe) London, 9 Nov. 1997.

MCCALLUM, B.T., *Crucial issues concerning central bank independence*, NBER Working Paper Series, no. 5597 (National Bureau of Economic Research, Cambridge, Mass, 1996).

MCLEAY, E., *The Cabinet and Political Power in New Zealand* (Oxford University Press, Auckland, 1995).

MISHKIN, F.S./POSEN, A.S., "Inflation Targeting: Lessons from Four Countries", *Federal Reserve Bank of New York Economic Policy Review*, vol. 3 no. 3 (1997), 9–110.

MITCHELL, A., "The New Zealand Way of Committee Power", *Parliamentary Affairs*, vol. 46 no. 1 (1993), 91–100.

MOORE, C.H., *The Federal Reserve System: A History of the first 75 Years* (McFarland & Company, Inc., Publishers, Jefferson, NC, 1990).

MORAN, M., "Monetary Policy and the Machinery of Government", PA, vol. 59 (1981), 47–61.

MULHOLLAND, R.D., *Introduction to the New Zealand Legal System* (8th edn., Butterworths, Wellington, 1995).

MÜLLER, W., "Ministerialfreie Räume", *JuS*, vol. 25 no. 7 (1985), 497–508.

MULLINS, E.C., *A Study of the Federal Reserve* (Kasper and Horton, New York, 1952).

MÜNCH, I.V./KUNIG, P. (eds.), *Grundgesetz-Kommentar*, Vol. 3 (3rd edn., C.H. Beck, Munich, 1996).

MUNG, M.C./ROBERTS, B.E., "The Federal Reserve and its Institutional Environment: A Review", in Th. Mayer (ed.), *The Political Economy of American Monetary Policy* (Cambridge University Press, Cambridge, 1990), 83–98.

NEDERLANDSCHE BANK, DE, *Hoedster van de gulden* (4th edn., Amsterdam, 1988).

NELL, J., "Central Banks and the News", *Central Banking*, vol. 6 no. 4 (1996), 79–83.

NEWTON, M., *The FED* (Times Books, New York, 1983).

NEUMANN, J., "Commenting on Beaufort Wijnholds/Hoogduin: Central Bank Autonomy—Policy Issues", in J.O. de Beaufort Wijnholds/S.C.W. Eijffinger/L.H. Hoogduin (eds.), *A Framework for Monetary Stability* (Kluwer Academic Publishers, Dordrecht, 1994), 103–7.

NGUYEN, L.M., *La Constitution de la Vème Republique* (4th edn., Les Editions S.T.H., Paris, 1989).

NOLAN, C./SCHALING, E., *Monetary Policy Uncertainty and Central Bank Accountability*, Bank of England Working Paper Series no. 54, Oct. 1996.

NORTON, J.J.N./WALKER, G.A., *European Monetary Union: An Historical Perspective*, paper presented at the European Monetary Union Special Workshop London, 26/27 Jan. 1996.

OFFICE OF THE STAFF DIRECTORS FOR FEDERAL RESERVE BANK ACTIVITIES, BOARD OF GOVERNORS OF THE FED, *The Role of Directors of the Federal Reserve Banks and*

Branches in the Functions and Responsibilities of the Fed (2nd printing, Washington, DC, Feb. 1989).

OLIVER, P., "The French Constitution and the Treaty of Maastricht" (1994) 43 *ICLQ*, 1–25.

OZKAN, F.G./SUTHERLAND, A., *A Model of the ERM Crisis*, CEPR discussion paper no. 879 (Centre for Economic Policy Research, London, 1994).

PATMAN, P., "The Federal Reserve System: A Brief For Legal Reform" (1996) 10 *St. Louis University School of Law Journal*, 299–326, reprinted in Joint Economic Committee Congress of the United States, 94th Congress 2nd Session, 3 Jan. 1977, App. I, 143–61.

PENNANT-REA, R., "The Bank of England: Yesterday, Today, Tomorrow", in R. Roberts/D. Kynaston (eds.), *The Bank of England* (Clarendon Press, Oxford, 1995), 217–24.

PERNICE, I., "Das Ende der währungspolitischen Souveränität Deutschlands und das Maastricht-Urteil des BVerfG", in O. Due *et al.* (eds.), *Festschrift für Ulrich Everling*, Vol. I (Nomos, Baden-Baden, 1995), 1057–70.

PIERCE, J.L., "The Federal Reserve as a Political Power", in Th. Mayer (ed.), *The Political Economy of American Monetary Policy* (Cambridge University Press, Cambridge, 1990), 151–64.

—— "The Myth of Congressional Supervision of Monetary Policy", *Journal of Monetary Economics*, vol. 4 (1978), 363–70.

PIPKORN, J., "Legal Arrangements in the Treaty of Maastricht for the Effectiveness of the Economic and Monetary Union" (1994) 31 *CMLRev.*, 263–91.

PIRIS, J.-C., "After Maastricht, are the Community Institutions More Efficacious, More Democratic and More Transparent?" (1994) 19 *ELRev.*, 449–87.

PLESSIS, A., "Banque de France", in M. Pohl/S. Freitag (eds.), *Handbook on the History of European Banks* (Edward Elgar, Aldershot, 1994), 204–8.

PÖHL, O., "Towards Monetary Union", in *IEA, Europe's Constitutional Future* 38 (1990).

POSTHUMUS MEYJES, H.C., "Nieuwe kleren voor het buitenlands en veiligheidsbeleid. Een beschouwing over de tweede pijler van het Europese Unie-Verdrag", *SEW*, vol. 45 no. 10 (1997), 365–9.

POULLAIN, L., "Für eine 'demokratische' Autonomie", in D. Duwendag (ed.), *Macht und Ohnmacht der Bundesbank* (Athenäum Verlag, Frankfurt a.M., 1973), 36–52.

POTACS, M., "Nationale Zentralbanken in der Wirtschafts- und Währungsunion", *EuR*, vol. 28 no. 1 (1993), 23–40.

PRAKKE, L./DE REEDE, J.L./VAN WISSEN, G.J.M., *Van Der Pott—Donner: Handboek Van Het Nederlandse Staatsrecht* (13th edn., W.E.J. Tjeenk Willink, Zwolle, 1995).

PRÉLOT, M., *Institutions politiques et droit constitutionnel* (11ème ed., revue et mise à jour par J. Boulouis, Dalloz, Paris, 1990).

PROST, S., "Die Deutsche Bundesbank im Spannungsbereich anderer unabhängiger Organe und Institutionen", in E. Büschgen (ed.), *Geld, Kapital und Kredit, Festschrift zum siebzigsten Geburtstag von Heinrich Rittershausen* (Pöschel, Stuttgart, 1968), 110–26.

QUADEN, G., "Indépendance et responsabilité des banques centrales: l'expérience des banques nationales", *Réflets perspectives de la vie économique*, vol. 30 no. 3 (1991), 133–45.

RANDZIO-PLATH, C., "Democratic Accountability of the European Central Bank", *Central Banking*, vol. 8 no. 3 (1997/8), 22–5.

RAWORTH, P., "A Timid Step Forwards: Maastricht and the Democratisation of the European Communities" (1994) 19 *ELRev.*, 16–33.

REDON, M./BESNARD, D., *La Banque de France* (3rd edn., série Que Sais-Je, Presses Universitaires de France, Paris, 1996).

RESERVE BANK OF NEW ZEALAND, *An Introductory Guide*, available from URL http://www.rbnz.govt.nz/ (last accessed Jan. 1999).

—— *Briefing on the Reserve Bank of New Zealand* (Reserve Bank, Wellington, 1996).

REUSS, H.S., *Making the Fed More Accountable*, Opening statements by the Chairman of the House Committee on Banking, Finance and Urban Affairs, for hearings on HR 8094, a bill to promote the accountability of the Fed , 10.00 a.m., Monday 18 July 1977.

REY, J.-J., "Indépendance et responsabilité: le projet de Banque centrale européenne", *Réflets perspectives de la vie économique*, vol. 30 no. 3 (1991), 147–60.

ROBERTS, R./KYNASTON, D. (eds.), *The Bank of England—Money, Power and Influence 1694–1994* (Clarendon Press, Oxford, 1995).

ROBERTS, S.M., "Congressional Oversight of Monetary Policy", *Journal of Monetary Economics*, vol. 4 (1978), 543–56.

RODGERS, P., "Changes at the Bank of England", *Bank of England Quarterly Bulletin*, vol. 37 no. 2, 241–7.

ROGOFF, K., "The Optimal Degree of Commitment to an Intermediate Monetary Target", *Quarterly Journal of Economics*, vol. 100 (1985), 1169–90.

ROUBINI, N./SACHS, J., "Government Spending and Budget Deficits in the Industrial Countries", *Economic Policy*, no. 8 (1989), 99–132.

RUSSEL-JONES, N., *1992—The Changing Face of the Financial Services: A Eurostudy Special Report* (Eurostudy, London, 1992).

SAGER, L.G., "The Sources and Limits of Legal Authority", in A.B. Morris, *Fundamentals of American Law* (Oxford University Press, Oxford, 1996), 27–56.

SAINT PHALLE, TH. DE, *The Federal Reserve. An Intentional Mystery* (Praeger, New York, 1985).

SAMM, C.-TH., *Die Stellung der Deutschen Bundesbank im Staatsgefüge* (2nd edn., Duncker & Humblot, Berlin, 1971).

—— "Verfassungsgarantierte Bundesbankautonomie", *WM* (1984), Sonderbeilage No. 5/1984.

—— "Die Unabhängigkeit der Bundesbank—Verfassungsauftrag oder ordnungspolitische Chance?", in H.J. Hahn (ed.), *Geldverfassung und Ordnungspolitik* (Nomos, Baden-Baden, 1989), 143–67.

SARGENT, N.J./WALLACE, N., "Some Unpleasant Monetarist Arithmetic", *Federal Reserve Bank of Minneapolis Quarterly Review*, vol. 5 (1981), 1–17.

SARTORI, G., *The Theory of Democracy Revisited* (Chatham House Publishers, Chatham, NJ, 1987).

SAYERS, R.S., *The Bank of England 1891–1944*, 3 Vols. (Cambridge University Press, London, 1976).

SCHMIDT, R., *Grundlagen und Grenzen der Unabhängigkeit der Deutschen Bundesbank*, in E.v. Caemmerer *et al.* (eds.), *Festschrift für Pan J. Zapos*, Vol. II (Ch. Katsikalis Verlag, Athens, 1973), 655–80.

SCHOENBROD, D., *Power Without Responsibility: How Congress Abuses the People Through Delegation* (Yale University Press, New Haven and London, 1993).

SCHOKKER, E., "De autonomie van de Centrale Bank; een vergleijking tussen Nederland en de BRD", *Maandschrift economie*, vol. 48, no. 1 (1984), 41–55.

SCHOTSMAN, R.J., *De Parliamentaire Behandeling van het Monetaire Beleid in Nederland Sinds 1863*, Diss., University of Brabant 1987.

SCOTT, R., "Ministerial Accountability" [1996] *PL*, 410–26.

SHAW, J., "European Union Citizenship: the IGC and Beyond", *European Public Law*, vol. 3 no. 3 (1997), 413–39.

SIEBELT, J., *Der juristische Verhaltensspielraum der Zentralbanken* (Nomos, Baden-Baden, 1988).

SMAGHI, L.B., *The Democratic Accountability of the European Central Bank* (EMI, Frankfurt a.M., May 1998).

SMALE, P., *Audits of the Federal Reserve System: Past, Present and Proposed*, CRS Report for Congress, 24 Jan. 1995, Congressional Research Service, Library of Congress, Washington, DC.

SMITS, R., The European Central Bank: Institutional Aspects" (1996) 45 *ICLQ*, 319–42.

——*The European Central Bank- Institutional Aspects* (Kluwer Law International, London, 1997).

SPINDLER, J.v./BECKER, W., STARKE, O.-E., *Die Deutsche Bundesbank* (4th ed., Verlag W. Kohlhammer, Stuttgart, 1973).

SPITZ, E., *Majority Rule* (Chatham House Publishers, Chatham, NJ, 1984).

STADLER, R., *Der rechtliche Handlungsspielraum des Europäischen Systems der Zentralbanken* (Nomos, Baden-Baden, 1996).

STARKE, O.-E., "Das Gesetz über die Deutsche Bundesbank und seine wichtigsten öffentlich-rechtlichen Probleme", *DÖV* (1957), 606–12.

STEFFANI, W., "Das Demokratie-Dilemma der Europäischen Union. Die Rolle der Parlamente nach dem Urteil des Bundesverfassungsgerichtes vom 12. Oktober 1993", in W. Steffani/U. Thaysen, *Demokratie in Europa: Zur Rolle der Parlamente*, ZParl, Sonderband 1/95 (Westdeutscher Verlag, Opladen, 1995), 33–49.

STERN, K., *Das Staatsrecht der Bundesrepublik Deutschland*, Vol. 2 (C.H. Beck, Munich, 1980).

STUDT, D., *Rechtsfragen der europäischen Zentralbank* (Dunker & Humblot, Berlin, 1993).

TAYLOR, G., *The Federal Reserve System* (Chelsea House Publishers, New York, 1989).

TIETMEYER, H., "The Role of an Independent Central Bank in Europe", in P. Downes/R. Vaez-Zadeh, *The Evolving Role of Central Banks* (Central Banking Department, IMF, Washington, 1991), 176–89.

——"Zur politischen Fundierung des monetären Integrationsprozesses in Europa", in O. Due, *et al.* (eds.), *Festschrift für Ulrich Everling*, Vol. II (Nomos, Baden-Baden, 1995), 1575–84.

UHLENBRUCK, D., *Die verfassungsmäßige Unabhängigkeit der Deutschen Bundesbank und ihre Grenzen*, Diss., Cologne, 1967.

USHER, J.A., *The Law of Money and Financial Services in the European Community* (Clarendon Press, Oxford, 1996).

VAUBEL, R., "Eine Public-Choice-Analyse der Deutschen Bundesbank und ihre Implikationen für die Europäische Wirtschaftsunion", in D. Duwendag/J. Siebke (eds.), *Europa vor dem Eintritt in die Wirtschafts- und Währungsunion* (Duncker & Humblot, Berlin, 1993).

VELTHOVEN, B.C.J. VAN/SCHAIK, A.VAN, "De zelfstandigheid van de Nederlandsche Bank inzake het monetaire beleid in historisch, politiek-economisch perspectief", in H.W.J.

Bosman/J.C. Brezet, *Sparen en Investeren Geld en Banken* (H.E. Stenfert Kroese B.V., Leiden/Antwerpen, 1987), 366–97.

VIBERT, F., "Memorandum submitted to the Treasury and Civil Service Select Committee", in Treasury and Civil Service Committee, *The Role of the Bank of England* (House of Commons Paper. Session 1993–4; 98–I, vol. 2), Report, together with the proceedings of the Committee. HC Session 1993–4 (HMSO, London, 1993), app. 29.

VICKERS, G., "Accountability", in L.H. Browder Jr., (ed.), *Emerging Patterns of Administrative Accountability* (Mr Cutchan Publishing Corp., Berkeley, 1971), 28–46.

VILE, M.J.C., *Constitutionalism and the Separation of Powers* (Clarendon Press, Oxford, 1967).

VONDELING, A., *Nasmaak en voorproef* (Uitgeverij De Arbeiderspers, Amsterdam, 1968).

VRIES, J.DE, *De Nederlandsche Bank- Geschiedenis Nader Beschouwd* (Martinus Nijhoff, Leiden/Antwerpen, 1992).

—— "De Nederlandsche Bank", in M. Pohl/S. Freitag (eds.), *Handbook on the History of European Banks* (Edward Elgar, Aldershot, 1994), 743–8.

WADE, E.S.C./BRADLEY, A.W., *Constitutional and Administrative Law* (11th edn., Longman, London and New York, 1993).

WADE, W./FORSYTH, C., *Administrative Law* (Clarendon Press, Oxford, 1994).

WAGNER, R.E., "Public Choice, Monetary Control and Economic Disruption", in P. Whiteley (ed.), *Models of Political Economy* (SAGE Publications, London, 1980).

WAHLIG, B., "Relations between the Bundesbank and the Federal Government", *Die Bank*, vol. 6 (1995), 52–61.

WALSH, C.E., "Optimal Contracts for Central Bankers", *The American Economic Review*, vol. 48 no. 1 (1995), 150–67.

WANDEL, E., *Die Entstehung der Bank deutscher Länder und die deutsche Währungsreform 1948* (Fritz Knapp Verlag, Frankfurt a.M., 1980).

WASSERMANN, R. (principal editor), *Kommentar zum Grundgesetz für die Bundesrepublik Deutschland*, Vol. 2 (Reihe Alternativkommentare, Luchterhand, Neuwied, 1989).

WEATHERILL, S./BEAUMONT, P, *EC Law* (2nd edn., Penguin Publishers, London, 1995).

WEBER, A., "Die Wirtschafts- und Währungsunion nach dem Maastricht-Urteil des BVerfG", *JZ*, vol. 49 no. 2 (1994), 53–60.

WEIKART, TH., "Die Änderung des Bundesbank-Artikels im Grundgesetz mit Hinblick auf den Vertrag von Maastricht", *NVwZ* (1993), 834–41.

WEINTRAUB, R.E., "Congressional Supervision of Monetary Policy", *Journal of Monetary Economics*, vol. 4 (1978), 341–62.

WERRES, TH., "The Deutsche Bundesbank and its Relationship with the Federal Government", in *Europe's Economy in the 1990s* (AGENOR Research Unit's European Research Project on Autonomy Phase I, 1989–1990, Vol. II, Brussels, 1989).

WHITTLESEY, C.R., "Power and Influence in the Federal Reserve System", *Economica*, vol. 30 (1963), 30–43.

WIJK, H.H.VAN, *De Nederlandsche Bank: functie en werkterrein* (Nederlands Instituut voor het Bank- en Effectenrecht, Amsterdam, 1988).

WILSON, J.Q./DIIULIO, Jr., J.J., *American Government: Institutions and Policies* (6th edn., Heath, Lexington, Mass./Toronto, 1995).

WOLFF, H.J./BACHOF, O./STOBER, R., *Verwaltungsrecht* (10th edn., C.H. Beck, Munich, 1994).

Wood, G.E., "A Pioneer Bank in a Pioneer's Country", *Central Banking*, vol. 5 no. 1 (1994), 59–74.

Wyatt, D./Dashwood, A., *European Community Law* (3rd edn., Sweet & Maxwell, London, 1993).

Zijlstra, J., *Per Slot van rekening: memoires* (Contact, Amsterdam, 1992).

Zöller, A., *Staatsbank der DDR und Deutsche Bundesbank. Ein Vergleich*, Diss., University Würzburg, 1991.

Zuleeg, M., "Demokratie in der Europäischen Gemeinschaft", *JZ*, vol. 48 no. 22 (1993), 1069–74.

REPORTS

Banque de France, *Annual Report 1995* (Direction générale des Études, Banque de France, Paris, 1996).

——*Monetary Policy Results in 1997 and Outlook for 1998*, available from URL http://www.banque-france.fr/ (last accessed Oct. 1998).

Board of Governors of the Federal Reserve System, *83rd Annual Report 1996* (Washington, DC, 1997).

——*Monetary Policy Report to the Congress Pursuant to the Full Employment and Balanced Growth Act of 1978*, 22 July 1997.

——*Strategic Framework 1997–2002*, Washington, DC, Dec. 1996.

Committee of Governors of the Central Banks of the European Economic Community, *Report on the Questions Posed by the Committee "ad hoc" Chaired by Premier Werner of 1 August 1970* [1970](OJ C136/21).

Committee of Governors of the Central Banks of the Member States of the European Economic Community, *Draft Statute of the European System of Central Banks and of the European Central Bank*, Agence Europe, Doc. no. 1669 and 1670 of 8 Dec. 1990.

——*Annual Report (July 1990–December 1991)*, Apr. 1992.

Committee for the Study of Economic and Monetary Union, *Report on Economic and Monetary Union in the European Community* (Office for Official Publications of the European Communities, Luxembourg 1989) (Delors Report).

Deutsche Bundesbank, *Banking Regulations 2* (Frankfurt a.M., 1996).

——*Annual Report 1996* (Frankfurt a.M., 1997).

——*Stellungnahme des Zentralbankrates zur Konvergenzlage in der Europäischen Union im Hinblick auf die dritte Stufe der Wirtschafts- und Währungsunion* (Frankfurt a.M., 26 Mar. 1998).

European Central Bank, *The Single Monetary Policy in Stage Three: General documentation on ESCB Monetary Policy Instruments and Procedures* (Frankfurt a.M., 1998).

European Commission, *Economic and Monetary Union* (Office for Official Publications of the European Communities, Luxembourg, 1996).

European Monetary Institute, *Role and Functions of the European Monetary Institute* (Feb. 1996).

——*Payment Systems in the European Union* (Frankfurt a.M., 1996).

——*Progress Towards Convergence 1996* (Frankfurt a.M., 1996).

——*The Single Monetary Policy in Stage Three—Specifications of the Operational Framework* (Frankfurt a.M., Jan. 1997 and Sept. 1997).

Europees Monetair Instituut, *Convergentieverslag- Verslag krachtens artikel 109J van het Verdrag tot oprichting van de Europese Gemeenschap* (Frankfurt a.M., Maart 1998).

Final consolidated report to the temporary committee of the European Parliament on the follow-up of recommendations on BSE (COM/97/509 Final).

First Report from the Treasury Select Committee, *Barings and International Regulation*, Session 1996–7, HC 65.

First Report from the Select Committee on Treasury, *Accountability of the Bank of England*, Session 1997–8, HC 282.

Independent and Accountable, A New Mandate for the Bank of England, Report of an Independent Panel Chaired by Eric Roll, Centre for Economic Policy Research, London, 1993.

Nederlandsche Bank de, *Jaarverslag 1996* (Kluwer, Deventer, 1997).

——*Kwartaalbericht September 1997* (Kluwer, Deventer, 1997).

Third Report from the Select Committee on Treasury, *Accountability of the Bank of England*, Session 1997–8, HC 571.

Report of the Committee on the Working of the Monetary System, Cmnd. 827, Aug. 1959.

Report to the Council and Commission on the Realisation by Stages of Economic and Monetary Union in the Community of 8 Oct. 1970 ([1970] OJ C136/1) (Werner Report).

Reserve Bank of New Zealand, *Annual Plan 1997* (Wellington, 1997).

——*Annual Report 1997* (Wellington, 1998).

Statement by J.L. Jordan, President of the Federal Reserve Bank of Cleveland before the Committee on Banking, Finance, and Urban Affairs, US House of Representatives, 19 Oct. 1993, reprinted in *Federal Reserve Bulletin*, vol. 79, no. 12, Dec. 1993, 1110–20.

Treasury and Civil Service Committee, *The Role of the Bank of England* (House of Commons Paper. Session 1993–4; 98–I, vol. 1 and 2), Report, together with the proceedings of the Committee. HC Session 1993–4 (HMSO, London, 1993).

Vers un Système Européen de Banques Centrales, Rapport du groupe présidé par Jean-Victor Louis (Editions de l'Université de Bruxelles, Brussels, 1989).

Wogau, K. v. (Rapporteur), *Report of the Committee for Economic, Monetary and Industrial Policy on the national central banks in the perspective of the 2nd and 3rd stages of EMU*, European Parlament, Session Documents (1.12.1993, DOC-EN\RR\240652).

OTHER ITEMS

"Accidental Hero", *The Economist*, 21 Sept. 1996, at 42.

Baratta, M.v. (ed.), *Der Fischer Weltalmanach 1997* (Fischer Taschenbuch Verlag, Frankfurt a.M., 1997).

"Blair's Banker", *The Banker*, June 1997.

Brüggemann, G., "Wenn Greenspan redet, hält die Welt die Luft an", *Die Welt*, 24 July 1997.

Calmfors, L., "An Accountable Bank", *Financial Times*, 23 Feb. 1998.

Chote, R., "Victims of 'Groupthinking'", *Financial Times*, 7 Sept. 1998.

Dodges, J.M., *Central Banking and Banking Supervision*, Memorandum of 1 Nov. 1945.

Duisenberg, W.F., Introductory Statement delivered to Hearing at the European Parliament's Sub-Committee on Monetary Affairs on 18 January 1999.

"Dutch Resist 'Deal' on Bank Job", *Financial Times*, 31 Jan./1 Feb. 1998.

"Ein Kompromiß bei der Amtszeit Duisenbergs macht den Weg frei für die Wirtschafts- und Währungsunion", *Frankfurter Allgemeine Zeitung*, 4 May 1998.

"Executive Agencies Within the EC: The European Central Bank—A Model?", Editorial Comments (1996) 33 *CMLRev.*, 623–31.

"Finanzen: Ist-Daten von 1997 sollen entscheidend sein. Waigel, Tietmeyer und Lamfalussy skizzierten ihre Vorstellungen zur Einführung der Europawährung", *Deutscher Bundestag*, WIB Heft 22/6 Dec. 1995.

Le groupe permanent pour une Europe Démocratique, "L'Europe Attend", *RMC*, no. 404 (1997).

Letter of the Chancellor of the Exchequer Gordon Brown to the governor of the Bank of England, 6 May 1997, reprinted in *Bank of England Quarterly Bulletin*, vol. 37 no. 3 (1997), 244–5.

"MPs seek veto on Brown's Appointments", *The Independent*, 5 Sept. 1997.

Nederlandsche Bank, de, NV, *Bank Act 1948 and Articles of Association* (1994 edn.).

Oxford English Dictionary, Vol. 1 (Clarendon Press, Oxford, 1970).

Remarks by Miguel Mancera (Conference proceedings), in Capie, F. *et al.*, *The Future of Central Banking* (Cambridge University Press, Cambridge, 1994), 315–22.

Remarks by A. Greenspan Chairman of the Federal Reserve System at the 1997 Haskins Partners Dinner of the Stern School of Business (New York University, New York, 8 May 1997).

Remarks by Chairman A. Greenspan at the 15th Anniversary Conference of the Center for Economic Policy Research at the Stanford University (Stanford, California, 5 Sept. 1997).

The Role of the Bank of England (House of Commons Paper. Session 1993–4; 98–I, vol. 2), Report, together with the proceedings of the Committee. HC Session 1993–4 (HMSO, London, 1993).

Memorandum submitted by the Banque de France, in Treasury and Civil Service Committee, app. 5.

Memorandum submitted by the Netherlands Central Bank, app. 10.

Memorandum submitted by the Reserve Bank of New Zealand, app. 17.

Memorandum submitted by the United States Federal Reserve System, app. 20.

"Tietmeyer: EZB-Mitglieder persönlich verantwortlich", *Der Tagesspiegel*, 28 Nov. 1997.

"Trichet Outlines Vision of 'Open and Democratic' Independent Central Bank", *Financial Times*, 8/9 Jan. 1994.

"Waigel Backs Down on Gold", *Financial Times*, 4 June 1997.

Webster's Third New International Dictionary (Merian-Webster Inc., Springfield, Mass., 1986).

CASES

European Court of Justice

Case 26/62, *Van Gend en Loos* v. *Nederlandse Administratie der Belastingen* [1963] ECR 1.

Case 138/79, *SA Roquette Frères* v. *Council* [1980] ECR 3333.
Case 70/88, *European Parliament* v. *Council* [1990] ECR I–2041.
Case C–300/89, *Commission* v. *Council* [1991] ECR I–2867.
Opinion 1/91 [1991] ECR I–6079.
Case C–65/93, *European Parliament* v. *Council* [1995] ECR I–643.
Case C–21/94, *European Parliament* v. *Council* [1995] ECR I–1827.
Case C–41/94, *Council* v. *European Parliament* [1995] ECR I–4411.

France

Décision no. 92–308 DC of 9 Apr. 1992, RUDH 1992, 336.
Décision no. 92–312 DC of 2 Sept. 1992, RUDH 1992, 341.
Décision no. 92–313 DC of 23 Sept. 1992, RUDH 1992, 344.
Décision no. 93–324 DC of 3 Aug. 1993, JORF 1993, 11014.

Germany

BVerfGE 14, 196.
BVerfGE 62, 169.
BVerfGE 89, 155 (for an English translation see [1994] 1 CMLR, 57 *et seq.*
BVerwGE 2, 217.
BVerwGE 41, 334.
Hess. VGH, Beschluss of 22 Sept. 1986 (8 TG 1524/86), WM (1986), 1312.
VG Frankfurt a.M., Urteil of 19 May 1989 (VII/3 E 636/86), WM (1989), 1416.

UK

R v. *Secretary of State for Transport, ex parte Factortame Ltd.* [1990] 2 AC 85 and *ibid. (no. 2)* [1991] 1 AC 603.

USA

Reuss v. *Balles*, 73 FRD 90 (DDC 1976). (584 F 2d 461).
Merrill v. *Federal Open Market Committee et al.*, 413 F Supp. 494 (1976), and 565 F 2d. (1977).
Riegel v. *Federal Open Market Committee*, 656 F 2d 873 (1981).
Melcher v. *Federal Open Market Committee et al.*, 644 F Supp. 510; 836 F. 2d 561 (DC Cir. 1987).
Committee for Monetary Reform v. *Board of Governors*, 766 F 2d 538; 47 US App. DC 48.
A.G. Becker Inc. v. *Board of Governors of Federal Reserve System*, 502 F Supp. 378.
Humphrey's Executor v. *United States*, 295 US 602, 55 . Ct. 869 (1935).

Index